A Nation by Design

A Nation by Design

Immigration Policy in the
Fashioning of America

Aristide R. Zolberg

RUSSELL SAGE FOUNDATION
New York, New York

HARVARD UNIVERSITY PRESS
Cambridge, Massachusetts
London, England
2006

Library of Congress Cataloging-in-Publication Data

Zolberg, Aristide R.
    A nation by design : immigration policy in the fashioning of America /
Aristide Zolberg.
        p. cm.
    Includes bibliographical references and index.
    ISBN 0–674–02218–1 (alk. paper)
        1. United States—Emigration and immigration—Government policy.
    2. United States—Emigration and immigration—History. I. Title.

    JV6483.Z65 2006
    325.73—dc22   2005044742

Contents

Acknowledgments

Given that the idea for this book emerged when my daughter, now a career woman with two children, was in the sixth grade, proper acknowledgments would fill a small volume on their own. I shall therefore limit myself to principals, with a number of student research assistants credited in endnotes in the appropriate chapters.

At the very beginning, while still at the University of Chicago, I was encouraged by my colleague Gerhard Casper at the Law School to submit a paper for a U.S. bicentennial conference chaired by historian William McNeill and the late Ruth Adams. My original undertaking was published in their coedited work *Human Migration* (Bloomington: Indiana University Press, 1978). I was then diverted for a decade to the study of international refugees, of which the major product was *Escape from Violence* (coauthored with Astri Suhrke and Sergio Aguayo; New York: Oxford University Press, 1989). Subsequently, I resumed work on the American experience at a time when immigration once again moved to the fore, and I benefited from the assumption of leadership of U.S. policy by Doris Meissner, head of the Immigration and Naturalization Service, who helped me understand the complexity of the task at hand in controlling immigration. Undoubtedly, the experiences of my family, myself, as well as my in-laws, the Lenchners, helped me develop an insider's perspective into this sphere of policy. My son Dan's membership in the family connects our collective experience with the earliest phase of American immigration history involving Africa.

I am grateful for the intellectual guidance and stimulation of Richard Alba, Alex Aleinikoff, Rainer Bauboeck, Philip Gleason, Josh De Wind, Nancy Green, Gary Gerstle, Mae Ngai, Dimitri Papadimitriou, Michael Teitelbaum,

David Reimers, and Peter Schuck. The late John Higham encouraged me to pursue the nation-making approach. Kenneth Prewitt and Ira Katznelson lived up to the old saying "A friend in need" by stepping in as the deadline approached and I was partly incapacitated.

This work could not have been done without the administrative and financial support of Jonathan Fanton, as president of the New School; trustee Henry Arnhold, who made it possible for me to establish a broad-ranging center on international migration at the New School (the International Center for Migration, Ethnicity and Citizenship, or ICMEC); and especially the Russell Sage Foundation, whose invaluable one-year residential fellowship made the difference between a bunch of ideas, piles of information, and a draft manuscript of several chapters. Since this is my first major publication since being appointed to the Walter Eberstadt chair, I take the opportunity to thank Walter for his generosity and thoughtfulness and hope he will enjoy the book.

At a more down-to-earth level, I also benefited from the invaluable research and administrative assistance of Kerry McNamara, Peter Benda, Philip Triadafilopoulos, William A. Gordon, Alison Clarkin, Brad Usher, Agnès Callamard, Dan Mulcare, Robert Melville, Rachel Schwartz, and Myra Waterbury, who, in the face of an emergency, performed well above what is expected from an administrative assistant.

The book is dedicated to my wife, Vera, with love and gratitude for a half-century of wonderfully constructive affection and companionship, trusting that it will meet her distinctive intellectual, aesthetic, and moral standards.

A Nation by Design

Themes and Perspectives

A nation of immigrants, to be sure, but not just any immigrants. From the moment they managed their own affairs, well before political independence, Americans were determined to select who might join them, and they have remained so ever since. Immigration policy, broadly conceived in this book to encompass not only entry but also related processes that affect the nation's composition, thus emerged from the outset as a major instrument of nation-building, equivalent in the fashioning of the United States to the amalgamation of diverse regions in the making of the United Kingdom, France, or Spain. Although as historical constructs all nations in some sense make themselves, the very nature of the immigration process provided the Americans with unusual latitude in doing so, and hence theirs may properly be termed "a nation by design."[1]

In the Old World, the people came with the territory: the construction of "France" is the history of the royal state's territorial expansion from the Paris region and of the concurrent transformation of the successively incorporated populations into *français;* in the same vein, in their aspiration to forge Britons out of the pieces being assembled by way of dynastic manipulations, the rulers of the United Kingdom had little choice but to work with the English, Welsh, Scots, and Irish.[2] In contrast, from the very outset, by way of its state and federal governments, the self-constituted American nation not only set conditions for political membership, but also decided quite literally who would inhabit its land. Long before what is conventionally regarded as the beginning of national immigration policy, the Americans undertook to violently eliminate most of the original dwellers, imported a mass of African workers whom they excluded from their nation altogether, actively recruited Europeans they

1

considered suitable for settlement, intervened in the international arena to secure freedom of exit on their behalf, elaborated devices to deter those judged undesirable, and even attempted to engineer the self-removal of liberated slaves, deemed inherently unqualified for membership. Immigration policy not only emerged as a major instrument of American nation-building, but also fostered the notion that the nation could be designed, stimulating the elevation of that belief into an article of national faith.

The American experience of nation-building is exceptional not only in comparison with the Old World prefabs, but also in relation to the other overseas nations of European origin where, throughout their formative years, immigration remained largely governed by the imperial governments or, in the case of the precociously independent South American states, was for a protracted period hardly governed at all.[3] As against this, American grievances regarding British immigration and naturalization policy were voiced for several decades before 1776, and their inclusion in the Declaration of Independence, which forms the core of Chapter 2, provides clear evidence of the founders' understanding that immigration was bound to play a key role in the building of the American nation. Duly noted in accounts of the founding, but as a side issue, the Declaration's grievances regarding immigration and naturalization belong in the foreground because these matters were regarded by both British imperial authorities and the American leaders as key processes that shaped basic features of the colonies' existence: the size of their population, its composition, and the rules for membership in the body politic. Rather than isolated skirmishes, the confrontations over these issues were vital episodes in the larger war over sovereignty, and amounted to an epochal struggle over the structure or design of American society. In short, the American colonies amounted to a congeries of disparate population fragments that had come into being largely as intentional and unintentional by-products of migration policies tailored to the pursuit of imperial objectives; to turn these elements into a unified society, and one that would provide the social underpinnings of a republic, was an immensely ambitious task, which required among other things a fundamental modification of ongoing immigration policies and related practices.

My account thus challenges the widely held notion that until the late nineteenth century, the United States maintained a laissez-faire stance in the sphere of immigration. As will be elaborated in Chapter 6, the conventional narrative was largely shaped by the protracted confrontation over immigration that spanned the first two-thirds of the twentieth century. This gave rise to a full-blown *Historikerstreit,* in which contending historians justified their respective positions by situating the founders on a continuum ranging from "openness" or "generosity" to "restrictionism." Marcus Lee Hansen's classic interpretation, elaborated before his death in 1938 and subsequently edited by Arthur M. Schlesinger Sr., prudently but deliberately comes down somewhere in the middle: "So the United States began its career with no encouragement to immigrants except that offered by its opportunities, and with no barriers except those confronting native and foreigner alike."[4] Echoed in the influential synthetic overview published in 1960 by Maldwyn Jones, this interpretation of the policy baseline as benevolently neutral, but marred by occasional eruptions of "nativism," has become canonic, and nativism itself has become a distinct object of study.[5] With regard to the first century, its adoption was facilitated by the near-absence of federal legislation on the explicit subject of immigration. While historians have accepted this as a given, from a perspective informed by theories of state—and nation—formation, this absence constitutes a puzzle: given the evident concern of the founders with the subject, why was so little legislation enacted?

A reexamination of the record with this in mind reveals that the absence of federal legislation does not reflect a lack of interest in regulating entry, but was attributable to the overriding of immigration policy by what was then the central issue of national politics, the matter of states' rights in relation to slavery. In effect, immigration policy could only be dealt with at the state level. Indeed, a considerable amount of regulation was enacted by port-of-entry states, amounting in toto to a national immigration policy; however, much of this was in turn invalidated by the courts on the grounds that it exceeded state authority. Although Gerald Neuman has reconstructed the record of state action, he has done so from an exclusively juridical perspective and has not paid much attention to the actors who challenged the states' actions and their motivations.[6] Such an inquiry in fact provides considerable insight into the political dynamics underlying immigration policy at a crucial turning point, half a century after independence, when the United States truly became a nation of immigrants.

The American "design" became more explicit as the founders sought to regulate immigration and naturalization so as to foster the transformation of a loose aggregate of political entities, some formed along the "family farm" path, others more properly colonial and stratified along racial lines, into a politically integrated white republic. As elaborated in Chapter 3, emerging as the key theorists in this field, Tench Coxe, Thomas Jefferson, Alexander Hamilton, and James Madison engaged in elaborate explorations of the relationship between population, land, and labor to determine what immigration policy would best serve broader goals of nation-building and economic development. On the political side, in his famous debate with Edmund Burke, Tom Paine set forth a radically innovative "civic" model of the nation as an alternative to the "ethnic" body politic, and this in turn provided the theoretical foundations for the country's first naturalization law. My analysis engages a collegial debate with Rogers Smith; although he rightly emphasizes the egregious shortcomings of American citizenship with regard to race, he gets so carried away by his critique that he fails to give proper weight to the innovative character of what was done. From a contemporaneous international perspective, the more striking fact is the law's *inclusiveness*, indicated by the absence of religious or national origin qualifications.[7] This constituted an obvious invitation to non-British nationals and, on the religious side, to Roman Catholics and Jews.

The concerns expressed at the moment of political emancipation adumbrate a lasting feature of the fledgling new republic, rooted in its peculiar colonial origins: although regulation of the movement of persons across a state's borders and access of aliens to citizenship by way of naturalization were recognized by contemporaneous legal and political thinkers as established practices, in the United States they achieved unprecedented practical and theoretical prominence because foreign immigration—as against mere transfers within the empire—made a much greater contribution to its population than had ever occurred in any European nation, or than any political philosopher envisioned might take place in a constituted community. Paradoxically, while the location of the United States on the western side of the Atlantic somewhat insulated its political development from European ideological currents and the effects of international tensions, thereby lending it a peculiarly insular character, the prominence of international migration rendered it unusually cosmopolitan, and promoted its role as an advocate of freedom of exit (Chapter 4).[8]

Nevertheless, observing the United States half a century after independence, Alexis de Tocqueville saw it as a fully formed "Anglo-American" society, and at this time Americans hardly thought themselves "a nation of immigrants." Despite the prevailing immigrationism, annual arrivals amounted to only one-fourth of 1 percent of the white population and contributed less than one-tenth of its spectacular demographic expansion (nearly 3 percent a year!). Chapter 3 demonstrates that this was not happenstance and that, in effect, the largely ignored federal Passenger Act of 1819, together with state regulations governing ports of entry, created a rudimentary system of "remote control," whereby the United States sought to select immigrants by projecting its boundaries into the source countries.[9]

However, in a thoroughly pessimistic footnote inserted on the eve of publication of *Democracy in America* in 1835, Tocqueville observed that the situation he reported on so optimistically had begun to change, and that the country's two large port-of-entry cities, Philadelphia and New York, were being invaded by a "dangerous" population of poor blacks and poor Europeans who "bring to the United States our greatest vices, and lack any of the interests which might offset their influence." As demonstrated in Chapter 5, this reflected his Whig friends' sense that the United States faced an unprecedented "immigration crisis" occasioned by an abrupt and considerable rise of arrivals from Europe, of whom an increasing proportion were perceived as significantly different from the established population, in that they were not "British" but largely Irish and German, as well as Roman Catholic to boot. Induced by the continuing expansion of the "great transformation," this human wave propelled immigration to the top of the political agenda, lining up the new capitalists eager to maximize their labor supply against defenders of the traditional boundaries of American society, whom historians subsequently labeled "nativists," and urban wage workers, who perceived immigrants as a threat to their living and an obstacle to the organization of a labor movement. The immigration crisis reached all the way to the U.S. Supreme Court, whose rulings in turn shaped the strategies of both camps and thereby determined the course of policy. The confrontation over immigration eventually interacted with the crisis over slavery to destroy the "second party system" and bring on the Civil War.

Ultimately, the "nativists" lost out to the capitalists, and consequently Tocqueville's nightmarish footnote moved into the text, transforming the established "Anglo-American" nation into a unique "nation of immigrants." This outcome inaugurated the protracted hegemony of economically driven policy, further elaborated during and after the Civil War, and expanded to encompass the recently opened West Coast. The vast increase and growing heterogeneity of the immigrants, now including Chinese, once again precipitated a crisis (Chapter 6). In keeping with the general trend of American political development during this period, within a single decade the ambiguous and administratively awkward jurisdictional equilibrium between levels of government in the sphere of immigration decisively shifted toward the national, as measures favored by most states but barred from enactment by the pre–Civil War Supreme Court now became national policy. The availability of a large and ethnically variegated labor force, with a substantial component of "birds of passage" on both coasts, imparted a distinctively segmented structure to the American industrial labor market and largely provides the answer to Werner Sombart's notorious question, "Why is there no Socialism in the United States?"

Nativism Reconsidered

Our understanding of the onset of federal regulation after the Civil War is largely shaped by the late John Higham's *Strangers in the Land,* which has deservedly achieved classic status and remains, after half a century, the most distinguished work on the subject.[10] Focusing on the period 1880–1925, Higham constructed a narrative in which the United States moved from openness to steadily growing restriction, culminating in the imposition of the national origin quotas and wholesale Asian exclusion. However, in his preface to a later edition, Higham himself reflected that "I would . . . if I were writing today, take more account of aspects of the immigration restriction movement that can not be sufficiently explained in terms of nativism." In his postscript to a revised second edition, he suggested that the "nation-building" framework I had adumbrated in preliminary articles would be particularly helpful.[11] His generous encouragement convinced me to undertake the present work, despite my long-term professional involvement in quite different fields.

Tacitly underlying Higham's conceptualization of nativism is the "frustration-aggression" syndrome derived from psychoanalytic theory by way of Theodore Adorno's *The Authoritarian Personality* and Gordon W. Allport's *Prejudice.*[12] Highly influential among American intellectuals in the 1950s, this syndrome also inspired Richard Hofstadter's analysis *Anti-intellectualism in American Life,* "conceived in response to the political and intellectual conditions of the 1950's," notably McCarthyism.[13] Underlying Higham's history of immigration policy is the idea that Americans, frustrated by the disruptions that accompanied industrialization and urbanization, projected their anger upon strangers. Translated into pressure on decision makers to restrict immigration, this collective disposition was alleviated only when the international situation provided alternative outlets in the form of external aggression, notably the Spanish-American War and World War I; but these were temporary alleviations, and afterward immigrants became once again the main target.

The basic problem with this approach is that there is no way of independently charting the level of frustration of a society except by using aggressive behavior—that which is to be explained—as the indicator, nor can the level of aggressivity be independently established with respect to particular groups and at different times. The result is such inherent covariance between cause and effect as to suggest we are in the presence of a tautology. Whose frustrations, when, and how deep? While suggestive overall, a psychopathology-inspired approach is inadequate because it cannot account for particular policy outcomes at specific times. Why immigrant strangers rather than other objects? If "nativism" and the restrictions to which it gave rise were rooted in a projection of insecurity in the face of change, how come when insecurity reached a new high in the post–World War II period, it produced McCarthyism instead, while immigration policy was in fact liberalized?

Whereas "nativism" is credible as an expression of frustration, what sort of stance would be "normal"? Given the historical baseline preceding the advent of restriction, it tacitly appears to be open immigration. But surely it is unrealistic to expect the United States to maintain its previous stance in light of the global transformations of the period, which vastly enlarged the worldwide pool of potential immigrants. The moment that constitutes Higham's starting point marked what is being increasingly recognized as the onset of globalization, when a number of factors changed more or less simultaneously to vastly enlarge the migratory flow, drastically altering the situation the United States faced. To begin with, Europe's demographic transformation spread to the Continent's least developed regions, the railroad revolutionized inland transportation, while the advent of iron steamships, whose carrying capacity was nearly tenfold that of sailing vessels and which reduced the Atlantic crossing from approximately one month to one week, transfigured overseas travel. Simultaneously, Asia and Africa were incorporated into the global political and economic system, and the recently formulated theory of evolution was combined with ideological rationalizations of imperialism to produce scientific racism. But if the external conditions of the late nineteenth century must figure in the explanation of the emergent American immigration policy, then in retrospect, it stands to reason that the conditions of the preceding period should be taken into account for the earlier phase of policy as well.

Most important, the psychopathological approach minimizes the rationality of the behavior of groups and classes with respect to the consequences of immigration. Higham himself seemed to be aware of the problem, as he pointed out the role of employers in resisting restriction, of labor in fostering it, of business cycles upon the receptivity of legislators to group pressures, and of the relatively autonomous role of the American executive branch in the entire process of policy making. However, he stopped short of taking into consideration that during the period with which he was concerned, employers not only resisted restrictions, but also were in fact fostering the expansion of immigration, thereby in effect generating the very conditions that stimulated "nativism." This contradiction, which has recurred in various forms throughout American history, often producing "strange bedfellows" on both sides of the confrontations over immigration, is at the heart of the present account.

Economic grounds for promoting or opposing immigration are easily conceived as "rational." This is much less the case with regard to the cultural considerations that underlie "nativism." Yet this might be thought of as the shrill expression, based on prejudicial assessments, of commonplace concerns with maintaining the receiving society's established identity. Viewed in the perspective of nation-building, a process common to both settled and immigrant societies, nativism can be thought of as representing the conservative position on an "identity" continuum, which allows for other positions ranging through the acceptance of shifting boundaries as a concomitant of historical change—where I would roughly place myself—all the way to the advocacy of radical transformation. Rather than thinking of "Americans" as going "nativist," one should think of such episodes as confrontations between different actors who position themselves variously on the "identity" dimension, much as economic actors do with regard to economic issues.

Another constraint arises from the unidimensionality of the concept of "restriction." Accounts of the more recent period generally highlight the persistence of restrictions until the 1950s, a return to greater openness from 1965 to 1990, and a neorestrictionist swerve in the 1990s. However, this again distorts reality in a number of ways. While the prohibition of Asian immigration together with the draconian reduction of European admissions and the notorious nationality quotas imposed in the 1920s certainly amounted to "restriction," this was only part of the story: concurrently, the United States was deliberately stimulating the expansion of immigration from Mexico and promoting massive internal migrations, notably the movement of African Americans from the South, which together blatantly contradicted the restrictionists' nation-building objectives. Conversely, the "liberal" legislation of 1965, which abolished the discriminatory European quotas and the remnants of Asian exclusion, and opened the door to their expansion, was coupled with measures explicitly designed to minimize "brown" immigration from Mexico and "black" from the Caribbean. And while there was surely a resurgence of restrictionism in the 1990s, the most interesting aspect of *that* story is its failure to achieve its most explicit objectives, the control of illegal immigration and a substantial reduction of legal immigration, both driven by shrill concern over the impact of immigration from the "South" on the character of the American nation.

Under the unprecedented conditions emerging in the world at large at the turn of the twentieth century, the imposition of limits on the immigration flow arose as a pressing imperative. Limits in turn implied selection; but on what grounds should this take place? Spanning an entire generation (Chapters 7 and 8), debate over this question was settled only in the aftermath of World War I, when, in one of the most spectacular displays of legislative power on record, with two waves of its magic wand the U.S. Congress sought to restore America's northwest European identity by making immigration from southern and eastern Europe disappear, much as it sought to do with alcohol. But whereas legislative action managed to reduce alcohol consumption by only one-third, in the sphere of immigration it was miraculously effective, and by 1930 the United States in effect proclaimed to the face of the world, "We are no longer a nation of immigrants." It maintained this position even after the advent of the New Deal and when some of its European cousins undertook to persecute others, who thereby became desperately in need of havens (Chapter 9).

A largely neglected aspect of the history of this period, even by recent institutionalist scholars of American political development, is that the implementation of restrictionism entailed a vast expansion of the American state's capacity to regulate movement across its borders, and the deployment of this capacity within the territory of other sovereign states so as to achieve the elusive "remote control" to which regulators had long aspired. However, even at this time American policy was by no means consistently "restrictionist." Responding to pressures from powerful agriculture interests for an ample supply of cheap labor, as well as from equally powerful oil interests concerned with establishing better relations with postrevolutionary Mexican governments, the legislators resisted closing the country's "back door," despite their explicit commitment to preserving the "original American stock" from contamination by Mexicans who, by their own standards, were even more objectionable than the southern and eastern Europeans they were keeping out.

In sharp contrast with the unswerving earlier march from open immigration to restriction, the reformers of the post–World War II decades dispersed along winding trails. One led to a redesigned main gate that fulfilled the aspirations of Americans (issued from the "new immigration") for status equality in the cultural sphere and enabled them to bring in their relatives; another to a revolving back door that continued to provide agricultural entrepreneurs with temporary labor; and the third to a side entrance for various groups loosely labeled "refugees," used by the U.S. government as a Cold War weapon as well as by influential ethnic communities unable to bring in populations of special concern through the main gate. The restrictionist régime was dismantled, giving way to a shifting bundle of disparate policy components (Chapter 10). The new policies reflected the broader transformation of postwar American society: dramatic changes in the size and distribution of the population as a whole; a shift in the boundaries of identity to encompass the "new immigrants," notably by way of the acceptance of Catholicism and Judaism as "American religions"; the emergence of a postindustrial economy; the beginnings of the civil rights revolution; the restructuring of political alignments; and the rise of the United States to world power.

It is noteworthy that at the very moment of these reforms, the foreign-born fell to their lowest proportion of the American population since Tocqueville's visit nearly a century and a half earlier, confirming that the restrictionists of the earlier part of the twentieth century had achieved their principal objective: the United States was no longer a nation of immigrants. Despite their protracted confrontations in the postwar years, defenders of the status quo and reformers were in agreement on keeping things that way. In this perspective, it is quite unexpected that in the last third of the twentieth century, the country's foreign-born population tripled in size and underwent a startling change of composition. Not surprisingly, even as it materialized, the new immigration stimulated an expanding debate over its desirability and consequences, recalling the confrontations of a century earlier, with social scientists and public intellectuals once again playing a prominent role in the production of updated ideologies (Chapters 11 and 12).

Very much in keeping with the established "strange bedfellows" pattern, the resulting alignments cut across the usual conservative-liberal divide; but in sharp contrast with the 1920s, an immigrationist coalition of capitalists and recent ethnics gained the upper hand. With regard to post–World War II policy developments, I had the benefit of a vast secondary literature, which is properly acknowledged at the appropriate points; but on the historical side, I relied especially on the several works of David Reimers, and on the political science side, on Daniel J. Tichenor's Ph.D. dissertation, completed in May 1996 and published in 2002.[14] On the period 1980–2000, our interpretations are in broad agreement; however, I focus my explanation more sharply on the surprising outcome—why reasonable expectations of a reenactment of the 1920s restrictions were not fulfilled.

Theorizing Immigration Policy: A Global Perspective

Although this book is concerned exclusively with American immigration policy, I consider the subject in a comparative perspective with a globalist bent, by way of a hybrid theoretical framework tinkered out of insights drawn from sociology, political economy, and cultural anthropology, as well as political science.

The starting point for theorizing about immigration policy is an understanding of the distinctiveness of international migration itself as a social phenomenon. In short, "international migration" entails not merely movement from one place to another, but derives its specificity from the organization of the world into a congeries of mutually exclusive sovereign states, commonly referred to as the "Westphalian system."[15] It involves the transfer of a person from the jurisdiction of one state to that of another and the eventuality of a change of membership in an inclusive political community. Accordingly, international migration is an inherently political process, and the relevant policies encompass not only the regulation of outward and inward movement across state borders—including of persons who are not, or declare that they are not, migrants—but also rules governing the acquisition, maintenance, loss, or voluntary relinquishment of "membership" in all its aspects—political, social, economic, and cultural.

Migration policies vary enormously, both historically and between states in a given period. As commemorated by the biblical narrative of the flight from Egypt, states traditionally prohibited the exit of economically valuable populations and resorted to draconian means to implement this policy, such as the imposition of galley slavery in seventeenth-century France to prevent Huguenots from departing for Protestant states, or shoot-to-kill border policing by the German Democratic Republic from its inception to its demise. But states have also acted ruthlessly to push out religious, ethnic, or social groups they considered undesirable and incapable of being subjected or transformed. All these stances coexisted in various parts of the world throughout the nineteenth and twentieth centuries, suggesting no overall historical trend toward convergence. A similar range of variation can be found on the entry side. States have raided others to abduct valuable populations; encouraged and facilitated the importation of slaves; and stimulated immigration by providing subsidized travel, lands, security, and easy citizenship, or by promising jobs; but they have also prohibited settlement and acted ruthlessly to prevent it. Positive or negative stances with regard to both exit and entry are usually defined in relation to specified categories of persons established on the basis of a wide array of criteria, including objective socioeconomic and cultural attributes (degree of skill, education, and wealth; religion, language, nationality, and race), as well as their putative moral or political disposition (judged likely or unlikely to commit crimes, or to support or oppose the régime). As a result, emigration and immigration policies often amount to complex arrays of disparate regulations and practices, with "laissez-faire" seldom a mark of indifference. States also exhibit considerable variation regarding modes of relinquishing and acquiring "membership," including not only formal citizenship but also political, social, and cultural rights.

How are we to make theoretical sense of this variation? At the most general level, "Whether migration is controlled by those who send, by those who go, or by those who receive, it mirrors the world as it is at the time."[16] Or, as suggested by a committee of the International Union for the Scientific Study of Population, the world can be conceptualized as a "global population system" in relation to which sending and receiving states, much as the migrants themselves, figure as "utility-maximizing" agents that respond to changing world-historical and local conditions by modifying their comportment—in the case of states, their policies regarding exit and entry.[17]

However, two qualifications are called for. As the complexity of contemporary debates on immigration policy in the affluent liberal democracies indicates, "utility" encompasses not only a population's economic value, but also its putative value in relation to cultural and political objectives. Moreover, "utility-maximizing" cannot be mechanically transposed from individuals to states. As executors of policies, states do not function as autonomous actors (even in the loose sense in which we consider individuals to do so), but rather as instruments manipulated by internal actors who have gained the upper hand in this particular sphere at a given time. Legal and administrative institutions, as well as "political traditions," which constitute the legacy of earlier policies, also play a significant role in shaping current responses.

In recent times, migration policies have been shaped by the dynamics of world capitalism, on the one hand, and of the international state system, on the other, within the context of epochal population dynamics.[18] Since the global population system and the system of states are both finite, migration policies are extremely interactive: any emigration always entails immediate immigration somewhere else; conversely, the possibility of immigrating affects decisions to emigrate; and the closing or opening of a particular national gate affects the potential flows into other states.[19] However, in contrast with the sphere of international trade, for example, far from being founded on recognition of this interactivity, state policies regarding emigration and immigration have been notoriously unilateral; as noted by Hannah Arendt, for example, "sovereignty is nowhere more absolute than in matters of emigration, naturalization, nationality, and expulsion."[20] This highlights the theoretical significance of even slight departures from the "sovereignty" baseline observable today, notably with regard to asylum.[21]

For the purpose of analytic clarification, exit and entry policies might be arrayed along an axis demarcated by negative and positive poles. Given the considerable variation in exit policies that can be observed historically, their impact on the formation of migration networks, and their interactivity with immigration policies elsewhere, it is evident that a comprehensive theory pertaining to the role of states in regulating international migration must cover the exit side as well. One basic proposition is that the possibility of preventing "exit" is a requisite for the effective exercise of most types of "predatory rule."[22] In the early modern era, under prevailing conditions of demographic scarcity, for the European mercantilist/bellicist state, the acquisition and retention of human capital for economic production and war comprised a basic source of power; from this perspective, the most important form of control pertained to outward movement. Accordingly, unauthorized emigration was tantamount to treason, and punishable by death or enslavement. The continuing significance of this policy stance is highlighted by its resurgence in the twentieth century as the hallmark of "totalitarian" states with command economies.[23]

The leading patterns of forced exit, including deliberate expulsions as well as escape from persecution or violence, stimulated by what is now generically termed "ethnic cleansing," can also be accounted for by the dynamics of state and nation formation within a bounded international system.[24] However, given this book's exclusive concern with the United States, I shall focus here on the entry side only. Although considerable attention has been devoted to variation among the contemporary immigration policies of capitalist democracies, the most striking fact about them is that, on a hypothetical continuum ranging from "open" to "closed" borders, they are clustered very narrowly around the "closed" pole.[25] While post–World War II policies constituted a liberalization in relation to the extremely restrictionist régime established in the first quarter of the century, the contemporary régime retains a "near-zero baseline" with regard to the supply of entries in relation to the demand for them as well as in relation to the size of the resident population—current annual U.S. immigration, for example, amounts to approximately one-third of 1 percent. As the theorist of international trade Jagdish Bhagwati observed in the early 1980s, the process of international migration is characterized by "disincentives" rather than "incentives," which led him to hypothesize quite correctly that if the socialist countries were to let people out, "the effective constraint on the numbers migrating would soon become the immigration legislations of the destination countries."[26]

The restrictive immigration régime prevails worldwide because it constitutes a sine qua non for maintaining the "Westphalian" international state system, as well as the privileged position of the "core" states amidst highly unequal conditions.[27] Economic modeling suggests that the hypothetical elimination of borders would stimulate worldwide economic growth, but also result in an equalization of conditions and hence produce a vast redistribution of income to the benefit of the populations of poorer countries. In effect, borders serve to prevent labor from commanding the same price everywhere, and also prevent people from the poorer countries from gaining access to the bundles of "public goods" dispensed by the more affluent states, which now constitute an important part of their populations' income.[28] It is also widely believed that restrictions on access to membership constitute a sine qua non for democratic governance, which requires at least some minimal degree of "community." Although the matters of precisely what level of immigration might be allowed and what priorities might be established are hotly debated, there is broad agreement that under present world conditions, the level would at best fall far short of the demand for access.[29]

Political Economy and Identity Politics

Consequently, the process of immigration policy decision making in a given state is driven by two very different sets of considerations, each of which relates to a distinct sphere of social interaction. In the perspective of capitalist dynamics, immigrants of any kind—including refugees—are considered primarily as "labor." Accordingly, immigration policies are shaped by the prevailing "class compromise" and the specific configuration of economic interests in the country in question, in keeping with the imperatives of prevailing technological and economic conditions.[30] Immigrants are characteristically welcomed by employers because they reduce the unit cost of labor (that is, lower wages) and also increase its elasticity; conversely, they are characteristically resented by resident workers as unfair competitors willing to accept lower wages (which constitute an improvement over their income in the country of origin) and below-standard conditions. At worst, they may not only lower wages but also altogether displace natives. However, even the most profit-driven capitalists are unlikely to favor a *huge* and *sudden* increase in labor supply, as that would occasion major social disruptions; hence, in contemporary capitalist democracies, arguments on behalf of "open borders" appear perennially as the playful musings of free-market ideologues, such as Julian Simon in the *Wall Street Journal,* but almost never in actual policy debates.[31]

These considerations, usually cast in a Marxian framework, have given rise to a considerable body of work accounting for the tendency of advanced industrial societies to recruit "guest workers" from less developed countries.[32] An alternative explanation was provided by the theory of labor segmentation, whereby under conditions of the welfare state the upper strata of the workforce are assimilated into "fixed" capital, leading to the institutionalization of a distinct "flexible" segment, for which again "guest workers" of one sort of another are very convenient.[33] In the United States, this analysis is applicable not only to the importation of Chinese workers to the West Coast from 1850 on, and of Mexican workers in World War I and World War II, as well as in the 1950s, but also by extension to the long-standing tolerance of "regular irregular" (in other words, undocumented) workers from the same neighbor. However, in recent years matters have been complicated by the reliance of some labor unions on such workers for the survival of their industry.

Still in the economic sphere, immigrants are also consumers of goods and services, both the ordinary kind that one buys and the "public goods" that are automatically available to all residents. Whereas they tend to be welcomed by sellers of individual goods and services—for example, real estate agents in port-of-entry cities—from the perspective of public goods the situation is more complex. Recent U.S. debates regarding the "balance sheet" of immigration in relation to welfare highlight the difficulty of establishing whether immigrants contribute more in taxes than they consume in public services or whether they are "free riders"; and the subject is understandably much hotter in European countries with more extensive welfare states.[34] Moreover, because different units of aggregation are used to draw up a balance sheet of the various costs and benefits involved, immigrants may be "good" for the whole economy, but "bad" for a particular locality or social group—or vice versa (for example, they may reinvigorate declining "rust belt" cities). Incidentally, similar considerations are applicable also to international-level assessments of the economic value of particular human flows by sending and receiving countries as a whole.

However, all types of immigrants—including even temporary workers—also constitute a political and cultural presence, which evokes a distinctive dimension of consideration pertaining to the putative impact of immigration on the host country's "way of life," "cohesiveness," or, in current discourse, "identity." Although the process in question is well evoked by classical sociology's concept of "integration," from Émile Durkheim through Talcott Parsons, I shall use the term "identity axis." In almost any immigration situation, there are significant groups among the hosts who believe that newcomers in general, or particular groups among them, would jeopardize the established national ways. In the United States alone, just about every cultural attribute imaginable was found objectionable at one time or another, notably "race," as constructed in the nineteenth and early twentieth centuries, referring to not only "Asiatics" and blacks but also "mixed-breed" Mexicans, different European nationalities, and Jews; religion, notably Roman Catholics from the eighteenth century until quite recently; and language, starting with German speakers at the time of the founding and again in the early twentieth century, and Spanish speakers today. Similar hostile responses have surfaced elsewhere, notably toward Jews from eastern Europe in most of western Europe yesterday, Arabs and Muslims more generally throughout Europe today, or when "Oriental" Sephardic Jews began arriving in Israel in the 1950s and when Ethiopian Jews began arriving later on.

Although reactions such as these are attributable in large part to prejudice and xenophobia that tend to exaggerate the problematic aspects of the situation, it should be recognized that the settlement—or prospective settlement—of any substantial group of people whose culture diverges markedly from the hosts' is likely to call the established "cultural compromise" pertaining to religious, linguistic, and racial diversity into question, and hence is a legitimate source of concern.[35] The key questions are always "How different can we be?" and "How alike must we be?" and, when they are answered, how the answers are to be implemented organizationally and materially.[36]

As it enters into play with regard to immigration, "identity" centers on nationality.[37] Originating largely in the course of efforts to institutionalize "predatory rule" in late medieval European states, modern nations have succeeded in socializing their populations to perceive one another as fellow members of intimate, family-like bodies, with a common ancestry and a common destiny. Although the formula for identity is usually founded on some objective characteristics of the society, such as the language actually spoken by much of the population and the religion many of them share, the culture of the rulers is usually accorded pride of place. However, political culture and ideological orientation may be invoked also, as in the United States and France following their democratic revolutions, or in the confrontation between "the West" and "the East" in the Cold War decades.[38]

Much less noted by writers on nationality and nationalism is that the formation of identity always involves a negative aspect as well. As conceptualized by the anthropologist Fredrik Barth, it entails the elaboration of a boundary between "us" and "them": thus, we are who we are by virtue of who we are *not*.[39] In this light, nationality involves the delineation of a boundary, denoting simultaneously inclusion and exclusion. Whatever the objective realities may have been in the early modern era, princes and their serving intellectuals emphasized similarities within the national borders and differences between the nation and its neighbors.[40] Although the negative "others" are commonly close neighbors with whom perennial wars are fought, from whom "we" must distinguish ourselves by any means possible, they can also be remote aliens, regarding whom little is known and therefore much can be invented. Groups originally recruited as low-skilled "workers" are especially likely to belong to the "non-us" world, a difference that is functional to their subjection within a status hierarchy; but this "wanted but not welcome" syndrome creates problematic situations if and when the workers begin turning into permanent settlers, akin to the dynamics of "liminality" analyzed by Victor Turner.[41]

Differing assessments along these lines precipitate confrontations not only between "natives" and "foreigners" but also among the "natives" themselves, between those who perceive the newcomers as a threat in relation to what is deemed a fragile status quo, and others more confident in the society's ability to weather change, or who welcome the diversity the newcomers would contribute as an enrichment. These alignments are probably related to a more comprehensive cultural cleavage that is emerging as the contemporary equivalent of the older rift between religious and secular camps, and encompasses other "cultural" and "moral" issues such as abortion, feminism, gay rights, or the death penalty. However, the camp of those positively disposed toward immigrants may also include "natives" who are not particularly open to change, but who feel an affinity with particular groups of newcomers, notably fellow religionists or ethnics. This sometimes involves the national community as a whole, with respect to populations located in other states who are regarded as "external nationals," on whose behalf the state may devise a "law of return" or some other unusually generous immigration policy.[42]

Refugee policy has tended to be driven by strategic considerations arising quite directly from the dynamics of the international political system: providing asylum to the victims of one's enemies was consistent with the imperatives of realpolitik in that it demonstrated the antagonist's evil ways and undermined its legitimacy. Concomitantly, refugees tended to be ranked high on the positive side of the "identity" axis throughout western countries; this was almost by definition, as in earlier times they were welcomed exclusively on the basis of religious or political affinity with the receivers, and therefore were not strangers but brothers and sisters in need. Under these conditions, statecraft and humanitarianism went hand in hand. By the same token, states were not inclined to help victims not "like us": proletarian Communards had almost no place to go after their defeat in 1871, and Jewish victims of Nazism were denied havens as well.

However, in the post–World War II period the international community began moving toward a more cosmopolitan approach, eventually extending refugee status to all those, anywhere in the world, who are outside their country and without government protection as consequences of "reasonable fear" of persecution. Concurrently, the superpowers expanded the domain of their strategic confrontations to encompass many regions of the Third World, contributing to a vast enlargement of the refugee pool. Although the overwhelming majority remained in their region of origin, some came knocking at the door of the affluent countries, and the fact that an increasing proportion of those who sought asylum were poor people of color—and thereby akin, from the perspective of the receivers, to immigrant workers—triggered alarm bells and prompted a reconsideration of established policies. This revisionism was facilitated by the end of the Cold War, which eliminated at one blow the "realist" foundations of the postwar refugee régime. The United States retained a refugee policy founded almost exclusively on "realist" foreign and security considerations until about 1980; although it then subscribed to the international régime, its actual policy continued to be driven by "realism," with some intrusion of constituency pressures (particularly with regard to eastern European Jews). The end of the Cold War, which eliminated at one blow the "realistic" foundations of the postwar refugee régime, has led to a sharp narrowing of the scope of the affluent democracies' refugee policy, including in the United States.

The persistent coexistence of these two very different dimensions of consideration and, concomitantly, of interests, the one pertaining to the putative or actual effects of immigration on material conditions, the other for cultural and political conditions, can be represented by cross-cutting axes, each with positive and negative poles, providing for a continuum of alignments from "for" to "against." Hence, it is possible to adopt a positive position on immigration with respect to one dimension, and a negative one in relation to another. This accounts for the often remarked upon tendency of immigration politics to straddle the ordinary "liberal/conservative" divide, and concomitantly the emergence of "strange bedfellow" coalitions for or against particular proposals. Successive attempts to resolve these disparate imperatives in the face of changing conditions shape immigration policy into complex and often inconsistent configurations, such as the segmentation of U.S. policy into a "main gate" dealing with general immigration, a side door for refugees, and a "back door" dealing with the procurement of temporary agricultural workers (Chapters 11 and 12).

Overall, in distinction from the prevailing view of American immigration policy as a single historical line weaving between openness and restriction at different points in time, I believe it has involved from the outset a combination of disparate elements designed to facilitate or even stimulate the entry of immigrants deemed valuable while deterring those considered undesirable, and occasionally even going beyond this to rid the nation of populations already in its midst. The result of deliberate efforts by policy makers responding to changing circumstances at home and abroad, these elements have intermittently crystallized into policy settlements anchored in concrete bureaucratic institutions, amounting to an "immigration régime." Once they have come into being, a protracted process spread over a half-century or so, these régimes acquire inertial power by way of the sheer weight of established institutions and of the interests of certain actors in preserving the status quo, turning attempts to change policy into an uphill struggle and thereby shaping the subsequent course of history, in keeping with the notion of "path dependency."[43]

This approach provides the framework for a revised understanding of the history of American immigration policy as beginning with the formation of an immigration régime in the 1750–1820 period, combining elements of colonial legacy with newly wrought bits of state and federal policy. Despite changing circumstances in both the United States and Europe, which triggered numerous policy initiatives, this foundational régime survived pressures to change throughout the antebellum period. Elaboration of a successor régime, designed to meet the challenges of the industrial age and of globalization, began as early as the 1870s but was not completed until the 1920s; in the intervening period, however, immigration was shaped largely in accordance with the residual older design. Efforts to substantially modify the second régime were launched as early as the 1930s, but largely failed until 1965, when the principal elements of a third edifice were set in place, with complementary pieces added over the next two decades. Once again, even as the régime was still being completed, challengers initiated efforts to replace it altogether. At the turn of the millennium, however, the outcome was by no means evident, as the imperatives of globalization pulled in opposite directions. While the formation of a North American economic zone fostered a consideration of modifications allowing for greater freedom of movement, the events of 9/11 abruptly revived obsolescent concerns over immigration as a threat to national security, and hence fostered a tightening of borders.

Political Process and Political Institutions

However powerful, the effects of social forces, external and internal, are not automatically translated into policy outcomes, but are mediated by political structures.[44] In the case of the modern United States, relevant considerations include the effects of formal political institutions in facilitating and constraining the elaboration of policy, notably the allocation of decision-making authority and power between levels and branches of government as well as the structures of representation and the electoral system. Proper attention must also be paid to the role of political parties and organized interests in decision making.

Each of the two dimensions represented by the axes also fosters a distinct mode of interaction between elites and the public, with concomitantly distinct outcomes.[45] Inspired by organization theory, Gary Freeman has suggested that "expansionist and inclusive" policies occur because, while the benefits of immigration are concentrated, notably by providing lower costs for employers in certain economic sectors and gratification for kin and coethnics of incoming groups, its costs tend to be diffuse, notably increased competition for jobs among some groups of the resident population and increased demand for certain services. Such a distribution tends to produce "client" politics, where small and well-organized groups intensively interested in a policy develop close working relationships with officials responsible for it, largely outside of public view and with little outside interference. Consequently, policy makers are more responsive to their immigration-advocating clients than to the more ambivalent or even opposed general public, whose utility-maximizing ability is handicapped by "serious barriers to the acquisition of information" about immigration and by a "temporal illusion," whereby the short-term benefits of immigration are easily seen whereas its long-term costs are denied or hidden. As a result, "[O]fficial policies tend to be more liberal than public opinion and annual intakes larger than is politically optimal"—in other words, the policies preferred by the median voter.

The situation with regard to "identity" is the reverse of what prevails in the economic sphere: the costs of immigration are diffuse, in the sense of a malaise pertaining to "threats to nationality," whereas the benefits are concentrated, in that certain ethnic groups increase their weight and hence "recognition" and potential political power in the nation. This may account for the reluctance of U.S. elites around the turn of the twentieth century to endorse immigration restriction, and for their eventual movement toward "universalism," notably with regard to the elimination of the national origins quotas directed against southern and eastern Europeans in the 1950s, when these groups became the mainstay of the urban wing of the Democratic Party but also provided new opportunities for the Republicans. Both dimensions make for "client" politics, but involve different sets of clients. The combination of business and ethnic groups as strange bedfellows into a "pro-immigration" camp is a characteristic U.S. outcome, partly a function of the rapid incorporation of immigrants into the body politic. More generally, the "concentrated-diffuse" measure is more heuristic when applied to disaggregated elements, and when a distinction is made between concentration within economic sectors and concentration in space.

While the distribution of costs and benefits of particular policies does shape political dynamics, policy issues do not arise in a vacuum but in a field structured by previous historical experiences, including ongoing policies in the sphere under consideration, which can be accounted for by way of path dependency. Contemporary American policy making takes place within the context of a prevailing worldwide restrictive immigration régime, which has to be explicitly accounted for. Another matter is that although Freeman speaks of "immigration policy" as of a piece, this ignores an important institutional reality, whereby all states today distinguish between "refugees" and "ordinary" immigrants, and in effect also between "settlers" and "workers." Accordingly, rather than a single overall dynamic, we should expect different processes to prevail in each of these policy areas.

Within the sphere of political economy alone, there is considerable variation in how the principal class actors are organized, and this in turn makes for major differences in the process and substance of policy: strong or weak labor unions, industrial or craft organization, the presence or absence of "peak associations" among workers and employers, and corporatist "social compacts" or unruly pluralism.[46] These structures account for not only variation in political dynamics, but also some variations in policy—such as the organization of formal guest worker programs in the more corporatist European countries (Germany, the Low Countries, and Sweden) as against employer-driven programs, often involving processes of marginal legality where unions do not participate in the making of industrial policy (France and the United States).

This is applicable to the "identity" dimension as well. For example, the ethnic organizations established by earlier immigrants in the United States achieved a degree of legitimacy as political interlocutors beyond what might be expected on the basis of their electoral weight, forming in the cultural sphere an equivalent of the "corporatism" that is sometimes encountered in Europe within the political economy sector, but is absent in the United States. Newer ethnic groups benefited in the 1970s from the technical and financial assistance of charitable organizations, notably the Ford Foundation, in organizing themselves along established lines, a development that distinctively shaped the subsequent dynamics of immigration politics (as detailed in Chapters 9 and 10). The standing of these ethnic organizations as "clients" is thus not merely a function of the concentration of benefits fostered by immigration policy, as demonstrated by the fact that in Europe, they have not become clients despite a similar concentration of immigration policy benefits.[47]

Some of these problems are addressed in a recent study by Keith Fitzgerald, inspired by the "structuration" approach of Anthony Giddens. Fitzgerald views the policy-making process as "episodic," with innovation commonly arising from improvised solutions to pressing problems.[48] The work is founded on a disaggregation of immigration policy into three segments, dealing respectively with permanent residents ("front-gate immigration"), refugees, and unsanctioned migrant laborers ("back-door immigration"), which display distinct policy dynamics that can be accounted for by contending theories of policy formation. Whereas policy regarding the "front gate" is shaped by the relatively free play of competing societal interests (political science's traditional "pluralism"), refugee policy is shaped by "realism" (in which the state looms as a major agent pursuing interests of its own), and "back-door" policy comes close to fitting classical "class-conflict" theories. While the disaggregation of "immigration policy" into discrete components does capture an often ignored feature of reality, in fact, all three modes of policy formation occur in each of the components; for example, while refugee policy has been driven to a considerable extent by foreign policy considerations, "pluralist" elements have come into play as well, notably by way of ethnic constituency pressures for and against the award of refugee status to particular groups. Moreover, the weight of "realist" considerations in the policy-making process is not a constant, but fluctuates with the salience of security concerns, notably the emergence of the Cold War, its waning, and the advent of 9/11.[49]

Together, these insights into the possible effects of political institutions and processes impart an indispensable concreteness to the macroanalytic considerations arising from the interaction of the political economy and identity axes within the global perspective set forth earlier. Social theory and history are both vital instruments if we are to understand how, even as it rose to world paramountcy and asserted itself as the leading conservative state, the United States redesigned itself as the first nation to mirror humanity.

Although my work has been cast all along in an historical perspective, this is my first attempt at producing a major study that engages in a direct dialog with historians, and on a key American subject to boot. With regard to primary sources, I would like to acknowledge a special debt to Edith Abbott, whose compilations of original material pertaining to American immigration up to the 1920s which I discovered in the University of Chicago library longer ago than I care to recall, very much inspired me to launch the present venture and pointed to likely sources of information. I have also relied heavily on secondary sources from a wide range of disciplines, including historical monographs and social science analyses. If, in the course of doing so, I often assess these works critically in order to account for the selective use I make of them, it will be understood that this is done in a collegial spirit and in no way reduces my gratitude to fellow scholars.

2

From Empire to Republic

Intoning the litany composed for them by Thomas Jefferson, the Americans assembled at Philadelphia relentlessly enumerate the wrongdoings of the man beneath the crown: "He has refused his assent to laws. . . . He has forbidden his governors to pass laws. . . . He has refused to pass other laws. . . . He has called together legislative bodies at places unusual. . . . He has dissolved representative houses. . . . He has refused . . . others to be elected." But the seventh time around, there is a shift in phrasing, as if to enhance the hammering's effectiveness by relieving its monotony, with the substantive issue now stated up front: "He has endeavoured to prevent the Population of these States; for that purpose obstructing the Laws for Naturalization of Foreigners; refusing to pass others to encourage their migration hither, and raising the conditions of new Appropriations of Lands."[1] Not content with bringing the unruly colonies to heel now, King George is determined to limit their population so as to minimize their future. Taking up the challenge, the colonists are equally determined to replace the immigration policy fashioned for a European empire with one of their own making, designed to serve an expansive American republic.

Duly noted in accounts of the founding, but as a side issue, grievances regarding immigration and naturalization belong in the foreground because these matters were regarded by both British imperial authorities and the American leaders as key processes that shaped basic features of the colonies' existence: the size of their population, its composition, and the rules for membership in the body politic. Rather than isolated skirmishes, the confrontations over these issues were vital episodes in the larger war over sovereignty, and amounted to an epochal struggle over the structure or "design" of American society. The American colonies amounted to a congeries of disparate population fragments that had come into being as the intentional and unintentional by-products of migration policies tailored to the pursuit of imperial objectives; to fuse these elements into a unified society, and one that would provide the social underpinnings of a "republic," was an immensely ambitious task, which required, among other things, a fundamental modification of ongoing immigration policies and related practices.

With these matters hotly debated for several decades before 1776, it is evident that American immigration and citizenship policy was in the making well before the country's formal independence. The concerns expressed at the moment of independence adumbrate a lasting feature of the fledgling new republic, rooted in its peculiar colonial origins: although regulation of the movement of persons across a state's borders and access of aliens to citizenship by way of naturalization were recognized by contemporaneous legal and political thinkers as matters of import, in the United States they achieved unprecedented practical and theoretical prominence because foreign immigration—as against mere transfers within the empire—made a much greater contribution to its population than had ever occurred in any European nation, or than any political philosopher envisioned might take place in a constituted community.

The particulars voiced in the seventh charge pertain to the positive side of immigration policy, that is, the provision of incentives to attract desirable settlers.[2] Foremost among the instruments devised by the colonies for this purpose was the naturalization of foreigners on much easier terms than in Britain itself. The object of a perennial tug of war between the colonies and the metropole ever since the late seventeenth century, the issue was propelled to the top of the political agenda in 1773 when Britain abruptly forbade its governors to assent to any new colonial naturalization acts. In the increasingly charged political context, the disagreement widened into a confrontation over sovereignty, as well as between the traditional conception of subjecthood and an emerging notion of republican citizenship.

The king's refusal to pass other laws "to encourage their migration hither" probably refers to the disallowance of a North Carolina act of 1771, which provided a four-year tax exemption for new settlers who came directly from Europe. The third grievance, "raising the conditions of new appropriations of lands," was prompted by an Order in Council of 1773 and related instructions issued the following year that effectively prohibited westward migration into the territories recently conquered from France, which the Americans eyed as their own. The policy fell especially hard on land speculators, notably Benjamin Franklin and George Washington. The Americans' anger was further exacerbated by London's ongoing attempts to discourage or even prohibit altogether the transatlantic migration of valuable British subjects, treating the colonies as if they had already turned into foreign lands, and thereby contributing to a self-fulfilling prophecy.

The founders were also inflamed by Britain's obstruction of the negative side of immigration policy, that is, measures enacted by the colonies to deter undesirables, which they resented as denying them the right of any community to self-protection. Prominent among these were perennial enactments to prevent the landing of convicts, inaugurated by the general court of Virginia as early as 1670, as well as regulations designed to keep out paupers. Most recently, the government also disallowed prohibitions of the slave trade imposed by South Carolina (1760), New Jersey (1763), and Virginia (1772); although these actions were largely motivated by fears that an unduly large proportion of blacks to whites would jeopardize colonial security, the British stance made it possible for advocates of American liberty, notably Benjamin Franklin and Thomas Jefferson, to answer charges of hypocrisy by asserting that slavery was imposed upon them by England.[3]

Empire Building in a New World

In the course of a century and a half of rule, the British Empire's migration policies and practices contributed to the formation of heterogeneous social fragments that, when assembled into a new state, encompassed a vastly broader diversity of racial, linguistic, and religious groups than existed in any kingdom of Western Europe. In the sixteenth century, North America had an aboriginal population of 2 to 5 million, but this declined precipitously after European contact.[4] For the period as a whole, net immigration from Europe into the original United States is estimated at 501,000, including 155,000 in 1630–1700 and 346,000 in 1700–1780.[5] A mix of free settlers and bound servants, the migrants were drawn initially mostly from England, but later on largely from the Celtic countries that were being amalgamated into the United Kingdom. There were also sizeable flows from the Continent, notably German speakers from a variety of principalities of the southwestern region of the Holy Roman Empire, as well as Swiss cantons. A population of mostly Dutch origin was incorporated by way of conquest as well. Concurrently, from the mid-seventeenth century onward, some 400,000 slaves were imported into the area from Africa.

These developments reflected policies designed from 1600 onward when, after successfully containing the Spanish Empire in Europe, the ascending northern powers were in a position to challenge more openly its monopoly in America. As they engaged in their moves and countermoves on the gigantic New World chessboard, France and England faced the same conundrum: in the islands and mainland regions to which they gained access, land was available in unlimited quantity almost for the taking, but labor was extremely scarce. A model developed by economic historians suggests that under circumstances such as these, if aspiring settler-landlords were to obtain income beyond what they could produce with their own hands, the workers they used must be prevented from moving and be forced to work—that is, they must be bound in some fashion.[6] In the absence of bondage, colonization of free or very cheap land would lead to the emergence of family farms, with some commercial exchange to meet local needs. This alternative outcome was especially likely in French and British settlements because of the paramountcy of the nuclear family in northern European cultures and the low density of native populations.[7]

The objective of overseas ventures was of course not to launch family farms but to develop colonies proper, that is, establishments designed to produce and export commodities that could be neither produced in Europe nor acquired by trade.[8] The leading colonial crop, from the twelfth century onward, was sugar, whose production required frost-free land and the organization of large plantations, as was done in the Caribbean; on the North American mainland, it was initially tobacco, to which rice and indigo were added later on, and eventually cotton.[9] To minimize the loss of human capital by way of emigration, at a time when population was reckoned to be scarce and hence highly valuable, ideally production was to be carried out by a non-European labor force under the supervision of a small number of Europeans. However, because Indians could not be enslaved in sufficient numbers to resolve the labor problem, workers had to be imported in large quantities.[10] The process of importation in turn made bondage even more imperative than suggested by the model because the workers must be acquired, transported over long distances, and marketed upon arrival; consequently, control over them must be maintained for a considerable period to recoup the considerable costs involved, be they borne by middlemen or by the eventual employer. Regularization of the system required the provision of a legal apparatus establishing title to the workers as "property," as well as the organization of some sort of police to back up the employers' claims and to enforce the harsh discipline required to exact labor from the workers under such conditions. This entailed active involvement by the state.

Overall, the French and British plantation experiences in the Caribbean and in the southern mainland were remarkably similar, especially with regard to the policies devised to resolve the problem of labor procurement. In the first half of the seventeenth century, as the slave trade was still under firm Iberian control, the northern colonists had little choice but to draw their labor force mostly from their own European population; but as the strategic balance changed to their advantage, they were able to turn to Africa instead.

Mercantilist preferences to the contrary notwithstanding, family farm settlements did emerge within the British and French American Empires as well, and in adjacent regions: New England and Canada—the region of Nouvelle France that is now the Province of Quebec.[11] However, although both settlements were launched in the early seventeenth century, by the time Britain conquered Canada in 1763, the huge province's population numbered only 79,094, as against some 600,000 New Englanders, including 245,698 in Massachusetts alone.[12] Given nearly identical rates of natural increase of about 3 percent a year, the disparity is attributable almost entirely to the much smaller net migration from France to Canada, the more surprising as in the middle of the seventeenth century, France's population amounted to some 20 million, approximately four times that of England and Wales, and in the early eighteenth century was still more than twice as large as that of all of Great Britain and Ireland.[13]

Conditions in early seventeenth-century England fostered a unique solution to the colonial labor problem, as the country was perceptibly more densely populated than ever before in human memory, and probably in history.[14] Although English policy makers generally subscribed to Jean Bodin's mercantilist doctrine, "One should never fear that there may be too many subjects or too many citizens, considering that there is neither wealth nor power but of men," colonial promoters argued that the country was too densely populated and that additional territory was necessary to support the surplus.[15] During this period England also experienced a spurt of industrialization and commercialization that produced greater collective wealth; but because the rate of economic growth did not keep up with the population increase, there was a decline in real wages. The transformation of the economy was accompanied by a wave of enclosures that threw part of the rural population off the land at the very time it was increasing, propelling a large number of the rural unemployed or underemployed to the cities, much as in the contemporary Third World.[16]

Although such an economic configuration provided the makings of a classic emigration "push," at the time "there is no evidence whatever that as a class the 'surplus' inhabitants had any yearnings for a new and perilous existence in the colonies."[17] Moreover, even those willing to take a chance did not have the means to cover the high transportation and relocation costs, amounting to approximately half the total annual wages of an unskilled laborer or one-third those of a skilled colleague; and because wages were close to subsistence, it was in effect impossible to forgo work for the lengthy period involved. In this context, the development of a system permitting the massive transfer of labor from England to its colonies by turning servants into a commodity emerges as a major economic innovation, on a par with the fateful organization of the African slave trade along these lines two centuries earlier.[18] The importance of this factor is highlighted by a comparison with France, whose attempts to develop a similar system were much less successful.

In its first two decades of activity, the Virginia Company undertook various experiments to adapt existing legal devices binding servants and apprentices to their English masters for the longer periods required to recoup the costs of transportation to the colonies.[19] A successful formula eventually emerged, whereby the workers were bound for a number of years sufficient to repay the investment, and sold outright to the planters for the duration of their contracts; routinized by way of printed forms with blanks for specifying terms of service, the traffic in servants constituted "the backbone of the whole migratory movement" to the English plantations. After the system was launched, Virginia's white population climbed from 2,500 in 1630 to over 10,000 ten years later.[20] Although African slaves became available from Dutch interlopers, their purchase price was higher than for whites, and the supply not assured; since the Netherlands had access to African slaves from the outset, it stands to reason that it was in England that a market in transatlantic white labor became most thoroughly institutionalized.[21]

In the second half of the seventeenth century, the English population's disposition toward emigration and the relevant policies were reshaped by the epoch's political upheavals, as well as by the imperial ambitions of successive regimes. The spectacular development of sugar on Barbados, as well as more general foreign policy considerations, promoted the Commonwealth's "Western Design" that culminated in the conquest of Jamaica from Spain in

1655. Concurrently England also challenged Dutch commercial supremacy, including its control of the slave trade; the Royal Africa Company was founded in 1660, and four years later England expelled the Dutch from the North American mainland. As England's economic transformation proceeded apace, industrial monopolies were severely shaken and wage laborers became more mobile; barriers to internal trade were removed, commercialization extended further. While these changes enlarged the pool of potential emigrants, they also stimulated demand for labor at home. The real wage began to climb, and by the early eighteenth century surpassed its previous peak.[22]

Although economic and strategic considerations called for the sustained development of colonies, their unquenchable thirst for English labor now competed with home needs. An ingenious alternative would be to supply the colonies instead "with the undesirables, vagrants, convicts or people like the Quakers who were thought to be making a nuisance of themselves at home. That they could and should do with such was a comfortable notion that made great headway."[23] However, transportation, which was prohibited as a penalty in its own right under English common law, came into widespread use as a form of commutation for capital punishment, and eventually as an interme-diate penalty between capital punishment and lesser sanctions such as whip-ping and branding.[24] The pool of candidates for transportation expanded rap-idly, as conditions fostered a growing number of displaced poor, whose efforts to survive by poaching and the like prompted enactment of a torrent of dra-conian "black laws" to protect the country's steadily privatized patrimony.[25] Urbanization also fostered the professionalization of crime. Penal transpor-tation was generalized in England around 1655 and soon extended to Ireland as well. To the felons were added Royalist prisoners from the Civil War, many of whom were Scots, as well as Irish Catholics forcibly removed from northern and eastern Ireland, where they were replaced by politically reliable Scottish Presbyterians.

The suggestion of a concerted imperial scheme to redeploy populations in accordance with specific objectives is by no means gratuitous, as the notion that by transporting Irish rebels the English government might simultaneously destroy Catholicism in Ireland and satisfy labor hunger in the colonies was duly recorded at the time by England's Venetian secretary as a policy under active consideration.[26] After the Commonwealth gave way to the Restoration, a similar fate was meted out to Quakers, Scottish Covenanters, and other rebels.

Overall, net emigration from England and Wales in the seventeenth century may have reached 700,000, including a considerable flow to Ireland; the estimate to the New World (including some Scots) is 378,000 for 1630–1700.[27] In keeping with the government's desire, nearly 90 percent of them went to the plantation colonies, between one-half and two-thirds of them as bound labor; however, because of high mortality rates from the passage and "seasoning," and also because of the high proportion of males and some return migration at the end of service, as of 1700 there were only 35,500 whites in the Caribbean and another 86,400 in the South, less than one-third the number who went.[28] Only one-tenth of transatlantic migrants, some 39,000 altogether, ended up in the northern settlements. Promoters of the Plymouth Company, reconstituted in 1620 as the New England Council, failed to attract investors to an unpromising region; however, that same year, a settlement was launched within the company's charted zone by a group that included religious separatists who had immigrated to Holland in 1608. Unable to overcome Dutch guild restrictions and fearing a resumption of war with Spain, the refugees obtained royal approval to lease land within the company's borders and then bought out the other investors. In the intervening years, another group of dissenters secured a patent for the adjacent territory to the north.

Within the framework of mercantilism, these settlements constituted "anticolonies" that developed along the alternative path resulting in the family farm outcome. "Considerably less than half" of the initial immigrants were indentured servants, and unlike in the plantation colonies, they did not function as specialized agro-industrial field hands but rather performed a multitude of tasks as members of the household economy, much as farm servants in Britain itself.[29] The distinctiveness of these settlements emerged very early on, and in turn shaped subsequent immigration by effecting a selection within the growing pool in England. Although the emigrants included few prosperous yeomen, there were almost no laborers; some 20 percent were "husbandmen," and many others craftsmen or small tradesmen, warranting overall description as members of the "middling classes" of English society.[30] In the 1630s, the Stuart regime's High Church policies together with economic maladjustment in the eastern counties fostered an emigration "epidemic" of over 15,000 people. Consequently, as early as 1640, New England's population of nearly 14,000 exceeded the 11,000 of the Chesapeake region.[31]

In contrast with the outflow to the plantation colonies, the British authorities viewed this emigration as a problem rather than as a solution.[32] The departure of moderately prosperous craftsmen, artisans, and farmers was contrary to economic sense because it simultaneously created a shortage of valuable human capital at home and provided the makings of a competitive economy abroad. There was also a danger in allowing the emergence of a "factious centre" with affinities to the Netherlands, which, albeit a fellow Protestant state, was England's commercial and colonial rival. Accordingly, a new law was enacted in 1637 to impose an oath of religious orthodoxy on all those planning to leave for America. Nevertheless, over the remainder of the century, some 25,000 additional emigrants moved to New England, including many religious dissenters. Although this was a small number in relation to emigration generally, their visibility was magnified by their relatively high social standing. The most likely explanation for the drain is that the state lacked the capacity or the will to extinguish the flow altogether: "In practice, the regulations were softened by the human frailty of the men entrusted with enforcement and by the ingenuity of those bent on invasion."[33] But it is also possible that the authorities remained somewhat ambivalent: after all, it was better for dissenters to go to New England than to make trouble at home or move to the Netherlands.[34] Thanks to a much healthier climate, there was little or no loss from seasoning; the sex ratio was more even; and because the availability of land and subsistence fostered early marriages, fertility was much higher than in Europe. Consequently, by 1700, the white population of Britain's northern mainland colonies (including Newfoundland) had grown to 135,100.

Religious dissenters were generally kept out of the colonies because of their putatively doubtful loyalty in relation to foreign powers that shared their religious orientation; this is why France prohibited the settlement of Huguenots in northern America and why England was equally determined to keep out its own Catholics from strategically vulnerable regions.[35] However, from the same strategic perspective, the Puritans were an asset rather than a liability because the religious radicalism that rendered them unbearable at home insured they would constitute a reliable outpost against the Catholic French. This rationale was applicable also to Quakers and to Scottish Presbyterians, who were even then being resettled in Ulster to bring the native Irish to heel.

As the century wore on, England's steadily growing naval supremacy opened the way to a more rational approach to colonization, which largely resolved perennial concerns over emigration. The turning point was the organization of the Royal African Company, which with the backing of the Royal Navy put an end to Dutch hegemony over the slave trade, and secured for Britain direct access to the African source. The availability of slaves quickly altered the balance of costs between African and European labor; by the same token, the metropole henceforth competed more effectively with the planta-tions for servants and apprentices.[36] In the southern mainland colonies, for example, the relative price of servants in relation to slaves went up by 57 percent between 1675 and 1690; the flow of white servants peaked in the 1660s and declined in the last two decades of the century, while the proportion of blacks rose rapidly from 5 percent of the population in 1660 to 21 percent in 1700. On this basis, one of the "new" economic historians has argued that the issue of labor supply largely resolved itself through the operations of the labor market.[37] To be sure; but it was a market whose "commodities" came into being thanks to forceful state intervention at the international level, and its collusion in the monstrous transformation of the common law into an instrument for securing total ownership of one human being by another.[38] And as the Caribbean colonies turned into increasingly efficient agro-industrial producers, the Puritan family farmers turned into Yankee commer-cial entrepreneurs, whose success was founded on the production of provi-sions for feeding the slaves and their supervisors.

Eager for additional settlers to open up the new inland territories at their disposal, British colonial promoters followed the Dutch and Swedish lead in exploring the possibility of enlisting German Protestants. Faced with general devastation at the end of the Thirty Years War (1648), some of the German-speaking mini-states—including Swiss cantons and principalities of the Holy Roman Empire—had sought to establish colonies of their own; however, be-cause opportunities for doing so in North America were rapidly foreclosed by Anglo-French dominance, their rulers accepted Dutch and Swedish offers of settlement.[39] After a bloodless conquest, in 1674 Britain gained permanent control over New Netherlands, whose population, including Dutch, French-speaking Walloon Huguenots and other North Sea Europeans from as far afield as Norway, was quickly anglicized.[40] Following in the wake of these developments, William Penn's visit to Germany in 1677 stimulated the cre-ation of an officially approved Frankfurt Emigration Society, which organized the departure of fifty emigrant ships in 1682–1684.[41] Anglo-Dutch entrepre-neurs based in Rotterdam, and familiar with the British market for servants, quickly took up the opportunity to convey Germans to their overseas desti-nations and eagerly promoted additional business.[42]

The recruitment of non-British subjects as servants was one thing; but for-eigners of greater substance would not come and invest without assurance that their property would be secure. This required action to eliminate their alienage, because under the common law, upon the death of an alien his property escheated to the Crown—or alternatively, in the colonies, to the proprietor or the charter government. The traditional solution in England was naturalization; but this could be accorded only by Parliament, which jealously guarded its authority so as to deter foreign immigration to England, feared as a threat to "the maintenance of its peculiar institutions in church and state and . . . the purity of the English race."[43] At best, the process was lengthy and expensive, and Catholics as well as Jews (until 1753) and other non-Christians were excluded by requirements of Protestant communion and oath to the Crown.[44] A lesser alternative was "denizenship," a more limited form of incorporation restricted to economic rights, notably to own land and to trade, which could be granted by royal prerogative; this was occasionally extended to Jewish traders for purposes of colonial development.

Since colonial charters customarily permitted the grantees to transport to America strangers not otherwise prohibited, local authorities subsequently assumed that these clauses empowered them to extend to such strangers the rights of subjects, at least within their own jurisdiction. Usually granted on an individual basis, colonial endenization or naturalization—the precise legal standing of these distinct practices was ambiguous—was sometimes extended to groups as well, and usually on more permissive terms than in England. Colonial legislation generally did not impose any residence requirement; and although they required that the applicants be free, so that the indentured were excluded for the length of their term, costs were within the reach of "those possessed of small means."[45] Although for the most part no oath to the Anglican Church was mandated, and rights were occasionally extended to alien Jews, Roman Catholics were almost universally excluded.[46] Initially, the British government appeared content to let sleeping dogs lie; but toward the end of the century, it was spurred to action by a concern that foreigners were encroaching upon British trade. Accordingly, in 1700 London issued an order-in-council that effectively blocked the granting of rights to groups and strictly limited the domain of the rights granted to individuals to particular colonies.

The Antinomies of Perfected Mercantilism

As the European states continued their rise to world hegemony, Britain fashioned itself into the dominant sea power while France battled its way to paramountcy on the Continent, turning into Leviathan and Behemoth, locked in a struggle to the death. In keeping with the tenets of mercantilism, the plantation colonies now vastly increased their slave imports while reducing their intake of white labor.[47] Concurrently, immigration from the colonizing nations proper declined substantially from the levels achieved in the middle part of the previous century.[48] In their island colonies, Britain achieved a ratio of slave imports to white immigration of nearly 10:1, France of over 30:1.[49] From a mercantilist perspective, the latter was as close as anyone had yet come to perfection; but hindsight makes us aware that such an extreme ratio invited disaster.

The white population of the future United States exploded from 223,100 in 1700 to 2,205,000 in 1780, with most of this tenfold increase attributable to an amazingly high rate of natural reproduction. The most carefully wrought estimate records a net migration of 336,800, of which over one-third was concentrated in the decade and half preceding the revolution.[50] Less than one-fourth of the newcomers were English; of the remainder, the leading groups were Scotch-Irish Ulstermen and Germans, followed by Scots proper, imparting to American society a precocious multiculturalism. The traditional explanation for the decline of English immigration is a weakening of the economic push.[51] Although this played a role, matters were not left to market forces alone: officials in effect regulated the English servant trade out of existence, as a consequence of which recruitment shifted to Ireland, Scotland, and foreign lands—so long as they were not Roman Catholics.[52]

A new labor system was devised for this purpose. In contrast with the mostly single and largely destitute servants, it involved families that borrowed part of the costs of their emigration on the security of a pledge of service. Upon landing, these "redemptioners," also called "free-willers," were given an opportunity to obtain the wherewithal to redeem the pledge from relatives or friends before being sold to an employer. Later on, mutual aid societies arose for this purpose as well.[53]

As noted earlier, eighteenth-century English migrants included a substantial number of convicts. Already a penalty under Scottish law, transportation was legalized in England in 1718 and subsequently emerged as the foremost punishment for Britain as a whole.[54] Repeatedly promoted as the "most humane and effectual punishment" in the British arsenal, and the only one that afforded the prospect of rehabilitation by way of exposure to a new environment, "It afforded a means of removing threatening offenders from the social mainstream, and without heavy reliance upon either the death penalty or imprisonment, thereby avoiding not only a bloodbath but the creation of a massive corrections system and a coercive force to staff it."[55] It was also a highly lucrative business: as numbers grew, government sold the convicts at a cheap price to entrepreneurs in the servant trade, who marketed them at a hefty profit to overseas employers, often without identifying their provenance. Whereas some American merchants profited, many employers quickly discovered they had gotten a bad bargain. Altogether, transportation added some 50,000 immigrants to the American colonial population in the decades prior to the Revolution, many of them hardened criminals rather than merely offending poor. Hence, it is no wonder that convicts emerged early on as a key issue in American immigration policy.

Although there had been a trickle of immigration to the mainland colonies from Ireland in the second half of the seventeenth century, large-scale movement began only in 1717–1718 with a first great wave from Ulster.[56] Ulstermen remained at the forefront for the remainder of the prerevolutionary period, accounting for 200,000 of the 280,000 Irish newcomers in 1700–1776; the remainder was divided about equally between Anglicans, many of them of English origin, and Catholics from the island as a whole.[57] Albeit organized by Presbyterian ministers, the initial exodus from Ulster was induced primarily by economic necessity rather than religious disabilities. Its immediate cause was the expiration of leases that had been granted on easy terms as an inducement to Protestant immigrants from Scotland so as to reduce the province's native Roman Catholic population to a minority. The Ulster Scots, who came to be known in America as "Scotch-Irish," now had to compete with Catholics for leases on the open market; but whereas the latter, confined to Ireland by imperial and colonial policies, had no choice but to settle for higher rents, the Presbyterians had the alternative of exit.[58] As the pool of potential emigrants grew following successive catastrophic harvests, more sought to leave; and since few could pay their own fares or go as redemptioners, Ulster moved to the fore as a major source of supply for the servant trade. Because Scotch-Irish immigrants were resented by New Englanders on both religious and economic grounds, the movement flowed mostly to Pennsylvania. The outbreak of a depression in the linen industry combined with an acute agrarian crisis induced another and yet larger wave of departures in the early 1770s. Given their vociferous anti-Catholicism and their frontier experience, the unruly Scotch-Irish could be turned into a reliable asset in the perennial confrontation with France.

By and large, Catholics remained excluded from the mainland colonies. Following the accession of William and Mary, the penal laws that deterred Catholics from acquiring real property and kept them out of the liberal professions were enforced with renewed vigor on both sides of the Atlantic; and the exclusion of Catholicism from the public realm, which meant in effect no churches and no clergy, in turn deterred colonial emigration by Catholics who had a choice in the matter.[59] On this the colonists saw eye to eye with the metropole, sometimes outdoing London in their enforcement zeal.[60] Although in the first three-quarters of the century some 10,000 Irish Catholics were transported to the American colonies as convicts, and an equivalent number landed within the flow from Ulster, overall the conjunction of British and colonial exclusionary policies proved remarkably effective. According to a survey undertaken shortly after independence by the American Republic's first Catholic bishop, his flock amounted to some 25,000 souls, about 1 percent of the white population, mostly poor southern Irish, small groups of Palatine Germans interspersed with Protestants from the same region, and a few hundred French-speaking refugees from Acadia.[61] Although a few individuals achieved prominence, including one as a signer of the Declaration of Independence, as a dispersed and still suspect minority Catholics did not figure as a significant component in the new nation.

Contrary to the British government's expressed preferences, English emigration rose again in the 1760s, when the combination of a new spurt of population growth, the accelerating tempo of enclosures, and a sharp drop of real wages generated a social crisis of unprecedented strength.[62] This was channeled into emigration because the North American colonies were no longer a wilderness but constituted thriving extensions of European society, with which there were now well-established linkages. The greatest of the colonial era, it adumbrated the emergence of a new pattern of transatlantic movement, "a shift to a more mobile, more skilled pool of people exercising some real choice."[63] The crossing to America was often the second stage of a migration that began with a move to London, much as occurs in the contemporary developing world.[64] With the massive departures of the second half of the seventeenth century long forgotten, the wave was further magnified in British eyes as unprecedented.

By providing the alternative of exit, the American colonies threatened to wreak havoc with the social discipline required by the imperatives arising from the new political economy. In a telling incident, in 1773, when the Scottish authorities undertook to prosecute the leaders of a strike in Paisley for unlawful combination, several thousands of the workers threatened to go off as a body to America.[65] Hence the emigration wave prompted the British state to devise more effective deterrents, and this in turn provoked the colonies further. The government's counteractions included the disallowance of the

North Carolina tax exemption for new settlers from Europe noted at the beginning of this chapter, which prompted the final portion of the seventh charge, added in Philadelphia. Fiscal concessions of this sort were among the earliest incentives enacted by the colonial legislatures to encourage immigration, along with land grants, cash bounties, and moratoriums on debt.[66] Beyond this, the government imposed explicit restrictions on emigration toward its own colonies, much as if they were already foreign states, with its concern spelled out disingenuously in the preamble to one proposal: "[T]he great increase of people in the . . . colonies has an immediate tendency to produce independency."[67]

European responses to Britain's attempts to recruit foreign immigrants and to the pull of opportunities generated by spreading information about its developing colonies were in keeping with the tenets of mercantilism. Enlisting the support of churches, the authorities in the most affected regions resorted to a combination of moral exhortation and legal barriers.[68] However, under catastrophic conditions such as prevailed in parts of the Holy Roman Empire, emigration might be envisioned as a solution rather than as a problem.[69] Altogether, between 1683 and 1783, about half a million German speakers left their homes for Hungary, Russia, and to a lesser extent Spain and France, as well as overseas British and French colonies. Although at the most 115,000 (less than one-fourth of the emigrant mass) landed in British North America, they constituted the colonies' largest and most distinctive foreign white community. The bulk settled in Pennsylvania, where the population of German-speaking ancestry accounted for 50–60 percent of the total in 1760, and 33 percent still in 1790.[70] German immigration was significantly more family oriented than its British counterparts, and although roughly half of each stream entered servitude upon arrival, the Germans did so mostly as redemptioners. Somewhat older and more skilled than British immigrants, the Germans were highly literate, as indicated by the fact that for the 1727–1775 period as a whole, 71 percent could sign the loyalty oath required of them upon landing, and by the end approached universal literacy.[71]

The incorporation of aliens remained problematic throughout the eighteenth century. Legally the issue was shaped by Parliament's claim to exclusive jurisdiction, which was confirmed by Edward Coke and William Blackstone; politically, by English hypernationalism, championed by the Tories. In 1709 the Whigs finally won their campaign for a general naturalization law, designed on behalf of Huguenot victims of Louis XIV's persecutions; but because this amounted to the proclamation of a more permissive immigration policy, which quickly attracted over 10,000 poor Palatines, the Tories repealed the law after they returned to power in 1710. Although as early as 1700, William Penn advocated a general naturalization law designed specifically for the colonies, Parliament failed to act. Meanwhile the colonies continued to grant local naturalization and "endenization." By the first third of the eighteenth century, this was used on a considerable scale everywhere except in New England, which struggled successfully to retain its English homogeneity.[72]

In 1740, Parliament enacted a general naturalization law covering the American colonies. Designed as an incentive to foreign settlement, the measure reflected the government's immigrationist stance, consistent with mercantilist principles: "[T]he increase of People is a Means of advancing the Wealth and Strength of any Nation or Country: And . . . many Foreigners and Strangers, from the Lenity of our Government, the Purity of our Religion, the Benefit of our Laws, the Advantages of our Trade, and the Security of our Property, might be induced to come and settle in his Majesty's Colonies, if they were made Partakers of the Advantages and Privileges which the natural born Subjects of this Realm do enjoy."[73] The law provided for naturalization without legislative action after seven years' residence; it required an oath of allegiance, a profession of Christian belief, and the sacramental test; however, reflecting colonial practice, Quakers and Jews were exempt, as were some other marginal Protestant sects.[74] The procedure was inexpensive and administratively simple. Parliament not only maintained the law in the face of restrictionist pressures, but in response to the exigencies of war, in 1761 it also extended naturalization to foreigners who were commissioned as officers in colonial regiments.

Nevertheless, in their efforts to entice entrepreneurs, most of the colonies continued to incorporate foreigners more swiftly by way of private measures and evaded the prohibition on group naturalization by playing fast and loose with the trade privileges inherent in British nationality. In 1759, for example, Pennsylvania enacted a statute providing that aliens who had died without going through naturalization processes were not liable to escheat.[75] Driven by competition among the colonies to attract desirable settlers by offering them favorable terms for acquiring land and trading, "The tendency toward generous naturalization policies . . . resulted in systematic deviations from English patterns that carried significant theoretical implications."[76] Although these were not articulated until the 1760s, the practices themselves softened the boundary separating ancestral members of the "English race" from adopted newcomers and thereby also adumbrated changing notions of membership.

American Perspectives

Driven as much by the dynamics of state formation in a conflictual international system as by their determination to prevent the colonists from encroaching on metropolitan interests, in the middle decades of eighteenth century the imperial authorities ventured beyond the traditional limits of parliamentary power to introduce "government in depth."[77] Within the established legislative framework, the crown naturally held the upper hand; unable to defend their interests, the colonists challenged the framework itself by invoking more general principles that established the legitimacy of their position. In the sphere of "migration and population," as in many others, the confusing jumble of contending concerns and interests that hitherto shaped policy preferences on both sides of the Atlantic was drastically simplified. Sharing a common understanding of the relevant social mechanisms, the London government and the colonial leadership elaborated mirror-opposite positions. Reframed in this manner, the debate over immigration inexorably evolved into a climactic dispute over sovereignty.

Both sides had similar notions regarding what sorts of people were desirable and undesirable; but whereas Britain was intent on ridding itself of convicts and paupers while seeking to retain the conforming and productive, the colonists were equally adamant to keep out the first and attract the second. Both sides shared a mercantilist understanding of population as the major source of wealth and power; but whereas this led Britain to try to keep the colonial population within bounds, it prompted the Americans to maximize their numbers by all possible means. Beyond this, from the perspective of Britain, the colonies were essentially economic undertakings, whose social, racial, or national makeup did not matter unless it occasioned problems of economic management or of external security. In keeping with Roman imperial tradition, diversity might even facilitate rule by dividing the colonists. But from the vantage point of the Americans, the colonies were communities in the making, whose heterogeneous composition might be a source of conflict and possibly lead to disintegration, the more so if they were assembled into a single political entity.

Britain's Refuse

The most evident undesirables were convicts. Despite the participation of American shippers and labor brokers in the profitable convict trade, their growing numbers were widely deplored and perennially evoked restrictive legislation. As early as 1751, Benjamin Franklin seized upon the popular issue of convicts to mobilize support for broader political demands. Recounting reports of horrendous crimes perpetrated by transported felons in various colonies, he sighs in the *Pennsylvania Gazette,* "What will become of our Posterity!"[78] Starting from the basic charge that the transportation of convicts is a source of growing criminality, he quickly escalates to the highest political plane: "Thou art called our MOTHER COUNTRY; but what good *Mother* ever sent *Thieves* and *Villains* to accompany her *Children;* to corrupt some with their infectious Vices, and murder the rest?" Strikingly anticipating Tom Paine's indictment of the king a quarter of a century later, Franklin levels a radical charge: England's transgression is tantamount to infanticide, and by killing her child, she disqualifies herself as a mother.[79] However, he is aware that matters are not one-sided, and adds that the blame must be shared by "those Merchants, who for the sake of a little paltry Gain, will be concern'd in importing and disposing of these abominable Cargoes."

In the same year, Franklin published a seminal essay on population, discussed shortly, which provided a framework used by other American thinkers of the revolutionary period in dealing with the subject and inspired Thomas Malthus. With demography evidently on the mind, he concludes his diatribe by linking transportation to the broader matter of population growth: "What must we think of that B———d, which had advis'd the Repeal of every Law we have hitherto made to prevent this Deluge of Wickedness overwhelming us; and with this *cruel* Sarcasm, *'That these Laws were against the* Publick Utility, *for they tended to prevent the* IMPROVEMENT *and* WELL-PEOPLING *of the Colonies!'* "

On this occasion, Franklin crafts two additional tropes that he would recycle over the next four decades along with the "evil mother." First, "We do not ask Fish, but thou givest us *Serpents,* and worse than Serpents!" The felons themselves are not to blame, because like venomous snakes, they behave in keeping with their unchanging nature. Switching registers to a coarse pun, he then asks, "In what can *Britain* show a more Sovereign contempt for us, than by emptying their *Jails* into our Settlements; unless they would likewise empty their *Jakes* on our Tables?" Later that year, he elaborates the serpent trope into a sarcastic suggestion. Feigning to concede that the American habit of killing rattlesnakes, "Felons-convict from the Beginning of the World," may be too cruel, he proposes "that this general Sentence of *Death* be changed for *Transportation.*"[80] Pretending also to accept the reformist rationalizations advanced on behalf of transportation to the colonies—"However mischievous those Creatures are with us, they may possibly change their Natures, if they were to change the Climate"—he concludes logically that the intractable reptiles should be sent to England for redemption.

Referring again to convicts in "A Defense of the Americans," written in 1759 under the guise of a letter from "A New Englandman" to the Printer of the London *Chronicle*, addressed in Franklin's colonial bumpkin persona as "Mr. Chronicle," he again insists on their unchanging nature but goes one step further, linking poverty and crime as two facets of the same defective makeup: "[T]he same indolence of temper and habits of idelness that make people poor and tempt them to steal in *England,* continue with them when they are sent to *America,* and must there have the same effects."[81] Hence, instances of redemption "are extreamly rare, if there *really* is a single instance of it . . . but of their being advanc'd there to the gallows the instances are plenty. Might they not as well have been hang'd at home?" Then, citing "a writer of that country" (his own words of 1751), comes the evil mother/toilet joke, once again. Seven years later (1766), following a parliamentary vote for extending the transportation system to Scotland—which eventually became law—the now London-based Franklin issues a "mock petition to the House of Commons" urging the repeal of all acts pertaining to transportation, or alternatively "that then the said Extension may be carried farther, and the Plantations be also by an equitable Clause in the same Bill permitted to transport their Felons to Scotland."[82]

By this time, from Britain's perspective, the problem of disposing of its proliferating convicts in the face of colonial opposition was no minor matter. In 1768, Captain James Cook was sent out by the Admiralty to explore the South Seas. Eventually he landed at what he initially thought of calling Stingray Harbor, but baptized Botany Bay instead to honor the achievements of the *Endeavour*'s gifted naturalists. In addition to their remarkable botanical observations, they also reported on social conditions, and their assessment that the aboriginal population would give no trouble proved decisive when the American colonists' triumph made it imperative to find an alternative dump for the United Kingdom's human refuse.[83]

On the scale of undesirability, "paupers" were a close second to felons. The distinction between the two categories was blurred, as British penal legislation was largely directed against the poor, and poverty itself was increasingly attributed to deficient moral character; sharing in their refusal to bow to prevailing social disciplines, paupers and felons simultaneously corrupted society and occasioned considerable public expense. With a precocious diagnosis of "welfare dependency" based on conveniently selected evidence, Poor Richard launches the first assault in the protracted American war on immigrants deemed unwilling to support themselves, and against the welfare state more generally. In the course of a transatlantic exchange on the subject of support for the poor, Franklin observes that whereas higher wages induce a decrease of industry among English immigrant workers, this does not hold for Germans—a rare instance in which the Germans, whom he usually badmouths, come out on top. As a good experimentalist, he reasons that since the two share a common ancestry and live in the same climate, the difference "must arise from Institution."[84] His prime candidates are the English Poor Laws, which he thinks might induce among the poor "a Dependance that very much lessens the care of providing against the wants of old Age." In further support of this inference, Franklin points out that on the Continent, the poor in Protestant countries are more industrious than those in Catholic countries, which have more numerous relief foundations, and he concludes by welcoming the new English practice of employing the poor in workhouses erected for that purpose.

Members of the lower classes who are lame, impotent, and infirm—a substantial proportion of populations at the time—were deemed undesirable as well because they constituted a burden to society, and in an age of devastating epidemics, the sick were genuinely dangerous. Since under the prevailing rudimentary regulatory regime it was almost impossible to inspect individuals and hold them accountable, colonial legislatures and port-of-entry bodies sought to deter their entry by imposing head taxes and security bonds, to be paid by shippers or prospective employers, and whose proceeds were sometimes used for the support of charitable institutions. However, these securities were systematically disallowed by London with regard to British subjects; and the colonists were often frustrated in their attempts to impose restrictions and conditions on foreigners as well.[85]

Population and Freedom to Leave

In 1716, evidence of a rapid increase in the number of Americans, derived from more reliable colonial censuses, was hailed by the Board of Trade as a vindication of Britain's colonial policy, and it recommended that this expansion be further encouraged; but after the board reported in 1755 that the mainland colonies had passed the 1 million mark, "Englishmen began to look at the colonial censuses and wonder if there might not be too many Americans."[86] In this light, Franklin's 1751 essay, *Observations Concerning the Increase of Mankind, Peopling of Countries, etc.,* can be read as a triumphant proclamation of America's dawning strength, and hence as a validation of its claim to westward expansion as well as to a distinctive place in the sun.[87] It is also a remarkable pioneering work of demography, viewing human population as subject to natural principles that govern the lives of animals and plants. In the Enlightenment vein, the essay's scientific demonstration was also harnessed to political contention. It begins with a scientific argument on behalf of statistics and appropriate rules of inference, which is immediately transformed into a political argument by using it to demonstrate American society's distinctiveness: differing from Europe in its nature, America warrants different laws as well. Because land is plentiful and cheap in America, marriages "are more general, and more generally early than in *Europe.*" Marriages that start earlier are also more fruitful. Given unions at twenty years of age and eight children, of whom half survive, "our People must at least be doubled every 20 years." This dramatic projection of the North American colonies' spectacular rate of population growth, unprecedented in European historical experience to date, proved broadly correct.

Franklin then turns to the implications of this growth for relations between the colonies and the Mother Country. Setting forth a precocious version of the "free land" model, he points out that despite this high rate of growth, labor remains scarce and dear because the availability of land provides to workers the alternative of family farms. This makes it impossible for the colonies to compete successfully with the Mother Country's manufactures. Franklin also denies that slaves make the colonies more competitive because they are expensive, and the rationale for their purchase arises only from the near impossibility of hanging on to white workers, who have the alternative of family farms. He finally comes to immigration proper. Reviewing conditions that depress population growth—in this pre-Malthus age, still dreaded as a catastrophic turn of events—he mentions among other things bad government and insecure property, the introduction of slaves (which induced a reduction in the number of whites in the English Sugar Islands), and then this: "The Importation of Foreigners into a Country that has as many Inhabitants as the present Employments and Provisions for Subsistence will bear; will be in the End no Increase of People; unless the New Comers have more Industry and Frugality than the Natives, and then they will provide more Subsistence, and increase in the Country." However, in that case there is a danger that the proliferating foreigners "will gradually eat the Natives out."[88]

As Franklin's readers undoubtedly noted, he specifies as a condition for this proposition that the receiving country "has as many inhabitants as the present Employments and Provisions for Subsistence will bear." Given his statement regarding the abundance of land, it is evident that this is not the case in the American colonies. However, he makes his own preferences quite clear: it is not necessary to bring in foreigners to fill up a temporary "vacancy" of population—such as might be occasioned by war, expulsion, immigration to the colonies, or the export of slaves—for if the laws are good, such vacancy "will soon be filled by natural Generation."[89] This anti-immigrationist argument would be restated almost literally by Jefferson three decades later.

In his conclusion, Franklin returns to natural laws, asserting that "there is in short, no Bound to the prolific Nature of Plants or Animals, but what is made by their crowding and interfering with each others Means of Subsistence." Much as in the absence of other plants, the earth might be gradually sowed and overspread with one kind only—we are still in the pre-evolutionary age as well—so "were it empty of other Inhabitants, it might in a few Ages be replenish'd from one Nation only; as for Instance, with *Englishmen*." England's population has already more than made up for colonial emigration, and in another century the colonial population will exceed England's, bringing immense new power to the British Empire. Despite the implicit assumption that the growing colonies will remain within the empire, the vision of a Britain overshadowed by its overseas offshoots could hardly be comforting to readers on the other side of the Atlantic.

For this glowing prospect to be realized, the conditions leading to colonial population growth must be met. This brings us back to current political issues: "How important an Affair then to *Britain,* is the present Treaty for settling the Bounds between her Colonies and the *French,* and how careful should she be to secure Room enough, since on the Room depends so much the Increase of her People."[90] But the Treaty of Aix-la-Chapelle signed in 1748 was inconclusive, and the year after Franklin penned these words the French responded to the westward movement of American traders by attacking their outposts and killing their defenders, prompting the lieutenant-governor of Virginia to dispatch young George Washington to protest their actions.

Commenting on news of an impending measure to impose restrictions on immigration to Britain's own colonies, Franklin asks in November 1773 why this is thought to be necessary now. One possibility is suggested by an item from a Scottish paper, reporting that 1,500 people emigrated from the Shire of Sutherland in the past two years, carrying with them £7,500, "which exceeds a Year's Rent of the whole Country," and urging that the sufferings the immigrants experience in America not only make this a matter of concern to the landed interest, but also warrant prohibitive action by the government in the name of the public interest.[91] Starting with the sarcastic response that the "humane Writer" might console himself with the knowledge that the misery in question is imaginary, for the emigrants undoubtedly made their decision on the basis of sound knowledge by comparing their situation at home with reliable accounts sent them by relations in America, Franklin goes on to assert, "If the poor Folks are happier at home than they can be abroad, they will not be lightly prevailed with to cross the Ocean."[92] This rational conceptualization of migration as arising from the decisions made by individuals in the light of information regarding conditions at the place of origin and at some putative destination constitutes the corner stone of contemporary social scientific theories of migration.[93] By the same token, those who shared Franklin's understanding expected that laissez-faire with regard to exit would be of benefit to the Americans.

He then considers in turn the necessity, the practicability, the policy (that is, the advisability), and the justice of the proposed law:

1. The law is unnecessary because population tends toward equilibrium: "If any Country has more People than can be comfortably subsisted in it, some of those who are incommoded, may be induced to emigrate." Note the strikingly modern assumption that it is possible to emigrate! However, as numbers dwindle—Franklin here contradicts his earlier contention that emigration does not occasion a reduction of population—competition for subsistence decreases; people are likely to stay home, even if they would not be as well off as if they migrate, because "the inbred Attachment to a native Country is sufficient to overbalance a moderate Difference." Eventually, the flowing of people brings about a leveling of conditions in various countries; "and where that Level is once found, the Removals cease." These dynamics have operated in all ages, "or we should not now have had so many Nations." Concomitantly, to call for a law to stop them "is calling for a Law to stop the Thames, lest its Waters, by what leave it daily at Gravesend, should be quite exhausted."
2. The law is impracticable because the state lacks the capacity to guard the entire coast, as would be required to turn Britain into a prison.
3. The law is inadvisable because, in keeping with Franklin's theory of population dynamics, immigration brings about an increase of the co-

lonial population, and thereby strengthens the empire as a whole—he still assumes, at least publicly, that the angry Americans will remain within it. Such national advantages more than balance "the Inconveniencies suffered by a few Scotch or Irish Landlords."

When he comes to justice, however, Franklin shifts abruptly from a mercantilist argument regarding population to the very different issue of the right of human beings to leave their country. As is evident from the context, the issue arose from sheer interest, the American desire to maximize the most desirable immigration. However, as is his wont, Franklin seizes the opportunity to move into the realm of high politics:

4. Beginning with a radical assertion of the right of expatriation, founded on the relativity of a subject's obligation to his sovereign—"I apprehend that every Briton who is made unhappy at home, has a Right to remove from any Part of his King's Dominions into those of any other Prince where he can be happier"—he immediately backtracks to less challenging ground: "If this should be denied me, at least it will be allowed that he has a Right to remove into any other Part of the same Dominions." The right of expatriation need not be invoked because moving to America is no different from leaving Scotland for England, a right that no one but the greediest of Scottish lairds would deny.[94]

By demonstrating that it is a *natural* right, Franklin raises the right to leave to the highest order of claims conceivable within the framework of contemporaneous English political discourse. However, the validity of this claim was moot because contradictory doctrines could be brought to bear on the subject.[95] Although Chapter 42 of Magna Carta specifies the right of "any one to go out from our kingdom, and to return," it sharply qualifies this right by adding "saving their fidelity to us." Moreover, Chapter 42 was omitted from all subsequent reissues of the charter, and the steadily growing assertion of state power in modern times fostered the doctrine of "perpetual allegiance," which removed the crucial element of voluntarism from feudal contractualism. The latter doctrine was confirmed by Blackstone as a ruling principle of English law in his *Commentaries,* published shortly before Franklin formulated his own argument. Liberal thought was a source of ambiguity as well. In his *Second Treatise*, John Locke observes that history provides many examples "of Men withdrawing themselves, and their Obedience, from the Jurisdiction they were born under, and the Family or Community they were bred up in, and *setting up new Governments* in other places," and goes on to assert that emigration is a natural right that everyone can exercise upon reaching adulthood.[96] However, this is qualified by way of the doctrine that citizenship is an irrevocable contract, so that the right to leave "is not a reserved right against government; it is one of those natural rights which the individual deliberately surrenders upon entering society."

Locke's assertion nevertheless opened a breach in the wall of "perpetual allegiance" with which his American followers were undoubtedly familiar. Additional arguments on behalf of the right to leave could also be drawn from international law, despite its generally statist orientation. Emmerich de Vattel, whose *The Law of Nations* was translated into English in 1760, goes farthest in specifying conditions under which a person has the right of expatriation: (1) if it becomes impossible to make a living, (2) if society fails to discharge its obligations to the person in question, and (3) if the majority of the nation were to alter the regime without his consent. The first will be recognized as precisely the argument Franklin formulated in 1773.

Actual practices were an additional source of ambiguity. Throughout the centuries, English monarchs perennially issued prohibitions on the exit of important classes of subjects, but otherwise restrictions were relaxed, "and it came to be understood that anyone could leave unless specifically forbidden, so that travel and emigration were *permitted* to English subjects as a matter of policy"; however, "the legal authority of the government to forbid this was not doubted, nor did the exercise of this privilege obliterate the allegiance which the emigrant continued to owe to the king."[97]

In this light, it can be seen that within the ideational and political context of the times, proclamation of the natural right to leave constituted an extremely radical step. Moreover, Franklin's suggestion that immigration to America is comparable to a move from Scotland to England adumbrated an ingenious way of getting around the stumbling block constituted by the "perpetual allegiance" doctrine: like Scotland before the Act of Union of 1701, the American colonies are "extrinsic dominions of the King," and hence bound to England only by "shared allegiance." Because allegiance and protection are reciprocal, default by either party releases the other from his obligation; hence, if the king can be shown to have harmed his subjects, then the Americans have the right to proclaim their independence.[98]

Less than a year later, Jefferson invoked the right to leave even more explicitly as a justification for severing ties with the evil mother. In *A Summary View of the Rights of British America* (1774), which outlined instructions for the Virginia delegates to the Continental Congress and became a prelude to the Declaration of Independence, Jefferson argues in a Lockean vein that by settling the country at their own expense, the first colonists became as free of British authority as the Saxons had become of German rule by migrating to England in ancient times. By the same token, their subsequent acceptance of British rule was a matter of consent, which could be revoked if conditions changed. Although Joseph J. Ellis has pointed out that this theory of expatriation "was utterly groundless as history" and conveniently overlooked considerable conflicting evidence, notably the charters and patents for which the early settlers applied before leaving England, in 1774 it was becoming ever more widely shared by Americans.[99]

Although Jefferson's explicit use of the "right to leave" to legitimize the rebellion was ultimately rejected by Congress, leaving no trace in the Declaration beyond the sentence "We have reminded them of the circumstances of our emigration and settlement here," his insistence on preserving the argument for posterity in his later reconstruction of events leaves no doubt of his own belief that the argument carried considerable weight.[100] Hence, as a doctrine that persuaded Jefferson to act and others to support him, it contributed significantly to the formation of the revolutionary outlook. Beyond its relevance to disputes over British emigration, the right to leave constituted a key element in the emerging American doctrine of citizenship by consent.

New Lands and Naturalization

The Treaty of Paris of 1763, which marked the apogee of British imperialism in North America, raised new issues that fed brewing tensions between the Crown and its American subjects. Whereas the Americans envisioned the newly conquered lands as an extension of the established colonies, over which they would exercise control, Britain instead proclaimed the vast trans-Appalachian territory an Indian reservation from which colonial settlers and land speculators were excluded.

In Canada, circumstances were conducive to a political accommodation between conquerors and conquered, despite the population's Catholicism.[101] Hence in sharp contrast with what occurred in postconquest Ireland and Acadia, under the Quebec Act of 1774 imperial governance was founded on a reinforcement of the economic power of Catholic landowners, protected by the retention of French law, and the organizational and spiritual power of the Catholic hierarchy, protected by freedom of religion. But from the perspective of the American colonists and especially the New Englanders, the Quebec Act was a nightmare come to life, "an insidious attempt by the ministry to introduce through the colonies' back door the evils of popery, civil law, and eventual absolutism."[102] Already battered by the 1763 proclamation, American interests were further hurt by the transfer of the huge area between the Ohio and Mississippi to Quebec's jurisdiction, which also had the effect of "raising the conditions of new Appropriations of Lands." Altogether, these grievances prompted the drafters of the Declaration of Independence to level yet another charge against the king:

> He has combined with others to subject us to a jurisdiction foreign to our constitution, and, unacknowledged by our laws, giving his assent to their acts of pretended legislation . . . for abolishing the free system of English laws in a neighboring province, establishing therein an arbitrary government, and enlarging its boundaries, so as to render it at once an example and fit instrument for introducing the same absolute rule into these colonies.[103]

As already shown, naturalization was closely related to land. Whereas in the first half of the eighteenth century the imperial authorities paid little heed to the colonies' local initiatives, in the light of the measures enacted by Parliament in 1740 and 1761 on behalf of America, questions began to be raised in London about the propriety of allowing the colonies to carry on.[104] As part of its hardening stance on legislative authority and population expansion, Britain nullified a 1759 Pennsylvania law designed to secure the property of nonnaturalized aliens by exempting them from escheat, as well as naturalization measures enacted by Pennsylvania and New Jersey; and, as noted earlier, in November 1773 Britain abruptly forbade colonial governors to assent to any more naturalization acts of any sort. This was a heavy economic blow to the larger landholding colonies—Virginia, New York, New Jersey, and Pennsylvania—as well as to individual speculators eager to "make a market" in land.[105] The New York Assembly, for one, defiantly continued to pass and repass private naturalization bills despite the governor's refusal.[106]

The grievance concerning naturalization, not referred to in the first Continental Congress's petition to the king (1774) or in the instructions prepared by Jefferson as instructions for the Virginia delegates to that body, first appeared in 1776 on a list that Jefferson compiled for the draft preamble to the Virginia Constitution Declaration of Rights, and was then carried over into his draft of the Declaration of Independence.[107] Beyond its relevance to the dispute over land and population, in the tense political atmosphere naturalization stood out in sharper relief as a prerogative of sovereignty, asserted by the colonies as a concomitant of self-government, but considered from the other side of the Atlantic as an act of defiance.

Colonial practices in this sphere further implied the emergence of a more inclusive and egalitarian notion of subjecthood.[108] Over time, the colonists' extensive experience of immigration and of the incorporation of aliens from diverse European countries fostered a view that community might be founded on a broader base than shared ancestry. While Benjamin Franklin and others reject the evil mother because she harmed her young, Tom Paine berates the very notion of "*parent* or *mother* country" as a phrase "jesuitically adopted by the king and his parasites, with a low papistical design of gaining an unfair bias on the credulous weakness of our minds." And he deftly throws out a promising substitute for the conventional imagined community: "Europe and not England, is the parent country of America" because "[t]his new world hath been the asylum for the persecuted lovers of civil and religious liberty from *every part* of Europe. Hither have they fled, not from the tender embraces of the mother, but from the cruelty of the monster."[109] Not being born of the same blood is not a liability, but an asset: Americans will constitute the first political community united by the choice of freedom over tyranny—or at least, whites "from *every part* of Europe" will do so.

The dawning of a more inclusive notion of community prepared the ground for the revolutionary idea of citizenship by consent. But while this development has been widely acknowledged as a signal historical turning point, less attention has been given to the fact that it entailed a concomitant shift from the traditional foundational reciprocity, the subjects' allegiance in exchange for the king's protection, to a new and more problematic relationship: the freely constituted community's commitment to admit newcomers to membership if they qualify. Consequently, as they proceeded to constitute themselves into a political body, the Americans faced an unprecedented question: if membership is not to be determined exclusively by tradition and birth, what criteria would be appropriate?

The Limits of Membership

By the standards of Europe, which educated colonials largely shared, on the eve of independence the American colonies constituted an assemblage of diverse communities that, if brought together into a single state, would constitute a uniquely heterogeneous mosaic. Although the American nation was represented by Louis Hartz, in a widely influential conceptualization, as issued from the emigration of a distinct "fragment" of English society, in reality by the late eighteenth century as much as half the colonial population traced its origins elsewhere.[110] Of the 3.9 million persons enumerated in the first national census of 1790—which excluded Indians—81 percent were white. Although an overwhelming 85.6 percent of them were native British subjects, born either in the British Isles or in North America, only 69.3 percent traced their origins to Britain proper, including 59.7 percent English, 4.3 percent Welsh, and 5.3 percent Scottish.[111] The remaining 16.3 percent came from Ireland, then still administered by England as a distinct colony with limited self-government, including 10.5 percent Scotch-Irish from Ulster and 5.8 percent from the southern provinces, encompassing both Anglicans (immigrants from England and their descendents) and Catholic "native Irish." Continental Europeans were also extremely diverse. The largest cluster were Germans, who amounted to 8.9 percent of the white population, slightly less than the Scotch-Irish; but "German" itself encompassed people from many different regions and countries, adhering to a variety of faiths, who shared not much more than a common language, and even that must be qualified in the light of dialectical variation. Other significant European "races" were the Dutch (3.1 percent of whites), French (2.1 percent), and Swedes (0.3 percent). Although nearly all were Protestant, this encompassed vast religious differences that were of considerably import at the time.

Among the white population, the proportion English varied from a high of 87.1 percent in Connecticut to a low of 25.8 percent in Pennsylvania, whereas the Celtic percentage ranged from a high of 42.9 percent in South Carolina to a low of 11.9 percent in Connecticut. Reflecting its "family farm" origins and subsequent efforts to restrict immigration, New England remained the most homogeneous region, both most white and most English. The middle colonies considerably more diverse. With 38.0 percent Germans and 2.8 percent others, Pennsylvania had the largest population of foreign origin; and its Celtic population outnumbered the English as well. New York had 15.9 percent Dutch, 9.1 percent German, and 4.2 percent French—mostly Huguenots—and nearly one-third of New Jersey's population was also of foreign European origin. Whereas after the conquest the Dutch were quickly anglicized, Germans speakers constituted a critical mass; supported by self-conscious leaders and support networks, they established a press in their own language and cultivated an extensive network of trade and religious communications via London and Holland to Germany itself, as well as across colonial boundaries throughout North America.[112] The Roman Catholic minority remained concentrated in the upper South, notably Maryland, but with a scattering of more recent newcomers in Pennsylvania as well.[113]

The sense of variety was heightened by the uneven distribution of the various groups among the colonies and their differing relationships, reflecting disparate modes of social organization.[114] The initial bifurcation between the "plantation" and "family farm" patterns of colonial development remained essential, providing the ominous combination of a congeries of "plural societies" founded on a racial division of labor coexisting in the same state with European fragments relieved of their feudal legacy.[115] However, by the time of the Revolution the "family farm" form had evolved well beyond agriculture to include patches of nascent industrialism and expanding cities with distinct laboring classes.[116] The proportion of blacks ranged widely from a high of 60.9 percent in South Carolina—akin to the situation prevailing in the "Sugar Islands"—to merely 2.0 percent in New Hampshire; albeit concentrated in the South, blacks also constituted 14.3 percent of New York's population and 9.8 percent of Rhode Island's, reflecting an agricultural sector operated by slaves in both states.

With the colonies beginning to view themselves as self-contained political communities, heterogeneity moved to the fore as a prominent concern. This was not an entirely new development: New England was always reluctant to take in non-English newcomers, New York behaved so harshly toward Palatines in 1709 that they moved to Pennsylvania, and there were occasional xenophobic outbursts in Pennsylvania itself, as well as protests against the permissive group naturalization of newcomers. In the same vein, Huguenots were harassed in Rhode Island and South Carolina, and in 1713 the Connecticut Assembly considered a bill to levy special duties on strangers, and adopted a measure directed against Moravians. As their disputes with the imperial government heated up, the colonists were not above complaining that foreigners, like slaves, were being imposed on them by Britain. Although by and large political leaders were disposed to inclusiveness, both by interest and by virtue of their ideological orientation, there were limits to be drawn. For example, in an afterthought to his 1751 essay on population, Franklin abruptly shifts to the subject of race.[117] Observing "That the Number of purely white People in the World is proportionately very small," he specifies that "white" excludes not only the black and "tawny"—Africans, Asians, and American Indians—but also Europeans of "what we call a swarthy complexion," not only Spaniards and Italians but also Russians, Swedes, and most Germans—"the *Saxons* only excepted, who with the *English* make the principal Body of White People on the Face of the Earth." In short, "white" for Franklin is limited to "Anglo-Saxon." Asserting that "I could wish their Numbers were increased," he goes on to suggest that America should take advantage of the opportunity it has, "by excluding all Blacks and Tawneys, of increasing the lovely white and Red."

Admitting the obvious, that "perhaps I am partial to the Complexion of my country," Franklin offers no justification for his preference than that "such Kind of Partiality is natural to Mankind." Two years later, however, he elaborates his views on the subject of Germans—presumably he has in mind the non-Saxon kind—and slaves. Despite their coarseness, his observations deserve to be taken seriously because the political disposition he attributes to these populations leads him to surmise their likely impact on American institutions, thereby revealing how he envisions admission to membership. Moreover, Franklin's beliefs were by no means idiosyncratic but reflected widely held views, including most notoriously those held by Jefferson three decades later, thereby testifying to their hegemonic status among the founding generation.[118]

Anticipating the social science literature on socialization, Franklin's attributions are founded on the notion that the political culture of individuals is molded by the distinctive institutions of the country in which they grow up. Writing to Peter Collinson from Philadelphia in 1753, he agrees with his correspondent "that measures of great Temper are necessary" with the Germans, "and [I] am not without Apprehensions. that thro' their indiscretion or Ours, or both, great disorders and inconveniences more generally may one day arise among us." As would be said about each subsequent wave of "new immigrants," Franklin asserts, "Those who come hither are generally of the most ignorant Stupid Sort of their own Nation." These characteristics render the newcomers credulous of knavery, but suspicious of honesty; and as few of the English know German, "and so cannot ·address them either from the Press or Pulpit,'tis almost impossible to remove any prejudices they once entertain."[119] Although Franklin's imputation of negative selection is contradicted by what we know of the German immigrants' objective characteristics, more recent arrivals did include a larger proportion of single young men and of families of modest condition than their predecessors, lending some credence to the notion of "deterioration."[120]

Franklin then makes an ominous inference regarding the dynamics of political culture: "Not being used to Liberty, they know not how to make a modest use of it." Hitherto submissive to civil authority and reluctant to participate in American elections, "now they come in droves," and as the first ethnic bloc, "carry all before them, except in one or two counties." This reasoning would be replicated almost literally by Jefferson in *Notes on the State of Virginia* three decades later, as well as by Alexis de Tocqueville in 1835 with reference to the wave of "new immigrants" who were flooding into Philadelphia and New York as he was putting the finishing touches to *Democracy in America*. He also agitates the specter of malintegration and of divisive language maintenance: "Few of their children in the Country learn English; they import many Books from Germany." Market conditions reinforced the spread of German as well, and the language was imposing itself in the public sphere also.[121] Should this continue, "[I]n a few years they will be also necessary in the Assembly, to tell one half of our Legislators what the other half say." In short, "[T]hey will soon out number us, that all the advantages we have will not in My Opinion be able to preserve our language, and even our Government will become precarious."

His concern about political stability made sense in terms of the Enlightenment understanding that languages embody specific cultural values and mold the outlook and comportment of their speakers accordingly: it follows that the presence within the same state of linguistic carriers of incompatible cultures will inevitably give rise to acute political contention.[122] Adumbrating another modern concern, maintenance of a distinct language constitutes a potential threat to national security, in that solidarities arising from the immigrants' roots may override those binding them to the political community in which they now live. The French, "who watch all advantages," are planning a German settlement in "back of us in the Illinoes [sic] Country, and by means of those Germans they may in time come to an understanding with ours." Already in the recent war, the Pennsylvania Germans adopted a neutralist stance "that seems to bode us no good."[123]

What is to be done? Franklin's correspondent of 1753 provides a categorical answer: the German stream should be diverted to other colonies. But albeit terming this proposal "very judicious," and despite his own expressed misgivings regarding Germans, Franklin concludes otherwise: "Yet I am not for refusing entirely to admit them into our Colonies"; as he explains later, "for they have their Virtues, their industry and frugality is exemplary; They are excellent husbandsmen and contribute greatly to the improvement of a Country." It will be remembered also that earlier, he had favorably contrasted the Germans' self-help with the "dependency" of British immigrants. Accordingly, he delineates the objective as maximizing the benefits of immigration while minimizing its disadvantages, and explains to his correspondent that in order to achieve this, "All that seems to be necessary is, to distribute [the Germans] more equally, mix them with the English, establish English Schools where they are now too thick settled, and take some care to prevent the practice lately fallen into by some of the Ship Owners, of sweeping the German Gaols to make up the number of their Passengers."[124]

Loath to pass up an opportunity to expand the colonies' productive and white population, Franklin the real estate promoter and physiocratic American nationalist thus inaugurates a series of fateful choices, when the lure of economic opportunity would outweigh the dictates of cultural conservatism. Albeit introduced by a minimizing "all that seems to be necessary," his proposal delineates a formidably comprehensive program that combines a selective immigration policy, designed to deter the landing of undesirables, with a proactive and well-coordinated immigrant policy, designed to incorporate culturally different newcomers by way of two major instruments, dispersed settlement and targeted education. This far-seeing agenda in fact entailed a higher degree of governmental intervention with regard to settlement and incorporation than the United States has ever engaged in to date, except on a very limited basis on behalf of Indochinese and Cuban refugees in the 1980s.[125]

With regard to the incorporation of those foreign immigrants who did come, in the absence of the unity that might be drawn from a common ancestry, political leaders would have to make do with other resources. As can be inferred from the comments of both Franklin and later on Jefferson, two of these were readily available: the English language, which was hegemonic everywhere except in Pennsylvania, and Protestantism. The revolutionary experience itself fostered the emergence of a third, democratic republicanism.[126] Together, these formed basic criteria for membership that, as formal or informal requirements, were promised a long career.

Persuaded that the regulation of access to membership begins with control over immigration itself, the revolutionary generation was aware that a fundamental decision had to be made regarding the slave trade. Franklin's opposition to the importation of slaves was founded both on moral objections to slavery and on practical considerations arising from its putative consequences. As noted earlier, he asserts in his essay on population that the introduction of slaves into the Caribbean Islands led to the disappearance of whites, and he objects to the peopling of America by anything but whites. As a London agent in 1770, when Granville Sharp's abolitionist campaign was beginning to get off the ground and was used to question the American colonists' legitimacy as self-proclaimed advocates of liberty, he undertook to deal more extensively with the subject.

A Conversation between an Englishman, a Scotchman, and an American, on the Subject of Slavery is designed mainly to silence anti-American critics by charging that it was England, after all, that launched the slave trade in North America, and then goes on to argue that slavery is not omnipresent in the colonies, and that many Americans abhor the slave trade as much as Granville Sharp.[127] However, Franklin minces no words regarding the undesirability of the slaves themselves: far from being mild tempered and tractable, the majority of Negroes "are of a plotting disposition, sullen, malicious, revengeful and cruel in the highest Degree." They are, in fact, very much like the refuse Britain is dumping in America: "[M]any of them, being mischievous Villains in their own Country, are sold off by their Princes in the Way of Punishment by Exile and Slavery, as you here ship off your Convicts." And as with the convicts, England is also to blame for tempting "prudent People" to give in to greed. The only solution is to "prevent this temptation" by prohibiting the trade altogether; "But this you will not allow us to do." In the absence of other forms of transatlantic movement from Africa, abolition of the slave trade meant that in the future immigration would be limited to Europeans only. Although this left open the question of what to do with the population of African origin already in the country, if Negroes were as Franklin said, then even if they were set free, they could not possibly qualify for membership in American society. What, then, was to be done with them?

3

An Acquisitive Upstart

"How far emigration from other countries into this, ought to be encouraged, is a very important question. It is clear, that the present situation of America, renders it necessary to promote the influx of people; and it is equally clear, that we have a right to restrain that influx, whenever it is found likely to prove hurtful to us."[1] Just as clearly, the opening sentences of Tench Coxe's paper, read before the Society for Political Enquiries at the house of Benjamin Franklin on April 20, 1787, highlight the basic flaw of the canonic accounts of immigration policy at the time of the founding and provide the needed corrective. Elaborated in the course of the protracted confrontation over immigration, they emphasize "neutrality": the United States neither encouraged immigration nor erected barriers against it.[2] In reality, it did both, actively seeking to attract valuable human capital but equally resolved to deter undesirables.

Coxe's measured tones notwithstanding, within the prevailing international context his immigrationist proclamation was highly provocative. In the same vein, Thomas Jefferson asserted, "The present desire of America is to produce rapid population by as great importations of foreigners as possible."[3] His friend James Madison similarly declared in the course of the naturalization debate at the Convention that America was indebted to immigration and advanced most rapidly where it was most encouraged, and subsequently anchored this to a doctrine, arguing that should an overcrowded country let its people go, part of the surplus "ought to be invited by a country greatly deficient in its population."[4] The hegemony of acquisitive immigrationism is confirmed by the fact that, despite the efforts of generations of restrictionists to find evidence of the founders' like-mindedness, they have not come up with anything better than Jefferson's qualified doubts about part of the flow, occasional admonitions against "encouragement by extraordinary means," and the enactment of measures to deter undesirables. Nevertheless, the latter must be taken into account as well.[5]

Drawing Them In

The founding generation's attempts to shape immigration must be understood in relation to the broader international context, within which the irruption in the Atlantic world of an underpopulated American republic in possession of an immense reserve of temperate lands, and determined to capitalize on this unique asset by marketing it to all comers, was a truly revolutionary event.[6] As demonstrated by the Scottish philosophers and the French physiocrats, and well understood by statesmen and men of affairs everywhere, the dynamics of political economy were determined by the ratio between land and population; and it was widely recognized that the Old World's established system was founded on scarcity of the first in relation to the second. Because of this, the lower orders had been subjected to rural dependency; and now that this population was increasing more rapidly while the amount of land remained fixed, they were being driven to become wage earners. This in turn constituted a sine qua non for the rise of manufactures and the expansion of national economic power. In this perspective, should a substantial part of the populace gain access to land overseas, both those who left and those who stayed behind would achieve a degree of economic autonomy that would radically undermine the established order.

Even more subversive was the assertion by the new state of its sovereign right to transform the subjects of European monarchs into republican citizens, and thereby free them of their allegiance and obligations to their erstwhile rulers. In light of the conventions that underlay the state system, this was construed as an outrageous violation of the law of nations, falling little short of a proclamation by the Americans of their right to appropriate manpower, which constituted the most valuable asset of any sovereign.

For the Americans, the major reference remained Great Britain, shortly to become the United Kingdom of Great Britain and Ireland. Linked by way of established networks into a transatlantic migration system, the two states were doubly at loggerheads. Britain's most urgent priorities were to stem the drain of valuable human capital to what was now an outright competitor, to rebuild in North America an empire that could withstand the upstart republic's suspected expansionism, and to dispose of accumulating human refuse. Emigration ground to a halt during the hostilities, but the reopening of the Atlantic after nearly a decade's interruption triggered a wave of departures comparable in size to those of 1770–1773.[7] The "great transformation" steadily broadened its domain and became more intensive, and the transatlantic networks established by the previous wave facilitated further overseas departures.[8] However, while the Revolution liberated Americans from the rule of a king who "endeavored to prevent the population of these States," it simultaneously freed the United Kingdom to erect more draconian obstacles to the departure of valuable population for what had become by virtue of the Articles of Peace a foreign state.

In 1785 Parliament extended to the United States the ban imposed in 1720 on the emigration of British seamen, artisans, and workers in key industries.[9] Three years later, it was extended to Ireland as well.[10] Together with the breakdown of established financial links, this fatally undermined the transatlantic market in bound servants within whose framework much of the immigration to the American colonies had taken place. However, it was ineffective as a barrier to the exit of persons who paid their own way, and there were many holes in the fence, notably by first sailing to Canada, Nova Scotia, or New Brunswick. Hence the problem of the American drain lingered on the British political agenda. A writer to the London *Sun* still complained some thirty years later, "The lower classes, and not a few among the higher, of our agriculturists and artificers, are in the full tide of emigration. America, by a principle not thoroughly accordant with the international law, receives them all, without hesitation, conditions, or enquiry." America has also become *"refugium pauperum et peccatorum,"* in utter contempt of British laws. "How long," he wondered, "is this unjust and injurious practice to continue? . . . The agriculture of that rival state,—for a rival she ever will be, with as much, at least, of inveterate envy as of honorable competition,—her manufactures, and her arts, are to be promoted by the drain of British population; and we passively look on, while our subjects are speeding from their native soil by shiploads, to enrich a foreign country,—a country with which we have not a common interest nor one common feeling,—a country with which we have had three wars in forty years,—a country with which we have no perpetuity of peace."[11]

Concurrently, Britain undertook to enhance the capacity of its remaining North American possessions to resist American ambitions. Reaffirmed by the American Revolution, the strange compact established by the Quebec Act of 1774 was further strengthened a generation later when the eruption of a "godless" revolution in France rendered Canada's Catholic elites totally dependent on their Protestant sovereign for protection. However, Britain also sought to foster the formation of an ethnic counterweight by implanting a politically reliable aristocracy of British origin, based on land grants, for which the most obvious source was the United States.[12] On this matter the antagonistic states were in tacit agreement, as the very characteristics that made the Loyalists undesirable to the Americans rendered them ideal as the foundation stone of British North America.

Estimates of the northward emigration have ranged as high as 100,000, and even the more conservative 50,000–60,000 currently accepted amounts to about 2 percent of the white population of the United States and 11–13 percent of the Loyalist mass; relative to population size, the flow was four to five times greater than the émigrés propelled by the French Revolution.[13] How much of the movement was attributable to deliberate actions on the American side is difficult to ascertain. The Congress as well as all the colonial legislatures required various kinds of loyalty tests and imposed disabilities on those who refused or neglected to abide by them, with sanctions ranging from confiscation of property to banishment; and at the end of the war, Massachusetts and several other states prohibited the return of Loyalists, even if they were born in America. The practice of political banishment was subsequently upheld by the U.S. Supreme Court in *Cooper v. Telfair* (1800).[14] Although after the Peace of Paris national officials agreed to forgive the Loyalists, this required state acquiescence, which was rarely forthcoming.[15] In the event, unlike the surviving French aristocrats, most of the American Loyalists never returned. The elimination of the counterrevolutionary camp considerably narrowed the range of disagreement over régime issues and thereby contributed to the republic's political stability.

Several thousand American Negroes, emancipated for their services to the Crown, went into exile as well, mostly to Nova Scotia. Rejected by the local Scottish settlers and unable to gain a foothold as farmers, they emerged as a problematic population, which along with others who ended up as "poor blacks" in London was subsequently relocated in Sierra Leone, a development that inspired American efforts to dispose of unwanted black freedmen as well.[16]

Too Few or Too Many?

What level of immigration did the American leaders think was appropriate, and how did their preferences relate to actual and potential flows? These are by no means anachronistic questions, as the founders were ardent quantifiers, particularly with regard to population matters. Besides Franklin (who achieved genuine distinction as a pioneer demographer), Jefferson, as well as Madison repeatedly bolstered their arguments with demographic projections of their own devising; and Dolly Madison even claimed later on that her late husband had anticipated several of the Reverend Thomas Malthus's ideas.[17] Most of the states instituted systematic censuses early on, and the founders projected their quantitative inclinations into the Constitution itself by providing for a decennial national census, designed to supply not only the head-counts necessary for implementing the representative system but also information for making sound policy in the national interest.[18]

The white population of the United States—the appropriate referent for considering the impact of European immigration—was known to be growing at an extremely high rate, confirmed by subsequent federal counts to exceed 3 percent a year for the country as a whole, approximately one and a half times the contemporaneous British rate, itself at an unprecedented high. Franklin had already demonstrated that this was attributable mostly to a phenomenal rate of natural reproduction, occasioned by the absence of what would soon come to be known as "Malthusian constraints." Under these conditions, he calculated, the white population of the United States would double in approximately thirty years even without any immigration whatsoever. Jefferson later corrected that for Virginia to twenty-seven and one-quarter years, and while Madison thought it might theoretically occur in as little as ten, he anticipated it would actually be achieved in twenty to twenty-five (this turned out to be approximately correct).[19]

Given this widespread interest in population, it is strange that initially no provision was made at the national level for statistical information on immigration properly speaking. Not only were there no aggregate figures on arrivals, but since all white residents were counted equally for the purpose of apportionment, the early censuses did not bother to distinguish between native- and foreign-born, thus making it impossible to infer immigration estimates indirectly. The first quantitative history of American immigration, published in 1856, set forth an estimate of 250,000 for the period 1781–1819.[20] This became a "stylized fact" that was enshrined in the U.S. Bureau of the Census's *Historical Statistics of the United States* a century later, providing the basis for the conventional wisdom that the volume of immigration during the period of the founding was "limited" and "hardly more than a trickle," and that "for several decades" it "remained less than before the Revolution."[21]

However, these judgments require revision in light of new evidence, gathered from ship lists and demographic projections, which raises the past estimate by about half, to between 366,000 and 400,000, of whom around 250,000 came prior to 1815.[22] Equally important, it is now well established that immigration fluctuated widely because of international events and restrictive state action on the European side; most of the immigrants arrived before 1800 and after 1815, and very few came in the intervening period, when the Atlantic was largely closed by embargoes and war.

Despite Britain's decision to extend to the United States existing prohibitions on the emigration of "artificers" and other valuable persons, departures resumed at a vigorous level after the Treaty of Paris of 1783; smaller flows left from the Continent as well, mainly northern Germany, resulting in about 14,000 immigrants a year for the remainder of the decade, of whom approximately 90 percent were British or Irish.[23] This was undoubtedly perceived as a high level, as it equaled or even exceeded the great wave of 1770–1775. Although the outbreak of war between Britain and France in 1792 impeded departures from the United Kingdom, reducing the yearly average for the 1790s to 9,790 and the British/Irish share of the total to 79.9 percent, by the standards of the time this was no "trickle." The visibility of immigration was enhanced by the fact that most of the newcomers landed in Philadelphia, then still the leading American port, and that arrivals were concentrated in the May–October sailing season. Although nearly all shortly moved on, the streaming in of as many as 2,000 foreigners a month into a city of 42,000 (1790 population) surely constituted a strange and impressive spectacle. From a demographic perspective, however, immigration remained a marginal phenomenon. Immigration in the 1780s amounted to a decennial addition of less than 5 percent to the white population, and accounted for merely one-sixth of its overall growth; and in the following decade, its contribution fell below one-tenth.[24]

As the Americans set about organizing their new government, they were well aware that the wave of settlers who had been attracted after the defeat of the French in 1763 stimulated an unprecedented expansion that lifted the American economy to a new plane.[25] Envisioning immigration primarily as a stimulus to demand for land, they did not worry about its impact on the republic's integrity because of its demographic marginality. How many might come? Although Jefferson reckoned "for example only" the demographic consequences of doubling Virginia's population of half a million by the sudden addition of an equal number of foreigners, he immediately conceded that such a mass "is a greater accession than the most sanguine advocate for immigration has a right to expect." Madison, who calculated that under the most favorable circumstances, a human population might naturally double in as little as ten years, suggested that Great Britain and Ireland "are capable of producing annually for emigration, no less than five hundred thousand," France no less than 1,250,000, and Europe as a whole no less than 7,500,000.[26] However, there is no indication that anyone took his estimates seriously, nor did he do so himself, conceding, "It is not meant that such a surplus could, under any revolution of circumstances, suddenly take place." In short, no one expected a sudden escalation, which was precluded by obstacles to departure on the European side, including state regulations but especially the limited capacity of Atlantic shipping and its relative inelasticity in the face of increased demand.

Accordingly, the most pressing issue was to insure that those who wanted to come were able to do so. From this perspective, the greatest problem was the British prohibition on emigration, which evoked considerable rancor. Shortly after the traditional prohibition was extended to the United States, Franklin sought to persuade an English friend who, like himself, began as a journeyman printer, and subsequently achieved worldly success as an MP (member of Parliament) and Printer to His Majesty, that the British should change their ways because they were harming themselves. "[Y]ou do wrong to discourage the Emigration of Englishmen to America," he explained, because, as demonstrated in his own writings on population, emigration "does not diminish but multiplies a Nation. You will not have fewer at home for those that go abroad."[27] However, Franklin's fertile mind quickly moved well beyond the demographic calculations of 1751, venturing boldly into unchartered terrain—the structural effects of democracy, the dynamics of immigrant incorporation, and even transnationalism: "[A]s every Man who comes among us, and takes up a piece of Land, becomes a Citizen, and by our Constitution has a Voice in Elections, and a share in the Government of the Country, why should you be against acquiring by this fair Means a Repossession of it?" A continued flow of English emigration will perpetuate English influence, along with the language—it will be good for publishing as well as for imperial politics. Not content to accentuate the positive, Franklin conjures up his own dreadful specter: why should England, by preventing its own emigration, leave America "to be taken by Foreigners of all Nations and Languages, who by their Numbers may drown and stifle the English, which otherwise would probably become in the course of two Centuries the most extensive Language in the World, the Spanish only excepted?" In an afterthought that was surely not lost on his correspondent, he suggested it does not really have to be the English; there are others in the United Kingdom who will do as well, notably the Scots and Irish.

In the same vein, seven years later Madison demonstrated the benefits of emigration for countries "whose population is full." This appeared in a newspaper article on "Population and Emigration," the first of a series elaborating and defending the republican camp's economic doctrine, prompted by the contrary strivings of the rising Hamiltonians.[28] Most astutely, he argues not only that free movement will make everyone better off, but also that migration from the British Isles to America will promote the development of their distinctive political economies in harmonious complementarity, and make it unnecessary and inadvisable for America to depart from its established economic ways.

Like Franklin, he begins by questioning the "constant sum" reasoning underlying mercantilist doctrine, whereby population transfers entail a loss for the source country and a concomitant gain for the receiver, and points out that emigration may even augment the source country's population: "The commercial nations of Europe, parting with emigrants, to America, are examples." Contrary to the assumptions of British policy, the emigrants will create a demand for products manufactured in the source country and simultaneously contribute to the production of exports to pay for them. "Where the settlers have doubled every twenty or twenty-five years, as in the United States, the encrease [sic] of products and consumption in the new country, and consequently of employment and people in the old, has had a corresponding facility." Since so much of the British commercial advantage is derived from emigration to America, it makes no sense to restrain the current. For good measure, Madison warns, "Other nations, who have to acquire their share in our commerce, are still more interested in aiding their other efforts, by permitting, and even promoting emigration to this country, as fast as it may be disposed to welcome them."

Freedom of movement not only is of benefit to sending and receiving states, but also "is due to the general interests of humanity." Since its course is "always, from places where living is more difficult, to places where it is less difficult, the happiness of the emigrant is promoted by the change: and as a more numerous progeny is another effect of the same cause, human life is at once made a greater blessing, and more individuals are created to partake of it." In short, freedom of movement provides for a better distribution of people in relation to resources and opportunities. In support of this point, Madison cites the exorbitant cost of supporting the poor in England and France—thereby unwittingly suggesting to Europeans the "dumping" solution that prompted the indignation of his fellow Americans. Freedom of emigration also promotes morality, since crowding fosters promiscuity and also makes it difficult to maintain a family: "Provide an outlet for the surplus of population, and marriages will be increased in proportion." As a concluding point, he suggests that westward migration has the same beneficial effect as international movement and, far from leading to population loss in the regions of origin, is likely "to quicken the aggregate population of our country." This constituted, in effect, a reaffirmation of the importance of independent agriculturalists as the foundation of the republican political economy.

Making a Market in Land

Upon signing the treaties implementing the 1783 Articles of Peace, the American states gained title under international law to immense reserves of undeveloped land; and the following year, Virginia's definitive cession to Congress of its claim to the huge "uncultivated" territory—by Europeans—north and west of the Ohio River created a national domain "to govern and, equally important from the viewpoint of the Confederation treasury, to sell."[29] Land sales indeed constituted the most opportune and politically least costly way of resolving the country's extremely high public indebtedness, as well as of financing government more generally. This required the organization of a national market in land and the stimulation of demand. Although the American population was growing, capital was in short supply, and therefore it was advisable to turn to Europe for additional buyers. George Washington and his circle also believed that the influx of European settlers would prevent the depopulation of the old states.[30] Since absentee landlords, associated with corrupt Crown practices, were unacceptable, and ownership should be tied to occupancy and fruitful use, the European buyers must be settlers. This in turn mandated attention to the property rights of aliens, as well as to procedures for naturalization.

The comprehensive régime elaborated by the founders to this effect clearly offered "encouragement" to immigration, but of a well-qualified sort. The connection between land and immigration is well illustrated by Tench Coxe's paper, presented around the time of the enactment of the Northwest Ordinance in 1787, which provided for the political and economic organization of the Virginia cession. Unlike monarchs, who arrogate land to themselves by right of conquest, republicans must justify their ownership on the basis of natural law: "Having obtained possession of a certain territory, any collection of men have a right to exclude all others from settling in so much of that territory as it is necessary for themselves. How much is necessary, ought, however, to be determined upon reasonable principles."[31] Societies vary considerably in the amount of land they require as a function of basic forms of political economy: "A nation of hunters requires large tracts for their support; husbandmen less; merchants or manufacturers still less." Because hunting, which Coxe's audience surely understood as a reference to the Indian way of life, is a morally inferior pursuit, "a nation of hunters can have no legal claim to the vast lawns and immense forests, which their habits lead them to desire." A case in point is Pennsylvania, which then contained at least 300,000 thriving inhabitants but would support no more than one-tenth that number if they depended on hunting. The right of ownership is founded on occupancy, and "[a]griculture, manufactures, and commerce may, therefore, properly be termed the only modes of occupancy, which the law of nature, in its reference to society, authorizes or allows." Practicing all three, the Euro-American collectivity is the legitimate owner of the land, and as such can decide whom to admit on its territory and whom to keep out.

However, disposal of America's most valuable asset must be organized in keeping with the imperatives of a republican political economy.[32] Paralleling ongoing changes in the labor market, the traditional régime governing land came to be viewed as incompatible with freedom, and land itself "more as a commodity to be sold for a profit and less as a family estate to be kept for posterity."[33] As indicated by the flood of petitions to Congress and to American officials, Europeans of substance who considered emigrating expected land grants, together with exemption from taxation and bounties; however, the revolutionary generation adamantly rejected grants as a path to aristocratic corruption, as well as ruled out by the government's need for immediate revenue.[34] The obligation of purchase also helped refute charges that the Americans were out to seduce European immigrants.[35] But the founders also pointedly rejected egalitarian distribution. The likely consequences of "free soil" were even then being made explicit by Adam Smith, whose conceptual framework they shared, as indicated by Franklin's already cited observations on the subject. It would not only drastically reduce the value of all real estate held by the states and the national government, as well as by the political class and their allies, but also undermine capital formation and wreak havoc with America's nascent industry by providing East Coast workingmen with an alternative from which they could be dissuaded only by an escalation of already high wages.[36] Squatting also threatened to foster the emergence of an abhorred "state of nature" in the West. Beyond this loomed the fear that a giveaway would unleash a lethal plebeian invasion by the land-hungry masses of Europe.

It was the urgency of deterring squatters as well as speculators that prompted enactment of the Ordinances of 1784 and 1785, which established the basic pattern for the marketing of public lands.[37] The requirement of a minimum payment of $640 for a section, equivalent to four or five family farms, foreclosed direct purchases by settlers of modest conditions and fostered instead undertakings by venture wholesalers, who made their profit by reselling smaller tracts.[38] Eager to stimulate demand, they quickly expanded their zone of prospection abroad and, in the face of British prohibitions on emigration, turned increasingly toward the Continent, thereby broadening the sources of American immigration. For example, in 1789 Gouverneur Morris acted as the agent of some American landowners in Paris; and developers of western New York sent out agents "to enlist the type of German farmer that had proved so successful in Pennsylvania and parts of the South."[39]

Since, under both common and Roman law, aliens could not obtain full property rights in land, the development of foreign demand required clear and firm assurances by way of a distinct legal régime. Hence in a signal departure from common law practice and in sharp contrast with the policy being established in British North America, resident aliens in the territories were authorized to purchase federal land without any waiting period and no risk of escheat.[40] But since property rights fell within the sphere of the states, which varied in their treatment of aliens, it was imperative to provide an internationally recognizable form of American nationality. Accordingly, the Constitutional Convention specifically empowered Congress to enact a uniform rule of naturalization, and President Washington placed the matter on the agenda in his very first message to the legislature, which acted promptly on the matter.

The new national government sought to enhance the prospects of settlement by eliminating Indian resistance, an activity that itself occasioned considerable federal expenditure and in turn rendered land sales more urgent. In 1796 the Federalists raised the floor price of the section to $2.00 an acre, thereby requiring a minimal initial outlay of $1,280, largely to stem large-scale emigration to the West, which they feared would deplete the labor force of the older communities of the East and reduce their own political influence.[41] However, their Republican successors were more responsive to perennial pressures to reduce the minimum size, especially as buyers were being attracted to the western districts of Upper Canada.[42] Accordingly, in 1800 the minimum was lowered to a half section (320 acres), and four years later to a quarter (160 acres), making it possible to acquire an average-size farm for as little as $80 cash, with the remainder payable over four years. Well publicized overseas, these developments constituted an irresistible and, in the eyes of many European officials, improper form of "encouragement" to immigration.[43]

Immigrant Labor

Aware of the accelerating industrialization of Great Britain, most of the revolutionary generation believed that the country's circumstances were ill-suited for such a development. For example, in his advice to emigrants, Franklin explained that America is ideal for agriculture, commerce, and simple transformation of raw materials, but warned that "great establishments of manufacture" are unlikely to succeed because they "require great Numbers of Poor to do the Work for small Wages; these Poor are to be found in Europe, but will not be found in America, till the Lands are all taken up and cultivated, and the excess of People who cannot get Land, want Employment."[44]

For most republicans, this promise of failure was a blessing because it provided assurance against corruption and decay. But in the famous "Report on Manufactures" of 1791 that constituted his manifesto, Hamilton took the republican theory head on and elaborated his own alternative, in which immigration figured as a crucial element. Proceeding to refute the conventional doctrine, he elaborated an "emerging market" thesis demonstrating that the creation of favorable conditions for manufactures would provide an incentive for investors to relocate from Europe to the United States.[45] Anticipating the usual objections, he also insisted that the development of manufactures would not retard the expansion of settlements because "the accessions of foreigners, who originally drawn over by manufacturing views would afterwards abandon them for Agriculture, would be more than equivalent for those of our own Citizens, who might happen to be detached from them."[46]

The secretary then turned to a discussion of how the constraints set forth in the "general theory" might be overcome. "Scarcity of hands" can be resolved in part by the use of machines, which will make it possible to hire women and children, and will also render labor generally more productive. Immigrants beckon as well: "Whoever inspects, with a careful eye, the composition of our towns will be made sensible to what an extent this resource may be relied upon. They exhibit a large proportion of ingenious and valuable workmen, in different arts and trades, who by expatriating from Europe, have improved their own condition, and added to the industry and wealth of the United States." Addressing widespread objections to wage work in manufacturing as an unsuitable pursuit for republican citizens, he points out further that the use of immigrants will leave Americans free to engage in more dignified pursuits.[47] Immigration will help resolve the "dearness of labour" problem as well: "The disturbed state of Europe, inclining its citizens to emigration, the requisite workmen, will be more easily acquired, than at another time; and the effect of multiplying the opportunities of employment to those who emigrate, may be an increase of the number and extent of valuable acquisitions to the population arts and industry of the Country."

Aware that this may sound callous, Hamilton sheds a crocodile tear: "To find pleasure in the calamities of other nations, would be criminal; but to benefit ourselves, by opening an asylum to those who suffer, in consequence of them, is as justifiable as it is politic."[48] Although he did not specify numbers, he clearly envisioned the situation that would in fact emerge in the first third of the next century, shortly after Tocqueville visited America, when immigration rose to much higher levels and a large part of the newcomers were confined to the seaboard cities by their inability to purchase land. Meanwhile, correctly anticipating that Congress would not implement his recommendation for attracting foreign artisans, Hamilton acted on his own and sent agents to Scotland and elsewhere to enlist knowledgeable workers.[49]

Although Hamilton's "system" was swept under by the panic of 1792, his suggestion that factories could be operated by immigrants, leaving Americans free to carry on more dignified activities, presaged the segmented labor market that formed a distinctive feature of American economic development in the age of mass migration.[50] The leader of the Federalist Party, which within a few years of the "Report" would enact the notorious Alien and Sedition Acts that established it as the fountainhead of "nativism," thus also deserves credit as the first explicit advocate of the mass immigration that decisively deflected the United States from its original course as an "Anglo-Saxon republic" toward reincarnation as a "nation of immigrants."

Prevailing conditions effectively ruled out autonomous emigration by the poor majority in the United Kingdom and continental Europe. The costs of transatlantic relocation were prohibitive, as they included not only the actual price of passage but also expenses for maintenance and forgone earnings during the several months involved. Because the sailing season coincided with the most active time for agriculture and urban outdoor work, the opportunity costs amounted in effect to the better part of a year's income. The poor could thus set out only if sponsored in some fashion, as provided by the indenture and redemptioner systems. However, the breakdown of established credit and commercial links in the wake of the Revolution destroyed the underpinnings of the British and Irish servant markets, and their reconstruction was severely hampered by the mercantilist measures imposed after 1783, as well as an egalitarian trend in public opinion that made short shrift of "servants," and the restrictive interpretations of American courts regarding contracts.[51]

Concurrently, on the American side, indentured servitude among the native-born declined from the 1760s onward as a consequence of economic fluctuations and rapid population growth. The domestic supply of wage workers increased somewhat following the emergence of a labor surplus in some rural areas, which drove those unable to make a living toward Philadelphia and other cities, and the resulting pool of free, floating, contractable laborers better served the needs of small manufacturers and master artisans.[52] Moreover, swept up by the whirlwind of liberty, in the wake of the Revolution white males "found it increasingly impossible to accept any dependent status whatsoever. . . . Americans began to think about indenture quite differently, as a form of involuntary rather than voluntary servitude and as essentially indistinguishable from slavery."[53] Disembarking immigrants were told by "agitators" that American soil liberated them of any previously contracted obligations, as was the case for slaves in Britain ever since the *Somerset* decision of 1772.[54] Disavowal of the traditional manner of importing servants can be inferred as well from the fact that Benjamin Franklin's 1784 "Information to Those Who Would Remove to America" makes no reference whatsoever to indenture as a possibility, even for the poor. From the employer side, the advantages of a free market in labor were reinforced by the outbreak of a severe depression in 1784.

Overall, legal developments in the postrevolutionary period indicate that while some forms of servitude for immigrants remained acceptable, they were steadily more circumscribed by a variety of qualifications, and a sharp distinction emerged between indentured servants and German redemptioners, significantly called "free-willers."[55] The German system was more acceptable because it usually involved indebtedness to a ship captain for all or part of the costs of a family's passage, which might be repaid in whole or in part upon landing, shortly thereafter by awaiting relatives, or by binding minors into apprenticeship under supervised conditions, usually within the community where their families settled.[56] Moreover, "[R]edemptioners were not the property of anyone when they entered the servant auction, and they assigned themselves to their chosen master."[57] How widely this was accepted is indicated by the fact that in 1792 George Washington proposed to the commissioners of the District of Columbia a detailed plan for the importation of German labor for construction work in the new federal city. Overall, about 45 percent of German immigrants arriving in Philadelphia between 1785 and 1804 bound themselves after landing to redeem their transportation debts; however, many others were "redeemed" by relatives or recently formed immigrant aid societies upon arrival.[58] The German system lingered on and even revived after the Napoleonic Wars, thanks in part to legislative ameliorations secured by German American societies.[59] However, in the face of the lure of America, many German states and principalities sought to prevent the drain of their valuable populations by criminalizing emigration.[60]

Keeping Them Out

Having asserted the parallel right "to restrain that influx, whenever it is found likely to prove hurtful to us," Coxe proceeded to elaborate the principle.[61] Whereas a "body of people" do not have the right "to exclude others from settling in a territory which it cannot legally occupy"—a reference once again to the legitimacy of white over Indian claims to land—"yet it will not be disputed, that it may wholly refuse or carefully qualify the admission into its own community." This is founded on "another original principle," well established in international law since its inception in the seventeenth century, namely, "its own preservation."

Reminding his audience that "[w]ith a most preposterous policy, the former masters of this country were accustomed to discharge their jails of the vilest part of their subjects, and to transmit ship loads of wretches, too worthless for the old world, to taint and corrupt the infancy of the new," he took the opportunity to demonstrate the difference that the achievement of sovereignty made: "It is not now likely that these states will be infected with the transportation of this sort, directly ordered from any other sovereign power. A state may banish its criminals; but it cannot, consistently with the laws of nations, obtrude them on another." Nevertheless, the danger persists because of opportunities to escape after the commission of crimes, or when the punishment is "indiscriminate exile." Hence, citing the Pennsylvania law that requires a foreigner "to be a good character" before he is admitted to citizenship, Coxe links regulation of admission into the *territory* and admission into the *community* as complementary elements of a comprehensive system of immigration control.[62]

Concern over convicts justifiably lingered on. No longer able to dump convicts in America, in 1776 the British government housed those awaiting transportation in old ships on the Thames and in southern naval ports, for possible use as labor in public works; however, this proved highly unpopular with local communities, which feared that the hulks would spread typhus.[63] Hence, as peace approached, Britain attempted to resume shipping to the United States by disguising the convicts as indentured servants. One load was successfully landed in Baltimore at the end of 1783, but the following year another was intercepted and ended up in British Honduras.[64] British North America afforded no alternative solution, as officials there were adamantly opposed to convicts as well. After contemplating the alternative of West Africa, the authorities settled on remote Botany Bay, Australia, because of its suitability as a naval base, which might be built by convict labor, and the first deportation fleet sailed out three years later.[65] Nevertheless, the Americans did not believe they had yet won this war. In 1787, Benjamin Franklin rehearsed his earlier proposal for transporting American felons to Scotland, and now added that they should be carried in American vessels, made idle by British restraints on trade. As an alternative, every English ship arriving in American ports "should be obliged to give Bond, before she is permitted to Trade, engaging that she will carry back to Britain at least one Felon for every Fifty Tons of her Burthen," thereby furnishing its government "with the means of 'better Peopling,' and with more Expedition, their promising new Colony of Botany Bay."[66] Albeit proposed here in jest, the use of a person-to-ton ratio for regulatory purposes was being devised as an innovative instrument for regulating all kinds of overseas movements, notably the transportation of Africans slaves as well as of British emigrants.

Responding to reports that convicts were being secretly introduced from the West Indies, in September 1788, the Congress, still operating under the Articles of Confederation, urged the states "to pass proper laws for preventing the transportation of convicted malefactors from foreign countries into the United States." Thus encouraged, several acted expeditiously and most of the remaining followed suit after the federal Constitution took effect.[67] This provided a precedent for collaborative action by the states, which under the new Constitution retained full authority in the realm of "police power," and the federal government, which was granted authority to legislate in the sphere of immigration (after 1808) but could not regulate "persons." Franklin's irony thus materialized into history, as American restrictions deflected some 150,000 felons to Australia over the next half-century.

The other urgent issue was paupers. Providing a foundational cliché of immigrant welfare dependency, Jefferson asserted in *Notes on the State of Virginia* that thanks to a well-established system of poor relief at the parish level, "you will seldom meet a beggar" from Savannah to Portsmouth; however, he grants that they sometimes do appear in larger towns, but "[t]hey are usually foreigners, who have never obtained a settlement in any parish. I never yet saw a native American begging in the streets or highways."[68] Yet there is no gainsaying that immigration did pose special problems in this sphere. As the population uprooted by the great transformation expanded, more of the lower classes entered into the pool of emigrants, including the "poor but honest," who could scrape together enough to pay the way of at least the principal male breadwinner.[69] Landing as free rather than bound workers, they were immediately exposed to the vagaries of the labor market, as well as to the whole range of ordinary life risks, without the benefit of obligated kin or even of the patriarchal support provided by the traditional order in their home community. Under these circumstances, institutions of public charity in the American ports of entry were recurrently overwhelmed. The problem was acknowledged even by a committed democrat such as the English refugee Dr. Joseph Priestley, who nevertheless dismissed it optimistically as "the most vicious in one country, and especially a distant one, being separated from their former connexions, and entering into new ones, of a better cast, may become reformed and useful citizens."[70]

However, echoing conventional views, policy makers believed relief recipients to be unfit for membership in a republic that was rapidly becoming market oriented, and foreign paupers were doubly objectionable because they imposed an extra burden on local authorities. In the final decades of the eighteenth century, the population supported under the various Poor Laws in England and Wales reached as high as 20 percent in hard times and seldom fell below 10 percent, and the precedent of transporting convicts suggested that the Crown would not hesitate to resolve its increasingly burdensome problem by dumping.[71] Albeit undoubtedly exaggerated, the belief had a basis in fact, as Poor Law authorities discovered early on that it was cheaper to pay a pauper's way to America than to support him and his family at home.

Accordingly, deterrent measures rapidly proliferated.[72] In response to the

1788 congressional call for action to deter convicts, Massachusetts integrated its convict statute with its Poor Laws.[73] Six years later, the state enacted a more draconian law providing for paupers to be deported "by land or water, to any other State, or to any place beyond sea, where he belongs," or if this cannot be done, incarcerated "and employed in the house of correction, or work-house."[74] Several states targeted "vagrants" as well, persons of no fixed abode who verged on the dangerous. Others were likely to be chargeable regardless of moral disposition because of their inability to work. As enumerated in various state laws, they included the sick, lame, maimed, or "impotent"; infants and the aged, with pregnant women sometimes added because they were not fit to work; and, finally, "idiots" and "lunatics."

The ports of entry faced the problem most directly. Given America's self-imposed constraint against barring "immigration or importation" prior to 1808 (discussed shortly), regulation was largely aimed at producing revenue to offset the costs incurred by city and charitable organizations. Most of the devices entailed some form of security to be put up by shippers on behalf of persons "likely to be chargeable to the community," which could sometimes be commuted into the payment of a much smaller cash fee. A flat head tax was sometimes added as well. These costs were passed on to the passengers themselves in the form of higher fares and thereby expected to eliminate or at least minimize the most destitute. Of the thirteen original states, all but Virginia, New Jersey, and Connecticut either reinforced existing colonial legislation or acted de novo before the end of the Napoleonic Wars. A second line of defense, adumbrated by Tench Coxe, was the imposition of a "good character" requirement for naturalization; and some further advocated high naturalization fees to prevent the poor from entering the body politic.

The most assiduous regulator was the State of New York, which faced the side effects of what was rapidly emerging as the nation's major port.[75] The existing bond of £50 pounds ($125) was doubled in 1788, with the liability period set at one year. In 1797, a year of recession, the bonding system was expanded to cover additional categories and the state imposed an additional tax on crew and passengers to defray the cost of a new hospital for indigent aliens. The following year, all aliens were made subject to bond, which was raised to $300 with an extended liability period of two years. This was commutable into a flat payment of $5.00 per passenger, except when it might be "injurious to the public interest," notably if there was reason to believe it might be used to dump a large number of paupers into the state.

To the extent that it was enforced, the commutation system would have the effect of inducing some screening of passengers by the carriers prior to embarkation. This in effect projected American immigration control abroad, a precocious form of "remote control."[76] However, there were built-in constraints against the imposition of effective deterrents. One can discern from the very beginning the makings of a clash of interests in the ports of entry between those benefiting from immigration as a growing component of shipping and as a source of labor, and those bearing the attendant social costs, notably municipal officials and philanthropic bodies. Competing for passenger traffic, the seaboard states faced a classic "prisoners' dilemma": all would be better off if they imposed restrictions, but each had an interest in lowering them to maximize its share of the traffic. New Jersey notoriously kept its landing requirements very low so as to attract traffic destined for New York, to which the passengers were then transported by lighter.[77] Arguing that the $5.00 flat payment harmed New York's competitive position, the city's merchants subsequently obtained its reduction to $3.00.

The Negro Problem

Republican revulsion against personal dependency focused most ardently on slavery. Despite their egregious shortcomings in this respect, arising from sheer class interest in the case of the Southerners but also from widespread doubt shared by Northerners as to whether Negroes—as they were generally called at the time—might ever qualify as autonomous citizens, the revolutionaries were nearly unanimous in their determination to end importations. Virginia had taken the lead in making a disavowal of the slave trade part of revolutionary ideology, both on principle and on security grounds, fearing that "unseasoned" slaves were more likely to rebel and respond to British promises of freedom.[78] As early as 1774, the Continental Congress urged a boycott of the British trade as well as total abolition, and a half-dozen states quickly complied. Yet Jefferson's charge that King George III "has waged cruel war against human nature itself" by enslaving innocent Africans and suppressed "every legislative attempt to prohibit or to restrain this execrable commerce" in men was notoriously eliminated from the final version of the Declaration of Independence, reflecting the divergent interests that would subsequently lead to a constitutional compromise on the matter.

Nevertheless, the egalitarian impulses unleashed by the Revolution prompted further challenges to the renewal of slave importations, coupled with security concerns, which became more urgent as the revolutionary wave spread to other lands. The assault now extended to slavery itself, at least in the North, where the institution was less deeply rooted in society and marginal to the economy; but even in the South, much of the revolutionary leadership advocated some form of gradual emancipation. Actual and prospective liberation in turn brought to the fore the issue of how ex-slaves might fit into American society. Moderate southern emancipationists such as Jefferson and Madison faced a dilemma: "Caught, as they thought, between the undeniable necessity of liberating their Negroes and the inevitability of disaster if they did, they clutched desperately at the hope that the problem, Negroes, would simply go away."[79]

This possibility arose quite literally, and as early as 1777, Jefferson tinkered with the idea of sending Negroes back to Africa as American colonists.[80] Hitherto rather vague, the notion took firmer root in the midst of the Constitutional Convention, when word came that the British abolitionists planned to launch a colony under British protection in Sierra Leone for unwanted free blacks in England and Nova Scotia, most of whom were of American origin.[81] A parallel notion was emerging among New England black communities. Initially aspiring to contribute to the emancipation of American slaves as well as to uplift African heathens, after the Revolution some black "colonisationists" adopted the language of nationalism as well. Persuaded that happiness and prosperity could not be achieved in America, a group in Providence, Rhode Island, launched an African Union Society that, upon hearing of the British plans, sent an exploratory mission of its own to Sierra Leone.[82] Taken together, the end of slave importation, the emigration or even deportation of free Negroes, and the requirement that candidates for naturalization be "free and white," which denied any free Negro immigrants entry into the political community, amounted to a project for reversing history so as to resolve a uniquely American problem, the transformation of a bundle of plantation colonies structured as plural societies into a section of a white republic.

Yet in the short term the balance of interests promoted continued importation. Although American slaves had a higher rate of natural reproduction than their West Indian counterparts, thousands were lost by way of British emancipation, while demand rose sharply between the end of the war and the late 1780s, and was subsequently reinforced by the invention of the cotton gin. Reluctant to import Virginia's surplus, considered a source of potential trouble, the states of the expanding Deep South insisted on continuing the trade with Africa. In the wake of the organization of representation on the basis of population, a radical departure from the parliamentary tradition of "virtual representation," slave imports mattered for the maintenance of the South's power in the political arena also.[83] This led to the notorious agreement for uniting slave and nonslave states into a national legislature, whereby non-naturalized foreign-born whites, even if bound to service for a number of years, were included in "the whole Number of free Persons," whereas slaves, even if American born, were counted as "three-fifths of a man." With regard to the slave trade, a compromise was reached on August 24, 1787, whereby the South withdrew its demand for two-thirds majorities on international trade, while the North agreed that "importation" would not be prohibited for at least another twenty years.

With historical attention understandably focused on slavery and the slave trade, little notice has been taken of the fact that the prohibition against barring "immigration or importation" prior to 1808 also provided assurance to the North that no barriers would be imposed on arrivals from Europe during the same period.[84] This would not only keep the North from falling behind the South in population for purposes of representation, but also possibly even undermine slavery by providing a pool of cheap labor that would provide an alternative to the peculiar institution. By the same token, the Constitution was made to contain a "negative pregnant" that negated the South's objectives: congressional power to regulate commerce now explicitly included authority to prohibit "migration or importation" as a whole or in part from 1808 onward.[85] Since Section 8 also empowered Congress "To regulate Commerce with foreign Nations," it further acquired the possibility of controlling "migration or importation" by indirect means, notably the regulation of shipping.

With regard to competition for political power between the sections, in the period before the deadline the South clearly achieved the advantage, as slave importations outnumbered European arrivals. Recent estimates suggest that at least 114,600 slaves were imported in 1776–1809, mostly after 1783, and that the traffic expanded after 1787 to improve holdings before the deadline.[86] It is further estimated that another quarter of a million slaves were imported illegally between 1808 and the Civil War.[87] In relation to the project of whitening America, this vastly outweighed the number of Negroes who returned to Africa.

To Make New Americans

As amply evident from the grievances voiced in the course of their struggle for independence, in the late colonial period the Americans favored an undemanding naturalization procedure that would attract valuable settlers by quickly extending to them the economic privileges attached to British nationality. This basic stance was reaffirmed after the war. Freed of the constraints imposed by the Crown, most of the states immediately eased existing procedures; the outlier was Pennsylvania, which lowered the waiting period to merely one month.[88] The sharp contrast with mercantilist Europe was widely broadcast by publicists such as Franklin, who pointed out that all the rights of a citizen could be obtained after one or two years of residence, and that the waiting period itself was not a heavy imposition, "there being no Restraints preventing Strangers from exercising any Art they understand, nor any Permission necessary." Several states granted aliens the right to own and inherit land, and even to vote. In keeping with the economic concerns mentioned earlier, upon acquiring the northwestern lands in the early 1780s, the Congress of the Confederation created a U.S. citizenship independent of state citizenship by incorporating long-term alien inhabitants, including French Catholics, free blacks, and individual Native Americans. The absence of explicit discriminatory qualifications established a baseline for further debates on the matter at the Constitutional Convention and in the first Congress.[89]

However, from a political perspective, the transformation of the colonies into an independent republic imbued naturalization with unprecedented and awesome significance. The procedure was no longer a gateway to British subjecthood but rather, as Coxe put it in his paper, provided "admission to a political fellowship," the body of republican *citizens*, a term that, in the English language, is an Americanism dating back to this period.[90] This fostered divergent considerations. On the one hand, the presence within the republic of an unintegrated population of resident strangers, as with metics in Athens or slaves in plantation colonies, was unacceptable, hence "admission to political fellowship" should be encouraged and facilitated. But on the other, the expectation that citizens would actively participate in the republic's political life counseled caution to insure that immigrants had it in them to become citizens.

The tensions generated by these contending imperatives are laid bare in Jefferson's *Notes on the State of Virginia*. In one chapter, he sets forth with evident satisfaction the generous conditions for access to membership in the Commonwealth of Virginia, which he had personally contributed to bring about: "A foreigner of any nation, not in open war with us, becomes naturalized by removing to the state to reside, and taking an oath of fidelity; and thereupon acquires every right of a native citizen."[91] However, in another chapter he sharply questions the wisdom of "great importations of foreigners," and in particular of admitting non-British immigrants into the Commonwealth's body politic: "Every species of government has its specific principles. Ours perhaps are more peculiar than those of any other in the universe. It is a composition of the freest principles of the English constitution, which others derived from natural right and natural reason. To these nothing can be more opposed than the maxims of absolute monarchies. Yet from such, we are to expect the greatest number of emigrants." As Jefferson saw it, the problem is one of political culture: "They will bring with them the principles of the governments they leave, imbibed in their early youth; or, if able to throw them off, it will be in exchange for an unbounded licentiousness, passing, as is usual, from one extreme to another. It would be a miracle were they to stop precisely at the point of temperate liberty. These principles, with their language, they will transmit to their children. In proportion to their numbers, they will share with us the legislation. They will infuse into it their spirit, warp and bias its direction, and render it a heterogeneous, incoherent mass."[92]

Perennially invoked by those opposing the incorporation of particular national or cultural groups, the statesmen's diatribe against continental Europeans casts a dark historical shadow over his republican celebration of openness. Yet he clearly does not believe that his opposition to "the expediency of inviting [immigrants] by extraordinary encouragements" contradicts the assertion of republican principles with regard to naturalization, which he firmly restates: "If they come of themselves, they are entitled to all the rights of citizenship." Moreover, he concludes with a "human capital" argument on behalf of selective immigration: "I mean not that these doubts should be extended to the importation of useful artificers. The policy of that measure depends on very different considerations. Spare no expence [sic] in obtaining them. They will after a while go to the plough and the hoe; but, in the mean time, they will teach us something we do not know."

The discordance in Jefferson's comments highlights a dilemma inherent in naturalization under the circumstances that the United States faced at the time of the founding, and thereby provides a guiding thread through the labyrinth of debates and policy. Underlying the American approach to naturalization was a radically voluntaristic version of social contract theory derived from the philosopher John Locke, expressed for example in the preamble John Adams wrote for the Massachusetts Constitution: "The body politic is formed by a voluntary association of individuals. It is a social compact, by which the whole people covenants with each citizen, and each citizen with the whole people, that all shall be governed by certain laws for the common good."[93] However, social contract theorists implicitly assumed that human beings naturally cluster into mutually exclusive voluntary assemblies and gave little heed to immigration. When the process imposed itself to their attention, the problem was resolved by shifting from a conception of society as a union of individuals to a body occupying a territory, as illustrated by Tench Coxe's emphasis on the legitimacy of American territorial claims.[94]

Although the voluntaristic element of citizenship figured in the doctrine of the French revolutionaries as well, by way of its association with substantial immigration it acquired in the American context a radical character it did not possess in settled European societies.[95] The modification of social contract theory to take immigration into account also led to an unprecedented emphasis on the Lockean doctrine of the right of expatriation, which in their initial moment of enthusiasm, the Americans asserted even on behalf of their own people.[96] Consequently, American voluntarism challenged head on the common law doctrine of "perpetual allegiance," which held that a subject was indissolubly linked to the sovereign and which constituted the foundation stone of the entire European state system.

Strangely, while rejecting the doctrine of perpetual allegiance, the Americans nevertheless retained the closely associated common law tradition of jus soli as the principal determinant of nationality—a notion that was not fully congruent with "citizenship." Jus soli, which arose from the principle that the land belongs to the sovereign, and hence those born on it owe him perpetual allegiance, was so very much associated with the Ancien Régime that it was explicitly rejected by the French Revolution on behalf of jus sanguinis.[97] In effect, the Americans reinterpreted the doctrine in the light of Enlightenment environmentalism: birth on American "soil," standing for social as much as physical milieu, afforded assurance of civic virtue. However, the new approach also provided the makings of a distinction, inscribed in political discourse from the outset and institutionalized in the constitutionally mandated decennial census in response to the mid-nineteenth-century immigration crisis, between persons of "American nativity," imbued with atavistic virtues that come from several generations of American nurturance, and Americans of "foreign parentage," who presumably lack these virtues even if born in the United States.

Our revulsion at Jefferson's disparaging remarks about continentals, of a piece with his even more egregious lucubrations on race, should not lead us to neglect his more general point that a broadening of the sources of immigration beyond the British Isles would induce a measure of cultural hetero-

geneity that he deems problematic for the republic's health. This was predicated on the notion, emphasized by Baron Montesquieu, that republics require
an especially high degree of social homogeneity to foster the common interest;
and for the same reason, since heterogeneity generally increases with size,
they must limit themselves to a small number. This meant not only reducing
economic inequality but also avoiding differences of religion and language.
The prevalence of this outlook is illustrated by Tom Paine's reference to it in
his debate with Edmund Burke: "If there is any country in the world, where
concord, according to common calculation, would be least expected, it is
America. Made up as it is, of people from different nations, accustomed to
different forms and habits of government, speaking different languages, and
more different in their modes of worship, it would appear that the union of
such a people was impracticable."[98]

Homogeneity was deemed especially urgent in the American situation because citizens were entitled to extensive political participation. In the sphere
of religion, whereas the variety of Protestant sects established in the United
States was perceived as falling within the bounds of manageability, Roman
Catholicism was perceived as lying beyond them. With regard to ethnicity,
the various groups of "Britons" or "Anglo-Saxons" were constructed as similar,
but sharply distinct from "Celts" and continental races, except for the original
"Saxons," a flexible term that usually encompassed German and Netherlandish
Protestants. Within the white world, the leading marker of worrisome heterogeneity was language, a preoccupation that had moved to the fore in the
course of the Enlightenment when language came to be envisioned as the
formative carrier of distinctive values.[99] Jefferson's concern was not that
the presence of French or German speakers in Virginia would hamper communication, but that their languages were imbued with the values of their
respective societies of origin, and programmed speakers accordingly: "These
principles, with their language, they will transmit to their children." His views
were by no means idiosyncratic, as indicated by Benjamin Franklin's already
cited observations on the subject, nor were they peculiarly American, as demonstrated by the efforts of the French revolutionaries to eliminate provincial
languages, associated with the Old Régime, on behalf of French, the language
of the Revolution.

American leaders varied considerably in their assessment of whether the
political community was still safely homogeneous or verged on unsafe diversity, and this indeterminacy meant that the matter was open to debate and
could spawn divergent policies. At one pole was the serene vision evoked by

John Jay in *Federalist* No. 2: "Providence has been pleased to give this one connected country to one united people—a people descended from the same ancestors, speaking the same language, professing the same religion, attached to the same principles of government, very similar in their manners and customs. . . . To all general purposes we have uniformly been one people."[100] But this view was hardly shared by all, and the situation at the time of the first federal census lent considerable credence to Tom Paine's alternative characterization of the United States as "[m]ade up . . . of people from different nations."[101] For some, the situation was reassuring and hence allowed for some risk taking with regard to immigration; but this also allowed for the argument that the republic should avoid courting danger by moving away from the status quo.

Rogers Smith has suggested that the latter view prevailed, and that this "authorized the new American republicans to exclude aliens as well as home-grown undesirable 'others' from full civic membership, as the predominantly Protestant Anglophone male citizenry saw fit."[102] But that is questionable: most notably, they extended full citizenship rights to Roman Catholics nearly half a century before the United Kingdom did so, as well as to Jews even before the French revolutionaries.[103] Given concerns over language, it is also remarkable that applicants for naturalization were not required to know English.

Under the circumstances, this constitutes an unexpected outcome, which must be accounted for. One possibility, suggested by the substantial reduction of the residence requirement in the first decade, is that the founders' conception of naturalization differed sharply from what later came to be taken for granted. Rather than the capstone of a process of integration, it was seen as an instrument for integration; rather than a status bestowed upon the newcomers after they demonstrated their qualifications for membership, it was a secular ritual akin to baptism, a sacrament that conferred on them qualities they hitherto lacked and rendered them capable of becoming Americans. Asking, "How the new citizens can best be rendered useful members of the community that adopts them," and, "How this can be effected, without endangering the happiness and safety of the original citizens," Tench Coxe answered, "The sooner the new citizens are fully incorporated with the society to which they acceded, the sooner they become useful members." By virtue of this inclusion, "they then grow attached to their new country: they consider themselves as part of it: they adopt the opinions and affections of their new brethren, and soon forget that they have adopted them, and imagine they are natural." This was in keeping with the widespread belief that, contrary to European visions of degeneracy, the American environment was imbued with regenerative powers verging on the miraculous, as demonstrated among other things by the population's spectacular rate of natural expansion. From that perspective, crossing the Atlantic was akin to traversing the mythical pool fed by the fountain of youth, a metaphor itself inspired by baptism. Inclusion of itself endowed newcomers with a republican soul.

Not surprisingly, Coxe anticipated objections stimulated by two distinct dangers: (1) "if the mode of access was rendered too easy, foreign powers . . . might make use of that method, to interfere in the public measures"; and (2) "the new citizens, infected with ancient prejudices and attachments, might employ the privileges they had acquired, to the injury of the country that had adopted them." But the first of these, he astutely demonstrates, is nullified by the very nature of democracy: "[T]he election of public officers, is in too many hands for a foreign power to do much mischief. . . . It would be a very clumsy as well as a very costly scheme to send a colony to a republic, in expectation of overturning it, by means of the municipal rights imparted to them." As for the "Jefferson jeopardy," it is offset by the very process that brought the for-eigners to the new land: "Driven away by the perception of evils, [the emi-grant] cannot but wish to preserve the new clime from the same systems which rendered the old intolerable to him. Already acquainted with their pernicious tendency, he will more readily discover, and more anxiously pursue measures useful and salutary to his present country, than the native citizen, whose love of novelty may lead him into propositions, of which his inexperience prevents him from perceiving the danger."

Coxe evidently represented one side of an ongoing debate. Although nat-uralization itself was left to be decided by a future Congress, the issue of what rights it might provide arose in the course of the constitutional debates with regard to eligibility for office. There was considerable sentiment "that full political rights should be reserved to those whose loyalties could be trusted due to native birth or extensive domestic residence," indicating limits on vol-untarism and the persistence of "a belief in the power of place of birth and inhabitancy to shape one's sense of political identity and allegiance."[104] This is best indicated by the requirement of nativity plus fourteen years of residence for eligibility to the office of president. The significance of the further require-ment of seven years beyond naturalization for the House and nine for the Senate can be assessed from opposite perspectives: naturalization was not enough, but outright nativity, in keeping with British practice for Parliament, was definitely abandoned as a requirement. The winning side argued on grounds of both principle and interest. While Edmund Randolph stressed that the rights of naturalized citizens could not be restricted because many had come to the United States "trusting in the general invitation to the oppressed that the Revolutionary leaders had extended," Hamilton emphasized that "only by making foreign-born citizens equally eligible with natives for holding office could Europeans of property be induced to come."[105]

The issue of naturalization was complicated by the dualism of state and national citizenship. While the final version of the Articles of Confederation provided that free inhabitants of each state would benefit from the privileges of citizenship in all the others, the problem was, as Madison pointed out in *Federalist* No. 42, that states with the most open provisions thereby imposed their views on all others.[106] It was to overcome this that intersectional agreement emerged at the Convention to vest in Congress the power "[t]o establish an uniform rule of naturalization . . . throughout the United States." Its coupling with the authority to establish "uniform laws on the subject of bankruptcies" highlights the prominence of economic concerns in the overall process. Although the decision insured that the boundaries of the political community would henceforth be determined nationally, the Constitution also retained the distinction between citizenship in a state and in the United States, thereby allowing for some ambiguity.[107]

Washington asserted in his very first message to Congress that the matter of a uniform rule brooked no delay, and the ensuing debate confirmed that the central concerns were landholding and officeholding rather than voting, which sometimes was extended to noncitizens, and reflected sectional interests as well as regional differences in ethnic profile.[108] As one would expect, Pennsylvania and other "western" states advocated quick and easy naturalization as an incentive for settlement, especially of persons of property to whom citizenship would provide secure ownership rights. This stance also served the interests of ethnic minorities. In the national elections of 1788, Pennsylvania's German community, which had hitherto shied away from politics, demanded representation in proportion to its weight in the population, thereby prompting both the Federalists and the Anti-Federalists to nominate appropriate ethnic candidates. Voting as a bloc, the Germans sent three representatives to the new Congress, where they firmly supported the "liberal" side in the naturalization debate, thereby providing a precocious demonstration of the "feedback effect" of incorporation on immigration and naturalization policy.[109] The other side consisted of a coalition of unlikely bedfellows:

New England, reflecting the region's narrower view of national identity, and the South, which, albeit favoring immigration, was afraid that most of the new citizens would oppose slavery.

Naturalization emerged as a second-line defense against undesirable immigrants. In keeping with the established trend, the law enacted in 1790 provided that free white persons of satisfactory character would be eligible for naturalization after two years' residence in the United States, including one year within the state. With the historical gaze riveted on "white," little notice has been taken that the qualifier "free" also excluded white immigrants bound to temporary servitude until their term expired. The requirement of "satisfactory character," probably inspired by the Pennsylvania Constitution and referred to as a salutary precaution by Tench Coxe in 1787, was designed to exclude not only convicts and felons but also "paupers," considered malefactors in need of discipline. The very poor in any case were unlikely to muster the court fees that naturalization entailed. That being said, the procedure's accessibility was insured by the specification that it could take place in any common law court of record. The law also provided that the minor children of naturalized parents become citizens by way of jus sanguinis and, conversely, that the children of American nationals born abroad be considered "natural-born" citizens.

In keeping with the contractarian spirit of American republicanism, admission to political fellowship required an oath of allegiance to the U.S. Constitution, thereby highlighting its superiority to a mere government. Although the Naturalization Act of 1790 refrained from subjecting applicants to political vetting, it did specify that foreign-born persons who had left the United States at the time of the Revolution could not become naturalized without the express consent of the states. Directed at repentant British-born Loyalists, this exclusionary provision, enacted several years after the end of hostilities, constituted one more marker of the country's emerging assertiveness as a sovereign nation and distinctive political régime.[110]

Although the requirement of whiteness constituted a retreat from the more inclusive notion of national citizenship inscribed in the Northwestern Ordinance enacted three years earlier, it evoked no debate whatsoever. Perennially restated in subsequent legislation down to the Civil War, this provision excluded not only persons of African descent, notably the mulattoes from Saint-Domingue (now Haiti) who shortly streamed into the United States as refugees from the revolution, but also American Indians, who could become citizens only by treaty. "White" clearly meant white exclusively, and when Asians appeared on the scene in the 1840s, the courts quickly determined that they were ineligible as a matter of course.

In the end, we find ourselves once again staring at the proverbial glass: although the law confirmed the republic's racial boundary, the inclusiveness of all free Europeans, regardless of nationality, religion, language, or even gender, constituted a unique assertion of republican universalism, no less remarkable for being driven by interests as much as sheer principle. The most radical took a perverse pride in the challenge presented by America's heterogeneity. Tom Paine, having acknowledged that a heterogeneous union appeared "impracticable," especially to "a metaphysical man, like Mr. Burke," went on to assert that "by the simple operation of constructing government on the principles of society and the rights of man, every difficulty retires, and all the parts are brought into cordial unison."[111] From an international perspective, the provision of routine access to American citizenship constituted a radical political innovation that challenged head on the doctrine of "perpetual allegiance" and threatened to seduce subjects away from their sovereigns. Added to the marketing of land, this constituted provocative encouragement to immigration.

Americans and Un-Americans

Beginning in Washington's second term, the ascending Federalists imposed successively more demanding requirements for naturalization, and also enacted the notorious Alien and Sedition Acts of 1798, designed to deter nefarious foreign influences as well as to maintain political order by subjecting both aliens and their American associates to governmental surveillance, as well as criminalizing certain forms of political protest. James Morton Smith's classic account of these developments, in preparation at the height of McCarthyism, presents the episode as a largely irrational response to internal and international tensions, prefiguring McCarthyism itself.[112] This was further interpreted by John Higham as a precocious manifestation of "nativism," and more particularly of the antiradical strain of the disease: whereas some believe that immigrants threaten republican freedom by virtue of their submissiveness to despotism, others believe they do so by virtue of their revolutionary disposition, the two being possibly dialectically related as Jefferson thought to be the case.[113]

While Stanley Elkins and Eric McKittrick have downplayed the 1798 measures as incidental aberrations that were not central to the Federalist project, pointing out that they were passed by very small majorities and that President John Adams explicitly dissociated himself from them, they have in turn been criticized by Rogers Smith, who argues that the legislation was part of a struggle over citizenship central to the confrontation between the emerging political camps: whereas the Republicans remained committed to citizenship by consent with regard to whites—albeit also engaging in aggressive racism— the Federalists emphasized hereditary allegiance and "nativism."[114]

But why did "nativism" surface at this time and in this form? Less than a decade after it emerged from its war of independence, and while it was still completing the arduous task of launching its national institutions, the United States was severely disturbed by the widespread revolutionary upheavals that shook the Atlantic world as a whole, compounded by the outbreak of what quickly escalated into a global war.[115] States were impelled to deploy draconian security measures against internal and external threats perceived to be interactive. Internal mobilization was stepped up, and controlling the movement of goods, information, as well as people across international boundaries became a matter of great urgency. Concomitantly, nationality gained unprecedented importance as the foundation of internal political solidarity; and national origin came to supplant religious affiliation as an indicator of putative political orientation.

Although the fledgling American Republic managed to survive thanks to the determination of its leaders to stay out of the conflict—at least until 1812—as well as to a considerable measure of good fortune, notably geographic remoteness from the central European conflict, its trials induced an awesome political crisis and a resulting transformation. The European conflict's prominent ideological dimension contributed to a sharpening of disagreements over the character of the American political régime, and this was in turn projected into the sphere of foreign policy. The fissures that appeared in the wall separating the perilous outside world and the insular realm of safe domesticity prompted efforts to reconstruct a more solid boundary. A basic task was to distinguish more clearly between reliable or unreliable Americans, and friendly or dangerous aliens.

By the early 1790s the revolutionary generation was clustering into two distinct political camps, if not yet organized parties.[116] The Jeffersonians hailed the French Revolution as indicating the progress of America's most reliable ally toward constitutional and republican government, as well as providing an opportunity to expand commercial exchanges that would loosen the British stronghold. As against this, the industrial- and capitalist-minded gathered around Hamilton were committed to a rapprochement with Great Britain and viewed the radicalization of the French Revolution through the eyes of the British political leadership, that is, as a threat to international peace and to established régimes everywhere. Much as the British government responded to mounting pressures for reform, inspired as much by the American Revolution as by the French, by elaborating a more authoritarian state, the Federalists believed that world conditions made it imperative to insulate the national government from popular pressures and to enhance its capacity to defend itself against foreign and domestic threats.

Although Americans commonly spoke of providing "asylum" to oppressed Europeans, in the 1790s the term took on a new and more literal meaning. The violent political upheavals in France, western Europe's most populous state, produced tens of thousands of émigrés. Some 8,000 landed in Britain, and nearly 2,000 in the United States. The latter were joined from 1798 on by whites and mulattoes escaping the slave uprising in nearby Saint-Domingue, eventually totaling well over 20,000.[117] Most of the French clustered in East Coast cities, and particularly the capital, Philadelphia, where they constituted a highly visible community of over 10,000.[118] Concurrently, the anti-Jacobin reaction in Britain drove many political radicals to America; as with religious dissenters in early colonial times, voluntary exile was often an alternative to criminal prosecution. After 1798 the United States also became a haven for defeated partisans of the French-supported United Irishmen insurrection, the most serious challenge to British imperial rule since the American Revolution itself. Ulster Presbyterians predominated, but about one-fifth were Catholics. Long associated with crime, drink, and poverty, the image of the "wild Irish" was immediately politicized; and "while the Federalists believed that the United Irishmen were part of an international revolutionary conspiracy, the United Irishmen were equally convinced that they were facing a British-based counterrevolutionary plot."[119]

Unlike earlier victims of religious persecution, who were generally considered politically unproblematic by virtue of their shared religious identity with the host state, in the late eighteenth century even partisans of the Old Order inspired fear because they might be infected with the revolutionary virus; moreover, it was suspected that the refugee flows provided cover for spies and terrorists. Accordingly, the upheavals occasioned a spate of parallel enactments throughout the Atlantic world, foreshadowing the tightening of border controls and the concomitant generalization of passport and visa requirements in the wake of World War I and the Russian Revolution.

The most relevant developments occurred in Great Britain, which remained for many decades the leading reference for American lawyers and legislators. In 1793 Parliament enacted the first Alien Bill in recorded British history, which required shipmasters to report foreigners to customs officers.[120] The following year the act was extended to cover British North America, one of a number of measures designed to insulate the colony from subversion by the United States. In 1795, after the king was attacked on his way to Parliament, Britain also imposed drastic restrictions on the press, the right of assembly, and political party activity. On the French side as well, measures designed to control the movements of foreigners proliferated from the beginning of the French Revolution onward, and were consolidated in the comprehensive passport law of 1797, which was subsequently incorporated into the Napoleonic Code and served as a model for many other continental states.

Under these circumstances, it is hardly surprising that the Federalists undertook to strengthen border controls and that, since the twenty-year prohibition spelled out in the Constitution prevented them from restricting immigration proper, they turned their attention to naturalization as a second line of defense. Their success in preventing Albert Gallatin from taking his U.S. Senate seat in 1794, on the grounds that he had not complied with state naturalization laws, indicated that they were not beneath using citizenship laws to deny their opponents access to office as well.[121] Although Washington opened the year 1795 with a prayer "to render this country more and more a safe and propitious asylum for the unfortunate of other countries," later in the year he approved without comment a naturalization law that more than doubled the residence requirement to five years. The authority of the "father of our country" thus became available to opposing camps in later immigration debates.

Albeit initiated by the Federalist administration and aimed principally at democratic activists seeking refuge from British repression, the measure was also supported by congressional Republicans, who feared subversion by aristocrats from France or Saint-Domingue and, as suggested by Madison, from Britain as well after the revolution he expected would erupt there in the near future.[122] Advocates of the change argued that easy access to citizenship was dangerous and insufficient to prevent improper persons from being incorporated within the American nation; in addition to the usual vagabonds and fugitives, the present European war was "inauspicious for the indiscriminate admission of aliens." Some also wanted to harden naturalization requirements to make it more difficult for foreign ship agents to evade tonnage taxes.

The proposed waiting time ranged up to ten years, but five years was agreed upon as a compromise. The law also called for a "declaration of intention," both of becoming a citizen and of renouncing all foreign allegiance, to be sworn to in a state or federal court three years prior to naturalization. Upon final application, the alien must declare "on oath or affirmation" (presumably to accommodate Quakers or non-Christians) "that he will support the Constitution of the United States and that he doth absolutely and entirely renounced and abjure all allegiance and fidelity" to any other prince or state.[123] Finally, applicants must renounce all titles of nobility. This was a trade-off amendment engineered by the Republicans and explicitly endorsed by Madison, which carried 59 to 32. However, an amendment requiring applicants to renounce slavery was defeated 28 to 63 after Madison opposed it on the grounds that it would have a bad effect on the minds of the slaves. Despite Federalist efforts to the contrary, aliens already resident in the United States were "grandfathered" into the less demanding 1790 law.

The cleavage was sharpened by Washington's retirement and the escalation of international tensions, which also provided the Federalists with an opportunity to strike at their domestic opponents in the name of national security. The country's survival indeed appeared in jeopardy as the sudden emergence of a spate of popular societies suggested it was succumbing to the Jacobin virus.[124] The earliest was the German Republican Society of Philadelphia; although its leaders were American citizens, its name and composition suggested decidedly "alien" origins, and the society acknowledged that its meetings were conducted entirely in German.[125] Moreover, its brand of republicanism appeared to confirm Jefferson's prediction that a people bred in tyranny was likely to swing to rebellion, as witnessed by their proto-anarchist proclamation in December 1794 that "all governments are more or less combinations against the people; they are states of violence against individual liberty, originating from man's imperfection and vice."[126] At least nine other republican societies were formed before the end of the year, twenty-three the following, and, at the suggestion of the newly arrived Jacobin envoy, Citizen Genêt, a number of them included the innovative term "Democratic" in their name. They were blamed for the "Whiskey Rebellion," an extensive anti–excise tax movement that swept western Pennsylvania in 1794 and so enraged Washington that he ordered the mustering of a national force to quell the uprising.[127]

The Federalists' near defeat in the 1796 presidential election, which they blamed on the support their opponents obtained from recently naturalized citizens, notably Irish, in the key states of New York and Pennsylvania, further affirmed their resolve to buttress their position by arresting or at least delaying the "feedback loop" that naturalization provided.[128] Still mostly Ulster Presbyterians, but with an increasing contingent of Catholics, the Irish had been arriving at the rate of 3,000–4,000 a year since the late 1780s; as more of them remained in the cities, they were both more visible and more influential than before, particularly in Philadelphia and its suburbs. Repeated Federalist attempts to deny the franchise to aliens precipitated a scramble to naturalize, and the Irish constituted over half of those who did so in Philadelphia in 1789–1806.[129] Although they strongly supported the constitutional movement, afterwards they broke with the Federalists over the rapprochement with Britain. Moreover, under the Pennsylvania Constitution of 1790, aliens could vote after two years' residence on the condition of paying their state and county taxes at least six months prior to the election. This was commonly done with the help of Republican merchants in exchange for electoral support. One especially provocative consequence of the alien vote was the election of Israel Israel, a Jew prominently involved in one of Philadelphia's democratic societies, to the state senate in 1797.[130]

In the course of their rapprochement with Britain, the Federalists stopped complaining about British restrictions on exit and even declared repeatedly that they would not encourage the Crown's subjects to break the laws prohibiting emigration. Washington, who had earlier collaborated in a scheme to bring skilled artisans to Virginia in defiance of British laws, severed his connection with the venture in 1791 because it was undignified for the president of the United States "to entice the subjects of another nation to violate the laws." Even more explicitly, in November 1794, precisely as John Jay completed negotiations for the eponymous pathbreaking treaty with Britain, the president stated in a letter to his envoy that "I have established it as a maxim neither to invite nor to discourage immigrants."[131]

In 1797, the congressional Federalists proposed a $20 federal tax on certificates of naturalization, justifying the move as a revenue-producing measure, as a way of preventing the naturalization of undesirables, as providing "some security for the attachment of persons to the Government of this country," and as a deterrent to immigration.[132] While the Federalists thus appeared to contradict the immigrationist arguments set forth by Hamilton in 1791, these had in fact lost much of their persuasiveness since the financial panic of 1792.[133] Although the tax failed to pass, the debates it generated are highly revealing. The Republican opposition insisted that it was unduly prohibitive, as it amounted to double the cost of a lawyer's license. Echoing Tench Coxe's reasoning of a decade earlier, Albert Gallatin, now leader of the Republicans in the House, also argued that if the concern was the republic's security, it would be unsafe to have so many living as foreigners in its bosom. "These men, speaking the same language and having the same manners, after they had been in the country ten or fifteen years, would look upon the refusal to admit them to the common right of citizens, except upon the payment of twenty dollars, as unjust and oppressive." Another member charged that the proposal "looked like entering into a treaty offensive or defensive with the Monarch of Britain, to prevent his subjects from leaving him and coming hither." However, Robert Harper of South Carolina retorted, times had changed: "There was a moment of enthusiasm in this country, when this was thought to be right—when we were not satisfied with giving to immigrants every blessing which we had earned with our blood and treasure, but admitted them instantly to the rights of citizenship. An experience of ten or fifteen years . . . had convinced us we were wrong." He concluded by suggesting the United States should do away with naturalization altogether, and allow for the acquisition of citizenship by birth only. Echoing Jefferson's reasoning, Harrison Gray Otis, the prime mover on the Federalist side, warned, "In Europe today, a revolution of manners, of the most formidable nature, threatened the subversion of all sound principle, of all social order." The proposed tax "would tend to foreclose the mass of vicious and disorganizing characters who could not live peaceably at home, and who, after unfurling the standard of rebellion in their own countries, might come hither to revolutionize ours." He singled out for special attention the "hordes of wild Irishmen" whose compatriots back home were even then uniting across the religious boundary to mount what was, as mentioned above, the most serious challenge to British rule since the American Revolution itself.

After the measure failed, he took the lead in launching a more comprehensive effort the following year.[134] As outlined in the recommendations of a Federalist House committee on May 1, 1798, the program included (1) a further doubling of the residence requirement for naturalization, (2) empowering the president to remove suspicious aliens during the present emergency (generally referred to as the "Alien Friends" proposal), and (3) empowering the president to apprehend and remove enemy aliens in the event of war ("Alien Enemies"). Although President Adams insisted that these laws were not part of his program, he did not actively oppose them and promptly gave his final consent.

Considered first, the naturalization measure dealt most explicitly with boundary making. Although there were proposals from the floor of the House for limiting citizenship to the American-born, as well as to bar naturalized citizens from holding national office altogether—as in 1790, reference was again made to British practices to this effect—or even from voting, these amendments were ruled out of order as subject to constitutional doubt and a proposalemerged to once again more than double the residency requirement to a total of fourteen years. Although the proposal squeaked by on a 41 to 40 vote, indicating that a number of Federalists found it too extreme, and not-withstanding Republican efforts in the Senate to reduce the requirement by half, the House version prevailed, and the bill was signed into law on June 18. The opposition's sole success was in exempting aliens who established residence before 1795. However, most of the "wild Irish" had arrived more recently and were thus subject to the harsher rule.

Borrowing a leaf from the recent British alien registration, which was re-ferred to in the course of the debate as an appropriate model, the law also subjected all aliens to national surveillance.[135] Acknowledging the necessity for such a law, the House Republicans focused on the removal of discretionary sanctions against American citizens aiding or abetting such aliens, or inter-fering with enforcement of the law, as well as on securing due process for the aliens themselves. Thus modified, the law survived as a recurrent feature of wartime policy.[136] Ironically, since the United States did not go to war with France, it was not used by the Federalists but implemented for the first time a decade and a half later by a Republican administration against British aliens.[137]

Frustrated by the constraints that the "Alien Enemies" Act imposed on pres-idential discretion, Otis and other hard-liners lashed out at such "alien friends" as the "wild Irish" and English "Jacobins" by way of extraordinarily harsh emergency measures. Their proposal, again modeled on British measures, not only made every alien in the United States liable to arbitrary arrest and de-portation, in peacetime as well as in war, but also penalized American citizens for "harboring, entertaining, or concealing" such aliens without the express permission of the authorities. "Buried in the heart of this bill was a bold attempt to purify the national character by isolating all aliens from American society and from each other."[138] Whereas the Republicans initially succeeded in watering down the proposal, after the "XYZ Affair"(involving allegations of the attempted bribery of a United States mission by French Foreign Minister Talleyrand) exploded in April 1798, anger at the French prompted the House to accept the more draconian version pending in the Senate, which also tightened up the surveillance already provided by the new Naturalization Act.[139] Again, although President Adams subsequently disclaimed responsibility for the act, he did not attempt to veto it and the measure became law on June 25, 1798, effective immediately for a two-year period.[140] Three weeks later he also approved the Sedition Act, which made it a crime to utter or publish "any false, scandalous, and malicious writing" against the government or the Congress, "with intent to defame . . . or to bring them . . . into contempt or disrepute."[141]

Although the "Alien Friends" Act was never officially invoked to effect deportation, this was not for lack of trying by the Adams administration, especially against United Irishmen in New York and Philadelphia, prominent Frenchmen, and even American dissidents of questionable nativity. Concurrently, the United States redoubled its diplomatic efforts to dissuade the British government from banishing Irish political prisoners who survived the insurrection's defeat to America. The legislation possibly induced some of the aliens who might have been targeted by its provisions to find other havens.[142]

Considered together, these measures amount to deliberate efforts to erect an internal boundary, not simply between natives and aliens, as suggested by historians of nativism, but somewhat more ambiguously between "Americans" and "Un-Americans." All natives were not equally American, nor all aliens equally un-American: the boundary builders placed on the one side well-behaved native-born and immigrants, and on the other disturbing aliens and Americans who adopt alien ways. For example, the democratic societies, which campaigned vigorously against the Alien and Sedition Laws, were repeatedly denounced as "alien" despite the fact that their membership consisted overwhelmingly of "natives": in the eyes of Federalist writers, they functioned through the "dark and silent system of organized treason and massacre, imported by the UNITED IRISHMEN," or, alternatively, were dominated by Jews and part of a conspiracy of the "tribe of Israel" to control American politics.[143]

By the same token, some foreigners were more "alien" than others: the Germans were a mixed lot, but the Irish were repeatedly singled out for opprobrium. Imported from Britain, Irish stereotypes were evidently well anchored in American discourse, as revealed on the opening page of what is generally considered the first American novel, *Modern Chivalry,* published in 1792 by Hugh Henry Brackenridge. After elaborately introducing his hero, Captain John Farrago, a Don Quixote–like character, the author turns to his

Sancho Panza, an Irishman named Teague Oregan [*sic*], with the terse comment: "I shall say nothing of the character of this man, because the very name imports what he was."[144] And in 1799, the year after the Irish rebellion, New York experienced the first of many violent confrontations between "Americans" and Irish immigrants, resulting in the death of one man and the arrest of several others.[145]

The Immigrant Feedback

Ironically, the measures regarded by the Federalists as a sine qua non for the perpetuation of their rule contributed instead to their premature downfall. Invoked by Kentucky and Virginia as grounds for nullification—at the initiative of Jefferson and Madison respectively—the Alien Laws also drove many immigrants more firmly into the arms of the Republican Party and prompted the states it controlled to enfranchise aliens after only one or two years' residence. Large numbers of immigrants, hitherto uninterested in naturalization, "immediately lined up at the registry offices."[146] Jefferson made the authoritarian and xenophobic character of the Federalist administration one of his major campaign themes in 1800, and the weight of the Irish immigrant vote in pivotal New York was probably decisive in his victory.[147] However, the Federalists "were no less obtuse and no less clumsy" in their dealings with the Germans, who were their natural allies.[148] Their military buildup and especially the taxes it required, together with their restrictive Americanness, stirred up a near-uprising in the rural counties of southeastern Pennsylvania, whose clumsy repression by military force drove the Germans also into the Republican camp. Concurrently, younger members of the German community undertook to wean their coethnics from the proto-anarchist doctrine voiced in 1794 and expressed in perennial tax rebellions, and to Americanize them by constructing German-language commentaries on constitutionalism that drew upon German history and traditions.[149]

As it was, the "Alien Friends" Act expired in mid-1800, and the Sedition Act at the end of the Adams administration in early 1801. By this time, the international crisis had begun to recede as well: the radical phase of the French Revolution was brought to an abrupt end by Napoleon Bonaparte's coup d'état of November 1799, and the following year the defeated Irish were deprived of their parliament and forcibly incorporated into the United Kingdom. The waning of tensions enabled the United States to resume, for the time being, the more neutral stance advocated by Washington in his Farewell Address.

Calling upon the country to live up to its vocation as an asylum for oppressed humanity, in his first message to Congress President Jefferson firmly recommended a revision of the Naturalization Law in a more generous direction. His own preference was for a return to 1790. However, Hamilton counterattacked on behalf of the Federalists, citing the doubts Jefferson himself had expressed in *Notes on the State of Virginia* against his present stance, and insisting on the "impolicy" of admitting foreigners to the suffrage immediately because of the resulting "classes and antipathies." Granting that the present fourteen years had been adopted "under peculiar circumstances," he suggested not less than five.[150]

Rogers Smith agrees with Hamilton that Jefferson had changed his position, and suggests that in the course of their struggle with the Federalists, "Republicans quickly realized that immigrants often felt more affinity for the partisans of small farmers and democratization than for mercantile and financial elites. Hence they reversed course on immigration, abandoning the qualms Jefferson had expressed during the 1780s."[151] But, as pointed out long ago by Frank George Franklin, Hamilton misrepresented Jefferson's position in *Notes on the State of Virginia* by omitting the conclusive "If they come of themselves, they are entitled to all the rights of citizenship." Jefferson's views were mixed all along, and, like Washington, he thereby lent himself to citation by opposing camps; but he was also an opportunistic party leader who did not hesitate to mobilize immigrants on behalf of his cause. The five-year waiting period was endorsed by the congressional Republicans as well, along with a requirement that "good character" be demonstrated by the testimony of two witnesses who were American citizens, and the bill was approved by about two to one in both houses.

In time, the five-year rule came to be considered the "liberal" norm, to be defended against perennial attempts by anti-immigrant forces to return to fourteen or even move to twenty-one years, subjecting aliens to a period of resocialization equivalent to the time it took male Americans to reach the age of full citizenship. Yet although there is no gainsaying that the five-year waiting period rendered naturalization more accessible than in any European state, it also moved away from the radical conception set forth during America's moment of enthusiasm as a baptism into citizenship, toward a more conventional notion of naturalization as the capstone of a process of resocialization.

Overall, these developments highlight the paradoxical dynamics of immigration in American political development. The institutionalization of a relatively open stance toward political incorporation by way of a combination of easy naturalization for newcomers and the benefits of jus soli for their American-born offspring allows for the entry of "strangers," identified on the basis of religious affiliation or ethnic origin, into the body politic. This is most likely to occur whenever immigration increases significantly beyond some established level, commonly accompanied by a broadening of its sources, usually as the result of a combination of social and political upheavals in the world at large, and economic demand on the American side. In turn, this development tends to precipitate a reactive movement to define the boundaries of "Americanness" more restrictively by excluding the newcomers, with concomitant efforts to enact supportive legislation. However, actual policy outcomes depend on institutional factors that have little or nothing to do with immigration proper, notably constitutional constraints and the configuration of party alignments.

However, the time gap between the onset of the objectionable stream and the mobilization of reaction into an effective nativist movement allows for a sufficient buildup of the group in question to provide the makings of an effective political actor, which can undertake to undo or at least reduce nativist achievements. This explains why the Federalists did not go all the way. Indeed, after the catastrophe of 1800, younger Federalists courted the Irish as ardently as the Republicans did; in Philadelphia, they "reversed themselves completely, and included in their party structure a 'committee to aid the naturalization of foreigners.' "[152] Other political conservatives would eventually learn that lesson as well.

4

The American System

In the first decades of the new century, successive Republican administrations set in place the elements of what amounted to a comprehensive population policy in which, as set forth in the doctrine elaborated by the founders, immigration was relied upon for a modest contribution to economic development and nation-building. Assumed to be responsive to emerging market forces on both sides of the Atlantic, it was nevertheless looked upon as a process subject to governance. Regulation of entry remained largely a state affair, but the national government played a coordinating role and in 1819 Congress adopted a comprehensive Passenger Act, whose significance as a foundational element of immigration policy has been underestimated. The measure constituted a bold regulatory innovation that afforded the United States a degree of "remote control" over immigration in order to attract suitable European immigrants of all nationalities by minimizing the dangers of the Atlantic crossing while simultaneously deterring the prospectively burdensome from embarking. Its revaluation is in keeping with the findings of a new generation of historians, who have challenged the conventional wisdom that, following the defeat of the Federalists in 1800, the central government sank into relative insignificance.[1]

This regulatory component was complemented by a market-oriented land policy calculated to make purchases more accessible to settlers of modest means. Concurrently, the national government undertook sustained diplomatic efforts to overcome European suspicions of the new state's acquisitiveness, as well as to reduce legal obstacles to exit. Matters came to a head in the wake of the "panic" of 1819, which constituted the first of a series of crises that punctuated the development of American immigration policy. Albeit principally concerned with incorporating European newcomers, American political leaders also sought to divest their society, and particularly the régime's key state, Virginia, of a growing free Negro population. Its limited size notwithstanding, their experiment in ethnic cleansing by returning Negroes to Africa must figure in any comprehensive account of the role of international migration policy in American nation-building.

A Democratic Republic

Despite the founding generation's determination to stay out of the global conflict, after a number of attempts to defend American interests by diplomatic means and pressure that ended in humiliating failures, the Republicans declared war on Great Britain. Although the decision to resort to force was slow in coming and American opinion on the subject was divided and confused, the experience had a profound transformative effect on both the doctrine and substance of the country's political economy and character.[2] As Gordon Wood has put it, "A new generation of democratic Americans was no longer interested in the revolutionaries' dream of building a classical republic of elitist virtue out of the inherited materials of the Old World. . . . Instead it would discover its greatness by creating a prosperous free society belonging to obscure people with their workaday concerns and their pecuniary pursuits of happiness."[3] A distinctive society emerged, combining a rapidly emerging market economy with liberal political structures, and harboring a middle-class culture derided by European elites as uniquely vulgar.

The war also stimulated the formation of a more expansive nationalism. Albert Gallatin's policy of financing it by issuing huge sums of U.S. Treasury certificates initially brought the national government to the edge of bankruptcy, but the conflict's favorable outcome saved the day and also enhanced the government's authority and political weight. Although the precocious invasion of Canada by an inadequate American force and the foray into Texas by a few hundred volunteers in aid of revolts against Spanish authority, tacitly approved by the government, were both abysmal failures, they reflected intimations of "Manifest Destiny." These were decisively enhanced by Andrew Jackson's victory at New Orleans in 1815, which "riveted imaginations on the southwest and aroused further interest in the Floridas, and even Texas."[4] Concurrently, it became ever more imperative to get Indians out of the way.

In keeping with their reorientation, the Republicans were highly responsive to the aspirations of the business community, an ironic fulfillment of Alexander Hamilton's strivings by his political opponents. The Madison administration took a number of crucial steps toward what was to become the "American system," including a commercial convention with Britain and the chartering of a second national bank, and in his inaugural address of 1817 James Monroe pledged "the systematic and fostering care of the government for our manufactures," including the procurement of additional labor so as to lower the high wages that placed manufacturers in a disadvantageous position. Concurrently, there was a growing belief that America's internal market was incalculably more valuable than anything abroad, which entailed the development of transportation infrastructure, signaled by the enactment of the Erie Canal bill in 1817.[5] By and large, the going was good. In the immediate postwar period, the rise in export values and monetary and credit expansion led to a boom in urban and rural real estate prices, speculation in the purchase of public lands, and rapidly growing indebtedness by farmers for projected improvements, which in turn stimulated prosperity in cities and towns; banks continued to expand as well, including the Bank of the United States, which acted as an expansionary force by facilitating credit.

As even restrictionist historians concede, the reorientation of the political economy reinforced the established immigrationist outlook.[6] There was no debate on the subject because the Federalist opposition was in tune with the Republican stance. The federal government was especially committed to the protection of U.S. shipping, which was able to exploit the window of opportunity provided by the global war thanks to the abundance, cheapness, and proximity of timber, which more than made up for the high cost of labor.[7] Benefiting from favorable conditions, American shipping began to be organized into lines, plying regular trade and passenger runs between the United States and Liverpool as well as Le Havre, France. From the beginning, passenger traffic supplemented manufactured goods as a source of revenue on the westbound passage, much as it did for British ships; concomitantly, the shipping industry emerged as a major actor in the sphere of immigration policy.

Little needed to be done about immigration after the war because ongoing social processes on both sides of the Atlantic fostered a desirable outcome. As of 1815, arrivals from Europe added to about a quarter of a million altogether since the end of the Revolutionary War, with the largest yearly levels occurring as far back as the 1790s. Between 1800 and 1810, they averaged only 8,400 a year, with the United Kingdom share of the total declining further to 72.5 percent (51.0 percent British, 21.5 Irish) and the Caribbean again becoming an important source (14.1 percent).[8] During the war, arrivals dwindled to almost nothing, but they climbed to unprecedented levels when peace returned.[9] Hezekiah Niles, editor of Baltimore's eponymous political economy weekly, announced in late June 1816, "The British and other newspapers teem with noises of the emigration of their people to the United States."[10] As the end of the season approached, he opined, "From the facts that are known to us, we venture an opinion that 50,000 persons will have emigrated to the United States, from Europe, during the year 1816," and went on to calculate that such a number would create wealth to the extent of $10–11 million if employed in agriculture, but as much as $15 million in manufacture ("the women and children assisting"), plus, in either case, furnish a home market equal to one-seventh of America's exports.[11]

Although his estimate was somewhat inflated, numbers did rise to at least 30,000 in each of the two following years, and possibly even higher in 1819.[12] The United Kingdom share of the total climbed back to 77 percent, but the Irish now outweighed the British, with 39.2 and 37.7 percent respectively. The wave also restored "Germans"—a term that covered the Low Countries (Netherlands and Belgium)—as the leading continental group (11.1 percent). Yet as Niles suggested, immigration was merely "[a]s 'a drop in the bucket' when viewed in relation to the whole body of the people. Not missed in the countries they came from, nor *felt* here; except in some small circles of the community."[13] The white population was now estimated at 6.6 million, more than double the 1790 level.[14] Annual immigration of 30,000 thus amounted to an addition of only one-half of 1 percent, and to merely one-sixth the contribution of natural increase. As President Monroe observed, commenting on the returns from the 1820 U.S. Census, "At the first epoch, our population did not exceed three millions. By the last census, it amounted to about ten millions, and, what is more extraordinary, it is almost altogether native; for the immigration from other countries has been inconsiderable."[15]

Although many of the newcomers traveled on, sizeable numbers stayed in the cities, which grew apace: Philadelphia, from 42,000 in 1790 to 91,000 in 1810 and 112,000 ten years later; New York, which forged ahead as a hub for long-distance sailing routes to Europe and the South, as well as for short-distance steam navigation to the Northeast and Southwest, and subsequently the Northwest by way of the Erie Canal, at an even faster clip, from 33,000 to 96,000 to 123,000.[16] Between them, the two major ports received about half of all newcomers; nevertheless, as of 1820, New York City's 3,834 foreign-born constituted a mere 3.1 percent of its population, and although the numbers doubled by 1825, they still amounted to only 4.61 percent.[17]

Niles's comments reflect considerable acquisitive satisfaction, with a strong measure of nationalist vindication. Speaking of the "teeming" European notices of emigration mentioned earlier, he observes, "The persons alluded to are chiefly farmers and mechanics—to add to the labor, and of consequence increase the wealth of our country in peace, and hold the nerve to assist in defending it in war." Even the Irish are now welcome: "We know that the Irish emigrants much aided to fill the ranks of the army during the war, and they fought gallantly for freedom, feeling that they had a share in the contest as their own." A couple of months later, notwithstanding an economic slowdown, he remains enthusiastic: "We have no reason to fear an excess of labor for many years to come. Our cities are crowded and business is dull, but the interior presents a vast and almost exhaustless field for industry. . . . Let them come. Good and wholesome laws, opened to honest industry, will *tame* even Mr. Peel's *'untameably ferocious'* Irishmen; as well as suppress *English* mobs, crying out for *employment* and *bread,* without the use of the *bayonet.*"[18]

Surmounting European Obstacles

The major obstacle to the achievement of American aspirations was located in Europe itself, where states erected ever-higher barriers to exit. In the context of a protracted global war, the threat posed by the American magnet was exacerbated by the monstrous manpower requirements of the new mass armies as well as, in France and Britain, expanding navies. Prohibiting propaganda by the promoters of emigration, and issuing their own counterpropaganda in the form of pamphlets describing the horrors of American life, European seaboard states collaborated to prevent embarkation by pushing emigrants back at their borders.[19] This was true even of the Netherlands, the major embarkation outlet for Germans, because its merchants and ship owners found the emigrant traffic unprofitable as the trade with America was not very large. Hence, sailings were infrequent and destitute passengers had to be supported from the time of their arrival until an opportunity for embarkation arose.[20] Governments further discouraged emigration by making it more difficult to dispose of property, preventing the sending of financial aid to those who were left behind, and cutting off emigrants from their prospective inheritance. Although the Congress of Vienna (1817–18) settling the Napoleonic wars and establishing the German Confederation specifically authorized the departure of the inhabitants from territory ceded by France (including most of present-day Belgium) for a period of six years and provided for free emigration from any German state to any other—which included the Netherlands—this required the payment of a large tax.[21] Although these measures were directed mainly against propertied emigrants, since few such were disposed to leave in any case, the net effect was to reduce emigration among those America most desired, the "middling classes" of society.

The matter was of special concern to the United Kingdom, not only on ordinary mercantilist grounds but also from a security perspective, as the Americans were suspected of entertaining designs on their northern neighbor. This also dictated efforts to populate British North America as rapidly as possible. Observing the substantial influx of skilled British artisans into the United States despite the prohibitions on their exit, the British consul in Philadelphia, Phineas Bond, suggested as early as 1788 an alternative strategy that would "restrain for the present and finally annihilate" the traffic altogether: raise the standards of comfort on passenger ships to such a high level as to make the cost of the crossing prohibitive for the emigrants and simultaneously unprofitable for the shipper.[22] The centerpiece of his proposal was the imposition of a limit on the number of passengers in relation to the tonnage of the vessel.

The notion of such a regulatory mechanism was evidently in the air, as it was set forth the same year by British abolitionists as a way of "meliorating" the slave trade out of existence. Shortly thereafter, the Highland Society seized upon the device to stem the exodus of their tenants, uprooted by a crisis of subsistence induced by the conversion of agricultural lands into sheep walks, to British North America.[23] But the Colonial Office, which reckoned on the Scots to constitute a counterweight to the French Canadians and a buffer against American encroachments, forged ahead with the relocation anyway.[24] The Society then secured an order enjoining the Treasury to survey "the causes of emigration and the means of preventing it." When the report concluded that emigration was a beneficial adaptation to new circumstances and that colonization projects helped direct its course to British possessions rather than the United States, the Society turned to Parliament, where a more traditional orientation toward the social order still prevailed. In June 1803, it approved a bill prepared by the Lord Advocate for Scotland providing a variety of safety measures as well as medical services on emigrant ships and, most prominently, implementing Bond's proposal by limiting the number of passengers to one per two tons on British ships, and to an exorbitant ratio of one per five tons on foreign vessels.[25]

The Passenger Act of 1803 has generated considerable interest as an historical turning point signaling the advent of "humanitarian" concerns or even of a "collectivist" outlook in British public policy more generally; but what matters here is that it was "cradled in mercantilism. . . . [I]f emigration was inevitable, British shipping and British North America, rather than American shipping and the United States," should gain whatever benefits it brought.[26] The preamble and final provisions are quite explicit, and British Foreign Minister Lord Castlereagh subsequently admitted in a letter to U.S. Secretary of State John Quincy Adams that the act's real purpose was to deter emigration to the United States, a concern rendered more urgent by the election of Thomas Jefferson, which "reawakened fears of American designs upon the ill-defended northern provinces."[27] Ironically, the passenger law not only emerged as a major target of American efforts to promote freedom of exit on behalf of desirable immigrants, but also provided a model for their own strivings to deter undesirable ones.

The measure was a strikingly modern bureaucratic device, as it is much more efficient to control the loading of a limited number of ships concentrated in ports than to police the movements of a large number of persons scattered throughout the realm. As adumbrated by Consul Bond a decade and a half earlier, the imposition of much greater space requirements on foreign than British vessels (by a factor of 2.5) was designed also to affect the direction of emigration, because at this time British North America (St. John, Quebec) and the United States were usually reached by traveling on a vessel of the appropriate nationality.[28] It was politically timely as well, as the recent proclamation of the "right to leave" in France and American criticism of the Crown's determination "to enslave its own people" made it difficult to continue denying freedom of movement to British subjects.[29] Although in the short term the Passenger Act's impact was mooted by the resumption of international conflict, after the Atlantic reopened it probably did exercise some deterrent effect on British emigration, as suggested by the figures cited earlier. Although both emigrants and shippers quickly learned that it was possible to sail to a British North American port on a British ship, and then go on to an American destination by sea or by land, the measure severely hampered attempts to revive the British servant trade.[30]

The centrality of the British act in American political perceptions is demonstrated by the vehement outpourings of Hezekiah Niles. In the tradition established by Benjamin Franklin, Tench Coxe, and James Madison a generation earlier, he persistently criticizes nations that erect obstacles to departure and seeks to demonstrate that this is against their own interest. In October 1816, he feigns surprise at the fact that although "every laboring individual . . . who leaves England, relieves the public of the necessity of supporting an individual . . . political jealousy checks humanity and even overpowers self-interest, and emigration is obstructed." A year later, he reports the scandalous case of a wife and five children supplied with ship fare by an Irish immigrant but turned ashore "to starve, unprotected, because they could not produce a certificate from the clergyman and resident magistrate that they were at *liberty* to emigrate!"[31] Reminding him of the fable of Saturn devouring his own children, the British "had rather that their people should perish at home, than suffer them to emigrate, and possibly, strengthen the power and add to the resources of another country." He is also highly critical of the British doctrine of "perpetual allegiance," which held that America's routinized and accessible naturalization law violated the law of nations, and thereby in effect also registers his approval of the American policy.[32] On the Continent, also, "measures have been taken to circumscribe emigration" despite the "oppressions of the middling classes" and "the privations of the poor"; "but still it is powerful, and will increase."[33]

Yet at the official level, considerations of prudence arising from the requirements of American foreign policy weighed toward the adoption of a more subdued stance, so as to allay European suspicions fostered by the activities of transatlantic recruiters, and to forestall even greater restrictions on exit. For example, Freiherr von Fürstenwärther, an emissary sent out by the German Diet in 1817 to investigate the redemptioner system, and whose mission generated considerable attention in Europe as well as America, reported that Secretary of State John Quincy Adams told him "in substance" that the U.S. government, knowing the European states did not favor emigration, "had not directly encouraged the same. Should the German princes alter their policy [of prohibiting departure], the U.S. might be more disposed to co-operate with them" on the matter of the redemptioners, "more on account of sympathy for the immigrants themselves" than out of concern for the economic welfare of the United States.[34] Although Marcus Lee Hansen proclaimed that this "embodies the first formal expression to the immigration policy of the nation," the envoy himself commented, somewhat skeptically, "For, be it principle and conviction or national vanity, people have, or affect in general in America, a great indifference to foreign immigration, and seem to be of the opinion that the population of the United States would increase enough without the same."[35] The secretary's prudent wording has been interpreted as an expression of caution "to avoid embroiling us with countries in Europe," and Adams himself went on to reaffirm the American régime's immigrationist stance: "Neither the general government of the union, nor those of the individual states, are ignorant or unobservant of the additional strength and wealth, which accrues to the nation, by the accession of a mass of healthy, industrious, and frugal laborers, nor are they in any manner insensible to the great benefits which this country has derived, and continues to derive, from the influx of such adoptive children from Germany."[36]

The restrictionists of the 1920s made much of a declaration by Secretary of War William Crawford in 1816 to the effect that it was better "to incorporate, by a humane and benevolent policy, the natives of our forests . . . than to receive, with open arms, the fugitives of the old world, whether their flight has been the effect of their crimes or their virtues." Crawford had been the caucus candidate of the young Republicans against Monroe, but this very statement reportedly cost him the nomination.[37] A senator from Georgia characterized as a strict Jeffersonian, Crawford represented agrarian resistance to the business-minded "National Republican" tendency of Adams; but his declaration also reflected the growing uneasiness of the South in the face of a process that inevitably altered the sectional political and economic balance to its disadvantage.

Americanization

John Quincy Adams was not concerned with economics alone, but went on to state a contract-like relationship between the American community and newcomers, which established the moral and political foundation of immigration policy during these formative decades. Lecturing the German on the contrast between a land of privileges and a land of equal rights, from which one of his class should expect no favors, he explains that the newcomers "come to a life of independence, but to a life of labor—and if they cannot accommodate themselves to the character, moral, political, and physical of this country, with all its compensating balance of good and evil, the Atlantic is always open to them, to return to the land of their nativity and their fathers."[38] Adams concludes with a statement of the awesome obligations the Atlantic passage entails, in terms that delineate with considerable precision the crystallization of a distinctive American political culture and expectations of a thorough resocialization:

> They must cast off their European skin, never to resume it. They must look forward to their posterity, rather than backward to their ancestors; they must be sure that whatever their own feelings may be, those of their children will

cling to the prejudices of this country, and will partake of that proud spirit, not unmingled with disdain, which you have observed is remarkable in the general character of this people, and as perhaps belonging peculiarly to those of German descent, born in this country. That feeling of superiority over other nations . . . arises from the consciousness of every individual that, as a member of society, no man in the country is above him; and, exulting in this sentiment, he looks down upon those nations where the mass of the people feel themselves the inferiors of privileged classes, and where men are high or low, according to the accidents of their birth.

The "European skin" to be shed marks not only status distinctions but also nationality. The protracted period of international conflict, culminating in outright war, further promoted sentiment of belonging to a distinctive "nation," and upon coming to power, the Republicans incorporated not only many elements of their Federalist opponents' economic doctrine but also much of their Americanism, enhanced by the relative hiatus in immigration: "A society accustomed to constant infusions from abroad found time to adjust itself to conditions where its people were home-born and home-bred."[39] The emergence of a distinct nationality was indicated by the almost complete victory of the American version of the English language over British English, as well as German and Dutch; the nationalization of Protestant denominations; and the proliferation of national symbols and public holidays.[40] Paralleling the shift that occurred in the course of the French Revolution, whereas a generation earlier Americans translated their political message into German so as to reach non-English speakers, they now expected Germans to translate themselves into Americans.[41] With slave imports legally prohibited after 1808, Americanization was beginning to progress among the black population as well.

Like all forms of identity formation, the development of nationality is a dialectic process, involving simultaneously a crystallization of the "us" and a reinforcement of the boundary between "us" and "others." This placed the burden of incorporation squarely on the shoulders of the newcomers, almost to the point of turning them into supplicants, and raised the possibility that some candidates for membership in the new nation might be held at arm's length or rejected altogether. Deeply rooted anti-Catholic prejudices were quickly revived after the war in the face of increased arrivals from Ireland, and the persistence of distinct communities was regarded with suspicion.[42] For example, Niles's comment on a congressional grant to a group of Napoleonic bigwigs in 1817 echoes Jefferson's in *Notes on the State of Virginia*: "I very much question the policy of any act of government that has a tendency to introduce and keep up amongst us a *foreign* national language or dialect, manners or character, as every large and compact settlement of emigrants from any particular country, must necessarily occasion." While welcoming immigration on economic grounds, he also views it as a source of problems: "I still assert and will maintain it, that the people of the United States are yet wretchedly deficient of a NATIONAL CHARACTER, though it is rapidly forming. . . . Its progress, however, is retarded by the influx of foreigners, with manners and prejudices favorable to a state of things repugnant to our rules and notions of right." He returns to the subject again four years later, focusing even more sharply on the persistence of foreign languages in Pennsylvania and Louisiana.[43] Fortunately, the situation is rapidly changing for the better: with regard to the Germans, "Commerce and the progress of the arts have made it more and more necessary for them to mix with their much more numerous fellow-citizens who speak the English language, and to read the books and papers printed in it. Most of the young persons, if now tolerably educated, can read and speak that language." While the older generations hang on to German, "It is out of the question to expect that the German can ever be the prevailing language in the United States." The French are less problematic because they do not live in compact bodies. Commenting on an order of the Louisiana Supreme Court to impose an English-only policy in the judicial process, which generated protests as an abuse of authority, he grants that this may require legislative action, but insists that "if it is rightfully done we must approve it, as hastening the period when one part of the people will not be called *French,* and the other Americans—when the latter appellation will belong to every citizen of the state."

Another impediment to national integration is the formation of ethnic political blocs: "If a citizen of the United States, born in England, Ireland or Scotland, is a candidate for office, the custom too generally is for *all* his 'countrymen' to support him, thereby maintaining an interest separated from that of the people at large: and in some of our public offices also, when the head of it happens to have had the place of his birth in a foreign country, we find that nearly all his subordinates are of his own class. This sort of clannish spirit begets one of opposition, lessens the public liberality, and militates against the public harmony." Niles concludes with a warning to naturalized citizens, suggesting that despite a return to relatively easy terms for acquiring citizenship, the internal boundary elaborated by the Federalists outlived their reign: "I never yet acted against a person because he was not a native born American

. . . but must frankly confess, that I have been sometimes almost tempted to wish that the rule of too many of them was enforced against themselves. Their conduct is highly indelicate, and a very improper return for the courtesy extended to them in permitting them to elect and be elected to office. As there is no man living who is a greater friend to emigrants than I am . . . it will be understood that I only deprecate the existence of a German interest, an English interest, Irish interest, French interest, or Scotch interest, in the U. States. I want only an *American* interest."

More persistent than any particular "nativist" outburst, "Americanism" was here to stay as a feature of the political landscape, manifested among other things by the persistence of a distinction between native and naturalized citizens, which prompted a group of 500 "Adopted Republican Citizens of the city of New York," probably Irish, meeting at Lyon's Hotel on Mott Street in 1809, to unanimously adopt a resolution "upon a subject which, for years, we have acutely felt and deeply deplored."[44] Having come here to seek asylum, "we pleasingly anticipated, from those who avow themselves the friends of freedom, exemption from that religious persecution and civil tyranny, whose inexorable reign had forced us from our native country. Alas! How greatly were we mistaken! How egregiously have we been disappointed! Our constitutions and governments are indeed free, but between these admirable institutions and ourselves a tyranny is intervened, much less tolerable than that from which we fled. . . . Are not we, who are citizens by all the solemnities and obligations of law, treated as aliens—stigmatized as foreigners? . . . Are we to be told, in this enlightened age, that the *law* is *not* to govern; that the essence of well-ordered society is *not* a government of laws, but a government of the worst passions?" Matters were made worse by the War of 1812, which "heralded the end of the Revolutionary period of liberal attitudes toward noncitizen voting."[45] Beginning with Louisiana in 1812, most newly admitted states confined the franchise to citizens, and a number of early states revoked the practice of granting it to aliens; and the Hartford Convention of twenty-six Federalist delegates from northeastern states, called secretively by the Massachusetts legislature in December 1814, advocated among other things the barring of naturalized citizens from holding civil office in the federal government.[46]

The Invention of Remote Control

In January 1818, Congress adopted a motion to investigate the possibility of limiting the number of persons carried by incoming ships according to the tonnage of the vessels.[47] Reported on March 10, and briefly debated the following December, the act "regulating passenger ships and vessels" became law on March 2, 1819, effective September 1 of the same year.[48] The measure prohibited ships of any nationality entering an American port from carrying more than two persons for every five tons of registry, and required them to deliver to the Department of State "a list or manifest of all the passengers taken on board," including each one's name, occupation, and place of origin. It further specified water and food requirements for Europe-bound ships departing from the United States.

The initiative for this signal national enactment came from Pennsylvania and Maryland representatives, prompted by German immigrant aid societies, themselves mobilized by von Fürstenwärther, to ameliorate the redemptioner system, which at the time encompassed two out of five emigrants from "Germany," including the Low Countries.[49]

Although the envoy—who himself subsequently settled in America—concluded that the redemptioner system did not hinder social mobility, he did report that the emigrants were subject to considerable abuse and exploitation.[50] Shipping arrangements led to unsafe overcrowding, as agents sought to minimize transportation expenses, and the brutal market practices of purchasers in transporting the servants inland as well as commonplace reference to redemptioners as "Dutch slaves" played into the hands of anti-emigration propagandists throughout Europe.[51] The extent to which the problem received national attention is indicated by the fact that, even as the matter was pending in Congress, Pennsylvania and Maryland enacted statutes requiring the registration of all deeds of bondage upon arrival with the aid of a person fluent in both German and English, limiting the period of adult servitude to a maximum of four years, and affording the servants access to the courts.[52]

American views of the redemptioner system itself were mixed. Overall, it was welcomed by American shippers and labor brokers, as well as by employers; commenting on the German report in the *North American Review*, Edward Everett even argued that it might provide a means of eliminating black plantation slavery.[53] As against this, the hostility to any form of white bondage that had arisen after the Revolution grew apace, as revealed for example by the petition addressed by a labor broker to the U.S. Senate in 1819 for aid in recovering escaped German "slaves" he had "purchased" in Philadelphia for resale in Tennessee or Alabama, because the Ohio courts refused to enforce the legally established contract.[54] The legal foundations of bondage were further undermined by the steadily progressing movement against debtor's prison.[55]

The 1819 law stood as the sole federal enactment pertaining directly to European immigration until the late 1840s. In the more general perspective of American development, it can be seen as a block in the building of the "American system," in keeping with the ongoing nationalization of major elements of economic policy. This aspect was emphasized by U.S. Supreme Court Chief Justice John Marshall five years later in *Gibbons v. Ogden,* the landmark 1824 decision that established federal paramountcy in the sphere of international commerce, when he referred to the 1819 act as an example of the legitimate exercise of congressional power in the sphere of commerce with foreign nations.[56] The chief justice also took the opportunity to affirm congressional authority in the sphere of immigration properly speaking. As he reasoned it out, since the Constitution restrained Congress from prohibiting "migration or importation of such persons as any of the states may think proper to admit" until 1808, it followed, "so far as an exception from a power proves its existence," that Congress was now free to act.

It is thus reasonable to interpret the Passenger Act as an indication that "the national government was beginning to recognize that the problem of immigration was broader than mere state interest and control."[57] Once the law's constitutionality was affirmed, its existence delineated a legal framework within which the states and the national government could henceforth act in complementary fashion to regulate a complex social process that by its very nature transcended the limits of authority allotted to each level under the Constitution. In that sense, the law signaled the completion of the legislative task initiated in 1808 with respect to "importation."

But what was the act meant to achieve, and to what extent did it succeed? In his sustaining opinion, Marshall characterized it as a "wise and humane law," which "provides for the safety and comfort of passengers, and for the communication of everything concerning them which may interest the government, to the Department of State."[58] But that was hardly all. Our understanding of the measure's substantive significance and impact has been hampered by considerations arising from the debate that raged in the first half of the twentieth century. *The Atlantic Migration* insists that the 1819 law was "a regulatory, not a restrictive measure."[59] Unfortunately, this insistence obfuscates the issue. In light of the British use of passenger regulations to restrict departures, a mechanism that the authors of the legislation explicitly cited as their inspiration and that was even then the subject of exchanges between Secretary of State Adams and the Foreign Office, and referred to in congressional proceedings, it is reasonable to infer that the American Passenger Act was indeed very much designed to "check the flow," or at least part of it deemed undesirable. Like its British counterpart, "The passenger law does not avow its purpose. Its effect, if enforced, would be to reduce the number of passengers per ship, thereby raising the price of passage. This would necessarily reduce the number of immigrants because many could not afford the increased rates."[60]

Why 2.5 tons per passenger? As the committee rapporteur explained it in Congress, Britain had recently reduced the minimum from 5 tons to 3; therefore, 2.5 tons "would afford every necessary accommodation."[61] This was in fact misinformation; as will be elaborated in the next chapter, Britain maintained a 5-ton requirement for U.S.-bound ships, but had recently lowered it to 1.5 for the traffic to British North America. Whether inadvertent or willful, the error helped justify a level that would significantly reduce the carrying capacity of all U.S.-bound ships embarking passengers on the Continent, but simultaneously give American ships an edge over their British competitors. Immigration restriction, yes, but business is business. Students of the redemptioner system have long been persuaded that the act contributed to its demise, and even the leading proponent of a purely "market" explanation for the disappearance of immigrant servitude agrees that the market in redemptioners "suddenly collapsed, never to recover," in 1820.[62]

In conclusion, the 1819 law undoubtedly constituted restrictive regulation, designed to achieve the often-voiced preference for free immigrants from the middling classes of European society; most likely, it was a device for extinguishing the remaining segment of the servant trade by rendering it uneconomical, as well as for deterring paupers subsidized by European poor law authorities. Hostility to Germans, Irish, and Roman Catholics generally probably came into play as well, but this cannot be established for certain on the basis of the available evidence.

The First Immigration Crisis

Completed in March 1819, the Passenger Act was scheduled to go into effect in September; but in the intervening period, the United States experienced a dramatic immigration crisis. This was the first in a series of episodic events, which have shaped immigration policy as intermittent attempts to manage crises precipitated by the conjunctural fluctuations of the developing international capitalist economy. These arise from the unavoidable lag between the onset of an immigration flow in response to a favorable conjuncture, and its self-sustained expansion after the conjuncture has taken a turn for the worse. The lag in turn exacerbates the maldistribution of the costs and benefits of immigration between the private and public sectors. While the going is good, the business community reaps the most immediately tangible benefits of immigration as a source of additional labor supply that keeps down inflationary pressure on wages, and as a source of additional demand for housing and consumer goods. But when the crisis erupts and many of the newcomers lose their jobs—usually more quickly than better-anchored natives or earlier immigrants—the costs of relief are passed on at least in part to the collectivity. The rising costs of relief in hard times require the establishment of priorities, and hence leads to a sharpening of the distinction between the "deserving us" and "intrusive them."

The first signs of trouble surfaced in 1818, when the American hunger for manufactured goods occasioned a sharp deficit in the balance of trade, further aggravated by abundant crops throughout Europe and a business contraction in Britain, which drove down demand for American agricultural products.[63] Accordingly, in the summer of that year, the Bank of the United States was forced to launch a series of deflationary moves. A further drop in cotton prices precipitated a full-scale panic in the spring of 1819, even as an unprecedented number of Europeans were embarking for America, many of them enrolled by labor brokers reckoning on a steadily expanding demand. Economic distress was suffered by all groups in the community; but with well over a quarter of the labor force in New England and the mid-Atlantic states now working in small factories, making everything from shoes to textiles—about one-third of them women and children—the most dramatic outcome was the advent of large-scale unemployment in the cities, and the concomitant swelling of the ranks of "paupers" dependent on relief.

Arriving immigrants were confronted with economic devastation; overextended brokers, unable to secure funds to maintain servants for whom there was no market, often "set them free to shift for themselves."[64] Unable to turn back or to go on, most of the newcomers remained confined in the port-of-entry cities, where they were of necessity even more dependent on rudimentary welfare institutions than natives.[65] In New York, where from the turn of the nineteenth century onward the foreign-born constituted about one-third of poorhouse inmates, in the summer of 1819 "the calls upon charity became insistent."[66] Yet the sailing season was still at its height, and the tide continued to pour in at a rate of about 2,000 per week for the country as a whole, according to contemporary observers, with perhaps another 1,000 a month entering by way of Canada.[67] Whereas at the beginning of the year the Managers of the Society for the Prevention of Pauperism in the City of New York stated confidently, "Our situation is peculiarly healthy and no local objection, either physical or moral, exists to arrest the approach of foreigners," later on they were "compelled to speak . . . in the language of astonishment and apprehension," listing "emigrations to the city from foreign countries" as the leading source of pauperism, clamoring for relief by way of more effective restrictions on the landing of indigents, and asserting, "This inlet of pauperism threatens us with the most overwhelming consequences."[68] The municipal authorities immediately attempted to enforce more vigorously existing state legislation that required each master of a vessel to report his passengers at the mayor's office, and authorized municipal officials at their discretion to demand a bond not exceeding $3,000 for each alien likely to become a public charge; and they also collected a head tax from passengers and crew for the purpose of financing medical facilities.[69]

By 1825, when immigrants constituted 4.6 percent of the city's population, they amounted to 40 percent of almshouse admissions.[70] The situation worsened when the state further tightened local residence requirements, stipulating that nonresident paupers be returned to New York City if they had first entered the state through that port. This was followed by another state law requiring counties to assume responsibility for technically nonresident paupers. Consequently, despite vociferous protests, the city was saddled with the full burden of the immigrant poor, at a time when assistance, hitherto viewed as an unquestioned obligation of Christian charity to the community's unfortunate, was coming to be regarded instead as a morally suspect contribution to the perpetuation of willful idleness and dependency.[71] The city's increasing ethnic diversity further undermined traditional community ties and obligations; in short, "Old New Yorkers found it difficult to apply Christian benevolence to ragged, uncouth, 'different,' and seemingly immoral newcomers."[72]

In the face of the new situation, Niles sharply revises his position on immigration: "We have always until just now greeted the stranger on his arrival here with pleasure. . . . Now, however, our population in most of the maritime districts and in some parts of the interior also, seem too thick—there are too many mouths to consume what the hands can find business to do; and that hitherto sure refuge of the industrious foreign emigrant, the western country, is overstocked by the domestic emigration."[73] America faces a familiar danger, but in a new form. While still trying to prevent the emigration of valuable subjects, Britain once again is seeking to dump its refuse overseas: "It is reported, that to relieve themselves of the support of their paupers, many such will be sent to the United States by the church-wardens etc., of England!" This insidious policy requires vigorous countermeasures on the American side: "It will therefore become the state authorities to be careful to take the proper securities of those who bring passengers, that they will not become chargeable on the public."

Allowing for a share of anti-British exaggeration, the reports about the church-wardens did adumbrate an emerging pattern, as Poor Law authorities discovered that by sponsoring the emigration of an adult male, they might permanently relieve themselves of the burden of supporting an entire family, since the sponsored emigrant would eventually provide remittances for the removal of his kin.[74] It was estimated in the late 1820s that the cost of removal of a family of five from the United Kingdom and its resettlement in British North America was not quite double the cost of a year's maintenance by the parish.[75] Although emigration of this kind was probably limited, "in some years it accounted for a not inconsiderable proportion of the departures from certain localities."[76]

These initiatives accorded with a momentous reorientation of British emigration policy, whose full impact was to be felt only after 1825. The 1811 census revealed that the country's population was growing at a higher rate, and the accelerating migration from the rural areas to the cities suggested the emergence of a sizeable "surplus" population in many parts of the country, whose transformation into unruly urban "mobs" was dangerous. Accordingly, the Colonial Office entertained ingenious schemes for "shoveling out paupers" while simultaneously populating the newly acquired imperial possessions with British subjects, especially vulnerable British North America. However, many of the uprooted voted with their feet for the United States instead, taking advantage of subsidized fares to leave the United Kingdom, but continuing southward on their own, and thereby lending credence to American suspicions and fears.

Under these circumstances, deterrence was propelled to the top of the American policy agenda. Raising the alarm, a Bostonian wrote the governor of Connecticut in 1821, "The poor come in shoals from Nova Scotia and Ireland, and we must find some means to reduce the number, or we shall all be candidates for the almshouse."[77] Matters were rendered even more urgent by information that other European states were moving in the same direction. Immigrationism had never amounted to mere laissez-faire, and the 1819 crisis sharpened its selectivity. While the national government sought to deter some by way of its shipping regulations and to attract others by way of its land policies, the principal port-of-entry states armed themselves with legislation designed to screen out paupers and convicts, as well as to compensate the receiving communities and philanthropic bodies for some of the social costs imposed on them by the screen's imperfections. Between 1819 and 1822, eastern seaboard states that lacked such protection, from Maine to Florida, enacted measures to the same effect. In the face of continued evasion of its laws, in 1824 the State of New York devised a more effective system for controlling the landing of aliens, extended the bond requirement to include all passengers, and raised sanctions for violation. The new law also empowered the mayor to order the deportation of indigent U.S. citizens landed in its port, and for whom no surety could be required, to the place of their last settlement.[78]

Overall, American immigration policy was being shaped by three major actors. One was the shipping industry, foreign as well as American, which sought to maximize traffic and profit, and to minimize barriers and costs imposed by national, state, and local authorities. Another was the seaboard states, which sought to improve their control apparatus in order to prevent the landing of undesirables, as well as to exact income from the passenger traffic for general purposes and to finance specific relief institutions. But whereas they had a common interest in selective restriction, they also competed to secure passenger traffic. Under these conditions, one would expect the emergence of a broadly similar regulatory stance, coupled with considerable instability regarding specific provisions. Moreover, since state enactments impinged on commerce with foreign nations, a subject the Constitution attributed to Congress, ship owners were in a good position to challenge them by way of the courts. Although they began to do so almost immediately, the states retained the upper hand until 1849, and lost it then mostly because the regulatory issues in question had a bearing on the vital issue of states' rights and slavery.[79]

The third was the national government. The linkage established at the founding between public land and immigration policy was reinforced in the wake of the crisis, as the national government undertook to organize an orderly transatlantic market in land by clearing the wilderness of its original inhabitants, rendering regions secure for European settlement, and providing the necessary infrastructure—military and political as well as physical—that steadily lowered transaction costs. Dependent on land sales for a significant share of its revenue until about 1840, and expending a large part of it in turn to remove Indians, it acquired a concomitant interest in maximizing demand for the product it had to offer; and this was itself partly determined by the level of immigration. The relationship between the two was emphasized by a Belgian analyst of the causes of emigration who, writing in 1846, concluded that "institutions made by men," notably "the two laws, of public lands and of naturalization, have a combined influence upon the whole matter of emigration."[80] The national government's interests largely coincided with those of the western states, as well as with those of the shipping industry. Accordingly, the policy arena came to be dominated by powerful institutional actors committed to the maintenance of an open-door policy for Europeans, regardless of short-term economic conditions or perennial concern over the disintegrative effects of cultural heterogeneity.

Land policy evolved rapidly to make purchase more accessible to the "middling classes" that were being displaced by developments in Europe. Already in 1817, the minimum parcel size was reduced in certain sections of the township from 160 acres to 80, the size of an adequate family farm.[81] Annual sales, which had been rising since the end of the war, doubled in 1818, reaching nearly 3.5 million acres, the maximum for a single year to date; and as demand drove the average price well above the previous level, revenue trebled. However, after another good year, the market collapsed, and federal receipts from land sales in 1820 amounted to only about 15 percent of the 1818 level. Accordingly, even as the panic prompted a reinforcement of barriers against needy immigrants, land policy was rendered more attractive to foreigners as well as Americans. The credit system, blamed for speculation and the ensuing panic itself, was abolished in 1820; but the same law generalized the 80-acre minimum and reduced the floor price from $1.64 to the initial $1.25 per acre, where it remained for several decades, so that a family-sized farm could henceforth be purchased for the round sum of $100 cash. In the late 1820s, the efforts of eastern businessmen to restrict sales so as to confine labor within their region were offset by the determination of western states to rapidly fill vacant lands. Reflecting the growing weight of the latter in the legislative process, the Preemption Act of 1830 authorized settlers established on the public domain as of 1829 to enter up to 160 acres at the minimum price, and in 1832 the minimum size was reduced further to a quarter of a quarter of a section, 40 acres.

As the Belgian analyst observed, "[T]he two laws, of public lands and naturalization, have a combined influence." During this period, "Nearly all of the agitation on the subject of naturalization had for its object the removal of restrictions upon aliens"; although the procedure was already quite easy, minor adjustments were enacted in 1824 and 1828 to facilitate it further, notably reducing the waiting period for filing a declaration of intention, required for eligibility to purchase federal lands, from three years to two.[82] In addition, the various levels of government rendered land purchases more accessible to foreign newcomers. In the sphere of property law, which was reserved to the states, the old common law doctrine that considered aliens as without heritable blood and as incapable of transmitting land by descent or by purchase—a tradition that was even then being reinforced in British North America by legislation to keep out U.S. settlers—came to be "everywhere modified and meliorated, and in several of the new States, by a wise forecast, was entirely swept away."[83]

In his September 1819 analysis of the immigration crisis, Niles reported skeptically that some Americans thought immigrants might amount to half a million over the next five years, not counting those entering by way of Canada or Nova Scotia. According to the newly established federal recording system, arrivals numbered 8,385 in 1820, about one-fourth the number estimated for the previous year, with the Irish in the lead (43.1 percent), and declined further to 6,354 in 1823.[84] Even if allowance is made for arrivals by land from British North America and for imperfections of the reporting system, there is little doubt of a substantial drop. The contribution of deterrent regulations to this decline remains moot, as they cannot be disentangled from the effects of the unfavorable American conjuncture, word of which was rapidly carried to Europe. The drop may have also reflected the effects of an economic upswing in the United Kingdom, coupled with the imposition of greater controls on exit from the Continent. With the redemptioner system swept away, recorded immigration from Germany fell most abruptly, from 968 in 1820 to 148 in 1822. It is noteworthy that this coincided with the advent of opportunities for Germans to migrate eastward, to open new lands in the realm of the czar.

However, in the second half of the decade, recorded migration returned to its immediate postwar level. The upswing was probably attributable to American recovery, combined with the onset of another economic downturn in the United Kingdom. Moreover, British capitalists themselves increasingly voted for the United States with their investments, and most of the colonial emigration schemes designed to deflect emigration from the United States to British North America were abandoned, leaving only those aimed at populating Australia and balancing Dutch speakers in South Africa. The stepped-up flow of British investment together with an increase in domestically generated capital prompted American statesmen and entrepreneurs to undertake monumental public works like the Erie Canal, which opened in 1825, and to launch "great establishments of manufacture" that required an immense supply of cheap labor that under prevailing American circumstances could be obtained only by way of large-scale immigration from Europe.

African Colonization

One day after approving the passenger legislation, President Monroe also signed "An Act in Addition to the acts prohibiting the Slave Trade." Providing for the stationing of a naval squadron in African waters, the measure transferred responsibility for Africans rescued from captured slavers from the states to the federal government and authorized the president to remove them from the United States to Africa, where an agency of the national government was to be established for receiving them.[85] Much like the Passenger Act, this was in keeping with the nationalizing trend, prompted by the desire of the states to pass on an irritating problem to the national government. But the new law also was a step toward realization of the "compelling fantasy" of removing Negroes from the United States.

Since the 1780s, the project for returning Negroes to Africa had been bogged down in jurisdictional disputes between the states and the national government, and also hampered by protracted international disputes over navigation as well as international conflicts. Meanwhile, enthusiasm for colonization was further stimulated by the Haitian Revolution as well as the "Gabriel Plot" that shook Virginia in 1801 (discovery of an alleged plan for a slave uprising, prompting between 16 and 35 executions) and enhanced racial fears throughout the South. Envisaging transportation as an alternative to execution, the state governor, James Monroe, asked the national authorities to inquire into the possibility of shipping the rebels to Sierra Leone; however, Britain adamantly refused. Virginia then considered establishing a free black colony of its own in recently acquired Louisiana; and when this scheme in turn failed, it enacted a law restricting the right of masters to manumit slaves by making such actions contingent upon the speedy removal of freedmen from the state. Meanwhile, the "problem" grew in size: whereas in 1790 there were fewer than 60,000 free Negroes in the United States, by 1820 they numbered a quarter of million, and many whites in the North, objecting to freedom at their expense, turned to colonization as the solution as well. Some Negroes joined in also. In 1811, the black captain Paul Cuffe sailed to Sierra Leone on a trading and emigration mission organized with the support of his white

Quaker friends, and upon his return attempted to revive the moribund Negro emigration societies in the northern seaboard cities.

The end of the Napoleonic Wars prompted renewed efforts to transform desire into reality. In 1816, the Virginia General Assembly passed a resolution urging the state's executive "to correspond with the President of the United States," the former state governor, "for the purpose of obtaining a territory upon the coast of Africa, or at some other place, not within any of the states or territorial government of the United States, to serve as an asylum for such persons of color, as are now free . . . and for those who may be hereafter emancipated within this commonwealth."[86] Its sponsor, Charles Fenton Mercer, then teamed up with the Reverend Robert Finley, director of Princeton's new theological seminary, and Francis Scott Key to enlist Henry Clay, Daniel Webster, Bushrod Washington, General Andrew Jackson, and other illustrious Washingtonians in launching the American Society for Colonizing the Free People of Color in the United States (ACS).[87] Finley also contacted Paul Cuffe, who had recently returned from another trip to Sierra Leone, for information about the colony as well as the possibility of establishing a distinct American settlement in its vicinity. In a bid for the support of moderate Southerners, the society explicitly disclaimed any opposition to slavery and emphasized that colonization was only for free Negroes.

Nevertheless, despite its distinguished sponsorship, the ACS project evoked skepticism among many whites, as illustrated by the comments of Hezekiah Niles. Much like Jefferson, Niles was a supporter of gradual emancipation, but thought that free Negroes had been so debased by the experience of slavery that they would not function effectively in the emerging society.[88] Voicing his commitment to "any rightful and reasonable scheme that could be adopted to ameliorate the conditions of our black population, or lessen their number," he expresses uneasiness with the removal policy, but believes it necessary. However, he concludes that colonization is both impracticable because of its extremely high cost, and inefficient because in the best of cases it will not make Negroes disappear.[89] Yet, "while I profess myself without any hope of success in the colonization project I freely acknowledge that I have nothing better to offer. I am only afraid that, by having our attention directed *abroad,* we may neglect our means at *home.*" In a later issue, Niles unveils his own preferred solution, paralleling Virginia's: emancipate the slaves but force the free states to accept this population. Over the long term, European immigration will resolved the problem, as the "black color will disappear" by being reduced to an innocuous minority.[90]

Provoked by Niles's criticism, the editor of the *Delaware Watchman* elaborated the positive case for colonization.[91] His initial metaphor reveals how the issue of slavery was intermingled with gender and morality: "We would wish now to act as a mother, who, from some circumstances of past error in conduct, making the even disgraceful and unfortunate, had brought into the world an offspring which, she deemed it dangerous both to herself and her issue to keep about her person; and yet would not abandon it to mere chance; —she places it at a secure distance, where she nourishes and protects it in infancy." He states the problem in familiar terms: the black population is growing, yet " 'tis utterly and obviously impossible, that the negroes should . . . be admitted to a full, free, and equal participation . . . as it is to change the whole of their skins from black to white." Even if whites and Negroes were alike to begin with, time "has, *in effect,* made them two distinct orders of mankind, which cannot now, I think, by any human effort, be peaceably and quietly amalgamated." And if Negroes were to be emancipated and educated, but still deprived of social and political rights, "a convulsion must sooner or later follow, dangerous as well to the whites as to themselves." Hence, removal is necessary. Challenging the estimate set forth by Niles, he doubts that 15,000 will volunteer at once; one might start with 1,000 for each of three years, which would cost only $750,000. Moreover, this could be advanced to the colonists in the form of a loan. And once colonization gets underway, Negroes will leave willingly without imposing any expense on the government, much as European immigrants now freely come "from misery and oppression, to happiness and liberty" in America.[92]

In May 1818, Congress endorsed the ACS petition, asking the U.S. government "to use its authority to negotiate treaties for the territory of the proposed colony, with native tribes of Africa and/or European governments that claim certain portions of the shores of that continent." Like Sierra Leone, the colony would also serve as a haven for slaves liberated from illegal slave ships, hitherto left to the states within whose jurisdiction they chanced to be found. Although the society claimed its emissaries had secured British cooperation in locating a suitable settlement in the neighborhood of Sierra Leone, in the end the Americans were left to fend for themselves.[93] After the 1819 act was passed, the ACS urged President Monroe to interpret it as a grant of authority to purchase territory outright, and hence the political establishment continued to play a determinative role in the settlement of "Monrovia" and its consolidation with others into "Liberia."[94]

However, the society's explicit disclaimer of any opposition to slavery fed the suspicions of free Negroes in the North, who denounced the undertaking early on as a deportation scheme and blamed the ACS for a new wave of anti-Negro sentiment, manifested in attacks on black churches.[95] Charging that "any plan of colonization without the American continent or islands, will completely and permanently fix slavery in our common country," in response to an address by the society's agents, the "people of color of the city and country of Philadelphia" resolved that "how clamorous soever a few obscure and dissatisfied strangers among us may be in favor of being made presidents, governors, and principals in Africa, there is but one sentiment among the respectable inhabitants of color in this city and country, which is, that it meets their unanimous and decided disapprobation."[96] Some free blacks even argued that their ancestors had come by choice as free immigrants.[97] Whatever emigrationist sentiment persisted aspired to a Negro land in the American West or was reoriented toward Haiti; and, later on, Upper Canada arose as a possibility as well.[98]

However, in the South, "free Negroes who were weary of fighting a hopeless battle resigned themselves to colonization."[99] As it was, the ACS was shortly wracked by internal divisions as well as by external problems. Despite the development of a network of local branches from 1825 onward, as of 1830 only some 1,400 had immigrated to Liberia under its sponsorship, mostly free Negro families living in southern cities, notably Richmond.[100] In the 1830s, the national and state societies were polarized by the outbreak of the bloodiest slave revolt the South had yet experienced and the rise of the abolitionist movement, which from the outset militantly opposed colonization as a scheme that benefited slaveholders. This led to the virtual destruction of the society in the South, while the northern branches were reduced to little more than debating societies. Among northern blacks, the convention movement, launched in 1830 by a gathering in Philadelphia to discuss the possibility of emigrating to Canada arose as an alternative to emigration to Africa, and resistance developed in the South as well.[101]

Nevertheless, the colonization movement survived throughout the antebellum period, mainly thanks to occasional grants from Virginia, Maryland, and other southern states for organizing the removal of manumitted slaves, as well as to indirect support from the national government, which maintained official agencies in Liberia and provided naval protection. Some moderate whites in the North continued to support the movement as well, among them Abraham Lincoln, who in the 1850s endorsed colonization as one of the elements of a peaceful resolution of the sectional conflict. Black interest in emigration, including among Canadian fugitives, revived under the leadership of Martin Delany in the 1850s as a proto-nationalist venture, but initially with the aim of settling in the Western Hemisphere rather than Africa.[102] At Lincoln's request, in 1862 Congress gave the president authority to resettle the slaves of rebellious whites, emancipated under the Confiscation Act, outside the United States; but although negotiations got underway for locations in Liberia, Haiti, and Central America, attention shifted shortly to the mobilization of free blacks into the Union Army.[103]

Over the half-century of its existence, the ACS collected $2.5 million from private and public sources. It resettled over 1,000 captives from slave ships and sponsored the transportation of 12,000 Negroes, most of them recently manumitted from large estates in the Deep South, under conditions close to deportation.[104] An ambiguous venture from the start, colonization contributed little to the resolution of America's growing slavery crisis but confirmed the boundary delineated in the naturalization law of 1790: the body politic was to be free and white.

5

Tocqueville's Footnote

Alexis de Tocqueville's hosts, half a century after independence, did not think of themselves as a "nation of immigrants." Reflecting the prevailing self-image, the Frenchman characterized them as a thoroughly formed "Anglo-American" people, whose political culture was founded on a collective character molded in the course of many generations of shared existence. However, in his chapter devoted to "the accidental or providential causes which contribute to the maintenance of democratic republicanism in the United States," Tocqueville does deal with contemporary immigration and its impact.[1] A first reference, within the text itself, reflects the optimistic conclusions he reached on the basis of his observations. All forms of government are dependent for their stability on general well-being, and this is particularly true of democracy because of the risk that a resentful people will overthrow the state; fortunately, "the material causes . . . which can foster well-being, are more numerous in America than in any other country in the world at any time in history," as if God had kept a part of the earth in reserve for the very purpose of this experiment. The vital element is the almost limitless availability of land, which allows for a "double migratory movement": the American is constantly relocating westward, where he "becomes a rich landowner," while the European emigrant, "arriving without friends and often without resources," and obliged to sell his labor in "the great industrial zone stretching along the Ocean" in order to survive, "always lands in a country that is but half-full, where industry is short of hands." Hence, he "becomes a prosperous worker; his son goes off to seek his fortunes in an empty country," and consequently "misery is unknown to native and foreigner alike."

However, changes intervening shortly after his visit prompted Tocqueville to thoroughly revise his assessment in a pessimistic vein. His afterthoughts are consigned to a footnote in a later edition.[2] The text to which it refers emphasizes the fortunate consequences for American republican institutions of the absence of a large hegemonic capital city, vulnerable to mob rule. But the footnote sounds the alarm:

> America does not yet have a great capital, but it already has very large towns. In 1830 Philadelphia numbered 161,000 inhabitants, and New York 202,000. The lower classes that inhabit these two cities constitute a populace which is even more dangerous than its European counterpart. They consist in the first instance of free blacks, condemned by law and by public opinion to a state of hereditary degradation and misery. One also encounters in their midst a multitude of Europeans whom misfortune and misconduct drive, day in, day out, toward the shores of the new world. These men bring to the United States our greatest vices, and lack any of the interests which might offset their influence. Living in a country of which they are not citizens, they are ready to take advantage of all the passions that agitate it. Indeed, in recent times, serious riots have been seen to erupt in Philadelphia and in New York.

Although these disturbances have evoked little concern because the cities in question do not govern the American state, Tocqueville concludes with an ominous warning: "I do not hesitate to predict that this is what will cause them to perish, unless their government succeeds in creating an armed force which, subservient to the wishes of the national majority, can be made independent of the people of the cities and able to restrain their excesses."

The nightmarish footnote was prompted by a profound transformation of the Atlantic migration system in the second quarter of the nineteenth century, which simultaneously fostered the American Republic's spectacular economic growth and challenged its original political culture. Immigration contributed to the formation of a distinctive societal segment, sharply differentiated from the "Anglo-Americans" by their ethnic origins, religion, and class. This development provoked increasingly vociferous negative reactions, subsumed under the label "nativist," that were channeled into a widespread and powerful political movement that interacted with the steadily sharpening confrontation over slavery to destroy the established party system and usher in a period of instability culminating in the Civil War. It also prompted the elaboration of intellectual constructions that provided the underpinnings for policies seeking to reinforce the external border to minimize the intake of the undesirable and unfit, and reinforce society's internal boundaries to prevent or at least delay the incorporation of immigrants deemed threatening to its preservation.

Yet we are left with a major historical puzzle: how come a force powerful enough to wreak havoc with deeply entrenched political institutions failed to stem the tide that brought it to life and provoked its outrage? A number of historians have suggested that the nativists did not even try to close the door: because, in contrast with a later period, they reckoned they lacked support for this objective; or because nativism was directed more against Roman Catholicism than against immigration per se; or yet because they were mostly concerned to limit the newcomers' political influence. Tyler Anbinder, for example, comments, "While arguing that immigration laws also required modification to prevent the importation of paupers and criminals, Know Nothings never actually sought restrictions or quotas on the flow of immigration."[3] This is a misleading, anachronistic perspective, as the establishment of quotas in the 1920s was the culmination of several decades of restrictive measures explicitly designed to reduce immigration by other means, including a variety of taxes and categoric prohibitions. A reexamination of the evidence with this corrective in mind reveals that many of the initiatives undertaken by the nativists in the middle decades of the nineteenth century were indeed designed to reduce incoming numbers, and that their advocates were often quite explicit about their intent. And although Dale Knobel insists that nativism was not primarily a response to an upsurge of immigration, but rather expressed concern to maintain personal independence and republican self-government, he does support the present point, in that "nativist mayors, councilmen, governors, and legislators did a good deal to implement nativist ideology."[4]

The record of legislative enactments at the state and national levels indicates that the nativists scored some important victories but failed to achieve their ultimate objective of significantly reducing immigration because the channeling of anti-immigration sentiment into policy was hampered by two major obstacles. One arose from the perennial dialectics of American immigration politics: spurts of massive and different immigration trigger nativist reactions, but nativism in turn stimulates the political mobilization of immigrants. As the second party system took shape, the Democrats developed an organizational commitment to the defense of immigrant interests, and since they held the upper hand in Washington throughout most of the period, this severely hampered anti-immigrant action at the national level. A second obstacle was the emergence of a powerful new actor. Immigration made possible the managerial revolution in American business, a process Alfred Chandler has felicitously termed the emergence of "the visible hand," and this hand in turn

firmly intervened to keep the gates open by exploiting constitutional arrangements, which subjected the regulation of immigration to an institutional
Catch-22.[5] Whereas the states were prohibited from intruding into the sphere
of international commerce, the national government was prohibited by considerations arising from the issue of slavery from regulating the movement of
individuals. This delineated spheres of mutually exclusive authority over immigrants that provided ample opportunities to challenge the constitutionality
of regulatory actions.

The Transformation of American Society

Tocqueville's ominous afterthoughts were prompted by the spectacular expansion of immigration that got underway shortly after his return to France.
From 1820 to 1830, the country's white population increased by nearly 2.7
million to reach 10.5 million; recorded immigration contributed a mere 5
percent of the growth, and in the year that brought Tocqueville, newcomers
numbered only 22,633, amounting to approximately one-fourth of 1 percent
of the white population.[6] Although the U.S. Census did not yet distinguish
between natives and foreign-born, it is estimated that the latter constituted
slightly less than 5 percent of the white population; and even in New York
City, by then the principal port of entry, they amounted to only 7 percent.[7]
However, in the course of the 1832 sailing season, recorded arrivals escalated
to 60,482, nearly three times the ongoing level and twice the previous maximum. Of the 34,193 whose country of origin was recorded, only 5,331 came
from Great Britain; 12,436 were Irish, and 10,194 German. Although most of
the Irish still originated in the island's northeast, by all reports they were now
mainly Catholic.[8] This was but the vanguard. New annual records were set in
1834, 1836, 1837, and again, after a brief respite attributable to the latter
year's financial panic, in 1840, when the number reached 84,066. For the
decade as a whole, recorded immigration amounted to approximately 15 percent of total white population growth, over twice the 1820s level. Altogether,
in the ten-year period beginning 1832, the United States officially received
over 650,000 immigrants, of whom only one-fourth were of British stock. To
these should be added a substantial number who landed surreptitiously to
evade regulations or entered by way of British North America, the bulk of
whom were Irish Catholic. The annual flow from Europe passed the 100,000
mark for the first time in 1842 and, after a two-year recess, again in 1845.
However, the rate of increase of immigration since 1832 was approximately

the same as that of population, so the contribution of immigration to white population growth remained stable at about one-sixth.

These developments lent themselves to wide-ranging interpretations. From one perspective, changing conditions now fostered an unmanageable "torrent."[9] As against this, it was possible to argue as late as 1845 that foreigners constituted "comparatively small and decreasing numbers," and that immigration "must be limited by the capacity of the vessels employed in bringing passengers, while our entire population goes on increasing in geometrical progression, so that in one century from now, we shall have a population of one hundred and sixty millions, but a few hundred thousands of whom at the utmost can be citizens of foreign birth."[10] In the event, the catastrophic prediction proved the more accurate. Striking one year after the two were issued, the tidal wave rapidly escalated, reaching 414,933 in 1854. Altogether, it deposited nearly 2.5 million people in the United States within a nine-year period, adding nearly 13 percent to the country's white population. The well-documented concatenation of depression, famine—the potato failure was the most dramatic, but there was also a severe shortage of cereal crops—and political upheavals that ravaged all of northwestern Europe in 1846–1850 enlarged the domain of emigration to encompass all of southern Ireland, a broader swath of the German lands, and France, Belgium, the Netherlands, as well as the edges of Scandinavia, and it also fostered the triumph of emigrationism among the relevant governments.[11] Reflected in the simultaneous uprooting of entire families, including more of the poor who hitherto could not afford to relocate overseas without assistance, the urgency of departure resulted in higher mortality aboard ships and more parlous conditions among the surviving immigrant masses.[12]

Immigration was now so prominent and worrisome a phenomenon that it prompted the introduction into the 1850 U.S. Census of an unprecedented distinction between native- and foreign-born. The count revealed that the proportion of foreign-born among the white population reached 11.5 percent for the nation as a whole, and 15.5 percent in the Northeast. The absolute number of foreign-born nearly doubled in the next decade, so that by 1860 the proportions were 15 and 22 percent respectively.[13] By 1855, when New York City's population reached 629,904, 51 percent were foreign-born, a more than sevenfold increase in their proportion since Tocqueville's visit, and a fourfold one since his footnote.[14] The phenomenon was no longer limited to the eastern seaboard, nor was it exclusively urban.[15] Except for northern New England and the South, the proportion of foreign-born outside the various states' large cities ranged between 10 and 20 percent, rising to 34 percent in Wisconsin and to a record 63 percent in newly opened California.

Moreover, as the 1860 Census report observed, "The European class would be far more numerous were their descendants also included." Although the census did not formally distinguish among "native-born" between those of "native" and "foreign" stock until 1890, the distinction itself emerged several decades earlier. Non-British immigrants constituted over 75 percent of arrivals in the 1830s and an even higher proportion later on; and the 1850 Census pointed out that of the foreign-born, only approximately one-fifth were of British "founding stock." The largest non-British groups remained the Irish, who peaked at 58 percent of arrivals in 1851, and the Germans, who did so at 50 percent in 1854. By 1860, among the foreign-born nationwide, the Irish were the most numerous, amounting to 39 percent, followed by the Germans with 31 percent, while the British-born "founding stock" fell to 14 percent.[16]

The contribution of immigration to economic development was so much taken for granted by American men of affairs that the question was seldom argued explicitly; and the validity of the prevailing view has been sustained by economic analyses of the consequences of transatlantic population movements in the first half of the nineteenth century.[17] The nexus of economic and social changes amounted to an American version of the "great transformation" that swept Great Britain earlier in the century and was even then spreading to much of Europe.[18] The contribution of immigration was critical since, as Tocqueville observed, the structure of American landholding was not conducive to the transformation of rural masses into factory labor. For example, Lowell's pioneering integrated textile mill, the Boston Manufacturing Co., initially secured a large permanent labor force by recruiting unmarried New England farm girls, but by the 1840s they were being replaced by Irish immigrants.[19] Europe contributed not only manpower but also capital, which during the 1830s entered the United States in unprecedented quantity as investments in canals, railroads, land, and state bonds; net liabilities to foreigners, mostly British, rose from $75 million in 1830 to $292 million in 1839. The lack of coal was overcome in the 1830s, and the railroad, in whose construction immigrant labor played a critical role, together with the telegraph, simultaneously transformed the processes of distribution, with the changes in production and distribution reinforcing one another and resulting in enlarged and more integrated enterprises.[20] The American economic revolution was already underway when the European economy went into depression. Although previous conjunctural downturns in Europe induced downturns in the United States as well—most recently in 1837—this did not occur in the late 1840s, partly because of the discovery of gold in California, but also because the unprecedented upsurge of immigration had a stimulating effect on housing starts. Hence the period 1849–1856 was one of nearly continuous boom, interrupted only by brief slumps in the latter half of 1851 and again in the fall of 1854.[21]

The railroad, which both contributed to the revolution of American capitalism and was its leading manifestation, rapidly emerged in the policy arena as a major actor favoring a high level of immigration on several grounds. The European flow not only supplied the huge pool of low-wage workers necessary for its rapid development, but also increased its passenger clientele, especially in newly developing regions, where the companies also sold land to Americans and newcomers. The federal government had been granting land to the states all along for the establishment of right-of-ways, initially roads and canals and later railroads. Resuming their increase in the late 1820s after several years of decline and stagnation, federal land sales surpassed the 1818 maximum in 1833, and rose to over 20 million acres in 1836. Altogether, from 1820 to 1841, receipts from land sales constituted over 11 percent of total federal revenues; but as of the mid-1830s, they amounted to approximately half of the federal government's income from all sources.[22] A new policy was inaugurated in 1850, when land was allotted to Illinois and other states straddling a projected line from Chicago to the Gulf of Mexico for the express purpose of turning it over as a subsidy to a private company, by which it would be sold.[23] In this manner, the Illinois Central, chartered in 1851, obtained over 2.5 million acres toward the construction of a line from Chicago to Cairo, Georgia, which was completed in 1856. In the face of sluggish sales, in 1855 the company adopted a more active stance: "[A]dvertising matter was printed in several languages and agents sent to Europe to induce foreigners to immigrate and purchase."[24] Shortly afterwards, the company organized a separate land department with its own marketing organization in the United States and abroad. Others followed suit; altogether, between 1850 and 1857, 21 million acres were granted in this manner to subsidize the construction of new lines throughout the Mississippi Valley.

Albeit less affected by the managerial revolution, the shipping industry also underwent a spectacular expansion. Total carrying capacity increased fivefold, from 1.2 million gross tons in 1830 to 5.5 million in 1861, a figure that was not surpassed until 1902; at this time, American ships carried two-thirds of U.S.-bound commerce.[25] Concentrated in the period 1847–1857, the boom entailed the construction not only of more ships, but of much larger ones as well; average capacity grew from 400 tons in 1820 to 1,250 by 1854.[26] Although the jewel of the merchant marine was the sleek and fast packet ship, which achieved toward the end of the era of sail a near-monopoly of fine freight and cabin-passenger trade, its mainstay consisted of combination traders, full of line and much slower, designed to carry cotton bales to Europe and from 300 to 600 immigrants in the 'tween [sic] decks on the westbound voyage.[27] Packets turned to the emigrant traffic as well when their monopoly began to be challenged by steam, as illustrated by Herman Melville's narrative of the experience of his alter ego, Wellingborough Redburn, in 1839.[28] The vessels launched at the height of the boom "were designed for emigrants, as carriage of emigrants had become the greatest single source of revenue for owners."[29] Like the railroads, American shipping companies also developed an extensive network of recruiting agencies in Europe.[30] Hence at the height of nativist fervor, railroads, factory owners, and shippers formed a stalwart alliance in defense of the established immigrationist policies.

As a consequence of these developments, between 1825 and 1855, the workforce in New York City and the urban sector of American society more generally shifted from "mechanics" to wage workers; and as the latter were overwhelmingly foreign-born, the emergence of a proletariat was dramatized by the alien character of the new class.[31] As the nativists charged, the foreign stream severely undermined the position of native-born skilled workers, and that period is "among the few times it has been possible to detect . . . a negative impact from immigration," with the Irish crucial to the process.[32] In 1850–1860, of the vast majority who landed in New York City, some 65 percent left immediately for the hinterland; however, the Irish were more likely than others to remain in the seaboard cities as "hands."[33]

Tocqueville's somber afterthoughts were very much in tune with the growing misgivings of his Whig informants, whose viewpoint he shared on many issues.[34] Under the impact of these startling changes, the diffuse reservations that had been voiced perennially regarding the cultural and political impacts of immigration were given a more reasoned form by Protestant intellectuals and emerged as a prominent element of American social and political discourse. As Matthew Jacobson has suggested, "Whereas the salient feature of whiteness before the 1840s had been its powerful and cultural contrast to nonwhiteness, now its internal divisions, too, took on a new and pressing significance."[35]

A contributing factor was that, notwithstanding their fervent nationalism, educated Americans remained largely imbued with the culture of Britain, sharing as a matter of course its deeply imbedded prejudices toward the Irish. Each eagerly awaited shipment of reviews brought with it reactions to the invasion of the ancestral island by the "simian race," echoing and reinforcing the dismay provoked by the spectacle of Irish hordes in New York, Boston, or Philadelphia.[36] As a new unruly working class, they were frightful; but as Roman Catholics, the Irish—to whom were added many of the Germans— were outright dangerous. Romanism had long stood as the negative pole in relation to which Puritanism defined its own moral disposition, and this remained true of the more attenuated version of the Puritan tradition embodied in the culture of the nineteenth-century Whigs, punctuated as it was by recurrent evangelical efforts to bring about moral renewal.[37] Anti-Catholicism was fueled as well by the controversies surrounding Catholic emancipation in Britain in the late 1820s.

Beyond this, the ideological war launched by the Holy See against political liberalism in the wake of the revolutionary upheavals of 1830, whose manifesto was issued in 1832 as the encyclical *Mirari Vos,* provided realistic grounds for suspicion that Catholic immigrants constituted a manipulable mass that might be used to undermine the world's only liberal republic. As Daniel Walker Howe has put it, "[C]oncern that the Church of Rome was less than enthusiastic about free institutions cannot be dismissed as irrational Protestant bigotry; Gregory XVI and Pius XI were not John XXIII"—nor even John Paul II.[38] Further worries arose from the designation of America as a Catholic "mission country" by the Austrian-sponsored Leopoldine Society, a development that Samuel F. B. Morse identified as a direct threat to national security.[39] The Mexican attack on the Alamo in 1836 suggested that Catholic power also loomed as a strategic impediment to the fulfillment of Manifest Destiny. Catholicism loomed as a potential threat from the revolutionary side of the political spectrum as well since, as Thomas Jefferson had reasoned, men socialized under authoritarian rule were likely to confuse freedom with license. At a moment when the Jacksonian victories ushered in the reign of popular democracy, the irruption into the British political arena of a radical Irish mass movement led by priests afforded the makings of another American nightmare.

It is therefore necessary to move beyond the reduction of "nativism" to "paranoia" and view the developing conflict as a confrontation between distinct collectivities, in the course of which they became transformed into societal groups organized to act in line with their divergent perceptions.[40] Ongoing changes stimulated the further development and proliferation of trade, political, and patriotic societies, which were organized primarily for participatory citizenship but, perceiving immigration as threatening individual independence and republican self-government, eventually took on a markedly "nativist" orientation.[41] The Irish, in particular, came to be viewed as an alien race who were located on the other side of a boundary delineating American identity, and whose intrusion therefore raised an unprecedented problem of incorporation. This was found not merely at the level of popular belief; for example, progressive mental health practitioners came to view the Irish, due to innate characteristics, as more susceptible to insanity and less responsive to therapy, who must therefore be institutionally segregated lest they worsen the condition of native patients.[42]

The Irish, for their part, had long lived within a Protestant state under conditions that fostered dependence on the Catholic Church as their major societal institution and on priests for their leadership, somewhat paralleling the situation of African Americans in the postemancipation period with regard to their ministers. They quickly became aware of the overwhelmingly Protestant character of American institutions as well, notably public schools and charitable organizations.[43] As in Europe, the conflict was particularly acute in the sphere of education for the lower classes, which was then undergoing transition from a limited philanthropic undertaking into a massive governmental service.[44] The initial solution was to demand parity—use of the Douay Bible alongside the King James Version in schools, hospitals, and poorhouses—and when this failed, strict enforcement of separation of church and state, in accordance with the Constitution. When this in turn got nowhere, Catholics opted for cultural separatism, involving the elaboration of a fully self-contained subsociety anchored in the parish, the school, and attendant social services, eventually reaching up toward a full-scale system of colleges, professional schools, and hospitals, all of which are still in existence today. In doing so, they took advantage of the freedom of association Tocqueville so much admired. It was quite natural for new arrivals to regroup into friendly societies along lines of ethnic and geographical origin, the more so as the existing native associations that served as their models were often exclusive; and in the face of perennial violent confrontations, these initiatives often extended to the creation of armed militias.[45] Within the context of established suspicions, these developments provided further evidence that Catholics were out to create a foreign body within American society. In the pursuit of their objectives, Catholics benefited from the battle-hardened leadership of John

Hughes, appointed in 1850 as America's first archbishop—a move naturally perceived by the other camp as providing yet further evidence of the pope's malevolent ambitions, confirmed by Hughes's explicit commitment to the massive conversion of Protestants.[46]

Tocqueville's dark vision of mob violence could have been stimulated by any one of a number of social and political disturbances, news of which was probably relayed to him in France by his Whig friends. After a generation of relative civil peace, in 1834 violence swept across the country, prompting the prominent theologian William Ellery Channing to comment that "society was shaken to its foundations, all its joints loosened, all its fixtures about to be swept away."[47] At least twenty-four ethnic conflicts of national importance have been recorded in that year alone.[48] The violence continued into the following year, exacerbated by the onset of a depression, and the division between natives and immigrants crystallized as well. In New York, sensing an impending defeat in the municipal elections of the spring of 1835, the Whigs egregiously exploited the growing anti-Catholic bigotry.[49] Following their loss and the dismissal of Whig officials by the newly elected Democratic Common Council, in June 1835 some of the Whig leaders called a meeting of all "Native Americans" to keep foreigners from depriving them of jobs and homes, and demanded a revision of the naturalization laws to require twenty years' residence for the suffrage. The presence of this provocative protagonist on the political scene precipitated renewed rioting, stimulating on one side the organization of an Irish militia and on the other the launching of a new political party, the Native American Democratic Association, which eventually entered into an alliance with the Whigs to contest statewide elections. The following year, they nominated as their candidate for mayor the prominent artist and inventor Samuel F. B. Morse, hitherto an ardent Jacksonian; another party leader was Mordecai Noah, a native-born Jew and the editor of the *Evening Star*. Morse was soundly defeated, dragging the upstart party down with him.[50] Now clearly the party of immigrants, the Democrats maintained control over the city for much of the next decade as the newcomers continued to pour in.

Ideology and Partisanship

The concerns provoked by the strange new situation stimulated the articulation of ideologies seeking to identify its causes and dynamics, as well as to provide guidance for appropriate action.[51] One of the earliest was set forth by

Morse in two series of articles published in 1834 and issued as books the following year.[52] Albeit laden with rantings, they must nevertheless be taken seriously as the political arguments of a committed democrat. Excerpting Jefferson's warning from *Notes on the State of Virginia,* he begins the series dealing more specifically with immigration much as in Tocqueville's footnote, with the observation "that the American character has within a short time been sadly degraded by numerous instances of riot and lawless violence in action, and a dangerous spirit of licentiousness in discussion." But in sharp contrast with the aristocratic observer, he firmly denies that this turmoil is attributable "to the natural tendency of Democracy," nor can he accept the notion "that the American character has suddenly undergone a radical change from good to bad." Hence, the cause must be extrinsic: it is "FOREIGN IMMIGRATION."

What is at stake is no less than America's unique world-historical mission. The struggle between liberty and despotism, which has been going on since the Reformation, reached a new stage with the emergence of the American Republic, identified by the despotic powers as their most dangerous antagonist, as for example in a lecture delivered in 1828 by Frederick Schlegel, confidant to Prince Metternich. Hence it is a prime target for subversion; but since the Holy Alliance "cannot send her armies," it relies on popery, "the promoter and supporter of arbitrary power," as indicated by the launching of the Leopoldine foundation. Emphasizing the large proportion of newcomers who are Roman Catholic, and hence under priestly control and subject to manipulation, he dismisses the possibility "that by the act of coming to this country, and being naturalized, their darkened intellects can suddenly be illuminated to discern the nice boundary where their ecclesiastical obedience to their priests ends, and their civil independence of them begins."[53] Not only do these priest-led ignorant masses organize themselves into "foreign bands" for the purpose of influencing our elections, but also "[a] portion of foreigners have had the audacity to attempt the formation of themselves into a separate MILITARY CORPS" named after O'Connell, who has "thrown a firebrand into the Slavery question." That many of the Catholic newcomers vote for the Democratic Party is hardly comforting, since it makes sense for a clique seeking to subvert a régime to penetrate it by posing as apparent allies. Echoing Hezekiah Niles and others, Morse inveighs against hyphenated identities: "I hold no parley with such contradictions as Irish fellow-citizens, French fellow-citizens, or German fellow-citizens. With as much consistency might we say *foreign natives,* or *hostile friends.*"

He then systematically reviews the ongoing debate over naturalization and rejects arguments that a lengthening of the residence requirement is contrary to the rights of those concerned. While in the period of the founding naturalization laws had to be designed to attract immigrants, this is no longer necessary today, and they should instead pay heed to national security: "When the country is invaded by an army, it is not the moment to indulge in pity toward the deluded soldiers of the various hostile corps, who act as they are commanded by their superior officers. . . . Innocent and guilty are brought over together. We must of necessity suspect them all."

One suitable response is to withhold naturalization from immigrants altogether, while extending citizenship to their descendants born and bred in the United States, in accordance with the jus soli tradition of Anglo-American common law. Whether or not naturalization takes place, the right of suffrage should be withheld from the foreign-born altogether. Moreover, in order to prevent the formation of hyphenated identities, associations dedicated to the maintenance of foreign culture should be prohibited.

Anti-Catholicism was but one element of a more comprehensive ideology. As Daniel Howe has shown, the Whigs embodied an outlook akin to Max Weber's spirit of capitalism, combining a religious sensibility derived from Puritanism, revived by the second Great Awakening, with "a vision of America as an economically diversified country in which commerce and industry would take their place alongside agriculture." They also sought to mobilize a recently enlarged electorate by appealing to Yankee Protestant natives and immigrants of British origin, who still constituted a substantial part of the newcomers. Overall, "[T]he affluent were attracted to Whiggery by the party's economic program, poor men more often by its ethnic identification."[54] These affinities have been confirmed by Michael Holt's extensive study of the party: in the North, Whigs and Democrats attracted different constituencies, both in terms of their relationship to the expanding market economy and of identity, and the rivals "often chose one party simply because the hostile group supported the other."[55] Yet while the Whig rank and file were overwhelmingly nativist in their outlook, the party's commitment to a business-minded economic program dictated adherence by its leaders to the established immigrationist policy, making for a dilemma that plagued the Whigs from the mid-1840s until their demise a dozen years later.

The elements of a solution were adumbrated by Alexander H. Everett, editor of the *North American Review,* at about the time of Morse's newspaper series, on the basis of the sensationalist and associationist psychology that was also the source of contemporaneous reformist experiments in treatment of the mentally ill.[56] The Irishman is as he is through no fault of his own, but as a consequence of the "ceaseless and disorganizing exactions of provincial vassalage" and "misgovernment" to which he has long been subject. However, his degradation is such that "[t]here is no charm in the middle passage to remove from his character the impress of recklessness and ignorance." What is needed is a thorough program of moral reconstruction: "It is necessary to implant in him a taste for many of the gratifications of life to which he has hitherto been a stranger, and to enlarge the scope of purposes beyond the mere support of a reckless and precarious existence. Without this previous discipline, the increased facility of satisfying his animal wants, so far from supplying a stimulus to increase exertion, will be found to afford the strongest solicitation to renewed and indolent indulgence." The stimulation of new aspirations will lead the immigrants in turn to submit willingly to the redemptive discipline of work. They were still "redemptioners," after all; but while a thriving industrial society can be entrusted to generate constructive stimuli and thereby overcome the political difficulties arising from the immigration of economically desirable cheap labor, to achieve this it must not allow itself to be burdened by the additional problem of paupers and convicts, such as Britain was willfully dumping into its hands. Hence Everett recommended strengthening restrictive regulations such as already existed in New York, which would also make it possible to provide appropriate relief to genuinely needy immigrants.

Initially, immigration also posed a challenge to the Democrats, who were emerging as, among other things, the party of workers in northern urban areas. In the early 1830s their electorate still consisted mostly of native Americans, many of them "mechanics" active in workingmen's organizations, who regarded the large influx of cheap labor as a threat to their income and status. For example, the New York Workingman's Advocate argued in the mid-1830s that a high tariff was useless to the worker because no tariff could arrest the growth of an excess supply of labor, which must of necessity reduce wages and bring about conditions in America similar to those encountered in England. The 1834 congress of the short-lived National Organization of Trade Unions also expressed concern with competition from convict labor, women, children, and immigrants.[57] Limiting the damage by restricting immigration presented itself as an obvious solution; but another was to even out chances by providing for American workers an equivalent to the "exit" available to their European counterparts, by way of cheaper or altogether free public land.

Aspiration to life as an independent farmer was the widely shared aspiration of an indigenous working class that had gained access to political citizenship and was not yet proletarianized. Both alternatives in fact surfaced within the New York Democratic camp in the mid-1830s: the one was advocated by Samuel F. B. Morse's Native American Democratic Association, the other by the Equal Rights Party, a radical Democratic faction also known as the Loco-Focos.

As it was, whatever negative dispositions were manifested toward immigration at the rank-and-file level, these were overridden by the Democratic Party's overwhelming organizational interest in recruiting the new arrivals. Although both parties attempted to do so, the Democrats, as defenders of the interest of the common man, less marked by adherence to a traditional vision of the American moral order, and committed to separation of church and state, were more attractive to poor immigrants in general, and to Catholics in particular; and by virtue of its strength among natives of Dutch and German descent, the party adapted itself more easily to a culturally heterogeneous clientele. The distinctive ethnic orientations of the two parties functioned as a self-fulfilling prophecy.[58] For the time being, the necessities of coexistence with a northern urban wing also constrained southern Democrats from acting on their misgivings concerning immigration as a source of reinforcement for the antislavery camp.

In the sphere of immigration, the Democratic Party naturally came to reflect the interests of newcomers, among whom the desire for family reunion tended to override concern with labor-market competition that might counsel the adoption of a restrictionist stance. This was broadened to solidarity with the larger ethnic group, as its expansion would facilitate the creation of appropriate community organizations and, in a democracy with liberal naturalization laws, constitute a source of increasing political power that could be deployed to render the receiving society more hospitable. As cultural pluralism grew, the positive pole of the political-cultural axis of immigration and citizenship policy came to life, with a decisive impact on national policy. In the twenty-six years from 1835 to the Civil War, the Democrats had a majority in the Senate in all but four years (1841–1845) and in the House in all but eight (1841–1843, 1847–1849, 1855–1857, and 1859–1861), thereby providing very limited opportunities for the enactment of anti-immigrant policies at the national level, despite the popularity of nativist sentiments in the country at large.

Restricting Immigration: The Limits of National Policy

Attempts to restrict immigration focused on the two well-established policy devices: prohibiting the landing of certain categories, and imposing taxes or passenger regulations designed to reduce carrying capacity and inflate ticket prices. The restrictionists also sought to reduce incentives by modifying land policies, and to limit the political impact of immigration by raising requirements for naturalization and erecting new barriers to political participation. However, they encountered severe institutional obstacles to the achievement of their objectives.

Deterring Undesirables

The problem of destitution among newcomers had long been on the agenda, "[b]ut it remained for the nativists to play up the foreign-pauper scare for all it was worth."[59] The flow of unprecedented magnitude overwhelmed the cities' limited social services and lent support to the belief that immigrants were especially burdensome; for example, the proportion of foreigners among admissions to the New York Alms Houses nearly doubled from around 40 percent in 1830 to almost 80 percent in the 1850s.[60] The nativists also exploited the widely publicized notion that European governments sponsored the departure of persons who could not have sailed of their own accord. *Niles' Weekly Register* proclaimed vehemently in mid-1830, "John Bull has 'squeezed his orange,' but insolently casts the skins in our faces."[61] Although the recently adopted official British policy of sponsored emigration pertained only to its own colonies, this made no sense in light of past American experience, as indicated by the reasoning of a Massachusetts legislative committee concerning the effects of the new Poor Law of 1834: "Can it be for a moment supposed that England intends this to burden her colonies, or that her colonies would quietly receive and provide for such accessions to their populations?" There was little doubt that Britain intended to take advantage of the Canadian loophole in the American fence, as indicated by a report from Albany, New York, in 1830: "It is said that from 7,000 to 8,000 paupers have arrived in Canada during the present season, to be dropped into the United States. How much are we indebted to John Bull for such acts of kindness—such reliance on our charity?"[62]

By the mid-1830s, even those committed to an immigrationist stance advocated more vigorous intervention to minimize the negative side effects of the process. This would also resolve the normative contradictions associated with immigration, as by its determination to exclude paupers, the United States simultaneously asserted that the problems it posed were not of its own making, and affirmed to the world the foundations of its social contract. Inextricably intertwined, these considerations provided the makings of a bipartisan consensus on the necessity of more vigorous governmental intervention to counter "dumping." But the seaboard states faced the inherent administrative problems of operationalizing categories such as "convicts" and especially "paupers" in relation to the mass of passengers, and of devising mechanisms for deterring their landing. Each of them was also pressured by actors with opposite interests: on one side, the welfare establishment as well as law enforcement authorities faced with mounting costs, and on the other, the shippers who thrived on bringing in as many aliens as possible. And finally, as noted earlier, as competitors for passenger traffic they were trapped in a prisoner's dilemma.

The regulatory system instituted in the early decades proved largely ineffective. The bonding system instituted by the states as well as passenger space regulations were easily evaded by smuggling passengers into the country on lighters, or by landing them outside major ports, notably in Perth Amboy, New Jersey. Professional bondsmen took over the task of supplying securities at a discount, and enforcement was so lax that by 1828 the effective price of bonds in New York had fallen to as little as $2.00 for a whole shipload.[63] Most important, the future of state regulatory activity proved altogether doubtful. Affirmation by the U.S. Supreme Court in 1824 of the national government's supremacy in the sphere of international and interstate commerce, including navigation, provided grounds for contesting the constitutionality of state bonds and head taxes. A challenge was launched as early as 1826 in response to an action of debt instituted by the State of New York to recover penalties under the bonding act passed two years earlier; and although the defendant was precluded for technical reasons from attacking the act on constitutional grounds and found liable in 1828, another challenge began to wind its way through the courts the following year, even as pressures for more vigorous state intervention increased.[64] As problems mounted and the shippers appeared likely to succeed, the eastern states were impelled to cooperate and launched a drive to secure a national solution. However, their initiative was countered by a de facto coalition of immigrant-hungry Westerners and southern guardians of states' rights, at a time when the issue of police powers, propelled by the conflict over slavery, was moving to center stage.

The shipper-engineered challenge, *City of New York v. Miln*, again arising out of an action by the state to recover debt, finally reached the U.S. Supreme Court in 1834. When first argued, with Chief Justice John Marshall still at the helm, it was believed that four out of seven justices considered the law to be unconstitutional as a regulation of international commerce. However, because two of the putative majority were absent from the Court, Marshall in effect foreclosed a minority victory by the unprecedented ruling that the Court could not hand down a decision since its practice was not to deliver judgments in constitutional cases unless four judges concurred in making it a majority opinion. The case was still pending in the spring of 1836, when the Massachusetts legislature, having established that the recently enacted British Poor Law was even more threatening than the old Speenhamland system (established in 1795 in the face of rising bread prices whereby a laborer would have his income supplemented to the subsistence level by the parish according to the price of bread and the number of children in his family, but which was alleged to encourage dependency and unemployment) because "the plan of His Majesty's poor law commissioners, recommending the emigration of their poor, has not only reached its maturity in positive enactment of law, but has actually come into operation," instructed the Commonwealth's representatives and senators to use "their endeavors to obtain the passage of a law by Congress to prevent the introduction of paupers into this country, or to favor any other measures which congress may be disposed to adopt to effect the object."[65] Accordingly, on July 4, 1836, the Senate of the United States directed the secretary of the treasury to collect facts on the "deportation" of paupers from Europe to the United States. Conducted over the next year by U.S. consuls and duly reported to the Senate in 1837, the investigation produced ambiguous results: outright deportation was very rare, but sponsorship of some sort was fairly common. In any case, urgent national action was called for because there was no prospect of securing a change of policy on the part of the countries of origin.

Even as Congress contemplated further action, the Supreme Court finally issued its decision in *Miln*. Contrary to earlier expectations, the Court, now headed by the Maryland Catholic Roger Taney, ruled 6 to 1 in favor of the constitutionality of the New York statute on the grounds that it was "not a regulation of commerce, but of police; and that being so considered, it was passed in the exercise of a power which rightfully belonged to the states." Justice Joseph Story was the lone dissenter.[66] The Court's pronouncements, which provided the most comprehensive statement of constitutional doctrine in the sphere of immigration to date and which determined the shape of policy for the remainder of the antebellum period, demonstrate that the common historical wisdom, which attributes the absence of federal regulation of entry prior to the Civil War to the persistence of a consensus on immigrationist laissez-faire, is based on a profound misunderstanding. Although the case dealt with immigration, Taney seized the opportunity to affirm the doctrine of states' rights. Adumbrating the Charles River Bridge case handed down later that year, *Miln* signaled a reversal of the Court's steadfast support of the growth of national power.[67] The Jacksonian justices shared in the new consensus regarding the need for more active governmental intervention to restrict paupers and convicts; and by upholding state regulation and grounding it on their reserved powers under the Tenth Amendment, while concomitantly putting Congress on notice that federal action must be limited to passenger legislation, they also indicated how this should be done.

The opinion was delivered by Justice Philip Barbour of Virginia, another recent Jackson appointee. Citing Emmerich de Vattel, the standard authority on international law, Barbour asserted that the power to regulate entry was a concomitant of sovereignty, originating in the law of nations, and hence pre-existed any written constitution or statute; by the same token, "the lord of the territory . . . has, no doubt, a power to annex what conditions he pleases, to the permission to enter." The American states thus possessed this authority before adoption of the U.S. Constitution, and since it lay in the realm of police, it was not taken away from them in 1787. So long as they were on ships, immigrants fell within the jurisdiction of the federal government, which legitimately controlled navigation—notably by way of the Passenger Act of 1819; but once they landed, they ceased being passengers and became persons, hence falling under the jurisdiction of the states.

This provided in effect a recipe for elaborating a comprehensive regulatory system. Moreover, by commenting explicitly on the substantive problems that prompted New York to enact the measure under consideration, the Court lent its support to the formulation of a national immigration policy by way of concerted state action. Noting that the section of the act in question was "obviously passed with a view to prevent her citizens from being oppressed by the support of multitudes of poor persons, who come from foreign countries without possessing the means of supporting themselves," Justice Barbour affirmed, "There can be no mode in which the power to regulate internal police could be more appropriately exercised. New York, from her peculiar situation, is perhaps more than any other city in the Union, exposed to the evil of thousands of foreign emigrants arriving there." Moving beyond the realm of economic costs toward broader political and security concerns, in his peroration the justice characterized restriction of entry as the moral equivalent of quarantine: both are appropriate precautions against "pestilence." In an even more emphatic concurrent opinion, Justice Smith Thompson further legitimated the complementary division of authority over immigration by reminding the Court that in September 1788, a year after ratification of the Constitution, Congress passed a resolution urging the states to enact laws prohibiting the entry of foreign convicts.[68] Referring to the entire corpus of relevant state law, he concluded, "To pronounce all such laws unconstitutional would be productive of the most serious and alarming consequences; and ought not to be done, unless demanded by the most clear and unquestioned construction of the constitution."

Miln immediately pulled the rug out from under pending congressional action to enact a national law prohibiting the landing of paupers. Although Secretary of the Treasury Levi Woodbury duly reported to the Senate on "deportation," no further action was taken by that body. The House had also appointed a Select Committee on Foreign Paupers and Naturalization Laws. Its report, dated July 2, 1838, included a letter from the economic theorist Friedrich List, U.S. consul at Leipzig, stating, "Not only paupers, but even criminals, are transported from the interior of this country to the seaports, in order to be embarked there for the United States," and suggesting that consuls be empowered to regulate immigration at the point of departure.[69] This constituted a precocious insight into how "remote control" might be extended, but was not operationalized until after World War I. On the basis of this report, the Committee on the Judiciary was instructed—*Miln* notwithstanding—to prepare a bill prohibiting the entry of paupers; but its very severe proposal was not acted upon.[70] Although further bills designed to deter the immigration of undesirables were initiated in most of the remaining antebellum Congresses, none became law.

With constitutional doubt removed, state and local authorities acted with deliberate speed. In New York City, where the panic of 1837 provoked riots among the unemployed, the Council secured depositions from Irish immigrants to the effect that they had been induced to emigrate by the Dublin representatives of New York shippers. Recently elected Mayor Aaron Clark warned that undesirables, evading state regulations by landing in Jersey City, were continuing to pour into the city; beyond overtaxing relief facilities, they were a source of moral and political peril as well. His analysis of the displacement effects of immigration was calculated to arouse the deepest fears of a sedentary urban populace: "They drive our native workmen into exile, where they must war again with the savage of the wilderness—encounter again the tomahawk and scalping knife—and meet death beyond the regions of civilization and home." New Yorkers were imperiled even if they remained at home: "I cannot doubt that all our citizens, both natives and those we have adopted, must abhor to see this blood-bought land of liberty and hope, forcibly made the common resort, and finally the general residence, of the drones, lazzaroni, conspirators, agrarians, revolutionary incendiaries, and fugitives from justice, of various parts of the old world." The mayor therefore proposed confining arrivals on their vessels until arrangements to forward them beyond New York City were completed. Meanwhile, he intended to require of them the maximum possible commutation fee, $10 per capita. Further plans included negotiations with New Jersey for relevant action, extension of the term of residence required for naturalization, as well as enlargement of the city's police force.[71]

The proliferation of state measures indicated a shift toward greater and more uniform selectivity, and the expanded categories enumerated in them anticipated those incorporated into the comprehensive federal immigration laws enacted after the constitutional doctrine changed in the wake of the Civil War. The New Jersey loophole was closed when that state imposed a head tax on all immigrants, ranging from $1.00 to $10, depending on the degree to which they appeared likely to constitute a public charge.[72] Massachusetts enacted a new and more comprehensive passenger law shortly after the *Miln* decision as well, with Maine following suit a year later, much as New Jersey had done in relation to New York.[73] The tidal wave of the mid-1840s fostered efforts to close loopholes by replacing selective bonds with generalized head taxes, and by enforcing regulations on those entering by land or sea from British North America as well, which again faced shipper-engineered court challenges. Goaded into action by local and state welfare agencies, the Senate and the House once more began gathering information from American consuls on the process whereby undesirables were being shoveled out.

Passenger Legislation

Miln's vindication of federal authority to regulate persons on ships also revived interest in passenger legislation as a device for immigration control. In the spring of 1847, the New York State Legislature enacted a concurrent resolution urging that, whereas the regulation of international commerce was constitutionally in the hands of Congress, and as steerage passengers had become "a large and lucrative branch of such commerce, profitable in proportion to the number of persons who can be induced to take passage on board of each vessel," the state's representatives and senators should work to secure a more humanitarian passenger law.[74] Quickly passed and without divisions in either house, the resulting Passenger Act of February 22, 1847, was the first national measure dealing directly with immigration since 1819. Its major innovation was the imposition, in addition to the established minimum volume requirement of 2.5 tons per passenger, of a space requirement expressed in "superficial feet."[75] Scheduled to come into effect on May 31 of the same year, that is, as soon as the new requirements could be communicated to European embarkation points, on March 2 the law was rendered even more severe by the provision that children over one year be counted as full passengers.[76]

The same problems of interpretation arise with this as with the 1819 act. It cannot be gainsaid that this was a humanitarian measure, designed to reduce the horrors occasioned by a sudden increase in the demand for passage without a concomitant increase in available space, and the eagerness of shippers to embark all they could. The law was supported by the Irish Emigrant Society of New York, and Herman Melville, whose position on immigration was "If they can get here, they have God's right to come, though they bring all Ireland and her miseries with them," probably had it in mind when he commented in 1849, "Of late, a law has been passed in Congress, restricting ships to a certain number of emigrants, according to a certain rate. If this law were enforced, much good might be done; and so also might much good be done, were the English law likewise enforced, concerning the fixed supply of food for every emigrant embarking from Liverpool." However, he added, knowingly, "But it is hardly to be believed, that either of these laws is observed."[77]

But the law also clearly accorded with restrictionist objectives, in that it would have the effect of lowering incoming numbers by reducing the carrying capacity of the existing fleet and raising prices. There are numerous indications that the American actions, which were quickly broadcast throughout Europe, were very much perceived as deterrents. Hansen, who explicitly denies the legislation's restrictionist intent, nevertheless reports German rumors to the effect "that the new American law amounted to a prohibition on immigration." Many flocked to get in under the May 31 deadline, and north German shippers sailed to Quebec to avoid the new regulations altogether.[78]

Similarly, in the United Kingdom, "The harsh penalties and evident deter-mination of the Americans frightened shipping agents into raising U.S. fares so high that the poorest and most debilitated of the 1847 emigrants were diverted, almost without exception, to British North America."[79] Since the passenger law was proclaimed after the beginning of the 1847 season, its full impact was not appreciable until 1848, and the statistical record points in the appropriate direction: recorded landings rose from 154,416 in 1846 to 234,968 the following year, but although conditions in Europe deteriorated further in the next winter, arrivals in 1848 decreased slightly to 226,527.[80]

Nevertheless, much as Melville anticipated, the new passenger law was a pyrrhic victory for whatever combination of humanitarian and restrictionist concerns that brought about its speedy enactment. Even as seaboard states struggled to cope with the growing influx, the shippers, alarmed by the di-version of traffic to British North America, prevailed upon Secretary of the Treasury Robert Walker to interpret the new regulations loosely and quickly secured enactment of a new law of their own design "to provide for the Ven-tilation of Passenger Vessels and for other Purposes."[81] Although the provision of ventilation hatches suggested concern with passenger comfort and safety, the measure's main provision was to abolish the minimum volume require-ment altogether, and the net consequence of its "superficial" space require-ment was to significantly increase the legal carrying capacity of ships, and to allow for the construction of large three-decked vessels with two steerages, one above the other.[82] Although such ships were not yet in operation, the economically advantageous design had already been formulated; and in the construction boom that followed, large three-deckers prevailed.[83] Contrary to the effect of the 1847 law, the new arrangements contributed to an observed drop in steerage fares from Liverpool from £5 to £4 or even £3.[84] That the shippers had gained the upper hand is confirmed by the enactment of yet another passenger law in 1849—the first one referring to Pacific as well as Atlantic traffic—which further liberalized regulations and dropped the re-quirement of additional passenger space for ships passing through the tropics.[85]

The confrontation over welfare came to a head as well. Despite the *Miln* decision's legitimation of bonding as an exercise of state police power, ship-pers naturally persisted in their attempts to minimize its impact.[86] To avoid forfeiting the bonds in case immigrants became ill or destitute, they sponsored the construction of cut-rate commercial hospitals and poorhouses, in which individuals were incarcerated under conditions considered dreadful even by the generally low standards of charitable establishments. Hearings held in New York indicate that the shipping industry's camp was thereby reinforced by builders and institutional operators who shared their interests, and that many of the inmates were later surreptitiously unloaded into public facilities as long-term residents. Hence the states sought more reliable income in the form of head taxes and health fees, to be collected from all immigrants prior to landing, usually in combination with additional bonds for those who appeared likely to become public charges, usually referred to at this time as "defectives."[87]

Fees and head taxes imposed on entire shiploads as a condition for landing were more difficult to evade than selective bonds and other such regulations; and although the cost could be passed on in the form of higher fares, acute competition for the immigrant trade rendered this inexpedient.[88] Hence the shippers turned once again to the courts. Originating as local actions in 1841 and argued in various terms of the U.S. Supreme Court beginning in 1846, *Smith v. Turner* and *Norris v. City of Boston* were decided together on February 7, 1848, in what came to be known as the *Passenger Cases*.[89] As with *Miln,* the constitutional significance of these cases transcends the sphere of immigration. Contemporary comments by participants, including Daniel Webster, indicate a clear understanding that the New York and Massachusetts immigrant laws paralleled enactments whereby southern states prohibited the landing of free Negroes in their ports, so that the outcome of the *Passenger Cases* would determine the validity of the latter as well.

In a 5 to 4 split, the Supreme Court declared that the New York and Massachusetts laws interfered with immigration and thereby infringed upon federal authority in the sphere of interstate and international commerce. The arguments advanced on behalf of the states left no doubt that the measures under consideration were designed to serve as instruments of a restrictionist immigration policy. Counsel for Boston argued that the 1837 law was not made for the purpose of regulating foreign commerce; essentially a "poor law," it did not affect "imports" since men are not articles of trade. The exaction of revenue in the form of head taxes on passengers was justified under the police power, which implies the right to provide for the expense of its execution. States must have the right to control "mercenary shippers" who are the instruments of a conspiracy by England, Ireland, and Germany "to poison our morals and increase our burdens." As argued by Justice Barbour in *Miln,* much like "pestilence," the danger must be confronted on shipboard rather than after landing.

The substantive aspects of the matter were emphasized by the other side as well, indicating that all those involved understood the cases as a confrontation between proponents and opponents of immigration. In the New York case, Justice John McLean, one of the majority, began by asserting, "To encourage foreign emigration was a cherished policy of this country at the time the Constitution was adopted," and further pointed out, "As a branch of commerce the transportation of passengers has always given a profitable employment to our ships, and within a few years past has required an amount of tonnage nearly equal to that of imported merchandise."[90] In the Massachusetts case, Justice Robert Grier characterized the American position even more pointedly as immigrationist with regard to economics but restrictionist with regard to culture: "It is the cherished policy of the general government to encourage and invite Christian foreigners of our own race to seek asylum within our borders, and to convert these waste lands into productive farms, and thus add to the wealth, population, and power of the nation."[91] In relation to this, the imposition of a head tax by seaboard states that did not want immigrants was tantamount to the power of preventing persons from reaching states of the interior that did.

With respect to the key contemporaneous issue of constitutional law, the outcome was ambiguous. The *Passenger Cases* "did not repudiate" the police powers doctrine affirmed by *Miln* because "a truly exclusive federal power over interstate and international migration would have been highly threatening under antebellum conditions."[92] However, the Court did qualify it by prohibiting the states from excluding undesirables, be they foreign paupers or free Negroes, outright or indirectly by taxing entries. With regard to immigration policy proper, while declaring head taxes in this form unconstitutional, it did sustain the exercise of police power to alleviate burdens ensuing from the entry of destitute or "defective" immigrants by measures such as had been used repeatedly to deter immigration, but only so long as the financial transactions involved were conducted after the passengers were landed.

The clarification prompted the seaboard states to quickly enact a modified system of bonds and commutation fees designed to be as effective as head taxes or hospital fees for generating revenue; however, as in the past, they also continued to compete for passenger business, and hence many of them retreated even before the midcentury crisis was over.[93] While imposing some limits to state action, the *Passenger Cases* did not broaden federal authority in the sphere of immigration. Consequently, as one senator wryly pointed out to another who complained about the landing of convicts, "[I]t was easier to make a speech than to introduce a bill to meet the difficulty that would be comfortable to the Constitution. . . . The states had authority and had acted. . . . Where was the jurisdiction in Congress? He was opposed to immigration, but did not know how to frame a bill not in conflict with state authority, state rights, and state jurisdiction."[94]

Land Policy

The conflict over immigration spilled over into the determination of public land policy as well, focusing on the "homestead." The linkage between the two spheres had long been evident to restrictionists—who perennially resisted measures allowing resident aliens to hold and transmit real property, or granting them privileges such as the right of preemption on the same terms as citizens, enacted by the Democrats in 1841—and simultaneously sought to render naturalization itself more difficult.[95] The rationality of their strategy was confirmed by the Belgian analyst cited in Chapter 4, who observed, "If they wish to check the immigrant invasion, the Americans should modify the laws regulating the sale of their public lands" as well as naturalization.[96]

The land confrontation was generally shaped by a combination of class and sectional interests, pitting eastern capitalists, fearful of losing their labor supply, against the eastern "common man" and the West; the South, initially divided on the question, coalesced in opposition to homesteading as it became increasingly convinced that the westward movement of farmers opposed to slavery would upset the political equilibrium. The stimulating effect of homesteads on immigration surfaced in the course of the 1852 debates as a leading argument against it, along with unconstitutionality, loss of revenue, and emigration from the East Coast. Initially, even steadfast advocates of homesteading urged caution with respect to aliens. Horace Greeley and his National Reform Association, acknowledging that "it is not just to tax a Maine farmer ten or twenty dollars in order to extinguish Indian titles, pay for surveys, etc., so as to give an Irish or German immigrant a farm for nothing," proposed restricting noncitizens to less desirable land; and his political ally, William Henry Seward, thought land should be granted only to foreign political exiles rather than ordinary immigrants.[97] A limited homestead bill was passed by the House but defeated in the Senate; with respect to immigration, the House measure was more restrictive in that naturalization rather than a mere declaration of intention was required. By 1854, the issue of aliens had become fully embroiled with that of "free soil" and emerged as one of the main subjects of controversy; many Southerners were now arguing that homesteads should be reserved for native-born Americans only, whereas Westerners and their allies on the whole advocated no citizenship qualifications whatsoever.[98]

Although it has been suggested that the nativist argument with respect to homesteading was merely a cover for class interest because " '[k]eep the public domain for Americans' was a far better slogan than 'Keep enough labor in the East to hold wages down,' " when businessmen opposed homesteading because they feared a loss of labor, their spokesmen did not hesitate to say so explicitly.[99] Those who invoked the "American" argument were concerned with politics rather than economics. For example, Representative Bowie of Maryland justified his opposition to the 1852 bill as follows: "[T]hough this bill may not contain provisions which will now admit all future emigrants from Europe, yet, let it become a law, and it becomes a wedge by which our public domain will be forced open to them. . . . Mr. Chairman, can anything be more dangerous than the infusion of an undue proportion of a dissimilar people among our own? . . . Is there no danger of European ascendancy in American councils?"[100] To a southern ear at this time, "European ascendancy" evoked the specter of Catholicism and the putative antagonism of new immigrants, particularly Germans, to slavery, which promoted the section's growing opposition to both homesteading and immigration in the latter part of the decade.[101]

The loss-of-labor argument receded from the debate at about the same time as the nativist argument moved to the fore because of the emergence of a new vision prompted by Whig modernizers who embraced homesteading early on, in the mirror opposite of the southern outlook, as a weapon in the war they were beginning to wage against slavery. Moreover, from the perspective of men attuned to the expanding geographical and organizational scope of American capitalism, homesteading no longer meant a loss of labor in the East. As Seward was to state it a few years later, its lure would result, on balance, in an increase of the national labor supply, because a significant proportion of the newcomers who aspired to launch farms would be forced to remain in the cities and work in order to earn the wherewithal to do so.

Naturalization

The most common proposal regarding naturalization, advanced by Morse as early as 1834 and taken up by the Native American Association in 1837 as well as by the American Republican Party in 1843, was to lengthen the residency requirement from five to twenty-one years, the hallowed gestation period for legal majority and, in the case of native white males, to exercise voting rights. This would have brought about a segmentation of the population into separate bodies with vastly differential rights, akin to the arrangements prevailing in colonial "plural societies," anticipating the conditions imposed on workers from China on the West Coast as well as on African Americans in the South after the Civil War, and *braceros* in the twentieth century. Although some ambiguity persisted regarding the authority of the states to *lower* naturalization requirements below the national level, it was quite clear that they could not be *more* demanding, and hence any state law imposing a twenty-one-year requirement would be found unconstitutional.[102] The change therefore required congressional action. Proposals to that effect were introduced in every Congress except the 30th (1847–1849) and the 32nd (1851–1853); but because of Democratic control, most of them failed to gain referral to committee or, if considered at the committee stage, were reported out with negative recommendations.[103]

For example, in June 1844, Peter Sken Smith, a leading American Republican from Philadelphia, sent Whig leader Henry Clay reports of a mass rally urging a change in the laws and denouncing the House Judiciary Committee for bottling up petitions on the matter. Initially, the Whigs were reluctant to go along; but after experiencing an electoral disaster in November 1844, which they attributed to newly and often illegally naturalized immigrants, they agreed.[104] However, in January 1845, the House Judiciary Committee reported out a bill to establish a uniform rule that explicitly rejected any radical change in the residence requirement, as this "would in effect operate as a denial of the privilege altogether." Citing Jefferson, they also took the opportunity to reassert the principle expressed by the Declaration of Independence's grievances: the object of naturalization laws is not only to increase population, but also "to assert the great principle of expatriation, and the right of every man to leave the country of his birth for the one of his choice."[105] In response to a resolution from the Massachusetts legislature urging an immediate review of the naturalization laws, the Committee again asserted that "no alteration of the naturalization laws is necessary for the preservation of the rights, interests, and morals of the people, or from the guarding of the ballot-box against improper influence."[106] Later in 1846, the committee rejected another proposal to extend the period because "[t]he longer the probation, the greater was the inducement to fraud," and because the very increase in immigration made it impolitic to maintain a large part of the population in a state of alienage. Although some Democrats occasionally attempted to reduce the period from five years to the original two, this too got nowhere.

Unable to lengthen the waiting period, Whigs and nativists perennially sought to restrict the political incorporation of immigrant newcomers by tinkering with their voting rights, which fell under the jurisdiction of the states. One possibility, adumbrated in Morse's proposal, was to impose a delay *following* naturalization, rising again as high as twenty-one years; others involved the regulation of voting itself, mostly by way of advance registration based on proper documentation of eligibility. Proposals of both kinds proliferated throughout the period, with mixed results.

The Know-Nothing Showdown

As the tidal wave continued into the early 1850s, the "visible hand" not only intervened time and again to keep the floodgates open, but also reached out beyond them to beckon for more. The consequences exceeded the catastrophic vision conjured up by the native Americans in 1845. Relative to total population, 1854 remains the record year for U.S. immigration, with recorded arrivals amounting to an increment of 1.6 percent, the equivalent of 4.4 million people in 2000, roughly four times the millennium year's actual level, including estimated undocumented immigrants. Even leaving aside the Chinese, who were beginning to land in larger numbers on the West Coast, most of the immigrants in 1854 were alien in religion, language, or both, with fewer than one out of seven of "founding stock."

The massive influx had a significant impact on the American labor market. The 1850s was an inflationary decade because of the California gold strikes, the vast influx of foreign capital, and subsequently the Crimean War, which increased international demand for grain; but whereas the cost of food went up as much as 40 percent over four years, real wages declined.[107] The squeeze affected more people because a larger proportion of the population, U.S.-born as well as immigrants, were now wage workers; and since the boom years were punctuated by slumps, more of them experienced unemployment as well.

Concurrently, the societal "cords" that held the Union together "snapped under tension as the sections drifted apart," and the party system that had provided stability for a generation collapsed.[108] This was triggered by the sudden expansion of the slave segment of the American polity, beginning with the annexation of Texas in 1845; followed by the compromise of 1850, which opened to slavery the territories acquired from Mexico; and the Kansas-Nebraska Act rammed by the Democrats through Congress in 1854, which repealed the Missouri Compromise of 1820. Hitherto loose transsectional coalitions bound by personal loyalties to leaders, but with somewhat differing ideological orientations—the Democrats were mildly populist, the Whigs more property-minded—both parties, in turn, were overwhelmed by the national tension. Whereas the northern Democrats were abruptly reduced to minority status within a largely southern party that ultimately weathered the storm, on the Whig side, not only did the southern wing massively defect in 1852 and subsequently disappear altogether, but also the party in the North broke down almost simultaneously, a development that cannot be accounted for by sectional tensions. According to David Potter, the inability of the Whigs to consolidate themselves as the dominant party in the North on the basis of their antislavery position, as William Henry Seward attempted to do in New York and Abraham Lincoln in Illinois, was attributable to "the rising tension in American society between immigrant groups . . . and native elements."[109]

By the time they entered the electoral arena, the bulk of the Irish and German newcomers had developed strong ties to the Democratic Party. Although some Whigs competed with the Democrats for their support, notably Seward as governor of New York in the 1840s, the party's conservative political tradition and the Puritanism of many of its supporters imposed constraints against the advocacy of substantive policies attractive to immigrants. On the other hand, both opponents of slavery and nativists "had reason to doubt that they could gain their objectives inside the party as well as they could outside of it," the first because business ties between textile manufacturers and suppliers of their raw materials imposed "an embarrassing affiliation with Cotton Whigs," the second because of the prominence of men like Seward, who either condemned nativism or avoided it on grounds of electoral strategy.[110]

The combination of what Michael Holt has termed "the politics of impatience" with a particular institutional configuration accounts for the spectacular rise of the "Know-Nothing" movement at this time. Ever since the early 1830s, the conflict over immigration had been kept within bounds by the operation of the party system; conversely, its breakdown provided an opportunity for new political entrepreneurs to exploit a broad "uneasiness about the powerlessness of the people to control the meteoric social and economic changes transforming their environment and threatening their most cherished values."[111] The nativists were now able to exploit the backlash against the immigration tide and evidence of rising Catholic power, notably the appointment by President Franklin Pierce of James Campbell as postmaster general and chief dispenser of Democratic spoils.[112] The leaders of the native fraternities made their move in the summer of 1852 and united in mid-1854 under the aegis of the Order of the Star-Spangled Banner (OSSB), a secret society founded in New York in 1849, which contributed to the success of a reform organization in the aldermanic election of 1853 and in May 1854 dramatically captured the mayoralty of Philadelphia with a majority of over 8,000.[113] In the wake of that victory, delegates from thirteen states convened in New York to set up a national organization; designating themselves as the American Party, they were dubbed "Know-Nothing" by Horace Greeley and quickly took up the nickname as a badge of honor. Concurrently, passage of the Kansas-Nebraska Act caused many antislavery Democrats to bolt their party, and this in turn provided antislavery Whigs with potential allies should they abandon theirs.[114] Such interparty rallying occurred in disparate fashion under a variety of labels, among them "Republicans"; and the new organizations coalesced at the national level under that name in July 1854, at about the same time as the Know-Nothings. Not only did the launching of the two coincide in time, but there also was considerable overlap between them, both at the level of the electorate and among local, state, and national representatives elected in 1854.[115]

As of mid-1854, when ships were dumping unprecedented numbers in the ports of entry, it appeared "that the Catholic or immigrant question might replace the slavery question as the focal issue in American political life," as indicated among other things by the fact that Democratic U.S. Senator Stephen A. Douglas "began assailing the Know-Nothings, rather than the anti-slavery groups, as the principal danger to the Democratic party."[116] The movement's rapid ascent was further stimulated by the recession induced by a summer drought, which triggered a panic on the New York Stock Exchange in the fall. Even as newcomers crowded into the labor market, railroad construction ceased, and the discharged workers poured into the cities.[117] Between June and the end of October, Know-Nothing became the popular rage; membership soared from some 50,000 to over 1 million; by February 1855 it had 150,000 members and 1,000 local chapters in New York State alone; and in September 1855 is reconstituted itself as the American Party.

In the fall 1854 elections, Know-Nothings scored astonishing successes in municipal, state, and congressional elections, prompting Edward Everett to paint their success as "the most astonishing result ever witnessed in our politics."[118] They obtained 63 percent of the vote in Massachusetts, indicating nearly unanimous support outside the Irish minority; over 40 percent in Pennsylvania; and even 25 percent in New York. A sizeable minority of the men elected to the House of Representatives were Know-Nothings, while others were antislavery men elected with Know-Nothing support: "Confusing though it may be, it was possible to say that the anti-Nebraska men held a majority in the House and also that the Know-Nothings held a majority in the House. At that juncture, it seemed clear that anti-slavery would be strongly linked with nativism, and the only question, apparently, was which of these forces would be predominant in the coalition." Given further Know-Nothing triumphs in other New England states as well as in New York, Pennsylvania, California, and the South in 1855, a year marked by bloody anti-Catholic riots as well, "it seemed entirely plausible for the New York Herald to predict that the Know-Nothings would win the presidency in 1856."[119]

Amidst these dramatic changes in the political configuration, Congress undertook once again to revise passenger regulations. The immediate trigger was communication by Britain of the report of a Select Committee that, working in close cooperation with the corps of executive officers established under earlier passenger acts, recommended a consolidation of regulations and an increase in the minimum space requirement. Since by this time three-fourths of the emigrant traffic from the United Kingdom was being carried in American bottoms, the report pointed out that the effectiveness of regulations depended on close cooperation between the two countries.[120]

In response, Senator Hamilton Fish of New York secured the appointment of a Select Committee, headed by himself, on Sickness and Mortality on Board of Emigrant Ships. A New York City Whig and former governor, Fish had long been concerned with immigration, and was among those urging congressional action in 1844–1845 against the dumping of paupers and convicts.[121] The Committee reported on August 2, 1854. Pointing out the difficulties of reconciling the divergent interests of passengers and ship owners, as well as of citizens of the United States and of other countries, and concluding that it was "worse than useless" to have unenforceable laws as was presently the case, they advocated a law that left the details of arrangements to be determined by the shippers themselves, but would induce them to safeguard passengers by making unsanitary ships unprofitable. Borrowing a leaf from a British regulation of 1801, whereby carriers chartered by the government to remove emigrants and convicts to the South Seas were reimbursed only for passengers disembarked alive at the end of the journey, the Fish Committee proposed fining carriers for deaths incurred in the course of passage.[122] Given mortality rates amounting to as much as 20 percent on a bad voyage, this would provide an incentive to reject as passengers all persons deemed ill or weak, surely a substantial proportion of those leaving Europe at the time.

New York merchants quickly mobilized against the bill and sent a protest delegation to Washington. Meanwhile, the U.S. Treasury began to seize ships under a surviving clause of the 1847 act when excess passengers numbered over twenty.[123] Fish then agreed to provide for the remission of penalties incurred by shippers under the existing law in exchange for their consent to his proposal. However, further consideration was delayed owing to Fish's ill health. By the time the second session of the 33rd Congress opened in January 1855, the financial panic and nativist victories had intervened, and constituency pressures for action to stem the tide were mounting. Early in the month, New York City's nativist mayor petitioned President Pierce for urgent national measures to prevent "dumping." Provisions prohibiting the landing of convicts, paupers, and "defectives" were added to the pending passenger bill, and Rep. Benjamin Fuller of Maine, who had opposed homesteading three years earlier because it would stimulate immigration, introduced a proposal similar to Fish's in a consolidated revenue bill. Parallel development took place in the Senate.[124] However, strong opposition arose on the grounds that Congress could not intervene in the sphere of police powers reserved to the states, and it was thus evident that national action to restrict immigration could occur only by way of passenger legislation.

This is where the key role of the business community in countering nativist restrictionism emerges most visibly. On February 15, 1855, the Senate's Committee on Commerce reported out a passenger bill initiated by New York's other Whig senator, William Henry Seward, which differed significantly from the one proposed by the still absent Fish.[125] Explaining that it had been drafted under the guidance of Secretary of the Treasury Thomas Corwin "to obviate the difficulties arising from misconstruction of existing law under which many vessels were seized," Seward asked for immediate consideration. In the course of debate over the propriety of rushed proceedings, he further defended his measure on the grounds that it was exactly as framed by the Treasury Department following the intervention of the New York merchants. The latter's resolution against the Fish proposal was brought up in the House, whose Committee on Commerce also recommended expeditious passage of Seward's bill. However, a measure tailor-made for the shipping industry evidently had no chance of passage in a Congress attuned to nativist concerns. The proposal was sent back to committee, which returned a compromise incorporating aspects of both the Fish and Seward proposals. This was speedily enacted without further debate or division and signed into law on March 3, 1855.

The new Passenger Act was the most significant victory for restriction to date at the national level. Its most striking aspect, least noted by historians of immigration, was comprehensiveness as a regulatory instrument. Repealing all previous passenger legislation, it covered all traffic under both sail and steam, in every conceivable type of vessel, plying the Pacific as well as the Atlantic, and even outbound ships operating on behalf of the African Colonization Society. Requirements pertaining to passenger comfort were raised considerably by reinstating the 1847 system combining both volume and superficial feet, as well as specifying minimum distances between decks.[126] Over the shippers' vehement objections, the law also imposed a "death tax" of $10 for every person above age eight who succumbed to disease in the course of passage, the proceeds of which were allocated to state boards for the care of immigrants. Nativist concerns surfaced explicitly in the form of a clause prohibiting the distribution of these funds "to any board, or commission, or Association, formed for the protection or advancement of any particular class of emigrants, or emigrants of any particular nation or creed," such as the Irish and German societies that hitherto shared in the proceeds of commutation fees in many states.[127]

The restrictionists apparently won, but their victory was hollow, as the sanction side suggests the measure was a mere palliative. The standard fine remained $50 for each excess passenger, as established in 1847 and 1848; but the maximum discretionary prison term was reduced from one year to six months, and nonpayment of the "death tax" was sanctioned by a fine only. Most significantly, the controversial 1847 clause providing for seizure when excess passengers numbered over twenty was repealed along with the act in which it was contained; and although the new law empowered the government to pursue actions for violation of previous regulations and specified that shippers remained liable for penalties they had incurred under them, its final provision stated, "The Secretary of the Treasury may, in his discretion . . . discontinue any such prosecutions, or remit or modify such penalties." In fact, the record indicates that from the time of passage "there was 'doubt as to the applicability of the penalties to the case of a vessel arriving from abroad,' and subsequently it was held that the law never applied to steamships"; moreover, the government never collected any of the penalties it imposed.[128]

Yet the game was hardly over and its outcome still uncertain since the full impact of the nativist surge would be felt only in the next Congress. Meanwhile, a great deal could be achieved in the country at large, given that about one-fourth of the states now had "American" governors. Local and state governments, controlled by Know-Nothings or seeking to forestall the new party's progress by preemptive moves, initiated ever more vigorous efforts to reduce the entry of undesirables and also launched a war against the enemy within by preventing the formation of autonomous immigrant social organizations and promoting assimilationist incorporation.[129] In the heat of victory, the New England states enacted a spate of measures requiring reading of the Protestant bible in public schools, prohibiting the use of public funds in sectarian schools (meaning Catholic establishments), requiring church property to be held by lay trustees rather than bishops, imposing the inspection of convents, and barring the teaching of foreign languages in public schools. In the absence of a federal measure, Massachusetts armed itself with a law authorizing any justice of the peace "to cause any pauper to be removed to his place of last abode beyond the seas."[130] At least thirty-five Irish immigrants are known to have been deported in 1855, including an unwed mother torn from her U.S.-born daughter and a mentally ill man, "long resident in this country . . . who up to the period when Heaven mysteriously deprived him of reason . . . contributed his measure of taxation for the support of the State."[131] New York also considered deportation, but its commissioners of immigration opined that "this direct power is not granted by the existing laws of the State, and is perhaps a regulation of the intercourse with foreign nations, not within the competence of the State legislature."[132] Petitions were therefore once again addressed to Washington for a national law to that effect, where they were joined by similar pleas from Rhode Island, New Hampshire, and others.[133] Governor Henry J. Gardner of Massachusetts and William T. Minor of Connecticut ordered the disbanding of militias organized by the foreign-born, despite an Irish American protest pointing out that these had come into being "fully as much owing to the separate organization of native Americans as to any disposition on the part of either Irish or Germans to isolate themselves."[134] In the same vein, the U.S. Government itself brought action against a dozen Irish-born naturalized citizens in Cincinnati for their membership in the Robert Emmett Club, on the grounds that by participating in a secret society pledged "to uproot and overthrow English government in Ireland," they violated an 1818 law prohibiting the "preparation" on U.S. soil of "any military expedition or enterprise" against a state "with whom the United States are at peace." Although the case was dismissed in 1856 because of insufficient evidence, the presiding judge sternly warned the defendants, "There can be no such thing as a divided national allegiance."[135]

The main Know-Nothing policy objective, as stated in their national platform, was still the twenty-one-year residence requirement for naturalization. Although this remained elusive because the representatives elected in November 1854 would be seated only in December 1855, and the Senate remained under Democratic control, steps were taken at the state level to render the process of naturalization more arduous as well as to delay voting by new citizens. Massachusetts, Connecticut, Rhode Island, and Maine all enacted laws prohibiting state judges from participating in any aspects of the naturalization process, thereby forcing applicants to turn to the less accessible and more expensive federal courts; Maine and Massachusetts also required immigrant voters to present their naturalization papers to town officials three months before election day. Following up on proposals advanced earlier by the Whigs, they also sought to "clean up the ballot box" by imposing literacy tests and registration laws.

Many of these initiatives required constitutional amendments, which had to be approved by special majorities in two successive legislatures. Measures to that effect were initially passed by the Whig-controlled Connecticut legislature in 1854, in Massachusetts the following year, and finalized in the latter state in 1857 thanks to Republican support. Connecticut and Rhode Island gave initial approval to constitutional amendments that would have mandated a twenty-one-year waiting period for voting after naturalization. In 1855, the Massachusetts Know-Nothings also got through the first step of a constitutional amendment permanently barring all immigrants from either voting or holding office; but they failed to gain approval the following year, despite softening the proposal to a twenty-one-year waiting period. They then got it through by reducing the waiting period further to fourteen years; but by 1857 many Republicans objected to the fourteen-year delay as bigoted and inexpedient, as it would drive Germans out of the party. A two-year delay was finally enacted in 1859 and ratified by the voters that same year. In New York, a coalition of Americans and Republicans enacted a registry law in 1859, but with loopholes that limited its effectiveness. In Ohio a deal was struck between Americans and Republicans on a constitutional amendment imposing a one-year waiting period on voting for naturalized citizens; however, Governor Salmon Chase worked to kill the amendment for fear it would antagonize German support; instead, he backed a requirement of lay boards for church property, which would please German Protestants.

Turning of the Tide

In the nine-month interim between the end of the 33rd Congress and the beginning of the 34th in December 1855, the configuration of political and economic factors that shaped immigration policy continued to evolve rapidly, and the immigration situation itself changed dramatically, as the tidal wave abruptly receded. The 1855 season brought only 197,337 Europeans, less than half the previous year's level, with the two largest groups accounting for most of the decline: the Irish, who had peaked at 221,253 in 1851, were already down to 101,606 in 1854, and now fell to 49,627, while the Germans dropped even more precipitously from 215,009 to 71,918 in a single year. Unbeknownst to contemporaries, the new lower level would persist for the remainder of the decade; about 1,750,000 arrived in the first half, but only 850,000 in the second.

How did this sudden change come about? Economic conditions in the months preceding the recovery undoubtedly dissuaded some from embarking for the United States. The nativist surge, news of which was quickly relayed to Europe by recent arrivals, and the recently enacted state and federal legislation undoubtedly exercised a deterrent effect, even prompting some immigrants to return.[136] Moreover, the Crimean War by now affected the countries that supplied the bulk of emigrants and tended to reduce exit. The absence of Russian wheat from the market revived agricultural prosperity throughout western Europe, and ships not engaged in importing necessities from America were quickly diverted to the Mediterranean for export and troop transport. The British government engaged in a massive recruiting campaign for its expeditionary force that, particularly in Ireland, provided an alternative to emigration, and similar considerations applied to France and the German states as well. Emigrants from the United Kingdom were now also drawn to Australia, where gold was discovered in 1851, while continentals were being wooed by a number of Latin American countries.[137]

This turn of events, plus the fact that the American economy again surged forward, stimulated by the unusually high European demand induced by the Crimean War, which also induced a huge boom in shipbuilding, reinforced the shipping industry's immigrationist stance.[138] Inbound U.S. vessels normally filled their decks with immigrants; but as their number rose in 1855 and 1856 while immigrants declined, they must have been running half-empty. Conditions of passage undoubtedly improved, but profitability tumbled. With the resumption of economic activity, business probably deplored the immigration drop as well, particularly in the face of a renewed surge of labor organization.

Meanwhile, the political situation continued to disintegrate. Although the Democrats lost control of the House, there was no clear alternative; following the opening of the 34th Congress in December 1855, it took the House two months and 133 ballots to elect a speaker, and even then by a plurality only. The victor, Nathaniel Banks of Massachusetts, who was completing his transition from the Democratic to the Republican Party by way of Know-Nothing, "personified the link between nativism and anti-slavery, but also the greater appeal of anti-slavery."[139] In the emerging alliance between the two movements in the North, the Republicans were gaining the upper hand. In February 1856, the sectional tensions that surfaced within Know-Nothing the previous year tore the party asunder into "North Americans" and "South Americans." The latter immediately nominated Millard Fillmore, with Andrew Jackson Donelson of Tennessee as vice president, while the North Americans scheduled a convention of their own for June, immediately prior to the Republican one. In the intervening months, they were induced by their new allies to nominate "a stalking horse, who would withdraw in favor of the Republican nominee at the strategic moment." On June 16, they chose Banks; two days later, the Republicans nominated John Fremont, who was anything but a Know-Nothing and even rumored to be a secret Catholic; and on June 19, Banks withdrew on behalf of the latter.

Under the changed circumstances, it is not surprising that the 34th Congress contributed nothing further to the redirection of American immigration policy. Petitions once again flowed in from the states, but they got nowhere because, in the assessment of a contemporaneous observer, "Party lines are more tightly drawn, and there is little use of asking political opponents for votes in Congress."[140] Nativism's last hurrah was the long-awaited bill prohibiting the entry of foreign paupers and convicts. Authored by Rep. Fuller of Maine, the same who had steered the passenger law through the House the previous year, it was reported out by the Committee on Foreign Affairs on August 16, 1856.[141] The 152-page document reprinted evidence of dumping from as early as 1832 and restated all the familiar themes, but also revealed how the issue of states' rights hampered action in the sphere of immigration policy. Among other things, it countered a communication from the government of Württemberg denying the right of the United States to deport paupers with the assertion that this was founded on the right of self-defense under the laws of nations; and given "the inherent right of every community to protect itself against all public evils," in this instance "the power exists somewhere either in the states, or in the general government, or in both of them." But where, exactly, remained problematic. Granting differences of opinion as to the power of Congress, the report emphasized that each level of government must act in its own sphere; Congress "can and ought to exert its authority to prevent the further introduction of those who exercise such influence upon society . . . but beyond this it can accomplish but little." Hence it went on to recommend more vigorous action by the states, which "with a few exceptions . . . have been as remiss as congress in the discharge of their duties on the subject." In their view, deportation of undesirables was a proper exercise of state police powers, as stated in *Miln* and in more recent cases involving runaway slaves.

Beyond this, reflecting ongoing developments at the state and local level, the committee adumbrated a comprehensive program of political management for a country that had been transformed into a segmented society paralleling Benjamin Disraeli's recently formulated "two nations," the one made up of mostly native Anglo-American "mechanics" and independent farmers, the other of immigrant urban wage workers, Irish or continental. The states must equip themselves to maintain public order and undertake a vigorous policy of Americanization. With respect to the first, the committee recommended a reform of the criminal system in order to achieve "the more prompt conviction and more certain punishment of all offenders," the establishment of institutions for the incarceration of juvenile delinquents and vagrants, and the creation of proper workhouses for the poor on the English model. Concomitantly, the states must be compensated by the national government for the additional expenses that such programs entailed.

Beneath the extreme language, one can identify a sweeping cultural strategy amounting to the elaboration of a comprehensive apparatus of resocialization, which adumbrated the distinctive hallmark of American education in decades to come.[142] The Committee began by recommending the rigid enforcement of liquor licensing laws and their restriction to American citizens, following Pennsylvania's lead. It further urged concerted action to destroy foreign organizations, as was being done in Massachusetts and Connecticut, so as to "discountenance the *esprit du corps* [sic] now so studiously cultivated among foreigners in our large cities, which is calculated, if not designed, to keep them foreigners in feeling, sentiments, and habits." Finally, "and most important of all," the Committee advocated "the adoption and enforcement of a truly American policy on all subjects—one which will tend to cultivate and develop an undying attachment to our country, its history, and its institutions, and to inspire a profound veneration and respect for the examples of our patriotic revolutionary ancestors." Subsequently reported as a bill, the recommendation for prohibiting the landing of foreign criminals, paupers, and "defectives" did not proceed beyond the Committee of the Whole on the State of the Union; revived in the next session, it again failed.[143]

Thus, in 1856–1857 as in 1854–1855, the gates were kept open by a de facto coalition of strange bedfellows: business-minded immigrationist Northerners, be they still Whigs or already Republicans; Republicans and surviving Democrats seeking to court immigrant constituents; and Southerners, be they Democrats or "South Americans," whose paramount objective was to forestall federal encroachment in the sphere of states' rights. The drop in immigration and the economic recovery did little to allay the nativist fury, with widely scattered mob attacks on immigrant neighborhoods culminating in the lynching of twenty Germans in Louisville, Kentucky, on August 5, 1855.[144] Yet by mid-1856 the Know-Nothing Party, swept up by the Republican tide, collapsed as suddenly as it had arisen. Historians who otherwise disagree with each other concur that the new party was able to absorb the Know-Nothings "without any formal concessions that would have forfeited the immigrant support also vital to political success. The Republicans were able to eat the cake of nativist support and to have too the cake of religious and ethnic tolerance."[145]

Seward's position rested on interest as well as principle, and this was also true of the prosperous Whig lawyer from Springfield, Illinois. Lincoln, whose clients included a railroad that was in the immigration business since 1850, campaigned for the Senate in a state with a very large foreign-born population, and his commitment to the development of the new territories on the basis of free labor implied a reliance on immigration. As champions of capitalist transformation, the Whigs who founded the Republican Party were, if anything, even more firmly immigrationist than the party leadership as a whole.[146] Whereas Seward's prominent role in the confrontation probably cost him the Republican nomination in 1856, the more prudent Lincoln "kept very silent in public about his disapproval of Know-Nothingism" and subsequently repudiated it only "by indirection," suggesting that foreign-born whites be given priority over native-born blacks with respect to territorial land grants.[147] But in 1859, asked by a group of German Americans for his opinion on the Massachusetts constitutional amendment that delayed voting for two years after naturalization, he expressed firm opposition on the grounds that, having "some little notoriety for commiserating the oppressed condition of the negro . . . I should be strangely inconsistent if I could favor any project for curtailing the existing rights of *white men,* even though born in different lands, and speaking different languages from myself."[148]

Nevertheless, nativism did not disappear as a political current but "went into the Republican party, just as it had come out of the Whig party." This was a crucial process for the course of American history, because by way of this sub rosa union, "The Republican party received a permanent endowment of nativist support which probably elected Lincoln in 1860 and strengthened the party in every election for more than a century to come."[149] In the same vein, the defeat of the Know Nothing immigration policy at the national level should not be allowed to overshadow the significance of its accomplishments at the state level, which can be seen in retrospect as preliminary steps toward a major change in the established immigration and citizenship régime.

Reining in the sense of outrage prompted by the nativists' egregious prejudices, one comes away from this period with a disquieting sense of their insight into the awesomeness of the looming transformation of American society. To the extent that the boundary of the nation's original identity was delineated by the Protestant tradition as incarnated in the English language, and involved a construction of the Catholic world as the significant negative other, the change involved nothing short of a transgression of the established boundary by the intruding negative. From the founding onward, repeated warnings had been issued against the formation of separate clusters, but an Irish and German Catholic world established itself within a single generation as a major component of American society, autonomous and largely self-contained, with a strong identity of its own and elaborate institutions to nurture it. Despite the efforts of those who would maintain the old America, the door was kept open in the face of the powerful social forces that uprooted the multitudes of Europe and, as a result Tocqueville's footnote moved into the text, transformed the bounded community of "Anglo-Americans" into a more diverse and segmented "nation of immigrants."

6

Seward's Other Follies

In his December 1863 message to Congress, President Abraham Lincoln called for the establishment of "a system for the encouragement of immigration." He pointed out that although incoming numbers had recently increased, "there is still a great deficiency of laborers, in every field of industry, especially in agriculture and in our mines." This could easily be overcome as "tens of thousands of persons, destitute of remunerative occupations, are thronging our foreign consulates and offering to emigrate to the United States if essential but very cheap assistance can be afforded them."[1] In the wake of this pronouncement, Secretary of State William H. Seward intervened decisively to obtain congressional approval of a scheme that established, in effect, a partnership between the American Emigrant Company and the national government to import labor from Europe. The company planned to collect from employers funds to advance the fares of workers, who would in turn contract to reimburse their debt after entering the U.S. market; a sine qua non was legislation to make the contracts enforceable in American courts.[2] Endorsed by Chief Justice of the U.S. Supreme Court Roger Taney, Secretary of the Navy Gideon Welles, as well as a long list of governors and senators, the American Emigration Company was widely publicized by American consuls throughout Europe, suggesting to prospective immigrants that it was an official agency of the U.S. government.

Concurrently, plans were moving ahead to complete the transcontinental route authorized by the Pacific Railroad Act of July 1862. Shortly after construction of the western segment got underway, its contractor sent to San Francisco for a gang of Chinese to break a strike by white workers, and the Central Pacific's labor force quickly turned predominantly Chinese. Paralleling developments on the East Coast, a de facto partnership was formed between Chinese merchant associations and the Pacific Steamship Company, subsidized by the U.S. government to carry the mail, to organize the massive importation of men from China. Here, the sine qua non was American intervention to persuade the reluctant imperial authorities to let their people go. An agreement to that effect was shortly secured as part of a treaty dictated by Secretary of State Seward in 1868. In an ironic indication of the changing times, Seward's principal agent was Anson Burlingame, the recent U.S. ambassador to the Sublime Porte, as China was termed at the time, who had made his political début as a Know-Nothing congressman.

Seward's initiatives inaugurated a more proactive era in immigration policy, in which the massive procurement of foreign labor from a diversity of sources came to be firmly acknowledged as an essential feature of the country's maturing industrial capitalism, and hence an "affair of state."[3] The reorientation was embedded in a spate of national enactments, culminating in major laws of the 1880s. Usually interpreted as marking a turning away from openness, these measures take on a different significance when considered within the broader context of American policy, which also included active state intervention to promote immigration. Most of them merely recapped the regulations hitherto imposed by the seaboard states, and this was even true of the ten-year prohibition on Chinese immigration enacted in 1882, which accomplished what California had repeatedly legislated, only to be told by the courts that its actions were unconstitutional.[4] This was in keeping with the more general transformation of the national government into a more forceful actor, with greater capacity to help the country's entrepreneurs realize the enormous potential of a continental economy. The new age also demanded the systematic elaboration of regulation into a stable and predictable administrative régime. While the initial impulse came from the leading sectors of the business community, Alfred Chandler's "visible hand," as nationalization proceeded the dynamics of immigration policy were rendered more complex by the emergence of organized labor as a highly concerned party with a distinctively negative voice on the subject.[5]

Part and parcel of an expansion of the capitalist economy to a global scale, the vast broadening of the sources of immigration brought in populations originating beyond the boundaries of what white Americans conceived of as their ancestral lands. Consequently, Seward's initiatives and its sequels also reawakened concerns over the impact of immigration on the character of the nation. The resulting confrontations produced disparate policies that, together, contributed to the development of an enduring, racially based distinction between immigrants eligible to become Americans and others to be kept at arm's length.

The Visible Hand Reaches Out: The Atlantic Side

The transformation of the American economy proceeded apace in the midst of political crisis. The panic of August 1857, touched off by overspeculation in railroad securities and real estate, marked the onset of an eighteen-month recession, but recovery then set in quickly. Reacting to the bad economic news and possibly the restrictionist enactments, Atlantic immigration dropped by half, from 251,306 in 1857 to 123,126 the following year. It remained down despite the recovery, leading industrialists to call for greater numbers and to reason that immigration's economic value outweighed the social costs it imposed. For example, the New York Association for Improving the Condition of the Poor, which represented the voice of industry, now reported that although the proportion of foreign-born among people on relief had climbed to an unprecedented 86 percent, this should not be a source of concern:

> We need labor. The modern Macedonian cry is, "Come and help us." Every honest, industrious man who comes to the country, whether poor or rich, is an addition to its strength and wealth. Unique, therefore, as is the fact under consideration, it is not less owing to our national policy, than to the peculiar position of our city as the gateway, or grand entrepot, of the marvellous exodus from Europe, which has brought with it, not only the wealth, and skill, and labor which we want, but also a vast amount of impotent and thriftless poverty we do not want. But as the one cannot be obtained without the other, should we not be content to accept the one with all its drawbacks, for the sake of the other? For while the burden of this poverty falls most heavily on New York, it is obviously attended in a commercial or pecuniary view, by counterbalancing advantages.[6]

Faced with a revival of trade unionism, employers also quickly discovered the value of labor importation as a weapon in industrial disputes. The first known concerted action to this effect was undertaken in 1858, when a group of iron molding firms in Albany, hit by three simultaneous strikes, issued a circular to employers of labor throughout the country urging the organization of a league for the purpose of importing substitute workmen from Europe.[7]

In 1859, the value of the products of industry exceeded for the first time those of agriculture, a development that was of course even more marked in the North. Although business conditions faltered with the coming of the war, government spending quickly stimulated the economy and fueled a growing demand for labor. This was rendered more acute by the deflection of manpower into the federal army, which grew from 186,751 in 1861 to 918,121 in 1863.[8] Meanwhile, the conflict drove European immigration further downward, "for every letter and every newspaper told of the disaster," to a mere 81,200 in 1861 and 83,710 the following year.[9] Labor unrest grew, as real wages did not keep up with inflation; in 1862, violence erupted among Irish workers in the coalfields of eastern Pennsylvania (the "Molly Maguires"), while the inequities of a draft law that allowed buying out and was administered by local Republicans provoked resentment among urban workers, culminating in the bloody four-day New York City riots of July 1863.

In an effort to stimulate immigration, in 1862 Congress reenacted the Homestead Law, which had been vetoed by President James Buchanan two years earlier, with a provision extending the privilege to resident aliens who had filed a declaration of intention.[10] Widely publicized by diplomatic and consular representatives in Europe, the measure probably accounted for a near doubling of European arrivals in the following season, to 163,733.[11] A variety of proposals emerged within Congress in response to Lincoln's appeal, ranging from limited measures such as the establishment of a national information program modeled after those launched by immigrant-hungry western states, to more proactive ones that provided incentives such as draft exemption and a lowering of residence requirements for naturalization; official sponsorship by way of cash assistance for passage and advance land grants, following Australian practice; and the chartering of a national immigration company.

The rhetoric that animated them indicates a renovated vision of the role of immigration in the country's development from which memories of Europe's nefarious dumping schemes and of the political dangers arising from a massive influx of heterogeneous newcomers were expunged. As the Senate's Committee on Agriculture confidently asserted, the United States was a nation of immigrants, which could take the side effects of immigration in stride:

> The advantages which have accrued heretofore from immigration can scarcely be computed. . . . Though a seeming paradox, it nevertheless approaches historical truth, that we are all immigrants. . . . The advantages of foreign immigration, as between the United States and the people of Euro-

pean countries, are mutual and reciprocal. . . . Such is the labor performed by the thrifty immigrant that he cannot enrich himself without contributing his full quota to the increase of the intrinsic greatness of the United States.[12]

Although the Committee deplored that, with regard to the facilitation of emigration, "very little is done by the government to promote this most desirable end," it rejected proposals for government-sponsored massive "importation" on the grounds that such schemes entailed considerable financial costs and extensive bureaucratic operations; that they would attract "the idle, very poor, or vicious" rather than "the thrifty"; and that foreign governments would undoubtedly act to "prevent the great depletion of labor that would result." The incorporation of a national immigration company was rejected as well because a private corporation "will necessarily look to their own pecuniary interests, and in the effort to advance these will neglect or sacrifice the interests of the immigrants." Instead, they proposed a very limited program establishing a commissioner of immigration within the Department of State, charged with gathering information regarding needs and conditions in various parts of the country, and with broadcasting this throughout Europe. Passed on March 2, the bill provided, in addition, for the creation in New York of a U.S. Emigrant Office, headed by a superintendent of immigration.[13] As late as March 21, Senator John Sherman insisted "that this was all the government could do."[14]

However, in mid-April the House's recently established Select Committee on Foreign Emigration recommended approval of an altogether different proposal that, as the accompanying comments made clear, had been devised by Secretary of State William Seward because the Senate bill fell short of what the administration had in mind.[15] Pointing out that the major obstacle to immigration stemmed from the fact that many who were already disposed to come lacked passage money, the secretary insisted that such persons were particularly desirable because "[b]eing entirely dependent on labor, they would necessarily become on their arrivals in the United States, and for a time, at least, remain laborers, and they would sagaciously seek the fields here which offer them the most abundant fruits." Should the labor supply be thus vastly increased, "persons who are exempt from want, and who could bring with them wealth, capital, art, and skill, would soon be seen to follow the humbler laborers into a field so inviting to enterprise." The growing demand for industrial labor in the older states had created a shortage in agricultural labor among the newer ones, and competition for labor was rendered more acute by the recent abolition of slavery. As for industry, "With abundance of capital and inexhaustible supplies of material, we want only cheaper labor and skill to establish our manufacturing interest on a firm and enduring foundation."

Since direct government assistance for transportation would be costly and likely to antagonize foreign powers, Seward proposed instead a two-part "commercial" policy: "The end may be partially effected by an increase in the number of vessels engaged in the conveyance of immigrants, and in part by adopting some system which would enable the immigrant to make the passage by the use of credit under an effective obligation to repay the cost out of the early avails of his labor when he shall have reached the United States." To this end, "[I]t might be expedient to provide some system by which the emigrant could pledge" to a future employer, in exchange for passage money, "a portion of the wages which he expects to earn after his arrival in the country"; as for those intending to settle on the land, he proposed issuance of a certificate for an allotment under the recent Homestead Law, which "might be signed away to whoever advanced the money for their voyage." Finally, the efforts of "classes of capitalists" as well as of state and territorial governments must be coordinated "under the direction of the government of the United States" by a commissioner within his own department. Secretary of the Interior John Usher endorsed Seward's proposal and pointed out that thanks to this scheme, the immigration pool could be broadened to include "the Latin races" of central and southern Europe, which were particularly suitable for agricultural labor; but he advised the House that it would be preferable to issue assignable land certificates only after actual entry.

The Select Committee recommended adoption of Seward's credit system, providing that "contracts may be made whereby emigrants shall pledge the wages of their labor to repay the expenses of their emigration," and creating authority "for the enforcement of the contracts" under U.S. and state law. While rejecting—for reasons that were not indicated—the Interior Department's separate bill pertaining to assignable land certificates, it did provide for the operation of transportation contracts as liens upon any land the immigrants might acquire. The Committee appeared to have in mind direct governmental assistance also, as the system was completed by a provision whereby "baggage and personal effects of every kind may be pledged to the Commissioner for the purpose of covering the expense attending the emigration of any person," and authorizing their sale in case the terms of the pledge were not met. The Committee further recommended that newcomers be draft exempt "during the existing insurrection."

The proposal sailed through the first two readings on the same day, and was approved by the House on April 22.[16] A concerted campaign was launched on its behalf over the next two months. The House ordered 10,000 extra copies of the report to be printed for widespread distribution, and the *New York Times* published a number of articles advocating an increase of immigration and the assumption by the national government of a promotional role to this effect. In this and other respects, the paper was very much Seward's voice. Nevertheless, the proposal evoked opposition in the Senate, which, on June 27, under the leadership of Senator Sherman, reinstated and passed its own more limited measure; however, a few days later, the House bill prevailed in conference.[17] Passed without division in either house on July 4, 1864, the Act to Encourage Immigration was approved by President Lincoln on the very same day. Although the system it established was "commercial," in that credit for transportation was provided by the private sector, the national government was deeply involved by providing the legal authority necessary to back this up, and by way of the creation of an administrative apparatus that gave the appearance of official sponsorship. The ambiguity was compounded by the sanction the law bestowed to the American Emigrant Company and the enlistment of consular officials as well as of the new Bureau of Immigration in its service.[18] Even the American press henceforth commonly referred to the activities of "Federal recruiting agents."[19]

A remarkable feature of the law was the inclusion, as its last clause, of a demurrer to the effect that "nothing contained herein shall be deemed to authorize any contract contravening the Constitution of the United States, or creating in any way the relation of slavery or servitude." The system did differ from ancestral forms of European indenture as well as from contemporaneous arrangements in the colonial world involving "coolies"—of which more later— in that the wage pledge was limited to one year, the contract was not a marketable instrument, and violation of its terms by the immigrant did not constitute a criminal act. However, it bore a striking resemblance to the "redemptioner" system the Passenger Act of 1819 had contributed to eliminate, and subsequent developments indicate that the defensive tone of the assertion was prompted by objections to the scheme as a violation of the moral norm that legitimated the ongoing war.

In the event, the American Emigrant Company did not succeed in raising the capital to which it aspired, nor in securing funds for assisted passages on a large scale.[20] Arguing that this was because mere financial liability for violation of contract "is nothing to this class of men," the Company therefore urged passage of additional legislation to fine workers who violated their contracts, and to grant the commissioner greater law enforcement authority, constituting in effect ominous steps toward bound labor.[21] In keeping with the trend toward comprehensive business organization, the company also sought to acquire control over all aspects of the importation process and secured an amendment to the Connecticut statute of incorporation enabling it "to own and operate steamships for the purpose of transporting emigrants, and to act as agents for the sale of lands and to own and sell livestock." This would make sanctions for contract violations even more imperative.[22]

Although a bill to that effect was passed by the House in mid-1866, it evoked vociferous opposition in the Senate, whose Committee on Commerce recommended instead repeal of the original measure. Explaining that the Act to Encourage Immigration had been thought innocuous until the proposed additional provisions revealed its full implications, the committee spokesman denounced it in no uncertain terms: "It smacks so nearly of that trade which was African, and was forbidden in the Constitution of the United States, that we objected to it at first on that ground. Then it was so closely allied to the coolie business that the committee was astonished that the Senate ever gave it a moment's consideration."[23] Another senator denounced it as "more monstrous . . . in character than the negro slavery that we have abolished" in that it involved the "hunting up of white men" and the subsequent use of "the right arm of the law to compel their execution under the stars and stripes." It was a plan "cunningly devised, by which capital is to seize labor, by which labor is to be turned up in its vise and held as if poverty were a crime." Although the motion to repeal the original act was tabled, the proposal to expand its scope failed as well.

It is by way of this controversy that organized labor made its historical entrance into the arena of immigration policy. In the course of the war, the labor movement met with increasing success; the number of local trade unions in the North grew spectacularly from 79 at the end of 1863 to 270 a year later; many of them organized nationally; and, after several attempts, the National Labor Union was launched in August 1866.[24] This coincided with the onset of an eighteen-month recession and the reappearance of large-scale unemployment for the first time since 1857. On most economic matters, the national craft unions continued to act as autonomous bodies; but the 1867 convention decided that the matter of labor importation, notably the provision of strikebreakers by the American Emigration Company with the assistance of American consuls, warranted action by the national body itself.[25] The convention passed a resolution urging repeal of the 1864 law and even appointed a delegate to the congress of the International Workingman's Association in Basel, Switzerland, with instructions to secure the cooperation of other national bodies in fighting contract labor and importation for the purpose of strikebreaking. Although the emissary did not go abroad on this occasion, others would attend similar gatherings later on.

These actions reveal a precocious awareness that the development of a transatlantic labor market created for American workers problems of which their overseas brethren had little or no understanding, and in relation to which their interests might fundamentally differ. Whether or not it took the form of actual contracts or was directly associated with strikebreaking, "importation," in the sense of overseas recruiting by private firms, continued to evoke protest from American unions as an unfair practice that afforded capitalists a decisive advantage. Over the long term, the experience fostered among American unions not only an antagonistic stance toward immigration more generally but also a fundamental ambivalence toward working-class internationalism.[26]

In the event, the 1864 law did not live up to its promise. Having doubled in one year following the enactment of homesteading, immigration took three years to do so again after 1864, and there was a sharp drop in 1868. How many of the arrivals were assisted under the act's provisions cannot be ascertained, and little use was made of the courts to enforce contracts.[27] In light of earlier experience with redemptioners, it is doubtful that juries would have reliably ruled on behalf of the creditors. In practice, the American Emigrant Company ended up operating merely as a travel broker, packaging the various land and sea components of voyage from the interior of Europe to the interior of America; but it was merely one of many such middlemen, along with railroads, shippers, and land companies, which together fostered a steady rationalization of massive transatlantic relocation in the latter decades of the nineteenth century.[28] This sometimes involved overseas contracts, particularly when the newcomers were being brought in to replace strikers; but more commonly, recruitment took place after they landed.

Finally, on March 9, 1868, the Senate's long-standing opponents of the law successfully attached a rider providing for its repeal to a consular and diplomatic appropriations bill.[29] The amendment was passed without division, the House concurred a few days later, and the repeal was signed on March 30.[30] Pressure from labor reportedly played a role in this outcome, and the postwar recession may have also tempered the enthusiasm of importers and their clients.[31] An attempt a few months later to revive the bureau itself fell by the wayside as well.

Nevertheless, a variety of bills to provide aid and encouragements to immigrants continued to be presented to Congress.[32] Most explicitly, the legislators urged the United States to declare that "the right of expatriation is a natural and inherent right of all people, indispensable to the enjoyment of the rights of life, liberty, and the pursuit of happiness . . . in recognition of which principle this government has freely received emigration from all nations and invested them with the rights of citizenship."[33] Prompted most immediately by charges of treason brought by the British government against Irish-born naturalized U.S. citizens involved in Fenian activities, on the grounds that they were still British subjects, the statute disavowed "[t]he last vestiges of the common law doctrine of perpetual allegiance" that had generated so much heat at the beginning of the century, and "gave clear expression to the liberal conceptions of civic membership."[34] Congressional discussion also referred to the desirability of removing obstacles faced by emigrants.[35] The same committee that recommended against reviving the Bureau of Immigration made an explicit connection between the two issues, pointing out in its report, significantly entitled "Encouragement of Emigration," that special measures to that effect were no longer necessary because, by way of the steamship and the telegraph, "distance is annihilated," and because the forthcoming proclamation on expatriation—to be implemented by means of bilateral conventions and treaties—would free all Europeans who wished to leave. Once legal impediments to mobility were removed, the European push and the American pull could be relied on to provide all the immigration the country needed.[36] Laissez-faire would work, but only if it was fostered by sustained governmental intervention.

The Invisible Hand Reaches Out: The Pacific Side

From an immigration perspective, the conquest of California was a revolutionary event that opened up for the first time since the abolition of the slave trade a second entry gate, connecting the United States with the huge population pools of Asia. As early as 1848, far-seeing policy makers envisioned the massive importation of Chinese laborers to build a transcontinental railroad as well as to launch the newly acquired land's agriculture.[37] A few hundred Chinese arrived in California as "forty-niners," rising to 2,716 in 1851 and 20,026 the following year.[38] At the outset, this was an overwhelmingly male population, engaged almost entirely in mining, largely as independent prospectors. As many went on to Australia or returned to China, the net balance of Chinese in the United States rose slowly, reaching about 35,000 in 1860 according to the U.S. Census and 47,000 by local estimates.[39]

China's seaborne migrations increased dramatically following the empire's forcible incorporation into the European-dominated world economy.[40] As of the mid-nineteenth century, emigration remained officially forbidden, but the Ch'ing authorities lacked the capacity to enforce the prohibition. Moreover, at the end of the Opium Wars (1839–1842 and 1856–1860), the European powers, eager to procure workers for their expanding mines and plantations in the tropical belt, insisted on including in the treaties they dictated provisions removing barriers to emigration and allowing foreign entrepreneurs to operate freely in the "Treaty Ports" of the South China Sea. This enabled the launching of an extensive network of labor recruitment and shipping involving both European and Chinese entrepreneurs, who established themselves in the new migration centers abroad as traders and labor brokers. Chinese miners and other enterprising individuals on the lookout for new opportunities also quickly responded to news of the discovery of gold in California and Australia.[41]

Unable to meet the costs of relocation on their own, Chinese workers usually set out as "coolies," a form of term bondage that resembled the extinct European indenture system and that was also widely used for the procurement of South Asians.[42] Unruly competition among Chinese suppliers, foreign agents, and navigation companies fostered an escalating spiral of coercion and violence, with many of the migrants victims of kidnapping and the ships amounting to floating prisons. Although American merchants based in China viewed the coolie traffic as a "dirty and disgusting sort of slave trade business," they were not above engaging in it themselves if the price was right. As the traffic expanded throughout the 1850s, they played an important role in the transportation of coolies to the New World, often sailing under South American flags to avoid regulation.

Throughout the colonial world, a basic condition for the operation of indentures was recognition of legal servitude and the enforcement of worker obligations by local authorities. But since this was not practicable after California was admitted to the union as a free state, an alternative emerged whereby Chinese emigrants borrowed the cost of their ticket and contracted for its repayment from their earnings in the United States, without being bound for a fixed period of years.[43] The "credit-ticket" system rendered them highly dependent on the Chinese merchant associations based in San Francisco. Known as the Six Companies, organized on the basis of regional origin, these functioned both as labor brokers and benevolent associations, controlling the laborers on the job by insuring that their wages were paid by the American employer to a Chinese labor boss or bookkeeper, who retained the appropriate debt installment on behalf of the lender. The system was sanctioned by requiring a certificate that the debt had been discharged in full in order to buy a return ticket to China, enforced by the Pacific Steam and Mail Company, which had an effective monopoly on passenger transport. By entrusting initial procurement and subsequent enforcement of work discipline to Chinese intermediaries, the system afforded signal advantages to American employers; and given perennial concern over "paupers," it insured that the immigrants would not constitute a burden on American society when no longer needed.

Although hostile prejudices toward the Chinese were established among white Americans well before contact occurred, they were exacerbated and acquired a distinct structure in California; as with African slaves, the unfree status of the "coolies" fostered racial prejudice toward the Chinese as a whole.[44] Albeit victims of extreme exploitation, they were regarded as responsible for their own degradation: there must be something in the Oriental mind and disposition that fostered a willingness to submit to bondage, a "fact" that in turn fostered the belief that the Chinese were inassimilable and must therefore be excluded. By the same token, opponents of exclusion insisted that most of the Chinese who came to the United States were not "coolies" but voluntary immigrants. These considerations have shaped the historiographic debate as well.[45]

The confrontation over Chinese immigration involved the shaping of California's moral economy, in relation to which the racial boundaries of the labor market arose as a central issue.[46] In effect, the California pioneers reenacted the great colonial debate between advocates of a free agrarian society and plantation entrepreneurs, here transferred to the development of mining. Following the discovery of gold, miners who identified themselves as "the laboring poor" insisted, in the spirit of Jacksonian democracy, that a claim was the birthright of every American, much like a homestead, and that titles must therefore be allotted in keeping with the working capacity of independent owner-producers, operating without servants.[47] Moreover, the privilege should be restricted to American citizens. As against this, capitalist entrepreneurs aspired to launch large-scale operations for which extensive claims and an abundant supply of cheap labor were required.[48] Accordingly, in 1852, Senator George Tingley sought enactment of a law to make ten-year contracts entered in China enforceable in California courts.[49]

Initially the independent miners mainly sought to prevent the importation by "monopolies of capitalists" of slaves or free Negroes under indenture. A clause prohibiting the admission of Negroes was widely supported by the 1849 constitutional convention, but ultimately rejected because of fear that its inclusion might lead Congress to deny approval of the charter; instead, the matter was left to be dealt with by the legislature later on.[50] As early as 1850, the state enacted a prohibitive foreign miners' tax, designed mainly to keep out Mexicans, but the Chinese quickly surged to the fore as the populace's main vexation. Constructed in California to occupy the antagonistic position assigned to free blacks on the East Coast, they were even depicted to look like Negroes.[51] The moral economy dimension clearly comes through in the complaint of a miner's convention in 1855:

> The American laborer claims the *exclusive privilege* and *right* of occupying and working the immense placers of our State. . . . If [the Chinese] are excluded from the mines, our own laboring classes will for a long series of years have the advantage of capitalists. Our laborers wish to keep up the value of their toil to a fair standard of competition *among themselves,* but you allow capitalists to import Chinese labor upon them, and the equilibrium is destroyed, capital is triumphant, and the laboring poor of American must submit to the unholy sacrifice.[52]

The perspective of the "laboring poor" was represented by the Democratic Party, which dominated state politics throughout the 1850s.[53] In 1852 the miners sought to prohibit the entry of Chinese into the state altogether, but failed; however, they did succeed in blocking enactment of a bill designed to facilitate the importation of "coolies" and also secured an increase in the tax on foreign miners, making employers liable for its payment; this also provided the state with about one-third of its annual budget.[54] While miners of European origin could overcome the tax by becoming citizens, under the prevailing legal interpretation the Chinese were presumed ineligible and hence permanently liable. In 1854 California Chief Justice Murray, a member of the Know-Nothing Party, ruled that an 1850 law excluding Negroes and Indians from testifying against whites applied to the Chinese as well, because by virtue of their common Asiatic origin, Chinese are like Indians.[55] In 1855 a committee of the legislature recommended that foreigners ineligible to citizenship be excluded from the mines altogether, but relented when it was pointed out that this would occasion a considerable loss of revenue and hamper trade with China; instead, they doubled the miners' tax. In 1855 as well, ships were required to pay $50 per landed passenger ineligible for citizenship. Although this was declared unconstitutional by the California Supreme Court because it interfered with international commerce, the legislature recidivated with another measure declaring that no Chinese or Mongolian should be permitted to enter the state, with fines and imprisonment for transporters.

At the international level, despite widely publicized denunciations of Asian labor migrations as "a new system of slavery," initially the concern of western governments was mainly to prevent their nationals from supplying "coolies" to competitors.[56] The issue imposed itself on the attention of U.S. officials in 1852, when a group of Chinese passengers aboard the *Robert Browne* rose up in mutiny, killing its American captain as well as some of the crew, and later running the ship aground on an isolated island off the coast of Japan. While seeking redress in Chinese courts, the American ambassador, himself a planter, warned Washington of the threat to the cotton trade from the use of cheap Chinese labor in foreign countries, and suggested that the United States should therefore prevent the use of American shipping for this purpose. However, no action followed.[57]

In the second half of the 1850s, Chinese officials began to put pressure on western states to provide better conditions for emigrants as a condition for the further development of trade and diplomatic relations.[58] Distinguishing between the "coolie trade" and the "voluntary emigration of Chinese adventurers," the American consul in Kwangtung suggested that while regulations for furnishing voluntary labor "may be a subject for future treaty stipulation," the coolie traffic should be immediately condemned "as a matter of humanity and policy." In 1859 the U.S. attorney general ruled that the remedy had to be instituted by Congress.[59] Three years later, following another mutiny on an American ship, it duly enacted a law prohibiting the transport of involuntary Chinese passengers in American vessels, and subjecting U.S. ships departing from China to inspection by an American consul.[60] This confirms John Torpey's insight that "remote control" originated in response to Asian immigration several decades before it was implemented on the Atlantic side.[61]

By establishing that all the Chinese landing in California were certifiably free, the new law opened up the possibility of more systematic procurement. Despite rabid popular opposition to Chinese workers, California's capitalists and merchants continued to promote the advantages of this "womanlike labor."[62] In 1862, a Joint Select Committee of the Assembly recommended that no further restrictions be placed upon Chinese immigration because it did not involve slavery or "coolieism"; although the Assembly rejected the recommendation and adopted instead a long memorial to Congress on the evils of unassimilable immigrants and the dangers of introducing a system of labor very similar to slavery, this was blocked in the Senate.[63]

Demand for Chinese labor surged following the organization of the Central Pacific Railroad by Collis Huntington and Leland Stanford in 1861. Although in his inaugural address as governor of California in 1862, Stanford asserted, "To my mind it is clear, that the settlement among us of an inferior race is to be discouraged by every legitimate means," profitability once again outweighed such concerns, and the following year the Central Pacific's own E. B. Crocker sent for some fifty Chinese to break a strike. After the conflict was settled, he kept them on, and soon issued a call for another 5,000, and eventually over 20,000 more.[64] As demand rose, Chinese merchants and white firms in San Francisco, operating as agents of the Central Pacific, undertook direct recruitment in the mountain districts of the Pearl River Delta.[65]

The Chinese issue was broached at the national level as early as December 1867, when U.S. Representative Johnson of California introduced a resolution in the House urging the Judiciary Committee to inquire whether Congress was empowered to enact legislation to prevent the immigration and importation of Chinese and Mongolians.[66] After the resolution failed, he offered it again the following January, expanding it to inquire whether the Civil Rights Act of 1866 and the proposed amendments to the Constitution could confer citizenship to Chinese born in the United States. Again, no action followed. In 1869, Johnson proposed yet another resolution specifying that "in passing the resolution for the fifteenth amendment . . . this House never intended that Chinese or Mongolians should become voters," but the House voted 42–106 against it.

In March 1868, the very same month that Congress repealed the 1864 Act to Encourage Immigration, and even as frustrated Californians were bringing their struggle on behalf of exclusion to Washington, Anson Burlingame, in his new capacity as representative of the Chinese Empire, signed a treaty elaborated by Seward, with labor procurement as its central concern.[67] Written unilaterally, the treaty can be taken as a faithful representation of U.S. objectives, as conceptualized by a far-sighted statesman of American capitalism. It asserted the right of the Chinese to expatriate themselves and to immigrate freely into the United States, but specified that the right of entry should not be construed to entail the right to acquire citizenship by naturalization; it also restated the terms of the 1862 U.S. legislation condemning involuntary immigration, and committed China to prohibit involvement of its own subjects in the coolie traffic. The provision pertaining to expatriation merely applied to China the general American policy proclaimed in the 1868 law to that effect.

The coupling of an insistence on the right of expatriation and the promotion of importation with exclusion from naturalization indicates that the design assumed Chinese workers would not be incorporated into American society, and hence envisioned, at least tacitly, the formation of an institutional limbo, populated by a mass of permanently segregated noncitizen workers, neither slave nor free. It constituted an idiosyncratic solution to the recurrent dilemma posed by the contradiction between economic rationality and racial exclusiveness: the erection of an internal boundary between the general population and a special category of human beings, identified as "workers" rather than as persons on the basis of membership in an ascriptive racial or nationality group and of the conditions governing their entry.

A dispatch to Seward from Burlingame's successor as U.S. ambassador cited a Californian correspondent's support for the "more liberal treaty" that was pending on the grounds that the additional labor it would provide "will make this State blossom like the rose, and turn its desert places into grain fields, tea, rice, sugar, coffe[e], and cotton plantations, and vineyards and orchards." After his arrival in China, the envoy reported further on the advantages of Chinese immigration in terms that echoed the secretary's own earlier arguments on behalf of the importation of workers from Europe: "[T]hey make profitable many of our resources which would otherwise remain undeveloped."[68] Around the same time, in response to charges that cheap and dependent Chinese workers would displace whites, the *Sacramento Union* argued that unemployment among the latter stemmed from their loss of a healthy work ethic and denounced special taxes on the Chinese as similar to the tactics used in the Middle Ages to persecute Jews.[69] At the national level, having initially derided the treaty, the editor of *The Nation* subsequently changed his mind, explaining that notwithstanding prejudice and prohibitory legislation, capital would continue to attract Chinese because they "will work harder and for less wages, and are more tractable" than Irish and German workers, and would also meet the acute need of American farmers for cheap servants.[70]

The matter of citizenship came to a head when radical Republicans set out to challenge racial barriers to naturalization as incompatible with their basic political doctrine. Concern with the Chinese in this respect first surfaced in 1866, when a senator from West Virginia pointed out that naturalization "involves not only the negro races, but other inferior races that are now settling on our Pacific coast."[71] The following year, naturalization arose as one of the leading issues in the California elections; afraid of what Congress might do, both the Democratic and Republican platforms declared their opposition to admitting the Chinese for citizenship, and both houses of the California legislature therefore rejected the Fifteenth Amendment by large majorities.[72] In 1870, in the course of debate over a bill to reduce naturalization fraud by requiring hearings in large cities to be held in federal courts, Senator Charles Sumner proposed an additional section providing "that all acts of Congress relating to naturalization be, and the same are hereby, amended by striking out the word 'white' wherever it occurs so that there shall be no distinction of race or color in naturalization."[73] As indicated by the declarations of those who opposed it, Sumner's proposal was defeated on the explicit grounds that it would grant citizenship to American Indians and Chinese; instead, the law of July 14 extended eligibility to persons of African nativity or descent alone, leaving Asians in effect excluded, albeit with some residual ambiguity.[74]

However, recent developments amounted to the creation of an unfortunate loophole: thanks to the recently adopted Fourteenth Amendment, which insured national and state citizenship to "All persons born or naturalized in the United States and subject to the jurisdiction thereof," persons of Chinese ancestry could become citizens by way of birth on American soil. The obvious remedy was to reduce the likelihood of such births by restricting the immigration of Chinese women. A first step was an 1870 law prohibiting the landing of any Asian female without first presenting to the commissioner of immigration evidence that she was a voluntary immigrant and a person of good character, reinforced in 1874 by the addition of "lewd or debauched women" to the categories of immigrants requiring a $500 bond.[75]

The treaty was reflected in a rapid escalation of recorded Chinese arrivals from an average of 4,300 for the 1861–1867 period to 6,707 in 1868, 12,874 the following year, 15,740 in 1870, and with intervening fluctuations to a new high of 20,292 in 1873, and yet another of 22,781 in 1876. Within California, as of the early 1870s, the Chinese constituted only about 9 percent of the total population; but since nearly all of them were adult males, they amounted to one-fifth of the economically active and probably one-fourth of all wage workers.[76] Increasingly pushed out by industrialization, independent white miners blamed the Chinese for their misfortune. Matters were exacerbated by the completion of the transcontinental railroad in 1869, which brought about a massive influx of white workers, mostly recent immigrants, while surplus Chinese were being dumped on the urban industrial labor market. Thanks to the scarcity of labor, California's white workers had gained victories such as the eight-hour day earlier than the rest of the country; but these precocious achievements were now jeopardized by the availability to employers of the Chinese alternative.[77]

Interest in Chinese workers was now shared by all sections of the country. The South had considered the possibility in the late 1850s, but at the time this had been overshadowed by talk of reopening the slave trade.[78] After the Civil War, southern planters quickly grasped the value of importing "another racial group engaged in menial labor in order to bring recalcitrant freedmen to terms."[79] However, there were some drawbacks: albeit "docile and thrifty," the Chinese would never go into debt to the proprietor, and in contrast with Mexicans, Central Americans, or Negroes, whom a proprietor had no trouble maintaining "in constant servitude," they could not be compelled to remain after the contract expired. Despite the opinion of the commissioner of the Bureau of Immigration that the "introduction of new races bound to service and labor, under contracts similar to those in the West Indies, is contrary to the true interests, as it is to the laws, of the United States," Chinese sugar workers were brought in from Cuba in this manner the following year to man plantations in Louisiana.[80] Alerted by the U.S. consul in Havana that this was contrary to the 1864 act prohibiting importation involving slavery or servitude, the attorney general ordered an investigation, which led to charges against an American captain for unlawful transportation. When the radical Republicans howled "slavery," Seward reassured them that the Chinese came voluntarily, and the charges were eventually dropped.[81] In 1868, a group of promoters sought to organize a joint stock company with a capital of $1,000,000 and voted to invite Cornelius Koopmanschap, one of the principal importers of Chinese into California, to attend their Memphis convention; however, the scheme was aborted because impoverished planters did not have the financial means to get the undertaking off the ground.[82] The following year, however, several hundred Chinese were recruited for work on the Alabama-Chattanooga railroad as well as to operate cotton mills.[83] In 1870, a contingent of seventy-five Chinese was brought all the way from San Francisco to North Adams, Massachusetts, by way of the recently completed transcontinental railroad, to break a strike staged by mostly Irish and French Canadian Knights of St. Crispin; later in the same year, two carloads were brought in the same manner to the Passaic Steam Laundry in New Jersey: and a similar episode was reenacted in 1872 at a cutlery in Beaver Falls, Pennsylvania.[84]

Although the practice remained limited because of its high cost and was abandoned in 1873, when depression reduced labor demand and rendered white workers more tractable, it propelled the Chinese issue to the national level and made Chinese immigration a prominent grievance of organized labor until well into the twentieth century.[85] From the late 1860s on, demands for Chinese exclusion were voiced in the annual congresses of various state and national labor organizations, including a convention of Negro workers; and in 1873 it was endorsed by the International Workingman's Association as well.[86]

The confrontation was not simply between capital and labor. The use of Chinese workers was believed to give larger entrepreneurs with overhead capital an edge, and because Chinese businessmen could more effectively exploit their countrymen within the confines of the enclave economy, they began to compete successfully in certain mass-production sectors, particularly cigar making and garment manufacturing. Hence, small white businessmen drifted toward the exclusionist camp as well, leaving "monopolists" as the only defenders of the Chinese.[87] With outright exclusion beyond California's reach, the state and localities cranked out punitive ordinances imposing obstacles to their landing and to their economic activities, only to have them challenged by the Six Companies and found unconstitutional because they violated guarantees provided by the Burlingame Treaty, which itself loomed increasingly as the major bone of contention.[88] The law prohibiting the landing of females was also found unconstitutional by U.S. Supreme Court Justice Stephen Field, sitting in his capacity as circuit court judge; but in the face of disagreement from his colleagues, he engineered a quick U.S. Supreme Court ruling on the questions raised.[89] In 1876, the Court unanimously invalidated the bond on the grounds that a bonding statute was not a proper exercise of state police power because "its manifest purpose is not to obtain indemnity but money."[90]

The California Republicans' identification with the railroads and other "monopolies," as well as their advocacy of continued Chinese immigration, emerged as major political liabilities. In 1868 President Ulysses Grant carried the state by only a few hundred votes, in 1873 an independent reform party secured control of the legislature, and two years later the Democrats triumphed throughout the state. Accordingly, in 1876 the Republicans broke with tradition and declared their support for Chinese exclusion, now arguing that they alone could deliver it by obtaining a revision of the Burlingame Treaty.[91]

The Regulatory Imperative

Beginning in 1875, within a single decade the ambiguous and administratively awkward jurisdictional equilibrium between levels of government in the sphere of immigration was decisively altered to the benefit of the national government. The change was part and parcel of the episode of state formation prompted by the onset of industrialization, involving the expansion of federal judicial power and the articulation by the Supreme Court of a nationalist doctrine that "recognized the continental scale of the new economic order and facilitated a concentration of governing authority."[92] Much like state building more generally, the recasting of immigration policy was a patchy process, implemented by way of a succession of Supreme Court decisions and congressional enactments, and prompted by the need to resolve institutional problems of long standing as well as by new problems arising from the changing scale and character of immigration itself.

The growing American demand for labor induced major changes in the technology of ocean transportation, and this in turn facilitated the further expansion of European overseas migration. Although the use of steam in navigation originated at the beginning of the nineteenth century and in fact preceded the railroad, its general application to ocean crossing occurred only in the 1860s, following the replacement of the wheel by the screw and of wood by iron, which together facilitated the building of much larger and faster ships.[93] Steam took over rapidly, from 31.5 percent of the passenger traffic arriving in New York in 1860, to over half in 1865 and over 90 percent in 1870. In 1856, transatlantic sailing vessels carried on average 247 passengers, as against 232 for steam; but in 1870 the relationship was reversed, and by the 1880s a single steamship might pack as many as 1,500.[94] Since shorter crossings enabled more frequent sailings and hence a higher return on capital investment, competition drove to ever-greater speed. Around midcentury, under the best of circumstances, the fastest sailing ships made the crossing in three weeks, with the average still around one month; but as early as 1871, the fastest crossing under steam took only eight to ten days, with an average of around twelve. As of 1873, there were already seventeen companies operating 173 steamships between Europe and New York, averaging around 3,000 tons each and totaling over 500,000 tons, and the industry subsequently underwent spectacular expansion, especially after the emerging German industrial giant entered into the fray.

Brinley Thomas has suggested that, reversing the dynamics of the earlier period, in the second half of the nineteenth century Atlantic migration was determined by the American pull rather than by the European push.[95] Although his proposition is difficult to verify, it is evident that the volume of immigration was highly responsive to variations in the American business cycle. Atlantic immigration quickly recovered from the sharp drop of 1868, reaching approximately the same level in 1873 as in the record year 1854, but the "panic" of 1873 once again awakened concern over a sudden labor surplus and precipitated an outcry over the "dumping" of convicts and paupers by European states, leading to renewed congressional calls for remedial action.[96] In 1877, when the United States experienced its worst depression as well as its largest strike wave to date, business misgivings extended to the intrusion of a new breed of labor "agitators."[97] However, matters appeared to take care of themselves, as annual entries declined rapidly to about 130,000 in 1878, the lowest level since 1863. Economic recovery once again fostered talk of a labor shortage, but immigration quickly escalated, exceeding the previously established record in 1880 and reaching 749,363 in 1882, a number that would turned out to be the century's maximum.

These fluctuations notwithstanding, the contribution of immigration to American population remained quite stable; thanks to continuing high fertility and a falling death rate, as of 1880 the proportion foreign-born among the country's white population was 15 percent, precisely what it had been on the eve of the Civil War. This remained unevenly distributed, ranging from a high of 24.6 percent in the West to a low of 4.2 percent in the South; but the percentage in the Northeast was only 19.7, slightly lower than in 1860, an indication that many of the newcomers were steadily moving inland in response to opportunities in both the agricultural and industrial sectors.

In contrast with the period immediately preceding the Civil War, Atlantic immigration played little or no role in determining national party alignments during Reconstruction, and was not used as a rallying point for political mobilization. Men of affairs appeared to be generally satisfied with the arrangements governing the flow, aptly characterized by one congressman in 1870 as "free trade in men."[98] The Republicans, mindful of the demise of their Whig predecessors, routinely solicited immigrant support and indeed obtained it from many groups, except for the staunchly Democratic Irish. Until 1882, arrivals from the United Kingdom remained the most numerous, and in contrast with the middle decades of the century, among them those of British origin, whom Charlotte Erickson aptly dubbed "invisible immigrants," exceeded the Irish in every year but one (1867). The second largest category were Germans, more heavily Lutheran than in earlier decades because of a shift to northern Germany as the principal region of departure. Most of them, along with fellow Lutherans from Scandinavia, moved directly to the Midwest, where they formed the original white settler population; hence, there were no opportunities for cultural clashes with established "Anglo-Americans." From the vantage point of intellectuals perennially concerned with such matters, the overall cultural character of European newcomers at this time was quite satisfactory: immigration "was simply recombining in the United States the strains which had earlier blended in English blood," fashionably referred to as the "great Gothic family."[99]

By way of this definitional legerdemain, the boundary of American identity shifted to encompass the Germans of concern to Benjamin Franklin and Thomas Jefferson, as well as Scandinavians. In the new record year, 1882, two-thirds of total white immigration was reassuringly "Gothic": 33 percent German, 14 percent Scandinavian, 14 percent British, and about another 5 percent of British stock from Canada and Newfoundland. Of the less desirable remainder, the two largest groups were the familiar Irish and their New World equivalent, the equally Catholic French Canadians, amounting to about 10 percent each. A mere 7 percent originated in non-German central Europe or in eastern Europe, and another 5 percent in southern Europe; but this "new" immigration was highly visible and evoked concerns that quickly propelled it to the fore of policy debates.

Nationalization of immigration policy was initially propelled by the West Coast's problems. In the face of repeated judicial defeats, the Californians had no choice but to bring their struggle against the Chinese into the national arena, and did so with considerable acumen, shrewdly identifying potential allies and varying their strategies accordingly.[100] Their task was facilitated by the deterioration of the Chinese image in public opinion under the impact of dramatic events, notably the massacre of American missionaries in Tientsin (1868), a coolie revolt in Peru (1870), and famine in China (1879), which raised the specter of the swamping of America by a tidal wave of starving humanity reminiscent of the Irish of an earlier generation, but commensurate with a population of 400 million. Concurrently, the proliferation of China-towns rendered the disturbing Oriental presence more visible throughout urban America at a time when the identification of filth as a source of disease provided scientific fodder for xenophobia. Americans, like Westerners else-where, increasingly viewed the Chinese through the lenses of the fashionable German theory of culture, according to which the social character of a people

was as immutable as its physical aspect.[101] Within this climate, the advocates
of manpower importation were driven to the defensive.

One urgent objective remained closure of the native-born Chinese loophole.
After President Grant, in his annual message to Congress of December 1874,
asked for legislation to fight the evils of Chinese immigration, of which the
worst was the importation of "lewd women," congressional activists seized the
opportunity to deal with broader issues. The rapidly enacted law of March 3,
1875, constituted the first national measure to control immigration by direct
means since the prohibition on slave imports. In a similar vein, it forbade the
"involuntary" immigration of contract workers generally referred to as "coolies," whose status was to be determined by U.S. consuls in Oriental ports of
embarkation; the "importation" by third parties under some sort of contract
"of women for the purposes of prostitution," regardless of race or place of
origin; and, more generally, the immigration pure and simple of such women
as well as of convicts.[102] Placing every incoming Chinese female under suspicion, the new law had the effect of reinforcing the exclusively male composition of the Chinese population and thereby, in combination with anti-
miscegenation laws, of minimizing its natural reproduction.

While American diplomats advocated maintenance of the status quo on the
grounds that "when the call for labor [in the Pacific states] ceases to be an
urgent one, the Chinaman will stop his migration in that direction," politicians
of both parties were pressed for immediate action.[103] In the closely contested
national elections of the next two decades, western electorates became steadily
more prominent in the calculations of national parties; and with the Chinese
now clearly ruled out as a prospective electorate, they were free to engage in
a bidding war for their exclusion.[104] The National Democratic Convention of
1876 adopted an anti-Chinese plank as a matter of course, while on the Republican side, despite resistance from transportation and industrial interests,
as well as from stalwart radicals, the California delegation was able to impose
a plank calling on Congress to investigate the effects of Chinese immigration.
Accordingly, in February 1877 a joint committee recommended a modification of the Burlingame Treaty to allow the United States to restrict immigration.

In the wake of the great railroad strike of 1877, the San Francisco Workingman's Party, akin to the New York Loco-Focos of the 1840s, staged a
successful political revolt that gave them control of the local Democratic Party
and thereby established their temporary dominance over California politics.
The state now served as an institutional base from which to press for exclusion

of the Chinese from the labor market altogether by way of a radical provision of its new constitution prohibiting their employment by corporations. Although the railroads quickly reestablished their political hegemony, the San Francisco labor vote remained the key to state politics; the outcome was a less radical labor movement, which gained permission to exclude the Chinese from the West Coast industrial labor market.[105] It is in this sense that the Chinese constituted what Alexander Saxton has termed an "indispensable enemy," reinforcing the position of white craftsmen in the Far West and thereby channeling the development of the regional labor movement toward a craft-based "business" unionism limited to skilled workers.

The western states pushed for nationalization of the issue on revenue grounds as well. As receivers of an increasing share of the incoming population, they were dissatisfied with the fiscal features of the ongoing system, whereby tax revenues from immigration went to eastern ports of entry alone.[106] Accordingly, they proposed replacing state bonds and commutation fees with a uniform national tax, whose proceeds would be allocated to the places of actual settlement. Although President Grant and Secretary of the Treasury Charles Conant supported these initiatives on the grounds that the subject of immigration was self-evidently a national matter, the national tax was naturally opposed by the State of New York as well as by leading immigrant societies on the East Coast, which shared in the revenues generated by the ongoing arrangements.

As before, port-of-entry states were facing a prisoners' dilemma: all of them had a common interest in maintaining a head tax of some sort, but each of them individually had an interest in lowering that tax so as to attract immigrant traffic from its competitors. Accordingly, New York lowered its commutation fees in 1871, and the following year, Massachusetts dropped them altogether. Shippers and the business community steadfastly maintained their traditional opposition to head taxes as well.[107] There matters stood until 1875, when shipper-originated challenges to New York and Louisiana laws reached the Supreme Court. Argued in January 1876 and decided in March, the two cases were merged as *Henderson v. Mayor of New York*.[108]

The decision was in keeping with the general trend of the age, when the Supreme Court affirmed the principle that government might act positively to foster economic development, and stepped in with little hesitation to eliminate state laws that impeded the formation of an integrated national economy.[109] Speaking for a unanimous court, Justice Samuel Miller deplored the long-standing jurisdictional ambiguities in the sphere of immigration, as well as the contingent aspect of earlier outcomes, notably the death of Chief Justice John Marshall before the conclusion of *Miln*. The Court was therefore determined to seize the occasion to establish a clear doctrine on sound footing. Conceding that the State of New York had a legitimate right to protect itself against the evils of immigration, he nevertheless pointed out that "it is a strange mode of doing this to tax every passenger who comes from abroad" because a state cannot invade a domain of legislation reserved by the Constitution exclusively to Congress. Immigration is a case in point, not only because passenger transportation is part of U.S. commerce with foreign nations, but also because immigrants qua labor constitute a factor of production and hence are inherently a component of commerce.[110] And finally, because the regulation of immigration constitutes an international process, it "ought to be the subject of a uniform system or plan" such as can be achieved only by way of a single law applying to the entire country.

Henderson had catastrophic effects for New York, as incoming ships immediately ceased paying fees while the commissioners of emigration retained the obligation to provide services for arriving immigrants. In the short run, the problem was met by emergency appropriations; but in the longer term, the solution was either to secure federal funds to operate the state's immigration machinery, or to transfer the whole matter into federal hands, prompting a reversal of the state's traditional stance. Concurrently, welfare officials enlisted the support of their counterparts in other states on behalf of nationalization of immigration, economic, and social policy. Although steamship companies and industrial interests remained opposed, and the only satisfaction New York obtained from Congress was an act to legalize the collection by state officers of head moneys due at the time of the *Henderson* ruling, the commissioners of emigration did secure the support of President Chester Arthur, who in his message to Congress of December 1881 recommended appropriate federal legislation.[111]

The coincidence of this development with the emergence of other pressing immigration issues, as well as the onset of another recession, thrust the entire subject into unaccustomed congressional limelight. In 1879, following a violent confrontation in San Francisco, Congress easily passed a bill (155–72 in the House, 39–27 in the Senate) limiting the number of passengers who could be transported by any ship coming from China to fifteen. After this was vetoed by the president as amounting to an abrogation of the Burlingame Treaty as a whole, which lay beyond congressional authority, the State Department dispatched a commission to China to obtain its cooperation in limiting the outflow of "lewd women, criminals, diseased persons, and contract laborers." Chinese officials agreed to restrict exit of the first three categories but pointed out, with respect to the last, that since "the emigration of Chinese to the United States for purposes of labor is provided for in our treaties," they would merely see to it "that each person goes of his own free will and accord."[112] However, the United States asserted its right to exercise discretion in the matter of immigration more generally and insisted it must obtain a modification of the treaty with regard to quantity and specification of where the Chinese might go. The compromise agreed upon in November 1880 allowed the United States to regulate, limit, or suspend the immigration of Chinese laborers but not to prohibit it altogether; and the restrictions applied to laborers only.

The revision constituted a major turning point in national immigration policy, in that the U.S. government in effect intervened to bring about a modification of the institutional context to the advantage of the exclusionists, whose victory was now a matter of time. In March 1882, Congress voted to suspend the importation of Chinese labor for a twenty-year period (29–15 in the Senate, 167–66 in the House); vetoed by President Arthur as in violation of the revised treaty, the bill was immediately reenacted with his approval for ten years, but with an additional section specifying that hereafter no state or U.S. court shall admit Chinese nationals to citizenship. A twenty-year exclusion was again enacted in 1888, but changed to ten four years later, and this was done once more in 1902. Two years later it was made applicable to all U.S. island territories as well, with recently acquired Hawaii as the principal target.

Because categoric restrictions proved in practice difficult to enforce, Congress relentlessly attempted to close every possible loophole. A particularly significant amendment enacted in 1884 required certificates of identification from the Chinese government to be verified and visaed by a U.S. diplomatic official at the port of departure, yet another precocious attempt at remote control. This also made it difficult for Chinese residents, even U.S. citizens, who traveled to China to return. The 1892 law further imposed on Chinese a unique registration requirement documenting their right to reside in the United States, which rendered all persons of Chinese descent, regardless of status or nationality, vulnerable to police harassment and arbitrary deportation.[113] Finally, in 1895 the U.S. government undertook to challenge the application of jus soli to persons of Chinese origin. In his plea to that effect before the Supreme Court, Solicitor-General Holmes Conrad insisted that the

U.S.-born Chinese "are just as obnoxious as their forebears"; pointing out that jus soli would make a Chinaman eligible for the presidency, he reasoned, "If so, then verily there has been a most degenerate departure from the patriotic ideas of our forefathers, and surely in that case America citizenship is not worth saving." Although the Court nevertheless upheld the jus soli tradition, the draconian measures directed at excluding Chinese women and the effective segregation of the resident Chinese male population insured that very few would in fact be in a position to benefit from the ruling.[114]

Together, these measures constituted a half-hearted attempt to undo the effects of the original importation policy. Paralleling efforts in the earlier part of the century to minimize the population of African origin by returning freed slaves to Africa, this willful reduction of a national group stands to date as the only successful instance of "ethnic cleansing" in the history of American immigration. The population of Chinese origin shrank from a peak of 118,746 in 1900 to a low of 85,202 in 1920; although numbers then slowly increased, as of 1940 there were still fewer Chinese in the United States than at the beginning of the century.[115]

Another piece of the established immigration régime came crashing down quite unexpectedly in 1880 when, as the result of yet another suit from the shipping industry, the Federal District Court of New York held that the 1855 Passenger Act did not apply to steamships, which now carried the entire passenger traffic. Steamship companies effectively blocked remedial action throughout the remainder of the 46th Congress (1879–1881). In the absence of valid regulations, conditions rapidly deteriorated, as indicated by the fact that the number of persons landed from Europe nearly doubled over the next two years while the total tonnage of incoming vessels remained unchanged.[116] A new effort to enact appropriate legislation was underway in early 1881, at the initiative of western representatives and with the support of immigrant societies, when New York exacerbated the crisis by threatening to close down the country's principal immigrant depot at Castle Garden unless federal aid were forthcoming.[117] Consequently, in his message of December 1881, in addition to the suspension of Chinese immigration, President Arthur also called for legislation regulating general immigration and providing for the care of arriving immigrants. Congress acted with unusual speed to impose stricter passenger requirements, only to have this defeated by the steamboat companies and replaced by a law more acceptable to them.[118]

The New Yorkers now took the lead. On June 19, 1882, the House Commerce Committee reported out a comprehensive bill that included the (1) collection of a 50 cent head tax by federal officials from each alien passenger coming in from a foreign port and paid into the U.S. Treasury for the purpose of regulating immigration and caring for the immigrants; (2) authorization to board vessels and examine the passengers in order to prevent the landing of foreign convicts (except those guilty of political crimes), lunatics, idiots, or other persons deemed likely to become a public charge [henceforth, "LPCs"], and provision for their return "to the countries from whence they came" at the expense of the owners of the vessel; (3) assumption of federal responsibility for the reception and care of arriving immigrants, but with administration of the facilities contracted out to state and local agencies; and (4) deportation of any excludable persons who might have slipped through, as well as those who became a public charge after arrival, with expenses to be paid out of the immigrant fund.[119] The bill sailed quickly through both houses, with omission of the provision imposing the costs of returning LPCs on the shippers, and limiting deportability after landing to nonpolitical convicts, and was signed into law on August 3, 1882.[120] Although the new law expanded the nationally excluded classes from the two provided for in the 1875 law (immoral women and convicts) to four (mental defectives and LPCs), this was in keeping with established port-of-entry practices. Important administrative innovations were the imposition of a head tax on the immigrants themselves, rather on the shippers, and reinstatement of deportability for the first time since the 1798 Aliens Act.[121]

No Coolies from Europe

After the violent strikes of 1877, politicians from both parties were prepared to make concessions to labor leaders, who were moving beyond the Chinese issue and seizing upon immigration more generally as a matter of vital interest.[122] The trade organ of the iron industry observed in 1881 "that no one could read the labor papers during the recent elections and not see in them a latent intention of making immigration an issue in the future," but that "[a]s yet the precise aims of such agitation were not clear."[123] However, a closer reading indicated that the agitation was being focused on "assisted immigration."[124] Although after 1868 the U.S. government no longer lent its authority to the systematic importation of contract labor from Europe, nothing prevented individual employers and workers from entering into such arrangements. While overseas contracts properly speaking, involving travel advances or outright subsidies, were limited to highly skilled workers and hence relatively rare, many strikes were lost when employers brought in gangs of new-comers "contracted" after they landed in New York.[125] A major battlefield was Pennsylvania's anthracite coal basin where, after the miners established closed shops in the late 1860s and were able to use strikes to manipulate coal prices, the railroads forced their way into controlling the mines and effectively de-stroyed the union by way of suspensions and lockouts, transforming com-munities into company towns privately policed by Pinkerton's Detective Agency and doubling the labor supply by massive recruitment of newcomers from central, southern, and eastern Europe.[126]

The demand for legislation against assisted immigration was first voiced in 1881 by cigar makers and glass workers within the framework of the new Federal Organization of Trade and Labor Unions, and was subsequently taken up by the Knights of Labor as well. The election of a sweeping Democratic majority in the House of Representatives in 1882 provided an opportunity for action. A bill "to prohibit the importation and migration of foreigners and aliens under contract to perform labor in the United States" was introduced in January 1884 by Martin Foran, a newly elected former union official from Cleveland and probably the first congressman issued from the ranks of or-ganized labor. Referred to the newly constituted Committee on Labor, the bill was reported out positively on February 23 with an amendment exempting skilled workers destined for new industries, as well as professional actors, lecturers, and singers. The bill was passed by the House on June 19, after a brief debate and another amendment specifying that the measure would not prohibit contracts entered into after landing. The vote was an overwhelming 102 to 19, with nearly unanimous support from the Democrats, who argued in their fall campaign, "If it became necessary to protect the American work-ingmen on the Pacific slope from the disastrous and debasing competition of Coolie labor, the same argument now applies with equal force and pertinency to the importation of pauper labor from southern Europe."[127] After repeated postponements and further amendments exempting domestic servants, rela-tives, and personal friends, the bill was passed by the Senate 50–9 on February 18, 1885, and signed into law at the end of the month.

Although the Foran Act merely prohibited immigration that involved formal contracts entered into abroad, its promoters were evidently seeking to achieve broader objectives. It is noteworthy that the committee report cited earlier provided very little evidence that this objectionable mass was being brought to the United States under contracts of the sort the law would prohibit. The only fully documented cases pertain to contracts between firms in Kent, Ohio, and Baltimore, and glassblowers in Belgium and Germany respectively; all other references are inferential only.[128] In his initial report on behalf of the House Committee on Labor, Foran insisted that the object of the bill was not to restrict voluntary immigration but "the immigration or rather the importation of an entire class of persons, the immigrant who does not come by 'his own initiative, but by that of the capitalist.' "[129] To a contemporary audience, the description that followed undoubtedly evoked the highly publicized coolie trade, with which the report repeatedly made explicit parallels:

> This class of immigrants care nothing about our institutions, and in many instances never even heard of them; they are men whose passage is paid by the importers; they come here under contract to labor for a certain number of years; they are ignorant of our social conditions, and that they may remain so they are isolated and prevented from coming into contact with Americans. They are generally from the lowest social stratum, and live upon the coarsest food and in hovels of a character before unknown to American workmen. Being bound by contract they are unable, even were they so disposed, to take advantage of the facilities afforded by the country to which they have been imported. They, as a rule, do not become citizens, and are certainly not a desirable acquisition to the body politic. When their term of contract servitude expires, their place is supplied by fresh importations. The inevitable tendency of their presence amongst us it to degrade American labor and reduce it to the level of the imported pauper labor.

To forestall charges that this was selfish legislation to the advantage of a single class, the report went on to suggest, much as was argued by anti-Chinese activists in California, that the issue pitted also smaller capitalists against the "monopolies."[130]

Immigrants and Sojourners

Foran characterized the imported laborers as mostly "degraded, ignorant, brutal Italians and Hungarians" who "are not freemen, and very many of them have no conception of freedom."[131] Even if they came voluntarily, they "would not be a desirable acquisition to our population."[132] Although the same had been said of Foran's own Irish forebears earlier in the century, a distinctive negative was now added: the newcomers were mostly single men who hoarded their meager earnings and returned to Europe within four or five years, with no intention of becoming U.S. citizens. The issue was thus not only contracts, but also that they were *sojourners* rather than *immigrants,* a status that rendered them similar to the Chinese coolies whom the United States had already excluded. Foran's formulation was by no means idiosyncratic. T. V. Powderly, master workman of the Knights of Labor who would later serve as commissioner-general of immigration, complained similarly, "These imported men show no disposition to become citizens of this country, but, on the contrary, seek to obtain a certain sum of money . . . and with it return to Italy or Hungary," and concluded that they "are brought into competition with skilled as well as unskilled labor, and it is fast becoming as bad as the competition of the Chinese in the West."[133]

Despite its grossly racialist formulation, this was an accurate observation, as Atlantic immigration was indeed undergoing an unprecedented differentiation into two segments, the one a continuation of the traditional pattern of familial relocation and settlement, the other an incipient stream of international migrant workers. The trend was amplified over the next decades, and on the eve of World War I, the annual number of southern and eastern Europeans departing from the United States amounted to 38 percent of landings. The major exception were Jews from the Tsarist Empire, whose rate of return was negligible; and when they are omitted from the count, the proportion of "sojourners" rose to approximately half.[134]

Although the Foran Act has entered history as one of organized labor's first victories in the national legislative arena, as a measure designed to prevent immigration from injuring workers it was ineffective. Overseas contracts such as it prohibited were in fact rarely used in strikebreaking, violations were almost impossible to identify, and initially no funds were provided for enforcement. The problem was not so much "contracts" as the unique difficulties that American workers faced in their attempts to control access to the labor market. This critically shaped the development of organized labor and provides much of the answer to Werner Sombart's question, "Why is there no Socialism in the United States?"[135]

The availability of a large force of ethnically distinct "birds of passage" imparted to American capitalism an acutely segmented structure, which emerged as one of its distinctive features.[136] Rather than fellow victims of exploitation, the newcomers came to be seen as irremediably malleable tools of the bosses; and given the impossibility of mobilizing them effectively, the goal was therefore to keep them out—a perverse variant of Hirschman's alternatives of "exit" and "voice."[137] The resulting strategy was to organize unions on the basis of craft, thereby excluding uninitiated and unskilled newcomers—including, later on, northward-bound black migrants from the

South—from the most prized segment of the labor market.[138] As Samuel Gompers reminisced in 1919, the experience of California's cigar makers alerted their colleagues elsewhere to the danger of "chinaization" and prompted them "to give early and hearty endorsement to the movement for a national organization of labor unions, for the help of all wage earners was needed in support of Chinese exclusion."[139] The fledgling Federal Organization of Trade and Labor Unions shortly turned its attention to the new immigrants from southern and central Europe, charging that most were "birds of passage" who bore a family resemblance to the Chinese, and were therefore equally unacceptable. Organized labor would subsequently respond much in the same way to the black migration from the South as well. Although it might be possible to keep European "birds of passage" out of the country altogether, as was being achieved with the Chinese, this required a vast broadening of the restrictionist coalition, which for the time being lay beyond labor's reach.[140]

The precocious elimination of the Chinese did not afford labor control over the market in the West either. Launched on its career as an agricultural wonderland, California generated a massive need for cheap farm labor. Initially, the demand was met by Chinese already in the state or introduced surreptitiously, so that as of 1886, they constituted seven-eighths of the state's agricultural force.[141] California farmers steadfastly opposed exclusion; and when this proved unavoidable, they focused their efforts on finding substitutes. As Mary Coolidge put it bluntly in 1909, "The history of general labor in California since about 1886 is the story of efforts to find substitutes for the vanishing Chinese."[142] Unable to compete for the new immigrants from Europe, they took a leaf from the experience of Hawaiian planters and turned to Japan and, after the Spanish-American War, to the newly acquired Philippines.[143] In most respects, the experience of the Japanese as a group initially wooed and later excluded paralleled that of the Chinese, except for the fact that most of them initially came as families and hence produced American-born progeny.[144] But a more permanent solution emerged around the turn of the twentieth century as Mexican *campesinos* and *peones,* much like their European counterparts, were uprooted by a growing inability to eke out a living from the land. Stimulated in part by the onset of Mexico's rapid population growth, from an estimated 7.8 million in 1850 to 13.5 million in 1900, the crisis was exacerbated by the policies of the Porfirio Díaz government, which nationalized communal lands to provide attractive conditions for foreign investments in commercial agriculture.[145] The influx of American capital into mining, com-

mercial farming, and transportation rapidly transformed Mexico's hitherto isolated northern states into "the Border," connected by rail to the labor-hungry
southwestern states.[146] As Mary Coolidge astutely observed, "[W]hile the
Immigration service makes desperate efforts to catch a few Chinamen crossing
over without certificates, the pauper Mexican Cholos, by the hundreds, freely
come and go under contracts of labor."[147]

Mexican immigration retained elements of its distinctively colonial origins
throughout much of the twentieth century, thereby institutionalizing the segmented structure of U.S. immigration and immigration policy despite the
eventual elimination of "birds of passage" from the Atlantic side. Once the
migratory system was in place, the availability of labor stimulated new agricultural undertakings, notably long-staple cotton in the arid Southwest, cen-
tering on the "El Paso del Norte" entry point (Texas, Arizona, and New
Mexico). As early as 1908, an analyst for the U.S. Bureau of Labor observed,
"Within less than a decade there has been a large increase in the amount of
Mexican labor employed in the United States; but more marked than the
growth of numbers has been the increasing range of its distribution"; whereas
hitherto Mexicans were seldom found more than 100 miles from the border,
"Now they are working as unskilled laborers and as section hands as far east
as Chicago and as far north as Iowa, Wyoming, and San Francisco. The number of different industries dependent upon Mexican labor is increasing."[148]
Despite the 1885 law prohibiting the immigration of contract workers, American employers regularly sent their Mexican or Mexican American labor bosses
deep into Mexico to recruit their workforce; in the same vein, in 1909 Presidents William Taft and Porfirio Díaz signed an executive agreement authorizing the migration of additional Mexican contract workers to man the nascent
sugar beet industry in Colorado and Nebraska.[149] As many as 500,000 Mexicans may have entered the United States between 1900 and 1910; and although they too were "sojourners" rather than immigrants, their comings and
goings contributed to substantial settlement.[150]

7

"An Intelligent and Effective Restriction"

The desirability of limiting immigration in some fashion was very much in the air even as the Statue of Liberty was being inaugurated in New York Harbor in 1886. Congress received over fifty petitions to that effect in 1888, and two years later the Senate established a standing Committee on Immigration while the House created a Select Committee on Immigration and Naturalization. The two bodies shortly undertook a joint investigation of the adequacy of existing controls with a view to extending and reinforcing them.[1] In 1890, the horrors of immigrant life in New York City imposed themselves on the consciousness of the reading public by way of the shocking revelations of Jacob Riis's *How the Other Half Lives,* while in the Midwest, renewed fear of "Papist devilry" drove the god-fearing folk into the arms of the newly founded American Protective Association.[2]

In the face of the accelerating expansion of international population movements worldwide and the rapid escalation of numbers pouring into the United States to unprecedented size, "regulation" evolved imperceptibly from its earlier meaning of deterring undesirables from entering through an otherwise open door, toward the notion of imposing limits on the overall flow, and thus turned into "restriction." The subject was taken up by a new breed of policy-minded intellectuals who, terming themselves "social scientists," devised innovative proposals for reducing immigration's deplorable consequences while retaining the benefits, and elaborated discourse to that effect for use by policy makers. In 1888, the American Economic Association, founded three years earlier by progressive professionals opposing unfettered laissez-faire, sponsored an essay contest on "The Evil Effects of Unrestricted Immigration" and awarded the prize to Edward Webster Bemis, associate professor at the newly founded University of Chicago, who had gone on the lecture circuit with a scheme purporting to eliminate the least desirable newcomers by subjecting all adults to a literacy test. Thanks to closely knit networks, his proposal quickly penetrated into the political arena. In January 1891, the prestigious *North American Review* brought out "The Restriction of Immigration" by Massachusetts U.S. Representative Henry Cabot Lodge, who earned Harvard's first Ph.D. in political science, and who endorsed the literacy test as the best solution to the immigration problem.[3] The article was made part of the *Congressional Record* the following month, in the course of debate on the federalization of immigration control, which itself became law in March 1891.[4]

The protracted campaign for the literacy test is etched in historical memory as a prelude to the radically restrictive and racially oriented immigration laws of the 1920s. However, this constitutes a reductionist interpretation of complex policy developments spanning three decades. To begin with, the imposition of limits on immigration was well-nigh inevitable because a concatenation of changes associated with the globalization of capitalism and the demographic revolution in the final decades of the nineteenth century induced a sudden and worldwide escalation in the number of people on the move internationally and the distances they covered. But while limits were in the cards, the means for their achievement were by no means preordained. The need to distinguish between these two aspects is revealed by later developments: limitation was to be a constant of immigration policy in the United States and the entire world of advanced industrial societies throughout the twentieth century, while the level of admissions considered acceptable and the devices for implementing it varied considerably. Equally important but much less noted in the historical literature was the elaboration of "remote control," whereby the United States managed to project its restrictive capacity preventively to the place of origin.

The choice of a literacy test was in keeping with the aspirations of the progressives, who promoted reforms "that would accomplish at least two analytically distinct goals: the establishment of *social justice* and the imposition of *social control*," and who sought "to impose uniform living habits on a culturally diverse population whose behavior seemed to threaten the morality and health of the community."[5] It should therefore be thought of as part of a bundle of contemporaneous campaigns constituting an ideologically mixed bag on behalf of mandatory school attendance, voter registration, and literacy requirements, as well as racial segregation, sterilization of the mentally defective, and the prohibition of alcoholic beverages. As an instrument of social control, the literacy test was inherently ambiguous. Of itself, it was hardly invidious, since such a device was widely advocated by reformers for all Americans as a condition for membership in the political nation by way of the vote.[6] Nevertheless, its advocates were fully aware that its restrictive effect would fall mainly on "new immigration" from eastern and southern Europe, and it thereby served the purposes of outright nativists who opposed this immigration as detrimental to the national identity.

Yet despite the enthusiastic reception Bemis reported for his proposal and its rapid endorsement by the intellectual establishment as well as by leading politicians, it took thirty years for the literacy test to become law. Why the lengthy delay? In his classic account, John Higham attributed it to fluctuations of the collective anti-immigrant fever occasioned by the constantly shifting relationship between American anxiety and alternative opportunities for its externalization, such as the Spanish-American War. Tacitly founded on the psychoanalytic theories of the 1950s, this explanation surmised a fixed quantity of hostility, displaced from one object to another according to circumstances, as in a hydraulic mechanism. A more persuasive account is that, as in the past, the vagaries of the legislative process largely arose from the contest between the "visible hand" seeking to maximize its labor supply and the defenders of the established boundaries of national identity. As it played itself out in the political arena, the confrontation was mediated by the party managers' pursuit of the immigrant vote, a factor the contemporary political scientist John Hawks Noble thought might be gotten around precisely by choosing the test as the instrument of restriction.[7] Recent research confirms that the importance of this factor was enhanced by the evolution of party politics toward the "fourth electoral system."[8] Two nonelectoral actors assumed prominent roles in the policy-making process as well. Organized labor, which had long clamored for a voice in the immigration sphere, gained access to the Office of the Commissioner of Immigration. This constituted in effect a corporatist arrangement, generally more characteristic of European than American approaches to the settlement of class conflict.[9] Concurrently, the "Jews" gained access to the Office of the Secretary of Commerce, which supervised the commissioner of immigration. Reflecting the launching by prominent Jewish financiers and businessmen of a number of national organizations to protect their co-religionists' interests, this was also an innovative corporatist arrangement, but in the sphere of ethnic rather than class politics.

The Globalization of International Migration

American thinking about social issues in the Progressive era was very much shaped by the shared concerns of European industrial societies.[10] These "Atlantic crossings" also held for immigration, whose vast expansion precipitated heated debates over appropriate policy responses. In he late 1880s, the British geographer E. G. Ravenstein enunciated comprehensive "laws of migration" that provided a seminal framework for analyzing the fledgling subject.[11] His key insight, elaborated by subsequent generations of social scientists into more complex theories, was that economic development accentuated the unevenness of material conditions across territorial space, and that individuals relocated to maximize their income in light of the available information regarding opportunities, taking into consideration the costs of moving. There was indeed a growing gap in the making between a small group of capital-rich, technologically advanced, and strategically powerful countries—European or of European origin, plus Japan—all of which also engaged in colonial expansion, as against the rest of the world, whose internal conditions were henceforth largely determined by transnational processes originating in the leading countries.[12]

The great transformation's continued ravages among the early industrializers of northwestern Europe and its expansion to Europe's "backward" southern and eastern regions, where the enclosure drama was reenacted on altered terrain, occasioned an enormous "push" leading to vast internal and international population movements.[13] Improvements in the production and distribution of food brought about a decrease in the death rate, and thereby stimulated unprecedented population growth; but since the larger population shared finite land resources, the proportion of landless laborers increased.[14] As the ownership of land became more concentrated and production more specialized, and with a shift from traditional tenancy to short-term wage work, social ties and shared interests binding landlords to workers were severed, leaving large numbers without housing or sustenance. The expanded rural population also rendered crop failures more devastating. As capital moved to more rewarding urban sites and fled some regions altogether, the countryside was deindustrialized; chances for village work disappeared, and the pay rates for rural goods declined, reducing the ability of country workers to get by in the local cottage economy.[15] Similar forces were unleashed in parts of what would later be called the "Third World" in consequence of indigenous attempts to catch up as well as more intrusive penetration by the industrializing countries, which between 1876 and 1915 appropriated one-quarter of the globe's land surface.

The "push" forces coincided with the "pull" generated by the vigorously growing agricultural and industrial sectors of the economic leaders. Eschewing craftsmen and women, and prohibited from employing children, employers were eager for less skilled, less expensive, more docile, and more disposable labor. In this perspective, necessitous migrants from less developed regions within the state or abroad were most welcome. Thanks to the rapid spread of literacy, combined with the advent of cheap printing, the telegraph, and photography, the uprooted themselves quickly learned where their quest for work was likely to be most rewarding, and the formation of a worldwide network of cheap mass transportation made it possible for them to get there. By virtue of these developments, for determined emigrants, destinations became increasingly interchangeable.

Much as had occurred in Great Britain, the Low Countries, and western Germany earlier in the nineteenth century, developing states came to view emigration as a welcome solution and eased mercantilist-era legal and administrative barriers.[16] For example, Spain maintained tight restrictions on exit through the 1850s, then relaxed them somewhat, and as of 1903 governmental permission was no longer required.[17] Following the founding of the Council of Emigration in 1901, Italian officials recognized the immense economic returns from temporary emigration to North America, amounting to an estimated $60 million in remittances annually from 1901 to 1914; protected against foreign competition, Italian shipping companies thrived on the traffic.[18] Japan's modernization from above similarly led the authorities to abandon their traditional policy of retention and to encourage emigration as a safety valve and source of public income.[19] Accordingly, by the turn of the twentieth century, Japanese workers constituted two-thirds of the sugar plantation workforce in Hawaii and were found among the Pacific states of South America as well. An exception was Russia, whose rulers eventually let go of minorities, notably Jews, but adamantly opposed the departure of Great Russians. European colonial governments also organized massive population transfers, by far the largest of which originated in the Indian subcontinent.[20] Although none were directed toward North America, around the turn of the century Indians began appearing in British Columbia and California, and some 7,000 arrivals were recorded in the United States before they were excluded in 1917 by the Literacy Act, as will be discussed shortly.

Concurrently, the onset of the transformation of the European periphery's empires into unified nation-states, modeled on western European experience as imagined and recorded by state-serving intellectuals, fostered more systematic pressures on minorities, often resulting in outright persecution. This produced additional massive movements of groups that were expelled or forced to flee from their homelands.[21] Although some of the larger minorities managed to gain their independence, the problem was often reenacted within the successor state, where remnants of the former majority were turned into a minority, along with "misfits" who belonged nowhere. These were culturally distinct populations so scattered that they could not possibly carve out a state of their own and hence, as Hannah Arendt pointed out, were more estranged and vulnerable than any others: the Jews, numbering some 5.6 million east of Germany in the 1870s, and the Roma.[22] Forced migrations arose throughout the western regions of the weakening Ottoman Empire as well, involving Muslim minorities in the new Christian nations, and Christians in the Turkish heartland, notably Armenians. Economic necessity and nationalist transformation sometimes combined, notably in the massive migration of the Jews from central and eastern Europe.[23]

The expansion of both voluntary and forced population movements was vastly facilitated by the availability of rapid and inexpensive steam-powered mass transportation on land and water. Around the turn of the twentieth century, railroad expansion was especially dramatic in the European periphery.[24] Similar developments took place in Latin America, Asia, and— somewhat later—Africa. On the New York run, the steerage price went down from about $40 in 1870 to $20 around the turn of the century, and dipped yet lower in depression years such as 1894, when the fare from Ireland dropped to $8.75.[25] As before, much of this was financed by remittances and prepaid tickets sent home from overseas, but now on a much larger scale. Like the railroads, the shipping companies helped to develop markets by moving closer to places of origin, and the two modes of transportation were integrated into well-established itineraries. For example, a German observer noted that the recently developed rail and steamship networks allowed an Italian to get to North or South America for less than the rail fare to East Prussia. The Hamburg-Amerika line, in particular, contributed to Jewish emigration by elaborating a web of agents in Russia and eastern Europe and alleviating the difficulties that observant Jews encountered when leaving their communities by providing them with kosher food.[26]

Overall, emigration from Europe to the major overseas receivers (Argentina, Brazil, Canada, and the United States) grew from 3.6 million in 1871–1880 to 12.9 million in 1901–1910, totaling 42.1 million from 1871 to 1914.[27] The United States was by far the leading destination, receiving more than six times as many immigrants as second-ranking Argentina.[28] However, in relation to population size, immigration was much larger in Canada, whose 400,870 arrivals in 1913 amounted to an addition of 5 percent to the country's population in a single year, over three times the U.S. record of 1854. There were also sizeable international flows toward the economically advanced northwest European countries, amounting to some 2 million foreign residents in northwestern Europe on the eve of World War I. The composition and size of the flows changed markedly as well. Ranked in terms of relative contribution to overseas movement, in 1871–1880 the top four European emigration countries were Ireland, Britain, Norway, and Portugal; but in 1913 they were Italy, Portugal, Spain, and Britain. However, while the annual rate of exit for Ireland in 1871–1880 was 661 per 100,000, for Italy in 1913 it was 1,630, nearly three times higher, and the top four all had an emigration rate above 1,000.[29]

In the United States, despite Chinese exclusion, the head tax, and various other deterrents discussed shortly, the record 1882 level was exceeded in 1903 and entries reached 1,285,349 in 1907. One needed not be a dyed-in-the-wool "nativist" to wonder how long things could go on in this manner, as continued growth at the ongoing rate implied a doubling of the annual average intake every twenty years.[30] On the eve of World War I Italy led the pack, followed by the Austro-Hungarian and Russian Empires, Canada, "other southern Europe," and Britain, now down to sixth place. In ethnic terms, the largest groups were Italians (some 3 million), Jews (2 million, mostly from the Russian Empire), and Poles (1 million). Return migration constituted a growing share of total movement; a rough estimate for 1908–1923 suggests that departures amounted to 35 percent of arrivals, with wide variation among groups, ranging from a high of perhaps 50 percent for Italians to a low of 15–20 percent for Jews before the tsarist pogroms and 4.3 percent afterwards.[31] While departures had little effect on perceptions of the magnitude of immigration, the high return migration among the "new" immigrants as a whole added to their undesirability from a nation-building perspective.

The Construction of a Restrictionist Rationale

Within the globalizing world, the responses evoked by the new situation were highly interactive, as the closing of one door deflected migrants toward others, who in anticipation of this or in reaction to it imposed barriers of their own. America's turn to a restrictive policy thus appeared natural and logical because it was grounded in an internationally shared understanding of the new trends and their implications for the receiving countries' economic, social, and political health. As early as 1888, Richmond Mayo-Smith cited in support of restriction that this was unlikely to give offense to European states because everyone recognizes the right of a nation to protect its home industry, and "The protection of its labor by shutting out the labor of other countries would be but a step further in the same direction." Moreover, "No one has disputed the constitutionality of our anti-Chinese legislation," and in fact "there is a great and increasing feeling that that was wise legislation." Beyond this, many of the European states "would gladly see the precedent established to restrict immigration," presently under consideration in England and France.[32] Indeed, despite Britain's commitment to economic liberalism, immigration restriction was on the political agenda from the mid-1880s onward, and in 1906 Parliament enacted a highly restrictive law that effectively closed its gates throughout the early decades of the twentieth century. A signal development was the legitimation of restriction within the framework of liberal political philosophy by Henry Sidgwick in 1891, on the basis of a distinction between the "national" and "cosmopolitan" ideal.[33] Germany imposed severe requirements for immigration in the 1880s, and a rationale for their further reinforcement was set forth in 1892 by the sociologist Max Weber, who demonstrated that the economic benefits Polish workers conferred to agricultural employers were outweighed by the integration problems they created for the German nation as a whole.[34]

This also prompted administrative innovations that American immigration control advocates quickly added to their arsenal of proposed control devices.[35] As early as 1879, the German imperial government imposed a passport requirement on persons coming from Russia and demanded that travelers present themselves to German representatives in that country to have this document visaed prior to departure. In the course of persistent attempts to control the flow from Poland, in 1908 all foreign workers were made to carry an identification card. During the depression of the 1890s, France mandated registration by all foreign residents wishing to pursue an income-generating occupation, and in 1906 Britain revived Napoleonic-era passport controls at entry to implement its new law.

In a world sharply divided between haves and have-nots, and at a time when population size was reckoned as a vital component of international power, the decreasing fertility of the haves came to be viewed as a dangerous form of "unilateral disarmament."[36] Rapid population expansion in the world at large was expected to produce a Malthusian crisis of subsistence, for which the only remedies would be armed conquest or migration, which in this perspective came to be seen as an insidious form of conquest. By 1900, there was an "almost neurotic awareness of this process," expressed most egregiously by way of warnings regarding "the yellow peril," a term popularized by Kaiser Wilhelm following the Boxer Revolt of 1900.[37]

The "dwarfing of Europe" attracted considerable attention in the United States, even though its population was still expanding, because it signaled a dramatic shift in the relative importance of white and colored populations at a time when "racial" differences were being essentialized. This pertained to intrawhite distinctions as well. For example, in an essay entitled "Immigration and Degradation," General Francis A. Walker, president of MIT, pointed out accurately that between 1790 and 1830 the country's population experienced spectacular growth "wholly out of the loins of our own people," but then went on to assert gratuitously that it was the onset of massive immigration around 1850 that depressed native reproduction: Americans "became increasingly unwilling to bring forth sons and daughters who should be obliged to compete in the market for labor and in the walks of life with those whom they did not recognize as of their own grade and condition."[38] A decade later, Charles Franklin Emerick, the author of "A Neglected Factor in Race Suicide" argued in a similar vein that immigration contributes to "degeneracy" by way of a proliferation of ethnic groups whose reluctance to intermarry reduced the white birthrate.[39]

Responses to the perceived challenge were shaped by an almost universal belief in the atavistic dispositions of various "races," shared by not only those who scorned the new immigrants but also many who emphasized their positive qualities.[40] Formalized into an academic subject in the early decades of the twentieth century as "national character" or "the psychology of peoples," it was a construct for dealing with the external world devised as far back as Herodotus but was given a more rational form in the Enlightenment and vastly elaborated in the late nineteenth century, when the steadily expanding domain of international interactions evoked the systematic cataloging of "others" by specialized intellectuals, and rising tensions prompted rulers to deploy unprecedented efforts to insure the loyalty of the masses by fostering the adoption of the national identity as an intimate part of their being.[41] Within this mode of thought, nations and related historical entities are constructed as collectivities verging on living organisms rather than mere social aggregates; in a Lamarkian mode, in the course of secular interactions with particular physical and social environments they develop distinctive "character" traits, which mold individual members of the group and somehow enter into their "blood," so that they will survive a change of environment or even of national membership. The differences of language, religion, social practices, dress, food, and physical appearance that distinguished the newcomers from the population of old American stock were exaggerated, drastically simplified, and elaborated into a hierarchical sociobiological construct that emphasized, within the white or Caucasian race, a profound race-like divide between the superior "Anglo-Saxons," "Nordics," or "Gothics" and the inferior remainder.[42] Challenging established boundaries of identity, the "new immigration" set off contentious debates over whether the newcomers could ever change enough to cross them, or whether the boundaries themselves should be relocated to accommodate the newcomers.[43]

The starting signal was given by the most public of the political economists, General Francis A. Walker. As superintendent of the tenth U.S. Census (1879–1881), Walker had turned the enumeration into "almost an encyclopedia of population, products, and resources," a feat that gained him international recognition as a statistician of the highest order.[44] Among other things, he elaborated the differentiation between U.S.- and foreign-born, which had been instituted in 1850 and reinforced in 1870 when the Census asked further whether father and mother were of foreign birth, by requesting their countries of origin.[45] Walker had strongly opposed Chinese exclusion, but later explained that in retrospect he "came heartily to rejoice" in it, "first, because it was a striking proclamation of the right and the duty of a nation to defend itself against what was believed to be a corrupting and degrading immigration, from whatever quarter; and, secondly, because that measure irrevocably committed the entire Democratic party . . . without whose consent a law restricting immigration might possibly be passed, but without whose support such a law could not possibly be maintained on the statute-book long enough to be of any use."[46] A contributing factor to his turnabout may have been the election of Hugh O'Brien, an Irish Catholic, as Democratic mayor of Boston in 1884. In 1887 he warned of the danger to American workers arising from the shift of European immigration to labor accustomed to a lower standard of living, and he proposed as a means for reducing this flow the imposition of $10 head tax, which would have increased the cost of transatlantic passage by half.[47]

The following year, in his prize-winning article, Edward Bemis adopted a more comprehensive approach, in keeping with a modern economist's conception of the national interest, with the rationalization of immigration so as to maximize the acquisition of human capital as his explicit objective.[48] Following an historical overview, he introduces a shocking statistic: thanks to the unprecedented magnitude of immigration, as of 1880, one half of the white population of the United States was of foreign birth or parentage. Relocation of "natives of foreign parentage" into the problematic category, made possible by the Census provisions noted, not only greatly magnified the national predicament but also tacitly negated the tradition whereby birth on the national territory signified unquestioned membership in the American community. Moreover, Bemis willfully exaggerated the size of the problem: as of 1890, even after an additional decade of immigration, residents of foreign birth or parentage still amounted to only one-third of the white population rather than half.

Echoing the popular views of Foran and Powderly, but casting them in a more measured academic tone, Bemis asserts, "In much of this immigration there is great good, but in another large portion there is equally great evil." First was the "moral evil," demonstrated by the overrepresentation of the foreign-born in insane asylums, poorhouses, and almshouses, and among those convicted of crimes. To this long-established litany, he adds a new element: it is the foreign-born "who indulge in most of the mob violence in time of strikes and industrial depressions." Drawing his examples throughout from southern Italians, Bohemians, and Hungarians, he then goes on to suggest that these troubles are specific to the new immigrants, a majority of whom are "illiterate and ignorant in the extreme," and arise from the overwhelmingly male composition of the flow—in the coded discourse of the times, they are Chinese-like sojourners. Deplorable enough in themselves, their moral inadequacies further occasion "political evil." Lacking adequate political socialization in republican institutions, and subject to manipulation "by the boodle and saloon element," the immigrants "stand in the way of needed improvements in legislation and administration, and by their votes keep our worst men in power." This is especially true of cities, where the proportion of foreign-born is much higher than in the country at large.

Conducting his analysis within the framework of the nascent welfare economics, Bemis asserts that because of their poverty and absence of skills, the newcomers "lower the standard of living and wages," increase unemployment, "and through this incalculable injury to our wage-earners depress their purchasing power, and consequently affect the prosperity of all other classes." He reckons that whereas individual firms find cheap labor profitable in the short run, "in the end it reacts on the employing class, since the consequent lower standard of life calls for fewer purchases of goods." This jeopardizes economic development: "Invention is thus repressed, for new machinery is only profitable where there is a large consumption." Thanks to the greater availability and cheapening of transport, even the poorest and least skilled can now come, precisely at a time when, according to the statistician Richmond Mayo-Smith, as the result of mechanization the United States no longer needs as much unskilled labor as before, and in any case can supply all of it by way of the natural increase of its now much larger population.

Concluding that "some far more effective restriction than the mere rejection of paupers and criminals" provided for in existing laws is needed, before proposing his alternative, Bemis systematically reviews arguments on behalf of open immigration and finds them wanting. To begin with, restriction is not "unchristian" because the effect of an overly heavy burden would be to lower "our national life, and consequently our power as a civilizing agency in the world." Moreover, America's readiness to take on all those uprooted in consequence of Europe's inequality and authoritarianism has the perverse effect of delaying reform of economic and political conditions in the countries of origin. Restriction is said also to constitute "a violation of a natural right to migration," but this is clearly not the case, "since until recently nearly all nations have controlled emigration and immigration" and the United States already restricts the Chinese, "which the supreme court does not pronounce unconstitutional." Although restriction does entail a change from "the political sentiment of our fathers that it is our mission to be a 'refuge to the oppressed of all nations,'" this is warranted by "totally changed conditions" since the days of Thomas Jefferson, notably the waning of public lands and economic evolution. Finally, the contention that restriction would inflict "an economic injury" on the nation is invalid because only a small portion of the incoming tide are bearers of significant human capital, and they are not to be excluded.

How is restriction to be effected? In the wake of the violent confrontations of 1886 in Chicago's Haymarket Square, some would exclude known anarchists, or others "who would refuse the oath of allegiance to our laws." However, not only would it be difficult to test incoming immigrants for their opinions, but also a preferable objective is to remove the conditions that make anarchy possible by educating the ignorant already here and preventing the landing of others. One way would be to raise the immigrant head tax from the 50 cents provided for by the law of 1882 to $50 or more, along the lines of what had been proposed by General Walker. However, such a measure is unlikely to be adopted because "The wage-earners of this country . . . would probably oppose it as a capitalistic and class test." Hence, he proposes an alternative: "Admit no single person over sixteen, and no man over that age who cannot read and write in his own language." Granting that this "is no sufficient test of one's fitness for good citizenship," he contends that the test would nevertheless effect an appropriate selection because the literate usually "demand and enjoy a somewhat higher standard of living." In a bold step toward remote control, he envisions having this administered before embarkation by consular staff or the steamship companies, and requiring its successful completion for the issuance of an immigration visa, so as to minimize the problems arising from rejections after landing. Should the test prove insufficient to keep out the ignorant, positive skill requirements might be imposed as well.

Although the literacy test's advocates characterized their position as a "middle course" between laissez-faire and more draconian prohibitions already in the air, notably "making race the test of fitness" for Europeans as for the Chinese, everyone concerned was well aware of its contribution to the achievement of this objective.[49] Bemis himself, while insisting that the nefarious economic consequences of unlimited immigration overshadow all others, and provide sufficient and urgent grounds for instituting a much more selective policy, nevertheless asks, "America has shown wonderful power of assimilation, but does it not look as if she were now receiving a heavier burden than she can wisely or even safely carry?" Granting that "the grandchildren of these people might make thrifty, intelligent citizens," he nevertheless suggests that in the intervening period, the country's standard of living will be reduced; and if so, "Does not the experiment of civilizing these thousands cost too dear if obtained at such a cost?" The test would not exclude many Swedes, Germans, English, or Scotch, or most of the Irish—now evidently on the right side of the identity boundary—"and we do not want to exclude them"; but "the Italian, Hungarian, and Polish emigration would fall off fully fifty per cent." A few years later, Noble suggests, "A race restriction, drawn so as to correct the ethnic changes in the new immigration, would have a good effect," but insists that "it is possible to obtain the effect by some less clumsy and offensive law than the indiscriminate exclusion of certain races as races,—a measure which no party manager could omit to oppose" because of the value of the foreign vote, which also precludes the use of such measures as the ability to speak English. Following Bemis, he goes on to demonstrate the effectiveness of the literacy requirement by calculating that it would exclude an estimated 75 percent of the Poles, Italians, and Hungarians, as against only 3 percent of the Irish, 2 percent of the English, and merely 0.1 percent of the Germans.

In support of his stance, Bemis invoked the work of another of the new social scientists, the statistician Richmond Mayo-Smith, who in the same year authored his own series of articles on "Control of Immigration" in the *Political Science Quarterly,* which were subsequently expanded into *Emigration and Immigration: A Study in Social Science,* which emerged as the progressive camp's authoritative work on restriction.[50] Formulating his arguments in the social Darwinist discourse that was emerging as the hegemonic framework of American social thought, Mayo-Smith thereby reveals its significance in the formation of the modern restrictionist outlook more generally.[51] Whereas for Bemis the problems posed by the new immigrants stem from deficiencies in human capital, for Mayo-Smith the unsuitability arises from their very being.[52] Competition is the sine qua non of civilization, but the wrong dose and the wrong kind are destructive; whereas in the past, the difficulties of international migration operated to insure a "natural selection" of the fittest, this is no longer the case because of the easing of conditions as well as the passing of the frontier. Unskilled immigrants are no longer needed, and reliance on them to cheapen the costs of labor is a clear instance of destructive competition that "makes commodities cheaper, not by increased industry and ingenuity, but by reducing the civilization of the community. Such a result is not only a wrong to our laboring class but is suicidal to ourselves." Venturing well beyond Bemis, Mayo-Smith warns, "The thing we have to fear most is the political danger of the infusion of so much alien blood into our social body that we shall lose the capacity and power of self-government, or that the elements of our national life shall become so heterogeneous that we shall cease to have the same political aspirations and ideals and thus be incapable of consistent political progress."

Tackling the "abstract right of immigration," he opposes the principle that a nation that has more land than it really needs has "a cosmopolitan duty to admit other persons to the soil if they desire to come," as enunciated by Sidgwick, a Spencerian version of obligation whereby "[t]he duty of every nation to humanity is to see that the higher civilization does triumph over the lower."[53] Moreover, "as a country progresses . . . [i]t no longer possesses the purifying power" of its pioneering days. The "struggle for existence" is now almost as severe in the United States as in Europe, and hence "[i]t is no kindness to these men to encourage or permit them to come." Because of the lag in information, the lower classes of Europe will not learn of the change of conditions and its consequences "for a great many years." Hence, in the intervening period, "If they are being led astray, we must interfere to prevent it." General Walker himself went on to elaborate his views in a more Spencerian vein as well, stressing the parallel between conservation and restriction as about-turns from traditional policy whose time has come.[54] Sticking to his guns, he rejects the literacy test as unwieldy and too easily falsified, as well as ineffective for keeping out "the anarchist, the criminal, the habitual drunkard," and advocates instead a $100 deposit—as against his earlier $10 tax—refundable upon the immigrant's departure within three years, or alternatively, for those wishing to remain in the country, presentation of evidence "that he is at the time a law-abiding and self-supporting citizen."

Explicitly racialist arguments on behalf of restriction were being elaborated as well. "The disorder which occurred at New Orleans in March, 1891, was like an alarm bell," John Hawks Noble reported a year later in the *Political Science Quarterly,* the organ of Columbia University's recently launched Academy of Political Science, "rousing every one to the danger of the possible growth of a large foreign class in this country, and since then the press has teemed with discussions of the social problem thus thrust into prominence."[55] The "disorder" was the lynching by the White League—a local organization akin to the Ku Klux Klan—of eleven immigrant Italian prisoners accused of conspiring to murder the city's Irish American police chief.[56] Six were about to be released after being found not guilty or by virtue of a mistrial, while five were still awaiting their day in court. Their swarthiness undoubtedly contributed to the crisis. Subsequently, a grand jury convened to weigh charges against eight survivors failed to return a single indictment, but concluded its work by calling for restrictions on immigration. By a twist of ideological legerdemain, the danger was made to arise from the victims rather than the perpetrators.

The same year, in an article on "Lynch Law and Unrestricted Immigration," Representative Henry Cabot Lodge characterized the actions of the New Orleans crowd as "not mere riot, but rather that revenge which Lord Bacon says is a kind of wild justice," but characterized the acquittals and mistrials as "a gross miscarriage of justice" since the Italians were undoubtedly active in the Mafia.[57] Although he begins by asserting that the inclination to criminal violence is not a particularity of certain "races" but arises "from the quality of certain classes of immigrants of all races," he then decisively shifts to "races" as the problem, citing a U.S. State Department report according to which "the immigration of those races which had thus far built up the United States, and which are related to each other either by blood or language or both," is declining, while that of "races totally alien to them" is increasing. The alien races are poorer and more ignorant than their predecessors, and also contain a high proportion of "birds of passage" who display no interest in becoming American. Hence, "Surely the time has come for an intelligent and effective restriction of immigration" to be achieved, first through inspection and certification by American consuls in the country of departure, and then by "some such fair and restrictive test as that of ability to read and write." Lodge observes in passing that the problem of low-quality immigration is by no means peculiar to the United States and has triggered calls for deterrent action in ancestral England as well.

Within the social sciences, the most explicit formulation of the racialist argument was elaborated by University of Wisconsin sociologist E. A. Ross, who alerted the country in popular articles as well as scholarly tomes to the "deterioration of popular intelligence" by reason of the changing racial stock. Others contributed as well: Frederick Jackson Turner viewed southern Italians and eastern European Jews as the very opposite of the frontier type he admired; K. Von Holst, founding chair of the History Department at the University of Chicago, argued in his revisionist *History of the American People* that the arrival of German and Irish Catholics in the 1840s created a legitimate issue for Know-Nothing agitation, and that the newest immigrants' socialist inclinations constituted a similar threat; John W. Burgess, founder of Columbia University's faculty and School of Political Science, imparted to his students—among them, Theodore Roosevelt—the notion that political forms were conditioned by ethnic factors, and asserted in 1906 that the changing composition of the American population would inevitably lead to a deterioration of the political régime.[58]

Not everyone was swept up by the restrictionist wave, and the nascent social sciences were not entirely one-sided. Even as racialist arguments moved to the fore, Columbia University anthropologist Franz Boas, himself a German Jewish immigrant, was undertaking their first systematic refutation.[59] The Washington-based statistician Roland P. Falkner pointed out as early as 1904 that many of his colleagues were basing their evaluations of the impact of immigration on sloppy statistical inferences, notably a comparison of present and past inflows that failed to take into consideration population growth as well as the high incidence of return migration, and wondered if it is not the case that "the doubts now expressed, whether the nation can successfully absorb the immigrants of to-day, will prove quite as unfounded as those which found expression some fifty years ago, when the first great influx of immigration occurred?"[60] Walker's theory of "population decline" was systematically refuted in 1912 by E. A. Goldenweiser, an official of the U.S. Bureau of the Census (which Walker had previously headed), who characterized it as "so overstrained and far-fetched as almost to appeal to one's sense of humor."[61] Tackling the widely held view that "recent immigrants, and above all illiterate immigrants, cling to the great cities," Walter F. Willcox pointed out that most of them arrive in cities, and that it takes them a while to disperse from these centers; as for the "swarming" proclivities of illiterates, the evidence provided by the Immigration Restriction League "is so slight as to require little analysis." What evidence there is indicates, in fact, that "illiteracy in any class of the population is more prevalent outside of cities than in them."[62]

In a most bizarre development, Richmond Mayo-Smith himself challenged the validity of the national integration component of the restrictionist ideology he helped to construct. His altered position was presented in a set of two 1894 *Political Science Quarterly* articles, which presented a rosy scenario whereby diverse immigrant elements "shall gradually be fused into one nationality, or one body—the American people." Both the physical and social environments constitute powerful assimilating forces, as demonstrated by the unchallenged paramountcy of the English language and of American political institutions, which will tame even the most dangerous.[63] In assessing the magnitude of the task, Mayo-Smith now moves the second generation into the "assimilator" camp because "they are not to be looked upon as wholly foreign, for they have been subjected to the influence of American life." His main policy prescription is therefore that school be conducted exclusively in English in order to reinforce the second generation's assimilationist role. What role he might have played as the policy debates on immigration and the literacy test heated up is impossible to establish, because he "suffered a nervous collapse" in 1901 following a boating accident, and died a few months later "as the result of a four-story fall."[64] However, his ambivalence outlived him, notably in a series of articles on assimilation by Sarah E. Simons that were published in the *American Journal of Sociology* in 1901–1902.[65]

Mobilization of the social scientists was intensified around 1908, when a congressional stalemate on immigration policy led to the creation of an Immigration Commission, which launched the most systematic gathering of information supportive of restriction to date; and this in turn prompted the preparation by the other side of an equally methodical critique of the Commission's evidence. Yet although the materials generated in the course of the protracted controversy constitute immensely valuable historical documents, the outcome was hardly a function of the validity of the information arrayed by the opposing camps. The American public, that is, readers of magazines, journals, and occasional books who also supplied most of the membership of civic associations, consisted overwhelmingly of middle classes rooted in the "old immigration," and hence were much more receptive to the arguments of the restrictionist social scientists, whose work systematized diffuse prejudices and provided concomitant responses, than to their critics, most of whom were excluded from the power networks, in many cases by reason of their Jewish origins.

"To Hell with Jews, Jesuits, and Steamships!"

With this outrageous outburst upon hearing that outgoing President William Taft had vetoed a general immigration law recodifying all previous legislation and providing for a literacy test, the Immigration Restriction League's Prescott Hall was paying a warped tribute to important elements of the coalition that successfully deterred the most egregious restrictionist projects for nearly a quarter of a century.[66] The hegemony of restrictionism within elite and mass opinion was not readily translated into policy because, as Daniel Tichenor has emphasized, legislative outcomes were a function of the votes each side could muster in congressional showdowns and the pressure they could exert on the executive.[67] The obstacles included electoral-minded party leaders, especially within the Democratic camp; business special interests; and emerging ethnic organizations concerned with the discriminatory impact of the literacy test on segments of the new immigration of special concern. The turning point that finally allowed for the restrictionist breakthrough was a shift in the position of the Democratic South on immigration, followed by cataclysmic changes in the international situation that radically heightened American nationalism.

Ironically, indirect evidence for the growing weight of nation-building considerations is provided by recent studies seeking to demonstrate the primacy of economic factors. For example, In her work on "the political economy of restriction," Claudia Goldin observes, "A large segment of rural America was against open immigration" at least by 1897, and goes on to suggest that this "probably has more to do with the history of nativist sentiment in America than with the particulars of immigration restriction of concern" to her study.[68] In the same vein, an econometric study of the political economy of immigration policy among the five principal New World receivers from the 1860s to the 1920s concludes that overall, "There is no compelling evidence that xenophobia or racism was at work in these economies, once underlying economic variables are given their due," but with regard to the American case, the authors are forced to qualify this conclusion out of existence and to conclude that Goldin "is not wrong when she attributes the passage of the literacy test to other (non-market) factors."[69] Yet another recent attempt to explain the sea change in policy by way of econometric models also finds that they "perform rather poorly."[70] As against this, positive evidence regarding the dominance of identity considerations is provided by a quantitative analysis of congressional voting to override President Woodrow Wilson's veto of the Literacy Act in 1915, which found that the lower the wage increase in the district in preceding years, the more likely the representative was to vote for closing immigration, but that the percentage of foreign-born in the district was an even more powerful determinant of a pro-immigration stance.[71] This pattern in fact probably emerged from the start, as suggested by Noble's 1892 comments—a subject to be elaborated shortly.

Following Henry Cabot Lodge's endorsement of the literacy test, a group of his Harvard classmates organized the Immigration Restriction League (IRL) to promote the measure among opinion leaders and the public at large.[72] Maintaining a "semi-conscious ambiguity" of their motivations in order to reach a wider audience, the IRL mostly emphasized immigration's negative economic impact.[73] However, the business community was hardly persuaded. On one aspect of economic analysis, Mayo-Smith turned out to be as wrong as could be: far from rendering unskilled labor obsolete, industrialization fostered a massive demand for it; and conversely, the availability of what was in effect an unlimited supply of such labor—welcomed by Andrew Carnegie as a "golden stream"—contributed to the development of a highly successful form of industrial production, founded on an acute form of labor segmentation.[74] However, there were some fluctuations and deviations from the business camp's overall immigrationist stance, attributable to short-term calculations arising from particular economic conjunctures and especially the belief shared by lesser fry that unlimited immigration gave an unfair competitive edge to large firms.[75] As leaders of middle-class society, many small businessmen also considered the new immigration primarily in a social perspective as a threat to the integrity of traditional American communities.

The steady flow of cheap, ethnically distinct, unskilled immigrant workers undermined labor's efforts to organize. The working class as a whole—consisting, around 1910, of some 40 percent of the national workforce employed in manufacturing, mining, construction, and transport—straddled the segmentation, but its skilled upper component consisted largely of natives or "old" immigrants, whereas the lower semiskilled and unskilled one was filled by newcomers. Although American workers were as militant as any in the world of industrial societies, their mobilization took place "within the middle class bias of the U.S. political system," a process manifested in the emergence of the American Federation of Labor (AFL), whose accommodation to existing political arrangements "developed from the politics of a split labor market, which displaced the politics of class during the industrializing period."[76] Recent research has confirmed contemporaneous reports of an overall increase of real wages in manufacturing in the pre–World War I decades, but not for lower-skilled workers. Not only did immigrants compete with natives (and previous immigrants) in unskilled jobs, but they also displaced urban natives in the Northeast and induced their westward migration in search of better opportunities.[77] Union membership—merely 4 percent of the nonagricultural workforce in 1896, and still only 9 percent in 1910—was drawn almost exclusively from the skilled component; although members of craft unions were in fact the least likely to suffer from the new immigration, they nevertheless generally came to regard it as a weapon wielded by the bosses for their undoing.[78]

Accordingly, in his belief that labor would oppose restriction on grounds of class solidarity, Bemis was as mistaken as Mayo-Smith was with regard to the decline of demand for unskilled workers. Hitherto concerned mainly with Chinese and contract labor, in 1896 Terence Powderly led the Knights of Labor to adopt the principle of qualitative restrictions more generally and endorsed a legislative proposal to limit the importation of French Canadian workers into New England manufacturing. Following his services in the Republican campaign, he was appointed commissioner general of immigration, the first in a long line of labor leaders to hold the position. The AFL endorsed the literacy test in 1897 by a vote of five to one; however, this hid from view the ambivalence of the rank and file, "torn between the desire not to deny to others the right which they or their families had enjoyed and an awareness of the growing danger to their jobs."[79] Overall, John Bodnar has suggested, "Skilled workers could overcome ethnic differences in the formation of narrow craft unions, but larger working-class unity with most unskilled newcomers proved impossible."[80]

After a somewhat passive interlude on the subject of European immigration during the subsequent period of economic expansion, the AFL resumed a more actively restrictive stance around 1905, following a considerable decline of membership induced by the business camp's aggressive anti-union campaign and the further growth of immigration. Himself a Jewish immigrant from Britain, AFL President Samuel Gompers advocated total exclusion of the Chinese and the selective restriction of Europeans who behaved like Chinese, who in his view constituted a steadily growing proportion of the incoming mass. The literacy test would serve this purpose, and from 1905 onward, the AFL voted resolutions in its support on no fewer than ten occasions, with much broader support from a craftsman membership that was turning into a privileged minority within the American industrial working class and increasingly feared radicalism as much as their employers.[81] Gompers adamantly held on to his stance within the National Civic Federation, the corporatist body launched by J. Pierpont Morgan and Mark Hanna at the turn of the twentieth century, despite attempts to sway him by featuring antirestrictionist luminaries such as Walter Willcox at Federation conferences.[82] As within the business camp, there were exceptional situations, notably among unions that came to terms with newcomers or that were dominated by them; moreover, ethnic solidarity with the targets of exclusion sometimes outweighed calculations regarding their detrimental effect on wages. In particular, the heavily Jewish Ladies Garment Workers, then the fifth largest AFL affiliate, remained on record as late as 1912 in opposing "any policy that would 'prevent the victims of political, religious, and economic oppression from finding a place of refuge in the United States.' "[83]

The world of labor was also swept up in "Atlantic crossings." The AFL's representative, Morris Hillquist, together with the Argentines, raised the issue of immigration at the Amsterdam congress of the Socialist International in 1904, but discussion was postponed to the Stuttgart congress four years hence.[84] Meanwhile, Karl Kautsky argued in *Die Neue Zeit* on behalf of uniform social legislation in sending and receiving countries as the preferred solution, while Otto Bauer pointed out in his work on the nationalities question that although immigration was organized by capitalists to put pressure on salaries, a distinction should be made between unfree workers, who benefited only capitalists, and free workers, who raised productivity and hence lowered prices, which benefited workers as well. With regard to the United States, the leadership suggested that the AFL exaggerated the danger posed by incoming Europeans, who were increasingly class conscious. At the Stuttgart congress, Hillquist acknowledged that free immigrants might be integrated into the labor movement, but insisted that races and nations incapable of assimilation be excluded, notably the Chinese and Japanese, along with strikebreakers. Endorsed by the South Africans, his resolution was amended to include a provision against discrimination; however, in the ensuing debate, Bauer insisted on total freedom of circulation for workers originating in modern industrial states. The matter was referred to a committee charged with drafting an immigration resolution for the next congress; but things did not look promising for the overseas immigration countries, which failed to gain representation in that body. It is no wonder that American labor shortly turned its back on internationalism altogether.

Party Politics

The significance of the foreign vote has to be understood within the framework of the "fourth electoral system" that emerged from the political "de-alignment" of 1893–1896. This constituted a revulsion against parties from which they emerged weaker and less stable; however, the electorate remained partisan, and another change in alignments occurred in the early 1930s.[85] The distribution of the popular vote between the parties at the national level had remained remarkably close after 1874, but each party now depended on a stable margin in different regions of the country, with close competition between them limited to the belt of populous states reaching from Connecticut to Indiana, excepting only Pennsylvania; upper New England and the West were safely Republican, whereas the Democrats were strong throughout the South. Thanks to their gains in the state legislatures, the Democrats won control of the Senate in 1893 for the first time in a generation. Although they were now poised for a breakthrough, this was thwarted by the severe shock of the 1893 depression that, by virtue of the country's much greater industrialization, occasioned unprecedented urban unemployment. The state and local elections of 1893 not only reversed the Democratic tide but also began a process of massive electoral transformation, extended and confirmed in 1894, when the Republicans won the congressional elections by a landslide.[86] The new 54th Congress contained 245 Republicans (+121, the largest gain ever) as against 204 Democrats (−118) and 7 Populists (−1); the reversal was most dramatic in the Midwest, which changed from 45 Democrats and 44 Republicans to 86 Republicans and 3 Democrats, and remained within the Republican camp for the next generation.

In short, the Democrats declined everywhere outside the South, while the

Republicans established their dominance in the most heavily industrialized and urbanized areas, including the Pacific states after 1900. Whereas in the late nineteenth century German and Irish ethnics constituted important sources of Democratic support, in the period 1900–1928 German association with the Democratic turnout was indeterminate in four out of fifteen elections, and otherwise significantly negative. The only ethnic group to resist Republican blandishments was the Irish Catholics, who thrived politically within the confines of their cities.[87]

The displacement of competitive situations by party dominance, together with more stringent voter registration laws that by the end of the nineteenth century required full citizenship in most states, fostered a sharp decline in electoral participation, particularly in the Republican-controlled regions.[88] Within the new configuration, the Democratic Party in the North maintained its traditionally positive stance toward immigrants. Initially, the Democratic South maintained an immigrationist stance as well in the hope of enlarging its white population; however, in 1907 the immigration bureaus established to recruit Europeans were held to violate the contract labor laws. Its interest in immigration thereby wiped out, the South provided especially fertile ground for the emerging intrawhite racism: "When in these years eminent philosophers and historians confused Darwinian biology with their own notions of 'racial' superiority, Southerners must have thought that at last the world had recognized their ante-bellum Anglo-Saxon defense of slavery."[89] On the Republican side, matters were more complex. Cultural conservatism and antiradicalism weighed in favor of limitation, as exemplified by Henry Cabot Lodge, and philanthropic overload did so for the reform-minded as well; but this was contradicted by the imperatives of class interest and electoral opportunism. Hence, it was difficult to muster a congressional majority on behalf of explicitly restrictive legislation. The coalitions assembled to that effect tended to be unstable and ran into difficulty at the presidential level, where party leaders engaged in a somewhat different calculus.

The Emergence of Ethnic Lobbies

The turn to restriction also prompted the formation of defensive lobbies among those targeted, notably the Jews. Europe's "new" anti-Semitism, which shifted from guilt for the killing of Christ to racial degeneracy and the infectious danger this posed for the social and political health of host nations, came into its own in the United States as well with the massive arrival of destitute

Jews from the confines of eastern Europe in the late 1880s.[90] Disturbed by their characterization as "orientals" incapable of assimilation, which suggested kinship to the Chinese, a prominent Jewish attorney alerted the readers of the *New York Times* as early as 1901 to the troubling possibility of a similar categoric exclusion.[91]

In keeping with the established pattern of philanthropic organization along sectarian lines, from the outset affluent Jews provided for the welfare of their own community. In response to the tightening of regulations, in the early 1890s, the associational leadership, mainly of German origin, promised to take care of impoverished newcomers in exchange for a liberal interpretation of antipauper provisions so as to allow them in. They also sought American intervention in Russia and Rumania to end the persecutions that induced massive emigration.[92] In 1898, in the wake of the organization of the IRL, New York financier Oscar Straus and others induced German, Irish, and Italian community leaders to join him in launching the Immigration Protective League (IPL), which proposed distribution of the new immigrants throughout the country as a way of reducing congestion and attendant problems on the East Coast. The policy was subsequently implemented by the Hebrew Agricultural and Industrial Aid Society (HIAS) with assistance from the Austria-based Baron de Hirsch Fund. Building on previous networks, in 1906 a group of prominent Jews founded the American Jewish Committee (AJC), initially designed to prevent infringement of civil and religious rights and to alleviate the consequences of persecution, but later mainly focused on immigration issues. Largely self-financed thanks to the affluence and generosity of its board, the AJC quickly emerged as a major player in the struggle against restriction because of the widespread belief that it spoke for and perhaps controlled Jewish immigrant voters. Shunning anything that might smack of "agitation," its leadership operated discreetly in the corridors of power. Concurrently, another group, connected with the Paris-based and Rothschild-sponsored *Alliance Israélite Universelle,* launched the National Liberal Immigration League (NLIL). Courting financial support from non-Jewish businessmen such as Andrew Carnegie by emphasizing the nation's need for labor, they obtained subsidies from shipping companies and broadened their leadership to include representatives of German and Irish ethnic organizations. The NLIL launched strikingly modern campaigns to mold public opinion by way of mass meetings and press propaganda, and engaged in congressional horse-trading through its unofficial agent, Boston's notorious James Michael Curley. Shunned by the AJC because its tactics were overly "conspicuous," the organization went out of existence in 1915 following its president's business bankruptcy as well as revelations by the AFL of the sources of its financing.[93]

The Catholic stance on immigration was more complex. Irish Catholics figured prominently in the struggle against restriction in their capacity as leaders of urban political machines, and as the core of the northern Democratic electorate.[94] The church hierarchy leaned in the same direction. James Cardinal Gibbons, archbishop of Baltimore and the country's leading Catholic prelate, had been concerned with immigration since 1888, when he organized a Southern Immigration Association to divert Catholics from northern cities to the South; responding to the AJC's approaches, he went on record against restriction in 1912 and again in 1915.[95] Archbishop John Ireland of New York also condemned the prejudicial attitude of old-stock Americans. However, the hierarchy's interventions in this domain were limited because Catholics from eastern and southern Europe, as well as Quebec, raised thorny problems of accommodation within their hitherto Irish- and German-dominant organization, making them wonder whether these flows "aided or damaged the church."[96] For example, in 1905, a group of parish priests wrote to President Roosevelt urging him to pursue restriction because "they found it impossible to keep in any relations with the church the mass of Catholic immigrants, especially the Italians."[97]

The Course of Policy

Writing in 1925, a leading immigration official[98] asserted that the years 1891–1893 constituted a turning point in the development of regulation.[99] A comprehensive federalization law, creating a new superintendent of immigration within the Treasury Department and providing for permanent inspection stations at the land and sea borders, was enacted in March 1891. Reacting to the successful use by the Chinese of the federal courts to challenge the administration of the exclusion laws, the measure also established that the decisions of immigration inspectors were not subject to judicial review and were final, except for appeals to the secretary of the treasury. Ironically, because the Chinese were handled under a separate régime, they retained the possibility of judicial review.[100] Although the bill reported out by the House's Committee on the Judiciary also provided for consular inspection of excludable categories abroad, this was later dropped.[101] Another "remote control" bill was passed by the Senate in July 1892, but no further progress was made until the next session.

The 1891 law also institutionalized more firmly one of the oldest traditional barriers, the exclusion of "paupers or persons likely to become a public charge," known in the trade as the "LPC clause."[102] This created a persistent Catch-22: applicants must demonstrate that they would not become a public charge, but could not do so by indicating that a job was waiting, as this would be evidence of a "contract," which was prohibited under the 1885 law. Unless they had independent means, they must provide "affidavits of sponsorship," notably a statement by American relatives of their willingness to support the immigrant for at least a year, together with evidence of their ability to do so. "Affidavits" subsequently turned into a vocable of awesome mystery in many European languages. The growing concern with immigration was reflected also in additional questions on the 1890 U.S. Census.[103]

Concurrently, objecting to the lax ways of New York's Board of Emigration commissioners, Washington assumed sole jurisdiction over the country's major port of entry and undertook to construct a new reception station off-shore. Initially an attempt was made to use Bedloe's (now Liberty) Island, but the great sculptor Frédéric-Auguste Bartholdi himself objected to the dese-cration of the Statue; Governor's Island was ruled out as well because of preemptive moves by other agencies, so the choice fell ultimately on Ellis Island. Construction of a sprawling wooden edifice began in 1890 and was completed in record time; in the intervening period, reception took place in the crowded old Battery Barge office. Following the 1892 opening of the new station, while first- and second-class cabin passengers were perfunctorily proc-essed aboard in New York Harbor, the steerage masses were transferred to makeshift barges, taken to Ellis Island for processing, and then herded into pens for transfer back to New York or beyond. The station inherited a corrupt administration, and conditions were exacerbated by the ferrying back to New York, where the newcomers were routinely preyed upon by swindlers.[104]

While the 1892 national Populist convention, meeting at Omaha with a strong southern contingent, added its voice to the fast-growing restrictionist camp, on the East Coast, the public was being frightened by news of an extensive epidemic of cholera in the Middle East and the confines of Europe, notably in Russia, the source of tens of thousands of Jewish immigrants landing in New York City, among whom typhus had already broken out earlier in the year.[105] Although by April the epidemic had been successfully con-tained, the precedent prompted the imposition of a strict twenty-day quar-antine over the entire port of New York. The following December, in his message to Congress, President Benjamin Harrison apologized to the Italian government for the New Orleans lynchings but also announced a continuation of the quarantine on immigrant vessels and the urgency of authority to prohibit immigration from "diseased countries." Senator William Eaton Chandler of New Hampshire, chairman of the Immigration Committee, proposed a one-year suspension of the entire flow, deemed by Secretary of State Thomas Bayard not to violate treaty obligations; however, this was dropped in favor of the president's more limited request. Signed on February 15, 1893, the law generated the Marine Hospital Service, which would later evolve into the U.S. Public Health Service.

Meanwhile, the literacy test was facing greater difficulties than its initiators anticipated. In the fall of 1892, Lodge secured the addition of illiterates as an excluded class to a bill designed to facilitate the enforcement of the existing immigration and contract labor laws as well as to make transportation companies liable for the return of excludables. Although his amendment was dropped from the final version, which was signed into law on March 3, 1893, two decades later Isaac Hourwich asserted, "Freedom of immigration was rejected as a general principle of American law by the act of 1893, which established the present inquisitorial procedure for the admission of immigrants."[106] The National Board of Trade subsequently considered Lodge's proposal, but stopped short of recommending its adoption, despite the onset of the most acute depression to date. Remote control was running into problems as well. A bill providing for the inspection of immigrants by U.S. consuls was passed by the House in July 1894 but struck out by the Senate following Secretary of State Walter Gresham's opinion that U.S. consular offices abroad would not be able to discharge the duties placed on them, even with a tenfold increase of staff; instead, it substituted a bill to exclude anarchists.[107]

Concurrently, the U.S. Supreme Court elaborated what Peter Schuck has termed "the classical conception of immigration law," which reinforced the juridical foundations of controls on admission. Reasserting the principle it enunciated as far back as 1837, but now with the federal government in mind rather than the states, the court proclaimed in 1892, "It is an accepted maxim of international law, that every sovereign nation has the power, as inherent in sovereignty, and essential to self-preservation, to forbid the entrance of foreigners within its dominions, or to admit them only in such cases and upon such conditions as it may see fit to prescribe."[108] In another decision in the same vein a year later, "Due process in deportation was smashed on the rock of judicial decision . . . never to be put together again" when the Court stated that deportation did not constitute punishment but was merely an administrative device for returning unwelcome and undesirable aliens to their own countries.[109]

Lodge pursued his crusade on behalf of the literacy test in the Senate, to which he was elected in 1894. Speaking on behalf of a bill designed by the IRL, reported out on February 18, 1896, he made clear that the issue was identity rather than economics. Emphasizing the "racial" differences between the old and the new immigration, he assured his colleagues, "This measure, if adopted, will exclude a large portion of the present immigration, and with few exceptions will tell exclusively on the most undesirable portions of immigration alone."[110] The senator went on to invoke the French sociologist Gustave LeBon's warning against imprudent racial mixtures: because of limits on any race's capacity for assimilating and elevating an inferior one, the lower race will prevail if it is too large. Rejecting consular inspection as difficult to implement and objectionable to foreign governments, he defended the test on practical grounds as the most effective device under existing circumstances. The supporting documentation provided, among other things, governors' replies to inquiries by the IRL indicating little demand for immigrants of any kind and a definite preference for northern Europeans, as well as caustic assessments of the new immigration by the relevant American consuls. Discussion of the bill was not yet concluded when the House approved overwhelmingly (195–26) its own version of the test, which exempted female illiterates "in view of the conceded scarcity of female white servants in nearly all parts of the country."[111]

The lopsided vote indicated that agrarian Democrats were now as sympathetic to restriction as their Republican counterparts. This reflected an alignment in the making, cutting across the two parties, of a pro-restriction economic "periphery" versus the country's dynamic "core," which included the industrial areas where most of the new immigrants lived and worked.[112] However, reflecting the new political realities, some of the Republican senators urged postponement of further action until after the fall 1896 elections because the measure might antagonize their immigrant constituents. Ohio Governor William McKinley and his manager Marcus Hanna "embarked on a pragmatic course toward a coalition of business and labor in the nation's major cities, where most of the votes lay."[113] Rejecting Lodge's demand for a gold plank in the party platform on behalf of eastern banking interests, they yielded to him on the test, but simultaneously waged an unprecedented campaign for the immigrant vote by distributing pamphlets in a variety of foreign languages.

Following McKinley's presidential victory, the Senate quickly enacted its own version of the test, again overwhelmingly (52–10, 27 not voting). As hammered out by the final conference committee, evidence of literacy was required of all physically capable persons over sixteen years of age, with a number of exemptions, including wives, elderly parents, and minor children of qualified immigrants. A remarkable feature was the test's design as a virtual *rite de passage* into a new American identity, achieved by imposing the Constitution as its text.[114] The requirement that it be administered in English "or the language of their native or resident country," which was understood as referring to official national tongues, was changed to English "or some other language," in response to the efforts of Jewish organizations to secure the inclusion of Yiddish and Hebrew. The nature of their efforts suggests that they were now prepared to live with the test. The bill again provided for a rudimentary form of remote control, in that those who failed the test were to be sent back at the expense of the steamship or railroad company, which would have the likely effect of prompting them to impose a first run through the test as a prerequisite for embarkation. In a somewhat different vein, the law also prohibited the use of foreign migrant labor, with the debates making it clear that the target was French Canadians, in accordance with the long-standing wishes of organized labor.

The final conference report was approved by a strong majority in the House (217–36, 125 not voting), but a narrow one in the Senate (34–31, 25 not voting); the reason for the remarkable 21-vote shift to the "nay" side in the Senate, which included Lodge, was the prohibition on foreign migrant labor, which would have hurt the interests of New England industry.[115] The outcome boded poorly for overriding outgoing Democratic President Grover Cleveland's likely veto, which was indeed issued on March 2, 1897. In his veto message, the president rejected economic arguments on behalf of restriction but granted that it was warranted on political grounds, because of the "necessity of protecting our population against degeneration and saving our national peace and quiet from imported turbulence and disorder." However, he dismissed the test as an unsuitable device that might well be counterproductive: "[I]t is infinitely more safe to admit a hundred thousand immigrants who, though unable to read and write, seek among us only a home and opportunity to work, than to admit one of those unruly agitators and enemies of governmental control, who can not only read and write, but delights in arousing by inflammatory speech the illiterate and peacefully inclined to discontent and tumult."[116] That in effect disposed of the test through the next two congresses.[117]

In the intervening period, the Ellis Island station burned down right after expansion had been completed, destroying all records from 1855 to 1897 and returning the processing once again to the old Battery Barge office. Arising from the ashes was the first important government edifice to be designed by private architects on a competitive basis. Characterized by the *Architectural Record* as an "admirable" state-of-the art achievement, from another perspective it constituted a veritable Foucaultian panopticon, where immigrants were subjected to unprecedented moral and physical scrutiny.[118] Designed to accommodate up to 5,000 arrivals a day, the reception hall was fully electrified and sported interior plumbing with hot water, capable of subjecting the newcomers to 8,000 showers. Auxiliary structures were largely completed in 1901, and a steel and glass canopy was added two years later for the waiting lines outside. Construction of a large hospital for contagious diseases began on another part of the t island in 1904 and was completed in 1906; the structure was further expanded in 1908. Sleeping barracks accommodating up to 1,800, albeit under extremely crowded conditions, were built as well.[119]

The prospects for further restrictionist measures improved when Lodge's friend Theodore Roosevelt became president in September 1901, following the assassination of McKinley by Leon Czolgosz, a native-born self-styled "anarchist" of central European origin. Roosevelt espoused a more intense form of nationalism, expressed by way of fervor for the West and western life, a fashionable cultural trend that "proved extremely fruitful to Americans searching for both an identity that excluded the ever-rising tide of culturally alien immigrants, and at the same time, an Anglo-Saxon theatre in which Americans were the principal actors."[120] In his first annual message of December 3, 1901, "T. R." recommended a comprehensive law providing for the more effective exclusion of anarchists by way of "a more thorough system of inspection abroad and a more rigid system of examination at our immigration ports, the former being especially necessary." Stepping boldly toward selection on the basis of human capital, he also called for an educational test and the exclusion of persons below a certain degree of economic fitness. However, two days later Congress received the Industrial Commission's recommendations, which included an increase in the head tax and tighter health controls, but omitted the literacy test. The House bill implementing the Commission's proposals was amended to add it, but this was subsequently struck out in conference.

The Act of March 3, 1903, signed amidst preparations to affix a bronze plaque bearing the poem by Emma Lazarus to the Statue of Liberty's pedestal, codified immigration acts from 1875 onward, tightened existing regulations, doubled the head tax to $2.00, and imparted to immigration laws and regulations an exceptional status that deprived aliens of the due process protection hitherto provided by the Fourteenth Amendment to all "persons" (rather than "citizens"). It also required medical examinations abroad before embarkment, the first operationalization of remote control on the Atlantic side; although its constitutionality was immediately challenged by the shipping companies, the provision was sustained by the courts in 1909.[121] It also took a step toward the racialization of restriction by requiring ships to record in their manifest their passengers' origins according to a roster of "races and peoples" constructed by Victor Safford, surgeon general of the U.S. Marine Hospital on Ellis Island.[122] The inclusion of "Hebrew" as a category immediately evoked protests from the Jewish organizations, which insisted that "Jew" did not signify membership in a race or nationality, but a religious affiliation, and hence that its inclusion was unconstitutional. However, the measure failed to impose an educational test or the economic qualifications called for by the president.

Albeit perennially on the agenda, the literacy test did not make it through the Republican-dominated Congress during the remainder of Roosevelt's presidency. The return of prosperity made business once again hungry for labor; the National Board of Trade explicitly opposed the literacy test, while the National Association of Manufacturers (NAM) organized its own pro-immigration lobby, which not only opposed the test but also sought the relaxation of existing regulations; and California's farmers clamored for a suspension of Chinese exclusion as well as began to import Mexicans. Moreover, until the end of 1904, Roosevelt was reluctant to move in this sphere lest the likely resentment of immigrant and second-generation voters jeopardize his bid for reelection.[123] However, in the intervening period, the Supreme Court generally upheld broad federal authority over immigration, and, as Rogers Smith has pointed out, this stance "became more pronounced, not less, after some progressive Republicans joined the bench," notably Oliver Wendell Holmes.[124]

After immigration passed the million mark in 1905 and again the following year, the odd alliance of patricians and labor launched yet another attempt to enact the literacy test, which was incorporated into a Senate bill authored by Vermont U.S. Senator Charles Dillingham, approved in May 1906, and subsequently reported out favorably by the House committee. Once again, however, political considerations pulled the other way. Albeit reported to favor the measure at heart, Roosevelt refrained from doing so openly in the face of the forthcoming midterm elections and especially William Randolph Hearst's bid for the governorship of New York on the Democratic ticket. To secure the critical Jewish vote in New York City on behalf of the Republican candidate, Charles Evans Hughes, the president announced the appointment of Oscar Straus, president of the recently founded AJC, as the country's first Jewish cabinet member and dispatched him to corral votes on the Lower East Side.[125] As secretary of commerce and labor, Straus was also in a position to overrule unwelcome decisions by Immigration Commissioner Powderly.

Operating behind the scenes, the AJC mounted an intensive campaign against the pending Dillingham bill.[126] Fortunately, the Jewish cause coincided with the views of House Speaker Joe Cannon, who opposed the literacy test partly because of his hostility to organized labor, but also for fear of jeopardizing party support among naturalized voters.[127] In the end, Cannon engineered a compromise whereby Congress established a comprehensive Immigration Commission, doubled the head tax again to $4.00, and took a further step toward the nationalization of boundaries by instituting a federal Division of Naturalization with exclusive jurisdiction over the process.[128] Although immigration dropped from nearly 1.3 million in 1907, the historical record for the twentieth century, to less than 800,000 the following year, it is impossible to ascertain to what extent this was attributable to the tax and the accumulation of restrictive measures as against the onset of a recession.

The 1907 law also took another step toward remote control by authorizing the president "to call, in his discretion, an international conference . . . or to send special commissioners to any foreign country, for the purpose of regulating by international agreement, subject to the advice and consent of the Senate of the United States, the immigration of aliens to the United States," and "of providing for the mental, moral, and physical examination of such aliens by American consuls or other officers of the United States government at the port of embarkation." The latter provision was singled out for noteworthiness by political scientist Paul Peirce, who, three years later, commented in the *American Political Science Review* that "the mere enactment of this provision is prophetic of a time when our national measures for the regulation of immigration shall be far more generously supplemented by international cooperation" and that "the ultimate solution of the problem of immigration is not to be found in measures purely and strictly national." Anticipating the "root causes" debate that swept the international community in the final years of the twentieth century, he suggested that only by way of action at the international level is there hope to achieve "some amelioration of the conditions and some relief from the oppressions which have driven people from their native lands, and so some modification of the very causes of immigration."[129]

The "most far-reaching" instance of international cooperation to date, in his view, was the "amicable settlement of the question of Japanese immigration." Following a decision by the San Francisco School Board in October 1906 to exclude Japanese children from white schools, in the face of protests by the Japanese government the Roosevelt administration sought in vain to persuade the local authorities to relent. It then negotiated a "Gentleman's Agreement" whereby Japan agreed to restrict the movement of its nationals to the American mainland in exchange for a commitment by the United States not to enact a Chinese-style exclusion. However, agitation against the Japanese persisted; the white unions blocked their access to manufacturing, and their movement into specialized agriculture led to the enactment of the Alien Land Laws of 1913 and 1920, which severely restricted the possibility of buying land.[130]

The racialization of policy advanced further as well by way of a proposal from Senator Chester I. Long, head of the Senate Committee on the Census, to include European "races" in the 1910 enumeration.[131] In response, census officials engaged in a variety of experiments, including a classification of the 1790 population according to country of origin by way of surnames, and eventually decided to use the roster of "races and peoples" developed by Victor Safford for immigration purposes. Fiercely opposed once again by the Jewish organizations, the proposal was stricken out in conference thanks to the efforts of Colorado's U.S. Senator Simon Guggenheim, as well as New York Representatives Adolph Sabbath and Henry Goldfogle; instead, the U.S. Census was mandated to record "mother tongue," which those concerned with national integration believed would provide the appropriate information and was acceptable to the Jewish spokesmen. However, the Immigration Committee won the return match later in the year. Despite Senator Guggenheim's insistence that "the Jews are not a race. . . . [T]hey belong to the country from which they came just as much as other people who have come," and testimony to the effect that "the tabulating of the Jews as such . . . is strengthening the hands of the people who have oppressed them," they continued to be recorded as Jews for immigration purposes. Defending the classification, Senator Lodge took the opportunity to state that the omission of race from the Census "was a great mistake. It makes the returns almost valueless." It is noteworthy that the German Jewish elite's stance evoked protest from Zionists, who insisted that Jews are a "people" legitimately aspiring to nationhood.

The Consolidation of Restrictionism

Chaired by Senator Dillingham, the Immigration Commission was composed almost entirely of restrictionist-minded members of Congress, Republicans or southern Democrats, and prestigious public intellectuals of progressive stamp but on record as favoring restriction, including Cornell Professor Jeremiah W. Jenks, the outgoing president of the American Economic Association; and Charles P. Neill, a past professor of political economy at Notre-Dame and Catholic University, who currently served as the U.S. commissioner of labor.[132] With the aid of an extensive staff of statisticians, economists, and special agents, the Commission mobilized the country's foremost social scientists and political thinkers, mostly advocates of restriction but also some opponents, notably Franz Boas, who produced a study of body changes among immigrants indicating their successful assimilation.

The Commission's recommendations were grounded in a set of explicitly enunciated principles that straddled and linked the two perennial axes of American concern. Its findings, gathered into a comprehensive quantitative and qualitative survey of the nature, causes, and consequences of immigration as a forty-two-volume report, consolidated a vast store of hitherto unavailable facts and provided an authoritative analysis of these data that allowed of no other conclusion than that, however much ongoing flows might be contributing to the American economy, they severely challenged the country's absorptive capacity and entailed unacceptable social and political costs.[133] Hence, immigration must be limited.

Although the Commission has been deservedly demonized for its egregious stereotypes regarding nationality and race and its firm commitment to Asian exclusion, by early twenty-first-century standards its outlook would be located on the relatively "liberal" side of the immigration policy spectrum.[134] Rehearsing themes of the previous two decades, it envisioned immigration in a progressive perspective, as a social factor subject to manipulation and control by way of public policy in order to achieve "rational healthy development." Its executive summary begins with the balanced assertion that "[w]hile the American people, as in the past, welcome the oppressed of other lands, care should be taken that immigration be such both in quality and quantity as not to make too difficult the process of assimilation." Inaugurating the protracted debate over "refugees," the more extensive text insists that most of the current newcomers from Europe are not "oppressed" and explains that "emigration from Europe is not now an absolute economic necessity, and as a rule those who emigrate to the U.S. are impelled by a desire for betterment rather than by the necessity of escaping intolerable conditions. This fact should largely modify the natural incentive to treat the immigration movement from the standpoint of sentiment and permit its consideration primarily as an economic problem."[135]

Aside from the matter of the physically and morally unfit, immigration policy should therefore be based on the primacy of "economic' or business considerations touching the prosperity and economic well-being of our people." But in keeping with progressive doctrines, sheer growth is not enough; the objective must be "rational, healthy development," measured by the extent to which "there is a corresponding economic opportunity afforded to the citizen dependent upon employment for his material, mental, and moral development." Further, the Commission vigorously rejects economic growth brought about "by means which lower the standard of living of the wage earners," and insists that "[a] slow expansion of industry which would permit the adaptation and assimilation of the incoming labor supply is preferable to a very rapid industrial expansion which results in the immigration of laborers of low standards and efficiency, who imperil the American standard of wages and conditions of employment." Claiming that its investigations have uncovered an "oversupply of unskilled labor" throughout the country, which hampers industrial progress, in keeping with the theories set forth by Bemis and Mayo-Smith, the Commission urges that the further admission of such labor be restricted.

The problems resulting from the massive reliance on unskilled foreigners not only are economic but also pertain to national integration, because the population that is most suitable as hands is unfit for membership in the political community. Priority should therefore be given to the elimination of people who come "with no intention to become American citizens, or even to maintain a permanent residence here," and also "those who, by reason of their personal qualities or habits, would least readily be assimilated or would make the least desirable citizens." Once again, there are to be no "coolies" from Europe. Hence, in addition to the continuation of Chinese exclusion as well as of the "Gentlemen's Agreement" pertaining to Japan and its Korean dependency, the Commission urges a similar understanding with the British government to bar south Asians and a selective reduction of the European flow.

In order to achieve this, the commissioners list a variety of possible methods, including two innovative measures: a "limitation of the number of each race arriving each year to a certain percentage of the average of that race arriving during a given period of years," and an annual cap on arrivals in each port of entry. However, while suggesting that all these methods would be somewhat effective, the commissioners overwhelmingly favor the literacy test "as the most feasible single method of restricting undesirable immigration," with New York Representative William S. Bennett as the lone dissenter.

The Commission's work was broadcast to the general public in a book-length version coauthored by Commissioner Jeremiah Jenks and Professor William J. Lauck, a senior staff member, which went into six editions over the next fifteen years. Originally a hefty work of 496 pages, it was subsequently revised and enlarged under the editorship of Rufus Smith, reaching 717 pages by 1926.[136] An early review by Emily Greene Balch of Wellesley College in the *Political Science Quarterly* provides a good indicator of how the Commission's findings were perceived by progressives at the time and confirms its far from extremist character: "The pivotal point of the whole study is perhaps the conclusion that the chief ground for concern in regard to our immigration is not its political results, not any menace of crime, pauperism or disease, but its industrial reactions."[137] The authors' main theme, she points out, is that whereas in the past immigration made possible America's remarkable economic expansion, "the point of complete saturation has already been reached in the employment of recent immigrants in mining and manufacturing establishments."[138] Balch goes on, "[T]he next most striking point of the vast investigation under review is the proof of the ubiquitousness and at the same time of the segregation of the foreign-born." What she significantly terms "The native American attitude of ignorance and indifference" extends, according to the authors, "even to the native churches, and very few agencies have been established for the Americanization and assimilation of southern and eastern European wage-earners." Therefore, she concludes, "Together with a 'domestic immigration policy,' to borrow Miss [Frances] Kellor's phrase . . . our authors desire certain changes in our immigration laws." In keeping with the Commission, "they favor some measure of restriction, of a sort to protect native labor. They are uncertain, however, what form such restriction should take." Albeit silent on the proposals they do discuss, which were in fact those considered by the Commission, Balch observes that they fail to include a "very interesting one"—presumably one she herself favors—"to use a minimum wage-requirement as a sieve for immigrants," and adds, "The crux is to find a practicable form for such a policy."

She also suggests as "worth considering on the other side" a recent article by Isaac Hourwich in the *Political Science Quarterly* reporting the preliminary result of a critique of the Commission's findings and recommendations.[139] The statistician's study had been commissioned by the AJC in an attempt to minimize the Commission's impact on the course of policy. Astutely using the Commission's own data whenever possible, he systematically refuted the "popular delusion" that immigration displaces American workers by demonstrating that "[i]n the long run . . . supply and demand approximately balance each other," and concluded with a remarkably perspicacious insight into the global nature of economic processes, which might have been written by a contemporary free-marketeer. Even the complete exclusion of all immigration would fail to assure steady work to all the unemployed because of the vast labor reserves available to American capital, notably both white and "colored" farm laborers, and the untapped potential of labor-saving machinery. Moreover,

> it must be remembered that capital is international; production has advanced by such rapid strides in the United States because capital has had a sufficient supply of labor. . . . If . . . an artificial scarcity of labor were created . . . resulting in a rise of wages that could cut down the profits below the average of other countries, more American capital would seek investment abroad. The pace of American industry would slow up, and American capital would find new fields in the industrial development of foreign countries with cheap labor. American goods produced by better paid American labor could not compete in the world's markets with the products of Mexican or Siberian labor directed by American capital. This competition would eventually throw out of employment a certain number of American workmen, restoring the normal ratio between the active and the reserve labor forces, which is essential to our industrial system. This outcome could not be prevented by obstructing the movement of workers from one country to another.

In any case, the Immigration Commission's recommendation of the "illiteracy test" is unlikely to have any significant effect on the American labor supply. Making allowance for the likely exemption of females, it would bar no more than about 130,000 common laborers annually, and this loss would be more than offset by a likely reduction of the ongoing rate of return.

Dismissed by economists of the restrictionist camp as methodologically flawed, the Hourwich study nevertheless provided solid ammunition for defenders of the status quo.[140] Ultimately, however, the course of policy was not shaped primarily by economic considerations because, contrary to Hourwich's assertion that "the race question" was "not involved in the restriction of immigration from European countries," within the legislative arena it loomed increasingly large.

Speaker Joe Cannon was shorn of his powers in 1910 by a coalition of Democrats and insurgent Republicans, and the test now returned to the legislative agenda by way of the very body he had created as a dilatory maneuver. The AJC sought to avoid the transfer of immigration from the Department of Commerce to the newly created Department of Labor, which would establish the primacy of organized labor's perspective and, in a shift from past policy, endorsed mass protest meetings to that effect. Other targeted groups joined in as well, but Cyrus Adler observed that "the Catholic Church was practically not represented in any way."[141] In the meantime, Commissioner of Immigration William Williams sought to restrict the ongoing flow in the spirit of the Commission's recommendations by tightening the enforcement of existing regulations.[142] Recorded entries from Europe fell from 926,291 in 1910 to 764,757 the following year and 718,875 in 1911, but then climbed back to over a million.

Attuned to the mounting weight of the new immigrants in the electorate, in the 1912 presidential campaign, complicated by the split between Republicans and Progressives, all three candidates opposed the test. Nevertheless, after the election of Woodrow Wilson, Congress completed action on a general immigration bill sponsored by Senator Dillingham that recodified all previous legislation and limited admission to those able to read (but not necessarily write) "some language." Replacing "national language" to allow for the inclusion of Yiddish and Hebrew, the wording reflected the successful intervention of the Jewish organizations, which also managed to eliminate the requirement that immigrants produce a certificate of good character, which would have been difficult for Jews to obtain from tsarist authorities. Outgoing President Taft vetoed the bill, as he had pledged to do, prompting Prescott Hall's colorful outburst used as the title of this section. As justification for his action, the president submitted a letter from Secretary of Commerce and Labor Charles Nagel, whose objections largely reflected the concerns of the Jewish organizations over the increasingly explicit targeting of eastern European Jews among the unskilled nationalities to be excluded.[143]

The Senate voted to override the veto, but the House failed to do so by a narrow margin of 5 votes. The restrictionist camp had a solid majority in both parties but, reflecting the southern shift, was now particularly strong among the Democrats (139–57 to override, as against 70–56 on the Republican side). After the Democrats gained control of both branches of government in 1913, under new southern leadership the immigration committees imparted a more explicitly racist twist to their proposals, as indicated by efforts that attempted to impose an absolute prohibition on "members of the African or black race" but failed of passage; they also reenacted the literacy test, now refusing to exempt victims of religious persecution, undoubtedly with Russian Jews and Armenians in mind. The lineup in the House was 179–52, but with the South voting 68–5; in the Senate it was 72–18, with only 2 Southerners on the negative side.

Woodrow Wilson's own position was ambiguous. He had written disparagingly of the new immigrants in his *History of the American People* (1902), dubbing them even less desirable than the excluded Chinese coolies, but in the course of his ascent bowed to political necessity, and either rationalized or perhaps came to believe that in merging their national characters, the country's disparate groups might "blend away into a solid blankness, the same way that all colors, when mixed together, produce white."[144] While trying to dissuade nativists such as the Daughters of the American Revolution and refraining from endorsing the literacy test, he waged a campaign against "hyphenism," directed not only against those who denied full Americanness to some immigrant groups, but also against immigrants who sought to retain a measure of distinctiveness. Although he refused to sign the literacy bill on the grounds that it violated the tradition of political asylum and the principle of equality of opportunity by excluding those to whom elementary education has been denied, his peroration reflected his ambivalence. Granting that if Americans wish to reverse the country's traditional immigration policy, "it is their right to do so" and he would not stand in their way, but they have not done so yet: "I am willing to abide by the verdict, but not until it has been rendered." Wilson's next words could be taken as an invitation as much as a challenge: "Let the platforms of parties speak out upon this policy and the people pronounce their wish. The matter is too fundamental to be settled otherwise." The Senate again easily overrode the veto, and the House failed to do so by only 4 votes.

Meanwhile, the idea of national origin quotas was making its way. In June 1913 Senator Dillingham brought it into the legislative arena as an alternative to the literacy test, proposing to restrict immigration to 10 percent of the foreign-born from each country given in the most recent Census, but allowing a minimum of 5,000 to come from any land. Proportional restriction "which shall apply impartially to all races" was further promoted in 1914 by a missionary critical of the humiliating one-sided "Gentlemen's Agreement" imposed on Japan, as a way of overcoming the discriminatory exclusion of Asians.[145]

War and Security

The outbreak of World War I in 1914 stimulated a huge demand for American agricultural and industrial products in Europe, while at the same time depriving the United States of a major source of labor. Following the erection of barriers to the emigration of strategically valuable manpower and the assignment of European vessels to military tasks, arrivals from Europe dwindled from 1,058,391 in 1914 to a mere 197,919 the following year.

The expansion of the European war into a world conflict dramatically altered the concerns of the various actors, as well as their strategies and resources. The sinking of the *Lusitania* in May 1915, and revelations of spying and sabotage by the Central Powers (that is, the German and Austro-Hungarian Empires and their allies), brought the war closer to home and affirmed Wilson's pro-British inclinations. However, immigrant sympathies were often at odds with the presidential stance, exacerbating concern over the consequences of diversity for the national community. Germans tended to side with the Fatherland; Jews who originated in Austria-Hungary offered prayers for their beloved Emperor Franz-Josef, who was an enemy, whereas those who came from pogrom-ridden Russia cursed the tsar, who was a friend; the Irish hardly cheered for the British side; and the Italians, reflecting their country of origin's initial neutrality, were wary of engagement altogether.[146] The response was "Americanism," which called for action against not only persons of German and Austro-Hungarian origin but also "hyphenated Americans" more generally.[147] The security frenzy also induced a noticeable increase in mob violence against immigrants and minorities, including Jews, marked by the notorious lynching of Leo Frank in Atlanta in August, 1917.[148]

Despite altered conditions, congressional restrictionists adamantly pursued their objectives in anticipation of vastly increased immigration after peace returned. Accordingly, in early 1916 the House overwhelmingly approved a new bill incorporating a version of the literacy test similar to the one vetoed the previous year, but with an exemption for those fleeing from religious persecution, as advocated by the Jewish organizations.

The extent to which the idea of limited immigration had by this time become hegemonic is revealed by an editorial in the *New Republic,* the paragon organ of American liberalism.[149] Leading with the resigned observation that

"Freedom of migration from one country to another appears to be one of the elements in nineteenth-century liberalism that is fated to disappear," it goes on to rehearse the grounds for the change by setting forth the deleterious economic and political consequences of "excessive" immigration for an industrial democracy with an incipient welfare state.[150] Accordingly, the literacy test is to be rejected not because it is wrong to limit immigration, but because it would not effect an appropriate selection. Granting its effectiveness in deterring the "huge influx of aliens fleeing from the poverty that will oppress Europe" in the wake of the current conflict "and the wars of revenge that may follow," the editors insist that "it does not follow that it will achieve the ends which alone can justify a restrictive policy." Rebutting the contentions of the test's advocates, they assert that "the illiteracy of the minor Slavic races offers not the slightest proof of congenital inferiority"; and as for assimilability, they observe ironically that it is in fact "the English, Germans and French, not the Slovaks, Ruthenians and Lithuanians, who remain attached to their home land into the third generation." The key issue is the effect of immigration on American labor: "We ought to regulate immigration with respect to conditions of employment, not by crude and illusory tests applied mechanically at the ports of entry." Seizing the opportunity to promote their broader doctrine, the editors go on to point out that this "implies that we ought to have a national labor policy, of which our immigration policy would be merely a part." In this perspective, the chief defect of the literacy test is that it cannot be used to adjust the flow to the changing conjuncture.

However, neither the *New Republic* nor other opponents proposed a realistic alternative. As it was, the Senate approved its own version of the test in December 1916 by an overwhelming majority of 64–7, with 25 abstaining. Senator Dillingham had reintroduced his bill on behalf of a nationalities quota, but indicated that he would go along with the literacy device as being more feasible. Bowing to the inevitable, the Jewish organizations again intervened to limit the damage: the requirement was limited to reading only in English or, now very explicitly, "some other language or dialect, including Hebrew and Yiddish." Another concession was to drop the American constitution in favor of "not less than thirty nor more than forty words in ordinary use." As in the past, exemptions were provided for elderly parents and grandparents of qualified immigrants, as well as wives and unmarried or widowed daughters—but not sons. An element of manpower policy was incorporated as well by providing that certain categories of skilled workers might be excused if the United States declared a special need for them. The measure also reinstated the exemption for victims of religious persecution, broadened to cover "whether such persecution be evidenced by overt acts or by laws or governmental regulations that discriminate against the alien or the race to which he belongs because of his faith." However, attempts to extend this to persons persecuted on political grounds were unsuccessful; this was hardly surprising, since the targets of such actions were likely to be radicals, whom the United States was determined to exclude and, as the Jewish negotiator observed, few of whom were likely to be illiterate.[151] The test was part of a comprehensive measure that rehearsed all excluded categories, with a strengthened anti-anarchist clause and another doubling of the head tax to a hefty $8.00. It also expanded the Asiatic bar to include India, but a move to exclude blacks from the West Indies and Africa again failed.

President Wilson vetoed the measure a second time, insisting again that the literacy test in effect penalized a lack of opportunity in the country of origin. More surprising, given his earlier objection to the lack of exemption for victims of persecution, he now objected to the wording of the relevant clause in that it required U.S. officials to pass judgment on the laws and practices of a foreign government, thereby leading them to perform "a most invidious function" that might occasion diplomatic incidents. However, this time Congress overrode his veto by 287–106 in the House, and 62–19 in the Senate, and the literacy test finally became law on February 5, 1917, two days after the sinking of the *Housatonic* prompted President Wilson to address Congress on the severance of diplomatic relations with Germany.

Wartime security concerns also fostered an internationally interactive turning point for remote control, making it possible to fulfill the restrictionists' long-standing aspiration to police borders more effectively by way of advance inspection abroad.[152] On July 31, 1914, the German authorities imposed a visaed passport requirement on all foreign visitors; France restored passport controls from the revolutionary period that had been allowed to lapse, and also required foreigners above the age of fifteen to carry an identification card bearing a photograph; and on the eve of the war, Britain enacted a more draconian Aliens Restriction Act that impelled the elaboration of an extensive immigration bureaucracy "that helped strengthen the momentum for keeping passport controls in place after the war."[153] On the American side, the turning point was a July 1917 joint order by Secretary of State Robert Lansing and Secretary of Labor William Wilson requiring aliens coming to the United States to present visaed passports "and that in the process of securing the approval by American consular officials they should furnish quite detailed information concerning themselves, and also providing for the investigation of these cases, to as full an extent as possible, by diplomatic and consular officials stationed abroad."[154] The several departments concerned subsequently "exerted every possible effort to prepare a law that would more adequately deal with the subject," resulting in the Act of May 22, 1918, "To prevent in time of war departure from and entry into the United States contrary to the public safety." Together, the order and the law "established a system for the control of the travel of aliens more complete and more effective than any which had ever been put in operation by the United States Government." In August 1918 the Department of State created a visa office within its division of passport control, and the following year elevated it into a separate division with jurisdiction over the entire process.[155] In June 1920, the visa fee was increased fivefold from $2 to $10, and the 1918 measure was extended by a new act the following year.[156]

Paradoxically, the erection of barriers to reduce ongoing flows was coupled with measures to stimulate others. Seeking alternative sources of labor, as anticipated by Hourwich, American employers recruited African American sharecroppers in the South, thereby setting off the "great migration," and also turned to neighboring countries. To facilitate foreign labor procurement, they secured an exemption from the prohibition against advance contracts (the "fourth proviso") as well as from the hefty head taxes and literacy requirement imposed to deter undesirable immigrants (the "ninth proviso") on behalf of some 70,000 Mexican agricultural and railroad workers.[157] Thanks to these arrangements, Mexicans were brought as far north as the Chicago-Calumet region for work in the railroad yards and steel mills. The draft initiated in 1917 precipitated massive returns to Mexico because, although foreigners who had not declared their intention of becoming citizens were not subject to the draft, all were required to register, and the following year the registration requirement was dropped to induce more Mexicans to come.[158] These exemptions were extended to a variety of skilled and unskilled workers from Quebec and the English-speaking islands of the Caribbean as well. Yet although there were also numerous petitions to Congress on behalf of the importation of Chinese workers, these came to naught.[159]

Commenting on enactment of the literacy test as a relentless advocate of restriction, Henry P. Fairchild pointed out that "[w]hile ostensibly a selective measure, putting the finishing touch to our classification of undesirables," the literacy test "will affect so large a proportion of the ordinary immigration stream as to be really restrictive. In effect, therefore, it introduces a new principle," initially concealed by supporters on strategic grounds.[160] This was a step in the right direction, but hardly a sufficient one; "how long it will take to secure the passage of a frankly restrictive law, such as that urged by Senator Dillingham lineup . . . time alone can tell." Surmounting the obstacle of traditional principle surely mattered, but the discovery of substitute sources of labor undoubtedly helped as well. Together with the great internal migration from the South, the intra-American movements vastly reduced the dependence of American industry on European labor and thus considerably weakened the visible hand's incentives for keeping the Atlantic gates open.

8

A Nation Like the Others

In the aftermath of World War I, the United States loudly proclaimed to the world its determination to cease being a nation of immigrants. In one of the most spectacular displays of legislative power in American history, with two waves of its magic wand Congress sought to make immigration disappear, much as it had attempted to do with drinking by way of the Volstead Act. But whereas alcohol consumption was reduced by only one-third, in the sphere of immigration the transformation was radically effective.[1] In 1921, when civilian shipping resumed to its full capacity, the United States admitted 652,364 Europeans, more than half of the 1907 record; and the addition of millions of brutally uprooted political refugees to the steadily expanding pool of economic migrants suggested that the record would soon be surpassed. Instead, in the following years the 1921 figure was quickly cut in half, and then in half again, so that by 1929, the last pre-Depression year, European immigrants numbered only 158,598. This amounted to merely one-seventh of the 1907 level and a marginal one-tenth of 1 percent of America's continental population.

Beyond this, Asian immigration was in effect extinguished altogether and most of the now exceedingly scarce European admissions were reserved for the "original American stock," the white nationalities that had an opportunity to proliferate over three centuries. The legislation's draconian character is demonstrated by its immediate effect on immigration from Italy and Poland. In 1914, Italian arrivals reached 283,738; after the wartime interruption, the number quickly returned to 222,260, and there can be no doubt that it was well on its way to exceeding the previous record. Instead, entries were sharply reduced from 1921 on, and as a consequence of the quota imposed in 1924, the average annual level for the remainder of the decade was reduced to 14,969, a mere 7 percent of the 1921 level. The effect of restriction was almost as acute for Poles, many of whom were Jewish: 95,089 in 1921 as against an average of 8,111 for the postquota years, about 8.5 percent of the unrestricted level.[2]

Implementation of both components of restrictionism entailed a vast expansion of the capacity of the American state to regulate movement across its borders and its deployment abroad to achieve the elusive remote control to which regulators had long aspired. The ad hoc visa system instituted during the war proved inadequate, and in the early 1920s the State Department established itself as the lead agency in the sphere of immigration by creating an elaborate overseas bureaucracy capable of carrying out the complex administrative procedures that implementation of the restrictive legislation required. Remote control effected a sweeping and permanent reversal of the relationship between potential immigrants and the American state. Whereas previously there was a presumption of admissibility unless an immigration inspector established the contrary, now the burden of proof was placed on aliens to establish prior to embarkation that they were eligible for admission according to the newly imposed and highly selective criteria. The innovations also made it finally possible to harness the shipping lines to the implementation of border control.[3]

From the perspective of the European shore, it was clearly understood that these actions signaled the determination of the United States to transform itself into a nation like the others. Writing in the mid-1920s, Alexis de Tocqueville's compatriot André Siegfried opened his account of America Comes of Age by observing, "The essential characteristic of the post-war period in the United States is the nervous reaction of the original American stock against an insidious subjection by foreign blood."[4] The transformation proceeded swiftly. A year later, a scholarly analyst of population issues commented that "American fear of renewed immigration resulted in the quota laws, after which active interest in immigration problems in this country declined."[5] By 1931, when Frederick Lewis Allen published Only Yesterday, his celebrated chronicle of major social events of the postwar years such as the "Big Red Scare," the revival of the Ku Klux Klan, anti-Semitism, and Prohibition, he made no mention of either the speedy resumption of large-scale immigration after the war or of its near-elimination by the end of the decade.[6] The very subject had been relegated to long-term memory.

Late-twentieth-century awareness of the centrality of race in American development has stimulated a revival of interest in the racialization of the white population by way of the national origins quotas, leading to a spate of research that complements John Higham's *Strangers in the Land*.[7] However, the concomitant imposition of an overall quantitative limit on European immigration has been accorded secondary importance. This distorts reality, because whereas the national origins quota law evoked vociferous opposition on the part of the targeted groups, the quantitative limit attracted a much broader consensus and proved a more enduring element of American policy. For example, Max Kohler, engaged in the struggle against restriction from the beginning of the century, reflected in 1927 on the path leading from the Commission to "Quota Laws, based on racial distinctions and preferences, which I abhor," but conceded "that the War required new methods of restricting immigration."[8] When the United States abolished the national origins quota system four decades after its adoption and simultaneously relinquished remaining barriers to Asian immigration, it not only retained a quantitative limit on immigration from Europe, Asia, and Africa, but also simultaneously imposed one for the first time on immigration from the Western Hemisphere.

However, the new immigration policy also included a third component, which in effect contradicted the cultural imperatives that drove the other two. Even as they restricted the "new immigration" nearly to the point of extinction, the legislators acting on behalf of the "original American stock" refrained from closing the country's back door, in full knowledge that it allowed for a growing stream of Mexicans who, by their own racial standards, were more objectionable than southern and eastern Europeans because they were for the most part not even "white." The emerging distinction between a main gate tightly regulated in keeping with the "national interest," as determined by the guardians of the country's "Nordic" character, and an informally managed "back door" where agricultural employers ruled supreme, was thus institutionalized into a long-lasting feature of American immigration policy.[9]

The Drive to Isolation

It is no accident that the longtime promoter of immigration restriction, Henry Cabot Lodge, was also Woodrow Wilson's nemesis on the League of Nations. Both responses were hammered out within a worldwide climate of tightening borders and increasing restriction on the movement of persons, triggered initially by rising international tensions culminating in the conflagration, but reinforced afterwards by economic difficulties and political instability.[10]

Wary of "insidious subjection by foreign blood," the political establishment kept a sharp lookout for the resumption of immigration. In the year following the armistice, the anticipated flood failed to materialize, as much of the available shipping was dedicated to the return of American troops; instead, there was a large exodus of workers who had come to America on the eve of the conflict and been immobilized during the war. By one careful statistical reckoning, from 1915 to 1922 over half as many foreign-born left the country as entered, a trend especially pronounced for males and among the Balkan nationalities.[11] But arrivals from Europe reached a quarter of a million in 1920 and some 650,000 the following year, prompting the immigration commissioner of the Port of New York to proclaim that over 10 million were waiting to embark; and Wilbur Carr, head of the U.S. Consular Service, warned in an appendix to a congressional committee report that the United States was about to receive an unprecedented wave of Polish Jews who were "filthy, un-American, and often dangerous in their habits . . . lacking any conception of patriotism or national spirit."[12]

Conditions in postwar Europe were indeed conducive to massive uprooting. The sudden demobilization of an entire generation of young adult males and a lack of capital interacted to mire the former belligerents in deep economic doldrums. The Continent was also in the throes of an unprecedented refugee crisis. The doctrine of national self-government was applied with special fervor to the dismantling of the defeated Austro-Hungarian and Ottoman Empires, and by the successor states themselves against their minorities. Meanwhile, the only victorious empire, Russia, exploded into a revolution that generated political refugees as well as minority ones, and also experienced some dismantlement, giving rise to further successor states, Poland, the Baltic trio, and Finland, all of which also mistreated minorities in the name of nation-building. Contrary to the American Jewish organizations' optimistic expectations, the war had been calamitous for Jews in eastern Europe as well. After some in the westernmost part of the Russian Empire welcomed the German and Austro-Hungarian armies as liberators from oppression, the tsar ordered their massive deportation to the Polish section of the empire; conversely, many Galician Jews fled to western parts of the Hapsburg Empire in the wake of the Russian invasion.[13] In addition to the sequels of the conflict itself, the Russian Revolution and the postwar settlements generated tensions that produced more internationally displaced persons. The Jews, again, were caught in the middle, mistrusted by the Bolsheviks for their bourgeois inclinations, and by nationalists, notably in the Ukraine, for leaning toward the Bolsheviks; half a million fled westward to Poland, where their arrival precipitated sporadic violence. By the mid-1920s, estimates of European refugees ranged to nearly 10 million, including 1.5 million resulting from the "unmixing" of populations in Greece and Turkey at the end of their own war, 2 million Poles, over 2 million Russians and Ukrainians, and 1 million Germans.[14]

In the wake of the war, there was "a pronounced tendency to regard the regulation of migration as an international matter." Observing that "[t]he Japanese introduced the issue at Versailles," A. B. Wolfe, an American scholar writing in 1928, surmised that "it was probably one consideration which helped toward the decision of the United States not to enter the League of Nations."[15] A conference of the leading immigration nations was held in Paris in 1923, and another organized by the successor to the Second Labor International in Prague in 1924; a general international conference was convened at Rome in 1924, with representatives of fifty-seven countries, where "under the leadership of Italy, some outspoken demands were made for modification of national sovereignty in the interest of the establishment of some international authority to regulate migration and settlement"; another labor-sponsored meeting was held in London in 1926, and a Second International Immigration Conference in Havana in April 1928. In the intervening period, the International Labor Office established a Permanent Migration Committee for the study of migration problems.

On a closely related theme, the postwar years also witnessed a revival of Malthusianism. In *The Economic Consequences of the Peace,* John Maynard Keynes emphasized "an excessive population dependent for its livelihood on a complicated and artificial organization" as one of the major factors of instability in prewar Europe, leading a contemporaneous commentator to suggest that "[s]o prominent a place given to the Malthusian specter in the prologue of a book of this kind, so widely read at so psychological a moment, could not fail to bring home to thousands of readers the fact that the population problem is far more than an academic pastime."[16] This concern was echoed on the American side in works such *Standing Room Only?* (1927) by Wisconsin sociologist E. A. Ross, long associated with the restrictionist cause.

In this light, it is evident that the significance of American policy transcended immediate concerns with immigration proper, constituting a defiant assertion of the country's unbounded nationalism, manifested most immediately by the State Department's refusal to take part in the discussions of the resolutions of the Rome Conference at the 1928 Havana meeting "on the ground that participation in such discussion might give rise to misapprehension as to the fundamental position of the United States, which is that control of immigration is a sovereign right and that Congress has final authority."[17]

The Deepening Ideological Divide

The anti-immigration camp was reinforced by the fear of Bolshevik contagion and a yearning for a return to "normalcy," as well as the onset of postwar economic doldrums.[18] Immigrant workers figured prominently in the successful drive to unionize steel that got underway in the summer of 1918, and in the wave of strikes that swept the country the following year.[19] In early 1920, Attorney General A. Mitchell Palmer predicted that by May 1 the country would be locked in the convulsions of a "Red Revolution," and went on to arrest some 6,000 allegedly seditious men and women, most of them immigrants, of whom many were subsequently deported.[20] In June of the same year, Congress enacted a law that, for the first time, punished aliens for merely possessing subversive literature, advising rather than advocating and teaching revolution, holding membership in groups and societies as well as organizations, and showing sympathy and support for radical organizations by way of financial contributions apart from actual membership.[21]

The campaign against radicals was part of an array of reactionary developments, including rejection of U.S. membership in the League of Nations; the revival of the Ku Klux Klan, which advertised itself as a 100 percent American organization, targeting foreigners, Catholics, and Jews as much as African Americans; the enactment of Jim Crow laws throughout the South; the tightening of laws restricting Japanese land ownership in California; and the onset of more explicit social discrimination against Catholics and Jews in elite institutions, notably universities.[22] The constitutional amendment to prohibit the consumption of alcoholic beverages, passed over President Wilson's veto in 1917 and effective as of January 1920, also constituted a rejection of "foreign ways," with support from middle-class, white, Protestant, socially mobile, native or thoroughly assimilated voters, while opposition was provided by wage-earning immigrants or Americans of recent vintage.[23]

Higham asserted, "After the war, the dwindling company of progressive intellectuals played curiously little part in restriction controversies. Most of them wearily agreed with the popular demand for a more stable, homogeneous ethnic pattern," and more recent writers have generally confirmed this trend.[24] While this was true, it would be more accurate to say that a signal cultural divide was in the making. While accepting restriction as inevitable under existing circumstances, antirestrictionist intellectuals held on to and even elaborated their position, laying the groundwork for a "nearly complete repudiation of every scientific rationale for racism"; however, the change "was not nearly or widely enough disseminated" to affect policy.[25] Bereft of political support in Washington, they carried on a rear-guard action. On the other side of the divide loomed a phalanx of restrictionist-minded intellectuals, closely connected with the eugenicists on the one hand and the Republican congressional leadership on the other, broadly comparable to the emergence of a neoconservative intellectual network in the post-Vietnam era. Among other things, they systematically set out to legitimize their camp's position by providing revisionist accounts of how immigration was envisioned in American history. Publicizing hitherto ignored demurrers by the Founding Fathers, they also exhumed the protracted regulatory efforts by states and localities discussed in earlier chapters.[26]

In the new climate, it was no longer necessary to dissimulate frankly racist objectives beneath the cover of concern for the economic welfare of American workers. The restrictionist camp's intellectual standing was further bolstered by the recently acquired scientific status of its unfavorable assessment of the new immigrants, founded on "eugenics" and the quantitative measurement of intelligence by way of the "intelligence quotient" (IQ).[27] The network institutionalized in 1910 by the founding of the Eugenics Record Office at Cold Spring Harbor, New York, reached into the highest strata of society, including the most prestigious universities. Its leaders included Madison Grant, a lawyer and Park Avenue socialite who was chairman of the New York Zoological Society, a trustee of the American Museum of Natural History, as well as a member of the Galton Society, which met in the museum. Grant's vituperative oeuvre, *The Passing of the Great Race,* published in 1916 by C. Scribner's Sons, "the most genteel and the most tradition encrusted of all the publishing houses," sported a fulsome preface by the paleontologist Henri Fairfield Osborn, president of the museum and research professor of zoology at Columbia University.[28] Grant himself subsequently wrote a preface for another popular work in the same vein, Lothrop Stoddard's *The Rising Tide of Color against White World-Supremacy,* also published by Scribner's, and later coedited a compendium purporting to demonstrate the Founding Fathers' suspicion of immigration, again issued by the same distinguished publishing house.[29]

Eugenics and the IQ were promoted also by the American Psychological Association, which declared, on the basis of the mass testing of draftees it conducted during the war, that blacks were inferior to whites and new immigrants to old, sometimes even to blacks. Although their results indicated that the scores of the foreign-born improved the longer they lived in the United States, this was dismissed as an error in measurement. A leading academic restrictionist asserted explicitly in 1926 that the work of H. H. Laughlin "had such great influence that it is often considered the principal basis of the Act of 1924."[30] The eugenicist orientation also pervaded the Committee on Scientific Problems of Human Migration established by the National Research Council's Division of Anthropology and Psychology in 1922.

On the other side, the *New York Times* proclaimed in an editorial, "This new historic idea (racial determinism) runs counter to our spiritual convictions as to the brotherhood of all human beings and the identical preciousness of all human souls. It runs counter to the political dogmas of universal equality and the sanctity of the will of the majority. Spiritually and politically it is not democratic but aristocratic—though the aristocracy is that of biology." While acknowledging that "with Bolshevism menacing us on one hand and race extinction through warfare on the other, many people are not unlikely to give it an increasingly respectful consideration," the inference they drew was not the need for immigration restriction but rather for "a league or association which will unite the nation in defense of what is precious in the Nordic inheritance." The *Nation* commented similarly in 1921 on "the controversies here and there stirring over the true color and quality of the national genius. At one extreme are the rock-bound nativists, the besotted Anglo-Saxons, who point with rapture to the Puritan tradition and with pride to the older days of Little America before the Civil War. . . . Our hopes lie rather in our fusion of many cultures. We are still, for all the changes that have taken place in three hundred years, a laboratory for the Old World, where a great human experiment is being carried on."[31] Following enactment of the 1921 law, the magazine cited a National Industrial Conference Board study indicating that because of the high number of departures, net immigration "shrinks to almost nothing," and exclaimed, "Yet in the face of a situation like this the immigration restrictionists are demanding a still tighter law!"[32] The *New Republic* also denounced the 1921 law as an "arbitrary, unscientific act" and editorialized in 1924 that since "[n]either our past nor our present immigration policy has been based on any high moral principle," one should not look at the immigration bills awaiting further negotiation in the light of "abstract justice," and concluded, "Looked at from the coldest point of view of expediency, then, it remains true that there is no justification in fact for such discriminatory legislation as both houses of Congress have enacted."[33]

Within the academy, a new generation of social scientists such as Robert E. Park and Robert Redfield, as well as historians such as Carl Becker and Carlton Hayes, systematically criticized the eugenicist, racialist, and hyper-nationalist literature on which restrictionists rested their case.[34] The turn of the National Research Council's Committee on Scientific Problems of Human Migration toward eugenicism prompted the Laura Spelman Rockefeller Memorial Fund to shift its support to a group of scholars who formed a new Migration Committee within what became the Social Science Research Council (SSRC). This innovative interdisciplinary body was initially chaired by Edith Abbott, based in the University of Chicago's Anthropology Department, and included leading disciplinary figures such as Charles Merriam (the SSRC's founding president) and Frederick Ogg from political science, John Commons and Robert Foerster from economics, and Carl Wittke from history. Although the committee's research interests encompassed international migration worldwide, it resolved to give special attention to Mexican immigration to the United States and internal migration of African Americans because of their growing importance. The projects it funded, including studies by Manuel Gamio, Walter Willcox, and Harry Jerome, had a major impact in developing migration studies as a scholarly field.[35]

Legislating and Implementing Restriction

Postwar legislative developments were shaped by the reinstatement of Republican hegemony, interrupted by the unusual circumstances of the three-way presidential contest of 1912 and its sequels. Benefiting from a popular revolt against the incumbents, driven largely by a doubling of the cost-of-living index since the end of 1915, the Republicans regained Congress in 1918, when the Democrats lost 26 House seats, notably thanks to the defection of their Midwestern German voters. They went on to reconquer the presidency in 1920, and maintained their control over both branches of the national government for the remainder of the decade.[36]

Republican control of Congress was determinative; writing in 1946, a pioneer analyst of the American legislative process, Lawrence Chamberlain, observed, "One may argue that American immigration legislation would have been improved had the president been able to make his influence felt. For our purposes, that is a point on which an opinion need not be expressed. The record shows that whatever immigration policy we have is the handiwork of Congress and not of the executive."[37] A study of House roll-call votes on immigration in 1920 and 1924 reveals that partisanship weighed heavily in the outcome: in all instances, restriction was supported by Republicans from both rural and urban districts, as well as by rural Democrats, mostly southern. This left northern Democrats, who in the wake of the 1920 election were reduced to only 10 percent of nonsouthern seats, as the only source of opposition.[38] However, since many voters of recent immigrant origin defected from the Democratic Party, notably on foreign policy grounds, defense of their interests probably ranked low among the party's priorities, except in New York City.[39]

Initially, the National Association of Manufacturers (NAM) resisted draconian plans to suspend immigration altogether or limit it severely on the grounds that this was too inflexible to accommodate future needs.[40] A similar stance was adopted by a National Conference on Immigration convened in 1920 by the Inter-Racial Council, a coalition of big business executives; immigrant advocates such as Louis Marshall, Max Kohler, and Fiorello La-Guardia; and foreign-language publishers, whose board was chaired by General Coleman du Pont and whose president was the head of the National Founders' Association. The conference resolved among other things that "[w]e regard the literacy test as not only without merit, but as a direct injury to the interests of commerce, industry, and agriculture, and recommend its repeal." Immigration should flow freely, but with strict enforcement of the antiradical provisions. They also issued recommendations pertaining to incorporation, including the creation of a "Federal Board of Assimilation" as well as federal funding for improving the education of immigrant children. Acknowledging that the United States was experiencing "a condition of public unrest," they nevertheless rejected allegations "that propaganda conducive to such unrest is being carried on principally among our residents of foreign birth" and particularly through foreign-language publications.[41]

However, in the summer of 1920, the American economy experienced its first severe recession since the 1890s, lasting until the spring of 1922, and it was in the course of this that Congress enacted the first quantitative restrictions on immigration. The Republican convention that nominated Warren Harding for president endorsed a proposal to impose draconian limits on European immigration for a year.[42] Spurred on by favorable political prospects, the escalation of arrivals, and dire economic conditions, at the end of 1920 the restrictionists in the House secured approval of a bill introduced by the Immigration Committee's new chairman, Representative Albert Johnson, a long-standing anti-Asian activist from the State of Washington, for a fourteen-month suspension of all immigration, except for farm labor and immediate blood relatives. Among the explicit arguments on the bill's behalf was that a large percentage of incoming immigrants were Jews, who would be kept out by way of the farm labor qualification. However, the upper chamber approved instead a plan by Senator Charles Dillingham to radically restrict European immigration for fifteen months by applying the nationalities quota system considered by his commission in 1911. The cap would be set at 5 percent of the foreign-born of each nationality resident in the United States in 1910, as enumerated in the U.S. Census, for an estimated total of 592,000. Temporary visitors, citizens of Western Hemisphere countries, members of certain learned and professional classes, as well as domestic servants would be admitted outside the quotas.

In the end, Congress approved a compromise conference version that reduced the cap to 3 percent so as to limit European immigration to approximately 350,000 per year. Preference would be given to wives and minor children of naturalized citizens and "intentioners," legally admitted aliens who filed their intention to naturalize. However, President Wilson allowed the bill to die by withholding his signature. A "liberal" alternative, advanced by the National Committee for Constructive Immigration Legislation and endorsed by the Committee of One Thousand, whose signatories included Cardinal Gibbons, Adolph Sabath, and social activist Lilian Wald, would have allocated admission in proportion to the number of members of each nationality group who had become naturalized citizens, plus their American-born children.[43] It is thus eminently clear that the opposition accepted not only the principle of a quantitative limit but also the allocation of entries on the basis of nationality quotas of some kind.

Dillingham's proposal quickly moved through the new Congress—the Senate vote was 78 to 1, with 17 abstentions—and was approved in May 1921 by the incoming Republican president, hailed by the Immigration Restriction League as the first genuine restrictionist in the White House. The law exempted alien minor children of citizens, certain professional classes, and domestic servants, and granted preference within the quotas to close relatives of citizens and intentioners. Amidst proliferating proposals for more extreme measures, including one by Chairman Johnson to suspend immigration altogether for a period of three years, at its expiration the legislation was renewed twice and extended to 1924. There were also perennial moves to prohibit Japanese immigration, driving the Japanese government to impose new restrictions under the "Gentlemen's Agreement."[44] In 1922 Congress further protected Americanness by adopting the Cable Act (42 Stat. 1022), whereby an alien woman marrying a U.S. citizen no longer automatically acquired his nationality.

Thanks to the new law and postwar business doldrums, European immigration dipped by two-thirds from 652,364 in 1921 to a mere 216,385 the following year. The restrictionist scholar Roy Garis contended that "according to a careful estimate [the measure] kept from our shores 1,750,000 to 2,000,000 immigrants, few of whom we would have been prepared to receive and care for in a year of unemployment and readjustment."[45] However, arrivals then climbed back to 364,339 in 1924, approximately the maximum level attainable under the new law. Garis observed further that the percentage of English-speaking immigrants, which had dropped to 8.8 percent of the total in 1914, rose to 14.9 percent in 1921 and reached 28.3 percent in 1924, and he noted approvingly that adoption of the quota system also had the effect of inducing more of those admitted to remain permanently, thereby restoring a measure of social stability to American society.[46]

However, the new system wreaked havoc with ongoing regulatory practices. Admissions within each country's quota were allocated monthly upon arrival in the United States, on a first-come, first-served basis, prompting races between steamships to reach the ports and dump their passengers before numbers were exhausted. Visas were required, but the consuls were instructed to refuse them only "when informed that a sufficient number of aliens had been admitted into the United States to exhaust the quota of the country of which the applicant was a native."[47] The system created considerable duress for the immigrants, who might be refused entry because the quota filled by the time they arrived or because they failed to qualify on some other grounds, as well as difficulties for the shippers and the stateside American authorities, who had to assume responsibility for returning them.[48] It thus became evident that efficient operation of the new system required the distribution of entry permits in advance of embarkation, and that this in turn mandated the elaboration of a more extensive overseas bureaucracy.

Preserving the Back Door

In 1924, the United States received almost as many nationals of independent countries of the Western Hemisphere as Europeans: 342,557 altogether, including 200,690 from Canada and Newfoundland, the forgotten throng of American immigration history, as well as 89,336 from Mexico.[49] Writing in 1930, Paul Taylor pointed out that "Mexicans" constituted not only 74 percent of railroad maintenance workers on the southwestern continental lines, where they took the place of Greeks, Italians, Japanese, and Koreans, but also 39 percent of workers on local and eastern roads. He explained that the situation "shows in detail the results . . . of the slackening of European immigration, the exclusion of Oriental immigration, the drift of older immigration to other occupations." Mexicans were no longer restricted to the Southwest, and "[i]n the long run, there is probably about as much, but no more reason to regard the Mexican population as confined to a region than the Negro population."[50] His unselfconscious confounding of Mexicans and African Americans matched that of the 1927 Annual Meeting of the American Economic Association, where several speakers singled out Negro movement to the northern industrial districts and Mexican immigration as major economic consequences of restriction.[51] The two met in the Chicago-Gary region, where by 1928 the labor force in steel was 12.3 percent African American and 9.4 percent Mexican, and in meatpacking 29.5 and 5.7 percent respectively.[52]

Both movements were driven simultaneously by "push" and "pull." World War I stimulated a great demand for cotton, driving its price in the Delta to the all-time high of $1.00 a pound in 1919, but disaster struck the following year, when it fell to 10 cents. Consequently, "The Delta began struggling on and off with economic depression a decade earlier than the rest of the country," turning sharecroppers into a burdensome population that owners brutally drove off their land.[53] On the pull side, even as he fought immigration on cultural grounds, Henry Ford dispatched company officials to recruit African Americans in the South.[54] As a leading immigrant advocate reflected at the time, Negroes were "attempting to fill the role that the immigrant alien had been taking much better."[55] Overall, African American migration to the northern industrial states soared from 370,500 in 1910–1920 to 664,900 in 1920–1930, with New York and Illinois the leading receivers in both periods.[56]

Mexican immigration had been long in the making, with 173,663 entries recorded in the 1910–1919 decade, but estimates of actual movement across the largely unguarded border range two to five times higher.[57] Its subsequent expansion was governed by ongoing economic transformations and protracted revolutionary upheavals, notably the Cristero rebellion of 1926–1929 in populous central Mexico, with movement vastly facilitated by the spread of automotive vehicles and the concomitant construction of a network of roads in northern Mexico.[58] On the American side, demand expanded from Texas cotton producers to sugar beet growers throughout the upper Midwest, and in the wake of draconian restrictions on Asian immigration, it grew vastly in California as well. Since the war, it also encompassed the railroads and northern industrialists. Large numbers of Mexican strikebreakers were transported from the Southwest to the Chicago area during the steel strike of 1919, much to the dismay of the AFL, and in May 1923 Bethlehem Steel again hired a large contingent of Mexicans as a "short-term supplement" to its labor force in the Chicago-Calumet region.[59] Altogether, the 1920 U.S. Census enumerated about half a million Mexican-born residents, as well as a Mexican American population of some 800,000; the population of "Mexican origin," which combined the two categories, numbered 486,418 in the four southwestern states alone, but this was again a very likely substantial undercount. Total recorded entries for 1910–1929 exceeded 1.5 million; however, there was considerable return movement, so that net immigration for the period is estimated at only about 400,000.[60]

The term "back door" was itself coined by the frustrated cultural restrictionists, who sought in vain to limit the growing Mexican immigration by subjecting it to a quota. As Garis, their leading academic spokesman, pointed out at another congressional hearing in 1930, "mixed breed" Mexicans were even more undesirable than Polish Jews or southern Italians; hence, "to admit peons from Mexico . . . while restricting Europeans and excluding orientals is not only ridiculous and illogical—it destroys the biological, social, and economic advantages to be secured from the restriction of immigration."[61] He explained further that the lax ongoing policy flew in the face of scientific demonstrations that Mexicans were less intelligent than Negroes and French Canadians, "the Mexicans of the Northeast," who also came in freely to work in the timber and lumber industry at about the same level of pay.[62] Others were concerned that the growing settlements along the southern and northern borders might lead to secession; one commentator surmised in the late 1920s that "it was not impossible that, if these two over-the-border movements should continue . . . plebiscites of the sort which have been held in Upper Silesia and Transylvania would result in the transfer of a considerable portion of the territory of the United States to Mexico and Canada."[63]

On the Mexican side, successive régimes were ambivalent over emigration: while humiliating from a nationalist perspective, as well as a potentially dangerous source of democratic ideas, it also became the major outlet for uprooted "surplus" population and a source of much-needed remittances.[64] Hence, the government "did not always act vigorously to retain or return its citizens."[65] On the American side, the relevant interests easily secured suitable institutional arrangements. In the face of impending restrictive legislation, agricultural entrepreneurs mobilized to maintain the wartime exemptions, which were due to expire in February 1920. As the president of the South Texas Cotton Growers Association explained to a Senate committee a month before the deadline, more workers were needed than ever because recent advances in mechanization facilitated the expansion of farms.[66] With regard to the immediate issue, he pointed out quite logically that no Mexican worker would come if he had to pay an $8.00 head tax, because if he had that kind of money there would be no need to come. He also reassured those who worried about the presence of revolutionary-minded aliens along the border that "[t]here never was a more docile animal in the world than the Mexican." Conceding that in the present political climate, Congress might not be able to grant agriculture's request for continued exemptions, he suggested there was an alternative possibility: "If you gentlemen have any objections to admitting the Mexicans by law, cut them out and take the river guard away and let us alone, and we will get them all right."

The State Department joined agribusiness in arguing on behalf of continued exemption, on the grounds that the imposition of quotas would jeopardize Ambassador Dwight Morrow's ongoing negotiations on behalf of American businesses nationalized by Mexico's revolutionary governments.[67] When the restrictionists fell back on the argument that as "mixed breeds," most Mexicans were excluded by virtue of the clause in the 1924 act that prohibited the immigration of persons ineligible for citizenship, the government insisted on classifying all Mexicans as white. It was also evident to analysts that "from a practical administrative standpoint a quota system would be impossible to enforce" because the lengthy land border "could not be adequately policed. The pressure to bring Mexicans across the border would be so great and smuggling them in would become so profitable that a quota law would quickly become a joke."[68]

Accordingly, Mexico, along with the other independent countries of the Western Hemisphere, was exempted from the numerical limits and national origins quotas that henceforth governed European immigration, and movement was restricted only by the head tax, the literacy requirement, the "LPC clause," as well as the prohibition against contract labor, none of which was seriously enforced, and hence undocumented entry became the norm. From the perspective of American farmers, this was one of the features that made Mexican labor particularly desirable: "Time and again, in their deliberations, the growers have emphasized the fact that the Mexican, unlike the Filipino, can be deported. . . . The general attitude of the growers toward the Mexicans is summarized in a remark made by a ranch foreman to a Mexican: 'When we want you, we'll call you; when we don't—git.' "[69]

America Restored

Thanks to these developments, Atlantic and Pacific restrictions were no longer incompatible with economic rationality. As dissenting voices weakened further, the restrictionist coalition raised its sights to the genuinely reactionary objective of rolling back the ethnic makeup of the country's white population to its pre-new immigration configuration.[70] In a series of articles published in 1923, Secretary of Labor James Davis bluntly asserted, "We want the beaver type of man. We want to keep out the rat-type." In order to bring this about, he promoted the imposition of numerical quotas on all countries, with a selection based primarily on American manpower needs, to be carried out in the country of origin prior to departure. The proposed extension of quota limits to the Western Hemisphere, notably Mexico and Canada, reflected protracted efforts by AFL President Samuel Gompers to secure the administration's support in this matter.[71] In addition, the president of the United States should have the authority of suspending immigration altogether whenever the secretary of labor and the secretary of commerce "jointly certify that in their opinion unemployment in this country makes suspension necessary."[72]

In early 1924, House Immigration Committee chairman Johnson proposed decreasing the annual European quota from 3 percent to only 2 percent, and using the 1890 U.S. Census rather than 1920 as the baseline.[73] This would reduce European immigration to about 110,000 a year as well as further minimize the eastern and southern share. The baseline shift originated in a *Scribner's* article by Roy Garis, a professor of economics at Vanderbilt University who subsequently published a triumphalist history of restrictionism with a foreword by Johnson himself. Johnson's bill also prohibited the immigration of persons ineligible for naturalization, a provision targeting the Japanese and their Korean subjects, but did not apply the quota system to the Western Hemisphere. It was approved by an overwhelming 322–71 vote on April 12, with support from every section of the country except for a divided Northeast and vociferous opposition from the New York City delegation, led by Samuel Dickstein and Fiorello LaGuardia.

However, the opposition lacked an alternative plan. Harold Fields, head of the nonsectarian League of Foreign-born Citizens, urged the creation of a federal board of immigration comparable to the Interstate Commerce Commission, which would put American immigration on a "scientific basis [founded] upon the social and economic needs of the country." However, a labor-oriented policy held little interest for Jewish organizations, which carried considerable weight in the opposition camp, because Jews were unlikely to be eligible on the basis of manpower criteria.[74] Bowing to the prevailing winds, they merely fought a rear-guard action to retain 1920 or even 1910 as the basis rather than roll back to 1890.[75]

An altogether different formula was put forth in the Senate by Republican Senator David Reed of Pennsylvania. Sharing in the objective of limiting the new immigration but recognizing that the 1890 baseline was politically risky because of its flagrantly discriminatory character, he proposed instead an annual cap of 150,000, with admissions apportioned according to the number of inhabitants of each "national origin" present in the continental United States as of 1920. Senator Lodge, still around to witness the victorious completion of his decades-long struggle to preserve America's identity in his image, explained disingenuously that "there can be no question then of discrimination, because it will treat all races alike on the basis of their actual proportion of the existing population."[76] The formula was suggested by John Trevor, a close associate of Madison Grant, who was himself probably inspired by a recent publication of the National Historical Society, *America's Race Heritage,* and it was promoted by Henry M. Curran, commissioner of immigration at Ellis Island, as a policy that "mirrored America."[77] Up to half of each national quota was allocated to relatives of American citizens aged twenty-one or over, and for the remainder, preference was given to persons skilled in agriculture, again with Jews as the target.[78] Unmarried minor children and wives of citizens were admissible outside the quota, as were natives—but not naturalized citizens—of independent countries of the Western Hemisphere.

While it has been argued that the shift of the United States from debtor to creditor status in world capital markets induced a decline of the price of capital in relation to that of labor, fostering mechanization and lessening dependence on unskilled labor, this was a long-term factor more evident to historical analysts than to contemporaneous actors.[79] With recovery underway, despite the availability of other sources of labor, business spokesmen reasserted their traditional immigrationist stance, and as late as February 1923, representatives of fourteen industrial groups, headed by the general counsel of the NAM, testified before the Senate Immigration Committee to a shortage of labor in the major producing states.[80] What tipped the scales was that businessmen were not merely capitalists but also social elites, swayed by concern for cultural regulation as much as by balance sheet imperatives. They sought to keep "Bohunks," "Kikes," and "Dagoes" out of the country for the same reasons that they excluded them from their clubs and universities and devised restrictive covenants on real estate to keep them out of their neighborhoods, notably the new suburbs rendered accessible by the automobile. After the conference bill was approved, the NAM and the U.S. Chamber of Commerce acknowledged that national origin quotas were desirable for national integration, but thought the numerical limitation overly restrictive in the light of economic recovery, and recommended retaining the 1920 level.

On the ethnic front, the leading Jewish organizations bowed to the necessity of numerical restriction but fought the national origins baseline, going so far as to characterize it as violating treaties with almost every country of the world, "comparable with German behavior" in World War I.[81] However, they no longer wielded the same degree of political influence within what had become a more rural-centered Republican Party, and they were further constrained by their own self-imposed caution.[82] Battered by wartime hostility, German Americans basically kept quiet, whereas Scandinavians demonstrated their Americanism by joining the outcry against the new immigrants. *America,* the leading Catholic weekly, shifted decisively toward restriction in the course of the Red Scare, and by 1923 was referring to the new immigration as a handicap to Catholicism and to the nation.[83] African Americans, hitherto ambivalent at best on the subject of immigration, were overwhelmed by fear that postwar flows would jeopardize their race's hard-earned foothold in northern industry, and shifted decisively to the restrictionist side as well.[84] Other than those directly targeted, one of the few explicit sources of resistance to the dominant trend was the northern Baptists, whose 1925 convention protested the quotas and racial provisions of the National Origins Act on the grounds that they erected obstacles to the fulfillment of America's providential mission: "The Good News of the gospel is to all the people of the world."[85]

The final bill was approved by the Senate on April 18 by 62–6, with 28 abstentions, but no vote of record. President Calvin Coolidge declined to meet with objectors and signed the Johnson-Reed Act on May 26. The sociologist Robert Park observed that the law's effect "was to give a sort of sanction to the notion which has been persistently maintained in the case of the Negro, that certain of the racial and national groups in the United States were not only culturally but biologically, inferior to others."[86] A similar point has been made more recently by Mae Ngai: the use of "origin" rather than place of birth in effect reconstructed "nationality" into a category defined by bloodline and blood quantum, akin to "race" as used with regard to Negroes and Asians.[87] Accordingly, the move evoked vigorous critiques from a number of contemporaneous social scientists, notably Park himself and Franz Boas.

Did the restrictionists really mean to equate differences among whites with those separating the "races of mankind," as conventionally understood at the time? In retrospect, their position appears ambiguous. For example, Roy Garis conceded somewhat defensively in 1926, "Very few students of immigration who are advocates of restriction maintain that there is any difference of inherent racial qualities between the old and the immigration . . . other things being equal, or that one nationality is 'superior' to the other." But he then went on to explain that other things are not equal: the new immigrants are not as easily assimilated as the old because their numbers are much larger; they differ sharply in economic, political, and social background; they are unstable (that is, many return); and they are concentrated in poorly paid industries that seek unskilled labor. He further cited H. H. Laughlin of the Eugenics Record Office, who "substantiated the conviction that was becoming more and more fixed in the minds of those favoring restriction" that "by admitting strains far removed" from the original settlers, "the United States has already tended to become in certain sections like Central Europe, a collection of unassimilable blocs."[88] Paradoxically, the Jewish organization B'nai Brith in effect agreed, commenting that the quota law might even be beneficial for Jews because it eliminated American fears about the dangerous effect of a large unassimilated mass, and that "this is a more honest argument for immigration restriction than the Nordic myth."[89]

Nevertheless, the conventional distinction between race and nationality prevailed, as reflected in the determination to deal with nonwhite races by way of exclusion and with undesirable European nationalities by restriction. Yale sociologist Maurice Davie, who approved of the quota system imposed in 1921, urged in 1923 that since the principle of exclusion was applied to the Chinese, "[t]here is need at the present time of excluding other dark skinned races, a need which will undoubtedly increase unless some action is taken. . . . One would think that our Negro problem was already large enough without adding to it that way. . . . The barred zone should be extended to Africa and also the West Indies, especially to Jamaica and the Bahamas, to stop the coming of blacks from these quarters."[90] The descendants of "involuntary immigrants" were indeed disregarded from the "national origins" baseline because, according to Senator Reed, both blacks and whites "do not want to allow great immigration from African sources."[91]

Yet the law's ostracism was less extreme for people of African origin than for Asians. Johnson-Reed terminated one-sidedly the long-standing "Gentlemen's Agreement" between the United States and Japan, and, extending the practice instituted with regard to the Chinese, aliens ineligible for citizenship were not admissible at all even if they were nationals of a European or Western Hemisphere country; the U.S. Supreme Court established that this encompassed the Japanese (*Ozawa v. US*, 1922) and Asian Indians, hitherto ambiguously "Caucasian" (*US v. Thind*, 1923).[92] The racial status of Arabs gave rise to considerable debate, somewhat like the Jews; albeit "Asians" (or Africans), they were a "people of the Book," and most of those immigrating at the time were in fact Christian.[93] Filipinos were still considered U.S. "nationals," along with Puerto Ricans; however, their settlement on the mainland evoked considerable opposition, and in 1934 Congress established a ten-year transition period to independence, simultaneously declaring that for purposes of immigration, the Philippines immediately constituted a foreign country, with an annual quota of fifty, the lowest in the world.[94]

For persons of African origin, however, the determinative criterion was nationality, as for whites. In keeping with the general principles governing the Western Hemisphere, blacks and mulattoes from Cuba and Haiti were neither excluded nor bound by numerical limits, but governed only by "qualitative" restrictions, notably the literacy and LPC requirements, as well as payment of the head tax. The independent countries of Africa (Ethiopia, Liberia, and South Africa) were each awarded a minimal quota of 100, as were the former German colonies mandated by the League of Nations. Blacks living under colonial rule were eligible within the quotas of their respective imperial powers, and presumably at their discretion. Given the large British allocation and the relatively low demand for visas from the British Isles, this provided opportunities for blacks from the English-speaking Caribbean. In practice, by virtue of the qualitative requirements, strictly implemented by American consular staff, the law limited the award of visas to the more skilled and educated segments of the island population. This selective effect undoubtedly helps explain the remarkable upward mobility of black West Indian immigrants in the middle decades of the twentieth century.[95]

The quota system was scheduled to become operational in 1927. In the intervening period, the House's preconference version would go into effect: admissions were reduced to 2 percent of the population of each nationality as enumerated in the 1890 U.S. Census, thereby immediately slashing the southern and eastern European share. But how were the quotas to be established and implemented? "Origins," beyond place of birth of residents and their parents, were not recorded in the Census and lacked official standing. Although an "account of the diffusion of ancestral stocks in the United States" had recently been set forth in *America's Race Heritage,* even the measure's most ardent advocates conceded that the National Historical Society's compendium was inadequate and that a more reliable classification would have to be undertaken. This prompted the creation of an interdepartmental Quota Board, chaired by Dr. Joseph A. Hill, chief statistician of the U.S. Census Bureau and a follower of Francis Walker, who endorsed his theory of the depressing effect of immigration on the native birthrate.[96] Hill's starting point was a 1909 attempt by the Census Bureau to classify the 1790 population according to country of origin.[97] Although he conceded to critics that this exaggerated the English proportion because by that time many names had already been anglicized, he nevertheless retained this as his baseline. After it became evident that the proposed system would increase the share allocated to the ancestral countries of the earliest settlers at the expense of the later western European sources, Midwestern congressmen from heavily German and Scandinavian constituencies belatedly joined their East Coast colleagues representing the new immigrants in attempts to secure postponement of the national origins provision, hoping that the breather would provide an opportunity for its modification, if not outright repeal.

Concerned with immediate electoral repercussions, the Coolidge administration obliged. As critiques proliferated, Hill obtained a grant from the American Council of Learned Societies to establish a more reliable baseline with the assistance of Walter Willcox, the Cornell demographer on record as a critic of restrictions; Howard Barker, a genealogist; and Marcus Hansen, the immigration historian. A second postponement was enacted in 1928 because the computation of the quotas was "indefinite and uncertain," and finally, in February 1929, the Senate endorsed Hill's third plan. Although incoming President Herbert Hoover had told German and Scandinavian audiences during his campaign that national origins quotas were impossible to determine "accurately and without hardship," he proclaimed them effective on March 22 and the system finally went into effect on July 1, 1929.

Restriction was coupled with "Americanization," simultaneously a movement in the sociological sense and a concerted policy whereby the federal government assumed an unprecedented activist role with regard to the incorporation of immigrants.[98] Federal bodies involved included the Bureau of Naturalization in the Department of Labor, the Bureau of Education in the Department of Interior, the Committee on Public Information, and the Council of National Defense; under their leadership, more than thirty states enacted Americanization measures and hundred of cities followed suit. The Bureau of Naturalization's public school program continued into the late 1920s with the participation of some 3,526 communities and over 1 million individuals. The apparently compliant response of the targeted groups to these pressures is attributable not only to obvious disparities in power, but also to the fact that, however painfully demanding "Americanization" might be, it nevertheless constituted a genuine invitation, which ultimately held out the promise of incorporation and full membership for those who conformed.

The Triumph of Remote Control

In the course of the new régime's enactment, it became evident that its effective implementation demanded the elaboration of an extensive immigration bureaucracy abroad. The new law required not only unprecedented advance selection of authorized immigrants from among applicants, but also the maintenance of application files for those waiting for quota openings at a later time, the further formalization of the distinction between "immigrants" and "visitors," and the imposition of unprecedented controls on the latter so as to prevent them from turning into immigrants by overstaying. The necessity of an effective exclusionary device is revealed by the extent to which demand exceeded the quotas: for northern and western Europe, by about 3 to 1, but for southern and eastern Europe and the Near East, by a huge 78 to 1.[99] This required passports visaed in advance by U.S. officials, an approach under consideration for some years, as much in response to the changing international situation as to immigration problems proper.[100] Labor Secretary James Davis, whose department now housed the Immigration Bureau, endorsed the visa system in the belief that it would free the department of pressures: "If we halt these cases before they leave their native countries we will end the troubles at our ports of entry."[101] The shipping companies had become strong advocates of advance inspection as well, since this would eliminate the costly visa races and minimize their growing liability problems.[102] Finally, after five years of congressional efforts, the Rogers Act of 1924 combined the Diplomatic and Consular Services into a unified Foreign Service and established it on a secure professional basis, and a further reorganization was carried out in 1931.[103]

These developments were largely the work of the State Department's Wilbur J. Carr, a career civil servant who had labored for two decades to transform the consuls into a professional corps.[104]

From the restrictionist perspective, it was evident that remote control had been established in the nick of time. In the fiscal year ending June 30, 1928, the consulates issued only 369,562 entry permits. The quotas for all of the countries of Europe and the Near East, totaling 161,346, were completely used up; another 3,321 were issued for other countries, leaving 2,238 unused admissions, "made up almost entirely of quotas for African and Asiatic countries against which there is little or no demand." In the same year, the department also awarded 161,255 immigration visas to "nonquota nationals" (that is, Western Hemisphere immigrants), exempt categories (ministers, professors, and students), returning aliens, and relatives of immigrants; and another 97,756 visitor visas to tourists and businessmen. As an incentive for strict enforcement, the *American Foreign Service Journal,* a staff publication, regularly published "error scores" of the various consulates based on the ratio of visa holders denied entry at Ellis Island. As the Department suggested, the system also provided some security to the immigrants: whereas the overall rate of exclusion at U.S. ports of entry was 3.6 percent, the rate for those arriving with a visa was only 0.25 percent. The remote control system was shortly expanded to cover health inspection as well. In response to British complaints regarding the difficulties that ongoing practices imposed on the steamships sailing under its flag, an interagency plan was worked out whereby U.S. Public Health Service surgeons together with immigrant inspectors were sent on an experimental basis to the British Isles to act as technical advisors— without diplomatic status—"with a view to giving intending immigrants an examination abroad equal to that given at ports of entry."[105]

The new system was immediately effective: recorded immigration from Europe was reduced from 364,339 in 1924 to 148,366 the following year, and averaged about 160,000 over the next four. Writing in the *American Journal of Sociology,* Alcott W. Stockwell of the U.S. Immigration Service, Boston, suggested that the various steps from laissez-faire to restriction "present an object lesson of what might be termed sociological evolution, and serve to demonstrate the ability of the American democracy to work out its own salvation."[106] Within a year, Commissioner of Immigration at Ellis Island Henry Curran reported in the *Saturday Evening Post* that virtually all immigrants now looked exactly like Americans.[107]

Concurrently, Congress empowered Immigration Bureau employees to arrest without warrant aliens seeking to enter illegally or illegally in the United States; to board and search vessels within the territorial waters of the United States, and "within a reasonable distance from any external boundary of the United States," any railway car, aircraft, conveyance, or vehicle; and, within a distance of twenty-five miles from any external boundary, "to have access to private lands, but not dwellings, for the purpose of patrolling the border to prevent the illegal entry of aliens."[108] Nevertheless, there were worrisome reports of illegal entries by way of the northern and southern land borders as well as the Florida and Gulf Coasts, mostly from Cuba; overstaying was another path to unauthorized immigration, since visitor visas were much easier to obtain. In the years immediately following the passage of the quota laws, what one observer termed "conservative estimates" of illegal entries ran to 175,000 a year; "At one time it was estimated that there were a million aliens illegally in the country. In 1935, according to the best official estimates, the number of alien residents in the United States who had entered unlawfully was 400,000."[109]

As anticipated, the largely unguarded Mexican border emerged as the major problem. In 1918, to help enforce the new Passport Act, the U.S. Army had assigned cavalry units to patrol duty along the Rio Grande; however, "because they rode through less difficult stretches and could be evaded rather easily, additional men were needed in the outside force who were rugged enough to patrol hostile areas on flexible schedules so people trying to enter illegally would never know when or where they might be encountered."[110] Thanks to Passport Act enforcement appropriations, the force was able to recruit local ranchers and cowhands, including many hitherto employed as private gunhands. Subsequently mobilized into enforcing prohibition, it was formally organized into the U.S. Border Patrol by the Immigration Act of 1924; by this time it had grown to some forty officers, who adopted a uniform inspired by the Canadian Mounted Police. However, the principal targets were neither Mexicans nor Canadians but Europeans and Asians, and the small, untrained body spent much of its efforts enforcing prohibition rather than immigration. Mexican "wetbacks" (los mojados) were generally allowed to pass unmolested; but if apprehended, they were taken to the nearest Chamber of Commerce, which paid the required fees and forwarded them to the nearest entry point, where they were allowed to reenter legally.[111] Thanks to a $1,200,000 appropriation, the Border Patrol was extended over the next few years to cover Florida as well as the Canadian border. As of 1930, it numbered 875 men "to protect a front, land and water, of . . . approximately 8,000 miles," of whom

433 were deployed on the northern border, 319 on the southern, and 122 on the Florida and Gulf coasts. However, in testimony before a congressional committee, Commissioner General of Immigration Harry Hull pointed out that this amounted in effect to 40 miles of patrol per man on duty at any given time.[112]

Ironically, even as the main gate was being radically straitened, the Ellis Island reception center, shattered in 1916 by the explosion of a munitions barge on nearby Bedloe's Island, was rebuilt with a handsome self-supporting terracotta ceiling and a new tiled floor, which imparted to the hall a palatial and welcoming appearance commemorated in its late-twentieth-century restoration.[113] But after the institutionalization of remote control rendered the New York scrutiny superfluous, except for immigrants from nonquota countries in the Western Hemisphere, the facility functioned mainly as a deportation center, with a reduced force and maintenance budget. Rather than providing eager immigrants with the first glimpse of a fabulous American future, the great hall's splendor accentuated the bitterness of America's writ of rejection.

Aftermath and Depression

The Immigration Act of 1924 was as far as the moderate elements of the restrictionist coalition were willing to go, but attempts to substantially soften the law mostly failed as well. By the late 1920s, mainstream politicians had in effect reached a consensus on the new régime, as indicated by the nearly identical platforms of the Republican and Democratic Parties in 1928, which called for full implementation of the new laws, but with some consideration for the reunion of nuclear families.[114] Other than the potential immigrants themselves, the most negatively affected were the shipping lines, which were devastated by the abrupt loss of much of their steerage business; however, they soon recovered after hitting upon the idea of reconfiguring the vacated space and promoting affordable "tourist-class" trips to Europe for American college students and schoolteachers.[115]

A number of yet more draconian proposals, set forth while the economy was still in full swing, failed to move forward.[116] Although starting in 1928 consular officers issued to holders of immigration visas serially numbered identification cards to be countersigned by immigration inspectors at the port of entry, constituting a record of the alien's legal admission, the federal government lacked the authority to require U.S. residents to carry such documents, and a 1930 Michigan law to that effect was found unconstitutional. There were also persistent attempts to impose quotas on Western Hemisphere countries as a whole, or specifically on Mexico. Immigration from the latter was viewed as especially problematic, because its *mestizos*—according to Princeton economist Robert Foerster—would "lower the average of the race value of the white population of the United States."[117] Following the failure of Gompers to secure the inclusion of Mexico within the quota system, his successor, William Green, enlisted Mexico's leading trade union body in the elaboration of a "Gentleman's Agreement" whereby the Mexican government would voluntary limit emigration; but after two years of protracted negotiations, the arrangement failed and the AFL returned to its traditional stance on behalf of quotas.[118] Among its allies were the cotton growers of East Texas, intent upon minimizing competition from the Southwest.[119] As before, however, proposals to that effect were vociferously opposed by California's growers, who insisted that a quota was unnecessary because "[t]he Mexican is a 'homer'. Like the pigeon he goes back to roost" and "can be deported if he becomes a county charge."[120] The laissez-faire coalition also included Texas Representative John Nance Garner, selected by Franklin D. Roosevelt as his running mate in 1932. The State Department opposed the Mexican quota as well because it would "endanger our relations" with Mexico, and because it was difficult to target the southern neighbor without treating Canada in the same manner. To alleviate congressional pressures, the Hoover administration engineered the enactment of a law upgrading the penalty for aiding illegal immigration from a misdemeanor to a felony (signed March 4, 1929), and the State Department sharply reduced the attribution of Mexican immigration visas by strict enforcement of existing regulations: the LPC clause, the prohibition against contract labor, and the literacy requirement.[121] The chief of the Visa Office reported with evident satisfaction to a staff conference on immigration policy, which was gathered in New York City in December 1930, that thanks to these administrative measures, legal Mexican immigration was brought down from 40,013 in 1928–1929 to 11,801 the following year.[122]

As the United States slid into the Great Depression, there were persistent congressional moves to reduce immigration further or even suspend it altogether for the duration of the crisis. However, the State Department continued to oppose such draconian moves on diplomatic grounds, and as an alternative suggested extending the approach it had developed for reducing Mexican visas to the rest of the world.[123] Accordingly, on September 8, 1930, President Hoover issued an executive order prescribing strict application of the LPC clause to all visa requests, and uniformity in enforcement was insured by consular conferences held in the following months at the principal immigration centers in Europe.[124] Over the next five months, less than 10 percent of the quota was used because in addition to the executive order, consuls were instructed verbally to keep visas at that level, and in March 1931, the president reported that in the first five months, 96,883 otherwise eligible aliens had been denied visas.[125] In the first "national origin" year, 1930, the State Department issued 150,879 European quota visas (out of a possible 153,714), as well as 107,469 nonquota ones, for a total of 258,348 immigration permits; but in the first year after the new regulations came into force, the numbers were brought down to 48,528 and 45,999 respectively, for a total of 94,527, a cut of approximately 60 percent.[126] By 1934, its score of refusals had more than doubled to some 750,000, over half of them under the public charge provision.[127] A contemporaneous economist suggested that this temporary move was likely to become permanent, since once demand for labor resumed, "a new exodus of the southern Negro towards the industrial centers of the south and the north seems inevitable."[128]

The election of a Democratic House in November 1930 brought Samuel Dickstein, a stalwart opponent of the discriminatory features of the quota system representing New York's heavily Jewish Lower East Side, to the chair of the Immigration and Naturalization Committee. Early in 1932, he introduced a bill to check the State Department's power to deny visas to relatives by providing for an appeal to the secretary of labor, but was unable to move this beyond the committee stage. However, to ward off further attempts to constrain its authority, the department instructed its consuls to review all cases in which relatives of citizens and resident aliens had been refused visas on LPC grounds. By 1934, less than 2 percent of relatives, who made up some 60 percent of admissions, were being refused.[129]

With regard to Mexican immigration, not only were the restrictions imposed in 1928 further reinforced, but there is also evidence of what amounted to a deliberate "push-out" throughout the Southwest. Documented Mexican immigration was brought down further to 3,333 in 1931, lowered to 2,171 the following year, and kept at roughly that level for the remainder of the decade.[130] Moreover, according to the Census, the Mexican-born population in the four southwestern states (Arizona, California, New Mexico, and Texas), which numbered 616,998 in 1930, dropped to 377,433 in 1940, a net loss of about 240,000. Many of those who left were undoubtedly accompanied by their U.S.-born children, and overall estimates of the exodus of Mexican immigrants and Mexican Americans (1929–1939) run as high as 1 million.[131]

Was the exodus voluntary or forced? Mexicans had an extremely low rate of naturalization, both out of reluctance to "betray" their fatherland and because the surrounding American community rarely invited them to integrate and take the steps leading to citizenship; the costs involved undoubtedly acted as a deterrent as well.[132] Generally denied local relief, unemployed Mexican nationals had little choice but to return to their country of origin, and this held even for some American-born adults who were unaware of their rights as American citizens.[133] The Southern Pacific Railroad rose to the occasion, organizing massive removal at the modest cost of $14.70 per head; although they were told that they could return at any time, their passports or Mexican identity cards were stamped by the county welfare department, thereby establishing that they failed to meet the "LPC" clause.[134] Over 13,000 Mexicans living in Texas and New Mexico were "voluntarily repatriated" in this manner between 1931 and 1934, as were another 18,520 from Arizona.[135] Similar developments were reported as far north as East Chicago and Gary, Indiana. Although the more brutal practices were discontinued after the New Deal came into being, and in the case of Los Angeles, out of concern for public relations in anticipation of the 1932 Olympics, the exodus continued throughout the decade.[136]

"On the Acquiescence of This Government in the Murder of the Jews"

Displaying a prophetic acumen equal to his prediction that prosperity lay just around the corner, President Herbert Hoover declared in a campaign speech in October 1932 that the tightening of immigration was justified because "[w]ith the growth of democracy in foreign countries, political persecution has largely ceased. There is no longer a necessity for the United States to provide an asylum for those persecuted because of conscience."[137] Hoover's self-deluding statement echoed the conclusions reached by the League of Nations the previous year when, concluding that the sequels of the post–World War I refugee crisis were nearly resolved, it planned to close the Nansen Office created to protect "stateless" persons without nationality as the result of post-World War I and Russian Revolution expulsions and flight (including my own Polish-born parents, whose stateless status I subsequently inherited by virtue of Jus Sanguinis, in vigor in my native Belgium at the time. The Office was named in honor of the Norwegian polar explorer Frdtjof Nansen, a leading promoter of refugee protection.) by 1938.[138] In fact, it was already evident to anyone willing to look that democracy was hardly growing in Europe: Fascism had triumphed in Italy back in 1922, and the Decree of Public Safety issued by Benito Mussolini in November 1926 to consolidate his police state turned the trickle of political exiles into a massive exodus, mostly to France.[139] In 1923 Primo de Rivera established a military dictatorship in Spain, while Marshal Pilsudski did so in Poland three years later, as did General Gomez da Costa in Portugal; and by the time of Hoover's campaign speech, Lithuania, Rumania, and Yugoslavia had joined the dictatorial camp as well. Last but not least, a mere three months after the president's pronouncement, the Nazis came to power in Germany and immediately proceeded to purge "non-Aryans" as well as political opponents from the bureaucracy, teaching, and the professions. This marked the beginning of an unprecedented challenge to American immigration policy.

The episode has spawned an extensive literature seeking to explain precisely why immigration policy *failed* to change. After a quarter of a century of nearly total disinterest, public consciousness was awakened in 1967 by Arthur D. Morse's sensational *While Six Million Died: A Chronicle of American Apathy*.[140] Works by Wyman, Feingold, Stewart, and Friedman, already in the making, quickly followed.[141] Since then, the literature has continued to pour out, leaving no stone unturned and no participant unscathed.[142] Nor has the target been government alone: in 1984, for example, a report of the American Jewish Commission on the Holocaust leveled severe charges against the major Jewish organizations.[143] Always the same question: why wasn't more done? The query has been directed also at the other countries that were in a position to do something, notably Britain, Canada, and Australia.[144] The underlying premise is that many of Adolf Hitler's victims might have survived by fleeing, and some writers have gone so far as to suggest that the Nazis would not have resorted to the Final Solution at all had they been able to achieve ethnic cleansing by pushing out all those deemed undesirable. In this light, America's failure to open its door wider constitutes a significant contributory cause to the Holocaust. Seething with retrospective outrage, the explanations for American immobilism run the gamut of possibilities: the bureaucratic rigidity of State Department officials and their outright anti-Semitism; President Roosevelt's indifference and his subservience to political gamesmanship; the inability of Jewish American organizations to rise above their petty quarrels and their unduly cautious stance; and, beyond all these, the deep-seated xenophobia and anti-Semitism of the American people. As happens when history is turned into a courtroom, the accumulation of charges has also provoked the elaboration of an exculpatory counterposition. William D. Rubinstein, author of a sweeping case for the defense, grants that "in the early days of the Nazi period, intending refugee migrants to the United States were met with severe obstacles," but points out that "the existence of a strict quota also meant that the United States could not fail to admit *some* Jews (and others), regardless of the intention of America's nativists, while political pressure could—and eventually did—ensure that Jews were admitted up to the maximum quota limit."[145] Granting that "America's record in its reception of refugees from Nazi Germany was far from perfect," he nevertheless insists that "on any objective analysis, in the context of the evils of the Nazi regime as they were known at the time—and not with post-Holocaust eyes—it is far better than its critics maintain."[146]

As a "case study," the episode raises a question of central theoretical import for this book's argument: how come a policy that was the outcome of an ordinary political process became so rapidly and profoundly anchored as to weather a radical change of circumstances? In this perspective, the American response to the refugee crisis is a powerful demonstration of the process of "path dependency," whereby "once certain choices are made, they constrain future possibilities. The range of options available to policymakers at any given point in time is a function of institutional capabilities that were put in place at some earlier period, possibly in response to very different environmental pressures."[147] Or, as Paul Pierson has put it in a recent overview, "Specific patterns of timing and sequence matter; a wide range of social outcomes may be possible; large consequences may result from relatively small or contingent events; particular courses of action, once introduced, can be almost impossible to reverse; and consequently, political development is punctuated by critical moments or junctures that shape the basic contours of social life."[148] Seldom has a scientific formulation encompassed a greater tragedy.

Nazi Initiatives and Initial Responses

At the time of the Nazi takeover, Germany had 525,000 self-identified Jews, including nearly 100,000 recent immigrants, three-fifths of them Polish nationals and another one-fifth stateless, mostly originating also in historic Poland or Ukraine.[149] An additional 292,000 persons were of Jewish descent, amounting altogether to about 1.5 percent of the total population.[150] Concentrated in the larger cities, one-third in Berlin, the Jews were overwhelming middle class, largely engaged in trade and commerce as well as in the professions, notably law and medicine. The targeting of the Jews for persecution came as a shock, not only because such brutality in a land renowned for its great culture was inconceivable, but also because Jews were arguably better integrated in Germany than anywhere else in Europe and perhaps in the United States as well, as indicated for example by the fact that they constituted 2.6 percent of university professors, at a time when they had barely crossed the threshold of American elite institutions of higher education.[151]

Initially the overwhelming majority of the targeted population adopted a wait-and-see attitude, making the best of a bad thing, expecting that the new government would not last, or that, once having assuaged the yearnings of Nazi militants, it would turn to the more serious business of economic recovery. This would surely temper attacks on an economically valuable segment of the population, as Hitler's own economic experts, notably Hjalmar Schacht, president of the Reichsbank, advised.[152]

Nevertheless, in the first two years, some 75,000 persons left Germany, about four-fifths of them Jews. Thinking of the move as temporary, most of them relocated in a neighboring country—such as Austria, Czechoslovakia, or France—where by virtue of their relative affluence they were regarded as unproblematic visitors.[153] Only a small minority undertook to emigrate overseas, given the difficulty of doing so in the midst of a worldwide depression and Nazi prohibitions on exporting assets. The leading alternative to the United States was Palestine, the obvious choice for committed Zionists; but others went as well merely because it was available, prompting a joke recorded by Victor Klemperer in June 1933: "An immigrant to Palestine is asked, 'Are you coming from conviction or from Germany?' "[154] Movement to Palestine was facilitated by a "transfer" (*ha'avarah*) agreement that the Zionist leaders negotiated with the Nazis, whereby departing Jews were allowed to remove part of their property in the form of German goods.[155]

Despite America's consecrated self-image as a land of asylum, the only provision for refugees under the recently established régime was an exemption from the literacy requirement in case of religious persecution; but this was hardly relevant to educated Europeans, and in any case was applicable only to people who met all the other conditions for immigration. The quota system itself did not constitute an overwhelming obstacle, as it provided for the admission of up to 25,000 Germans a year; ironically, Jews rejected by the Nazis because they did not satisfy their criteria of because they were genuine Germans. The problem arose rather from the Hoover-imposed LPC clause noted earlier.[156]

Concern with the German situation was initially circumscribed almost exclusively to the Jewish community. At the highest levels, lucidity prevailed. As early as May 8, 1933, the secretary of the American Jewish Committee alerted his Executive Committee that "[W]hat has happened to the Jews in Germany (and indirectly to the Jews of the world) is worse than the expulsion of the Jews from Spain. It not only involves the possible extermination [sic] of 600,000 Jews, but threatens to react dangerously upon the political, social, and economic status of the Jews in other countries. . . . We have a tremendous job on our hands, not a passing episode. But one that threatens to be a problem for a long time. . . . Many civilized countries of the world will have to be enlisted to offer shelter to the refugees."[157] Shortly after Hitler came to power, Representative Dickstein introduced a bill to revoke the executive order of September 1930 tightening the LPC clause. However, Max Kohler, who had taken over as the American Jewish Committee's immigration specialist after the death of Louis Marshall, urged him to desist because, given the unemployment crisis, the initiative created "a situation where it will be charged that America's Jews want to sacrifice America's obvious and essential interests on behalf of their German coreligionists."[158] The other leading organizations concurred, and Dickstein gave up. Instead, he reintroduced his 1932 bill for a review process, but abandoned this as well in the face of State Department hostility.

Restrictionism remained firmly entrenched despite the fact that the Democrats controlled both houses from 1932 onward. Concerned most of all with building a coalition in support of his economic recovery program, President Roosevelt was intent on avoiding moves that might alienate crucial elements of his own party, notably the Southerners; and this was true also of the liberal bloc that labored on behalf of foundational New Deal legislation, notably the Wagner Act (1935).[159] Finding their path blocked in Congress, advocates of a more open door turned to the executive branch.[160] Committed to a rigid interpretation of its functions and to protection of the national interest narrowly construed, the State Department bureaucracy opposed special treatment for refugees on the grounds that this might antagonize the German government, and jealously guarded its recently acquired authority over the award of visas against encroachments by congressional advocates or by the Department of Labor, which housed the Immigration Bureau, reorganized in 1933 as the Immigration and Naturalization Service (INS).[161] The rivalry between state and labor was exacerbated by the fact that the latter was headed by Frances Perkins, one of the most liberal members of Roosevelt's cabinet. Although Secretary of State Cordell Hull was himself married to a Jewish woman, within the habitus of the foreign service, anti-Semitism was respectable and perhaps even mandatory.[162] An especially relevant case in point was Wilbur J. Carr, who in his capacity as assistant secretary of state for administration in the early 1930s was in a position to decisively implement his preferences.[163] Although the State Department also contained a few exceptional individuals, both Jews and non-Jews, who perceived the gravity of the situation early on and were determined to intervene, they faced an uphill fight within their own bureaucratic sphere.

Despite intervention at the presidential level by Judge Irving Lehman, brother of the New York governor, with support from Secretary of the Treasury Henry Morgenthau, the established LPC policy was maintained on the grounds that there was little need for change so long as the German quota remained unfilled, a state of affairs that was of course attributable precisely to the policy in question. The State Department also opposed a proposal by Judge Mack of Philadelphia to use a provision of the 1917 law allowing for the LPC requirement to be met by the posting of bonds, and after Perkins ordered her department to move ahead with the bonding procedure anyway, the State Department continued to delay its application.[164]

Refugee advocates were constrained from mobilizing public opinion on behalf of their cause by the pervasiveness of anti-Semitism, whose prevalence and depth are difficult to imagine today.[165] Among its most extreme manifestations were the rantings of Father Charles Coughlin, the Detroit-based "radio priest" who even in his early leftist phase, when he attacked Wall Street and preached that "the New Deal is Christ's deal," charged that the Depression was cunningly orchestrated by a sinister international Jewish directorate.[166] Coughlin was by no means a marginal character but a major public figure, invited twice to the White House by the newly elected Roosevelt, who was eager to cultivate Catholic immigrant communities and determined to emulate the priest's masterful use of the new broadcasting medium. Anti-Semitism formed a negative background that constrained decision makers from making choices that appeared *philo*-Semitic, and it severely handicapped the efforts of American Jews on behalf of refugees for fear of confirming reigning stereotypes.[167] Although by virtue of their numbers and urban concentration, the Jews of the "new immigration" achieved some political clout in states critical for Democratic success, notably New York, Illinois, and Pennsylvania, their representatives were afraid to undertake substantial modifications of the immigration system because they were persuaded "that a debate on the House floor could lead to an explosion against us."[168] As in Europe, the experience of anti-Semitism also contributed to the spread of Zionism, whose organizational expression was the American Jewish Congress. This was the source of a persistent dilemma: should efforts to secure asylum for the persecuted Jews of Germany be directed at the United States or at Britain, which guarded the door to Palestine? Jewish-dominant labor unions, such as New York's garment workers, as well as radical groups close to the Communist Party, were least constrained and immediately took a firm stand on behalf of liberalization of the immigration laws; however, their marginal position in the political arena minimized their influence on policy makers, and mainstream organized labor turned a deaf ear to their entreaties.[169]

Nevertheless, the various interventions did result in a slight loosening of red tape regarding immigration visas, including the possibility of issuing them to German refugees residing in other European countries, and more significantly in a liberalization of temporary visitors' visas. There were also successful efforts to admit a number of distinguished refugee scholars, scientists, and artists under a provision of the immigration law allowing for the possibility of acquiring foreign talent outside of quota limitations.

The Limits of International Intervention

At the international level, the Nazis' proclaimed objective of ridding Germany of the Jews confronted liberal states with a dilemma: wouldn't the provision of asylum to those deemed undesirable encourage the Nazis to pursue their project more vigorously? Often dismissed as an excuse for inaction, in retrospect this consideration is rendered more credible by its evocation at the end of the twentieth century with regard to "ethnic cleansing" in Bosnia.[170] At the outset, the League of Nations was immobilized by the requirement of consensus, which afforded Germany an effective veto; hence both the refugees and their hosts were left to their own devices. After Hitler pulled out in October 1933, the League did establish a "High Commission for Refugees (Jewish and Other) Coming from Germany," but to avoid antagonizing Germany, it was organized as an autonomous entity, located away from Geneva.[171] This also made it possible to secure American involvement, in keeping with indications from President Roosevelt that he was inclined to adopt a somewhat more internationalist stance while avoiding an all-out confrontation with the isolationist camp.[172] With the president's approval, the League appointed an American, James G. McDonald, a former official of Herbert Hoover's relief organization, as high commissioner.

Although the agency was able to effect some resettlement, McDonald resigned in December 1935 and registered a forceful and lucid protest over his lack of authority and means: "I am convinced that it is the duty of the High Commissioner for German Refugees, in tendering his resignation, to express an opinion on the essential elements of the talks with which the Council of the League entrusted him. When domestic policies threaten the demoralization and exile of hundreds of thousands of human beings, considerations of diplomatic correctness must yield to those of common humanity. I should be recreant if I did not call attention to the actual situation, and plead that world opinion, acting through the League and its Member-States and other countries, move to avert the existing and impending tragedies."[173] His successor, Sir Neill Malcolm, was more directly connected with the League and somewhat better funded, but nevertheless retained a narrow mandate dealing only with the formal protection of refugees who had left Germany. In early 1938 the League moved to consolidate the Nansen Office and the High Commission for Refugees (Jewish and Other) Coming from Germany, to which Austria had een added in the wake of the Anschluss, into a single organization.

The expectation of return, shared by many of the early refugees, was shattered by the proclamation of the Nuremberg Laws in September 1935, which indicated that their exclusion was permanent and precipitated a greater exodus as well as an escalation of visa applications. In response to entreaties from advocates, Roosevelt issued a directive to give refugees "the most humane and favourable treatment possible under the law." Accordingly, Carr's successor, George Messersmith, who had shown some sympathy for refugees while serving in Berlin, instructed the European consulates that the possibility of becoming a public charge "was not sufficient grounds for denial" of a visa.[174] The new policy resulted in a dramatic increase in visas granted under the German quota, from 6,978 in fiscal year 1936 (27 percent of the maximum possible) to 12,532 the following year (48 percent).[175] Concurrently, the president also extended the validity of visitors' visas issued earlier to persons who could not return to Germany.

As of the end of 1937, the Jewish exodus from Germany amounted to some 130,000; taking into consideration the fairly large number of deaths attributable to the population's age structure, this amounted to a little over one-fourth of the original number. Of these, about 38,400 went to Palestine, 35,000 to the United States (including extended-stay visitors as well as quota immigrants), and another 20,000 to South America (mostly Argentina and Brazil). The remaining 50,000 were scattered throughout Europe, including some 10,000 each in France, Britain, and the Netherlands. But in March of that year, the Austrian *Anschluss* added 180,000 persons to the pool of undesirable "non-Aryans" within what was now the "Greater Reich," prompting about one-third of them to flee abroad by the end of the year. The annexation of the Czech Sudetenland in the fall contributed another 30,000, of whom most escaped to nearby Prague. The Nazi government then decided to expel some 30,000 Polish Jewish residents who, unwanted by the Polish government (which in order to prevent their return cancelled the citizenship of persons residing more than five years outside the country), languished for several months in a no-man's-land. Distracted by his parents' predicament in Hannover, Germany, Herschl Grynszpan, a student in Paris, attempted to assassinate the German ambassador, but succeeded only in killing a minor official. This unleashed the state-organized terrorist retaliation of November 9–10, 1937, known as *Kristallnacht,* the night of broken glass.

The emerging situation was well captured by a grisly joke: the world was made up of two kinds of countries, those where Jews could not live, and those they could not enter.[176] Those already outside the Greater Reich turned into permanent refugees, and most of those still inside understood that they had little choice but to emigrate; and it was becoming evident that eastern and central Europe's 5 to 6 million Jews were in dire jeopardy as well.[177] France, which had arisen as a major haven in mid-1936 when Prime Minister Léon Blum's Popular Front came to power, began to close down after Blum was overthrown. His conservative successor increased the authority of border guards to keep refugees at bay and responded to the *Kristallnacht* exodus by creating detention centers. Nevertheless, he refrained from expelling refugees already in the country, and there was a continuous trickle of illegal entry as well, so that on the eve of the war, France hosted about 40,000 refugees from Germany and several hundred thousand from Spain after the onset of civil war in 1936. Most critical was the situation in Palestine, where in 1936 the Arabs rose up against expanding Jewish settlement. To pacify them, Britain reduced legal entries, which averaged 41,000 a year from 1933 to 1936, to between 10,000 and 12,000 after that.

Consequently, by 1938 the United States and the other democracies were faced with a refugee crisis of unprecedented character and magnitude, which forced them to confront their restrictive immigration policies head on. Roosevelt endorsed merging the small Austrian quota with the larger German one so as to provide more opportunities for newly vulnerable Austrians, an operation facilitated by the presence in the Berlin and Vienna consulates of sympathetic officials, who also initiated a more liberal policy regarding visitors' visas. For some months, the prominent journalist Dorothy Thompson, who was married to the novelist Sinclair Lewis, had been promoting the establishment of an international organization capable of dealing with the refugee problem on a broad scale. Thompson's proposal was opposed by the State Department, which advocated instead U.S. cooperation with an enlarged refugee bureau of the International Labor Organization. Nevertheless, it was taken up by President Roosevelt, reportedly on the advice of his confidant, Judge Samuel Rosenman, and with the support of Secretary Morgenthau.[178] Accordingly, on March 24 the president announced the convening of an international conference to establish a new ad hoc Intergovernmental Committee on behalf of refugees (IGC); however, he also indicated that the United States would not consider increasing admissions beyond the numbers prescribed by existing legislation, nor would it expect any other nation to do so. Moreover, Secretary of State Cordell Hull made it clear that in order to attract British participation, there was to be no discussion of Zionism or Palestine. Immediately afterwards, Roosevelt also appointed a Presidential Advisory Committee on Refugees, made up of representatives from the major religious communities and headed by former High Commissioner McDonald. Concurrently, Representatives Dickstein and Emmanuel Celler drafted a bill that pooled all the quota allotments and made them available to refugees regardless of nationality, as well as exempted them from the LPC requirement. However, the leading Protestant, Catholic, Jewish, and nonsectarian refugee aid agencies opined that the initiative jeopardized the scheduled international conference and persuaded the congressmen to desist.

Caught unawares, a reluctant State Department had twenty-four hours to plan Roosevelt's conference, which was scheduled to open in Evian-les-Bains, the French watering resort near Geneva, on July 5; "Considering that the Department did not really favor the President's idea in the first place, it is not surprising that the preparation lacked imagination and went little beyond the procedural."[179] Although the president's objectives remained nebulous, as an indication of the importance he attached to the meeting, he appointed as leader of the American delegation Myron C. Taylor, former chairman of U.S. Steel, with McDonald as an adviser. They were accompanied by unofficial representatives of thirty-nine private organizations, twenty-one of them Jewish. German and Austrian Jews, no longer under any illusion about their future, hoped the conference would help mobilize sufficient international funds to permit a total evacuation, which was estimated to require four years.

Thirty-three nations were invited, including all the European democracies, Canada and Australia, the Latin American states, and Italy; no call was issued to Germany, nor to Russia, Poland, Hungary, Rumania, Yugoslavia, Greece, Turkey, or Spain. Italy alone refused to participate, on the grounds that Germany had been kept out. Anti-Fascist Italian exiles hoped to benefit from this refusal, as their efforts to gain protection under the League had hitherto been defeated by Italian vetoes.

Mystified as to American intentions, the European states initially opted for routine representation by diplomats in neighboring posts. However, a five-point agenda sent out by the United States on June 16 clarified the president's objectives somewhat, suggesting that the conference should consider establishing a continuing body to cooperate with existing refugee organizations as well as deal with "the problem in the larger sense," and that it should make recommendations not only on all the specified agenda items, but further on "other points which may be proposed to it." This was interpreted by local diplomats to mean that Roosevelt was opening the conference door "to the whole existing or potential refugee problem outside Germany—that is, in Spain, Italy, Poland, Rumania, and Hungary."[180] Although the more comprehensive approach was strongly opposed by France and Britain, Norway and nongovernmental organizations that had been dealing with anti-Fascist refugees from Italy and elsewhere leaned toward broadening, and the prospect caused several of the participants to upgrade their delegation.

As the conferees prepared to meet, the New York State Encampment of the Veterans of Foreign Wars, holding its annual meeting in Albany, adopted a resolution stating that it "disapproved" of the action of President Roosevelt in permitting refugees to come to the United States.[181] This was very much in tune with the attitude of the more general public; according to a *Fortune* poll taken at the time, 67.4 percent of Americans said the United States should keep out German and Austrian refugees.[182] As against this, *New York Times* columnist Anne O'Hare McCormick insisted in her Independence Day piece that "[a] great power free to act has no alibi for not acting." Providing a haven for refugees "is not simply humanitarian. It is not a question of how many more unemployed this country can safely add to its own unemployed millions. It is a test of civilization."[183] In the same issue, the paper also reported that Rabbi Stephen S. Wise, a member of the President's Refugee Advisory Council, told the Detroit congress of the Zionist Organization of America, in his valedictory address as president, that Evian would be a "dismal failure" unless Britain was prepared to open Palestine to mass immigration of Jews from

Germany and Austria, and urged the American delegation to impress this on their British colleagues.[184] The Zionists unanimously adopted a resolution thanking President Roosevelt for bringing the conference into being and urging the establishment of a special commission to that effect.

On the eve of the opening, one delegate commented that the atmosphere at Evian was that "of a none too trustful poker game, particularly as between the three great democracies, the United States, the United Kingdom, and France," but with the object of the game "changed from money and arms to human beings." The motive power continued to be supplied by the United States, with the United Kingdom as the chief brake, and France trying to steer a middle course. In his opening statement, Myron Taylor argued on behalf of an Intergovernmental Committee, which would become a permanent continuing mechanism competent to deal with future refugees from other countries, to be established outside the League. As against this, Earl Winterton, on behalf of Britain, and Senator Bérenger, on behalf of France, insisted that the new body's domain be limited to refugees from Germany and Austria, and that it function merely as an advisory body to the League's high commissioner. Although the Americans preferred to have the presidency go to Bérenger so as to engage the Europeans into the project, Taylor was elected instead, indicating that the Europeans expected the United States to shoulder most of the responsibility for the new body and its policies.

From the outset, the sticking point was immigration. Winterton announced that his government was actively surveying possibilities of relocating refugees in its colonial and overseas territories, and in particular of settling a limited number of families in East Africa, while the American delegation reported that the recently consolidated German and Austrian quotas would be entirely filled in the current year.[185] Both the Belgian and Dutch delegates pleaded saturation, while Argentina insisted it had done as much as the United States, despite its much smaller population. The Australian representative issued the conference's most restrictionist response, pointing out, "As we have no real racial problem, we are not desirous of importing one by encouraging any scheme of large-scale foreign migration." Canada, in striking contrast, indicated that although it had been forced by the Depression to prohibit immigration in principle, it had made "a substantial number" of administrative exemptions on behalf of refugees.[186] The Dominican Republic stood out from the pack by pledging to take in as many as 100,000 refugees, but it was difficult to know whether this was a serious proposal. The League's high commissioner indicated his support for the IGC on the grounds that "it would have behind it the enormous prestige of the President of the United States of America and the American people," but also reported discouraging replies from the dominions and other overseas governments.

On July 8, the IGC held a hearing for some forty nongovernmental assistance organizations, mostly Jewish. Rabbi Jonah B. Wise promised the full cooperation of the American Joint Distribution Committee, while Dr. Arthur Ruppin reported on behalf of the Jewish Agency that Palestine had already absorbed 40,000 refugees but could take more, provided Germany let them take out some assets. Nahum Goldmann of the World Jewish Congress estimated that the IGC would have to provide for the emigration of 200,000 to 300,000 remaining Jews in Greater Germany within the next few years, and urged it to also consider the situation of the Jews in Poland, Hungary, and Rumania.[187] The conference also heard three representatives of Austrian Jewry, authorized by the Nazis as observers, to the effect that if the conference could arrange for the exodus of some 40,000 persons, the authorities would let them take out some of their property.[188] Back in New York, Evian was the subject of many Sabbath sermons; but concern remained focused on emigration to Palestine rather than the United States.

On Bastille Day, Evian adopted a final resolution constituting itself into a permanent body independent of the League, to be headquartered in London but headed by an American. Leaving the management of refugees already out of Germany to the League's high commissioner and the Nansen Office, the IGC would undertake negotiations toward the orderly resettlement of prospective refugees, but limit itself initially to Germany and Austria so as to discourage other states from imitating the Nazis. It was to report to a permanent committee of the thirty-two states attending the present meeting and would be governed by an executive committee of five states, chaired by Britain. Roosevelt announced the appointment of George Rublee, a distinguished seventy-year-old Washington lawyer, while Myron Taylor continued on as American representative on the Executive Committee. The conference also approved an optimistic resolution to the effect that the report of the technical committee "holds out that the prospects have increased for the reception of refugees," and recommending that governments "continue to study" these technical problems "in a generous spirit." However, as negotiations drew to a close, the *New York Times* reported under the headline "REICH POWER FELT AT REFUGEE PARLEY" that Germany was putting pressure on the Latin American states and its small neighbors to whittle down a proposed resolution, insisted on by France and Britain, asserting that involuntary emigrants *have the right* to export their assets.[189] Accordingly, the conference limited itself to urging the country of origin to "collaborate" in this matter.

Highly divided at the time, assessments of Evian remained so after the conference passed into history. The *New York Times* commented editorially that although "[i]t cannot be said that the conference solved the problem," nevertheless it "accomplished all that it could have been expected to do," and the editorial concluded by suggesting, "In a special sense it is up to the United States, which has taken a generous initiative, to set an example of prompt and generous action."[190] Bluntly summarizing the outcome, the *Christian Science Monitor* headlined "NATIONS LOATH TO GIVE ASYLUM TO JEWS."[191] In the same vein, Hitler remarked sarcastically in January 1939, "It is a shameful example to observe today how the entire democratic world dissolves in tears of pity, but then, in spite of its obvious duty to help, closes its heart to the poor, tortured people."[192] Jewish Americans were angered by the conference's failure to address the Palestine issue, and Evian came to be inscribed in their collective memory as the gateway to Auschwitz.[193]

Pointing to a contemporaneous punster's observation that Evian backward spells "naïve," one retrospective critic has provided a caustic summary of the proceedings: "Having established a precedent for inaction, the American delegation listened as one national representative after another disavowed the initiative in resolving the refugee problem."[194] But an analyst viewing Evian from the perspective of the development of an international refugee régime has suggested instead that, thanks largely to the skillful efforts of Myron Taylor, the conference constituted a turning point in American acceptance of cooperative responsibility for the solution of a European problem, as well as a stepping stone toward what would become a more solid international refugee régime after World War II.[195]

As it was, the IGC was quickly overwhelmed by developments arising from the briskly evolving international situation. Two months after mandating Rublee to undertake negotiations for orderly departure, Britain and France sought to appease Hitler by granting him the Czech Sudetenland, a move that sent many thousands fleeing toward Prague and added substantially to the population at risk within the enlarged Greater Reich. Then came *Kristallnacht,* prompting the *Los Angeles Examiner* to proclaim in a banner headline, "NAZIS WARN WORLD JEWS WILL BE WIPED OUT UNLESS EVACUATED BY DEMOCRACIES."[196]

Nevertheless, by the end of the year the Nazi government appeared to recognize the IGC as a bargaining agent.[197] Rublee finally reached Berlin in

January 1939 and reported optimistically to his governing body the following month that he had achieved an agreement with Hjalmar Schacht on a plan for the orderly emigration of most of the remaining Jews and non-Aryans from the Reich with part of their assets, leaving some 200,000 elderly persons to live out their lives peacefully within their homeland with the help of a trust fund to be established by Jewish organizations abroad. The scheme, which paralleled the ongoing *ha'avarah* agreement, was promptly approved by the State Department.[198] His mission accomplished, Rublee stepped down; his place was taken by Sir Herbert Emerson, the League's new high commissioner for refugees from Germany, thereby in effecting merging the two bodies. However, no progress was made toward implementation of the Rublee plan, and an attempt to enlist Mussolini's help came to naught as well; in fact, the Duce himself belatedly initiated Jewish persecutions. Schacht himself was shortly removed from his post, and captured German documents retrospectively confirmed that the Nazis saw the Rublee plan as a means of speeding up the exit of Jews and of securing some immediate economic gains, but were by no means committed to implementing the conditions specified.[199]

Accelerating Crisis

The refugee crisis grew throughout 1939 at an accelerating pace. On March 15–16, less than six months after Britain, France, Germany, and Italy signed the Munich Pact, Hitler annexed the rest of Czechoslovakia, adding another 400,000 Jews and anti-Nazis, including many recent refugees from Austria and the Sudetenland, to the pool of persons in jeopardy. There were additional anti-Semitic actions in Hungary and Poland, as well as in the Baltic states. In May the British government published a White Paper further restricting Jewish immigration to Palestine to 75,000 over a five-year period; however, perhaps to compensate for this move, it eased immigration into Britain itself. Consequently, by the outbreak of war Britain emerged as the third largest asylum provider, after Palestine and the United States.[200]

In response to *Kristallnacht*, President Roosevelt recalled his ambassador from Germany, extended the visas of some 15,000 German visitors, and pressed the IGC to undertake a survey of the "uninhabited areas of the world" that might provide resettlement for anywhere from 10 to 20 million displaced persons. A worried German ambassador to Washington reported "a hurricane of condemnation," stressing that "Even the respectable patriotic circles which were thoroughly . . . anti-Semitic in their outlook also begin to turn away from us."[201] Yet restrictive legislation came closer to passage than at any time since 1930, and an interfaith effort to enact a law to admit German children outside the quota, promoted by a blue-ribbon committee that included former IGC director Rublee, generated considerable enthusiasm in the country at large but failed to secure presidential endorsement. After being amended to grant children priority for admission *within* the quota rather than in addition to it, the "Wagner-Rogers" bill was opposed by its original sponsors and failed to come to a floor vote in either house.[202] A scheme to increase admissions by "mortgaging" quotas for later years failed as well. At the end of May, the plight of refugees filled every neighborhood movie screen, as the weekly newsreels featured the pathetic passengers of the SS *St. Louis.* Lured to Cuba by a corrupt diplomat with the promise that they would be allowed to wait there for American visas, they were in fact denied admission; prohibited from entering American waters, the vessel was escorted by the U.S. Coast Guard along the coast of Florida to prevent anyone from swimming ashore, and it ultimately sailed back to Europe, landing its passengers in Antwerp. An Alaskan Development bill that would open the territory to settlement by refugees, promoted by the Department of the Interior but opposed by the State Department, and another involving the Virgin Islands, got nowhere in Congress.[203] Nevertheless, thanks to the recent changes in American administrative practices, the German-Austrian quota was being filled as promised, and additional refugees were being admitted as tourists also. Richard Breitman and Alan Kraut therefore conclude that the period from March 1938 until September 1939 marked the most liberal phase of American immigration policy between 1931 and 1946.[204]

Altogether, about 127,000 Jewish refugees were admitted to the United States in 1933–1940, including immigrants and visitors who were subsequently allowed to stay. Was the glass half full or half empty? The number exceeded the refugees admitted to Palestine in the same period (65,900 Germans, Austrians, and Czechs, out of 208,600 recorded legal immigrants in 1933–1940, plus some illegals), and amounted to considerably more than any other country.[205] However, another 110,000 could have been admitted within the limits of the German quota alone in the years before it was filled. Totally ignored in Rubinstein's intemperate plea on behalf of a good western conscience is the fact that as of the end of June 1939, 309,782 nationals of the Greater Reich (including Austrians and Czechoslovaks) had applied for immigration visas, resulting in a waiting list that would have taken a dozen years to exhaust within the framework of the established quota system.[206] Finally, the masses widely understood to be at risk in Poland, Hungary, and Rumania, as well as nationals of those countries who had managed to move to western Europe prior to the extension of the Nazi Empire, were overwhelming kept out by virtue of the extremely small quotas for central and eastern Europe.

On August 23, 1939, Germany and the Soviet Union signed a nonaggression pact; one week later, Germany invaded Poland, which contained by far the largest Jewish population in Europe, and France and Britain declared war on Germany. By this time, approximately three-fifths of the Jewish population of pre-*Anschluss* Germany had gotten out, nearly half of them in the last two years. The 250,000–300,000 Jews remaining in Germany and Austria, as well as most of those in ex-Czechoslovakia, were now in effect confined. Following the division of Poland between the Nazi and Soviet partners, western Poland's massive Jewish population faced Nazi occupation as well, and from late 1939 onward, Nazi policies and practices in occupied Poland shifted perceptibly from persecution toward annihilation. While the possibility of westward movement was almost totally eliminated by the outbreak of war, a small number managed to escape to eastern Poland under Soviet rule, to the Soviet Union itself, or even to Japan.

The United States Faces the Holocaust

In the spring of 1940, Germany launched major offensives in the West, which shortly brought Denmark, Norway, Belgium, Luxembourg, the Netherlands, and northern France under its control; concurrently, it established its hegemony over the Balkans, either directly (Greece) or through allied régimes (Hungary, Rumania, and Bulgaria). The French Republic voted itself out of existence, and on July 10 Marshall Pétain became head of the French state; albeit formally neutral, the Vichy government collaborated with the Nazis in most spheres, notably in implementation of their anti-Jewish policies. However, for a time unoccupied France afforded a place of refuge and the possibility of exit to neutral Spain, or even overseas.

With Britain out of play, except with regard to Palestine, and the overseas dominions also at war with Germany, neutral America's immigration policy moved to the fore as a critical determinant of the fate of refugees outside occupied Europe. The outbreak of war stimulated renewed xenophobia, manifested in renewed attempts to restrict immigration and to exclude aliens from membership in American society, including a stark proposal by a Georgia congressman "[t]o deny admission into the United States to all immigrants and to deport all aliens."[207] President Roosevelt's interest in refugees was steadily overshadowed by an overwhelming concern with getting his program in support of Britain through Congress and getting the country ready for an impending war.[208] Immigration policy was steadily tightened up on security grounds, and refugees were deemed to provide particularly grave risks of infiltration, leading to a reversal of the permissive use of the German and Austrian quotas.[209] In June 1940, the INS was transferred from the Department of Labor to the Department of Justice, and a registration requirement was imposed on all aliens. On the other hand, in July 1940 Roosevelt created a President's Advisory Committee on Refugees, at whose behest the State Department instituted an "unblocking" procedure for the award of visas to refugees trapped by the collapse of France. In addition, the Committee drew up a list of 4,000 persons in special danger to be given visitors' visas, of whom 2,000 arrived over the next year.[210]

However, the president's most consequential move was the appointment of Breckinridge Long as the successor to Messersmith as assistant secretary of state for administration. A political appointee associated with Woodrow Wilson, Long has achieved historical notoriety as the bête noire of refugee policy for his extremely rigid stance on the subject of visas; this stance, blamed by many on his personal anti-Semitism, is better accounted for by an over-zealous concern with security, which he shared with Avra Warren, head of the Visa Division. Following the proclamation of National Emergency on June 24, 1941, the award of visas was centralized in Washington, where applications were subject to an elaborate security screening that prolonged the already arduous procedure; particularly problematic was a new policy of rejecting affidavits of support from anyone other than immediate relatives. Moreover, on July 10, 1941, all U.S. consulates in Germany were closed, making it impossible to obtain visas without first escaping the country. Although the President's Advisory Committee on Refugees met with Roosevelt on September 4 to protest the new procedures, his sole concession was provision for an appeal.[211] Combined with the shortage of transportation and the refusal of the shipping lines to accept German currency, the new procedures prevented thousands of otherwise eligible persons from entering the United States between 1940 and 1942, with often fatal consequences. Estimates of refugees who were in a position to leave Europe but prevented from doing so by U.S. obstacles range from 62,000 to 75,000.[212] However, even in this darkest period, the record is not completely one-sided, and the INS claimed that 34,000 more Jewish refugees were admitted to the United States during the 1940–1942 period under the various quotas.[213]

On June 22, 1941, Germany invaded the Soviet Union, rapidly bringing under its control eastern Poland, the Ukraine, and the Baltic states, most of which had large Jewish populations. With Jewish undesirables now rising to several millions and almost totally immobilized, in early 1942 the Nazis adopted a systematic program for implementing the "Final Solution," hitherto practiced *in loco,* by way of removal to industrialized death camps. Sketchy information regarding their existence reached Jewish American leaders as early as May and was confirmed at the end of July by a more reliable source. The recipients passed on the information to the government, but abided by the State Department's request not to make it public, pending official verification.[214] President Roosevelt spoke up about war crimes as early as October 7, but skeptical officials verified the information to their satisfaction only in late November. The tragic news was then widely publicized.

On December 17, 1942, the United States joined Britain and ten allied governments in exile in denouncing the Nazi extermination plot, but no action followed.[215] After meeting with Vice President Henry Wallace and Speaker of the House Sam Rayburn about the need to loosen restrictions on immigration and imports, President Roosevelt retreated when told that this would meet with considerable congressional opposition.[216] In the face of mounting public pressure, the British ambassador to Washington asked his government to cooperate with the Americans on refugee problems, and after trying to sidestep the issue, the State Department finally responded on February 25, 1943, on the eve of a massive rally organized by Rabbi Stephen Wise in Madison Square Garden under the slogan "STOP HITLER NOW!"[217] To avoid likely demonstrations, the conference was to be held in Bermuda, with refugee relief organizations limited to observer status. Myron Taylor, at this time special envoy to the Vatican, refused to head the U.S. delegation in the absence of a guarantee of effective action and was replaced by Harold Dodds, president of Princeton University.

The Bermuda Conference opened on April 16, 1943, which happened to be the first evening of Passover and also marked the onset of the final Nazi assault on the Warsaw Ghetto. It was agreed at the outset that it should not consider any actions that might detract from the war effort, in particular no negotiations with the enemy. The American delegation refused to discuss any changes in immigration law, while the British shunned any consideration of opening Palestine beyond the 75,000 specified in its 1939 White Paper. The American contingent included Representative Sol Bloom, the son of immigrant Polish Jews, who had risen by way of Tammany to chair the House Committee on Foreign Affairs; albeit denounced by Jewish critics as a State Department *shabbas goy,* willing to abide by its preference for limited action, he alone among the two delegations attempted to open the door to negotiations with the Nazis for the release of Jews; however, he was effectively checked by Dodds.[218] In the end, the conference limited itself to a consideration of financial measures to cover the cost of maintaining refugees in neutral nations, temporary havens where refugees might be transferred if and when shipping became available, and provisions for their repatriation. Widely indicted for "foundering in its own futility," it did initiate a plan for an expanded IGC with increased authority to deal with the problems created by the war.[219] The organization was revived in August 1943, but its initial plan for removing refugees from Spain to French North Africa was quashed by the military on the grounds that it would antagonize Muslims, and it remained of little practical value for the remainder of the war.

As the tide turned in favor of the Allies, pressure mounted to take more decisive action on behalf of rescue, as manifested by gigantic rallies in Madison Square Garden and Carnegie Hall and a proliferation of resolutions to that effect in Congress. However, Roosevelt acted only after being warned that further failure to do so would trigger a political scandal. Acting on the basis of intelligence that there was a possibility of evacuating some Rumanian Jews, the World Jewish Congress requested state and treasury approval for the transfer of "ransom money" to Switzerland. This was granted by the U.S. Treasury in July, but the State Department stalled until the end of the year. On November 3, the immigration bureaucracy finally ceased recording the Jewish identity of immigrants of various nationalities.[220]

Outraged by the State Department's persistent reluctance to carry out even cautious negotiations on behalf of threatened survivors, on January 16, 1944, Secretary of the Treasury Henry Morgenthau presented President Franklin D. Roosevelt with an eighteen-page memorandum prepared by his staff under the provocative title "Report to the Secretary on the Acquiescence of This Government in the Murder of the Jews."[221] At this time as well, summoned to defend the government's refugee policy and its stance at Bermuda, Long turned himself into a definitive political liability by mistakenly claiming that some 580,000 refugees had been admitted to the United States since 1933; in fact, there had been only 296,000 recorded arrivals from Europe, of whom only some 202,000 might qualify as refugees, including 138,000 Jews.[222] In response to these developments, Roosevelt loosened the State Department's grip on refugee policy by creating a War Refugee Board (WRB) as a joint operation of the Treasury, War, and State Departments; and within the State Department itself, visa operations were transferred to Assistant Secretary Adolph Berle, who subsequently initiated a more liberal administrative policy.

This constituted a definite shift in the American stance, which enabled children to leave Rumania for Bulgaria and Turkey, and also allowed refugees in Spain to be evacuated to North Africa. In a significant reversal of Bermuda, the administration also engaged in direct negotiations with Hungarian strongman Admiral Horty to dissuade him from turning over the Jews under his control to Germany, an intervention credited with saving about one-third of the targeted population.[223] About 1,000 Jewish survivors, in American custody in southern Italy, were relocated to an unused military installation in Oswego, New York, where they were detained for over a year so as to maintain the legal fiction that they were not in the United States even as visitors. These innovative actions confirmed the mounting weight of external policy considerations in the sphere of immigration, and established precedents for the adoption of exceptional policies on behalf of refugees in the postwar period.

In the same vein, in 1943 the president took on Congress in the matter of Chinese exclusion after Generalissimo Chiang Kai-shek indicated that such treatment was inappropriate for a wartime ally and was being exploited by Japanese propaganda. Promoted by a blue-ribbon association under the leadership of the popular novelist Pearl S. Buck, but opposed by the AFL and veterans' associations, a proposal to add persons of Chinese nationality or of Chinese descent to those eligible for naturalization, and providing for the admission of 105 Chinese a year as ordinary immigrants, became law in December 1943. Although the measure had limited practical effect, it constituted a significant breach in the racial foundations of American immigration policy and also confirmed the further emergence of foreign policy considerations in that sphere as a concomitant of the transformation of the United States into a global power. A similar measure was enacted on behalf of India in July 1946.[224]

Reviewing American immigration policy for the period 1924–1952 as a whole, Robert Divine concluded in 1957 that with respect to the refugee crisis, "The American record . . . is curiously mixed": while efforts to liberalize immigration law on behalf of refugees failed, the Roosevelt administration's administrative flexibility enabled the United States to absorb more refugees than any other nation."[225] Breitman and Kraut offer a similar assessment: within the context of a general failure of the West to live up to its values, "The American record was not the worst. But the United States failed to do even what its own immigration laws allowed."[226]

Why was not more done? Anti-Semitism within the State Department, within the Congress, and in the country at large all played a part; so did the divisiveness and pusillanimity of American Jews, as well as the president's perennial subordination of humanitarian measures to what he considered more vital political objectives, and later on to strategic imperatives. In the end, however, one thing stands out throughout: all the relevant actors took it for granted that the quota system was etched in stone. Albeit hardly a part of the Constitution, it had swiftly taken on an aura of legitimacy seldom achieved by ordinary legislation, as representing the American people's inviolable determination to no longer be a nation of immigrants. In the absence of a sufficiently powerful counterthrust, the bureaucracies governing the award of visas and admissions were left largely to implement their own preferences, which were restrictionist.[227]

As suggested at the outset, the episode is a tragic demonstration of "path dependency." Although the divisions among American Jews and their hesitations played a significant role, when the situation in Europe made it necessary to substantially alter American immigration policy, the obstacles advocates faced were so considerable that even a preternaturally united and committed community would have been stymied. Surreptitious action to land immigrants illegally, as in Palestine, was not feasible because the Atlantic was not the Mediterranean; it would have entailed logistically and politically complex operations, imperatively involving Mexico or Cuba. Alternatively, they might have tried to alter policy by extraordinary means, akin to the contemporaneous Ghandian civil disobedience movement, or to the civil rights movement of the postwar era.

This very possibility was indeed raised by the besieged Jews of Warsaw in a spring of 1943 message to Smull Zygelbojm, the Bundist representative to the Polish government-in-exile, demanding that Jewish leaders "go to all important English and American agencies. Tell them not to leave until they have obtained guarantees that a way has been decided upon to save the Jews. Let them accept no food or drink, let them die a slow death while the world looks on. This may shake the conscience of the world." Zygelbojm reflected to a friend at the time that "[i]t is utterly impossible, they would never let me die a slow lingering death. They would simply bring in two policemen and have me dragged away to an institution." Nevertheless, six months later he did carry out the mission they assigned him: "Let my death be an energetic cry of protest against the indifference of the world which witnesses the extermination of the Jewish people without taking any steps to prevent it."[228] Collective action along such lines would have satisfied the imperatives of moral commitment, but would it have succeeded in altering policy in time? We shall never know, because it was not tried.

9

The Ambiguities of Reform

American society's profound transformation after World War II, as well as enormous changes in the world at large, brought the regime established in the 1920s steadily into question. However, because of the peculiar configuration of American political institutions, defenders of the established identity boundaries initially managed to retain the upper hand, regardless of which party was in power in the White House or in Congress. There ensued a protracted confrontation between the conservatives and those seeking to shift the boundaries to encompass the European "new immigration" as well as Asians. Hardly noted in the extensive literature on the subject, however, is that the reformers now tacitly accepted the restrictionists' overall objective of keeping immigration within very limited bounds, and agreed that the "nation of immigrants" was a thing of the past. The face-off culminated in an historical compromise, a year after the enactment of the Civil Rights Act of 1964, whereby the main gate was redesigned to remove the features that humiliated Americans of the new immigration and enabled some to bring in their relatives, as well as to erase the last traces of Asian exclusion. But as this was being celebrated in a moving ceremony at the foot of the Statue of Liberty, much less was said of the fact that the long-awaited reform also imposed unprecedented restrictions on browns and blacks from neighboring countries.

While participating in the ongoing transformation of the American economy, agriculture sought to retain the advantages it had derived since the beginning of the twentieth century from the availability of a vast pool of cheap labor in Mexico and the Caribbean. Here also, the configuration of political institutions provided signal advantages to defenders of the status quo, and their ability to secure a largely free hand was reinforced by the marginality of the issue of agricultural labor for the overwhelmingly urban-based reformist camp. Accordingly, the back door persisted as a largely unregulated gate, which paradoxically contributed to the movement of American society away from the exclusively European identity of the architects of the back-door policy, who viewed themselves also as dedicated defenders of cultural traditionalism.

Quite unexpectedly, in the wake of the assumption by the United States of responsibilities incumbent upon its leadership role in the incipient Cold War, state interests assumed unprecedented importance in the determination of immigration policy as Washington found it necessary to provide entries in order to carry out its foreign policy objectives. In contrast with the Versailles era, international relations in the immediate postwar era rested on a somewhat bipartisan foundation, and despite bickering at the edges, these conditions by and large persisted throughout the Eisenhower years.[1] In the face of resistance by the guardians of the main gate, the foreign policy establishment secured the opening of a side entrance that, while serving their purposes, was also quickly seized upon to alleviate constituency pressures for letting in more "new" immigrants.

The resulting policy regime, which persisted into the dawn of the twenty-first century, reflects what Keith Fitzgerald has astutely termed the "improvisational institutionalism" that brought it about.[2] Although its segmentation into a main gate, side entrance, and back door appears at first sight quite incoherent, it is in fact no more so than any other policy sphere in a complex society. Once the baseline norm was changed from an open door to a closed one, the structure of immigration policy was radically altered as well: from a set of measures restricting access of particular categories through an otherwise open door, it turned into a set providing exceptional access through an otherwise closed one. This reflected the successful efforts of powerful political actors to achieve disparate objectives of special concern, a process that imparted to immigration policy as a whole a distinctly compartmentalized structure. That being the case, it is to be expected that the disparate elements will sometimes operate at cross-purposes, as demonstrated most dramatically by the unanticipated consequences of back-door policy, engineered to promote agricultural interests, and of the opening of a side entrance on foreign policy grounds, on the traditional design of American national identity.[3]

America Transformed

In the period of less than half a century between the enactment of the national origins system and its repeal, the social and cultural conditions that stimulated nativist hostility toward the new immigration and insured its success were altered beyond recognition. Most fundamental were dramatic changes in the size and distribution of the American population as a whole, as well as of its socially relevant components. Overall, population expanded by half, from 106.5 million in 1920 to 151.7 million in 1950, and then further to 180.7 million in 1960, almost entirely by way of internal growth, reflected most spectacularly in the "baby boom."[4] Thanks to the dramatic drop in immigration induced by American policy and the international situation, the share of foreign-born declined by nearly half, from 13.1 percent in 1920 to 6.9 percent in 1950, and bottomed out at 5 percent between 1960 and 1970, when U.S. society probably reached its record level of "Americanness."

As it expanded, the population became overwhelmingly urban and suburban, while its center of gravity shifted westward. Military service and the wartime demand for factory labor uprooted millions from rural areas and small towns, few of whom drifted back when peace returned; concurrently, Americans got into their cars and drove to their new houses in the suburbs, whose building was stimulated by subsidized mortgages under the "G.I. Bill of Rights" and by extensive road construction, also subsidized by the federal government on grounds of defense policy. Although all the regions shared in population expansion, thanks to internal migrations the West more than doubled its relative size, from 8.3 percent of the total in 1920 to 12.9 percent in 1950 and 17.0 percent in 1970, and in 1963 California bypassed New York as the most populous state.

Foreign-born whites and those of recent immigrant parentage remained the most urban Americans of all; and as the cities became more racially diverse, the ethnic boundaries that separated them from the mainstream were overshadowed by the more prominent one demarcating racial distinctions. Black emigration from the South resumed at an unprecedented pace during and after World War II, spreading from the older industrial areas to the new ones of the West Coast, where the black presence was hitherto minimal. Indicating growing African American determination to overcome discrimination, membership in the National Association for the Advancement of Colored People (NAACP) grew from 50,000 to 450,000, and in 1942 a group of union leaders launched the militant Congress for Racial Equality. A substantial segment of the rapidly expanding Mexican American population also relocated from the rural areas of the southwest to West Coast and Midwestern cities in response to new economic opportunities. In addition, half a million Puerto Ricans moved to the mainland between 1940 and 1960, settling mostly in northeastern cities.[5] Overall, the black and Hispanic population of the central cities rose spectacularly from 10 percent in 1940 to 33 percent in 1950, climbing yet higher over the next two decades as they continued to move in while whites moved out.

As the American economy entered the postindustrial stage, immigration no longer mattered as a source of manpower, except in agriculture.[6] Confirming the discovery of the 1920s, the native-born minorities, together with poor whites who migrated in droves from Appalachia and the Deep South, constituted a formidable "industrial reserve army," amply sufficient to meet the labor needs of even the most dynamic economic expansion. Overall, from 1947 to 1957 factory operatives fell by 4 percent, while clerical ranks grew by 23 percent and the salaried middle class increased by 61 percent. The shrinkage of the manufacturing labor force was particularly marked among the less skilled segments, in the textile, clothing, and steel industries, which in the past had been particularly open to immigrants and subsequently to American minorities.[7] In the mid-1950s, for the first time white-collar workers outnumbered blue-collar workers, a turn of events captured by academic analysts, notably the widely read *White Collar* and *The Organization Man,* as well as in the popular media, such as the Twentieth-Century Fox film, *The Man in the Grey Flannel Suit* (1956).[8] The transformation also entailed the entry of more women into the labor market.

The upturn of agricultural productivity was even steeper than for the non-farm sector, reflecting what has been termed "the third agricultural revolution," driven by mechanical innovations and the widespread use of efficient pesticides and fertilizers. Total farm production went up by one-half during the 1950s alone, while the number of farm workers decreased by 30 percent; as a proportion of the total labor force, they dropped from 17 percent in 1940 to 6.2 percent in 1960. Much of it involved the expropriation of small farmers to the benefit of large corporations, whose efficient operation depended on the availability of a massive force of migrant labor, especially for harvesting fruit and vegetable crops, which remained labor-intensive. As of 1960, there were some 2.5 million itinerant farm workers with an average annual income under $1,000, who were totally marginal with regard to labor laws and social benefits, and whose attempts to organize were suppressed, often violently.[9]

Although the bulk of the migrants were drawn from indigenous minorities, they were perennially supplemented by newcomers from Mexico and the West Indies as well.

These transformations reduced organized labor's concern with main-gate immigration policy. Within the industrial sector, the unions' most challenging problem was no longer the influx of foreign labor, but structural changes that hit the highly unionized sectors such as coal and steel hardest, as well as the movement of industry to the South and other regions hostile to organization. Moreover, they made little progress in signing up clerical employees, many of whom perceived union membership to be incompatible with middle-class status.[10] Consequently, while union membership continued to grow somewhat, it failed to keep pace with the expansion of the labor force, and the percentage of nonagricultural labor in unions fell from 33.2 percent in 1955—probably its historic high—to 28.4 in 1968. Daniel Tichenor has asserted that, thanks to the longtime opposition of the Congress of Industrial Organization (CIO) to the national origins quotas, its merger with the American Federation of Labor (AFL) in 1955 "brought about a momentous and enduring shift in organized labor's role in national immigration politics."[11] However, this must be qualified somewhat. Organized labor was nearly completely absent from the agricultural sector, a situation resulting in part from the flow through the back door, which in turn undermined its efforts to change the situation; hence it moved to the fore as a major contender in the emerging struggle over the back door and, as developments there affected the main gate, returned to the fray with regard to the latter as well.

Cultural norms and resulting attitudes were changing as well. Eric F. Goldman has argued, "All through the New Deal period and the war years, the powerful thrusts of minorities had been ramming more and more holes in the walls of discrimination," and the policies designed to keep minorities down were out of kilter with the times by the end of World War II: "By V-J, Jews seeking admission to professional schools had a ten-to-fifteen-per-cent better chance than the applicant of 1929. First-generation Catholics of eastern or southern European backgrounds reported far less difficulty in purchasing homes in upper-middle-class neighborhoods. During the four swift years of the war, Negroes for the first time knew the white-collar kudos of working as salesgirls in the swank department stores of the North, and Negro representatives on labor grievance committees were becoming accustomed to speaking up as freely as their white colleagues."[12] However, Sheldon Neuringer has asserted with equal confidence, "In the intervening years between 1924 and the early 1950's nothing had happened to weaken appreciably" in the minds of the majority of citizens and their congressmen the established notion "that there existed but one desirable national culture, the one that had been forged and nurtured by the original colonists and the nineteenth century immigrants from Northern and Western Europe."[13] Moreover, he insists that even advocates of "cultural pluralism" still agreed that some nationalities are more easily assimilated than others.[14]

Evocative of the old saw about the glass half full and half empty, these assessments are not necessarily contradictory. A survey conducted in November 1942 suggests that the boundary that had earlier delineated a white Protestant nation had shifted to encompass Catholics, but that the resulting amalgam distinguished itself sharply from, in ascending order of distance, Chinese, Jews, and Negroes. The full Americanization of Catholics was confirmed by the fact that two-thirds of the public said they would vote for one of them as president.[15] For the minorities on the far side of the boundary, the social and economic transformations discussed earlier, as well as the circumstances associated with World War II, constituted a mixed bag: they fostered majority hostility, occasioning some violent confrontations, but also greater tolerance conducive to integration. This was especially true of the nearly universal experience of male military service, which legitimized the right of all who served to receive equal treatment—even African Americans, who remained sharply segregated within the services.

Although strategic and political imperatives led to the formal ending of Asian exclusion in 1943, they also occasioned the relocation and large-scale internment of some 110,000 West Coasters of Japanese origin, including not only 40,000 foreign-born who remained alien by virtue of the prohibition on their naturalization but also their 70,000 American-born citizen children, on the grounds that "[t]he Japanese race is an enemy race."[16] Despite challenges on grounds of "equal protection," the policy was upheld by the U.S. Supreme Court in 1944. However, many of the interned were subsequently released on the condition of relocating away from the West Coast, a development that paradoxically facilitated their integration and hence contributed to a blurring of racial boundaries over the long term. On the other hand, sharp criticism of the internment policy by academic analysts as early as 1945 indicates a precocious commitment of part of the intellectual community to universalist norms.[17] Beyond this, as early as 1946, 50 percent of respondents in a broad survey thought the average Japanese living in the United States was "loyal," while only 25 percent thought them "disloyal"; and the favorable reception of

Go for Broke!, a 1951 film celebrating the heroism of a Japanese American regiment, suggests that attitudes among the general public underwent rapid change at the war's end.[18] As of 1946, 55 percent of Americans queried in a public opinion poll answered "yes" to the question of whether "Jews have too much power in the United States"; however, despite some rise in unemployment, "the post-war years did not produce any major anti-Semitic movements . . . and actually represented the beginning of the end for organized anti-Jewish agitation."[19] Another survey indicated that anti-Semitism was much stronger among the age group 35–49 than among those 21–34, suggesting it was a generational artifact that would eventually pass from the scene.[20]

These changes were attributable not only to wartime propaganda denouncing Nazi racialism, which was subsequently reinforced by revelation of the horrors of the Holocaust, but also to the more proactive stance adopted by Jewish organizations and numerous church bodies, the CIO's National Committee to Abolish Racial Discrimination, the NAACP, and the National Education Association in combating anti-Semitism and racism. During the war as well, the U.S. government provided unprecedented resources for research in this field, effecting little short of a revolution in the social sciences and leading to the elaboration of a multistranded antiracist doctrine. An early product was Gordon W. Allport's "scapegoat theory," published by the Anti-Defamation League of B'nai Brith's in 1948 as a "Freedom Pamphlet" and subsequently elaborated into his classic masterwork, *The Nature of Prejudice.* Another was the American Jewish Committee's massive investigation of the origins of racial and religious prejudices, resulting in Theodore Adorno's *The Authoritarian Personality* (1950), which argued that far from being an isolated phenomenon, anti-Semitism was part of a more general ideology of the Right and was the product of a distorted "passive-aggressive" personality.[21] In a similar vein, within anthropology, Ruth Benedict and Margaret Mead vigorously promoted "nurture" over "nature."[22] Traditional racial attitudes were challenged head on by Gunnar Myrdal in *An American Dilemma,* his report of the Carnegie Foundation's project on race relations, while Otto Klineberg's *Race and Psychology* provided in effect the official doctrine of the newly created United Nations Educational, Scientific and Cultural Organization (UNESCO), which contributed to the questioning of racialism in the United States.[23] Much of this literature was disseminated among a more educated general public by way of the new "quality" paperbacks. Anti-Semitism was tackled head on in the popular media as well, notably in Laura Z. Hobson's bestselling novel *Gentleman's Agreement,* published in 1947 by Simon & Schuster, the very firm that had actively promoted the restrictionist literature of the 1920s. The story was further popularized by a film, which captured the Oscar for best picture, "proving that anti-anti-Semitism was now not only acceptable, it was highly respectable."[24] The downgrading of prejudice to an aberration was eventually extended to the broader realm of historical interpretation, as suggested by the title of Richard Hofstadter's classic essay, *The Paranoid Style in American Politics*.[25]

The incorporation of Europeans of the "new immigration" into the white mainstream was fostered as well by negative developments, the rising presence of African Americans in the North and West, and to a lesser extent of Hispanics. Although Myrdal wrote in his 1942 introduction that he saw fundamental changes underway pushing practice closer to American ideals of equality, in the following summer, forty-seven American cities exploded in the bloodiest racial riots to date, a drama powerfully evoked in Ralph Ellison's 1952 novel, *Invisible Man*.[26] The Mexican American minority benefited somewhat from the promotion of Mexico to the status of "good neighbor," marked by an unprecedented invitation to the Mexican Army to parade in downtown Los Angeles in honor of the 1943 Cinco de Mayo. However, its increased visibility, fostered by large-scale migration from the border communities to urban California in response to the opportunities provided by war industries, as well as massive recruitment under the *bracero* program discussed shortly, evoked hostile reactions as well. Matters rose to a head one month after the parade when, following reports of an attack on a group of sailors by a Mexican gang, white soldiers and irate Angelenos invaded the *barrio*, beating Mexicans as well as blacks and Filipinos, who responded in kind.[27] In the postwar years, there was growing talk of "wetbacks," amplified by the popular media, and by the 1950s Mexicans largely replaced southern and eastern Europeans as the most immediately threatening immigration problem.

The slow but steady progress of domestic antidiscrimination legislation, largely attributable to an alliance between the NAACP and white liberals, with Jews very much in the vanguard, undermined the legitimacy of the discriminatory national origins system posted on America's door. In 1938, the State of New York adopted a constitutional amendment prohibiting discrimination on grounds of race or religion; in 1941, it established a Committee on Discrimination in Employment, which covered nationality as well; two years later, it enacted a law prohibiting defense contractors from refusing employment to qualified persons on grounds of national origin, race, color, or creed; and in 1945, it adopted the most comprehensive law in the nation, which banned all other forms of discrimination on these grounds as well. By 1951, six states and two dozen cities had followed New York's lead, and fair employment practices laws covered about one-fourth of the American population.[28] Under the leadership of Hubert Humphrey, mayor of Minneapolis, the Democrats committed themselves at their 1948 convention to enact laws against job discrimination, lynching, and poll taxes at the federal level as well, but the second Truman administration failed to deliver. That same year, the Supreme Court ruled in *Shelley v. Kramer* that restrictive real estate covenants, such as were featured in *Gentlemen's Agreement,* ran counter to the equal protection clause of the Fourteenth Amendment, and went on two years later to void state higher education laws that created separate but equal facilities.

Overall, by the time of the Eisenhower era, while Americans continued to make intrawhite distinctions based on "national origins," the boundaries between the groups had begun to blur, and the notion that ancestral origins determined different degrees of desirability and assimilability, which had brought the national origins system to life earlier in the century, had lost much of its erstwhile respectability and no longer played a significant role in the public sphere. Indeed, the issue of immigration itself had disappeared. The *Atlantic Monthly,* one of the two quality general magazines of the period, did not carry a single article on the subject between 1925 and 1953, and only three between 1953 and 1965; the other, *Harper's,* published two in the 1930s, two in the 1940s, and three in the decade and half between 1950 and 1965.[29] Surveys also indicated that the percentage of Americans who said they wanted fewer or no immigrant admissions declined dramatically throughout the 1950s, falling at the end to only one-third.[30] Reflecting on the situation from the vantage point of the mid-1980s, William Issel has suggested that although "[w]hite Americans who trace their ancestry to northern and western Europe continued to wield more power, privilege, and, consequently, prestige than other ethnic groups after 1945," by the 1950s "they increasingly sloughed off loyalties to ancestral homelands and replaced them with a religious identification to Protestantism."[31] Ethnic particularisms among Americans issued from the "new immigration" as well those who traced their origins to Ireland had become attenuated as well, giving way to more generalized identities as Catholics and Jews.[32]

Changing Political Configuration

However, the political arena evolved at its own pace. Despite the new interest of the foreign and defense policy establishment in shaping aspects of immigration policy, Congress retained the upper hand in this sphere.[33] A study of congressional voting from 1949 to 1954 indicates that alignments on the principal immigration measures were remarkably consistent, and closely related to a more general "civil rights" dimension, which ranked as the second most important factor throughout the period.[34] This reflected a marked disjunction between the outlook of the politicians who decisively shaped immigration policy by way of their control of key committee positions, and those seeking to reform it, largely in response to the growing electoral power of constituents issued from the "new immigration." These urban constituencies were crucial to the Democratic victories of 1940, 1944, and especially 1948, when they enabled Harry Truman to win despite the defection of four states with 39 electoral votes to Strom Thurmond's segregationist States' Rights Party. The ethnics' political clout was reflected in their increasing presence among officeholders as well. For example, eight Italian Americans were elected to Congress in 1948, twice as many as in any previous year, and they also gained more than twice as many seats in the state legislatures of the Northeast; the first Italian American senator, John Pastore, was elected in 1950 (Rhode Island); and Columbus Day made into a federal holiday in 1971. The change was even more dramatic with regard to presidential appointments; whereas of the 186 known federal judges named by Warden Harding, Calvin Coolidge, and Herbert Hoover, 170 were Protestant, 8 Catholic, and 8 Jewish, of Franklin D. Roosevelt's 197, 52 were Catholic and 8 Jewish, and of Truman's 127 (through the summer of 1951), 38 were Catholic as well as 12 Jewish.

David Plotke has suggested that in the postwar years, the Democratic order adopted a "defense of position" strategy, initially consolidating itself, and after Truman's surprising 1948 victory, launching a new offensive under the "Fair Deal" label; despite some setbacks, "the central results of the late 1940s was to confirm the key political and legal shifts of the 1930s, including the national state's regulatory role," and even major counterreforms such as the Taft-Hartley Act entailed a reluctant settlement with the Democratic order.[35] In the sphere of immigration, however, the situation differed somewhat, in that hitherto the Democratic order had not committed itself to a reformist program, except in the limited matter of Chinese exclusion. In this respect, the Truman administration went in fact well beyond the New Deal. By the mid-1950s, Democratic Party leaders outside the South stood out as militantly reformist in the sphere of immigration, twice as strongly as Republicans, and four times more than their own followers, with a greater distance between them than on any other issue studied. However, even among the Democratic leadership, support for increased immigration was only of the order of 36 percent.[36]

The fragmented structure of the American legislative arena enhanced the weight of idiosyncratic factors. From the end of the war to 1963, the course of immigration policy was shaped by two individuals. One was Representative Francis E. ("Tad") Walter, chairman of the Immigration Subcommittee of the House Committee on the Judiciary whenever the Democrats held the upper hand. Walter represented a mixed rural and urban Pennsylvania district, but with a larger percentage of old-stock Americans than other Democratic constituencies in the state. A veteran of two wars with close ties to patriotic organizations, he was a popular legislator who had excellent relations with southern Democratic congressmen, particularly Sam Rayburn, whom he hoped to succeed as speaker. While amenable to the usual congressional give-and-take on most matters, for reasons that appear to have had more to do with a desire to assert his power than with ideological persuasion or material interest, from the outset of his protracted tenure Walter insisted that maintenance of the national origins quota system was nonnegotiable.[37] The other key actor was Senator Pat McCarran of Nevada. His Irish Catholic origins notwithstanding, McCarran was a stalwart restrictionist who envisioned immigration as a national liability, except insofar as it supplied Spanish Basque sheepherders for his rancher constituents, on whose behalf he perennially engineered the enactment of special legislation.

Carving Out a Side Entrance

While defenders of the established immigration regime were motivated exclusively by domestic considerations, the situation in the world at large emerged as a major problem for the U.S. government as well as for Americans of the new immigration, driving congressional representatives of the relevant constituencies to constitute a more vigorous reformist camp. Although revelations of the scope of the Holocaust affirmed the resolve of some hitherto cautious Jewish groups as well, the most immediate issue arose from continental Europe's displaced population. According to the first comprehensive survey, some 30 million Europeans were uprooted in the six years of war. After the tide turned and the Allies expanded their territorial control, the prospect of millions of "displaced persons" (DPs) emerged as a critical military and humanitarian concern well beyond the capacity of the rudimentary international organizations formed in the interwar period. In the wake of British and American experience in the Middle East, in 1943 the United States took the lead in organizing the United Nations Relief and Rehabilitation Administration (UNRRA) to oversee most of the relief operations in postwar Europe.

Simultaneously, Europe as a whole, and the countries disadvantaged by the national origins system in particular, generated a huge emigration "push." Although the baby boom was nowhere as marked as in the United States, countries that still experienced a high rate of fertility and whose economies were severely weakened by a period of depression followed by war were unable to absorb all of those coming of age into their labor force. In addition to Poland and others in the East, whose populations were shortly immobilized by prohibitions on exit, they included the Netherlands, which at that time achieved the highest birthrate in Europe; the southern nations, Italy, Greece, Spain, and Portugal; and Ireland.[38] Although some had access to alternative destinations, the expansion of demand generated extremely long waiting lines extending in the most extreme cases to several decades into the future.[39] This was especially the case for Italy, which had a quota of 5,802, and Greece, whose quota of 307 was the smallest in Europe.

Accordingly, as the United States relinquished the last remnants of isolationism and undertook to reconstruct Europe into a reliable forward bastion of the "free world," foreign policy interests assumed unprecedented importance in the determination of immigration policy. Roosevelt's Immigration Commissioner Earl Harrison urged as early as 1944 that greater consideration be given to "international implications," notably by instituting more flexible quota regulations that would enable the United States to meet situations of an urgent nature. His successor, Ugo Carusi, concurred, asserting, "There is no reason why the new concept of international cooperation should not extend to our policy with respect to immigration."[40] In the same vein, even Yale's moderate restrictionist Maurice Davie asserted, "Immigration has . . . assumed new significance in connection with plans for establishing an enduring peace."[41]

Although the objective was repatriation, in the summer of 1945, faced with some 8 million DPs in Germany, Austria, and Italy, American officials began suggesting that resolution of the problem might require resettling some of them in the United States.[42] But this was much easier said than done. An analysis of wartime public opinion panels established by the Office of War Information indicated strong opposition to the admission of refugees and displaced persons, largely founded on the fear that this might cause unemployment. Even those favoring admission did not think a fuller acquaintance with the DPs' privations would persuade the other side to change their views and concluded that only a change in the definition of their interests, and of how they might be affected by various measures, would bring about a shift.[43] Polls at the end of the war suggested that the shift, if any, was very slight. In August 1946, 72 percent disapproved of President Truman's plan "to ask Congress to allow more Jewish and other European refugees to come to the United States to live than are allowed under the law now," and only 16 percent approved. Shortly afterwards, in response to a statement pointing out that "about one million Polish people, Jews, and other displaced persons must find new homes in different countries," 50 percent thought the United States should not take any, and of the 43 percent willing to receive some, the majority opted for much less than a quarter of the total.

Yet, while the Daughters of the American Revolution, the Veterans of Foreign Wars, and the American Legion publicly supported proposals to further limit immigration in order to protect returning veterans from competition, and while successive polls indicated that unemployment was the main concern, in contrast with the prewar period, neither the elimination of foreigners nor further immigration restriction appeared among the solutions advocated by the public more generally.[44] Moreover, there was broad support for measures to ease the immigration of the alien fiancées, wives, and children of members of the American armed forces (the "War Brides Act" of December 28, 1945), as well to exempt alien spouses from the "race" exclusion, making it possible for Japanese and other Asians to acquire U.S. citizenship by marriage, as was the case for others (Act of July 22, 1947).

As it was, contrary to expectations, the vast majority of European DPs returned to their home countries within a few months; nevertheless, at the end of 1945 the western Allies were left with about 1 million on their hands, mostly persons who refused to go back to regions occupied by the Red Army, as well as latecomers who continued to stream in. They constituted a heterogeneous lot, both nationally and politically, including forced laborers from a variety of Nazi-occupied countries; Balts who had moved to Germany when their lands were annexed by the Soviet Union; Ukrainians and others who fled before the Russian advance; descendants of German eighteenth- and nineteenth-century colonists *(Volksdeutsche)*, many of whom had welcomed the German armies as liberators and were now being expelled from central and eastern Europe in keeping with the Potsdam agreements; as well as some 100,000 Jewish death camp survivors. The situation was exacerbated in 1946 when the Soviet Union released tens of thousands of DPs within its jurisdiction, and thousands of Jews fled Poland following an outburst of deadly pogroms. *Volksdeutsche* continued to stream in as well; by 1950, some 8 million out of a potential 12 million had arrived in the western occupation zones of Germany, accompanied by another 1.5 million Germans fleeing the Soviet zone. Additional refugees were generated by postliberation conflicts as well, notably the civil war in Greece between Communist partisans and the returning royal government, and clashes within eastern and southern European states that resumed their elusive pursuit of ethnic homogeneity and geopolitically desirable boundaries.

In the context of the nascent Cold War, as the Truman administration undertook the reconstruction and rearming of Europe as its highest priority, the presence of a mass of DPs in Germany, far from being regarded as a deserved retributory hardship for the country that bore responsibility for the war, came to be seen as a threat to the social and economic stability of a strategically crucial region. Growing distrust of its erstwhile ally also led the United States to oppose the forcible repatriation of DPs to the Soviet Union. Accordingly, the administration took the lead in forming the International Refugee Organization (IRO) as the major instrument for resettling "the last million," a task that was expected to be completed by the end of 1951. Although the burden of resettlement was to be shared by all IRO participants, the United States must take the major portion because, as the author of the Marshall Plan explained, "You cannot assert leadership and then not exercise it." The organization's innovative procedures, which emphasized individual determination of refugee status, were carried over into the Office of the United Nations High Commissioner for Refugees (UNHCR), established by the UN General Assembly in December 1949.[45] Although the new organization's mandate was again limited to a three-year period, many assumed from the beginning that it would become a permanent agency; and although its domain was still confined to Europe, it pertained to a wider array of categories, and the notion of refugees as a distinctive group of international migrants driven by "well-founded fear of persecution" was formalized by way of a convention enacted in 1951.

Having largely failed to achieve their objectives before and during the war, in the aftermath of the Holocaust American Jewish organizations mustered unprecedented efforts to secure government assistance in relocating survivors. While the Zionist mainstream set its sights on Palestine as early as the summer of 1943, and concentrated on pressing for U.S. intervention to that effect, the more assimilationist groups worked on behalf of the resettlement of some of the survivors in the United States.[46] Seeking to accommodate both camps, in

August 1945 President Truman urged Britain to allow 100,000 Jewish DPs into their Palestinian mandate and later in the year issued a directive authorizing the attribution of visas that had gone unused from national quotas to DPs, as well as acceptance of LPC affidavits, hitherto limited to individuals, from voluntary organizations such as the Joint Distribution Committee. A total of 40,324 persons were admitted in this manner between 1946 and 1948, of whom the largest groups were Germans and Poles, about two-thirds of them Jewish survivors.[47]

However, this fell far short of Jewish needs, which were exacerbated by the refusal of Britain's new Labour government to open up Palestine, as well as of Washington's resettlement obligations to its allies. In the face of continued resistance to changes in immigration policy proper, reinforced at the end of 1946 by the election of the first Republican congress since the launching of the New Deal, President Truman turned instead to ad hoc legislation on behalf of DPs. Shifting strategy accordingly, the Jewish organizations organized an interfaith Citizens Committee on Displaced Persons (CCDP) to work on behalf of the legislation. With William Bernard as its executive director, the committee elaborated a proposal to allocate 400,000 visas, approximately the number unused during the war years, to "unrepatriable" persons over a four-year period, including an estimated 100,000 Jews. Constituting about half of the unrepatriable total, the number was deemed to represent a fair share because U.S. population amounted to about half that of the potential receivers as a whole.

While the American public remained heavily hostile to refugee admissions, by linking the issue to the emerging Cold War, the administration "provided a new basis for conservative support which was only marginally related to traditional interest group politics."[48] Introduced by Republican representative William Stratton of Illinois on April 1, 1947, the proposal received the support of the AFL and American Legion, which dropped its opposition after its national commander toured the DP camps at the administration's invitation. Following Secretary of State George Marshall's testimony, the House Foreign Affairs Committee agreed that "resettlement was the only feasible solution."[49] Nevertheless, as the legislation wended its way through a contentious Congress, where among other things it was denounced by a Texas representative as mainly of benefit to Jews who had been planted by the Soviets in the DP camps, admissions were scaled down by half to a mere 202,000 over a two-year period, with the visas to be "mortgaged" against future quotas of the appropriate countries, and with provisions designed to minimize Jewish admissions.[50] Congressional action was completed in June 1948, even as the Soviet Union and the United States confronted each other over the Berlin blockade, confirming the onset of a Cold War. As the final product awaited presidential approval, some Jewish groups blamed the stingy outcome on the CCDP's interfaith coalition strategy instead of protest action, and considered recommending a presidential veto; however, in the end they deferred to the committee, which decided that half a loaf was better than none.[51] It was by then evident that the Jewish vote might play a crucial role in the forthcoming presidential election. Contrary to his State Department advisers, who counseled against antagonizing the oil-rich Arab states, President Truman granted immediate recognition to the new state of Israel in May 1948, and he also signed the Displaced Persons Act "with great reluctance" on June 25, 1948, charging that it was both anti-Semitic and anti-Catholic.[52]

As it was, the measure brought about a rapid increase in quota immigrants to an unprecedented 197,460 in 1950; however, the "mortgaging" provision lengthened the waiting time for ordinary applicants from countries with small quotas, in the extreme case of Greece to as much as two centuries.[53] Following the Democratic sweep, those intent upon liberalizing immigration policy followed the new path traced by the DP law as an alternative to confronting the national origins system. Initially resistant, at the urging of President Truman, Subcommittee Chairman Walter allowed a bill initiated by Brooklyn Representative Emmanuel Celler for expanding the 1948 law to be reported out; and although Celler had sharply criticized the "mortgage" provision, he now accepted it as a condition for Walter's cooperation.[54] Signed into law in June 1950, the measure raised the total to 341,000; extended the cutoff date to June 30, 1951; eliminated the preferences for annexed countries and agriculture; increased the quota for orphans; and provided quotas for special categories. Altogether, 409,696 persons were admitted under the amended Displaced Persons Act, accounting for over half of the refugees admitted between 1946 and 1965.[55]

Manhandling the Back Door

In the early postwar years, the U.S. government collaborated in institutionalizing what amounted to a form of indentured labor.[56] Although in the wake of U.S. demobilization Mexican workers were massively dismissed and returned, the need for temporary crop workers shortly grew greater than ever because the mechanization of preharvest operations was far more advanced than of harvest itself. However, agricultural employers were not eager for continuation of the *bracero* program because, by virtue of the wage and benefit regulations mandated under the international agreement, *braceros* were more costly than domestic migrant workers, let alone illegals; moreover, the agreement continued to loom as an entry wedge for reformist regulation. With the return of peace depriving Mexico of its leverage, they secured a program more to their liking. Despite the opposition of organized labor and of the National Citizens Council for Migrant Labor, from 1948 on foreign workers were admitted exclusively under the proviso, at the discretion of the attorney general—up to 70,000 workers that year, including 50,000 Mexicans, 10,000 British West Indians, as well as 10,000 Canadians—and 113,000 in 1949. Many of the Mexicans entered initially as "wetbacks" *(mojados),* then were rounded up by the Border Patrol, taken back with the agreement of Mexico to recruitment centers south of the border, legalized under the proviso, and then "paroled" to their American employers, thereby endowing the latter with extensive authority over their persons.[57] When Mexico attempted to bargain for a better deal by holding back its workers, the patrol skipped the return routine altogether. The unregulated flow continued as well; although the harboring of an illegal alien was upgraded in 1948 from a misdemeanor to a felony, there was in fact no way of enforcing the law or any apparent interest in doing so.

The 1950 report of the Senate Subcommittee on Immigration, which established the basic framework of postwar policy—discussed further below—recommended permanent legislation to permit the admission of temporary agricultural labor in a nonimmigrant classification when like workers could not be found in the United States, as determined by the commissioner of the INS upon application by the employer and in consultation with appropriate agencies. To counter this proposal, sharply criticized by organized labor and its liberal allies, President Truman appointed his own Presidential Commission on Migratory Labor, which reported in 1951 that the *bracero* program and its sequels contributed to the influx of undocumented workers, and that these in turn lowered wages and worsened conditions for domestic migrants. To counter this, it recommended the imposition of fines on employers of illegal labor. As indicated by the Los Angeles riots, there was also mounting hostility throughout the Southwest to Mexican workers more generally, viewing them as the vanguard of undesirable "mixed-blood" immigration.[58]

However, the outbreak of the Korean War drastically altered the political configuration, as the draft call-ups combined with the economic stimulation occasioned by defense orders created an acute labor shortage in agriculture, or at least made the claim that there was one more credible, and also restored Mexico's bargaining power.[59] Hence the United States and Mexico rapidly negotiated a revival of the wartime agreement. In the course of congressional debate over implementing legislation, Illinois Democratic Senator Paul Douglas introduced an amendment penalizing employers of unauthorized labor, in keeping with the Presidential Commission's recommendation, and it was strongly supported by organized labor on both sides of the border as well as by the Mexican government.[60] However, the workers' interest in the matter was ambiguous since many preferred the wetback route because of the high cost of graft for being selected as a *bracero*—the going price was about 600 pesos, equivalent to about $50.[61] Emerging as a new political player in the sphere of immigration policy, the Mexican American community appeared divided on the subject: on the one hand, Representative Jose Estevan Fernandez of New Mexico thought Spanish-speaking Americans might not be able to provide proper identification and therefore would be rejected by wary employers, but the G.I. Forum, launched to fight discrimination against Mexican Americans who had served in World War II, supported the proposal.[62] Organized labor sought in vain to establish priority for Puerto Ricans, who were subject to American labor laws, as well as certification of shortages by the secretary of labor.[63]

Ultimately, employer sanctions were not included, prompting the Mexican government to withhold its agreement; however, it relented when President Truman, upon signing the new *bracero* law on July 13, 1951 (P.L. 78), promised to obtain separate legislation to that effect. In 1952, the United States duly enacted a law that prohibited aiding, harboring, and concealing illegals. Although this formally redeemed the president's pledge, the measure was a masterful confection of legal hypocrisy, in that it specified that "the usual and normal practices incident to employment shall not be deemed to constitute harboring." Affording employers total immunity, what came to be known as "the Texas proviso" further institutionalized the employment of unauthorized workers as an informal but vital component of the immigration regime.

Although most of the *braceros* and *mojados* returned to Mexico at the end of the season, over the years their comings and goings produced substantial settlement. In the course of repeated stays, some learned that immigrant status opened the way to more rewarding jobs or started families, and acquired the know-how to deal with the American immigration bureaucracy, availing themselves of a long-standing provision of the law providing the possibility of legalization after seven years' well-behaved residence, or by marrying an American citizen or legal resident. As well, employers encouraged especially valuable workers to return and sometimes undertook to sponsor them as immigrants.[64]

National Origins Redux

Provoked by steadily bolder questioning of the established régime, Senator Pat McCarran launched a vigorous counterattack by undertaking the first comprehensive review of immigration since 1911.[65] Issued on April 20, 1950, the McCarran Report bore the imprint of Staff Director Richard Arens, who was characterized by Marion T. Bennett, a former Republican congressman from Missouri, as a man "widely commended and decorated . . . by civic patriotic groups and with equal fervor denounced by anti-restrictionists and Communists," but described by New York Senator Herbert Lehman's legislative assistant as "one of the most prejudiced people I've ever known, a force for intellectual evil."[66] Arens worked in close consultation with officials of the Visa Division of the Department of State and of the INS, many of whom were stalwart restrictionists.[67]

The report formed the basis for bills submitted by the senator and Representative Walter in early 1951 with a call for urgent action to deflect the Truman administration's likely attempt to renew and broaden the DP legislation.[68] With regard to the main gate, it firmly advocated continuation of the national origins quota system. However, it paid tribute to changing times by downplaying the racial theories that provided its original rationale and justifying it instead as "a rational method of numerically restricting immigration in such a manner as to best preserve the sociological and cultural balance of the United States." The report nevertheless insisted that the quotas favored "immigrants considered to be more readily assimilable, because of the similarity of their cultural background, to those of the principal components of our population."[69] Moreover, critics were quick to point out that the leopard had not lost his spots: for example, the report emphasized the magnitude of Jewish immigration, pointing out that although Jews constituted less than 4 percent of the American population in 1937, they amounted to 14 percent of immigrants from 1906 to 1943.[70]

Although Senator McCarran insisted that his bill eliminated sex and race discrimination, it was in fact a mixed bag. With regard to sex, it was indeed progressive, as the nonquota status attributed to wives of citizens was now extended to husbands as well. As for race, while formalizing the end of Asian exclusion, it also confirmed the policy of tokenism by granting a minimal quota of 100 to the other countries of the "Asia-Pacific Triangle" and imposing a ceiling of 2,000 on the Asia-Pacific triangle as a whole (excluding China and Japan). Moreover, the bill maintained for Asians alone a determination of nationality on the basis of ancestral origin rather than place of birth. Most important, the bill imposed a token quota of 100 on all colonies, viewed as independent states in the making. This was evidently designed to minimize ongoing immigration from the British West Indies, whose residents were hitherto able to avail themselves of the generous quota allotted to Britain, for which demand from the British Isles itself was low.[71] Moreover, the restrictive postcolonial quota was applicable despite the West Indies' unquestioned location within the Western Hemisphere, whose independent countries were hitherto not subject to numerical limitation. The unprecedented targeting of black immigration for restriction was immediately denounced by New York Representatives Vito Marcantonio and Adam Clayton Powell, as well as by major African American organizations, whose leaders were expanding their base in connection with the nascent civil rights campaign.

The McCarran bill further reserved the first 50 percent of each national quota for immigrants with skills urgently needed by the United States and provided only 5 percent for "new seed" immigrants. On the horizon since the 1920s, skill preferences had already been incorporated into the DP legislation; however, the present proposal used it as a restrictionist device, as unused visas within the higher preference segments were not transferable and would thus fall by the wayside, occasioning a substantial reduction in overall immigration. In keeping with the emerging Cold War climate, the McCarran bill also placed unprecedented emphasis on national security considerations, providing for tighter regulation of naturalization as well as more draconian procedures for denaturalization and deportation. Representative Walter's bill largely paralleled McCarran's but was somewhat more palatable to immigration advocates because it made unused visa numbers in the higher preference categories available to lower ones or nonpreference applicants, thereby maintaining immigration at approximately the ongoing level.

Although the joint hearings held by McCarran and Walter in spring 1951 largely echoed the confrontations of an earlier era, a striking difference was the near-silence of employers and organized labor. In effect, European immigration was no longer relevant to the American economy; indeed, at its 1952 convention, the CIO denounced the bills, stating, "We are confident that in the present state of our economy the United States could admit each year a substantial number of immigrants without danger to the national economy or American wage scales and standards of living."[72] What mattered economically was the "back door."

Surprisingly, given the tangible rise of anti-Mexican sentiment throughout the Southwest in the postwar years, neither McCarran nor Walter sought to impose a quantitative limit on Western Hemisphere immigration. The Mc-Carran Report itself devoted only 2 of its 801 pages to the subject; echoing the frustrations of the restrictionists of the 1920s, it pointed out that the nonquota classification of natives of the Western Hemisphere had given rise to much controversy because many of these immigrants "are of stock similar to natives of southern Europe" and should therefore be restricted in the same way. While in the past the flow from Mexico fluctuated according to the business cycle and was restricted by intensive consular examinations, visas, and fee requirements, it was now on the rise again, and its size "indicates that this numerically unregulated immigration system presents one of the most questionable features of our immigration policy." Nevertheless, observing that the exemption from numerical limitation rests chiefly on "considerations arising from the geographical proximity of Western Hemisphere countries and considerations of friendly relations among them," it concluded that "it is impossible to protect land borders from illegal entries" and that this immigration should therefore continue to be regulated "by the qualitative restrictions in the law" alone.

But if it was impossible to control physical entry, as the report acknowledged, qualitative restrictions would have little deterrent effect; what, then, was the point? Albeit well-nigh useless with regard to border control, the system was highly effective as a deterrent to the incorporation of Mexicans, in particular, by way of naturalization. As noted earlier, the McCarran Report also recommended a continuation of special provisions for the recruitment of temporary labor. Overall, it thus tacitly validated the status quo along the southern border as a solution to the perennial "wanted but not welcome" dilemma. This was confirmed by a provision in the legislative end product prohibiting persons from "contiguous territories" from adjusting their status from nonimmigrant to immigrant, clearly designed as an additional obstacle to Mexican incorporation.

Absent the economic dimension, the conflict over main-gate policy was structured mainly along the integration axis, with an array of old-style "Americanist" organizations wearing the new garb of Cold War politics, as well as the Republican mainstream and southern Democrats, confronting a mixture of left-leaning Democrats such as the Americans for Democratic Action and ethnic organizations such as the American Jewish Committee, with considerable overlap between them. As noted, the antirestrictionist camp now included an African American voice as well. The reformers' overall position was set forth in *American Immigration Policy: A Reappraisal,* edited by sociologist William S. Bernard, who had served as executive director of the CCDP on behalf of the National Committee on Immigration Policy, a blue-ribbon coalition of Jews, Catholics, and liberal Protestants.[73] Challenging the national origins system on the grounds that southern and eastern Europeans had effectively demonstrated their capacity for integration into American society, the reformers argued that the rules governing the Western Hemisphere constituted a "fundamentally democratic procedure of selecting immigrants on the basis of individual fitness alone," which provided a desirable model for immigration more generally.[74] Inconsistently, they simultaneously invoked Western Hemisphere immigration as a negative reference by pointing out that it created more serious problems than the flow from Europe.[75] In keeping with the coalition's internationalist orientation, they proposed to allocate a portion of admissions in accordance with the emigration needs of the world at large, and urged coordination of American policies with international agencies.[76]

At the level of legislative strategy, disagreements arose from the partners' somewhat different priorities. Focusing on repealing the national origins system as part of their campaign to eradicate anti-Semitism, the Jewish organizations were less concerned with securing an increase in admissions because most of their European co-religionists had perished in the Holocaust or were confined behind the "Iron Curtain," while the Zionists thought it imperative to direct residual Jewish migration toward Israel.[77] Conversely, the Catholic partners were less concerned over the demeaning significance of the national origins system and more concerned with enlarging numbers, especially to satisfy the massive Italian demand. However, this could also be achieved by further enlarging the side entrance.[78]

The reform proposals finally materialized as substitute bills introduced by Emmanuel Celler in the House and Hubert Humphrey with former New York Governor Herbert Lehman in the Senate. Rather than challenging the system as a whole, they sought to alleviate the situation by extending nonquota status to the parents of citizens; moving the population baseline from 1920 to 1950, which would enlarge the quotas by a little over half and raise the share allocated to the "new immigration"; and allowing unused visas to be pooled for redistribution where needed. The bills directly challenged McCarran-Walter on the two racial issues, assigning Asians to the quota of their country of birth, and retaining the West Indians' status within the United Kingdom quota until independence, after which they would presumably obtain nonquota status on a par with natives of the other independent countries of the Western Hemisphere. However, neither bill ever made it out of subcommittee. Concurrently, with an eye on the forthcoming presidential campaign, President Truman denounced McCarran and Walter for their stalwart commitment to the national origins system and proposed to admit another 300,000 persons under a new DP law over the next three years, including especially Italians "to reduce the Communist threat."[79]

The Walter bill, with its reallocation feature intact, was approved by an overwhelming 206–68 on April 25, 1952. In the Senate, after an attempt to recommit failed miserably by 44–28, and a set of amendments by 51–27, the McCarran proposal passed by a voice vote on June 10. The conference report, which adopted Walter's reallocation feature, was then comfortably approved by both houses. It was now up to President Truman. Would he impose his veto? The ethnic organizations urged him to do so, with the exception of the Japanese American Citizens League, which accepted the quotas in exchange for the removal of lingering barriers to Asian naturalization. The administration itself was divided: whereas the Justice and State Departments recommended approval because the measure repealed Asian exclusion, the Department of Labor, the Mutual Security Administration (in charge of the Marshall Plan), and the Bureau of the Budget favored a veto. The president's own legislative strategist opted for this as well, reckoning that there were enough votes to sustain a veto but not enough to enact the liberal alternatives, which would then place the administration in a position to push through its proposal to once again extend and broaden the DP act.

On June 25, President Truman did veto the bill, citing maintenance of the national origins system as his main ground and asserting in no uncertain terms, "It is incredible to me that we should again be enacting into law such a slur on the patriotism, the capacity, and the decency of a large part of our citizenry." However, it was immediately overridden in the House by an even more overwhelming 278–113, well over the required two-thirds, and in the Senate by a much narrower margin of only 2 votes, 57–26 (13 not voting). The Democratic South, including newly elected Texas Senator Lyndon Johnson, voted with the Republicans, and only in the heavily immigrant

Northeast did a majority in both Senate and House, including newly elected Representative John F. Kennedy, vote to sustain the veto.

The Immigration and Naturalization Act of 1952 selectively repealed earlier legislation and became the basic law in this domain. Overall, it further institutionalized the distinction between the main gate and the back door, with regard to which it confirmed established arrangements. While preserving the quotas, it changed the formula for computing them from "a number which bears the same ratio to 150,000 as the number of inhabitants in the continental United States having that national origin . . . bears to the number of inhabitants in the continental United States in 1920" to one-sixth of 1 percent of the number of persons of that national origin in the United States in 1920, as computed for the 1924 act. Every independent country in the world was allocated a minimum quota of 100. Altogether, these provisions made for an increase of only a few hundred in total quota immigration. The law also introduced an explicit labor procurement element into main gate immigration by reserving the first 50 percent (first preference) for immigrants with skills identified as needed by the United States; but it simultaneously provided for the exclusion of persons seeking entry on the basis of skill if the secretary of labor certified that there was an adequate supply of such labor, or that their entry would have an adverse effect on wages or working conditions. Applicable to the Western Hemisphere also, this provision, as subsequently administered, instituted a negative certification requirement that rendered applications more difficult. The next 30 percent (second preference) were allocated to parents of adult citizens, and the final 20 (third preference) to spouses and children of legal resident aliens. Any unused remainder of the latter was made available to brothers and sisters, as well as adult sons and daughters of citizens (fourth preference). The law did ease family reunion somewhat by extending nonquota status to the children of citizens regardless of age, as well as to their husbands and spouses regardless of date of marriage.

Defenders of the national origins system emphasized that it legitimately sought to preserve the nation's sociological and cultural balance and that, contrary to the critics, it did not discriminate against Catholics, since many of the nonquota immigrants from Canada and nearly all those from Mexico belonged to that faith, nor against Jews, who were not identified as such but rather assigned to the appropriate nationality.[80] However, their main concern was no longer Catholics and Jews, but the preservation of whiteness. In this light, McCarran-Walter emerges as an updated barrier against what the conservative nation-builders viewed as the most threatening flows: Asians, West

Indians, and postcolonial peoples of color more generally. It also expanded the grounds for exclusion to cover a broader swath of "immoral," "subversive," and "narcotics" categories; as Arens explained, for the first time the law supplied the immigration service with adequate weapons to deal with Communist penetration and its plan of "conquest by immigration." The reformers' sole consolation was their success in blocking the appointment of Arens as INS commissioner of the new Eisenhower administration.

In retrospect, the McCarran-Walter law can be seen as primarily an exercise in symbolic politics, the last hurrah of a political generation that was passing from the scene. Although main-gate reform itself remained on the agenda, this was largely an exercise in symbolic politics as well, and it took a back seat to other means of satisfying constituency demand and meeting foreign policy objectives. Consequently, immigration for the decade as a whole amounted to about 2.5 million, by far the heaviest since the 1920s, but less than one-half of this (1,098,790) occurred within the quotas, and the bulk of the 1.4 million others belonged to nationalities that did not meet traditionalist identity criteria.[81] The modest share of quota immigration in the total reflected not only the rising importance of alternative entry gates, but also the fact that only 71 percent of the 1,547,500 slots provided for were filled. This was because, while demand from the less favored countries remained very high, the favored northwest Europeans used only 566,218 out of the 1,251,650 slots reserved on their behalf (about 45 percent). Quite dramatically, within a decade and a half after World War II, the traditional "push" gave way to a powerful "pull" to relieve labor shortages; not only did demand for American immigration visas decline sharply, but immigration to Europe itself also rose to unprecedented levels, thanks to a fundamental transformation of the economic and social configuration of the relevant countries. Beginning in the mid-1950s, most of the developed world, which now also included Japan, followed in America's footsteps, rising to unprecedented affluence and entering the postindustrial stage.

The Back Door Moves to the Fore

In his feisty way, President Harry Truman succeeded in getting the 1952 Democratic National Convention to endorse a call for revising McCarran-Walter and went on to make it a salient issue in the presidential campaign. This was in tune with the changing national mood; for example, on the question of whether more refugee admissions should be allowed, a 1953 survey indicated that the public was now almost evenly split.[82] At the campaign heated up, the president appointed a Presidential Commission on Immigration and Naturalization of his own. Headed by Solicitor General Philip B. Perlman and Earl G. Harrison, this was tantamount to a counter–McCarran Commission, whose composition insured a liberal recommendation. Although the Republican candidate, General Dwight Eisenhower, was initially silent on immigration, after being challenged he in turn denounced McCarran-Walter in no uncertain terms.[83]

Following extensive hearings encompassing 634 public leaders and social scientists, the commission issued *Whom We Shall Welcome,* which became the benchmark for reform efforts. Going well beyond the recent congressional proposals, it charged that the national origins system was founded on an archaic "melting pot" theory that took into account none of the sociological developments of the last thirty years, and proposed replacing it outright with a flexible allocation of visas every three years on the basis of a modified set of preferences that took into consideration political asylum, family reunion, manpower needs, and the needs of the free world, while also allowing for "new seed" immigration, without regard to national origin, race, color, or creed.[84] Combining the baseline proposed by Humphrey-Lehman with the equation introduced by McCarran-Walter, it proposed a ceiling on quota immigration at "1/6th of one percent of the U.S. population" enumerated in the 1950 U.S. Census, for a total of 251,162, some two-thirds above the established level. By a feat of numerological magic, the formula, originally pertaining to members of each national origin within the American population in 1920, thus evolved into the idea that 1 immigrant per 600 Americans constituted an appropriate level for annual *quota* immigration. Whereas the Commission itself recommended adding parents and grandparents to spouses and children as nonquota immigrants, and maintaining the Western Hemisphere outside the quota, in his testimony before the commission, Senator Lehman advocated a "blanket quota" of "one immigrant per 500 people," or "between 300,000 and 350,000 a year," a somewhat higher total than the Commission's, but one that included the Western Hemisphere.

This was the first time a proposal to that effect, hitherto associated with the most extreme restrictionists, was set forth by the liberal camp, confirming an emerging consensus on numerical restriction as the baseline of American immigration policy. Albeit sidelined, the reformers slogged on. On August 3, 1953, the last day of the first session of the 83rd Congress, eight Democratic senators, including Herbert Lehman and freshman John F. Kennedy, introduced an omnibus bill revising and replacing McCarran-Walter; and a parallel proposal based on *Whom Shall We Welcome,* but now encompassing the Western Hemisphere as well, was introduced in the House by stalwart Emmanuel Celler and New Jersey's Peter Rodino, a spokesman for Italian American concerns.

The significance of the liberal camp's tacit endorsement of the restrictionists' overall objective of keeping immigration within very limited bounds has been largely ignored by historians of immigration policy. The shift undoubtedly accorded with the wishes of organized labor, whose witnesses warned the Commission that in case procurement under the *bracero* program, the proviso, and the "wetback" system were denied to employers or became too costly as the result of regulation, they would seek to obtain their field hands by way of large-scale ordinary immigration from Mexico. But the determinative role of path dependency in bringing about the endorsement was substantiated in 1956 by Louis L. Jaffe, who participated in the drafting of the Lehman bill.[85] Pointing out that until 1921, unlimited immigration was the logical concomitant of "Manifest Destiny," which required men as soldiers and workers, and that the laws of the 1920s reflected the waning of those conditions, he reflected somewhat disingenuously, "It is a rather puzzling feature of the 1924 settlement that immigration from the Americas was not restricted at all." Since immigration designed to meet specific economic objectives requires a planned economy, which is not the case in the United States, "It must be concluded, therefore, that the economics of immigration are today marginal and relatively unimportant," and hence that immigration should be designed exclusively to serve family reunification and provide havens for political refugees. Implicitly, since Mexican immigration was essentially economic, it was unjustified. More explicitly, Sidney Liskofsky of the American Jewish Committee, which had steadily opposed national origins quotas, now thought most Americans agreed to the use of cultural-ethnic criteria for admission, and drew attention to sociologist Nathan Glazer's recent justification of this stance.[86]

Shortly to become famous by way of his coauthorship of *Beyond the Melting Pot,* Glazer pointed out in his contribution to the symposium (in which Jaffe appeared as well) that the great turn-of-the-century migration had the effect of making America "different," and commented,

> I would not undo that difference. But it is reasonable to suggest that one of the necessary decisions that must precede the formulation of a national policy on immigration is whether we want to become even more different or are satisfied with what we are. In 1921, the American people decided they

wanted to stop. . . . Nations have rarely been faced with the problem of deciding their ethnic make-up, but the United States was. I think the racist thinking that accompanied that decision was reprehensible. The decision itself, however, one can understand. American had decided to stop the kaleidoscope and find out what it had become.[87]

In 1956, "even more different" could only refer to browns and blacks from the Western Hemisphere. Promoted concurrently by the economic concerns of the labor-minded liberal reformers and the identity anxieties of the traditional restrictionists as well as many liberals concerned over the changing racial character of American cities, Mexican immigration was rapidly emerging as the major concern.

In his February 1953 State of the Union message, President Eisenhower conceded that the McCarran-Walter Act "does, in fact, discriminate," and recommended enactment of an immigration statute that would guard the national interest "and be faithful to our basic ideas of freedom and fairness to all." Although he sent a letter to Congress recommending appropriate action, the matter did not constitute a very high priority.[88] Meanwhile, far from reducing the movement of Mexican labor, which was widely acknowledged as the leading cause of the growing illegal flows and permanent settlement, American policies were stimulating its further expansion. By the time the *bracero* agreement expired at the end of 1953, the Korean "emergency" was over and the United States was in the throes of a postwar slump. Both Mexico, which faced rapid population growth and high unemployment, and the American growers wanted the flow to continue; but whereas the Mexican negotiators once again held out for employer sanctions, betting that the United States would bow to its demands on foreign policy grounds because the deteriorating situation in Central America enhanced the need for good relations with Mexico, the United States chose instead to play hard ball and in late January 1954 once again opened the border at El Centro, California, to enlist thousands of illegals under the "proviso."[89] Negotiations shortly resumed, leading to a new *bracero* agreement in mid-March, again without employer sanctions but granting Mexico the face-saving device of a Joint Migratory Labor Commission.

The issue of illegal Mexican immigration surged to the political fore as California Governor Earl Warren, President Eisenhower's close political ally, complained that the "wetback invasion" imposed an unacceptable welfare burden on his state and demanded federal reimbursement. Accordingly, on the advice of Attorney General Herbert Brownell, the president appointed his

West Point classmate General Joseph Swing, who had begun his career in the campaign against Pancho Villa and was now commander of the California-based 6th Army, as commissioner of the INS with the mission of regaining control of the border. In June 1954, after securing the cooperation of the growers by assuring them of an adequate supply of legal *braceros* under more favorable conditions, Swing launched "Operation Wetback," a massive roundup of deportable aliens in selected districts of California, Texas, and later Arizona. The target areas were flooded with advance announcements designed to encourage undocumented workers to leave on their own, especially because no provisions were made to deport their families.

The roundups tapered off in the fall as the growing season came to an end. As evidence of its success, the INS reported that the six-week operation netted 1.3 million departures; but since voluntary returns were not actually counted, the claim is difficult to assess, and skeptical observers have pointed out that there was no evidence of a mass exodus on the U.S. side, or of massive arrivals in Mexico. However, the INS reported that the number of apprehensions rose to an unprecedented 1,035,282 for the year as a whole, and in March 1955 General Swing announced that the "wetback problem" had been licked for the first time since the 1920s. Congress was sufficiently impressed to provide the Border Patrol with three aircraft and twenty-four new vehicles.

Under the circumstances, American farmers had little choice but to apply for legal *braceros,* whose procurement was now eased.[90] Accordingly, the program expanded further to an average of over 400,000 a year in 1956–1959; concurrently, INS apprehensions declined to 165,186 in the first post–"Operation Wetback" year, and bottomed out at a mere 39,750 in 1960, the lowest level since 1943. It is impossible to ascertain to what extent this reflected INS bureaucratic maneuvers or an actual decline in illegal entries.[91] Concurrently, the number of Mexicans admitted as immigrants grew rapidly, doubling from 9,600 in 1952 to 18,454 the following year, doubling again in 1954, and reaching an unprecedented 65,047 in 1956, establishing Mexico as the leading source of legal immigration (a position it maintained for the remainder of the twentieth century). Over 40 percent of the successful applicants had previous experience as agricultural laborers in the United States, a clear indication that the networks fostered by the *bracero* program and informal recruitment contributed to the growth of immigration proper. This triggered heightened concern in Washington, leading to the institution of a more restrictive visa policy, which quickly reduced admissions to 23,061 by 1959.

Meanwhile the growing mechanization of cotton harvesting, notably in

Texas, stimulated in part by the high cost of legal *braceros,* steadily reduced the need for stoop labor, so that the economic base for the *bracero* program was narrowed to California's fruit and vegetable growers. The matter surged to national attention on Thanksgiving Day 1960, when CBS telecast the harrowing documentary *Harvest of Shame,* movingly narrated by America's premier airwave journalist, Edward R. Murrow, which explicitly linked the *bracero* program to the plight of domestic migrants. The Eisenhower administration subsequently decided to discontinue the program, but in response to protests from the growers agreed to a six-month extension.

In the intervening period, with main-gate reform effectively ruled out, both the administration and the reformers fell back on the side entrance. In 1953, the administration requested authorization to admit 120,000 persons in each of the next two years to accommodate remaining German expellees, escapees from Communism, as well as emigrants from countries with large surplus populations and good friends in Washington, notably Italy, Greece, and the Netherlands. The measure was identified in a National Security Council memorandum as a device to "encourage defection of all USSR nations and 'key' personnel from the satellite countries" in order to "inflict a psychological blow on communism" and, "though less important . . . material loss to the Soviet Union" by draining away its professionals.[92] In the face of a threatened filibuster by McCarran, it was scaled down somewhat and its administration shifted from the DP Commission to the State Department's refugee program, with stepped-up security verifications.[93] Subsequent measures facilitated the immigration of additional Greeks as well as of southern Italians, on the grounds that post–Civil War and postearthquake devastation rendered them vulnerable to seduction by the Communist Party. Numerous Chinese sought to enter the United States as well after the Communist takeover of 1949; in 1950 alone, some 117,000 persons claiming to be the children of U.S.-born Chinese, and hence themselves "derivative citizens" not subject to quota limitations, applied for U.S. passports in Hong Kong, creating a huge processing backlog making for a four- to twelve-year wait.[94]

In 1956, the United States seized upon Soviet Secretary General Nikita Khrushchev's hint of greater freedom for the satellites to encourage oppositional initiatives in Hungary; however, the Soviet tanks rolled in on November 4, triggering the exodus of several thousand freedom fighters as well as others who took advantage of the temporarily open border. Unwilling to support the rebels because of the danger of a confrontation with the Soviet Union, the Eisenhower administration nevertheless authorized 5,000 admissions under the 1953 act. However, some 200,000 Hungarians managed to cross into Austria, which allowed them in only on condition of rapid resettlement. This was undertaken by the International Committee on European Migration and the UNHCR, with the United States and Canada each committing themselves to taking about 20 percent of the total.[95] As admissions available under the 1953 law proved insufficient, the administration resorted to an obscure provision of the general immigration law that gave the attorney general discretionary authority to "parole" any alien into the United States for reasons of emergency or if "deemed strictly in the public interest." Another 31,500 Hungarians were admitted in this manner, and two years later a new law allowed them to acquire immigrant status.[96] Albeit intended to deal with medical emergencies and judicial proceedings, "parole" was henceforth used repeatedly to admit nationals of Communist countries or groups of special interest to particular members of Congress.

Although Senator McCarran died in 1954, Representative Walter stubbornly carried on a defensive struggle on behalf of their legislative progeny. Despite increasing criticism nationally and even within his own constituency, Walter was reelected in 1954, with reinforced influence in the once-again Democratic Congress. However, from 1955 onward, the congressman began hinting that he was not wedded heart and soul to the quota system, and would support revision "if something fairer can be devised." Quick on the uptake, in February 1956, the president recommended a number of interim measures "to alleviate as much as possible inequities in the present quota system," notably a change in the population baseline from 1920 to 1950, thereby raising the limit from 154,657 to 220,000, as had been recommended by the Truman-appointed commission, with the possibility of pooling unused numbers for reallocation within each region. He further proposed creating a pool of 5,000 outside the national quotas for immigrants with special skills as well as canceling the "mortgages" that had accumulated under the several DP programs. However, Walter immediately denounced the proposals as little more than a "refurbished version" of those advanced by his perennial foe, Emmanuel Celler, and effectively discouraged the Eisenhower administration from tackling main-gate immigration until its final year.[97] Furthermore, Walter astutely exploited the growing concern over the Mexican "invasion" to justify his position on immigration more generally. In a Memorial Day speech, subsequently published in the *Congressional Record* and widely reprinted, he noted a "remarkable increase" in legal immigration from Mexico over the preceding two years and charged that if the Eisenhower plan were adopted, "it would be entirely safe to assume that by, say, 1980, we will have much difficulty making ourselves understood in the English language in some parts of the country."

Nevertheless, defenders of the national origin quotas and the immigration regime's residual racial restrictions were now very much on the defensive. Harry Rosenfield, executive secretary of the Truman Commission, suggested in 1956 that a vital change had taken place in the last four years: from a somewhat partisan, relatively localized issue, immigration reform had become a nonpartisan national issue, with a consensus that McCarran-Walter required revision.[98] Not only had labor shifted its position, but even among the Daughters of the American Revolution, there were suggestions that the national origins quotas were "illogical and absurd," and their "pseudo-scientific" pretense was widely discredited. Private bills to overcome the constraints imposed by McCarran-Walter proliferated as well, rising from 429 in 1945–1947 to 4,797 in 1953–1955 and 2,810 in the 1955–1956 session of the 84th Congress alone. The quotas were criticized on foreign policy grounds as well. For example, Donald J. Kingsley argued that while the image of the United States remained bright in Europe thanks to modifications in the DP legislation that opened the door to Greeks and Italians, with regard to Asia the persisting image was the gunboat rather than the Statue of Liberty. While the lifting of Japanese exclusion by McCarran-Walter was "a major step in the right direction," the remnants of discrimination against Chinese, in particular, were of great propaganda value to the Communists, and "We cannot afford them any longer."[99]

"An End to Anarchy"

By the early 1960s, David Reimers has suggested, the national origins system had come to be regarded by many Americans as on a par with deliberate segregation, that is, contrary to the spirit of the Constitution, and there were few who would defend it explicitly.[100] But in keeping with the rules of the Washington political game, since abolition of the quotas was politically valuable to the reformers, they could be made to pay to achieve their objective. The price, motivated by the conservatives' determination to limit the settlement of browns and blacks, was the imposition of an unprecedented numerical limit on the Western Hemisphere. The ease with which the reformers paid up reflected their long-standing ambivalence regarding the back door.

Although immigration reform did not figure in the 1956 campaign, in the wake of Senator John F. Kennedy's near-success in securing nomination as the Democratic vice presidential candidate, his aides identified it as a valuable campaign theme. Support for reform was naturally much stronger among the urban groups issued from the new immigration, whose fulsome support was crucial for Kennedy's ascent, given lingering suspicion of a Catholic candidacy in the Midwest, the South, and rural areas generally.[101] As the ageing Senator Lehman retired from the fray, Kennedy began assuming leadership in the immigration sphere, and in 1957 seized the opportunity to make his mark. Carefully avoiding a head-on clash with Representative Walter, he began by sponsoring a bill designed to let in the dependents of persons already admitted under the Refugee Relief Act, as well as to lift quota mortgages and regularize paroled Hungarians; however, in the face of Walter's disapproval, the latter was dropped. The outcome was the Act of September 11, 1957, which passed the Senate by a resounding 65–4, and the House by 295–98; even Walter, who was hospitalized at the time, indicated his support. The mortgage for-giveness provision, which released some 300,000 entries over the next several years, was perceived quite correctly by defenders of McCarran-Walter as "a major successful assault," which "went far to accomplish the objectives of the anti-restrictionists, falling short, however, of outright elimination of the quota system and national origins formula which it effectively diluted tempo-rarily."[102] Kennedy followed up with *A Nation of Immigrants,* which originated as a pamphlet commissioned by the Anti-Defamation League of B'nai Brith, following a preliminary outline prepared by historian Arthur Mann.[103] In 1959 the senator's staff prepared another proposal to replace the national origins system; although this stood no more chance of enactment than Humphrey-Lehman, it did serve as the basis for a comprehensive reform project prepared by nongovernmental organizations and subsequently introduced by Senator Philip Hart of Michigan.

The dynamics of international migration relevant to American policy had changed enormously since the national origins system was enacted, and even since the days of McCarran-Walter. While Europe dried up as a source of demand for entries, except for some family members in the southern coun-tries, the developing world made a dramatic entrance into the American orbit thanks to the combination of decolonization, which lifted barriers against exit; a high population growth; the undermining of traditional economies without sufficient development to absorb the generations coming of age; and the spreading transportation revolution, which enabled even extremely low-income masses to move over great land distances and across oceans. The population of the United States' southern and southeastern neighbors ranked among the fastest growing in the world.[104] Mexico shot up from 27 million in 1950 to 60 million in 1975, a rate of increase of approximately 5 percent a year, despite considerable emigration to the United States. The Central American countries (Guatemala, Belize, Honduras, Nicaragua, Costa Rica, and Panama) were also increasing steeply, from 9 million in 1950 to 18.5 million in 1975 (an increase of about 4 percent a year). The Caribbean Islands (excluding Cuba and the American possessions) rose somewhat more slowly from 9.1 million in 1950 to 14.5 million in 1975 (2.4 percent), but still substantially given considerable flows to Britain, France, the Netherlands, and the United States. Among the latter, the Dominican Republic doubled its population, from 2.3 million in 1950 to 4.7 in 1975. Cuba behaved much like the others, growing from 5.5 million in 1950 to 9.3 in 1975, despite considerable departures in the wake of its revolution. Worldwide, Asia of course provided the largest potential source; with China in effect closed to emigration, this meant the Indian subcontinent, Pakistan, India, and Bangladesh, which rose from 445 million in 1950 to 775 million in 1975 (about 3 percent a year). It also involved South Korea, which was intimately linked with the United States since the war, which grew more modestly from about 20 million in 1950 to 35 million in 1975. Africa, which loomed as a potential source for the first time since the slave trade, had very high rates of population growth as well; over the same period, Nigeria, for example, more than doubled from 30 million to 63 million (about 4 percent a year).

Much of the developing world was also highly vulnerable to refugee-generating conflicts; although most of the flows were regionally contained, some ran toward the United States or were drawn in more proactively by its policies. The most immediate instance of the latter was Cuba, in connection with which, for the first time since the United States began encouraging "defectors" as a weapon in its Cold War arsenal, implementation of the policy required the first massive provision of asylum on its own soil.[105] Immediately after coming to power, the Fidel Castro regime encouraged the emigration of upper- and middle-class Cubans as potential opponents; concomitantly, the Eisenhower administration welcomed the exodus as contributing to the delegitimation and destabilization of the regime. Initially, most of the Cubans came on visitors' visas; and after the United States broke diplomatic relations with Cuba in January 1961, the new Kennedy administration, taking advantage of the absence of a cap on Western Hemisphere immigration, quickly widened the door by waiving visa requirements altogether. By the end of the year, some 100,000 Cubans had fled to the United States, with over 70,000 registered in Miami alone. Regarded as temporary exiles who would return when the Castro regime fell or was overthrown, many of the refugees were enlisted into the Bay of Pigs operation to bring this about. Afterwards, the United States envisaged the refugees' permanent settlement.[106] The blockade drastically reduced flights, while Cuba closed its borders, leaving some 350,000 holders of visa waivers stranded under Castro's rule. Altogether, some 200,000 Cubans entered the United States from the beginning of the exodus to 1965; like the Hungarian parolees, most were eventually regularized as immigrants.

As anticipated, Americans of the "new immigration" provided substantial support for Kennedy, arguably accounting for his victory in decisive northern states, notably Illinois. Shortly after the election, the new president charged Abba Schwartz, a liberal Washington lawyer with long experience in refugee and immigration affairs, but acceptable to Walter, with the preparation of a comprehensive proposal in collaboration with his brother, Attorney General Robert Kennedy. However, he did not mention immigration in his first two State of the Union messages, possibly out of fear that stirring this hornet's nest would jeopardize higher priority objectives.[107] Impatient with Kennedy's delays, Congress once again enacted particularistic measures to alleviate constituency pressures; for example, in 1962, Senator John Pastore of Rhode Island, the first Italian American elected to the upper house, secured the admission of 16,000 southern European brothers and sisters (albeit reduced from an initial request for 65,000).[108]

Meanwhile, the administration tackled the back door. Responding to long-standing union demands, the Department of Labor launched an active campaign against the importation of temporary workers, but Congress again enacted a *bracero* program extension, this time for a two-year period, albeit with the requirement that they be paid prevailing wages and an employer fee of $15 per head. Inclined to veto the measure, President Kennedy ultimately refrained from doing so for fear of antagonizing Mexico at a critical time for relations with Latin America.[109] The program finally was allowed to expire at the end of 1964, but a limited supply of temporary workers could still be secured legally under the proviso according to need, as determined by the secretary of labor. Following the highs of the late 1950s, the *bracero* program shrank to less than 200,000 in its final year; concurrently, undocumented entries once again began to rise, as suggested by the growth of apprehensions from a low of 39,750 in 1960 to 51,320 in 1963.[110]

Foreign policy considerations undoubtedly weighed heavily as well in the liberals' decision to forego the ceiling on Western Hemisphere immigration that had been incorporated into the Humphrey-Lehman reform proposal a few years earlier. In March 1962, Senator Hart of Michigan, whose staff had migrated from Senator Lehman's office upon his retirement, introduced his own bill, inspired by Kennedy's 1959 proposal and further elaborated by concerned organizations.[111] Maintaining the Western Hemisphere's current nonquota status, it provided 250,000 admissions for the rest of the world on the basis of an innovative schedule of priorities reflecting internationalist norms: 50,000 admissions reserved for refugees, 120,000 allocated to sending countries in proportion to the emigration of their nationals to the United States during the previous fifteen years, and 80,000 to be distributed in proportion to the senders' population size, up to a maximum "bonus" of 3,000 per country. The unprecedented notion of harnessing U.S. immigration to the needs of other countries was immediately denounced by defenders of the status quo as totally inappropriate. For example, Marion Bennett pointed out that not only would the measure promote the immigration of southern Europeans, but also 12.45 percent of admissions would be allocated to Asian and African countries; although this was close to the proportion of the nonwhite population of the United States (11.4 percent in 1960), and hence in keeping with the conservative "mirror" theory, he warned that the putatively much higher birthrate of Asian and African immigrants would rapidly alter the country's racial composition, and he raised a deliberately fright-provoking question: "Can we have a nation on such a basis as suggested?"[112]

The administration's own proposal finally emerged on July 25, 1963, in the wake of an improved congressional majority and the death of Representative Walter, which freed the White House to tackle the national origins system head on.[113] Spokesmen emphasized that the project was designed not only to right past inequities, but also to put an end to the "anarchy" resulting from the restrictions imposed by the system and the special legislation enacted to overcome them. As in the Hart proposal, the administration's maintained the Western Hemisphere's nonquota status and extended this to the newly independent states of the Caribbean, thereby lifting the 100-lid clapped down on them in 1952. The annual ceiling for the remainder of the world was raised by a mere 10 percent to 165,000, but considerably more room was provided under it by moving parents of citizens to nonquota status. The remnants of Asian exclusion were to be eliminated immediately, and the abhorred quotas phased out over a five-year period. The measure established formal parity among source countries by limiting yearly admissions from any one of them to a maximum of 10 percent of the total, regardless of population size or demand level. While keeping the existing priority for qualified manpower, the proposal facilitated certification so that the category would be used more extensively. In a bow toward the internationalist outlook of the Hart proposal, it specified that up to 20 percent of entries could be reserved for refugees if needed, as decided by the president on the recommendation of a seven-person Immigration Board. The remaining preferences were allocated to relatives of citizens and permanent residents who did not benefit from nonquota status, notably brothers and sisters. Unused numbers in the higher preferences would be available for allocation to the lower ones. The president was also authorized to reserve up to half of the unallocated numbers for persons disadvantaged by changes in the system, notably hitherto privileged applicants from big-quota western European countries, including Ireland.

Albeit endorsed by bipartisan groups in the Senate and in the House, the Kennedy proposal nevertheless remained trapped in congressional gridlock. As anticipated, the powerful conservative chairman of the Senate Judiciary Committee, Senator James Eastland of Mississippi, adamantly resisted the elimination of racial barriers, especially as they pertained to black immigration from the West Indies, and mobilized his southern Democratic and conservative Republican allies on behalf of a Western Hemisphere ceiling. More surprising was the trouble in the House, where Democratic Representative Michael Feighan of Ohio, an administration supporter who had succeeded Walter as chair of the Immigration Subcommittee, was being recalcitrant because of a feud with the difficult Emmanuel Celler, chairman of the parent Judiciary Committee, and because he felt the White House had not consulted him sufficiently in the elaboration of its proposal.[114] Consequently, the Kennedy proposal had not moved forward in either house by the time of the president's assassination.

Lyndon Johnson, who had voted to override Truman's veto of the McCarran-Walter Act in 1952, was now eager to consolidate his support among big-city ethnics. Thanks to his command of the Senate, he was also in a better position than Kennedy to overcome congressional obstacles. A week after his first State of the Union message, he convened all the immigration policy players at a White House conference, at which he endorsed the Kennedy proposal pending before Congress but insisted that civil rights legislation must be given the highest priority. The Senate Judiciary Committee complied, thereby postponing hearings on immigration until early 1965. Meanwhile, trouble continued to brew in the House, where Feighan also questioned the continued nonquota status for the Western Hemisphere now that the West Indies were to be included. As a bargaining chip, he introduced a bill of his own that maintained the national origins quotas; albeit unable to get this reported out of the Judiciary Committee, he was able to block the administration's bill at the subcommittee level. This prompted Johnson to put his personal aide, Jack Valenti, in charge of negotiations.[115]

Despite scurrilous attacks on immigrants by Arizona Senator Barry Goldwater's running mate, William Miller, who castigated Johnson for opening the floodgates "for virtually any and all who would wish to come and find work in this country," and was in turn denounced by Senator Hart as a "Know-Nothing," the reformist camp emerged from the 1964 elections very much reinforced. The respectable media now swung definitively against the national origins quotas, including even the *Saturday Evening Post,* hitherto a stalwart defender of the system as a bastion of "Americanism."[116] Enactment of the civil rights legislation, which prohibited discrimination on the basis of "national origins" as well as race, deprived it of its last vestiges of legitimacy. Thanks to their strongest showing since 1936, the liberal Democrats were finally in a position to overcome the stranglehold of the Rules Committee and the southern-dominated seniority system, as well as to pack the relevant committees with people of their own. Three committed reformers were thus appointed to the Feighan subcommittee while, in the Senate, Edward Kennedy took over management of the administration proposal (S. 500) from Senator Hart. Following publication by the *Washington Post* of a Harris poll indicating that a solid majority of the public still opposed changing the law to allow more immigration, the administration sponsored a Gallup poll of its own, which demonstrated that half of the public favored abolition of the national origins system; however, it also confirmed that there was still overwhelming opposition to any increase in immigration.[117]

The hearings on S. 500 began on February 10, 1965, with Subcommittee Chairman Eastland deferring to Senator Kennedy who, mindful of the polls, stressed that except for the repeal of the national origin quotas, the administration's proposal was quite conservative. With regard to numbers, it "merely updates our present law to conform more fully with our actual practice," and there is no reason to fear a flooding of cities, as "the present level of immigration remains substantially the same." While still attributing first preference to manpower, the latest version increased the share allocated to relatives as well as to disadvantaged northwest Europeans, at the expense of refugees. This was obviously designed to broaden congressional support.[118]

Although the administration publicly opposed the Western Hemisphere ceiling, there were indications that if push came to shove, it would be willing to pay up. For example, provoked by Senators Sam Ervin and Everett Dirksen on the issue of Jamaica, Trinidad-Tobago, and the Western Hemisphere more generally, Attorney General Nicolas Katzenbach stated disingenuously that "as a practical matter . . . the pressure of overpopulation that leads to immigration" is not found in "most of the countries of this hemisphere," but that "[i]f there were great numbers" coming from that region, "then it would seem to me that the matter would have sufficient seriousness to attempt to restrict immigration from these countries." Although he insisted that such an eventuality had not yet arisen, the statement was a clear hint that a deal was possible. Senators Kennedy and Hart intervened along the same lines, as did Secretary of State Dean Rusk.

For the time being, Senator Ervin merely responded wryly that if it was true that those countries *lacked* population pressure, it was doubly unjust to discriminate in their favor as the administration proposed to do by granting them nonquota status, and further that the proposal could hardly be termed fair in that it did not take into consideration differences in the population size of source countries; nor did he fail to stress repeatedly the inconsistency of a law that gave preference to the highly skilled but would keep out "ditchdiggers" (as stated by Senator Robert Kennedy, appearing as former attorney general), when as a consequence of the termination of the *bracero* program and Secretary of Labor W, Willard Wirtz's reluctance to allow use of the proviso, it was precisely men willing to do that and gather crops who were in short supply. He also pointedly brought out the structural contradiction between a law designed to attract the highly skilled worldwide, and American policy toward the developing world: "Now, aren't we chasing ourselves in a circle . . . when we send the Peace Corps abroad in order to lift those people up, and we are spending money for helping undeveloped countries, and then we admit to this country their most skilled people, aren't we leaving them in the fix from which we are trying to extricate them?"

Organized labor remained mainly concerned with the back door. Testifying in support of the administration proposal in the spring of 1965, an AFL-CIO spokesman asked for a reduction of the attorney general's discretion with regard to temporary labor by making the criteria for determining a shortage more precise; and after Secretary of Labor Wirtz was overruled by Attorney General Katzenbach on a matter of importing West Indians to Florida, the AFL-CIO returned to demand an absolute prohibition of foreign farm workers and an upgrading of the secretary of labor's power. This in turn prompted

Senator James Eastland, the hitherto absent subcommittee chairman, to resume control in order to hear witnesses from the American Farm Bureau Federation and the National Council of Agricultural Employers, both of whom stated candidly that they had not planned to appear were it not for the AFL-CIO's recent demands. However, Senator Kennedy reassured them that the pending bill would not alter the existing situation.[119]

Bowing to Lyndon Johnson's power, Representative Feighan finally relented on the national origin quotas and the Western Hemisphere ceiling. In the course of the House floor debate, a Republican-sponsored amendment on behalf of a 115,000 ceiling, which Feighan now opposed, was adopted in a teller vote (156–164), but subsequently defeated in a roll-call vote after the administration applied considerable pressure on its own party (218–189, 25 not voting); however, despite this, the southern Democrats voted 55–35 for the amendment. Ultimately, the administration's bill was approved on August 25 by 318 to 95, with only one important modification, advanced by Feighan, extending the existing nonadjustment provision for persons from contiguous territories to the *entire* Western Hemisphere. This would subject West Indians to the existing regulation designed to prevent temporary Mexican workers from becoming permanent residents.

When the House bill was taken up by the Senate Subcommittee, Senator Ervin, with support from his Republican colleague Dirksen of Illinois, immediately introduced an amendment providing for a 120,000 ceiling on the Western Hemisphere, scheduled to go into effect on July 1, 1968, *unless* a Presidential Commission appointed for that purpose recommend otherwise by July 1, 1967, *and* Congress acted accordingly. Ervin's insistence on a ceiling was an old story; but the conditional formula reflected a recent deal with the administration, which reluctantly bowed to the inevitable.[120] Given widespread ambivalence on the subject within Democratic ranks, the price was not very high.

Despite the conditional formulation, the Western Hemisphere ceiling was here to stay, since it was most unlikely that a majority would be mustered against it over the next couple of years. The level was established slightly below ongoing average immigration from the region (130,000), but considerably below what it might be with the English-speaking West Indies—limited since 1952 to 100 each within the United Kingdom, but heavily oversubscribed into the tens of thousands—added on. Moreover, demand from that quarter was likely to increase, as the United Kingdom, to which West Indians had turned in larger numbers when the United States closed its door to them in 1952, had recently begun to restrict their entry.[121] Nevertheless,

America's neighbors remained somewhat favored in that, in relation to population size, the Western Hemisphere's annual quota was larger than for the rest of the world. Both the *New York Times* and the *Christian Science Monitor* endorsed the Western Hemisphere limit editorially, on the grounds that its adoption now might prevent the enactment of more stringent legislation later on.

In the home stretch, Senator Sam Ervin took wry pleasure in pointing out that between the old guard and the new there was now agreement on fundamentals. The bill was passed on September 22, by an overwhelming 76 to 18, with 6 abstentions. The conference committee's task was "not a difficult assignment because of the agreement in substance" between the two versions.[122] The tightening of the back door fostered even greater consensus in the House, where the yeas went up by 2, and the nays down by 26, for a final vote of 320 to 69.

Scheduled to go into effect on July 1, 1968, the new law retained the established distinction between the Eastern and Western hemispheres.[123] With regard to the first, it provided an annual quota of 170,000 admissions, with a maximum of 20,000 for any one country. The first two preferences, together with the fourth and fifth, attributed an overwhelming 74 percent of the entries to family reunion, including 24 percent for brothers and sisters of citizens, prompting the law to be nicknamed "the brothers and sisters act"; in addition, children, parents, and spouses of American citizens were admitted outside the quota. Another 20 percent was allocated on the basis of personal qualifications considered of value to the United States (third preference of 10 percent for professionals, scientists, and artists of exceptional ability; sixth preference of 10 percent for skilled and unskilled workers in short supply, as certified by the secretary of labor). The final 6 percent (seventh preference) was set aside for refugees, defined as people fleeing persecution from Communism or the Middle East, as well as victims of natural calamity, as specified by the president. With regard to the Western Hemisphere, the law provided for a ceiling of 120,000 to be imposed in 1968, unless decided otherwise in the interim; however, there was no provision for a schedule of preferences in allocating the visas.

The Best-Laid Schemes of Mice and Men . . .

Celebrated in a solemn signing ceremony at the foot of the Statue of Liberty on October 3, 1965, the legislation that abolished the national origins quotas was widely hailed as an achievement on a par with the previous year's Civil

Rights Act, signifying the raising of white Americans of the "new" immigration to equality with those of the "old." Providing another bit of historical vindication, in anticipation of the event, President Johnson declared Ellis Island to be part of the statue's National Monument. But the moment was clouded by a number of ironies. As it happens, at the very moment of reformist triumph, the foreign-born had fallen to their lowest proportion of the American population since Alexis de Tocqueville visited America, a mere 5 percent. By and large, this confirmed that the restrictionists had largely succeeded in their objective of reducing immigration to a marginal role in American existence.

Another irony pertained to the promise that the law would put an end to the reigning anarchy. By 1965, the boycott and sanctions that isolated Cuba from 1962 on fostered severe economic difficulties, and these in turn brought about deterioration in the material and political positions of the middle strata, prompting growing pressure for authorization to emigrate.[124] Having gained full control, Castro decided the moment was ripe to rid himself of the discontented, which would also liberate housing for reallocation to the party faithful, and announced that all those who wanted to leave Cuba were free to do so. Seizing the occasion of the signing ceremony to respond, President Johnson promised that "those who seek refuge here will find it" and declared, contrary to both the spirit and the letter of the new law, that he would use his parole authority to that effect. Following a short-lived boatlift, Cuba and the United States negotiated a massive program of orderly departures by way of "freedom flights." Foreign policy considerations fostered special terms for Dominican immigration as well.

Yet another irony pertained to the "back door." Although he was the first president to originate from the Southwest, Lyndon B. Johnson drew attention to the law's liberating effect with regard to immigration from Europe and Asia, passing over the likelihood that three years hence, it would impose unprecedented restrictions on immigration from the Western Hemisphere. Since the *bracero* program had been terminated a year earlier, many hoped that 1965 would also mark the beginning of the end of the "Harvest of Shame"; but INS statistics for that year indicated a near doubling of border apprehensions since President Kennedy's first message on immigration. There was every reason to anticipate that since legal temporary entry was all but eliminated, absent a tightening of the lax controls along the southern border, unauthorized entries would continue to rise and reach unprecedented levels. If the immigration gate were to be narrowed as well, the likely outcome would be an even worse anarchy than the one whose end was being celebrated. The prevailing silence on the subject in Washington suggests collusion among decision makers, encompassing both liberals and conservatives, to deliberately bury their heads in the sand.

As the Western Hemisphere Commission began its work in 1966, its members shared the working assumption that some sort of limit would have to be imposed, but asked for a delay because some opposed an outright numerical cap, and it was not clear how else the limit might be imposed; however, Senator Dirksen opposed an extension on the grounds that the limit was part of the deal to enact the 1965 law. Hence the Commission went out of existence and the ceiling went into effect as scheduled in 1968. In the absence of a preference system, all applicants except for immediate relatives were subject to rigorous labor certification. The queues became ever longer, and the regulatory process itself generated an incentive for illegal behavior. Reversing the old "Catch-22" whereby immigrants must demonstrate they were not liable to become a public charge but could not do this by demonstrating a job was waiting because this would violate the prohibition against contract labor, the certification now required nearly all Western Hemisphere applicants to secure a job offer. But this was of course hard to obtain without prior contact with an employer, and given the admission queue, the applicant would not be available to fill the position for two or three years. Hence the most rational approach was to enter illegally, secure a job, and spend the waiting period working in the United States. Given the spotty character of law enforcement and the absence of sanctions other than expulsion by way of "voluntary departure," and since most Mexicans thought of themselves as coming to the United States to work and not to live permanently, the risk was quite acceptable. Employers had every incentive to avail themselves of this boon as well. By all accounts, illegal entries rose rapidly.

In a further irony, the immigrants most negatively affected by the Western Hemisphere quota were Canadians, who were surely not the intended target. This was because as ordinary skilled and white-collar workers, many Canadian applicants failed to meet the Department of Labor's criteria for certification; and in the absence of per-country ceilings, Canadians were crowded out by Mexicans and others. Accordingly, Canadian immigration dropped from approximately 30,000 a year before the law went into effect to about one-fourth that level in the mid-1970s, while Mexican admissions rose to around 60,000. Most peculiarly, given that the law was so closely associated with the Kennedys, it also operated to the detriment of Irish immigration. As intended, the new family preferences fostered big increases in immigration from southern

Europe, many of whose nationals had come to the United States in the postwar years by way of the special programs devised on their behalf. However, as early as 1968 the Irish American National Immigration Committee complained that the measure unfairly limited immigration from Ireland because their nationals had come so long ago that few of their contemporary American descendants had close relatives on whose behalf they could exercise family reunion.[125] Taking advantage of the exemption from visitor visa requirements, many overstayed their legal three-month limit and illegally engaged in gainful employment; accordingly, in the early 1980s Irish American organizations formed an Irish Immigration Reform Movement (IIRM) to lobby Congress on behalf of legalization of their status and reform of the immigration system to facilitate their admission as permanent residents in the future.[126]

The greatest irony of all was that a law that expressed the nation's determination to maintain immigration as the marginal feature to which it had been effectively reduced in fact had the opposite effect. From 1965 on, legal immigration expanded much more than the builders of the new and improved gates said they anticipated: admissions increased from 3.3 million in 1961–1970 to 4.5 million in the following decade, and continued to rise afterward. Moreover, the new flows were very different from the old. By the mid-1970s, European immigration began to decline as the family reunion backlog was taken care of and most European countries themselves turned into receivers. Concurrently, immigration from the developing world (Latin America, West Indies, Asia, and Africa) climbed from an average of 42.6 percent of the annual total in the last years of the McCarran-Walter system (1960–1964) to 58.8 percent in the transitional period 1965–1969, then to 71.7 percent in 1970–1974, and stabilized at approximately 75 percent afterwards. Substantial enough to induce major changes in the composition of the American population, the phenomenon was strikingly similar to the influx of "new immigrants" that precipitated restrictionist agitation in the late nineteenth century.

10

The Elusive Quest for Coherence

Again, a Nation of Immigrants

While political attention was focused on devastating racial confrontations and an exceptionally divisive war, the United States turned once again into a nation of immigrants. Legal immigration expanded much more than the architects of the refurbished gates anticipated, from 3.3 million in 1961–1970 to 4.5 million in the following decade, a hefty 40 percent increase; by 1981 admissions reached over twice the 1965 level, with further growth in the offing, and it was also amply evident that the documented inflow was hardly the whole story.[1] Moreover, the bulk of the newcomers were located on the far side of the recently expanded boundary of American identity. Vastly overshadowing the transformation effected by the immigration that precipitated restrictionist agitation at the turn of the twentieth century, within one generation the new wave turned the United States into the first nation to mirror humanity.

Whether hailed or deplored, there is no gainsaying that this development was contrary to the tacit agreement to maintain immigration as a minor feature of American existence that underlay the 1965 reform. Was this happenstance, or the result of a deliberate change of policy? Some of the objectors have charged that the authors of the 1965 law had such an outcome in mind all along, and deliberately pulled the wool over their opponents' eyes.[2] However, the record clearly indicates that while the lawmakers did intend to eliminate the immigration system's discriminatory features, notably as they affected Asians and West Indians, they did not anticipate that incoming flows would expand as much as they did, nor that non-European sources would become as dominant.[3] Nevertheless, it is the case that a law designed to preserve the established profile of the American population inadvertently contributed to its radical modification. As intended, it allowed for the expansion of immigration above the statutory annual quota by exempting the admission of immediate relatives of citizens—their spouses, children, and parents—from numerical restriction. However, in combination with the preference provided for brothers and sisters *within* the annual quota, this gave rise to an unanticipated "chaining" effect: after they became citizens, the siblings' spouses were able to pass on immediate relative preferences to new families, and so on. Accordingly, the number of exempt admissions began to snowball: starting around 50,000, it reached over 150,000 in 1980, raising admissions by about half above the statutory quota.[4]

The 1965 law also contributed to a broadening of the sources of immigration. The bulk of admissions, allocated to family reunion, naturally replicated the ethnicity of their sponsors; hence the only openings for significant change were the employment and refugee preferences, which totaled 26 percent of Eastern Hemisphere admissions from 1968 to 1976, and the same proportion of worldwide admissions from 1976 to 1980. The "members of the professions of exceptional ability in sciences or arts" (10 percent) originated mostly from the Philippines, Korea, and India, and the "skilled or unskilled workers in occupations in which labor is in short supply" (another 10 percent) mostly from Mexico and the Caribbean.[5] Of the refugees (6 percent), from 1966 to 1981, three-fifths were eastern European and the remainder mostly Asian, initially overwhelmingly Chinese (including Hong Kong), and later also Vietnamese.[6] An additional source of diversification was the admission of large groups of refugees under special programs, which added about 20 percent to the immigration taking place under the 1965 law. Much as in the postwar period, these programs came into being principally in the service of foreign policy objectives, somewhat inflected by constituency pressures. Reflecting the changing geography of Cold War confrontations, the streams shifted from Soviet-dominated Europe to neighboring Cuba and Central America, whose proximity fostered uncontrolled additional movements, as well as Southeast Asia, hitherto altogether outside the domain of U.S. immigration. In turn, as permanent residents and eventually citizens, immigrants from the new sources could avail themselves of the family reunion opportunities provided by the 1965 law, and were much more likely to do so than European foreign-born, who had by then exhausted their pool of living relatives.[7]

The growing size of immigration and its changing makeup were inextricably interwoven. In the final decade of the old régime, 1951–1960, 60 percent of legally admitted immigrants were European or Canadian, with Germany as the leading source and Canada in second place; while Mexico ranked third, the next two were again European, the United Kingdom and Italy. In the transitional decade, 1961–1970, the European-Canadian portion declined to 46 percent but the top five sources remained unchanged, albeit with Mexico now in the lead. However, in 1971–1980, the European-Canadian component sank to a mere 22 percent of the total, and while Mexico remained the top source country, the next four were now the Philippines, Korea, Cuba, and India. Nevertheless, as of the early 1980s, legal admissions averaged about 600,000 a year, amounting to approximately one-fourth of 1 percent of the American population, precisely the level to which immigration had been reduced by the restrictive legislation of 1924; but this was roughly half again as much as the "1/6th of 1 percent" the architects of the 1965 reform thought was an appropriate level. Moreover, it was increasingly evident that this was accompanied by considerable unauthorized entry and settlement. A study based on the 1980 U.S. Census estimated that the United States had at least 2.1 million illegal residents, suggesting an annual net flow one-fourth the size of legal immigration, thus boosting the annual increment to about 800,000.[8] Altogether, the foreign-born population increased by half, from 9.7 million in 1960 to 14.1 million in 1980.[9] At a little over 6 percent of the population, the immigrant mass remained close to the Tocquevillian low and considerably below the record 15 percent level of 1890 and 1910; but from a demographic perspective, immigration's contribution to American population growth doubled, from about 10 percent in the postwar decades to slightly over 20 percent in the 1970s, and in sheer numbers, the foreign-born nearly equaled the historical record set in 1930.[10]

Overall, from the perspective of the mainstream, the return of immigration to the fore appeared as a disturbing challenge, which exacerbated the ongoing social crisis by swelling the ranks of the vociferous minorities and imposing additional burdens on the beleaguered welfare state. Dominated by undocumented border-crossing Mexicans, with the remainder consisting mostly of visa "overstayers" from widely ranging sources, including Caribbean Islanders as well as some Asians and Africans, in the eyes of many the unauthorized flow reinforced immigration's disquieting otherness.[11] Hence these developments stimulated an expanding debate over immigration's causes, desirability, and consequences, recalling the confrontations of a century earlier, with social scientists and public intellectuals once again playing a prominent role in the production of battlefield ideologies. Ironically, at the dawn of the Reagan era, which promised less government and reduced regulation, there was growing agreement that the system instituted in 1965 proved obsolete from the start, allowing matters to get out of hand, and a rising clamor on behalf of a more comprehensive and effective immigration régime backed by expanded federal services.

The search for a solution by way of a succession of commissions and task forces fostered the emergence of new political actors determined to shape policy, notably a spate of neorestrictionist groups and an array of ethnic organizations speaking in the name of the newcomers. Unexpectedly, states and localities reentered as significant players in the immigration arena as well by way of their involvement in the provision of social services. With immigration policy driven simultaneously by economic and identity considerations, alignments cut across conventional right-left divisions, following a "strange bedfellow" pattern that fostered legislative measures purporting to definitively overcome the problems plaguing the main gate, the side entrance, and the back door, and constitute a coherent immigration system.

Fixing the Back Door

As the leading source of both legal and unauthorized immigration, Mexico assumed singular significance, evoking that of Ireland a century and a half earlier, except that American fears now crystallized around language rather than religion. The remarkable expansion of Mexican movement was attributable to the formation of a transnational system, arising from an interactive combination of "demand-pull factors in the U.S., supply-push factors in Mexico, and network factors that bridge the border," which itself bore many parallels to the transatlantic configuration that emerged in the nineteenth century.[12]

On the push side, the basic factor was Mexico's demographic explosion; despite increasing emigration, the rate of population growth more than doubled from 2.5 percent a year in the postrevolutionary decades to 5.5 percent in the 1960s, boosting the total from 26.3 million in 1950 to 69.7 million in 1980.[13] Although economic development is usually accompanied by a decline in fertility, in Mexico this was delayed by the rural sector's unusual capacity for absorbing more labor, thanks to the egalitarian *ejido* land reform enacted in the 1930s, as well as the maintenance of a guaranteed price for corn.[14] By the same token, abandonment of this policy in 1973 in response to pressure from international economic agencies dominated by the United States triggered a massive uprooting of the rural population, now much more mobile thanks to a spectacular expansion of the road network, the progress of literacy to a nearly universal level, and the spread of communications.[15] Although the new development strategy entailed huge foreign exchange liabilities, in the 1970s these could be covered by petrodollar income arising from the oil crisis; however, the day of reckoning dawned in the early 1980s, and the government's decision to declare a moratorium on debt service payments precipitated a protracted thirteen-year crisis marked by recurrent negative growth rates of GDP and real wages.[16] Fertility did begin to drop, but the country continued to be faced with expanding waves of young adults seeking to enter the labor market. Most were drawn northward to new industry located along the border, often under *maquiladora* arrangements whereby components manufactured in the United States or other highly industrialized countries were shipped to Mexico for processing and assembly. Workers in this sector grew from some 100,000 in 1980 to 518,000 a decade later and rose to over 600,000 by 2000, producing additional employment in related services.[17] However, once uprooted Mexicans were on the move, it made sense for many to take a chance on the American side of the border, where opportunities were expanding as well, from the traditional migrant agriculture to the lower reaches of industry and services, and spreading steadily farther from its traditional base in the Southwest.

On the American side, within a political arena confronted with the need for urgent action to resolve the urban crisis, in the late 1960s and early 1970s there was little incentive to place immigration on the legislative agenda. Moreover, as one contemporaneous assessment suggested, "Congress and its members are believed to be particularly ill-suited to deal with immigration, as it is a 'no-win' issue for most candidates."[18] Nevertheless, in keeping with the long-established agenda of organized labor, the liberal camp remained committed to the control of illegal immigration and perennially sought to do so by imposing sanctions on employers who hired unauthorized foreign workers. Their resolve was reinforced and their cause legitimized in the late 1960s by the widely publicized struggle of the United Farm Workers (UFW), founded by César Chávez in 1963, to organize the overwhelmingly Mexican California grape pickers, whose strikes were repeatedly undermined by the recruitment of undocumented border-crossers from Mexico as well as the illegal use of legally recruited foreign seasonal agricultural workers ("H-2"), long provided for under the immigration law but now used more widely as substitutes for the abolished *braceros* as strikebreakers. In 1971, Representative Peter Rodino, a liberal Democrat from New Jersey who had played a lead role in the elimination of the national origins quotas and was now chair of the Immigration Subcommittee, once again undertook to enact employer sanctions.

However, a division now arose within the liberal camp between organized labor and the recently emerged national Hispanic organizations, which forcefully opposed sanctions. How they came to adopt this stance requires elucidation as, given the Chávez movement's ethnic identity, action against illegal immigration could hardly be viewed as anti-Mexican, and polls indicated that a majority of Hispanic voters supported sanctions as well as a secure form of national identification.[19]

The formation of Hispanic organizations and their emergence as full-fledged actors within the national political arena were stimulated by the mobilizational climate of the civil rights movement and reflected the growing numbers and increasing relative weight of Hispanics, especially of Mexican origin, in the American population, as well as their greater urbanization.[20] The oldest Mexican American political organization was the League of United Latin American Citizens (LULAC), traditionally representing the concerns of middle-class citizens in the Southwest, and paralleling the Urban League within the African American world; its ranks reinforced by veterans who took advantage of the G.I. Bill, in the post–World War II period it played an important role in the struggle against discrimination.[21] The 1960s gave birth to the more ethnic-oriented Raza Unida, which pressed for "Chicano" political and civil rights and fostered the formation of the Mexican American Democrats within the Texas Democratic Party, whose endorsements became essential for progressive "Anglos" seeking statewide office. However, because of their isolation and unfamiliarity with American institutions, Mexican immigrants tended to respond to Chicano activists but proved difficult to mobilize for electoral action.[22] In the early 1970s the Ford Foundation financed the development of more broadly based organizations, notably the Mexican-American Legal Defense and Education Fund (MALDEF), patterned after the NAACP's Legal Defense Fund, which assisted its beginnings, and the National Council of La Raza, launched to empower grassroots Chicano organizations by providing research and financial support.[23] The three developed an effective division of labor within the Beltway; as the chief Washington officer of LULAC explained to an interviewer, "Among us nobody can lobby like LULAC, litigate like MALDEF, or research like La Raza."[24] Following the precedent set by African Americans, in the 1970s Hispanics also gained a voice within the AFL-CIO by way of a Labor Council for Latin American Advancement.

Overwhelmingly U.S.-born and well-educated, and with little experience
of farm work, Washingtonian Hispanics opposed employer sanctions on the
grounds that they were likely to lead to discriminatory practices, and they
advocated instead more vigorous enforcement of existing labor laws.[25] Some
Mexican American politicians opposed sanctions as well, notably California
Representative Edward Roybal, reportedly on the grounds that "illegal aliens
cannot vote, but do get counted when grants are calculated or district lines
redrawn."[26] Liberal congressmen with substantial Hispanic constituencies
tended to follow suit. The split over sanctions surfaced within the labor world
itself, as unions in industries threatened by global relocation, notably the once-
powerful International Ladies Garment Workers and their male counterpart,
worried that they would jeopardize the use of undocumented immigrant
workers, which enabled clothing manufacturing to survive in the United
States.[27] The Republicans were also divided on the issue, but on different
grounds. Notwithstanding the economic benefits that illegal immigration afforded to growers and other employers, notably in California, it offended
partisans of law and order, the more so because of its largely nonwhite character; but advocates of tightened borders and identity cards were in turn
countered by libertarians, who generally opposed the expansion of policing.[28]
As it was, throughout most of the 1970s, recurrent House initiatives on sanctions died in the Senate, where agricultural interests asserted themselves decisively thanks to the political control exercised by Senator James Eastland of
Mississippi.[29]

In keeping with the general restructuring of American politics, the rapidly
growing Hispanic minority—with the exception of Cubans—gravitated toward the Democratic Party.[30] Hence, in response to constituency pressures,
in 1973 the party's congressional leadership undertook to seek remedial action
regarding the allocation of Western Hemisphere visas that, in the absence of
a preference system, rendered family reunion (other than for nonquota immediate relatives) more difficult than for the rest of the world. However, those
concerned over the growth of Mexican entries, which now used some 60,000
of the Western Hemisphere's visas annually, seized the opportunity to promote the imposition of a per-country cap, and in 1973 a bill combining the
two measures cleared the House by 336 to 30.[31] However, the Senate committee again sat on its hands. Demand mounted steadily, and by 1976 the
visa backlog was over two years long.[32] In 1975, the State Department
dropped its traditional opposition to a cap on Canada and Mexico on "Good
Neighbor Policy" grounds, reasoning that a uniform ceiling was preferable
because it would permit an equitable distribution of immigration from the

world at large, and because illegal immigration would persist whether immigration from Mexico was capped or not. The congressional stalemate was finally broken in mid-1976, and an easily passed bill was signed into law by President Gerald Ford, who criticized the rigid ceiling provision and promised to submit legislation to increase the Mexican quota.[33] Legal immigration from Mexico was immediately reduced by half, but given the ease of unauthorized entry, the consequences were obvious.[34]

While President Jimmy Carter broke symbolic ground by appointing Leonel J. Castillo, the first Mexican American ever elected to Houston municipal office and the administration's ranking Latino, as INS commissioner, his administration incorporated the liberal split on the back door. While Castillo advocated a large-scale legalization program for undocumented workers, Secretary of Labor Ray Marshall, a University of Texas labor economist close to organized labor, sought a more limited legalization program coupled with the establishment of mandatory work-eligibility identity cards, which Castillo opposed on civil liberties grounds.[35] Nevertheless, in 1977 the administration eventually came up with a comprehensive package, including increased annual quotas for Canada and Mexico to a combined 50,000, employer sanctions, elaboration of the Social Security card into a national identification document, reinforcement of border control, and a legalization program to clean the existing slate. However, the issue of sanctions was as divisive as ever.[36] Accordingly, wary of intraparty conflicts and with a tough presidential campaign in the offing, in late 1978 Senator Edward Kennedy, who assumed the chairmanship of the Judiciary Committee following Eastland's long-awaited retirement, together with Representatives Rodino and Joshua Eilberg, engineered a postponement of the whole immigration business by entrusting it to a Select Commission on Immigration and Refugee Policy (SCIRP), scheduled to report at the end of 1980.

Fixing the Side Entrance

Even though the new law purported to regularize refugee flows by providing for the admission of some 10,200 annually through the "Eastern Hemisphere" segment of the main gate, immigration by way of the side entrance expanded considerably and became vastly more diverse in the 1970s, as Cold War confrontations shifted from Europe to the Third World; concurrently, the growing controversies over foreign policy spilled over into refugee policy as well.

Despite its leadership in the establishment of an international refugee régime in the postwar years, the United States subsequently refused to accept oversight by international organizations regarding admissions on its own territory because of persistent opposition within the political class to anything that might be construed as an abandonment of national sovereignty. However, the political configuration changed somewhat in the 1960s as the civil rights revolution spilled over into the international sphere. Taking advantage of the reinforced liberal component within the Senate's Democratic majority, in 1968, Senator Edward Kennedy took the lead in securing ratification of the 1967 United Nations Protocol Relating to the Status of Refugees, which imposed on signatories the obligation to recognize as refugees people living outside their country of origin and unable to avail themselves of its protection, "owing to a fell-founded fear of being persecuted" by reason of race, religion, nationality, or political opinion.[37] But despite the ratification, subsequent Republican administrations carried on the ongoing policy of "calculated kindness," limiting admissions under the refugee preference or on parole to "victims of Communism," most egregiously refusing to take in Chileans fleeing the right-wing Pinochet coup engineered with U.S. support in 1973.[38] Ironically, "calculated kindness" itself, which hitherto had limited implications for immigration because so few were able to leave, suddenly began to produce substantial flows as, for a variety of reasons, some of the European Communist governments liberalized exit, while the emergence of new leftist régimes on America's doorstep and the sequels of U.S. involvement in conflicts in the world at large triggered massive flights of people with some claim to American asylum and assistance.

One of the first groups to secure the possibility of exit from the Soviet Union was the Jews.[39] Availing themselves of the expanding educational opportunities provided by the revolutionary régime, they had become considerably overrepresented among scientific and technical elites; but in the 1960s the ruling elite erected unprecedented barriers to their professional ascent and encouraged some to leave. This exceptional stance was rationalized on the basis of the régime's nationalities policy, whereby the Jews, like other Soviet citizens, were allowed to relocate in their national homeland, in this case Israel.[40] To reduce resentment and pressure from other groups, the Kremlin adopted a mixed strategy, simultaneously granting a limited number of visas and harassing applicants to discourage others; however, the strategy backfired as the issue of "refuseniks" provided a focus for mobilization at home and abroad.[41] In response to pressure from American Jewish organizations, as a condition for détente the Nixon administration called for a more generous exit policy that would also allow Soviet Jews to come to the United States. Eager to conclude the Strategic Arms Limitation Talks (SALT) and trade agreements, the Kremlin complied.[42] Exceeding the refugee allocation provided by the immigration law, exiting Soviet Jews were admitted to the United States under presidential parole. After Moscow backtracked, demanding that educated emigrants compensate the state for the costs of their training as a condition for departure, Congress enacted the Jackson-Vanek Amendment to the Trade Act of 1974, denying most-favored nation treatment to any "nonmarket economy country" that limits the rights of its nationals to emigrate.[43] Although most Soviet Jews went to Israel, a substantial minority settled in the United States over the next two decades; and in keeping with the chaining effect fostered by American legislation, the onset of a new stream quickly generated additional immigration.[44]

The largest source of new immigration attributable primarily to foreign policy was Indochina.[45] As late as 1973, the special assistant to the secretary of state for refugee and migration affairs assured Congress that although the Vietnam War was creating refugees, he did not "anticipate them coming to the United States . . . it would be our opinion that they could be resettled in their own country."[46] However, in April 1975, as the end neared, Secretary of State Henry Kissinger asked Ambassador Graham Martin to plan for as many as 200,000 Vietnamese exiles, and after Thailand and Malaysia made it very clear that they would accept refugees only on the condition that they would be quickly relocated, the Vietnamese were moved to U.S. bases in Guam. With the country in the midst of a recession and polls indicating opposition to massive Indochinese immigration, President Ford appointed an advisory committee to mobilize opinion leaders on behalf of a program to be carried out under presidential parole authority. No significant opposition surfaced, even from the antiwar camp, and less than a month after the final evacuation of Saigon, a grumbling Congress authorized federal aid to the receiving communities. About 130,000 refugees were resettled in the United States, as against 6,000 in third countries, mostly France. A subsequent law patterned after the Cuban Adjustment Act turned the Indochinese into permanent immigrants.

However, when processing was terminated in December 1975, there were still 80,000 Indochinese in camps throughout Thailand, and of the remaining 1.5 million military and civilian personnel who had served the anti-Communist régime, many were continuing to flee to neighboring countries. While the United States distanced itself from the region, a group of regional specialists within the State Department under the leadership of Philip Habib promoted additional resettlement, both out of obligation to former associates now in jeopardy and because the outpouring threatened to destabilize the region's remaining non-Communist countries. Forming an alliance with refugee-oriented nongovernmental organizations (NGOs), notably those laboring on behalf of Soviet Jews, they organized a blue-ribbon Citizens' Commission on Indochinese Refugees (CCIR), modeled after the one created on behalf of DPs after World War II.[47] Their moment came in 1978 when Vietnam's severe economic setbacks prompted the government to nationalize private trade, which under the circumstances amounted to "ethnic cleansing" directed against the Chinese minority and triggered a dramatic outpouring of "boat people."[48] The Carter White House immediately authorized parole for another 15,000 and appointed Habib to lead an interagency task force that recommended the resumption of massive resettlement, a policy endorsed by the National Security Council. Cambodia now began generating refugees as well amidst reports of horrendous exactions by the Khmer Rouge. Although the Carter administration was initially reluctant to take them in because this might interfere with its political strategy in the region as a whole, in the fall of 1978 Congress enacted a joint resolution directing Attorney General Griffin Bell to modify the policy.

Although the U.S. government had by now spent over $1 billion to relocate and assist some 170,000 Indochinese, the refugee crisis was further exacerbated by Vietnam's lightning offensive against Cambodian leader Pol Pot and the outbreak of war between China and Vietnam. Dramatic media coverage of the brutal *refoulement* of fleeing populations by Thailand and Malaysia provoked a groundswell of support throughout the West on behalf of a major rescue effort. In keeping with its overall commitment to the promotion of human rights, the Carter administration organized the Geneva conference of July 1979, resulting in an agreement among the industrialized nations to take on 260,000 Indochinese, but with the major share going to the United States.[49] However, tens of thousands of Cambodians along the Thai border were still in jeopardy; after United Nations High Commissioner for Refugees (UNHCR) negotiations for their repatriation failed, the CCIR and its congressional allies overcame the administration's reluctance, and some 30,000 Cambodians were paroled in as well.

Amidst these developments, Congress was steadily more determined to narrow the president's parole authority, both as a concomitant of its resolve in the wake of Vietnam to restrain presidential power in the sphere of foreign policy more generally, and to regain control over immigration policy. However, in the wake of the Indochina crisis, in accord with the Carter administration, Senator Edward Kennedy moved refugee policy to the top of the Judiciary Committee's agenda. Committed to bring it in harmony with international norms, the committee drafted a bill to increase the admission of refugees who met the international definition from the 17,600 currently provided for under the seventh preference, recently extended to cover the Western Hemisphere, to 50,000, but with presidential authority to admit a higher number should the need arise, in consultation with Congress. Parole authority was to be used only for individual cases, as originally intended. Given that some 8 million people met the international definition at the time, most of them in first-asylum countries awaiting resettlement, admissions must necessarily be selective; accordingly, the law specified further that preference should be given to people "of special humanitarian concern to the United States," with the precise allocation among groups to be determined by the president in consultation with Congress.[50] The proposal also established for the first time a statutory process whereby any alien physically present in the United States, irrespective of immigration status, could claim asylum on the grounds of meeting the refugee definition.[51] These "asylees" would be charged against annual refugee admissions, but on the basis of current applications—3,702 in 1978 and 5,801 in 1979—it was anticipated that they would amount to no more than about 10 percent of the 50,000.

The measure easily won approval by the Judiciary Committee (17–7) and, under the unusual partnership of Edward Kennedy and Republican Senator Strom Thurmond as floor managers, cleared the Senate by a unanimous 85–0. A parallel bill underwent a more bumpy ride in the House, but ultimately passed 328–47, albeit with an amendment requiring hearings when the level exceeded 50,000 and imposing a two-year waiting period before refugees became permanent residents.[52] A conference compromise reducing conditional entrance to one year and eliminating the hearings requirement was approved by a close 207–192 in the House, with residual southern Democrats joining most Republicans in voting against it. The coordinator for refugee affairs, created earlier by the Carter administration, was given increased authority as well, with the rank of ambassador at large. Concomitantly, the worldwide ceiling for ordinary immigration was reduced from 290,000 to 270,000, with the liberated seventh preference percentage reallocated to the second (spouses and unmarried children of permanent resident aliens), raising the family reunion share to 80 percent.

Rapidly accepted into the mainstream, as indicated by its unproblematic subsequent reauthorization by Republican-controlled congresses, the refugee law of 1980 consummated the reorganization of the main gate into two separate entrances. In one important respect, it exceeded the obligations imposed by the international refugee régime, in that while signatories must allow refugees to remain only so long as the conditions that drove them into flight persisted, the United States in effect integrated them into its immigration system by providing that they could shortly turn into ordinary immigrants, regardless of conditions in their state of origin. However, the provision "of special humanitarian concern to the United States" opened the selection process to bargaining by a variety of ideological and ethnic interest groups. As interpreted by subsequent administrations, it was applied almost exclusively to citizens of Communist countries and, within that, to groups that had strong domestic advocates, notably Soviet Jews and Indochinese. The asylum process and "Extended Voluntary Departure," which in effect replaced parole, were implemented in a similar manner. The 50,000 level specified in the law proved irrelevant, as the number admitted rose to 66,439 in the first year and then rapidly escalated to over 100,000, where it remained for the remainder of the century.[53] Far from a minor feature, asylum emerged as one of the most perplexing and controversial aspects of the entire immigration policy régime; by 1983, there were over 170,000 pending applications from fifty-three countries, and numbers continued to escalate. Since the law failed to provide for those who feared to return because of general conditions but were not specifically targeted for persecution, and hence did not meet UN Convention criteria, they remained subject to discretionary treatment by American authorities.

While the law was predicated on the possibility of selecting from the mass of refugees in the world at large a limited number for resettlement, even before the ink was dry, the United States faced two major crises in which it was in effect forced to assume the role of "first asylum" country. The first involved a dramatic resumption of the Cuban exodus. The interruption of the "freedom flights" in 1973 had stranded over 100,000 persons approved for departure, whose hopes fluctuated with the state of relations between Havana and Washington.[54] In response to friendly moves by the Carter administration, in 1979 Castro allowed Cuban exiles to visit their homeland, and some 100,000 rushed over in the first few months, renewing ties with relatives. Although the CIA predicted that Cuba might resort to large-scale emigration to reduce discontent occasioned by deteriorating economic conditions, and Castro himself recurrently threatened to unleash a torrent of people, the administration was taken by surprise when, in the course of a dispute with Peru over the right of its embassy to provide asylum to dissidents, Cuba withdrew its guards and some 10,000 persons invaded the embassy grounds. On April 19 Castro insisted that those wanting to leave must be taken directly to the United States and opened up Mariel Harbor to U.S. Cubans wanting to fetch their relatives; the exile community immediately organized a boatlift, and the transfers got underway the next day. Aware of widespread public opposition to rising immigration and the growing unpopularity of the Indochinese refugee program, the Carter administration was initially reluctant to provide massive asylum to the "Marielitos," but after California Governor Ronald Reagan seized upon the boatlift as a presidential campaign issue, the U.S. Navy began providing escorts and a reception center was opened in Miami. Then, amid reports that Castro was emptying his jails and mental hospitals, the administration again shifted position and finally brought the exodus to a halt. By this time, 130,000 Cubans had landed in the United States under presidential parole authority and been awarded the newly created status of "entrants." This was later extended, and in 1984 the Justice Department ruled that the Marielitos were eligible to become permanent residents under the Cuban Adjustment Act of 1966. Those who could not be immediately released to relatives were confined in military installations.

The misgivings induced by Mariel were compounded by a concurrent spurt of Haitian "boat people" who landed surreptitiously along the Florida coast.[55] Burdened with a long history of political instability, Haiti is the only Western Hemisphere country ranked in the World Bank's bottommost income category. Throughout the 1960s, François "Papa Doc" Duvalier was actively supported by the United States as a reliable ally against Cuba, despite the brutal character of his régime, which prompted the exodus of many professionals from the mulatto upper class to the United States.[56] Although conditions in Haiti improved somewhat as sugar production in the neighboring Dominican Republic, where many Haitians worked, expanded to pick up the U.S. market share vacated by the Cuban boycott, the reinstatement of protection on behalf of American domestic sugar growers in the 1970s had a catastrophic effect, triggering a larger stream of migrants from more modest strata, even as the new immigration restrictions on the Western Hemisphere came into effect.[57] Although American consular officers instituted more demanding procedures for visitor visas to prevent "overstaying," the main effect of this measure was to increase the flow of illegal entries. Asylum applications soared as well, but this was a largely fruitless procedure for nationals of non-Communist countries. In the wake of Mariel, the Congressional Black Caucus demanded that Haitians be treated the same as Cubans, thereby making its entrance as a positive actor in the immigration arena. Accordingly, those in the United States as of June 10, 1980 (later extended to October 10), were granted "entrant" status.[58] Although the Reagan administration reinstated differential treatment and began incarcerating arriving Haitians, whom the INS then proceeded to deport, the courts subsequently began ordering Haitian detainees paroled to community sponsors pending their appeal, and eventually most were released. Washington then secured from the Duvalier government the right to search Haitian vessels on the high seas and its agreement to stop unauthorized emigration as a condition for receiving aid. Coast Guard interdiction proved an effective deterrent to entry; although the INS insisted that boarding procedures provided for the possibility of filing asylum claims, of over 21,000 Haitians intercepted through 1989, only six were brought to the United States to do so. Although the Justice Department's 1984 ruling on behalf of Cubans further sharpened the invidious distinction between the two groups, most of the Haitians who reached the United States eventually obtained resident status under the "amnesty" program for illegal aliens in 1986.

Foreign policy objectives also contributed to the onset of substantial immigration from the adjacent Dominican Republic, albeit by way of the main gate rather than the side entrance.[59] Despite the country's poverty and the absence of quantitative restrictions on the American side, emigration had remained low through the 1950s because the long-ruling dictator, Rafael Trujillo, imposed an effective prohibition on exit by refusing to issue passports to his nationals. In the wake of the Cuban Revolution, the Kennedy and Johnson administrations adopted a strategy of "conservative preemption" by eliminating Trujillo and managing Dominican politics until the reliable Joaquin Balaguer was elected in 1966. As noted with regard to Haiti, the country initially thrived from the exclusion of Cuba's sugar from the U.S. market, but was concomitantly hard hit by the return of protectionism.[60] To reduce the mounting unemployment that was deemed a source of radicalization, the United States then instituted an exceptional immigration policy by liberally issuing visitors' visas to Dominicans, despite common knowledge that many would overstay. By the time the Western Hemisphere was brought under the preference system in 1978, there was a critical mass in the United States able to generate family reunion priorities and thereby contribute to a further expansion of the flow. By 1990, the small Dominican Republic ranked as the fourth largest source country and by far the largest in relation to population; remittances from the United States amounted to one-tenth of its GNP, nearly one-fourth of its foreign exchange, and approximately equaled the annual budget of its government.

The contribution of foreign policy to immigration from Central America was especially egregious, as the revolutionary and counterrevolutionary conflicts from which they stemmed were rooted in an explosive social configuration maintained with U.S. support, and the conflicts themselves were aggravated by American intervention.[61] Having access to the United States by way of Mexico, escaping Central Americans could ask for asylum at the border, enter surreptitiously and initiate an asylum request, or settle unobtrusively among the expanding Latino communities. Asylum claims climbed steeply in the 1980s and quickly overwhelmed the system, but foreign policy once again came into play with regard to their disposition.

The smallest and most densely populated country of Latin America, El Salvador was traditionally ruled by an alliance of coffee-growing oligarchs and the army, supported by the Catholic Church and the United States, which brutally repressed any stirrings of revolt among the peasantry. Following the failure of reformist efforts in the 1960s, a leftist opposition gained ground among the rural and urban masses. In response to the government's repressive violence, the Frente Farabundo Marti para la Liberacion National and the Frente Democratico Revolutionario launched an armed struggle. Determined to defeat the insurgency, the Reagan administration supported the center while trying to control the extreme right, and also channeled resources and support to the armed forces. The president sought to enlist support for his policy by agitating the specter of "feet people" who would run north in case of a Communist takeover; however, before it was contained the conflict produced some 500,000 internally displaced residents and over 1 million emigrants, mainly to Mexico and the United States.

Guatemala, the largest and most important country of Central America, with the United Fruit Company as its dominant landlord, underwent a Mexican-style revolution in 1944. Judging that the agrarian reform undertaken by Jacobo Arbenz threatened its interests, in 1954 the United States organized a covert operation to remove him. The ensuing corporatist state established by the landed oligarchy and foreign investors, with the army as the dominant political actor, emerged as one of the worst human rights violators in the hemisphere. In 1960 a group of leftist army officers constituted the nucleus of the first of a series of guerilla groups, which united in 1982.

Although it was unable to establish an urban base, the movement developed considerable strength among the mostly Indian peasant communities of the north and on the Pacific Coast. The army's successful counterinsurgency campaign created massive displacements and prompted the Carter administration to suspend military aid. As of 1982, it was estimated that between 30,000 and 100,000 Guatemalans had been murdered since 1966; 1 million were internally displaced; and 200,000 had fled abroad, of whom 46,000 were recognized as refugees by Mexico and most of the remainder became undocumented residents of Mexico and the United States.

The Mariel episode turned Cubans from welcome "defectors" into "bullets aimed at Miami" and led to a fundamental change of policy toward disaffected populations from leftist régimes. Polls indicated that 59 percent believed that the latest Cuban immigration was bad for the United States, and only 19 percent that it was beneficial, with resentment especially high among African Americans, who were experiencing high unemployment. A prolonged riot in Fort Chaffee, Arkansas, added to the general perception that the Marielitos were "bad" refugees; many proved hard to place, and the problem posed by released criminals rankled on for the remainder of the decade.[62] Consequently, while launching its war against the Sandinista régime that had recently come to power in Nicaragua, the Reagan administration carefully sought to "avoid creating a pathway to the United States" for those who sought to escape it.[63] Although the ensuing decade of violence and economic deprivation, punctuated by the Sandinistas' attempt to draft young men for war service, provoked massive internal displacement and drove an estimated half-million out of the country, very few admissions under the recently adopted U.S. refugee law were allocated to Nicaraguans, on the grounds that safe havens were available in neighboring countries. In contrast with its Dominican policy, the United States also imposed very demanding requirements on Nicaraguan visitors' visas, achieving a refusal rate of 70–80 percent. However, those who did reach the United States obtained preferential treatment in asylum procedures. Anticipating a favorable outcome, Nicaraguans were more likely than other Central Americans to file claims and were usually then released on their own recognizance. The rate of favorable rulings was higher than for others, and many of the unsuccessful applicants were granted Extended Voluntary Departure. As against this, Guatemalans and Salvadorans tended to request asylum only after being apprehended as illegal aliens; most of them were detained throughout the proceedings and were unsuccessful in demonstrating "well-founded fear" to the authorities' satisfaction.[64] Initially many of the unsuccessful applicants were deported, but the pace slowed down after a number of churches launched a "sanctuary" movement on their behalf. Despite all attempts to deter Salvadorans, they quickly grew into by far the largest Central American immigrant community in the United States.

Fixing the Back Door (Continued)

The Select Commission on Immigration and Refugee Policy (SCIRP)[65] became operational in July 1979 and completed its work at the end of February 1981.[66] A joint undertaking of the legislative and executive branches, it was composed of eight members of Congress drawn equally from both houses, and eight presidential appointees, including four cabinet secretaries and four public members who represented major Democratic constituencies.[67] Former Governor of Florida Reuben Askew served as chair until he was appointed U.S. trade representative, and was then replaced by Father Theodore Hesburgh, president of Notre Dame University, who had previously headed the Civil Rights Commission. The staff director was Professor Lawrence Fuchs of Brandeis University, a political scientist known for his research on the role of ethnic interest groups in American politics, who served on the executive board of MALDEF.

By the time SCIRP submitted its report in February 1981, Ronald Reagan had been elected to the presidency; but despite the change of administration, hailed as the dawn of a new era in American politics, the commissioners set the legislative agenda for an entire decade, leading to the enactment of major legislation in 1986 and 1990.[68] With refugee matters considered to have been largely resolved by the 1980 act, SCIRP devoted most of its attention to the perennial problems of the back door as well as to the restructuring of the main gate. Overall, it recommended "closing the back door to undocumented/ illegal immigration, opening the front door a little more to accommodate legal migration in the interests of this country, defining our immigration goals clearly and providing a structure to implement them effectively, and setting forth procedures which will lead to fair and efficient adjudication and administration of U.S. immigration laws."[69] To the question "Is immigration in the U.S. national interest?" SCIRP answered "a strong but qualified yes": strong "because we believe there are many benefits which immigrants bring to U.S. society," but qualified "because we believe there are limits on the ability of this country to absorb large numbers of immigrants effectively." The commissioners insisted, "This is not the time for a large-scale expansion in legal immigration—for resident aliens or temporary workers—because the first order of priority is bringing undocumented/illegal immigration under control, while setting up a rational system for legal immigration."

Most prominently, in keeping with the aspirations of Mexican American leaders and liberals generally, the Commission voted unanimously on behalf of the legalization of a substantial portion of the undocumented/illegal aliens now in the country. In an astute attempt to preempt negative reactions to what came to be popularly known as "amnesty," it began by asserting that this was motivated by a "strong desire to regain control over U.S. immigration policy," as well as an "acknowledgment that, in a sense, our society has participated in the creation of the problem." Control was to be achieved not only by expanding the Border Patrol and reinforcing the Immigration and Naturalization Service, but also, and especially, by imposing sanctions on employers of illegal aliens, in keeping with the longtime aspirations of organized labor and its supporters. The inclusion of additional recommendations, notably revisions of the H-2 program to provide additional temporary workers in agriculture, enhanced the possibility of horse-trading among the various interests concerned.[70] Although at the urging of Hispanic groups the Commission considered allocating larger quotas to Mexico and Canada, it ultimately recommended maintaining a uniform quota for all countries.[71]

The incoming Reagan administration was divided on pending immigration issues, as were Republicans more generally. On one side were those who adhered to the view set forth by free-market economists connected with the Council of Economic Advisers and the American Enterprise Institute, notably Barry Chiswick, that immigration was of net economic benefit to the United States, but could be made even more beneficial by shifting the priorities from family reunification to the acquisition of human capital.[72] As the former governor of California, Reagan himself was close to the fruit and vegetable growers, who remained the major beneficiaries of the ongoing system founded on undocumented immigrant workers, and continued to argue their need for foreign labor of some sort.[73]

The realities of agricultural employment were difficult to establish because data were variously collected by different agencies, resulting in what Philip Martin has termed "a harvest of confusion about who works on the nation's farms."[74] At the time SCIRP issued its report, about two-thirds of the farm workforce consisted of family members. Where operations were mostly family-based, as in the Midwest, hired workers tended to be of the same ethnic groups as the employers; but where workers outnumbered operators, as in

California, the employers tended to be white, while the hired workers belonged to minorities. Many of the crops that once relied on immigrant
workers, notably cotton, were now fully mechanized, but fruit and vegetable
growers as well as flower and nursery farms reported that 80–90 percent of
their workers were immigrants, and insisted that without an assured supply,
they would go out of business. Although such operations constituted only
about 75,000 out of the 818,000 farms that hired labor in 1987, they were
the mainstay of a crescent of states ranging from Arizona to Washington.
Western growers preferred the largely unregulated status quo, and their fierce
opposition to employer sanctions was shared in attenuated form by the business community as a whole, which viewed them suspiciously as a dangerous
extension of federal regulation, as noted repeatedly by the *Wall Street Journal.*

Labor analysts differed broadly regarding the market situation and its consequences. While some argued that labor-intensive industries were an anach-
ronism and hence there was no need for a pool of unskilled aliens, the costs
of whose presence fell primarily on low-income workers, others maintained
that mechanization was a gradual process that would slowly reduce the demand for alien labor without deleterious effects on the economy, as had already occurred in tomato and cotton harvesting. They pointed out further
that progressively fewer aliens were being employed in agriculture, and more
in lower-level industrial jobs, and that there was not enough credible evidence
to establish a cause-and-effect relationship between illegal migration and domestic unemployment. If so, there was no need for major changes in the
immigration system, and employer sanctions "may reduce the economic and
social well-being of the country, with adverse consequences for citizens as
well as for aliens."[75]

Although some in the incoming Reagan administration viewed immigration
primarily as an economic issue, others, notably Attorney General William
French Smith, envisioned it primarily from a law-and-order and identitarian
perspective. Overall, the administration was generally unsympathetic to "amnesty" and especially concerned that the newly legalized would gain access to
redistributive public benefits, which it was notoriously committed to reduce.[76]
Shortly after taking over, it established an interagency Immigration Task Force
of its own under Attorney General Smith. Reporting the conclusions of its
review of policy in a June 3 memo to the president, Senator Howard Baker
and Attorney-General Edwin Meese explained that immigration pressure, especially from Mexico, continued to rise at a time of inflation, unemployment,
and cuts in social programs, and that substantial illegal immigration of a level

equaling or even surpassing the legal side "is changing our population, particularly in the Southwest, where many communities will likely have Hispanic majorities in the next decades."[77] Pointing to a backlash in the making, exacerbated by the recent refugee crisis in Florida, they concluded, "Immigration is 'no win.' Improved policies cannot solve the problem, and will most certainly be criticized from one quarter or another." However, they went on to prepare the ground for the Task Force's recommendations.[78] The Task Force substantially agreed with SCIRP on the legalization of unauthorized residents currently in the United States, but with the effective date pushed back to January 1, 1977; however, they differed on employer sanctions and suggested the establishment of a national identity card. Selecting from among the options it laid out, on July 30 the Justice Department announced the administration would beef up the Border Patrol, strengthen the enforcement of federal labor laws, impose civil fines on employers of illegal foreign workers and require them to verify eligibility, launch an experimental program of guest workers at the 50,000 level for two years, and double the visa allocation for Canada and Mexico. When polls revealed sharply negative reactions to a national identity card, the idea was quickly dropped.[79]

As it undertook a major overhaul of the immigration régime, the 97th Congress was a newly divided body, with the Senate in Republican hands for the first time in a generation, and in which party control was being reasserted after two decades of looseness.[80] Alan K. Simpson of Wyoming, one of the two Republican senators on SCIRP and the new chair of the Immigration Subcommittee, emerged as a key player on immigration issues until his retirement in 1996. The son of a former governor and senator, educated entirely within the state, and whose previous political experience was confined to service in the Wyoming House of Representatives, Simpson was entirely new to the subject of immigration and had been appointed to SCIRP only after Senator Strom Thurmond declined.[81] Albeit recounting that he was moved by childhood memories of the mistreatment of Japanese internees relocated in Wyoming during World War II as well as by the exploitation of *bracero* workers, the senator was especially troubled by illegal migration, which he thought not only undermined domestic workers but also bred disrespect for the law and cultural separatism.[82] His outlook was shaped by his chief of staff's *éminence grise,* the neo-Malthusian demographer Léon Bouvier, detailed by the Bureau of the Census as a consultant to SCIRP.[83] Within the commission, Simpson had pressed unsuccessfully for an overall ceiling on immigration, designed to reduce the growing flow of immediate relatives of citizens.

In a dissenting appendix, he acknowledged that "15 percent of the population is of Hispanic origin" and that one could not "be insensitive to the contributions of these people," but insisted that present-day patterns of immigration differed significantly from those of the past, raising doubts as to "the degree to which immigrants and their descendants assimilate to fundamental American public values and institutions," and warned that "if linguistic and cultural separatism rise above a certain level, the unity and political stability of the nation will in time be seriously eroded."[84] Accordingly, the Task Force's endorsement of an increase in legal immigration, similar to the one recommended by SCIRP, prompted him to complain publicly about lack of support for his package from the White House.

Simpson's counterpart in the still-Democratic House was Representative Roman Mazzoli from Kentucky's third district, a Notre Dame graduate who had persuaded Father Hesburgh to assume the SCIRP chairmanship.[85] According to Simpson, it was a partnership made in heaven: "Mazzoli was from the third district of Kentucky and I was from Wyoming, so obviously we could handle it. No one else could. A California senator couldn't touch it with a stick, a Massachusetts senator, New York, New Jersey, forget it. They can't play with the issue. So we decided to play." However, Simpson was clearly the senior partner, as the bipartisan package they sponsored as a pair of identical bills included his overall immigration cap, which SCIRP had rejected.

"Simpson-Mazzoli" constituted an ingenious trade-off between liberals and conservatives across the two dimensions of interest that perennially structure immigration policy. It provided for employer sanctions; legalization of immigrants who had arrived before January 1, 1978; temporary residence for those who came between 1978 and 1982; and a slight expansion of the temporary workers program (H-2). The sanctions appealed to organized labor as well as to restrictionists seeking to deter illegal immigrants, especially Mexicans, whereas amnesty appealed to Hispanics and to civil rights liberals more generally, and the H-2 expansion to business. As noted, it leaned further toward restrictionism than SCIRP by also providing for a cap on overall immigration, including immediate relatives of citizens but not refugees. Set at 425,000, this was well below the ongoing level of 530,639 in 1980 and 596,000 in 1981.[86] The proposal also sought to prevent future "chaining" by eliminating the fifth preference allotted to brothers and sisters of U.S. citizens, which had the largest backlog, to the benefit of an increased quota for skilled immigrants.

The SCIRP recommendations and Simpson-Mazzoli were endorsed by much of the quality press, notably the *New York Times,* whose editorialist on the subject was awarded the 1982 Pulitzer Prize. Responses of interest groups were largely in keeping with their established positions. Although in the course of its public hearings in major cities, SCIRP discovered lingering black resentment of immigrants generally, within Congress the alliance that Hispanic and African American leaders had built up in the civil rights era held on.[87] Organized labor continued to be torn between its traditional class interest and the growing importance of its Hispanic membership.[88] Accordingly, as congressional action got underway, the garment unions officially supported employer sanctions but made them contingent on the enactment of amnesty; the AFL-CIO also advocated sanctions, but endorsed Hispanic demands for an antidiscrimination measure.[89] On the other hand, the UFW shifted its stance, having concluded that sanctions constituted a major obstacle to organizing the undocumented. Overall, labor now reserved its heavy artillery for temporary worker programs that, according to a study of the farm workers' unions completed around the time SCIRP got underway, constituted the most formidable threat to their future.[90] In 1981 labor launched a specialized lobby, the National Immigration Forum, which under the leadership of Frank Sharry built itself into a civil rights movement for newcomers and emerged as a leading opponent of the Federation for American Immigration Reform, the major restrictionist voice in the policy arena.[91]

Sporting the clever acronym FAIR, the latter organization was founded in 1979 by Dr. John Tanton, a semiretired ophthalmologist from rural northern Michigan and a follower of Paul Ehrlich, founder of Zero Population Growth (ZPG), of which he served as president from 1975 to 1977, and of Garrett Hardin, dean of neo-Malthusian human biologists.[92] Although by virtue of their advocacy of birth control education and abortion, partisans of population control are generally associated within the contemporary American political landscape with the liberal camp, as is the environmental movement generally, it should be remembered that conservationists and eugenicists figured prominently in the early twentieth-century nativist movement. Hardin, who launched his crusade on behalf of population limits as early as 1949, argued in his resounding essay "The Tragedy of the Commons," published in *Science* in 1968, that the population problem is as vital as the nuclear threat because a finite world can support only a finite population and the optimal level has already been exceeded. Because allowing individuals to pursue their self-interest will lead to disaster, limits must be adopted by the collectivity as a whole and imposed on individuals.[93] With zero growth as the objective, the annual U.S. new population allowance is 1.5 million, and no immigrants should be admitted so long as births exceed that number; and should the collectivity determine that some should be taken in anyway, notably refugees, then it must assume the concomitant obligation of deducting them from its birth quota. In the same vein, as ZPG president, Tanton insisted that the organization take a stand against immigration because this now constitutes the major cause of U.S. overpopulation. In the face of objections from some of the membership, he then left to found FAIR.[94] He subsequently joined California's Senator S. I. Hayakawa, who as president of San Francisco State University achieved national notoriety in the 1960s by his vigorous opposition to student protests, in promoting a constitutional amendment making English the official language of the United States and harnessed FAIR's resources to the campaign. When the FAIR board of directors objected, he left once more to found U.S. English, where his actions quickly prompted a wave of resignations as well.[95] FAIR carried on under the leadership of Executive Director Roger Conner, a lawyer of similar Michigan background, and subsequently Dan Stein, with substantial support from Cornelia Scafe May's Laurel Foundation, as well as from the Pioneer Fund, an organization dedicated to "race betterment."[96] Albeit maintaining a mainstream stance, FAIR developed connections with more explicitly racist groups such as San Francisco's STOP-IT.[97] After it established itself as the leading restrictionist lobby, the organization attracted many INS retirees, including former Commissioner Alan C. Nelson. While vigorously backing employer sanctions, to be implemented by way of national identification cards as well as tighter control of the border and stronger enforcement of the immigration laws, FAIR firmly opposed amnesty.

Prospects for enactment of the congressional package were iffy, because it required cooperation between normally opposed interests, which might agree on a quick trade-off but were unlikely to stay together for the long haul, as one or the other of the coalition partners might conclude along the way that it would be better off with the status quo. "Simpson" was easily enacted by the Senate on August 17, 1982, but with eligibility for legalization moved back to 1977 and amendments declaring English the official U.S. language, signaling the emergence of a related issue on the "identity" dimension.[98] "Mazzoli" evoked considerably controversy in the still-Democratic House, as the provision to cut out brothers and sisters was objected to by the most recent immigrant groups, Asians and Hispanics. The latter, represented by Ed Roybal of California, chairman of the Hispanic Caucus, and Robert Garcia of New York, also objected vehemently to employer sanctions. Labor-oriented representatives also opposed the introduction of temporary workers and joined forces with opponents of legalization. The bill was in effect sunk when Chairman Rodino announced that his Judiciary Committee would postpone its markup until after it passed the Senate and the unsympathetic House leadership then buried it for good by allowing it to come to the floor with almost unlimited amendments.[99]

Even as the debate got underway, external developments exacerbated the importance of immigration issues. In 1982, MALDEF won its first Supreme Court case, *Plyler v. Doe,* which ruled that the imposition by the State of Texas of a $1,000 school fee on the children of illegal immigrants violated the equal protection clause of the Fourteenth Amendment.[100] This suggested that even if U.S. employers and the market economy benefited from the abundance of low-wage illegal labor fostered by the porous border, the process imposed potentially heavy social costs on the public sector; from a broader nationalist perspective, the ruling further exacerbated the sense of a "loss of control." Concurrently, prospects for an expansion of the flow of Mexican undocumented were amplified by dramatic devaluations of the peso in February and December 1982.[101]

Reflecting where the two houses left off, Simpson and Mazzoli sponsored somewhat different bills in the 98th Congress, with Simpson again leaning in a more restrictive direction. The revised versions also responded somewhat differently to pressure from the growers: whereas the House bill boosted the existing H-2 program from 40,000 temporary foreign crop pickers a year to between 300,000 and 500,000, the Senate's granted agricultural employers a three-year transitional exemption from employer sanctions, during which a search warrant would be required to apprehend illegal aliens in an open field. "Simpson" again passed the Senate in May 1983, with Kennedy ultimately voting against it in accordance with the Mexican American position, along with conservatives who wanted a more restrictive measure and Westerners attuned to the growers' demand for more workers.[102] However, in the House, Speaker Thomas "Tip" O'Neill blocked action on "Mazzoli," anticipating that President Reagan might use the measure to trap the Democrats in the forthcoming campaign between general pressures to restrict immigration and the opposite concerns of their Hispanic constituents.[103] Widely criticized by the media, the speaker subsequently relented and scheduled a vote in early 1984.[104]

Meanwhile, in the face of mounting agitation against illegal aliens, which was especially acute in California, the western growers lifted their opposition to employer sanctions and focused instead on expanding the package to include a more generous temporary worker program.[105] Their campaign was a textbook case of effective lobbying. In the fall of 1982, Thomas J. Hale, a former president of the Grape and Tree Fruit League, representing the thousands of farmers who grow most of California's grapes, peaches, plums, and pears, began pulling western farm groups dependent on illegal immigrants into a "Farm Labor Alliance." The organization then raised a very large action fund by imposing a special assessment on every one of the millions of boxes of fruit produced by its members. Early in 1983, the Alliance retained prominent Washington law firms to deal with each of the major political parties. On the Republican side, the key adviser was James H. Lake, a top aide in three of Reagan's gubernatorial campaigns, with close ties to key Californians in the administration, White House Chief of Staff Ed Meese and Deputy Secretary of Agriculture Richard E. Lyng. To deal with the Democrats, the alliance retained the firm of former Party Chairman Robert S. Strauss; the partner in charge was Ruth Harkin, a former Department of Agriculture lawyer and wife of Representative Tom Harkin of Iowa, a member of the Agriculture Committee. Since the Senate had already passed a bill, the Alliance concentrated on the House, where under the guidance of Tony Coelho, a Californian who was chairman of the Democratic Congressional Campaign Committee, they were able to persuade another California Democrat, Leon Panetta, to champion their cause by way of an amendment providing for foreign workers. Panetta was a moderate-to-liberal representative who had ambitions for a leadership role; "If he put his name on the guest worker proposal, they knew it could not be a horrible, abusive type of program."[106] To complete the operation, the amendment was cosponsored by a Washington State Republican, Sid Morrison.

The Reagan administration's various components responded in keeping with their differing institutional concerns: the Department of Agriculture was strongly supportive and the Department of Labor strongly opposed, while the Department of Justice objected because the program would be difficult to enforce. However, Meese persuaded the objectors not to press their case, confirming the White House's stance of benevolent neutrality. Thanks to this, the Alliance easily secured the support of the House Republican leadership. In early 1984 the House Agriculture Committee approved a Panetta amendment authorizing the attorney general to admit foreign crop pickers on three days' notice; they would be allowed to stay up to eleven months and to move from farm to farm, but would be confined to a prescribed region. The anticipated level was about 250,000 a year.[107] The amendment was adopted by the House as a whole in June, with the Republicans voting 138 to 15 in favor but Panetta's fellow's Democrats, reflecting labor and Hispanic objections, 90 to 157 against.[108] Ultimately, the bill squeaked by on the eve of the Democratic presidential convention in a cliffhanging 216 to 211, with the Democrats almost evenly divided.[109] The last few votes necessary for a positive outcome were mustered by Jim Wright, O'Neill's heir-apparent, by way of an amendment moving the cutoff date to 1982 but with added limitations, including an English-language study requirement for legalization applicants. This was yet another manifestation of a growing concern over the integration dimension.[110]

A quantitative analysis of the House vote confirms that it was driven by the dynamics of the "strange bedfellows" configuration and highlights their complexity.[111] The study identified four sets of variables that might affect the vote: "nationalism" (akin to what I have termed "identity concerns"), economic interest (business and agriculture), minority concern with discrimination, and regionalism (for example, rivalry between the "Sunbelt" and "Frostbelt," notably over political representation by way of reapportionment). Overall, voting was affected by perceptions rather than by "real-world" conditions. Representatives from northern states supported the bill, while those from the Southwest tended to oppose it; areas with the lowest percentage increases in capital income since 1970 supported it also, as did those with the smallest reductions in levels of unemployment since 1975 and those experiencing deteriorating economic conditions, suggesting that economic distress fosters support for restrictive legislation. Representatives of minority constituencies tended to oppose the bill, while representatives from largely Republican districts (ranked high on the "nationalist" variable) tended to vote for it. Representatives from districts least affected by illegal immigration were most likely to vote for immigration control, suggesting that their voting was driven by identity concerns. As against this, those from Sunbelt states with large Spanish-origin constituencies, especially when they were themselves members of minorities, tended to vote against the bill because of employer sanctions, as they perceived that they would exacerbate anti-Hispanic discrimination, outweighing benefits that might result from other provisions.

In the event, the bedfellows' victory turned out to be quite hollow. As the conferees met on September 13 and October 4, prospects for an immigration law appeared bleak because the Democrats reckoned their campaign would fare better without one.[112] Ultimately the conferees were unable to resolve their differences over federal payments to the states, and Simpson-Mazzoli thus died a second time. Reflecting the inherent ambiguities involved, the measure's demise evoked widely divergent assessments. Oscar Handlin, the dean of liberal immigration historians, deplored the loss of "a more liberal measure than any we've had in 90 years," while Richard Wade, another eminent American historian, long associated with the Democratic Party, found the bill in essence "identical with the restrictive legislation of the 1920's."[113] Less extravagantly, the former executive director of SCIRP, Lawrence Fuchs, characterized the conferees' bill merely as "an improvement over earlier versions." Deploring "The Death of a Humane Idea," the *New York Times* laid most of the blame on Hispanic leaders and warned that theirs might be a bitter victory because in the face of mounting sentiment against illegal aliens, the new Congress was likely to enact employer sanctions without any amnesty. Caught short by the unanticipated willingness of their legislative allies to compromise with their opponents, the groups with most at stake in the outcome, fruit growers and Hispanics, read the writing on the wall: veto politics, leading to deadlock, had run its course, and in the next go-round they would have to accept the best possible arrangement within the package deal.[114]

Jump-starting a Corpse

Having risen to assistant majority leader, in April 1985 Senator Simpson unveiled a third revised edition of his proposal that changed the balance between its two elements in the direction anticipated by the *Times*.[115] The amnesty provision was curtailed by being made contingent on a showing of improved enforcement of the immigration laws, as indicated by a reduction in the number of illegal entries and overstayers. Employer sanctions were maintained, but the burden of verification was lightened, and penalties for violation reduced to civil. There was no temporary worker program, but agricultural employers were once again granted a three-year grace period free of sanctions. Kennedy tried to redress the balance, but largely failed.[116] In the intervening period, a Texas congressional election involving a challenger opposed to legalization attracted national attention; although he narrowly lost his bid, perception of a backlash against legalization led to a hardening of positions.[117]

Despite the electoral defeat of FAIR's senatorial voice, Trevor Huddleston, the shift of congressional advantage toward the restrictionist side was evident. As consideration began in the Senate, the Chamber of Commerce, which had opposed earlier versions and been denounced by Senator Simpson in 1982 for being selfishly concerned with profitability alone, now approved. The proposal also drew praise from Attorney General Meese and INS Commissioner Alan Nelson, who welcomed the postponement of amnesty, but it was criticized by the ACLU as "an unfortunate compilation of some of the worst elements of the original Simpson-Mazzoli bill," while LULAC and MALDEF said they would oppose the new version even more adamantly than the old.[118] At the committee stage, Simpson accepted amendments beginning legalization not later than three years after enactment, imposing criminal penalties for repeated employer offenses, and establishing an expedited procedure for recruiting alien workers under the H-2 program, without specifying a numerical limit. Meanwhile, the Alliance resumed its blitzkrieg on behalf of an extensive program of temporary workers, prompting Senator Simpson to complain that "their greed knows no bounds."[119] This was approved 12–4, with ten Republicans and two Democrats in favor; the four negative votes were all Democrats, including Kennedy.

When floor debate began in the Senate on September 11, California Republican Senator Pete Wilson championed a program along the lines advocated by the Alliance, providing for 200,000–300,000 workers a year, admitted for a period of nine months and confined to a particular region, with 20 percent of their wages held in a trust fund, to be distributed only after they returned home; President Reagan reportedly supported that provision more strongly than any other element of the immigration package.[120] Despite the opposition of Simpson and Kennedy, who charged the proposed system resembled the pass laws of South Africa, the Senate approved a bill providing for up to 350,000 "Wilson workers" a year. The delay for amnesty was reinstated as well, and the Senate also approved a provision requiring states to check the legal status of aliens applying for social benefits. Conservatives and liberals joined forces to enact another amendment, opposed by the administration, requiring federal law enforcement officers to obtain a warrant before searching open fields for illegal aliens. Federal aid to the states was set at $3 million over a three-year period. Thus amended, the bill was approved 69–30; 41 Republicans and 28 Democrats voted for it, and 19 Democrats—including all the liberals—and 11 Republicans against it. The Senate's action drastically reduced prospects for enactment of a law because liberal Democrats in the House remained adamantly opposed to temporary workers; reflecting Speaker O'Neill's continued opposition, the House sat on its hands throughout the first half of the year. Rodino decided that no further action would be taken for the remainder of the year, while the Democratic leadership entrusted to

New York's Charles Schumer the delicate task of working out a compromise on foreign workers with Leon Panetta and Howard Berman, who stood poles apart on the issue.[121]

As the year of the Statue of Liberty's centennial began, the administration remained torn between the imperatives of law and order and those of economic growth as envisioned by free-market advocates. Shortly before a meeting of the Mexican and U.S. presidents to celebrate friendly relations between the two countries, the INS publicized the upsurge of illegal entries occasioned by Mexico's deteriorating economy and linked the flow to crime and drugs as well as terrorism, prompting Mexican officials to denounce tighter border controls as an unfriendly gesture, while the Los Angeles County Board of Supervisors urged President Reagan to dispatch troops to the border. Later in the year, the INS commissioner himself hinted that the time might come when this would be necessary, a view echoed by Senator Wilson.[122]

On March 11, 1986, the president finally met with Simpson and Rodino, who now agreed to proceed, and on June 9 Schumer announced the compromise was ready. Guaranteeing to growers the foreign workers they demanded, but minimizing their extreme exploitation by providing an opportunity to become permanent residents and even citizens, it was a remarkable feat of congressional horse-trading, which secured the support of both the UFW and the Farm Labor Alliance and further enhanced the congressman's reputation as an astute operator.[123] The compromise was endorsed by the House Judiciary Committee on a vote of 19–15, with Mazzoli opposed, and the bill itself reported out 25–10, in time for the Independence Day recess. This was the third time in five years that a bill had gotten this far in the House.

As a prelude to the centennial celebrations, the media gave considerable attention to immigration. According to a *New York Times*/CBS poll, 49 percent of the public thought the level should be decreased, while 42 percent felt it should be kept the same or increased.[124] Not surprisingly, people of old American stock most strongly supported a decrease (50 percent) and recent arrivals least supported it (29 percent). All regions but the Northeast favored a decrease; conservatives did so most strongly (57 percent), moderates least (45 percent), while liberals fell in the middle (48 percent), confirming the ambiguity of immigration issues in relation to the left-right ideological continuum. Overall, the public supported the broad outlines of the original Simpson-Mazzoli package, but strongly disapproved of guest workers (58 to 36 percent).

Although the *New York Times*' Robert Pear interpreted the poll to indicate that "[t]here is strong and growing public support for new restrictions on immigration despite widespread sympathy for both legal and illegal immigrants as individuals," this was a questionable analysis. Pear supported his contention by contrasting the 49–42 percent division with 1965, when the proportions were 33 and 46 percent. However, the comparison was misleading because, as presented in the national media in 1965, the main issue was the abolition of the national origins quota system that discriminated against immigrants from southern and eastern Europe, who had by then entered the American mainstream; moreover, in the intervening period, legal immigration more than doubled and apprehensions of illegal border-crossers escalated more than tenfold.[125] A more appropriate inference was that after the refugee crisis of 1979–1980, a barrage of reports on illegal immigration, and the multiseason Simpson-Mazzoli playoffs, the proportion of "don't knows" in the polls decreased by about half, most of them probably shifting to the negative camp, but the percentage accepting the much higher level of immigration was only four points below 1965. As *U.S. News and World Report* concluded, there was no evidence of an upsurge of xenophobia comparable to what followed earlier waves of immigration.

But congressional actors do not operate on the basis of a long-term view, and what mattered was not "reality" but a particular reading of it imposed by high-stakes players. To insure action before the end of the session, the architects of the compromise urged the Rules Committee to bar hostile amendments so as to avoid upsetting the bill's "delicate balance."[126] Finally, on September 24, the Committee sent the bill to the floor, having barred from consideration a substitute amendment by Representative Daniel Lungren of California, the ranking Republican on the Judiciary Committee, to drop the Schumer compromise in favor of the Senate's "Wilson Workers," but agreeing to a provision set forth by the chair, barring the deportation of Nicaraguans and Salvadorans for eighteen months. Negotiations over the back door thus occasioned a modification of refugee policy, indicating that despite increasing segmentation, the several components of immigration policy remained linked by the nature of the process. However, Lungren successfully mobilized his party troops to prevent floor consideration of the thus-modified bill (202 to 180, with only 13 Republicans supporting the rule). With Congress scheduled to adjourn on October 10, Rodino declared he had no intention of asking for another rule, and the bill was once again dead. The administration now swung into action, with Meese urging the Rules Committee to send the measure back to the floor "in a way that allows the full House to vote its conscience," that is, with the possibility of amendments hostile to the Schumer compromise. In a surprise move on October 1, the Republicans tried to circumvent the Rules Committee and bring the bill to the floor; but this time it was the Democrats who managed to block the effort on a sharply partisan vote, 230 Democrats and 5 Republicans versus 167 Republicans and 10 Democrats. Again, the bill appeared dead because even if it were enacted by the House, time was needed to iron out significant differences with the Senate.

In a sudden change of tactics, despite a lack of final action by the House, Senate and House supporters worked out a compromise that they then used to persuade the Rules Committee to reconsider. In short, foreign workers were limited to a three-year transitional period; the work period requirement to qualify for amnesty was raised to ninety days in each of the last three years, leading to a transitional one-year status of "temporary resident," after which the workers would achieve permanent resident status; and the number eligible for the entire transition period was limited to 350,000. Whereas Representative Lungren found the new version acceptable, Senator Wilson still did not, but did not exclude a further splitting of the difference if the House were to enact the bill.[127] In a dramatic reversal, it did so by 230–166, prompting Senator Simpson's faux–country boy trope, "I guess we just jump-started a corpse." In keeping with the "strange bedfellows" pattern, the opposition was made up of liberal Democrats, who warned of discrimination, and conservative Republicans, who objected to the overly generous treatment of illegal aliens, future guest workers, as well as Central Americans.[128] For the first time, however, five Hispanic representatives out of eleven, including the chairman and vice chairman of the Hispanic Caucus, voted *for* the bill, out of fear "that any immigration bill in a future Congress would be even more restrictive and might omit the amnesty."[129]

Congressional adjournment was again postponed, and the conferees met to iron out remaining differences. Seeking maximum leverage as last-minute negotiations got underway, the administration publicly stated for the first time its objections to the Schumer amendment, which it characterized as a "well-intentioned" but "inequitable, ineffective, and costly scheme for meeting the needs of domestic agricultural employers."[130] Nevertheless, a final compromise was devised on October 14. At Senator Simpson's insistence, the conferees agreed not to bar the deportation of Salvadorans and Nicaraguans; with regard to sanctions, employers must verify the status of all new job applicants but were not responsible for judging the authenticity of the documents presented to them; employers would be subject to a civil penalty of $250 to

$2,000 for each illegal alien hired, but a "pattern of practice" would give rise to criminal penalties, with fines up to $3,000 and six months in prison; sanctions would go into effect six months after enactment without the "sunset" provision; however, the General Accounting Office (GAO) would report on their effects and, if they led to severe discrimination or problems for employers, Congress might reexamine and even repeal this portion of the law. With regard to legalization, the conferees adopted the House's more generous 1982 cutoff date; aliens must apply within an eighteen-month period starting six months after the bill became law; they would then move into the transitional status of "lawful temporary residents," and after a year be eligible to apply for permanent residence if they could demonstrate "minimal understanding of ordinary English" and a basic knowledge of U.S. history and government. It should be noted that these requirements were hitherto not imposed as a condition for immigration but rather on applicants for U.S. citizenship after five years' residence. The Schumer compromise survived in altered form, making illegal aliens who worked in agriculture for at least ninety days in 1985–1986 eligible for permanent residence after a two-year period as "temporary residents," an option available also to any seasonal farm workers admitted in fiscal year 1990–1993, should the domestic supply prove inadequate. To prevent a sudden swell in national welfare rolls, Congress denied most applicants access to federal needs-based assistance programs for a period of five years; however, because this might increase the burden of state and local social service programs, it provided grants to reimburse state authorities for certain expenses incurred on behalf of legalized aliens during the transition period.[131] The final measure also set aside 10,000 visas to be allocated by lottery for countries "disadvantaged" by the 1965 law. Initiated by Representative Brian Donnelly of Massachusetts on behalf of the Irish, it was hailed by New York's Senator Anthony D'Amato as "affirmative action" on behalf of Europeans more generally.[132]

What Representative Mazzoli called "the least imperfect bill we will ever have before us" was approved by a vote of 238–173. The majority included 7 fewer Democrats and 15 more Republicans than the previous House version; liberal Democrats objected, and members of the Hispanic caucus remained about evenly divided; free to vote their preferences, African American representatives were evenly split as well.[133] In the Senate, Simpson filed a precautionary motion to prevent a filibuster, and the bill was finally approved on October 17, 63–24. The majority included 34 Democrats and 29 Republicans; against it were 16 Republicans and 8 Democrats, including both conservatives and liberals. Senator Phil Gramm (R-Texas) denounced the amnesty provisions and the Schumer arrangements, while Senator Kennedy objected to the potential for discrimination.[134] On November 6 President Reagan signed the bill into law, but to overcome opposition within his team, indicated that he would significantly limit the power of the Special Counsel for Immigration-Related Unfair Employment Practices to investigate and prosecute discrimination.[135]

Waxing lyrical as befits the revival of a corpse, the New York Times hailed passage of the Immigration Reform and Control of Act of 1986 (or IRCA) as "Freedom Day." Having perennially allocated blame to various actors in the long-running production, it now dispensed lavish praise to Schumer, Mazzoli, Lungren, and many others, but above all to Senator Alan Simpson: "Ten and 20 years from now, when the children of Freedom Day hear his name, they'll think grateful, noble thoughts."[136] In the same vein, Lawrence Fuchs subtitled the paper on IRCA he presented at the 1987 American Political Science Association meetings "A Triumph for the Civic Culture," explaining that "there would have been no successful conclusion to the legislative effort . . . had not many of the key actors in the process . . . and especially Alan Simpson, be[en] free from particular constituent or interest group pressures to think about larger questions of what is usually called the national interest . . . the unifying political principles of equal rights based on the founding myth of the Republic, which gives the nation its sense of national purpose and identity."[137]

In the country at large, however, pronouncements ranged as widely as they had while the law was in the making. Hispanic leaders appeared still deeply divided; while some continued to denounce the law, the president of La Raza conceded that although he could not endorse it, it was "probably the best immigration legislation possible under current political conditions." Many in the know were skeptical; for example, Roger Conner of FAIR said that the bill "could be the turning point in regaining control of our nation's borders, or it could turn into an immigration disaster," depending on how both sanctions and amnesty were implemented and what, if any, steps were taken to reduce legal immigration.[138] The county executive of El Paso, Texas, who thought that amnesty would encourage others to come and that sanctions would hardly stop employers, predicted that "after the initial shock it will be business as usual on the border."[139] He evidently knew what he was talking about.

Fixing the Back Door (Concluded)

Albeit useful as a device for securing congressional votes, as a design for rebuilding the back door IRCA was inadequate because the two elements that made the package deal possible were structurally contradictory. As a foundation for the erection of an internal border, employer sanctions failed because they blatantly contradicted the interests of all employers, large or small, of old American or immigrant stock, and were harmful to some of the legal minority workers they were meant to protect. Simultaneously, for the Chicano community, marginalized throughout most of the twentieth century, legalization constituted a liminal experience of accession into the American nation, which vastly expanded its potential political power and afforded it an unprecedented voice in the determination of immigration policy. The elaboration of an internal border thus also contradicted the trend toward a more inclusive society, in which some of the rights traditionally reserved for citizens were extended to aliens, turning them into denizens.

Subject to the most intense monitoring in the history of immigration policy, IRCA's clearest achievement was the legalization of some 3 million immigrants, the bulk of them of Mexican origin.[140] Nearly 1.8 million filed applications under the basic program for illegals who have resided continuously in the United States since 1982 and another 1.3 million under the Special Agricultural Workers program (SAW). The INS opened 109 new offices, with an additional 980 sitesome 200 voluntary agencies and community organizations; those eligible as SAWs could also file at U.S. consulates abroad, as well as at some entry stations in California and Texas. Both programs were self-funded, with fees of $185 per adult and $50 per minor child, for a maximum of $420 per family; however, because of required medical inspections, photographs, and fingerprints, as well as self-promotion by enterprising lawyers, a typical family of four faced costs of $1,000 or more. Although the INS deliberately drafted the regulations so as to "ration" the benefits of legal status, its incentives for doing so diminished over time because of successful litigation on behalf of immigrants who stood to benefit from more generous interpretations of the law.[141] The big surprise was that applications under the SAW program numbered over twice the INS's highest estimate. After an initial review, the agency estimated that as much as one-third of the applications were fraudulent, as revealed by claims to have harvested strawberry trees. Lacking the funds and personnel to prosecute individual applicants, it attempted to deal with the situation by tightening procedures and slowing down approval, only to once again face court-mandated readjudications.[142]

By August 1992, 87 percent of the applications had been approved, 9 percent denied, and 4 percent were still pending. Of the 2.7 million newly legalized immigrants, 2.5 million had, after a slow start, also secured permanent residence ("green cards").[143] Residents of California were well in the lead, with 59.2 percent of the total, followed by a far second Texas (16.6), New York (6.5), Illinois (5.9), and Florida (5.6). Overall, an estimated 90.6 percent of the pre-1982 illegal population was legalized.[144] Fully 70 percent of applicants under the basic program and over 81 percent of SAWs originated in Mexico, as against an estimated 55 percent of the illegal population as a whole; Salvadorans came as a distant second (6.2 percent), with the rest of Central America and the Caribbean accounting for another 15 percent altogether, and the remainder widely scattered, but with Europeans and Asians somewhat underrepresented.[145] Whereas the Mexican and Central American applicants were overwhelmingly undocumented border-crossers (85 percent), the others were mostly overstayers (73 percent). The SAWs were largely male, the others somewhat less so (56 percent).

Although legalization and admission to permanent residence hardly transformed the immigrants' social and economic situation, the changes did afford them some tangible benefits. As of 1992, while the jobs they held were still among the poorest paying, "the picture was not uniformly bleak"; overall, "The advent of work authorization acted as a 'union card,' fostering widespread occupational mobility. Legalization also fostered widespread investments in education, training, and language skills, which—at least for Mexican men—reaped substantial wage gains."[146] Nevertheless, many remained severely handicapped by low education and poor English, and while over one-fifth attended some sort of school, notably the English-language classes mandated by the IRCA programs, and over one-tenth earned credits toward a high school or higher degree, after five years of legal residence, a disproportionate share of the legalized families remained below the poverty threshold and their prospects were worsened by the severe recession in California.[147]

One study of the applicants revealed "that one of the stronger incentives for legalizing, from the immigrant perspective, was the right to travel internationally," followed by the right to petition for relatives to immigrate," leading its author to conclude that "rather than fully integrating legalizing aliens into their identities as U.S. residents, legalization was a way to keep their ties alive with the country of origin."[148] However, this wrongly assumed that integration is a zero-sum process, whereby ties with the country of origin and incorporation into American society are mutually exclusive; in fact, the desire to bring in relatives provided strong evidence of the immigrants' intention of shifting their family's center of gravity toward the United States, a tendency even more marked when they became citizens. The number of naturalization petitions escalated, from a yearly average of 238,000 in 1981–1990 to a record 1,412,712 in 1997; in 1994 Mexicans surpassed Filipinos as the largest group of new citizens, and peaked in 1996 at 254,988, about one-fifth of those sworn in.[149]

As a deterrent to illegal entries, the law was a mixed bag at best. Implementation of employer sanctions was doomed from the start. Because immigrants were much more widely distributed than ever before, the new regulations entailed a wholesale transformation of American business practices, requiring each of the country's 7 million employers to maintain on file for three years new forms attesting that they had checked the work eligibility and identification documents of every employee. Matters were complicated by the existence of many variants of the alien registration card as well as the wide availability of fraudulent documents, notably Social Security cards.[150] On the governmental side, enforcement entailed a monumental and unprecedented joint undertaking by the Department of Labor and the Department of Justice, for which they lacked organizational capacity and failed to obtain adequate funding, in keeping with the White House's thorough lack of sympathy for any expansion of the regulatory apparatus. The program began with six months of "public education," followed by a one-year "warning period"; the first citation was issued in August 1987, the first "Notice of Intent to Fine" the following October, and the first actual fine levied at the end of the year against a Wendy's in Washington, D.C. At this time, it was estimated that one employer out of two was in full or partial compliance; a year later, between 78 and 87 percent of them reported familiarity with the regulation, but few were aware that the law also contained antidiscrimination provisions. Enforcement capability remained extremely limited: the INS aimed at 20,000 inspections in FY 1988 but completed only 12,000, and was stuck at that level the following year as well. While the 1982 eligibility deadline excluded the hundreds of thousands who entered later, there were no prospects of their massive roundup and deportation, and most were able to continue working because, thanks to a "grandfather clause," employer sanctions were not applicable to existing employees. By 1991, one of the commissioned reports noted, "Growth in the enforcement budget has halted due to government-wide stringency," and took it for granted that Congress was likely to "sunset" employer sanctions altogether.[151]

Employer sanctions appeared to have a harmful effect on Hispanic employment. In 1988, the GAO reported that while the data did not establish a clear pattern of discrimination, neither did they exclude it; however, in 1991 it concluded on the basis of more systematic evidence that the verification requirement occasioned "widespread discrimination against legal but foreign-sounding or foreign-looking workers" and suggested that its future "could be threatened" by this finding.[152] Studies conducted by MALDEF and the ACLU, as well as one commissioned by the State of New York, also found the verification requirement to be a source of discrimination, providing support for calls to repeal the verification requirement outright.[153]

Although employer sanctions had been touted ever since the 1950s as a decisive deterrent to illegal immigration, most analysts concurred from the outset that their effect was likely to be extremely limited, as the flow across the border was largely shaped by economic conditions on both sides, and these powerful "push" and "pull" factors outweighed the costs that sanctions imposed on either employers or workers.[154] As it was, apprehensions dropped sharply from 1.8 million in 1986 to 1.1 million the following year, and then continued to decline more slowly, falling slightly below 1 million in 1989.[155] "Line-watch apprehensions" along the border, which had risen to a record 946,341 in 1986, declined as well to 521,899 in 1989.[156] However, different methodologies produced contradictory assessments, including two studies commissioned by the U.S. government from the same think tank.[157] One reported that in the first three years, on balance, sanctions did appear to reduce the flow of undocumented immigrants, albeit by at most one-fifth; however, this did not signify a reduction in immigration, as "[s]ubstantial increases in applications for asylum . . . upward shifts in trends for applications for immigrant visas, and downward shifts in tourist and business visas issued in several countries, suggest that undocumented immigrants are searching harder for alternative, legal means of entering the United States."[158] It concluded that if the intent of employer sanctions was merely to curb the rate of increase in the flow, then the current level of enforcement was adequate, but that to generate a large decline it must be significantly increased.[159] The other study established on the basis of interviews with undocumented residents that entries in fact increased slightly after IRCA, and that those ineligible for legalization had no intention of returning home to Mexico or Central America but planned to increase the length of their stay in the United States so as to minimize the frequency of risky crossings. It concluded that the effect of employer sanctions was mainly to stimulate an expansion of the market in fake documents.[160] Concurring with these evaluations, the Department of Labor concluded that sanctions would neither significantly deter illegal immigration nor curb the growth in the underground economy, and that "[s]ignificant gains in the pursuit of both objectives requires a sustained and comprehensive efforts that includes border controls and the determined enforcement of all labor laws."[161]

A comprehensive overview of "line-watch apprehensions" and of the enforcement effort concluded that IRCA probably brought about a reduction in illegal Mexican immigration during the three years immediately after enactment, but that after 1989 it was again on the rise and that, overall, IRCA experience confirms the "curiously contradictory character" of U.S. policy toward illegal migration from Mexico, "emphasizing the appearance of control while in fact failing to stop substantial undocumented flows."[162] A more theoretical attempt to assess the effects of sanctions by modeling them as a "tax" on employers similarly concluded that they would have a significant effect on the real wages of legal low-skill workers only if enforcement was high, but pointed out that, given the scattered distribution of illegal workers in American industries and the limited personnel available for enforcement, the aggregate effect was likely to be negligible.[163] Ironically, the initial decline in apprehensions may have been occasioned simply by a reduction of the INS's capacity for border enforcement, as personnel were reallocated to other duties, notably employer inspections.[164]

Commenting on IRCA in 1989, Senator Simpson's chief of staff, Richard Day, suggested that if it proved ineffective, Congress would first try "to more strongly enforce employer sanctions," and if that did not work, "then I suppose there would be increased pressure for more drastic measures. I am sure there would be calls for more fences, ditches, or whatever and certainly for more Border Patrolmen." However, after IRCA's futility as a deterrent was established, Michael Fix, a senior researcher in the RAND-Urban Institute team, reflected that this hardly mattered, as employer sanctions were not meant to be effective, but rather "to create a symbol and perception . . . a political 'cover' for liberalizing our immigration laws."[165] These sharply diverging outlooks determined the order of battle for the next confrontation.

Fixing the Main Gate

While implementation of IRCA got underway, Congress tackled the remainder of the SCIRP agenda; but as it wended its way through the realm of the strange bedfellows, a project originally designed to restructure immigration into a zero-sum game by imposing an overall limit, and to shift it from a family allowance to citizens and permanent residents toward a neomercantilist device for the acquisition of human capital, was once again transformed by its inexorable political dynamics. Despite rising concern over immigration in the country at large, the alliance of old-time ethnics and expanding groups of recent vintage with free-market zealots proved unbeatable, enabling both those aspiring to bring in relatives and the procurement-minded to secure their objectives, at the expense of those seeking to limit or even reduce immigration.

Quite unexpectedly, European ethnics joined the call for expanded immigration as well. Although the notion of "illegal immigrants" evoked mainly images of Mexicans and Central Americans surreptitiously crossing the southern border by night, by this time they included some 100,000 Irish men and women, working for the most part in construction and child care, as well as many other Europeans. The lottery drew over 1 million applications in a one-week registration period, including hundreds of thousands from Ireland, and the Irish won over 40 percent of the special visas.[166] Although a second lottery was legislated in 1988, this did not assuage the Irish Immigration Reform Movement (IIRM), which achieved a more influential position within the Beltway by coalescing with others into a movement to help *all* countries— mostly European, but also African—disadvantaged by the 1965 act.[167]

Thanks to the Democratic reconquest of the Senate in 1986, Senator Kennedy was now again in the driver's seat. Although he sought to maintain a working alliance with Alan Simpson, the latter was still determined to institute a cap on immigration as a whole, while the Democrats continued to push for quasi-refugee status ("Extended Voluntary Departure") on behalf of the Salvadorans and Nicaraguans whom Simpson had managed to exclude from the final IRCA conference.[168] The jointly introduced S. 2104 met Simpson's long-standing objective by setting an overall cap of 590,000 on annual immigration, excluding refugees. In keeping with the traditional emphasis, 80 percent of the entries were allocated to family reunion. The entry of immediate relatives of U.S. citizens remained unlimited, but the number admitted in a given year would be deducted from the family visa allocation the following year so that, as the mass of immediate relatives grew further, as was likely when more immigrants of the latest wave became citizens, the number available for preference visas would substantially shrink. The cap would thus eventually take on a restrictive function, which would affect most severely the siblings of recent immigrants.[169]

The proposal's most innovative feature was an increase of independent admissions from the current 54,000 to 120,000, more than called for by SCIRP, of which 55,000 would be allocated on the basis of a system inspired from Canadian policy, providing "points" for education, skills in demand, age, working experience, and English-language proficiency. Although this appeared to be designed on behalf of labor procurement, Senator Kennedy made the provision's intent quite clear, pointing out that "America will open its doors again to those who no longer have immediate family ties in the US. For example, in 1986, because of the family restrictions, only 1,852 applicants from Ireland qualified for immigrant visas. . . . Similar statistics could be cited for many other nations that have sent large number of immigrants to the U.S. in the past."[170] In a provision promptly decried as a "fat cat" measure, individuals could also qualify for admission as independent immigrants by investing $1 million and creating at least ten jobs. The bill passed the Senate on March 15, 1988, after minimal debate, by an overwhelming 88–4. However, Rodino and Mazzoli refused to take it up in the House, thereby freezing movement until after the midterm elections.[171]

Although immigration advocates were now largely focused on the Reagan administration's harsh position on Central Americans, its forceful promotion of the market economy was conducive to viewing immigration more generally in a favorable light. From a largely liberal assemblage encompassing churches, synagogues, Hispanic and Asian groups, as well as civil rights organizations, the pro-immigration coalition expanded to encompass much of the business community and its allies, economists and conservative think tanks such as the Heritage Foundation, the American Enterprise Institute, and the Hudson Institute, whose 1987 report, *Workforce 2000,* funded by the U.S. Department of Labor, popularized the notion of a growing shortage of skilled labor. In the same vein, the Council of Economic Advisers declared that the economic contributions of immigration exceed its liabilities by lowering product prices and providing higher returns to capital.[172] However, while some free-market economists, notably Julian Simon, favored altogether unlimited entry, others such as Barry Chiswick and George Borjas charged that the current family- and refugee-oriented policy led to a decline in skills and advocated policy reorientation toward outright procurement.[173] Similarly, a comprehensive overview prepared by the Department of Labor for the first triennial presidential report on immigration mandated by the IRCA pointed out that immigration was somewhat of a "doubled-edged sword": although in their entry-level manufacturing and service jobs, immigrants usually complemented domestic workers, they became more competitive as they acquired greater proficiency in English and familiarity with the market, with other immigrants and ethnic minorities the most vulnerable.[174]

Kennedy and Simpson cosponsored a similar proposal the following year. As approved by the Judiciary Committee in June 1989, S. 358 once again imposed a cap on overall immigration, placed greater emphasis on human capital, and modified the allocation system to permit more immigration from Europe. However, it came under heavy fire from committee colleagues of both parties, who eliminated points for English proficiency, a remarkable move given the "English-only" movement that was gaining strength in the country at large, and loosened the cap to allow for steadily increasing numbers.[175] Ethnic groups that fought to increase the second preference and maintain the existing fifth preference (for brothers and sisters) intact succeeded in making this a condition for increasing "independent" visas and the imposition of an overall cap. This obviously entailed an increase in overall immigration, which was acceptable to Senator Kennedy but contrary to the long-standing objectives of Senator Simpson. Hitherto largely silent, the Bush administration warned Simpson against imposing a cap and scaling back family preferences, on the grounds that it would jeopardize its "pro-family" stance and raise the ire of Asians and Hispanics, and insisted, "The greatest danger . . . may be . . . identification with those whom the press calls the immigration 'restrictionists' or 'exclusionists.' "[176] Passed on July 13 by 81–17, the bill provided for a "flexible ceiling" of 630,000 and reserved 150,000 admissions for independent visas and families on a point system. It also required the Census Bureau to adjust total population figures so that illegal aliens would not be counted toward reapportionment of legislative seats.[177]

In the House, Howard Berman introduced a very liberal bill (H.R. 672) that, among other things, extended the privilege of unrestricted admission hitherto enjoyed exclusively by close relatives of citizens to those of permanent resident aliens, suspended the deportation of spouses and minor children of persons legalized under IRCA, and established a three-year pilot program allotting 55,000 visas on a lottery basis to applicants who scored a threshold number of qualifying points, mostly on the basis of work experience.[178] A companion bill was introduced in the Senate by Paul Simon, Democrat of Illinois, while New York's Charles Schumer added a draft providing among other things for "diversity" on behalf of underrepresented countries, designed to benefit Europeans mostly.

The House hearings, beginning in late September, elicited testimony from the usual suspects, which now included European ethnic advocates of "diversity," notably the IIRM and the American Committee on Italian Migration. Warning of the likely undesirable unforeseen consequences of the pending proposals, demographer Michael Teitelbaum referred in his testimony to "the Alice-in-Wonderland world that you live in, and I have lived in, of immigration advocacy," and circulated copies of a paper on the 1965 law by historian David Reimers, which pointed out that it had neither intended nor been expected to lead to substantial increased immigration from Asia and Latin America.[179] In the wake of the hearings, Bruce Morrison of lottery fame, who replaced Romano Mazzoli as subcommittee chair, crafted a bill of his own providing for 95,000 employment-based admissions, uncapping the second preference for family members of resident aliens, and allowing for as many as 100,000 more annual visas than Kennedy-Simpson, which cleared by a comfortable 23–12.[180] Although the White House went on record as preferring the Senate's version, the *Wall Street Journal* editorialists praised Morrison's for its potential contributions to American economic growth.[181] Leading the opposition, Lamar Smith failed to secure passage of an amendment reducing admissions to the Senate's level, and the bill finally passed on October 3, 1990, 231–192. His efforts to the contrary notwithstanding, the House also enacted a bill providing EVD for Central Americans, 258–162.

The Senate agreed in late October to a 700,000 annual level for each of the three years following enactment, after which it would be reduced to 675,000, with 480,000 for family reunification.[182] Senator Simpson finally gave in on Central American EVD as well as on amnesty for the spouses and children of aliens legalized under IRCA, but secured in return maintenance of special visas for investors of at least $1 million and at least ten U.S. workers, as well as a program for a pilot ID program based on drivers' licenses. The latter held up approval in the House, where on the next-to-last day of the session, Edward Roybal and his fellow California Representative Esteban Torres argued on behalf of the Hispanic Caucus that the provision was objectionable as the forerunner of a national ID system, and quickly won over their African American colleagues, who were angry at President Bush's veto of a civil rights bill, as well as some liberal Democrats and libertarian republicans.[183] Supporters of the overall bill then came up with a concurrent resolution to strip out the license provision from the conference report, which both chambers approved on the very last day of the session by a voice vote. The Senate and the House also agreed to provide 55,000 legalizations for each of the next three years to cover spouses and children of immigrants legalized under IRCA, provided they had entered the United States by May 1988. In response to criticism of employer sanctions, it reinforced the antidiscrimination provisions instituted by IRCA. While the compromise made the bill more acceptable to House Republicans, it remained objectionable to members from border states, who feared an influx of immigrants.[184] The House finally adopted the conference report on a bipartisan but heavily Democratic vote, and the Senate by a comfortable and thoroughly bipartisan 89–8, with 3 not voting.[185] The political alignment was similar as for IRCA, but with Hispanics and blacks less split.[186] On November 29, the measure was signed by President Bush as promoting both family values and American competitiveness.

To invoke another of Senator Simpson's tropes, Congress built a ceiling with a hole in it. P.L. 101–649 established an overall cap of 675,000 beginning in fiscal year 1995, including immediate relatives of citizens but excluding refugees, and increased the individual country ceiling slightly from 20,000 to 25,620.[187] Family reunion was allocated 480,000 entries, 71 percent of the total. While immediate relatives of citizens remained unlimited, the number admitted in a given year was to be deducted from the following year's allocation to relatives of citizens and permanent resident aliens governed by the preference system. However, the law also insured a minimum of 226,000 admissions for the latter so that, if over 254,000 immediate relatives of citizens were admitted in a given year, the cap might be raised the following year above 675,000. The preference system was somewhat modified as well, notably by reducing visas for siblings to reduce chaining, but raising those for the spouses and unmarried children of permanent residents from about 70,000 to 114,000.[188] Employment-based immigration was more than doubled, from 54,000 to 140,000, constituting 21 percent of the posttransition total, with a preference system of its own emphasizing human capital as well as capital *tout court,* and some protection for American workers.[189] The law also institutionalized the category "diversity immigrants" from underrepresented countries and enlarged it to 55,000, or 8 percent; applicants must have the equivalent of a high school diploma or two years' experience in a skilled occupation. This was likely to benefit eastern Europeans, who since the collapse of the Communist system were no longer eligible for refugee status but, as a consequence of prolonged exit restrictions, lacked relatives in the United States; it was also likely to benefit Africans. Ireland was guaranteed 40 percent of the "diversity" allowance during the transition period, but afterwards no country would receive more than 7 percent.

Various provisions regarding refugees were packed into the law as well: the number of asylees permitted to become resident aliens was raised from 5,000 a year to 10,000, and Salvadorans were granted an eighteen-month "safe haven" under a new Temporary Protected Status (TPS) clause, which advocates had been trying to secure on their behalf for several years, but scaled down from thirty-six months to assuage Senator Simpson. The act further institutionalized TPS as a distinct status, which the attorney general could accord to persons from countries subject to armed conflict, natural disasters, or other extraordinary conditions, who might not meet the "well-founded fear" standard of the international refugee convention.[190] Responding to the wishes of the electronic industry, the law also facilitated the temporary recruitment of highly skilled and managerial employees by easing regulations for the award of H1-B visas (awarded to highly skilled workers deemed in short supply), but capped them at 65,000 a year. On the control side, it authorized more INS and Border Patrol personnel—subject, of course, to budgetary action—provided for the improved maintenance of border fences, and instituted tighter procedures for deporting alien criminals.

Even as the measure was nearing completion, a Roper poll reported that 75 percent of the public said legal immigration should not be increased, and nearly half said it should be reduced; furthermore, a majority believed that legal as well as illegal immigrants displaced American workers, burdened the social welfare system, and threatened American culture.[191] Given the growing anti-immigration mood in the country at large, what accounts for enactment of a law moving in the opposite direction? Daniel Tichenor has pointed out that the measure "reflected an insulation of the policymaking process from restrictive-minded publics," and Reimers also suggests that Congress was more liberal than the public and responsive to special interests favoring immigration.[192] In a more nuanced vein, Debra DeLaet has observed similarly that "Congress initially attempted to address the public desire for restrictions on legal immigration and to assert the appearance of control," and that "passage of this liberal policy in spite of popular support for immigration restrictions can be attributed to interest group politics and liberal norms." The decisive factor was that "while public support for a reduction in legal immigration was broad, it was not well-organized. . . . In contrast, a liberal coalition of well-organized groups, including ethnic organizations, churches, and employer associations, articulated strong opposition to proposals for restricting legal immigration," and the incipient international human rights régime provided moral weight to their claims as well.[193] But if the main gate's design was indeed contingent on such an unusual configuration of interests, the restrictionists could be counted on to seize the opportunity of a change of circumstances to make another bid for a turn at the drawing board.

11

Why the Gates Were Not Shut

Immigration begets not only more immigration, but also nativist reactions. A quarter of a century into the new wave, a growing number of Americans grumbled ever more vociferously about the transformations it wrought, and many thought the gates should be substantially narrowed, if not shut altogether. Propelled to the center of media attention by a succession of dramatic incidents, immigration became a hot subject, debated by a proliferating cohort of experts at a level of acerbity unknown since the 1920s. However, the hostile national mood's impact on policy was mediated by political institutions, which constituted an arena where the interplay of the two dimensions of concern and interest emphasized throughout this work generated heavily contingent political outcomes.

For those determined to reduce immigration, family reunion policy emerged as the most relevant target because it reinforced sociological processes so as to foster a "chaining" effect. A statistical analysis confirmed that the single most important determinant of the size of a national flow was that of the relevant foreign-born community in the United States.[1] But pursuit of this objective was constrained by the inherent legitimacy of a family-oriented policy, notably for cultural conservatives with whom the restrictionists otherwise had much in common, as well as the effective defensive strategies of the threatened ethnic groups. As it was, the 1990 law, which originated as an attempt to shift the priorities from family- to employment-oriented criteria and to impose an overall cap on legal immigration, resulted instead in the cumulation of the two, holding forth the prospect of a further expansion of the intake.

Overall, however, it was illegal immigration that captured the headlines, especially the influx from the south. Yet the protracted efforts to deter unauthorized movement by imposing sanctions on American employers produced little more than a perfunctory law whose enforcement remained a largely dead letter, and the border itself remained a sieve. In what he aptly termed "the making of Amerexico," Peter Andreas argued in the early 1990s that "American policies have actually helped to create the very problem that U.S. officials are now struggling to solve" on both the supply and the demand sides, and that "[i]llegal immigration is a core link (even if an informal one) in the growing economic integration between the United States and Mexico—a link more important than NAFTA."[2] Border controls turned out paradoxically counterproductive as well. The going smuggler rate to Los Angeles was $700, to be paid whether the venture was successful or not; and since the money was usually borrowed, if caught, the border-crosser had an even greater incentive to try again in order to pay off his debt. IRCA contributed to the further growth of illegal movement as well: not only did the loosely enforced employer sanctions have little deterrent effect, but the newly legalized millions also provided a stronger and more stable community base to sustain and protect unauthorized newcomers. In the same vein, a U.S. commission concluded that the SAWs program "had unintentionally promoted more immigration by sending the message that being illegally employed in farm work in the United States would facilitate becoming a legal immigrant."[3]

All of these factors paled next to the effects of the North American Free Trade Agreement (NAFTA). Signed by President George Bush, Mexican President Carlos Salinas, and Canadian Prime Minister Brian Mulroney on December 17, 1992, the event concerned mainly relations with Mexico, as the United States and Canada had such an agreement since 1989. Pressures from international organizations had been driving Mexico into the neoliberal mainstream, as signified by its decision to join the General Agreements on Tariffs and Trade (GATT) in 1986, and forced its government to again devaluate the peso by nearly half in 1994, precipitating another huge drop in real purchasing power and further enhancing incentives to seek a living north of the border. NAFTA also required Mexico to abandon the protectionist agricultural policies that enabled subsistence farmers to stay on their land, thereby exacerbating the exodus. Designed to stimulate the rapid expansion of transborder economic linkages, NAFTA facilitated human movement as well. Already some 1,700 trucks crossed the Rio Grande bridge from Juarez every day, and they would eventually have access to every part of the United States and Canada.

Concomitantly, the Mexican diaspora vastly expanded its domain. As of the mid-1990s, Mexico accounted for 14 percent of legal immigration into the United States and close to 40 percent of undocumented arrivals; these immigrants were younger, less educated, and poorer than the U.S. population as a whole, and the more recent arrivals were less educated than their predecessors.[4] About 5 percent of the U.S. population was of Mexican origin, but the proportion rose to 20 percent in California. Mexican Americans still lived mostly in California, Texas, and Illinois, but nearly one-third of the newcomers were now going to other states.[5]

The sense of "invasion" was compounded by developments in the Caribbean.[6] In the mid-1980s, patrols by U.S. vessels in the Straits of Florida and the Windward Passage had reduced unauthorized immigration from Haiti and Cuba by as much as 90 percent. However, massive flight from Haiti resumed in the wake of the overthrow of President Jean-Bertrand Aristide in September 1991, and the following year interceptions rose to 31,041, prompting charges by the State Department and the INS that by sending their patrol crafts close to the Haitian shores, the Coast Guard was turning them into magnets for human traffic. The vast majority were returned to Haiti on the basis of perfunctory shipboard interviews by the INS, prompting the Haitian Refugee Center in Miami to sue the Bush administration for violation of the 1980 Refugee Act and international treaties regarding refugees. After a federal court issued an injunction against repatriation, the government established a refugee camp at Guantanamo Bay, Cuba; but screening interviews conducted there were challenged as well because they did not provide for lawyers. The situation shortly gained the attention of the Congressional Black Caucus and prominent African Americans. More attuned to these political allies than its predecessor, the Clinton administration concluded that the only alternative to massive asylum was the restoration of a more legitimate political regime in Haiti, which it brought about in 1994.[7] No sooner was the Haitian crisis over that the Cuban government once again loosened exit as a safety valve for mounting discontent; aware that Cuban Americans, sobered by the Mariel experience, were unlikely to send another flotilla, the regime encouraged the emigrants to float toward U.S. waters on makeshift rafts. Interceptions rose to an unprecedented 37,194 in 1994, propelling immigration into prime time once again and creating a disastrous situation for Florida's Democratic governor, who was seeking reelection in a difficult year.[8]

Although immigration policy did not rank highly among the Clinton administration's concerns, the subject was abruptly propelled into the headlines in January 1993 by way of an embarrassing incident involving Zoe Baird, the incoming president's nominee for attorney general, who was found to have employed an undocumented Peruvian immigrant as a child-sitter. Concurrently, a series of violent incidents revived concern over immigration as a security issue, dormant since the early years of the Cold War. That same month, a Pakistani gunman who had entered the United States on a temporary business visa in March 1991 and filed for asylum a year later, launched an attack on CIA headquarters. This was followed on February 26 by a bomb explosion in the basement garage of the World Trade Center, for which six Middle Eastern men were later convicted.[9] On Sunday, June 6, immigration burst out as a dramatic made-for-TV event when the freighter *Golden Venture* ran aground on a sandbar off Rockaway Beach in New York City. The ship, which had been at sea for three months, held a cargo of over 300 Chinese from the province of Fujian, including about 20 women, who had promised to pay $20,000–35,000 to professional smugglers based in Hong Kong and Taiwan. Quickly achieving iconic stature, the *Golden Venture* perennially reappeared on the screen when several of the survivors, detained in York, Pennsylvania, filed claims for asylum as victims of the Chinese government's one-child policy, eliciting support from churches and humanitarian organizations.[10] On April 19, 1994, a car bomb exploded outside the federal office building in Oklahoma City, killing 168 persons. Although this proved to be an entirely domestic tragedy, it triggered heightened concern with security that spilled into the immigration sphere and further reinforced the restrictionist mood.

In the intervening period, frustrated by the apparent ineffectiveness of the deterrent they devised in 1986, control-minded policy makers initiated more draconian proposals. With the public's increasingly negative mood and the decision makers' restrictionism feeding each other, there was every reason to expect that the framework created in 1965 would undergo a fundamental overhaul, with a drastic reduction of the intake in the offing. Nowhere did the transformations effected by the new wave provoke more acute reactions than in California, which felt particularly besieged and whose populist legacy facilitated the exploitation of immigration by opportunist politicians.

Yet in the end, the mountain gave birth to . . . more than a mouse, something like a hefty rat, but still a considerably smaller offspring than its dramatic travails presaged. While a number of anti-immigration measures were enacted at the state and federal levels, none of them substantially reduced either the legal or the illegal flow, and as the twentieth century approached its close, the wave rolled on, largely undisturbed. Under the circumstances, the most compelling question is, why were the realistic expectations of a reenactment of the 1920s not fulfilled? Although neither history nor the social sciences are well equipped to deal with negatives, I shall undertake to explain why the expected did not happen by first demonstrating that restrictionism was very much in the air, then reconstructing the legislative efforts it generated, and finally accounting for their limited success.

Stranger Encounters

As the century approached its close, Americans looked at immigration "with rose-colored glasses turned backwards."[11] While they continued to take pride in their past as a "nation of immigrants," in 1992 support for outright reduction climbed to an unprecedented 54 percent, the following year to 61 percent, and in 1995 to 65 percent, warranting the judgment that "sentiment against a continuation of current levels of immigration ha[d] returned to historic highs."[12] Those who thought immigration policies should be revised rose dramatically as well, from 48 percent in 1990 to 80 percent in 1992, with a majority disapproving of President Bill Clinton's handling of the subject and supporting a government-issued national identity card indicating a significant shift from earlier opposition to such a measure.

Although unemployment and economic pessimism were contributing factors, the fact that the turn to the negative occurred in the midst of a boom suggests that noneconomic considerations carried considerable weight.[13] One study established that restrictionism was related to more general conservative attitudes and to "an isolationist perspective along a broader array of international issues."[14] Another concluded that "the overall predictive power of economic motivations" was "modest," and that "opinions concerning the economic effects of immigration are best regarded as an amalgam of material concerns and more purely affective responses to particular ethnic groups," serving as "legitimating arguments for restrictionist policies in a culture that discourages open expressions of nativism or xenophobia."[15] Peter Burns and James G. Gimpel pointed out that "more respectable restrictionists never argue . . . on blatantly racist or nativist grounds," so that "[f]rom the content of elite discourse and from the rich academic debate on the costs and benefits of immigration, observers would likely conclude that the main rationale for restricting immigration was an economic one"; however, they believed instead that in the 1990s, racial prejudice played a much greater role than economic outlook in shaping attitudes toward immigration policy.[16]

The tendency of the "reducers" to target specific groups provides further support for this interpretation. In 1984, 51 percent thought Latin American immigrants were too numerous and a comparable 49 percent felt this way about Asians, but only 31 percent targeted Africans and a mere 26 percent Europeans; over the next decade, perceptions of oversupply rose across the board, but the ranking held fast.[17] Throughout the period, stable majorities or pluralities believed that immigrants generally tend to end up on welfare and use a disproportionately high share of government services; and between 1985 and 1993, appreciation of their positive contributions fell while perception of the problems they occasioned rose. Once again, these judgments varied considerably by group, as indicated by their scores on an index of desirability: in 1993, Europeans scored very high, Asians middling, and Latinos markedly low, with Haitians at the bottom.[18] Overall, white respondents were most likely to advocate reducing the level of immigration and to support delaying access to welfare benefits; African Americans were generally more liberal, but when questions were formulated specifically to raise the issue of economic costs, they tended to be more restrictionist; and although Hispanics emerged as more ambivalent, they by no means diverged from the pack.[19]

On the whole, the negative turn appeared to be stimulated less by direct encounters with the newcomers than by perceptions of their growing presence in the country at large, which aroused fears of an irreversible transformation of American identity. Jack Citrin and his associates have suggested that the influx of newcomers into a community tended to affect the level of anti-immigrant collective action, pointing out that the victory of Proposition 187 in California (discussed below) "spawned imitative proposals in other states with a large immigrant presence—such as Florida, Texas, and Arizona—but not in states with few immigrants."[20] However, the fact that a number of other high-immigration states, notably New York, New Jersey, and Illinois, did not experience a high level of anti-immigrant collective action, and that the growing hostility had a limited impact on national legislation, casts doubt on the validity of their proposition.

The effects of the growing immigrant presence on public opinion were not clearly one-sided. Initially, the new wave stimulated greater tolerance: whereas in 1965, 67 percent of Americans agreed that "[f]oreigners should give up their foreign ways and learn to be like other Americans," by 1981 the proportion had gone down to half. However, those viewing immigrants in a favorable light subsequently declined abruptly from 69 percent in 1990 to 61 percent in 1992 and 60 percent the following year. The limits of tolerance were manifest: whereas 53 percent in 1985 and 51 percent in 1993 agreed that "children of immigrants should be taught some subjects in their native language so that they can better understand what they are learning," in 1993 a whopping 66 percent disagreed with the proposition that "[i]n areas with a large number of immigrants from a particular country, public signs should be printed in their native language."[21] Contact with immigrants produced ambiguous effects, as suggested by another finding that whites living in close proximity to large Asian and Hispanic populations tended to have more favorable views of these two groups, and were more likely than racially and ethnically isolated whites to support increased immigration.[22] One helpful suggestion is that policies directed against immigrants were more likely to be adopted by "bifurcated" states," where a nonethnic white majority coexisted with sizeable minority populations, paralleling the composition of the historic Deep South. Most of the states that enacted "Official English" measures during this period were of the "bifurcated" type.[23] An analysis of 1994 opinion on immigration in the tradition of symbolic interactionism found that neither income nor race was statistically significant, but that pessimism regarding the national economy as well as political conservatism were related to anti-immigration. The single weightiest variable was support for a law making English the official language, pointing once again to the weightiness of perceptions of immigration as a cultural threat.[24]

To what extent did the negative turn reflect the changing opinions of people once favorably disposed toward immigrants, as against the accession of more anti-immigration cohorts to the ranks of opinion holders? While those born after World War II were found to be less prejudiced than their predecessors toward blacks, Hispanics, Jews, and Asians, the most recent cohorts showed no tendency to be less prejudiced than their elders. Outside the South, the 1961–1972 cohorts were more likely to hold negative stereotypes of Hispanics and Asians than their 1946–1960 predecessors, leading the authors to surmise that whereas prejudice toward blacks would continue to decline somewhat at the level of the nation as a whole by virtue of cohort succession in the South, this was unlikely to occur with respect to Hispanics and Asians.[25]

In conclusion, there is no doubt that in the early 1990s, the public mood became markedly less favorable toward immigrants and immigration, probably from a combination of shifting views among those who grew up before the onset of the new wave, and of the more negative outlook of those who came of age as it landed. Although there was a general decline of prejudice, some Americans opposed immigration on old-fashioned grounds, because the newcomers were largely Latino or Asian; others felt threatened by intruders on their economic turf; and for some, whose identity was being formed even as the new wave landed, immigrants replaced blacks as the "other." This was evidently stimulated by the dramatic increase in negative rhetoric about immigration in the public sphere.[26] In that light, however, the fact that the anti-immigration mood did not produce more drastic legislative action becomes even more puzzling. Gregory Huber and Thomas Espenshade have suggested that while the public's opinions on immigration were inconsistent, ambivalent, and weakly held, the attention of federal policy makers was captured by "vocal pro-immigrant interest groups."[27] But how could policy makers simultaneously contribute to the formation of anti-immigrant opinion among the public, and ignore it on behalf of the objectives of pro-immigrant interest groups?

The Great Immigration Debate

Immigration[28] will constitute "the next major post-cold war debate," the *New Republic* announced in 1993, and Michael Lind suggested in the *New Yorker* two years later that Ellis Island's past as an ammunition depot is "a nice bit of symbolism, for immigration is proving to be one of the most explosive issues of American politics in the nineties."[29] Echoing the public mood, the intellectual establishment quickly took up positions on both sides of the emerging divide and vied for the policy makers' attention by generating an array of proposals with appropriate rationales for action. Since no one explicitly advocated illegal immigration, the alternatives in that sphere pertained solely to the degree of enforcement and the means to be used; but with regard to legal immigration, the range of choices was much wider, involving overall numbers as well as the criteria for selection, with the latter becoming more critical should admissions be reduced.

In a survey of the preliminary lineup, Daniel Choi commented that "already the post-ideological ironies are piling up" and Peter Schuck observed similarly that, aside from "strangeball extremists" advocating a totally open or totally closed door, "the liberal-conservative axis is a poor guide to attitudes toward immigration."[30] This muddled state of affairs was hardly surprising, as it reflected the perennial tension between the distinct imperatives of capitalism and identitarian nationalism, producing the recurrent formation of "strange bedfellow" alliances. Adding to the confusion, the late twentieth-century lineup entailed a complete reversal of post–World War II positions in relation to the status quo: in the earlier period, given the restrictionist system in effect, advocates of more open immigration were the attackers, but now they were on the defensive, and it was those seeking to restrict immigration who were on the move and thereby captured the center of attention, reenacting the drama that took place at the beginning of the twentieth century. But while this gave them a significant advantage in the realm of discourse, with regard to policy theirs was an uphill fight because American political institutions are designed to make it easier to maintain the status quo than to innovate.

The restrictionists faced an unprecedented challenge in the ideological sphere because of the hegemonic position of free-market doctrine in late twentieth-century America, which made for a near-consensus among economists on the value of immigration as a device for acquiring human capital. The most vigorous statement of the ruling dogma was set forth by Julian Simon in a series of papers culminating in a book published in association with the libertarian Cato Institute.[31] Addressing "a national debate that has been going on for more than a century" regarding "how many immigrants, of what kinds, should the US admit each year," he answered unhesitatingly, "more than at present," but wanted them "chosen more for their economic characteristics and less on the basis of family connections," possibly by allocating admissions by auction. However, he stopped short of endorsing the *Wall Street Journal*'s "open borders" editorial stance, because "we have little understanding of how many people would choose to immigrate if the door were completely open, and even less basis for predicting how the mix of immigrants by skill and education would change." In any case, he deemed the "open borders" position politically unfeasible. Insisting that immigrants neither take jobs away from natives nor widen the national income distribution, Simon nevertheless acknowledged that the competition they impose drives down some natives' wages, albeit less than popularly imagined, and that the benefits and costs of immigration are unequally distributed, with the latter falling disproportionately on the locales of greatest settlement, notably by way of public services such as education.

The most vocal alternative was set forth by George Borjas, who emerged in the late 1980s as the main supplier of economic ammunition for the restrictionist camp.[32] Starting from the theoretically ingenious assumption that the United States in effect competes with the immigrants' home states and other potential immigration countries for their human and physical capital by "selling" visas, Borjas criticized current policy for its "extremely peculiar" pricing system: "We literally give visas away to persons who have close relatives in the country and, with a few exceptions, charge a prohibitively high price to persons who do not." Compounded by the "giveaway" to refugees, the pricing system's economic irrationality brought about a deterioration of the immigrant flow's skill composition. Although Borjas rejected the charge that unskilled immigrants undermine the current earnings and employment opportunities of natives, he insisted that they are likely to have a negative impact in the long run "because of their relatively high poverty rates and propensities for participation in the welfare system and because national income and tax revenues are substantially lower than they would have been if the United States had attracted a more skilled immigrant flow." In order to reestablish American competitiveness in the international market for skilled workers, he recommended adoption of the Australian and Canadian point system for awarding visas and suggested that they might even be bought and sold in an open market. Borjas restated his position even more provocatively in 1999, with a proposal for "taxing" yearly admissions by deducting the estimated number of illegal entries from the total allocation.[33]

Although as a *National Review* regular Borjas clearly located himself in the conservative camp, his economic arguments elicited sharply negative reactions from free market and libertarian circles, while his labor audience was limited because of his conservative identity. Overall, his findings echoed other research suggesting that immigration's overall impact on employment and wages was modest, but negative for some American workers, and that the illegal flow, in particular, tended to depress wages in a number of already marginal sectors of the economy. These effects led the labor-oriented economist Vernon M. Briggs Jr. to formulate a critique of ongoing policy very similar to Borjas's, but to conclude very differently that "[t]he real need is for an expanded national human resource development policy for citizen workers, not for a continuing increase in immigrants who are admitted mainly without regard to their human capital attributes."[34] The objective should be a targeted and flexible immigration policy designed primarily to admit persons who can fill job vacancies for which qualified citizens and resident aliens are unavailable, but not so many as to discourage them from investing in training and government bodies from providing resources for them to do so. However, Briggs's audience was limited because organized labor could no longer oppose even the illegal flow as harmful, given the crucial importance of newcomers in its strategy for renewal.

As the economic debate wore on, the emphasis shifted from the impact of immigration on the labor market to the costs it imposed on the welfare system. In a series of papers commissioned by Negative Population Growth and the Carrying Capacity Network, advocates of an outright moratorium on immigration, another economist, Donald Huddle of Rice University, ventured way out of the professional mainstream, claiming that post-1970 immigrants cost the United States a minimum of $42 billion annually in public service and displacement costs.[35] The "dependency" theme was easily enlisted into the service of broader arguments on behalf of restriction; for example, in a 1994 *National Review* article, Peter Skerry started by observing that "immigrants place enormous burdens on already strapped local and state governments" and are becoming more welfare dependent, and then went on to suggest that "while we don't know much about the cultural impact of all these newcomers on our nation's values and institutions, I would argue that such concerns are not necessarily racist or xenophobic, but reflect the legitimate anxieties that any nation would have as its way of life shows signs of changing."[36]

Albeit widely cited by congressional restrictionists, Huddle's estimates were dismissed as much too high by most other researchers, including not only liberal think tanks but also the National Research Council and even George Borjas.[37] A more balanced assessment pointed out, "Whether immigrants are seen as a net drain or a net benefit largely depends on two issues: the level of government at which the costs are assessed, and the types of immigrants being considered," and concluded that the costs of providing services fell mainly to state and local governments, because they are responsible for education, while taxes flowed largely to the federal government. These findings were subsequently incorporated in the Urban Institute's *Immigration and Immigrants: Setting the Record Straight*.[38] Emerging as the handbook of the liberal camp, it suggested that "undocumented immigrants, not legal immigrants, are the ones likely to generate a negative fiscal impact," and since measures undertaken to date to control illegal immigration "have been largely unsuccessful," the priority should go to "altering the policies for controlling illegal immigration, not a need for major overhaul of the country's legal admissions." A balanced appraisal by the Congressional Research Service (CRS) confirmed that the foreign-born as a whole were no more likely than the native-born to participate in the AFDC, Food Stamp, or Medicaid programs, but were more likely to use SSI and state assistance; and that, not surprisingly, the use of public assistance was highest among elderly aliens and refugees.[39] Addressing a matter of vital interest to legislators who would deny welfare benefits to legal immigrants, the CRS pointed out further that there were no constitutional obstacles to such measures because "[u]nder Supreme Court rulings, Congress may discriminate against or among aliens in federal benefits programs so long as the distinctions drawn are reasonably based."

Given the pro-immigration bias of free-market economics, environmentalism moved to the fore as an important source of respectable arguments on behalf of reduced immigration. FAIR's emergence in the early 1980s as the prominent restrictionist lobby has already been noted. In 1994, the Sierra Club, one of the largest and most influential environmental groups, long concerned with overpopulation, joined the pack by publishing *How Many Americans?*, whose coauthors Leon Bouvier and Lindsey Grant not only singled out immigration as the leading source of pressure on the environment, but also went on to argue that it threatened the survival of white America.[40] Displaying a front-cover endorsement from Richard D. Lamm, former governor of Colorado, and a back-cover one from Garrett Hardin, the book called for an outright population rollback. However, whereas Hardin had always insisted that his concern was exclusively with the quantitative aspect of immigration, Bouvier and Grant deplored its qualitative impact as well, emphasizing that the United States of 2050 "will be ethnically more diverse," and by 2100 "will be unrecognizable to Americans of today." Obviously designed to arouse reactive fears among white Americans, these projections were founded on a questionable assumption regarding social behavior and an unwarranted reification of census categories, which constituted such elementary errors that a professional demographer such as Bouvier could commit them only willfully. Ultimately rejecting the goal of "zero net immigration" as unrealistic, the authors proposed setting the annual level at 200,000, approximately one-fourth the ongoing intake, a number that emerged as the restrictionist norm, and urged serious efforts to end clandestine immigration altogether.

The Sierra Club's apparent endorsement of a restrictionist position with nativist overtones triggered a fractious internal confrontation. Although the board of directors sought to contain the damage by adopting a policy of neutrality on immigration, this hardly settled the matter. The restrictionist faction launched a successful drive to place a proposition to that effect on the ballot for the April 1998 election, and then waged a campaign for membership support with help from like-minded organizations including FAIR. This prompted in turn the elaboration of a competing proposition, affirming the need for global population stabilization but asserting that America's population problem cannot be solved by immigration controls, and that the club should therefore remain neutral on the subject. With a somewhat larger turnout than expected, the membership endorsed neutrality by 60.1 percent. However, "Sierrans for U.S. Population Stabilization" charged that the "establishment" manipulated the election process and violated the club's rules and bylaws, and their leader subsequently justified his faction's stance by pointing out that Hispanic members of Congress scored below the average Democratic member's score on the League of Conservation Voters charts.

With traditional concerns losing their urgency in the waning days of the Cold War, immigration was eagerly embraced by the security-minded as an hitherto ignored source of danger. In the early 1990s, a number of *Foreign Affairs* articles reviewing global population issues from a security perspective concluded that "the demographic significance of international migration has decidedly diminished" and that there was no cause for "exaggerated visions of global apocalypse."[41] However, in a work purporting to prepare policy makers for the twenty-first century, Paul Kennedy swept aside such careful assessments and singled out the "global population explosion" in his opening chapter as one of the most challenging issues.[42] In view of the imbalances in demographic trends between "have" and "have-not" societies, one should expect "great waves of migration" because "desperate migrants are unlikely to be deterred" by immigration policies. A year later, in a coauthored *Atlantic Monthly* article, Kennedy asserted, "Many members of the more prosperous economies are beginning to agree with Raspail's vision of a world of two camps, North and South, separate and unequal, in which the rich will have to fight and the poor will have to die if mass migration is not to overwhelm us all." The reference was to a conservative French essayist, Jean Raspail, who set forth his vision in a melodramatic 1973 novel, in which after a horde of Third World paupers from the shores of the Ganges commandeers a flotilla of derelict ships and sets sail for the promised land of affluent Europe, the white world is seized by a collective paralysis induced by the loss of its "racial will" to fight for survival.[43] Kennedy and his coauthor argued that "the pressures are now much greater than they were when Raspail wrote," not only because of the additional people on the planet, but also because of the communication revolution as well as the prospect of widespread chaos in the developing world, as sensationally depicted by Robert D. Kaplan in the same magazine earlier in the year. Such views were echoed, albeit in more moderate tones, in academic security-oriented discourse as well. For example, in 1992, MIT political scientist Myron Weiner proclaimed that because international migration was a source of conflicts within and between states, it is necessary to supplement the economic approach with a "security/stability" framework.[44]

Why did talk of a "crisis" benefit from such a receptive hearing? The works noted are contemporary expressions of the "fear of population decline" that has gripped the West since the beginning of the twentieth century.[45] As Amartya Sen has pointed out, however, the white "sense of a growing 'imbalance' in the world ignores history and implicitly presumes that the expansion of Europeans earlier on was natural, whereas the same process happening now to other populations unnaturally disturbs the 'balance.' "[46] However, there is no gainsaying that if world population is grouped into conventional "racial" categories, which is the common practice in public discourse among Europeans and their overseas offshoots, "white decline" is a genuine historical trend and the "deadline" has been moving up. In the United States, for example, whereas in the early 1980s demographers estimated that "non-Hispanic whites" would decline to 50 percent by 2080, a decade later the fatidic moment was moved up to 2050.

Yet although the impact of immigration on the racial composition of American society evoked widespread concern, the boundaries of acceptable public discourse in the post–Civil Rights era imposed constraints against the explicit expression of such views, and reduced them to *sous-entendus* (unstated understandings). This left the field wide open to invasion by the marginal right such as the AICF, whose alarming 1990 pamphlet, *The Path to National Suicide,* undertook to "break the silence" on the dangers presented by the flood of non-European immigrants pouring into the country and the prospect of a decline of the white population into the minority.[47] Invoking among others the conservative political theorist Alan Bloom, Lawrence Auster denounced the "new cultural revolution" that provides "a sanction for the widening attack on Western culture in our schools," manifested among others by the multicultural curriculum adopted by New York State in 1989, on the grounds— by the education commissioner's own admission—that "[t]he assimilationist ideal worked for ethnic peoples who were white but is not working nearly as well for ethnic peoples of color." To avoid its impending suicide, the United States must reduce the number of legal immigrants to perhaps 200,000 per year, and more should be done to stop illegal immigration, including denying automatic citizenship to the children of illegal aliens. A more cautiously worded cultural argument on behalf of restriction was set forth by George Kennan: "Just as water seeks its own level, so relative prosperity, anywhere in the world, tends to suck in poverty from adjacent regions to the lowest levels of employment. But since poverty is sometimes a habit, sometimes even an established way of life, the more prosperous society, by indulging this tendency, absorbs not only poverty into itself but other cultures in the bargain, and is sometimes quite overcome, in the long run, by what it has tried to absorb."[48]

The most notable attack on the mainstream perspective was launched by Peter Brimelow, a senior editor of both *Forbes* and *National Review,* initially in a 1992 cover article in *National Review,* subsequently expanded and published as a book by Random House in 1996 with the personal endorsement of its publisher, Harold Evans.[49] An overblown tirade that earned its British immigrant author the dubious distinction of being hailed as "the new Madison Grant," *Alien Nation* marked the ascent to respectability of an explicitly white-supremacist position that echoed the rantings of Brimelow's acknowledged mentor, the late ultra-Tory M. P. Enoch Powell, but had hitherto been confined in the United States to shadowy groups. Reminiscing that "[n]ot so long ago, the literature of egregious bigotry was treated like pornography," Jacob Weisberg suggested that *Alien Nation* may do for immigrant-bashing what Charles Murray's *The Bell Curve* did for racism, "make it respectable."[50] Widely reviewed in the foremost newspapers and magazines, the book propelled its author to immediate celebrity status as a quick-witted reactionary talking head, and sold over 60,000 copies.

The more interesting question is not why Brimelow, but why the considerate treatment he received? Although many proponents of restriction sought to distance themselves from the book, "one could sense a collective sigh of relief on the part of at least some restrictionists" for whom *Alien Nation* "opened up a space for expression on this highly volatile subject and has perhaps served to diminish somewhat the power the threatened charge of 'nativism' possesses in immigration-related discourse."[51] Indeed, while deploring Brimelow's scurrilous rhetoric and acknowledging his limited as well as often sloppy factual foundation, mainstream reviewers nevertheless recommended that he be taken seriously. For example, while charging that Brimelow profoundly misunderstands American culture, Michael Lind suggested in the *New Yorker* that the questions he raises about the effect of immigration on national culture "are not in themselves illegitimate." Jacob Weisberg observed similarly in *New York* that, although contrary to Brimelow's gloomy prediction, "America isn't a multicultural society," immigration is nevertheless a source of genuine problems, and hence, "We need to caulk the cracks along the border, downgrade the preference for non-immediate family and come up with federal help for immigrant-swamped regions."[52] In passing, Weisberg also wryly suggested a moratorium on right-wing Brits.

While distancing themselves from Brimelow's blunt racism, mainstream conservatives sought to reconcile the cultural anxieties they shared with their economically motivated support of immigration by emphasizing the imperative of assimilation. John O'Sullivan, under whose editorship *National Review* emerged at the vanguard of restrictionism, in effect an outlet for the Federation for American Immigration Reform and American Immigration Control Federation perspectives, insisted that the United States is not merely an "idea" but a "nation," whose identity "remains at the moment more cultural than ethnic," founded on "the universalization of British culture." He went on to argue "It is possible to become an American," no matter what one's genetic roots, "in a way it is not possible to become a Slovak or a Pole." Acknowledging his debt to Arthur Schlesinger Jr., Russell Kirk, Lawrence Auster, and Peter Brimelow, he rejected Horace Kallen's "cultural pluralism" as a "precursor doctrine of multiculturalism" and argued, "In real life, what was important was the assimilation to a WASP norm." Elaborating after the campaign for Proposition 187 got underway and criticizing conservatives who opposed it, he explained further "that a multiethnic society can succeed only if it is also a monocultural society." In a similar vein, Harvard's Stephan Thernstrom objected to Brimelow's assertions that recent immigration has been "huge" and that it is "systematically different from anything that had gone before," but invoked him in support of his own contention that "our society may be much less capable of absorbing newcomers than in the past" because "the melting-pot ideal has been under assault and the concept of 'Americanization' is frowned upon in enlightened circles."

A particularly coherent expression of this perspective was formulated by Linda Chavez. Rejecting "current talk of a new 'alien nation' " as "no less fantastic" than the "Passing of the Great Race" scare of the 1920s, she stressed, "Assimilation—not race—is the issue and deserves more attention and reinforcement than it currently receives in the public policy debate." Similarly, insisting on the legitimacy of cultural concerns, Nathan Glazer urged that they not to be abandoned to the Brimelows, and seized the opportunity to promote good old American pluralism: the "assimilatory powers of America" remain strong and most newcomers wish to be incorporated, but the process is being jeopardized by the extension of affirmative action beyond African Americans as well as the adoption of multiculturalism. Incorporation would function more effectively by reducing numbers, notably illegal immigration.[53] A rhetorically shriller version of this stance was subsequently elaborated by Samuel Huntington.[54]

Between Scylla and Charybdis

Thanks to the ongoing debate, as the Clinton administration was taking shape, the possible policy choices were clear, but it was much less evident how a Democratic president might make them without incurring heavy political costs. There was widespread agreement on the need to deter illegal immigrants, with only some of the Latino national organizations holding out in the name of civil liberties; but there were many options regarding appropriate means, notably whether to put teeth into employer sanctions and institutionalize government-issued identity papers. Positions on legal immigration ranged from maintenance of the status quo to drastic cutbacks; family reunion was the fat most accessible to trimming, but this would antagonize Latinos, who constituted a critical electoral prospect for the Democratic Party. There was a confrontation in the making over the rights of legal immigrants as well: whereas in the past quarter of a century, their social citizenship had steadily expanded to largely equal to that of the native-born and naturalized, there were growing calls to exclude them from most welfare programs.

The administration also inherited a huge bureaucratic mess. Shortly after it took over, the Committee on Government Operations issued a devastating critique of the INS, charging that the agency "has not done a good job" with regard to both border control and the provision of services to immigrants, thereby antagonizing both restrictionists and immigrant advocates. The findings of government auditors "have been so consistently negative and the problems so pervasive" that in its 1992 report the Department of Justice identified the INS as its "No. 1 'high risk' area." The problem originated at the very top: "Most Attorneys General not only don't know anything about immigration, they don't have the slightest interest" in the subject.[55] Although every area was found to be highly problematic, the main issue was that "we've effectively lost control of the southwest border." Despite an 82 percent increase in Border Patrol funding over the 1986–1991 period, the proportion of agent time devoted to control activities decreased from 71 to 60 percent, and they avoided patrolling areas known for high levels of illegal entry and drug smuggling, invoking a shortage of appropriate vehicles. The agency also ignored departmental requirements for employee screening, and consequently its staff was particularly vulnerable to corruption.[56] Moreover, the INS had no way of implementing deportation proceedings, or of detaining "the millions of aliens who are subject to detention or who have been ordered deported." A number of witnesses, including former Commissioner Leonel Castillo, also charged that the INS suffered from an "enforcement bias" that "had an adverse effect on the ability of the agency to provide quality services" in other areas, notably the processing of asylum applications, employment authorizations, naturalization interviews, and status adjustment requests, and that INS enforcement "had a terrible effect on the civil and human rights of Latino U.S. citizens living in the border region." Several of them suggested that the enforcement and service functions were so incompatible that serious consideration should be given to their separation. Independent researchers reached similar conclusions.[57]

Asylum policy turned into a battleground as well. In the face of indications that the growing number of applications reflected the increasingly routine use of asylum as a device for securing entry, as far back as 1981 the Reagan administration had undertaken to deter claims by requiring persons without proper documents to demonstrate "defensively" to an INS examiner that they should not be apprehended and deported because they qualified as refugees; and if allowed to enter, undocumented applicants were jailed pending their formal hearing. Initially the "defensive" requirement appeared an effective deterrent, as new asylum filings declined and the backlog shrank every year from 1984 through 1990. However, a series of court decisions to the effect that Central American claimants had been rejected in an overly summary fashion imposed additional procedural guarantees and abruptly expanded the backlog. This was of considerable benefit to marginal applicants because an unadjudicated affirmative claim "appeared to be a ticket to indefinite residence, along with an authorization to be employed, in the United States," which took on unprecedented value after the imposition of employer sanctions.[58] Following suggestions from human rights organizations, at the beginning of the Clinton administration the INS stationed some of its trained asylum officers at major airports to provide a preliminary screening so that those with strong claims might be released into the community pending their hearing. However, in the face of this, William Slattery, INS district director for New York, initiated in cooperation with FAIR a campaign to deter "defensive" asylum claims, arguing in a series of unauthorized television interviews that jailing was ineffective and expensive, and hence that the INS should regain authority for summary exclusion.[59]

Concurrently, the United States also continued to admit an annual quota of refugees from specified groups. Although under the 1980 law the government was obligated to make individual determinations of their qualification under the "well-founded fear" criterion, INS officials assumed that Soviet Jews,

Armenians, and certain Vietnamese automatically met the test. However, in the mid-1980s, the Reagan administration's attorney general Edwin Meese III began requiring that members of these groups also be subjected to individual examinations, thereby sharply reducing the proportion granted refugee status. In response, Senator Frank Lautenberg secured the enactment, by a spectacular 97–0, of an amendment to the Foreign Aid Appropriations Act of 1989 providing that people fleeing from Indochina as well as Jews and Evangelical Christians residing in the Soviet Union be awarded refugee status upon showing a "credible basis for concern about the possibility" of persecution, rather than the more demanding "well-founded fear." The amendment was subsequently renewed in 1990 and 1992 over objections from Senator Alan Simpson.

Shortly after assuming office, President Clinton ordered a review of immigration policy to be conducted by Vice President Albert Gore with members of Congress from both parties. As an indication of the administration's commitment to the upgrading of the INS, he appointed as commissioner an unusually experienced professional, Doris M. Meissner, who had served as a senior manager within the agency in the early 1980s and subsequently conducted research on immigration at the Carnegie Endowment.[60] Concurrently, the president appointed the Commission on Immigration Reform (USCIR) called for by the 1990 immigration law. Scheduled to begin reporting in 1994, it was chaired by former Texas Representative Barbara Jordan, who had gained considerable attention during the Watergate hearings, with Susan Martin, a well-known immigration analyst with experience in previous commissions, as her executive director. Although it included some avowedly pro-immigration members, the Commission's makeup afforded the prospect of control-minded initiatives.[61]

Reflecting the mood in the country at large, restrictionist proposals quickly surfaced in the new Congress, but made little progress as control of both houses remained in Democratic hands.[62] In July 1993 the president formulated a navigation plan designed to avoid both Scylla and Charybdis. Proclaiming, "We must say 'no' to illegal immigration so we can continue to say 'yes' to legal immigration," he asked Congress for an additional $172.5 million to cover the first phase of a multiyear plan "to protect our borders, remove criminal aliens, reduce work incentives for illegal immigration, stop asylum abuse, reinvent and revitalize INS, and encourage legal immigrants to become naturalized citizens."[63] The plan was inaugurated quite dramatically on the morning of September 19, when the INS chief of the El Paso district, Silvestre Reyes, launched Operation Hold the Line, which sought to put an end to unauthorized border crossing by imposing a Border Patrol blockade around the urban sections of the district, to be supplemented by a 1.5-mile steel fence along the border. This wreaked havoc with a series of events planned by the civic leaders of El Paso and Ciudad Juarez in anticipation of the approval of NAFTA on the theme "We are all *Fronterizos*," culminating in a "Day of Unity," when the two mayors were scheduled to sign a "Good Neighbors" convention. Instead, the mayors denounced the "Berlin Wall" as sending the wrong message to Mexico, and the celebrations were canceled.[64] However, Reyes himself parlayed his role into a successful election to Congress in 1996.

Operation Hold the Line was the preview of a more comprehensive border enforcement plan unveiled by Attorney General Janet Reno and Commissioner Doris Meissner in February 1994, involving the deployment of 5,000 agents, a 40 percent increase over the present number, along major crossing points in California, Texas, and Arizona, where the administration would erect more effective physical barriers as well. They also announced the installation of a computer system that would reduce the time for processing an alien by as much as 75 percent, and fingerprint identification technology that would flag criminal aliens and provide unprecedented data on recidivism.

The administration's tough stance, confirmed a few months later by the publication of its policy agenda, *Accepting the Immigration Challenge,* extended to asylum as well.[65] The goal was to achieve determination at the moment of entry, or at most within ten days, as against current delays of as much as eighteen months, and to render applications less attractive in order to reduce their number and prevent further backlogs. As elaborated by the administration's principal consultant, Professor David Martin, subsequently appointed general counsel of the INS, the plan provided for the expedited exclusion of "defensive" applicants, as urged by Senator Simpson, but leaned slightly toward the advocacy side by entrusting the process of determination to trained asylum officers rather than border inspectors, and providing for a review by officials of the INS. Priority was to be given to new applications, and work permits denied to new affirmative applicants unless the government took more than six months to resolve their case. Affirmative applicants without authorization to be in the United States (that is, undocumented border-crossers or visa overstayers who presented themselves voluntarily) who were turned down would immediately be put into deportation proceedings, much as defensive applicants. Published in the *Federal Register* in late March 1994, the Martin reforms evoked objections from human rights advocates, but were promulgated later in the year and took effect in January 1995.[66]

In its own interim report, issued in September 1994, the Jordan Commission endorsed the administration's innovative strategy for border control but opposed cutting welfare for legal immigrants. In an assessment prepared for the Commission, a team of social scientists reported that in its first year, Operation Hold the Line substantially deterred illegal crossings into El Paso, but that its effect weakened over time; it was strongest for workers from the immediate region but less effective for long-distance labor migrants who simply shifted to crossing points beyond the blockade.[67] One of the team members commented subsequently that Operation Blockade's success (the operation consisted of the reinforcement of border controls along the Rio Grande in the El Paso vicinity) demonstrated that "[c]ontrolling illegal immigration is a policy option the U.S. government has chosen not to pursue, partly because of lobbying efforts by myriad special-interest groups," thereby victimizing the communities that must care for the immigrants and the immigrants themselves.[68]

The Commission also stressed the need to revive employer sanctions and set forth "a measured strategy for developing a new system for verifying that individuals are authorized to work in the United States." Skirting the controversy surrounding the notion of a national ID card, it suggested that "the most promising option for alleviating the fraud and discrimination found in current verification procedures is a computerized registry based on the social security number," and it recommended launching a careful pilot project whereby employers could check the validity of these cards by telephone.[69] In contrast with the border policy recommendations, however, this "drew fire from both conservatives and civil libertarians."[70] More than three dozen prominent conservative figures, including Milton Friedman and William Kristol, immediately sent a letter to Republican members of Congress warning that the cost of a computer registry would run in the billions of dollars.

Trial Run in California

The need for vigorous action on immigration was suddenly made more urgent by developments in California, a vital element of Bill Clinton's victory. The widespread uneasiness provoked by the ongoing wave was hardly surprising, as this constituted an unprecedented experience for the West Coast. Throughout the first half of the twentieth century, most of the state's newcomers were old-time Americans, and even the European-born usually arrived after a period of seasoning elsewhere; Mexicans came as well, but were discounted as marginal "birds of passage," whose presence did not affect the community's identity. Things changed dramatically from 1960 onward, when the state's foreign-born population escalated from 1.3 million (9 percent of the total) to 6.5 million in 1990 (22 percent).[71] More immigrants, overwhelmingly Hispanic and Asian, landed in the 1980s than in the three previous decades combined, and California received nearly one-quarter of all those legally admitted in the United States. Over half of the 3 million illegals granted amnesty under IRCA resided there as well. The transformation was most dramatic in Los Angeles County, whose foreign-born population shot up from 11 percent of the total in 1970 to nearly 33 percent two decades later, turning the city into "a giant jigsaw puzzle" of mono-ethnic neighborhoods "that no one knows how to put together anymore."[72] Both the legal and illegal flows continued to increase in the 1990s despite the onset of a devastating economic crisis occasioned by the collapse of the real estate boom and the abrupt retrenchment of defense spending on aerospace. The weight of immigration was further enhanced by a shift in the balance of population movement, whereby in 1991–1992 California lost 41,000 more residents to other states than it received from them.

The emergence of immigration as a hot issue in the politically most important state was the result of a deliberate experiment to turn latent antiforeign sentiment into political capital, facilitated by the state's tradition of direct democracy. In 1984 voters approved by 71 percent a ballot initiative directing the governor to write a letter to the president expressing the state's opposition to the multilingual ballots mandated by Congress, and two years later, following a well-financed campaign by Palo Alto software millionaire Ron Unz, they adopted by 73 percent a constitutional amendment declaring English to be the state's sole official language. Albeit engineered from above, this clearly expressed widespread uneasiness in the face of the transformations of the cultural landscape. Although the Los Angeles riots of April 1992 were widely represented as a black-white conflict, the first victims were Latino residents, and a substantial number of Latinos and Asians were targeted later on, suggesting that the riots "provide stark evidence of the way in which immigrants provided the perfect scapegoat for American populations frustrated with developments in their society."[73]

Pete Wilson, the longtime mayor of San Diego, who throughout his two terms in the U.S. Senate relentlessly advocated an expanded guest worker program, was elected to the governorship in 1990 and soon talked about as a presidential candidate in the wake of Richard Nixon and Ronald Reagan. However, his prospects sank abruptly along with the defense industry and grew even gloomier in the wake of the riots, when he stood lower in the polls than any of his predecessors. His fate appeared sealed by the Democratic sweep of 1992, when Bill Clinton became the first Democrat to carry the state since Lyndon Johnson in 1964, and both Barbara Boxer and Dianne Feinstein were elected to the Senate. All bets for 1994 were now on State Treasurer Kathleen Brown, the "New Democrat" daughter and sister of popular governors.

Seeking to make a comeback, Governor Wilson seized upon illegal immigration as the scapegoat. With the benefit of research provided by FAIR, he proclaimed that the use of public schools and public hospitals by undocumented immigrants constituted a heavy burden for the state and local governments, with the educational cost alone estimated at some $1.5 billion annually.[74] Early polls indicated that the "unfairness" theme played particularly well with swing voters, notably white suburbanites, rural independents, and Democrats.[75] In August 1993 Wilson published a widely advertised "Open Letter" to President Clinton, in which he demanded sweeping measures against illegals and called for a constitutional amendment to repeal the Fourteenth Amendment's provision making everyone born in the United States a citizen, so that this might be denied to the American-born children of illegal immigrants. Subsequent polls confirmed that illegal immigration was a sure bet.[76] National prospects were promising as well: among adult Americans expressing an opinion, 47 percent favored a proposal to stop providing government health benefits and public education to illegal immigrants and their children, and a year later the proportion rose to 55 percent.[77]

On top of its other miseries, in January 1994 California was hit by a devastating earthquake. Initially running well behind his likely Democratic challenger, the governor seized the opportunity provided by the disaster to boost his job performance ratings and further improved his standing by securing a record-breaking federal aid package. Concurrently, Harold Ezell, a former regional chief of the INS, and William King, executive vice president of Americans against Illegal Immigration, launched a drive to place Proposition 187 on the ballot, with financing from the state Republican Party.[78] Cleverly dubbed "Save our State" (SOS), the initiative would deny social services, nonemergency health care, and education to illegal immigrants. It further required public educational institutions to verify the immigration status of both students and their parents in order to exclude illegal residents, and provided for the creation of a system to check the status of applicants for all state services.[79] Proposition 187 further required all service providers to report suspected illegal aliens to California's attorney general as well as to the INS, and made the manufacture, distribution, and use of false documents to obtain benefits or employment a felony. No ordinary law, it could not be amended by the California legislature "except to further its purposes" and then only by a recorded supermajority vote in each house or by another voter initiative.

Although critics were quick to point out that the goal was not really to rid California of illegal immigrants, and that it did not contain a single word against the employment of undocumented workers or about sanctions for employers who violated existing laws on the subject, Proposition 187 evidently struck a responsive chord as it immediately scored at the 62 percent level among prospective voters.[80] The subsequent campaign on its behalf triggered a huge backlash against immigrants generally and prompted a series of restrictionist initiatives by members of the state's congressional delegation.[81] However, in the *National Review* article noted earlier, Peter Skerry warned, "It would certainly be ironic if conservatives were so misled by a desperate politician who has been no friend of theirs. For while Wilson's proposals won't stem the tide of illegals, they will certainly alienate Mexican Americans and other Hispanics whom conservatives have been courting so assiduously for some years now."[82]

Despite a challenge from the right by Ron Unz, in the end Wilson easily won the nomination. Facing a quandary, as the polls indicated that most of their electorate endorsed the initiative as well, the Democrats called for vigorous border control and the enforcement of employer sanctions as more appropriate measures for controlling illegal immigration; however, their defensive stance in turn antagonized the Latino community, whose support was vital for Brown's chances.[83] As the election campaign itself got underway, support for Proposition 187 continued to climb, reaching around 70 percent in September. Since California was expected to be crucial for President Clinton's reelection, the initiative attracted considerable national attention.[84] But whereas its popularity at the grassroots level within the state was echoed by indications that an overwhelming majority of the national public thought the government was not doing enough to control illegal immigration, among the elite media there was a remarkable convergence from both sides of the spectrum against the proposal. For example, the measure was characterized by the *New York Times*' conservative columnist, William Safire, as a "nativist abomination" that would deny education to children of illegals and turn teachers into government informers, "and for what—to put hard-working immigrants in costly jails?" Meanwhile, in the liberal column slot, Anna

Quindlen dismissed it as "a simplistic answer to a complex problem" that "makes a mockery of everything that has ever lured people to this country," and in an editorial the paper itself characterized the initiative as "indecent."[85] The measure also evoked negative comments from *Time* magazine and was denounced by two leading Republican conservatives, Jack F. Kemp and William J. Bennett, as "fundamentally flawed and constitutionally questionable"— prompting Governor Wilson to respond, "Those are two guys who have been in Washington too long."[86]

As the elections neared, the Democratic administration "tried to help the anti-proposition forces without pitting Clinton against California's white middle class."[87] Conceding that it was not wrong for Californians to want to reduce illegal immigration, or to view this as a national responsibility, the president dispatched Attorney General Janet Reno to publicize the ongoing plan to beef up controls along the border. Shortly afterwards, the INS launched with considerably hoopla Operation Gatekeeper around San Diego, patterned after the previous year's El Paso initiative.[88] Dismissed by Wilson as "tinkering" and "a Band-Aid for a hemorrhage," it enabled the administration to announce soon afterwards that INS arrests—the conventional but inherently flawed index of illegal alien traffic—had been reduced by 30 percent. The administration also helped fund a study by the Urban Institute that found that while illegals drained about $2 billion a year from the budgets of major destination states, at the national level legal and illegal immigrants together contributed a $25 to $30 billion surplus by way of their tax payments. Wilson responded by demanding an immediate "down payment" of $1.8 billion to compensate California for the costs attributable to leaky borders. Proposition 187 intruded into the Senate race as well by way of an exchange of "nanny scandals."[89]

Opposition came mainly from the Latino community, with some Asian participation. Although mainstream Chicano organizations and politicians opposed mass demonstrations as counterproductive, some radical groups organized a mid-October march and rally in Los Angeles, which drew an estimated 70,000–100,000.[90] Departing from its usual avoidance of involvement in American domestic politics, the Mexican government entered the fray as well, instructing its envoy to assail the measure in a speech in Los Angeles and subsequently launching an advertising campaign to remind Californians of Mexican contributions to their state.[91] As polls indicated a softening of the affirmative camp, in late October Wilson stepped up his offensive, proposing that every Californian be required to obtain an official identity card for presentation when seeking a job, entering school, or applying for nonemergency health care, and calling on Washington to set up a national system to that effect. The governor's suggestion was immediately denounced by Ms. Brown as "Big Brother, big government"; by MALDEF in Los Angeles as "a form of fascism"; and by the executive director of the southern California branch of the ACLU as "the kind of thing they tried in South Africa." Even some of Wilson's allies privately expressed dismay.[92] In the final heat, while endorsing the governor for reelection, the *Los Angeles Times* called his support for Proposition 187 "hopelessly wrong" and called for its defeat, while Los Angeles Mayor Richard J. Riordan, the state's second most powerful Republican, crossed party lines to support Senator Feinstein over Republican opponent Michael Huffington.[93]

In the end, Proposition 187 carried by 59–41 percent, and both Wilson and Feinstein were comfortably reelected. Although approval by a hefty majority was widely interpreted as a dramatic manifestation of the new restrictionism, the deliberate engineering from above cast doubt on its significance as a measure of the public will. A study based on exit-poll data suggested that while support for Proposition 187 was an example of "cyclical nativism," provoked primarily by California's economic downturn of the early 1990s, "endogeneity" played a part as well, as the issue of illegal immigration was politicized by the gubernatorial and senatorial candidates.[94] Moreover, statewide support was markedly weaker than the 73 percent who approved the "English-only" Proposition 63 of 1986. Exit polls suggested that a good proportion of the supporters were aware that Proposition 187 would never pass constitutional muster, but viewed it as a "message" urging the federal government to do a better job of protecting U.S. borders: "To many it was not the *ends* that were critical, but the *means* that would get public dialogue flowing."[95]

Whereas support reached 63 percent among white voters, African Americans and Asians were evenly divided (47 percent) and Latinos strongly opposed (23 percent).[96] Latino support came from Latinos who speak English and are citizens, and whose integration fostered identification with whites.[97] However, while race/ethnicity weighed heavily in the electorate's choices, it was not determinative. Prop. 187 ran significantly better in counties with the highest percentages of Republican registration and behind in those with the lowest; but it was difficult to isolate the effect of partisanship from that of whiteness, as the Republican Party gets only a small share of the minority vote. Catholics were more opposed than Protestants, reflecting the public position of Catholic Church officials as well as the fact that Latinos are largely

Catholic. Among social characteristics, education emerged as most significant: whereas 66 percent of those with a high school education or less voted in favor, only 53 percent of those with a college education did so; but, as the *Los Angeles Times* pointed out, "Since the college educated were also less likely to be competing for the same jobs as the undocumented, it is hard to tell whether this is a matter of greater toleration or greater economic security." Attempting to sort out the weight of "nativism" and of economic considerations by using the vote for the earlier Proposition 63 in good times as a proxy for "unadulterated nativism," Karin McDonald and Bruce Cain established that economic insecurity contributed significantly to support for Proposition 187.[98]

Immediately after his reelection, Governor Wilson moved to bar illegal immigrants from receiving prenatal services and from entering nursing homes, thereby freeing what he claimed was $90 million a year in funds for legal residents; on the other hand, in an appearance at the Heritage Foundation in Washington shortly afterwards, he revived the idea of a Mexican guest worker program, albeit insisting that families would be excluded.[99] Although the enactment of Proposition 187 prompted zealots to enforce it according to their own lights, advocacy organizations immediately countered by filing suits in state and federal courts. A San Francisco superior court judge temporarily restricted the state from expelling an estimated 300,000 illegal immigrant children from public schools pending a hearing, and a similar order was subsequently extended to public colleges and universities. The Los Angeles City Council voted to join legal challenges and directed its employees to continue providing services to all in the meantime; and the city's policy chief also announced that although the initiative required local law enforcement officials to report to the INS any illegal alien arrested for other reasons, there would be no policy changes in his department. However, the board president of the Los Angeles Unified School District was threatened with recall and a number of other local politicians subsequently backed away from public opposition to Proposition 187. As widely anticipated, on November 21, 1995, U.S. district Judge Mariana R. Pfaelzer threw out most provisions of Prop. 187 as unconstitutional, either by virtue of *Plyler v. Doe,* or because they were preempted by federal laws, as was the case with the sections pertaining to law enforcement.[100]

Most ominously, as a political experiment, Proposition 187 revealed the strategic value of challenging the established boundaries of social citizenship. Although the measure's educational provision was obviously unconstitutional, it highlighted the fact that the Constitution does draw a clear line between citizens and aliens; in particular, the Fourteenth Amendment distinguishes between "the privileges and immunities of citizens of the United States," which include a broad range of substantive civil rights and benefits, and the narrower guarantee of "the equal protection of the laws" extended to all persons.[101] Pointing to Proposition 187's potential for restricting undocumented aliens' access to public services, Kitty Calavita suggested that this was similar to what occurred during earlier bouts of nativism, but that it now focused "almost single-handedly on immigrants as a tax burden, a focus that is unusual, if not unique in the history of U.S. nativism."[102] In fact, this was more of a reenactment of nativist history than she allowed, as the theme of "immigrants as a tax burden" preceded even American independence and played a key role in the first nativist era; but this time around, the theme's strategic value was enhanced by its congruence with a more general attack on the welfare state.[103]

By the same token, Proposition 187 revealed the value of citizenship to those it targeted, as more Latinos voted than in any previous state election.[104] The political integration of Latinos generally—except for Cubans—and of the Mexican-born in particular had hitherto proved a slow and uneven process.[105] The 1992 presidential electorate encompassed 4.2 million Latinos, constituting 3.7 percent, a record high and a 14.2 percent increase in Latino turnout compared to 1988, exceeding the 11.4 percent turnout increase for the electorate as a whole. However, Latinos still were overrepresented among nonvoters (14.6 percent) and had the lowest turnout of the four racial groups. Although this has been attributed to "culture," notably by John Tanton, who warned that immigrants bring with them a tradition of *mordida,* Susan Gonzaléz Baker has demonstrated that the low turnout is largely attributable to the Latino population's demographics—young, with less formal education and low income, characteristics associated with lower registration and turnout among the general population as well. Once eligible and registered, Latinos "demonstrate a healthy enthusiasm for the ballot box": their registration and turnout more than doubled from 1972 to 1992, a far greater rate of increase than for the African American population, and turnout in the 1994 congressional elections was two and a half times higher than in 1974. By virtue of their geographical concentration, these changes had a significant impact on outcomes at the state and local levels.[106] Revealing simultaneously the vulnerability of noncitizens to politically induced disasters and the political power of citizenship, Proposition 187 precipitated a rush toward naturalization. At the time, nearly 40 percent of the Latino population in the United States were foreign-born, and only 18 percent of those eligible had naturalized; for Mexicans, the proportion was only 15 percent. But the following year, application rates doubled nationwide and escalated fivefold in California and other key states; and nearly one-third of the new citizens were of Mexican origin.[107]

The Revolution That Failed

The California outcome was vastly overshadowed by the Republican conquest of Congress for the first time since 1952.[108] Immigration itself did not figure prominently in the Republican program; the 1992 platform did not address it, and as of mid-1994, some leaders favored the status quo (Jack Kemp and Phil Gramm), some advocated radical restriction (Bob Dole and Pat Buchanan), but most were "agnostic." However, in the face of growing demand for reduction among the general public, it was expected that the Republicans would move in that direction as well, and the success of Proposition 187 encouraged the restriction-minded to press forward in the new Congress.[109] Prospects appeared excellent, as the change of majority moved them into key committee positions while throwing the immigrant-minded lobbies, fashioned by the experience of operating in a Democratic legislative milieu, in total disarray. The House Judiciary Committee was now chaired by Henry Hyde, a conservative pro-lifer not previously interested in immigration, leaving Subcommittee Chair Lamar Smith a free hand. A conservative Texan who thought that the 1965 immigration regime had been "unduly influenced" by the civil rights struggle, and proclaimed, "The American people don't want immigrants coming here to live off the taxpayer," Smith had long striven to reduce family and refugee admissions while enhancing procurement of the highly skilled. He now hoped a bipartisan legislative solution could be forged so that immigration would not "become entangled with the 1996 presidential race."[110] Smith's position was reinforced by the presence on his subcommittee of John Bryant, another conservative Texan, as the ranking minority member, thanks to whom he had the votes "to do just about anything he wanted."[111] Moreover, early in his reign, House Speaker Newt Gingrich announced his support for legislative action in this vein and appointed a Congressional Task Force on Immigration Reform chaired by Elton Gallegly, one of the most strident restrictionists, whose California district had overwhelmingly supported Proposition 187. The Clinton administration chimed in with a declaration by the president in his 1995 State of the Union message that "in every place in this country [Americans] are rightly disturbed by the large number of illegal aliens entering our country," and that he would work with Congress to speed their deportation.[112]

Waving their much-touted "Contract with America," the Republicans undertook with deliberate speed to dismantle the welfare state. Under Newt Gingrich's forceful leadership, by the end of March the House had passed a welfare reform bill projecting savings of $17.5 billion over five years, achieved in part by denying most needs-based federal benefits to noncitizens. Senate Majority Leader Bob Dole initiated a similar measure, affording the prospect of a $15.8 billion haul by requiring, among other things, that the traditional "affidavits of support" provided by sponsors, hitherto ruled by the courts as not legally binding, be cast in the form of an enforceable contract and demonstrate ability to maintain the immigrant at an income 200 percent above the poverty line. This was approved by the Senate on September 19, 1995, by an overwhelming 87–12. There were also moves to make legal immigrants subject to "deeming," whereby their sponsor's income was taken into consideration in determining their own. While this ran counter the trend of recent judicial decisions, which steadily reduced the distinction between lawful alien residents and citizens, it revived and moved to the fore one of the oldest fundamentals of American immigration policy, emphasized from the founding onward, namely, the assurance of self-sufficiency as a condition for admission.

In the spring of 1995, the Jordan Commission issued its report on legal immigration, which prompted *St. Louis Post-Dispatch* columnist Stephen Chapman to comment that the body "created to make it politically easier for Congress to deal with the issue, has chosen to side with the exclusionists."[113] Tackling head on the key issue that SCIRP had skirted, the Commission, with only one dissenter, recommended elimination of the family-based admission categories that contributed to "chaining," notably brothers and sisters of citizens, as well as adult (married and unmarried) sons and daughters of citizens and permanent residents. Moreover, the admission of parents would require a legally enforceable affidavit of support.[114] This was expected to reduce annual admissions by nearly one-third to about 550,000, including 400,000 family members, 100,000 skill-based immigrants, and 50,000 refugees (not including asylum adjustments), with a transitional extra 150,000 to accommodate the existing backlog. It was evident that the narrowing of family reunion would affect most heavily recent immigrants, and especially Mexicans.[115]

The Commission's recommendations, together with those of the Gallegly Task Force, formed the basis of a bill introduced by Lamar Smith on June 22 with 38 cosponsors, including his subcommittee's ranking Democrat Bryant. As Frank Sharry, director of the National Immigration Forum (NIF), reminisced, "In the spring of 1995 we didn't think we could turn the restrictionist tide, couldn't stop the reform juggernaut, and it looked like something close to zero immigration was on the verge of being enacted. . . . Smith wrapped himself in the Jordan Commission's cloak and wanted to get the bill to the floor by the end of the year."[116] Gallegly also proposed allowing states to deny education to the children of illegals, as in Proposition 187, in anticipation of the overturning of *Plyler v. Doe* in the near future. Although he also sought to abolish birthright citizenship for the children of illegal aliens, this was a largely symbolic move, as its implementation would require a constitutional amendment nullifying the Fourteenth Amendment.

In the Senate, however, the Republicans faced internal difficulties. Alan Simpson, who returned as subcommittee chair, planned extensive hearings on a new bill focusing on illegal immigration, providing for tighter employer sanctions, hopefully jointly with Smith, with whom he enjoyed a warm working relationship.[117] However, Judiciary Committee Chair Orrin Hatch was on record as opposing sanctions, and Simpson's political effectiveness was open to question.[118] As markup time approached, a Family Immigration Coalition was assembled to block Simpson's measure. With the negative votes of Edward Kennedy and Paul Simon in the bag, only two more were needed; since the remaining Democrat, Dianne Feinstein, was doubtful as she had lobbied hard for membership in the subcommittee to demonstrate her toughness on immigration, they focused on finding a responsive Republican. Using the previous year's overwhelming vote for the Lautenberg Amendment as an arm-twister, they secured the support of Republican Senator Charles Grassley of Iowa, where the Lutheran church had resettled many Vietnamese.[119] The subcommittee approved the bill on June 14 with the support of Feinstein, who thereby earned her toughness points. Simpson then steered his bill through the Judiciary committee, reshaping it to make it more like the House's.

The "strange bedfellows" syndrome now entered into play with a vengeance. As Jack Kemp and William Bennett's opposition to Proposition 187 already indicated, responsiveness to the concerns of business interests led many Republicans to oppose a crackdown on illegals and their employers, as well as any drastic reduction of admissions. In the Senate, Hatch now joined Kennedy in urging the repeal of employer sanctions.[120] Governor Wilson himself spoke out in support of a new guest worker program and House Majority Leader

Richard Armey, an economist by training, hesitated to shut off "the supply of willing and eager new Americans," declaring that "If anything we should be thinking about increasing legal immigration." Speaker Gingrich, driven by the polls and conscious of California's importance to the party, was initially more supportive of Smith, but changed his mind after a meeting with representatives of caterers, fast-food establishments, and restaurant chains.[121] Beyond this, the party leadership was increasingly concerned that a blunt restrictionist stance would alienate Asian and Hispanic voters who, albeit heavily Democratic, were not as out of reach as African Americans. Moreover, a number of Republican governors warned Speaker Gingrich that the elimination of welfare benefits for legal immigrants would impose heavy burdens on their states.

With the prospect of a significant reduction of immigration in the offing, the concerned economic interests organized as "American Business for Legal Immigration" to lobby on behalf of the procurement of workers in high-tech fields. Seizing the opportunity, the libertarian Cato Institute brought them together with La Raza and MALDEF, their Asian-Pacific counterparts, as well as the now Hispanic-oriented AFL-CIO, all seeking to maintain existing family preferences.[122] Since most Democrats could be counted on to vote against restriction, the coalition focused largely on driving a wedge between Simpson and the Republican leadership. Key to their success was support from Michigan Senator Spencer Abraham. A Christian Arab American from the Detroit area, former deputy chief of staff to Vice President Dan Quayle, and elected to the Senate in 1994 as a defender of small business, Abraham thought Simpson "truly misguided" on free-market and ethnic grounds, and promoted the slogan "Immigrants yes, welfare no." Another important ally was Senator Mike DeWine of Ohio, an Irish Catholic pro-lifer who opposed the family cutbacks sought by Simpson because of their association with population-limiting organizations. Welcoming an unusual opportunity to cooperate, the Christian Coalition and the Catholic Bishops Conference joined in as well.

Leading the defense on the liberal side, the NIF sought to split the House bill into legal and illegal segments, anticipating that while the latter was certain to pass with a wide margin, the former could be blocked by a similar coalition of business interests, family-minded ethnics, and anti-abortion activists. With the Judiciary Committee sharply divided along ideological lines and several of the Democrats not reliable on immigration, they enlisted the support of its chair, Henry Hyde, a devout Roman Catholic who was notorious for his successful advocacy of an amendment prohibiting the use of federal welfare funds to pay for abortions. However, Lamar Smith kept things under tight control, offering business a compromise on employment-based visas if they would stop trying to split the bill. Business accepted the deal, leaving their coalition partners high and dry, except for small victories on asylum. Maneuvering continued into the fall, and Smith's rewritten bill was eventually approved by the Judiciary Committee on a largely party-line vote (21 Republicans and 2 Democrats versus 10 Democrats).[123]

Drawing on the support provided by the Jordan Commission, after completing his illegal immigration bill, Senator Simpson announced in November 1995 that "curbing, even stopping, illegal immigration is not enough," and introduced an Immigrant Reform Act. Much like Smith's, it reduced the intake by about one-third by drastically narrowing family admissions, as the senator had sought to do ever since his arrival on the scene in 1980. Contrary to the preferences of most Republicans, however, it also lowered employment-based recruitment by about one-third and imposed a $10,000 tax on every immigrant hired. The bill further strengthened provisions for deportation on grounds of "public charge" and provided for the creation of a national database to verify identities as well as summary exclusion. It also imposed a statutory ceiling of 50,000 refugees, less than half the number scheduled for admission in the current year—an approach "designed to cause the Lautenberg amendment to implode without being repealed"—and imposed a thirty-day deadline after entry for all asylum applications.[124] It was reported by the subcommittee on a 5–2 vote, with only Kennedy and Simon dissenting, and the two bills were then combined into one. In a *coup de théatre,* Senator Simpson then announced he would not seek reelection, thereby turning enactment of the proposal into his valedictory. Although he sought a committee markup before Christmas, Chairman Hatch held back until February 1996. In the intervening period, opponents of the asylum deadline addressed themselves to Spencer Abraham; although he himself was unwilling to take the lead in striking the deadline, he indicated he would support such a move and suggested DeWine as its initiator.[125]

On January 9, 1996, President Clinton vetoed the recently enacted welfare legislation, in part because it imposed restrictions on the eligibility of legal aliens for federal benefits and allowed the states to determine which aliens could receive them at the state and local levels. Scrambling for position, the administration initially supported most of the USCIR's recommendations for reducing family immigration.[126] However, at the behest of John Huang, Democratic National Committee vice chairman, the president announced on the occasion of a major Asian American fundraising dinner that he favored "suspending" sibling immigration rather than eliminating it. The administration also opposed Simpson's statutory cap on refugees on the grounds that this was related to the conduct of foreign policy, a presidential responsibility, and while endorsing summary exclusion, it objected to its mandatory application. It strongly opposed the deadline for asylum because this would make U.S. law inconsistent with its international obligations; moreover, since applications had fallen by 57 percent as a result of the Martin regulations, and the INS was now able to conduct interviews with 84 percent of new claimants within sixty days of their application, the deadline was an unnecessary over-reaction.

On the Senate side, the assault on restriction was launched in late February when Senator Spencer Abraham announced he would lead an effort to split Simpson's bill, in keeping with the strategy pursued by the strange bedfellows. Although Simpson sought to preserve his cuts in family reunion by restoring those in employment-based admissions, this merely angered the Democrats and affirmed their resolve to defeat him. This time, business remained faithful to its partners, and ultimately even Chairman Hatch voted with Abraham and DeWine against the frustrated loner from Wyoming on admission cuts, while reinforcing the coalition on behalf of welfare denial. DeWine's amendment eliminating the asylum deadline carried as well, with only Simpson voting against it; and another amendment striking summary exclusion failed on a tie vote, suggesting it might succeed on the floor. The bill was split on March 14, and Simpson had to choose between legal and illegal immigration, as he would not be given enough floor time to bring up two pieces of legislation before retiring.

The coalition was still seeking to split the House bill as well. A few days before the Judiciary Committee vote, Lamar Smith offered a deal to refugee advocates: if they gave up their opposition to a statutory ceiling, he would amend the bill so as to exclude the ex–Soviet Union Jews and others covered by the Lautenberg Amendment from the 50,000. Reckoning that this revealed Smith's desperation, they turned down the offer and the ceiling was killed. Meanwhile the opponents of a reduction in family immigration managed to bring the Christian Coalition into the fray and the bill was split by 238–183, a larger margin than immigration advocates had dared hope for.

Gallegly now reintroduced his amendment to permit states to exclude illegal alien children from school; thanks to support from Speaker Gingrich, it was approved 257–173, signifying in effect congressional endorsement of Proposition 187. However, employer verification evoked the usual resistance from business-oriented legislators; as Representative Sonny Bono, the entertainer turned restaurateur, explained in the course of a hearing, "All I wanna do is sell a plate of pasta. . . . Why do I have to be the bad guy?" Yielding to this plea, his colleagues approved an amendment providing that an employer would be deemed to have complied if there was a "good faith" attempt, notwithstanding a "technical or procedural failure" to actually meet the requirement. Quickly dubbed the "Sonny Bono" amendment, this amounted in effect to a reenactment of the old "Texas proviso."[127] Approved by an extremely broad 333–87 vote, the final bill retained the six-month deadline for asylum applications, summary exclusion, as well as antiterrorism provisions, and set the affidavit requirement for family sponsorship at 200 percent of the poverty level, which was estimated to preclude 44 percent of sponsors, thereby limiting family reunion privileges to the better off and in effect restricting legal immigration on a class basis. By the late spring of 1996, a trade-off between the Democratic president and the Republican Congress neared completion, providing for a crackdown on welfare and reinforcement of the "deeming" requirements in exchange for maintenance of the family reunion regime. This left the Gallegly amendment barring illegal children from the public schools as the only source of a likely veto.[128] The new measure cleared the House by a comfortable 228–101 on July 31, and the Senate on the next day by an equally overwhelming 78–21. President Clinton indicated he would sign the conference agreement into law despite his objections to restrictions on legal immigrants, for which he would send corrective legislation to Congress.

A signal turning point in both social and immigration policy, Title IV of the Personal Responsibility, Work Opportunity, and Medicaid Restructuring Act (P.L. 104–193) replaced Aid to Family with Dependent Children (AFDC), whose principal beneficiaries were low-income female-headed households, with Temporary Assistance for Needy Families (TANF), which promoted job preparation, work, and marriage, and was limited to a total of five years within an individual's lifetime. It confirmed the established ineligibility of illegal and nonimmigrant aliens for most welfare benefits. As for legal immigrants, it imposed greater responsibility on sponsors by expanding "deeming" requirements, making affidavits of support legally enforceable by government agencies providing means-tested social services. It also imposed stricter standards of eligibility for most welfare benefits and authorized states to deny legal immigrants access to certain types of assistance, including Medicaid and TANF. Refugees remained eligible for both in the first five years and afterwards at the state's discretion. The total cost savings to the federal government was estimated at $20–25 billion between 1997 and 2002, approximately 45 percent of the projected savings of the entire welfare reform bill.[129]

Concurrently, Congress completed its work on widely supported antiterrorism legislation, which included a House-imposed "expedited exclusion" provision more severe than that of the immigration bills, providing authority to remove any alien who had crossed the border without valid documents, even decades earlier, and allowing the State Department to designate "terrorist" organizations whose members and representatives were excludable from the United States. The law also toughened provisions regarding criminal aliens and added alien smuggling to the list of crimes to which the Racketeer-Influenced Corrupt Organizations (RICO) regime applies.

Whether deliberately meant to hurt immigrants or enacted merely on grounds of fiscal opportunism, the welfare measure severely narrowed the boundaries of social citizenship.[130] Yet some thought it did not go far enough. On the eve of the 1996 Republican convention in San Diego, FAIR organized a conference on "Immigration Reform Awareness Week" in the venue city, where grassroots immigration control activists had an opportunity to mingle with Peter Brimelow, John Tanton, and former Colorado Governor Richard D. Lamm.[131] However, to the restrictionist camp's consternation, pro-immigration Jack Kemp emerged as the party's vice presidential nominee, in effect constraining use of immigration as an issue.

Immediately before the August recess, Senators Hatch and Arlen Specter (R-Pennsylvania) had come up with a compromise on the Gallegly amendment by grandfathering illegal immigrant children enrolled in school by September 1996; however, the president reiterated his intention to veto the pending immigration measure if this was included. The showdown persisted, with the Republican leadership hoping that a Clinton veto would anger the California voters, while some of the California Republicans, feeling electorally vulnerable, urged the leadership to drop the Gallegly amendment. The conferees, of whom nearly two-thirds were from California, Texas, and Florida, then fashioned a harsh bill that included the most restrictive provisions of the House and Senate measures, but without the Gallegly amendment, which the House Democrats managed to exclude from the final version. The House approved the result on September 25 by 305 to 123, with all but 5 Republicans voting for it, along with 76 Democrats. The bill preserved the Senate's streamlined asylum and deportation proceedings and struck a compromise on employer sanctions; "deeming" for admission purposes was kept at 200 percent of the poverty level, but sponsors who fell between 125 and 200 percent were allowed to get a cosponsor to vouch for the remainder.[132] The Gallegly amendment was then approved as a stand-alone measure, 254–175, but with no prospect in the Senate.

While the immigration bill awaited action in the Senate, eager to recess for the campaign, Democratic strategists reckoned that if the president signed it, he would lose some of the liberal and recent citizen vote; and immigrant advocates hoped to kill it altogether because its welfare provisions were even worse than the welfare law's. As the deadline neared, the president adopted an unexpectedly tough negotiating posture, demanding the elimination of the new employment discrimination provision and of the deeming requirements, prompting Senator Simpson to quip, "The White House and its Democratic allies have moved the goalposts."[133] Finally Speaker Gingrich agreed to lower the sponsor income requirement to 125 percent as well as to drop other provisions pertaining to deeming, verification, and sanctions regarding naturalization. Incorporated into the Fiscal Year 1997 Omnibus Consolidation Appropriations Act, the Illegal Immigration Reform and Immigrant Responsibility Act of 1996 (IIRIRA) was signed by President Clinton on September 30.

Besides reiterating the welfare law's delegation of authority to the states to deny benefits to legal immigrants and stiffening sponsorship requirements, IIRIRA focused largely on enforcement, along the lines urged by the Jordan Commission. In addition, it stiffened civil and criminal penalties for illegal entry as well as for assisting it, and limited the ability of aliens to challenge INS decisions and deportation rulings in federal court. An important judicial innovation pertained to expedited removal, similar to the process instituted by the recent Antiterrorism and Effective Death Penalty Act.

Half Full, or Half Empty?

Assessments of the 1996 enactments largely concur that economic motives do not provide a sufficient explanation and that they can best be understood as reactions "against the 'browning' and 'yellowing' of America."[134] But given the salience of these identitarian concerns, it is striking that the measures in question did not reduce admissions outright, prompting David Reimers to conclude, "In all, it appears that the pro-immigration lobby won the 1996 battle. . . . If indeed, the problem is too many immigrants, then the restrictionists were thoroughly defeated."[135] "Thoroughly" is too strong; although the enactments did not reduce the legal intake, they did reverse the ongoing trend toward lower and more diffuse boundaries of citizenship by distinguishing its several domains along the lines drawn by T. H. Marshall, and imposing more demanding conditions for gaining access to them.[136]

The most evident innovation pertained to social citizenship, hitherto taken for granted as an entitlement available to legal immigrants in their capacity as "persons" by virtue of the Fourteenth Amendment. Lamar Smith's proclamation that "immigration is not an entitlement, it is a privilege" resonated with recent discourse on welfare in which, as suggested by Nancy Fraser and Linda Gordon, entitlement figured as a pejoratively charged ideological term, "associated most commonly with the conditions of poor women 'who maintain their families with neither a male breadwinner or an adequate wage.' "[137] The parallel was not an artifact of critical interpretation, but was enunciated quite literally in Smith's own admonition, "Just as we require *deadbeat dads* to provide for the children they bring into the world, we should require deadbeat sponsors to provide for the immigrants they bring into the country."[138]

While representing 9 percent of households receiving welfare in 1994, noncitizens accounted for 23 percent of the drop by 1997.[139] The noncitizens' level was higher than the citizens' in 1994, and despite the decline, remained higher in 1997; however, among poor households, the levels were the same in 1994 but by 1997 the immigrants' was below the citizens'. In addition, an Urban Institute study found evidence of "chilling effects" that discouraged nonnaturalized immigrants from claiming welfare benefits even when they remained eligible, and notwithstanding the exemption of refugees, the decline among them was as steep as for the noncitizen population as a whole.[140] The study anticipated that the "chilling effects" would be amplified as nonrefugee immigrants entering after 1996 would be ineligible for public benefits for at least five years.

As it was, with the robust national economy insuring higher state tax revenues and shrinking welfare rolls, in the wake of his reelection President Clinton was able to rally congressional support for restoring some of the benefits cut by the 1996 laws, and the Balanced Budget Act provided SSI payments to legal immigrants who were already in the United States and receiving benefits at the time the law was enacted. This was subsequently extended to cover food stamps for immigrant children and the elderly as well. Benefiting from the same favorable circumstances as the federal government, most of the immigrant-receiving states used their own resources to replace federal funds during the first five years, allowing time for many of the immigrants to become citizens.[141] These developments in turn prompted Representative Gallegly to publicize General Accounting Office (GAO) data showing that the proportion of recently naturalized immigrants receiving federal benefits during fiscal years 1996 and 1997 was higher than for native citizens, with the largest difference in California, and to introduce a measure denying public assistance benefits to naturalized citizens altogether. However, his proposal went nowhere.[142]

As anticipated, the courts intervened to alleviate the policy's impact as well. The New York Court of Appeals ruled in 2001 that the state may not deny Medicaid benefits to immigrants regardless of their date of arrival, and on June 25, 2001, the Supreme Court neutralized some of the harsh judicial regulations imposed by IIRIRA. Speaking for a 5–4 majority, Justice John Paul Stevens ruled that noncitizens who pleaded guilty to crimes before 1996 should not be automatically deported—albeit leaving in limbo those who did *not* plead guilty but were convicted—and in a second decision, the Court said the government could not detain immigrants indefinitely, even if they had committed crimes, if their home countries refuse to take them back.[143]

As noted, seasoned observers had surmised that the denial of welfare benefits to legal immigrants was likely to stimulate acquisition of U.S. citizenship, so that actual cost savings would be smaller than the measures' advocates had promised. In the event, the Clinton administration, very much aware of its electoral interest in the matter, actively promoted naturalization. Under the "Citizenship USA" crash program, part of an effort led by Vice President Gore to reduce bureaucracy, the INS cut the average wait for swearing-in after qualifications for naturalization were met from two years to six months; applications rose from an average of 300,000 a year before fiscal year 1994 to 1 million in fiscal year 1996, many of them from the pool of those amnestied in 1986. As the English and civics tests constituted intimidating hurdles, a 1994 measure exempted persons over sixty-five with twenty years' residence, as well as those suffering from certain disabilities; and the INS subsequently broadened the exemption by extending the language waiver to persons over fifty with at least twenty years' residence (and only fifteen for those over fifty-five), also allowing them to satisfy the civics component in their own language through an interpreter. Consequently, a spectacular 1.2 million naturalization certificates were awarded between October 1995 and September 1996, eliminating a massive backlog of nearly 500,000 cases.[144]

With respect to the civil rights dimension of citizenship, Stephen H. Legomsky has asserted that the statutes enacted in 1996 represent "the most ferocious assault on judicial review of immigration decisions" ever launched by Congress.[145] Together, the three laws changed established practices "by creating new removal courts that allow secret procedures to be used to remove suspected alien terrorists; by shifting the authority to make 'expedited removals' to immigration inspectors at ports of entry; and by setting unprecedented limits on judicial review of immigration decisions."[146] One provision of the IIRIRA, whose constitutionality was affirmed by the Supreme Court in 1999, strips federal courts of jurisdiction to hear legal challenges to deportation process and institutes a more restrictive regime that deprives lower courts of jurisdiction over resident aliens' claims of selective enforcement of immigration laws against aliens who belong to groups characterized by the State Department as terrorist or Communist organizations.[147]

The restrictionists also attempted to elaborate boundaries of cultural citizenship, a dimension altogether ignored by Marshall, with language as the marker, Spanish as the target, and the elevating of English to the unprecedented status of exclusive official tongue as the objective. By the mid-1990s, nearly half the states enacted laws or constitutional amendments to that effect, and a movement got underway in the 1980s to enact a national English language constitutional amendment as well.[148] Advocates also sought to reverse language legislation enacted in the wake of the civil rights movements, notably the requirement of voting facilities in languages other than English and the provision of bilingual education. Seizing the opportunity provided by Republican control of Congress, before leaving for the 1996 summer recess, the English language militants secured passage by the House of an English Language Empowerment Act. The first "official-English" measure at the federal level, it banned most federal publications in languages other than English, repealed bilingual voting rights, mandated English-only naturalization ceremonies, and shielded English speakers from "discrimination." Proclaimed by its Republican advocates as "essential to preserve the nation's 'common bond' and 'empower' immigrants by motivating them to learn the language," the measure was condemned by Democratic opponents "as divisive, mean-spirited, and potentially unconstitutional in its restrictions on minority access to government."[149] However, although the bill was championed by Speaker Gingrich with an eye to the fall campaign, the Senate, mindful of a veto threat by President Clinton, declined to consider the measure.

Nevertheless, despite the restrictionist rationale on behalf of the enactments, their effect in this regard was very limited. Assessment of the new laws' impact on immigration was no means an easy task because the principal players engaged in a protracted numbers game. The Clinton administration's

INS estimated that there were 5.1 million undocumented immigrants in the United States as of January 1997, reflecting a large inflow in 1988–1989, a steep decline in 1990–1992, and relative stability in 1993–1996.[150] It also reduced its estimate of the average net increment of unauthorized residents from 275,000 a year to 135,000, on the grounds that previous estimates of return migration were unduly low. Accordingly, as of 2000, there were 5.5 million unauthorized residents.[151] Given the Census Bureau's estimate of 3.8 million "residual foreign born" in 1990, this amounted to a net increase of 1.7 million for the decade, thus tacitly suggesting that despite all the criticism to which it was subjected, the Clinton-era INS achieved considerable progress in controlling the borders.

A year later, however, the Census Bureau, charged with achieving more accurate counts of elusive population groups to insure a fair, constitutionally mandated decennial reapportionment, estimated that the foreign-born population numbered 28.4 million, up from 19.8 million in 1990, with net immigration of all kinds thus amounting to 8.6 million for the decade as a whole.[152] Bureau specialists also agreed on a "consensus estimate" of 2.25 million unauthorized, nearly one-third above the INS figure.[153] In June 2002 the bureau announced the official result of Census 2000, according to which the foreign-born population of the United States numbered 31.1 million, an increase of 11.2 million over 1990.[154] Albeit somewhat lower than the research team's estimate, the official count nevertheless indicated average net immigration, legal and unauthorized, of at least 1.1 million a year for the decade as a whole. This clearly exceeded the previous historical record of 8.8 million established in 1901–1910. There was a large increase in employment-based immigration and a considerable decrease in refugees and asylees, in keeping with the strongly articulated preferences of the Republican Congress.[155] The main source of change regarding the latter was not legislation, but the continuing waning of the Cold War, which reduced Washington's incentives for generous action on grounds of foreign policy, leaving mostly groups that benefited from powerful domestic advocates.[156] However, with regard to the most hotly contested issue, family reunion, all efforts to the contrary notwithstanding, the only possible conclusion was, *plus ça change . . .*

But that was by no means the last word. In January 2003, the Bush administration's INS released its own revised estimate of a net addition of 5.5 million unauthorized immigrants in the 1990s, bringing the total as of 2000 to 7.0 million. Additions to the unauthorized population by way of uninspected border crossing or violation of visa terms amounted to 7.1 million, ranging from a low of 564,000 in 1993 to a high of 968,000 in 1999, with some 1.6 million leaving the pool by way of return, legalization, or death.[157] The report constituted a major indictment of INS performance during the eight Clinton years: the estimate of an annual net addition of 275,000 unauthorized, which their predecessors had reduced to 135,000, was too low rather than too high, and the numbers had grown under the Clinton watch. Moreover, the makeup of those who "left" the unauthorized pool indicates that control played a very limited role in bringing this about.[158] In short, the Clinton administration's highly publicized "Operations" were a total failure, and despite repeated assurances, the INS failed to bring unauthorized immigration under control.

While these estimates should be viewed skeptically, the most reliable data available indicate unambiguously that the restriction-driven policy enactments of the 1990s had little effect, as both the legal and unauthorized flows surpassed those of the previous decade.[159] Family reunion retained the upper hand and, since it was generated mainly by recent arrivals, it remained heavily Hispanic, with Mexico retaining the position it achieved in the 1960s as the largest source of legal immigration, as well as of unauthorized entry. Legal immigration continued to shift away from western Europe and even from the southern European countries on whose behalf the 1965 law was designed, toward eastern Europe, whose citizens were for the first time in many decades free to leave; Central and South America; Asia; and to some extent Africa, hitherto almost entirely absent from the scene. Poland and the ex–Soviet Union were now the leading European sources—although it should be noted that they were followed by the United Kingdom; the Caribbean and Central America grew over the 1980s; and Asia remained at the same level as in the 1980s, with the Philippines still in the lead, but with a shift away from Korea and toward China and India.

"It's Immigration, Stupid"

"Five years on, it takes some effort to recall the full fury of the anti-immigration hurricane that hit Washington in 1996," the *New York Times'* immigration specialist reflected in July 2001.[160] Remarkable for both its speed and amplitude, the swing was triggered largely by political rationality. As one commentator put it shortly after the elections, "Journalists transfixed by Republican battles over abortion are looking in the wrong place: It's immigration, stupid, that is emerging as the most divisive issue in the GOP coalition."[161] Not surprisingly, those believing themselves negatively affected by immigration were most keenly perceptive. Recalling Kevin Phillips's 1968 pronouncement that in American politics "demography is destiny," and his prediction that as the result of ongoing population changes, the Democrats' long-dominant Roosevelt coalition was giving way to an "emerging Republican majority," Peter Brimelow and Ed Rubenstein warned readers of the *National Review* that the Republican "Phillips Coalition" of the West and South was now itself being undermined by the immigration that got underway even as Phillips made his initial prediction.[162]

While Proposition 187 helped Pete Wilson secure his reelection, it jeopardized the Republican Party's future in California, and this was compounded by the policies subsequently enacted by the new Republican Congress. In 1996, Bill Clinton carried the state with 51.1 percent, a gain of nearly six points over 1992, while his Republican challenger, Senate Majority Leader Bob Dole, managed a mere 38.2 percent, a better showing than George Bush's humiliating 32.1, but nothing to write home about. And although the Republicans gained three congressional seats over 1994, the Democrats upped their share of the state's total congressional vote from 47.5 percent to 49.6. Most spectacularly, in the 46th district's highly publicized showdown, Loretta Sanchez, a Hispanic woman, beat the well-established conservative Republican Robert K. Dornan.

The Democratic surge in the politically most important state was largely attributable to mobilization of the Mexican American electorate. Electoral participation by Hispanic citizens rose from 41 percent in 1990 to 50 percent in 1994—a nearly 25 percent increase.[163] The 1996 naturalization wave produced 318,000 new citizens in seven southern California counties, a number equivalent to the population of the state's ninth largest city, and raised the Latino proportion of the potential electorate from 9 percent in 1994 to 13 percent in 1996.[164] Although the mobilization was clearly driven by outrage, it was considerably facilitated by the Clinton administration, very much aware of its interest in the matter. Proposition 187 and the 1996 laws caused a further surge of naturalization and voter registration, which further enhanced the weight of the new immigrant vote in the electoral balance. Since those who envisioned immigration as a threat to the American future already voted Republican, there was nothing to gain and something to lose from actively pursuing restriction.

Despite their evident Democratic bent, Hispanics were not completely beyond Republican reach; for example, in the 1997 Los Angeles mayoralty contest, when the Hispanic electorate for the first time surpassed the black,

Richard J. Riordan garnered 60 percent of their votes in his successful bid for reelection. However, Governor Wilson further alienated them from the Republican Party when, in response to the U.S. District Court's March 1998 ruling that core provisions of Proposition 187 were unconstitutional, he persisted in filing an appeal. In the intervening period, millionaire Ron Unz launched a new initiative to end bilingual education in the state.[165] While many delegates at the fall 1997 state Republican convention endorsed it, the chairman opposed it vehemently for fear it would further alienate Hispanic voters.[166] As it was, Proposition 227, dubbed "English for the Children," was approved in June 1998 by a hefty 60.9 percent of the electorate; and despite the state chairman's opposition, it evidently appealed to his rank and file, as Republican support rose to 77 percent.[167]

The 1998 state and midterm congressional elections were the California Republicans' Waterloo. Despite his attempts to distance himself from the legacy of Proposition 187 and avoid immigration more generally, Attorney General Dan Lungren, Wilson's appointed heir, lost the governorship to Gray Davis by a twenty-point landslide; the Republicans gave up all but two of the statewide posts; and their share of the legislature shrank to such an extent that California emerged as the nation's most Democratic state after Hawaii.[168] With term limits forcing the retirement of numerous incumbents, there was a substantial increase in the number of Latino candidates, and the Democratic surge swept them into office. Cruz Bustamente became the first Hispanic lieutenant governor, and Antonio Villaraigosa the first Hispanic speaker of a legislature that included seventeen Hispanic Democrats and one Republican; former State Senator Art Torres became chairman of the state Democratic Party. Democratic Senator Barbara Boxer was reelected by a whopping 53 percent majority, and her party also secured twenty-eight of the state's fifty-two House seats, a gain of three over 1996. California's new congressional delegation included five Hispanic Democrats but not a single Republican. These emerging political realities quickly fed back on policy making, leading to the curtailment of most of the measures provided for by Proposition 187.[169] Stalwarts subsequently tried to revive the initiative by elevating it into a state constitutional amendment to be placed on the November 2000 ballot, but did not succeed.

While clearly demonstrating the critical importance of the Latino vote, the elections also indicated that its potential was far from fulfilled. Hispanics now made up about 13 percent of the California electorate, up from 6 percent in 1990, whereas whites shrank from 85 to 64 percent; and their turnout was

4.3 percent higher than for a matched group of whites, at all levels of age and education. However, still only two out of five registered Hispanics voted, and it was estimated that 48 percent of those eligible to register had not yet done so.[170] The national implications were sobering as well, both because of California's weight and in view of the growing Hispanic populations in key states such as Texas, Florida, New Jersey, and Illinois.

In Washington, the most important unsettled issue remained the "chaining effect" occasioned by the established family reunion regime. Although Congress remained in Republican hands, the Cato Institute's Stuart Anderson told the *Washington Post* that since both houses had rejected cuts, "members are unlikely to revisit this contentious issue against next year," and even harsh critics of illegal immigration, such as Representative Dana Rohrbacher of California, now pronounced Senator Simpson's proposal to cut legal entries "very harmful."[171] Nevertheless, in its final report, issued in September 1997, the USCIR—with Warren R. Leiden once again dissenting—reiterated its earlier recommendations for narrowing family reunion so as to roll back annual admissions to about 550,000.[172]

In preparation for its report, the commission asked the National Research Council (NRC) to undertake a review of the economic, demographic, and fiscal effects of immigration under various scenarios.[173] The panel's assessment turned out to be broadly positive, providing solid material for partisans of the status quo while in effect pulling out the rug from under the USCIR's own feet. Should the flows (legal and illegal) continue at the ongoing level, the population would reach 387 million in 2050, with immigration accounting for two-thirds of the addition. Persons aged sixty-five years and older would approximately double, but would constitute a much higher proportion of the population were immigration to decrease. Asians would rise from 3 percent of the total to 8 percent, and Hispanics from about 9 to 25 percent; however, by the middle of the twenty-first century, ethnic and racial lines would be "even more blurred" as the result of increasing intermarriage between immigrants and natives. The panel was guardedly optimistic with regard to social integration generally, as initial findings suggested that "some recent immigrants and their children—especially Asian Americans—match native-born whites in education and occupation, although not in incomes, fairly quickly." No links were found between immigration and crime rates. While newcomers tended to cluster in homogeneous neighborhoods, as their socioeconomic status rose, "most immigrants disperse from the ethnic neighborhoods where they first tend to settle, and integrate with the overall population." Moreover, contrary to widespread opinion, English-language acquisition was proceeding apace.

With regard to the protracted debate over costs and benefits, the NRC concluded that immigration unquestionably produced net economic gains for the population as a whole, but that its fiscal impact was more mixed. Immigrants were more costly than natives during childhood, because immigrant families have a higher birthrate and because of bilingual or language-assisted education, but less expensive in old age, so that over a lifetime, the differences tended to balance out. In conclusion, "the long-run fiscal impact is strongly positive at the federal level, but substantially negative at the state and local levels," especially in heavily immigrant states. However, the NRC's assessment was hardly the final word on these matters.[174]

Albeit shared by policy analysts of every stripe, the USCIR's recommendation for narrowing family reunion failed to find takers in Congress, prompting Gimpel and Edwards to conclude, "In the absence of a truly national outcry demanding restrictions on legal immigration, the future of policy . . . rests largely in the hands of the Washington interest group community," and that the restrictionists "would not have the energy and organization to match their opposition anytime in the foreseeable future."[175] A somewhat more accurate interpretation is that, independently of the state of public opinion, the political climate changed because of calculations by Republicans and hitherto vacillating Democrats. Chastened by the most recent developments in California, the Republican 106th Congress was more reluctant than ever to tackle immigration issues. In the Senate, Simpson retired and the subcommittee chair was assumed by Spencer Abraham, who signaled his sharply different stance by appointing as his chief aide Stuart Anderson, the very man who helped cement the previous year's strange bedfellows coalition against the reduction of legal immigration.

With the Clinton impeachment trial overshadowing all other activity throughout most of 1998 and the economy escalating to unprecedented heights, immigration waned from the headlines and the mood shifted away from restriction. A 1999 Gallup Poll reported that only 44 percent of Americans favored reduced immigration as against 65 percent four years earlier, and that this was the lowest level since 1977.[176] Although an array of symbolic measures continued to be tossed into the legislative hopper, none got very far, except for an attack on the INS, whose survival became another bone of political contention between the Clinton administration and its opponents. In its final report, the USCIR advocated abolishing the agency altogether and assigning its duties to other bodies, prompting the House Appropriations Committee to direct Attorney General Reno to develop a restructuring plan by April 1, 1998.[177] Viewing this as a move to turn immigration into an issue in the forthcoming midterm elections, the administration strongly opposed abolition, arguing that the agency had recently achieved significant victories in tightening the asylum system as well as the border with Mexico, and hence deserved a chance to clean its own house. In keeping with this, a consulting firm recommended separating the service and enforcement missions within the existing agency.[178] Additional alternatives generated by the Immigration Subcommittee got nowhere because its parent committee had bigger fish to fry, notably impeaching the president of the United States, but it was evident that the agency was not much longer for this world, despite the unusually intelligent professional leadership of its latest head, Doris Meissner.[179]

Concurrently, as economic recovery continued, there were renewed demands for additional foreign workers, prompting the restrictionist Center for Immigration Studies to acknowledge that their camp was now "completely on the defensive."[180] With both parties vying for Silicon Valley contributions, there was considerable support within Congress for enlarging high-skilled temporary visas (H-1B) as well.[181] Torn between opposition from its friends in organized labor and the desire to please its other friends in Silicon Valley, the Clinton administration eventually endorsed the increase, but sought to strike a deal by coupling it with a measure granting legal permanent resident (LPR) status to half a million temporary protected persons from El Salvador, Guatemala, Honduras, and Haiti, under the 1997 law that accorded this to Nicaraguans and Cubans. In addition, it proposed making nearly 1 million illegal immigrants in the United States since the enactment of IRCA in 1986 eligible for legalization. Albeit endorsed by what the *Wall Street Journal* also termed an "odd-bedfellows collection of conservative, liberal, and labor groups," the Clinton proposal was opposed by most Republicans.[182] In May, the House Judiciary Committee approved the increase in H-1B visas, but beat back legalization; and in October, the Senate voted 96–1 to provide nearly 600,000 new workers for the high-tech industry over the next three years.[183]

With the unemployment rate at its lowest in thirty years, but also continuing evidence of union decline in the traditional industrial sectors, organized labor's reassessment of immigration issues, underway within garment manufacturing since the 1980s, reached the mainstream. In mid-1999, AFL-CIO President John J. Sweeney appointed a committee to review the federation's immigration policy, acknowledging that the current system for punishing employers of undocumented workers had failed and was often used to intimidate workers as well as interfere with unionization efforts. This was endorsed by the Executive Council In February 2000, preparing the ground for official endorsement at the AFL-CIO's biannual convention in December 2001.

As the 2000 presidential elections approached, it became fully evident that the decisive factor in bringing about a major shift in immigration policy was the rapidly rising value of Hispanic votes in the American political marketplace. In California, which emerged once again early on as the coveted prize, in late 1998 "virtually the entire statewide Republican elected establishment" lined up behind Texas Governor George W. Bush, who had just won reelection with 49 percent of his state's Hispanic vote.[184] While the *New York Times* correspondent commented, "Still, 2 of every 3 new Hispanic voters in Texas register Democratic," even a reader weak in arithmetic could infer that by the same token, one out of every three registered Republican, a proportion that held considerable promise.[185] From the outset, the Texas governor distanced himself from the restrictionist stance of his party's congressional wing and comfortably joined the company of the strange bedfellows. Announcing that he was "against the spirit" of Proposition 187 and would not have supported such a measure in Texas, he defended *Plyler v. Doe* by declaring, "I felt like every child ought to be educated regardless of the status of their parents."[186] A January 1999 poll indicated that Pete Wilson's presidential bid was supported by a mere 5 percent of likely voters as against 20 percent for Bush, and Wilson dropped out two months later.[187] In the course of his first swing through California as a declared presidential candidate the following June, one of Bush's stops was the Plaza de Mexico, a Hispanic area at the Del Mar Fair near San Diego, where he pointedly delivered some of his remarks in Spanish. Later on he said he would consider "guest worker programs and other ways for immigrants to come into the country," but would insist on immigration controls and a waiting period for citizenship. Without explicitly rejecting employer sanctions, he did so tacitly by endorsing strict border controls on the grounds that "it is far more compassionate to turn away people at the border than to attempt to find and arrest them once they are living in our country illegally."[188]

The rich political returns that Spanish brought Governor Bush prompted the California Republican Party to invest $10 million in an unprecedented campaign of commercials in that language, inspiring a journalist to predict that "the attention bestowed on Hispanic voters this year would equal that lavished on 'soccer moms' in 1996."[189] Analysts were quick to point out that the states with the largest Hispanic populations, California, Texas, New York, and Florida, accounted for 144 of the 270 electoral votes needed to win the White House. Although the Democrats evidently held the upper hand, the game was by no means one-sided; the Republicans were encouraged by one of their surveys, which showed that 45 percent of Hispanics are "hard core Democrats" and 35 percent hard-core Republicans, indicating a 25 percent "target group" of undecided voters, and prompting the pollster to conclude, "We have now moved from the Southern strategy we pursued for the last three decades . . . to a Hispanic strategy for the next three decades."[190] The California Republican finance chairman largely concurred, pointing out, "The explosive growth of the Latino population and the ever-increasing percentage of Asian voters in California is changing the dynamic," but cautioned, "It's also important not to misread the results of the 1990's: Pete Wilson did get elected twice."[191] However, that was long ago: a March 2000 poll indicated that 54 percent of Californians now considered immigrants a benefit versus 34 percent who saw them as a burden, and only 2 percent thought immigration an important issue, as against 20 percent in 1998.[192]

In the March 2000 primary, Vice President Gore, Arizona Senator John McCain, and Governor Bush each took about one-third of the California votes; in the hypothetical fall contest, Gore and Bush split even, thus enhancing the value of the Hispanic one-tenth of the electorate. Gore got half of the Hispanic votes in the primary, but in the hypothetical contest, Bush drew a respectable 3 in 10 Hispanic voters, well above recent Republican statewide showings.[193] In his victory speech, Bush proclaimed, "Legal immigration is not a source of national weakness; it is a sign of national success." He subsequently courted the business community by supporting the expansion of the H-2A program providing temporary workers in agriculture, as well of the H-1B visas, and then attended a Cinco de Mayo celebration in San Diego, addressed the National Hispanic Women's Conference in Los Angeles, and met with Latino leaders in Philadelphia and Cleveland. Asked whether English should be made the country's official language, he said he supported "English-plus, insisting on English proficiency but recognizing the invaluable richness that other languages and cultures bring to our nation of immigrants," and added, "In Texas, the Spanish language enhances and helps define our state's history."

Yet in its 2000 platform, the Republican Party still adopted a mixed stance, reflecting the persistent tension between business interests, electoral opportunism, and identitarian conservatism. While restating their support for increasing H-1B visas, expanding the H-2A program for temporary agricultural workers, and rejecting calls for a more vigorous implementation of internal controls by way of employer sanctions and identity cards, they endorsed the USCIR's recommendations for sharply narrowing family reunion.[194] With Al Gore running on a platform that called for "amnesty" and for punishing "employers who recruit undocumented workers in order to exploit them," while tacitly endorsing the family reunion status quo, it is not surprising that George W. Bush got only 42 percent of the California votes to Al Gore's 53 percent.[195] Nevertheless, the Texan did win about one-third of the Latino vote nationwide, prompting his pollsters to insist that he could and must increase that share to at least 40 percent in 2004, and Hispanic advocates to suggest that "a generous program for adjusting legal status would win the administration new supporters."[196]

Immediately following the election, after resisting the idea for months, the Republicans, under the leadership of Senator Orrin Hatch, submitted a proposal on pending immigration issues to the White House, and Congress inched toward an agreement that could be included in a comprehensive budget deal, clearing the way for adjournment. The Republican shift was attributed to a desire "to be in tune" with George W. Bush, "who has tried to cultivate good relations with Hispanics Americans," and to pleas from employers eager to hire them.[197] Negotiations continued down to the wire. Finally, on Thursday, December 14, Congress approved a measure whereby up to a million immigrants who entered prior to 1982 would be eligible for legalization, moving up the deadline from 1972, but not quite to the 1986 one requested by the Clinton administration. Spouses and minor children of U.S. citizens and legal permanent residents would be allowed to come to the United States and work or, if already in the country, would not have to return home and reenter when their visa was awarded, if they had been awaiting it for more than three years. An estimated 300,000–500,000 would benefit from this provision, and another 200,000 "green card" applicants (brothers and sisters, qualified workers) would be allowed to wait for their visa in the United States as well upon payment of a fine. Farmers' organizations and labor unions also struck a compromise on a proposal to gradually grant legal residence to undocumented workers in exchange for expanding and streamlining the program that brings seasonal workers from Mexico, from 40,000 to as many as 250,000, and give them an opportunity to earn legal residency gradually as well. However, Senator Phil Gramm opposed the legalization component and "scuttled the deal at the eleventh hour."[198]

Conclusion: National Design in a Globalizing World

From the very outset, Americans were aware that immigration was destined to play a unique role in their economic and political development, and hence devoted considerable attention to the elaboration of instruments for achieving their objectives. Immigrants were required as human capital and as a vital source of demand for the immense reserves of land the founders appropriated by driving out the first inhabitants and the British monarchy. The economic perspective prompted not only a wide-open door, but also efforts to change prevailing European exit policies. However, the newcomers would also contribute to an unprecedented political experiment, a republican nation based on civic virtue. These concerns fueled a protracted debate over qualifications for admission, and on who possessed them or was capable of being resocialized in the American mold. The resulting immigration and naturalization policies were boldly inclusive, in that membership in the American collectivity was open to members of all European nations, regardless of faith or inheritance, but simultaneously brutally exclusive, closed to the "red" race by what amounted in effect to ethnic cleansing, and to the "black" one largely by way of "social death," with stray attempts to resolve the anomaly of freedom by promoting their return to Africa.[1]

Membership in the civic nation also prompted the erection of moral boundaries by way of measures to prevent the use of America as dumping grounds for the refuse of European states, notably felons, paupers, and the insane, considered unredeemable by inheritance or disposition, much as with race. Political qualifications were imposed early on as well: unrepentant Tories who did not leave of their own accord were driven out, and following the outbreak of the French Revolution, so were those who took republicanism too far. For political reasons, arising largely out of the issue of slavery, most regulations pertaining to admission and membership were located at the state rather than federal level, with the notable exception of naturalization, which involved a defiant assertion of American sovereignty. Altogether, these measures amounted to a quite literal translation of the "social contract" from a theoretical construct into a set of laws and institutions that established a path-setting baseline for immigration policy.

By virtue of its historical antecedents and the cultural inheritance shared by the bulk of its white population, the civic nation took on an "Anglo" cast. From the turn of the nineteenth century onward, this underwent vigorous Americanization, stimulated by the renewal of conflict with Britain and facilitated by a prolonged period of low immigration, attributable to events in Europe and a lack of confidence in the new nation's future. Proceeding largely within the sphere of civil society, for example by way of the anglicization of worship in the Dutch Reformed and German Lutheran Churches, Americanization amounted to the injection of an element of ethnic nationalism into the civic model.[2]

From this baseline, immigration policy evolved in response to a series of crises, arising from the conjunction of changes in the configuration shaping the "push" in the world at large, and conditions within the United States governing the "pull," with each crisis prompting a redefinition of the qualifications for membership and the elaboration of instruments to insure the appropriate selection. The first arose shortly after Alexis de Tocqueville's visit, when the pool of potential European emigrants suddenly underwent a vast expansion. Familiarity with developments in the contemporary world help us grasp the brutality of this transformation and its impact: from the perspective of European political and economic elites, population turned abruptly from a scarce valuable into an embarrassing surplus and a source of potential "voice," in relation to which "exit" beckoned as a welcome solution.[3] The commercialization of agriculture and the onset of industrialization uprooted huge rural masses, and the invention of steam, initially applied to water transport but shortly to land as well, vastly increased their mobility and linked inland regions with Atlantic ports. Population displacement was further amplified by the devastating effects of the potato disease of the late 1840s, which occasioned famine not only in southern Ireland but also throughout northwestern Europe, including the Low Countries, northern Germany, and Scandinavia.

Although the relaxation of strictures against European emigration accorded with long-standing American aspirations and was a boon to shippers as well as land developers and nascent industrialists, the expansion of the pool of emigrants to encompass more of the poor and a broader range of nationalities evoked negative reactions from defenders of the established Anglo-American version of the civic identity, focusing on the southern Irish. According to prevailing perceptions, largely derived from Britain, the Irish constituted a distinctly inferior race and presented a clear and present danger to America because of their subservience to the papacy, which at the time was vehemently denouncing liberal republicanism. The confrontation between a sanctimonious mid-nineteenth-century Anglo-American Protestantism and a demonized Roman Catholicism strikingly evokes the late twentieth-century construct of a "clash of civilizations" between the West and Islam, and more particularly European reactions to Muslim immigrants. Beyond this, the massively uprooted poor were perceived as "paupers" who willfully resisted the imperatives of the nascent market economy and hence were not suitable for membership in American society, much as the "welfare abusers" of a later period.

Lasting for the better part of two decades, the immigration crisis interacted with the issue of slavery to bring about the demise of the second party system and thus contributed to the coming of the Civil War. Although the anti-immigrant movement secured substantial electoral victories in the early 1850s, in the end it failed to achieve its objective, in that the gates were not shut and the United States turned decisively into a "nation of immigrants." However, it did secure the enactment of some barriers to free entry at the state level and the consideration of restrictionist bills by Congress. Although most of the state measures were eventually determined to be unconstitutional and the congressional initiatives did not succeed, they provided models for national legislation in the post–Civil War years, and can thus be seen in retrospect as path-shaping elements pointing the way toward a more restrictive régime. Among them was the precocious institutionalization of "remote control," whereby the United States projected its borders outward to ports of embarkation abroad and enlisted private transporters as policing agents.

The Civil War and its aftermath inaugurated another thrust of acquisitiveness, as the American hunger for immigrants expanded further in the wake of the conquest and opening of the West, the development of railroads, the progress of industry and mechanized agriculture, and the passing of slavery. This was easily satisfied as the great transformation now swept up eastern and southern Europe, while revolutionary changes in the transoceanic transportation system considerably reduced the cost of relocation and procurement.

The addition of a Pacific component made the immigration pool truly global and concomitantly rendered the American dilemma between acquisitiveness and nation-building more acute, as Asians challenged established boundaries of membership in the nation. The ensuing half-century confrontation was akin to a prolonged boxing match in which each of the contenders won some rounds, but one was steadily weakened and finally dealt an unsurprising knock-out blow: first Chinese and then Asians more generally were altogether excluded, while southern and eastern Europeans were sharply curtailed. In keeping with long-standing precedents, the boundaries of the civic nation were tightened as well to exclude unacceptable radicals and those deemed irremediably unfit in light of notions drawn from eugenicist constructs then in vogue.

This was accompanied by negotiations resulting in a slight reformulation of the nation-building recipe, away from the literally assimilationist "melting pot" to allow for a modicum of "cultural pluralism," combining proactive Americanism of the "pledge of allegiance" variety, constituting a mandatory boundary-crossing *rite de passage,* with the legitimation of hyphenated identities celebrating the retention of distinct roots, albeit in domesticated form. The settlement of the 1920s was further institutionalized in succeeding decades: while the restrictionist legislation, together with the Great Depression and the closing of the Atlantic following the outbreak of World War II, produced a prolonged hiatus in European immigration, thereby marginally contributing to bring about the "Final Solution," the New Deal fostered the incorporation of the urban working class, largely of recent immigrant origin, into the American mainstream. The massive mobilization of World War II completed the job, as it "jumbled together farm boys and factory hands, old-stock Yankees and new immigrants, rich as well as poor, Protestants, Catholics, and Jews. Many young men who had never left their rural county or urban neighborhood confronted in the army more social, ethnic, and religious diversity than they had ever encountered, perhaps ever imagined. In the year that it took to train a division, and in the months of service that followed . . . human barriers were often breached and long-lived bonds between men created. Old stereotypes withered and once-improbable friendships flowered. . . . For millions of men born during and just after the Great War of 1914–18, their experience as GIs defined their generational identity as nothing else could."[4] National integration was further reinforced by the postwar G.I. Bill, which enabled a large part of the second generation to climb into the middle class. Concurrently, however, the great migration of African Americans from the South, the expansion of Mexican "guest worker" programs, and the activation of the Puerto Rican reserve, all of which were driven by a "wanted but not welcome" strategy of economic exploitation without integration, prepared the ground for new boundary challenges in the postwar period.[5]

Institutionally, the legislation of the 1920s reversed the baseline norm of American immigration policy, bringing it in line with the one prevailing in the Westphalian state system at large: whereas hitherto entry was open unless prohibited, it was now closed unless authorized. This had the unforeseen effect of fostering more organized efforts to secure inclusion among the approved categories and of promoting immigration reform as a political issue. Hardly noted at the time was that the strategy of remote control that the United States successfully operationalized for policing transoceanic immigration was inherently inapplicable to deal with Mexico, which now emerged as the leading source of newcomers.

The 1965 legislation represented first and foremost the coming of age of the early twentieth century's "new immigration" and the institutional consecration of a shift of boundaries, whereby the United States definitively abandoned attempts to constitute itself into a "WASP" nation and redefined itself as a pan-European one, pledging allegiance to the flag under a deity that was Catholic and Jewish as well as Protestant.[6] Although categoric prohibitions against Asians were lifted as well, there was little expectation that this would generate much of a flow. However, the legislation simultaneously erected an unprecedented barrier to the immigration of West Indian blacks and Mexicans, expressly identified as problematic from an integration perspective. Concurrently, considerations of foreign policy prompted a substantial intake of refugees, initially by way of ad hoc measures and subsequently in a more institutionalized fashion, with its compass shifting in accordance with the focus of American external concerns: from western Europe to eastern and southern Europe, and then to the Caribbean, Southeast Asia, and Central America.

In the light of the protracted history of Chinese exclusion on grounds of race, which was eventually extended to Asians of every kind, and the subsequent construction of the Japanese into a savage enemy people, it is remarkable how within less than one generation, Americans unproblematically accepted a shift of their national boundaries to encompass the growing presence of East and South Asians. Instead, as the new immigration wave unexpectedly expanded to surpass all previous ones, the erupting crisis centered on the Mexican presence, and more particularly on the proliferation of unauthorized residents as well as the rising prominence of the Spanish language, provoking an unimaginative revival of ancient nativist stereotypes such as the inanities of political scientist Samuel Huntington, for whom the latest newcomers are unpromising candidates for membership in the national body by virtue of their biological and cultural inheritance, much as the new immigrants of the turn of the twentieth century were for his intellectual ancestor Henry Cabot Lodge.[7]

The crisis once again took the form of a boxing match, but with the point count to date favoring the established immigrationist title-holder rather than the challenger. What accounts for the restrictionists' limited success? David Reimers and Debra DeLaet concur in attributing this to effective resistance by an unusual coalition of business, civil rights activists, and immigrant constituencies—what I have termed "strange bedfellows." However, this is an insufficient explanation, as business and immigrant constituencies were on the scene in the 1920s as well. One major additional factor is the differing structure of the political party system. The restrictions of the 1920s were enacted by a coalition of conservative Republicans, largely from Midwestern rural constituencies, and southern Democrats, who together gained the upper hand and, once having enacted a restrictionist régime, managed to fend off attempts to change it over the next half-century. The coalition persisted even after the passing of the Republican era, as the Democratic leadership of the 1932–1948 period, dependent on southern support for its social programs, largely refrained from challenging the immigration status quo and, when it did do so in the early 1950s, failed in its attempt. In addition, for much of the period in question, organized labor stood firmly within the restrictionist camp, acting in keeping with what it construed as its class interest.

As against this, in recent times, by virtue of changes in quantity and quality, "Immigration has been translated into a redistributive issue such that votes for and against immigration policies can be predicted by reference to political partisanship." In support of their contention that this increased partisanship has arisen from the changing nature of immigration issues, James Gimpel and James Edwards point out that it cannot be attributed to incidental factors, such as the shrinking number of southern Democrats.[8] A particularly noteworthy finding is that prevailing economic conditions within electoral districts had little impact on congressional voting, and where they did, what occurred was usually the opposite of what might be expected: high joblessness led to support for open immigration policies, probably because this tended to occur in urban districts with large immigrant populations. Commenting, "Ironically, the labor market position of many ethnics may be eroded by the liberal immigration policies that their representatives support," they observe that "in the clear choice between family reunification or economic advancement, many immigrants prefer family reunification first and foremost." Representatives of black constituencies also tended to vote for immigration, despite the competition it generates. Overall, "The modern view [since the 1980s] within the labor and civil rights communities is that workers' rights and civil rights are indistinguishable."[9]

However, if partisanship were determinative, then restrictionism should have triumphed in 1996. Because of their focus on roll-call analysis exclusively, Gimpel and Edwards overlook the significance of contention over immigration within the Republican Party, arising from its dual personality as the party of business and of cultural traditionalism. It is not labor alone that changed; in launching their struggle to defend the America that was, Republican restrictionists found themselves repeatedly ambushed by the Orrin Hatches and Sonny Bonos in their midst. Whereas in the early decades of the twentieth century American industrialists gave up on European immigration as a major source of labor supply, making do instead with African Americans from the South, while agriculturalists simultaneously accelerated their mechanization and turned to Mexico, in its final decades both, as well as the expanding service sector, stood firm on insuring a continuing supply of labor, for which Mexico constitutes the most convenient source.

The late twentieth-century political configuration also differed from the earlier one in that it afforded recent immigrants a greater measure of political power by virtue of their strategic location in key states. Ironically, despite efforts to exclude them from citizenship, Hispanics, and particularly Mexican Americans, also figure in the story as targets of political opportunity. The growing Latino presence in the political arena was startling: 54 percent of the adult Hispanic population voted in 2000, as against 40 percent a decade earlier.[10] Although their voting deficit persisted, this was largely accounted for by citizenship status; when adjusting for demographic differences, for the period 1990–2000 as a whole, the Hispanic average lag in turnout of 18 percent relative to non-Hispanic whites was slashed to only 3.8 percent, and between 1994 and 2000, to merely one percentage point. Among naturalized immigrants, when social background differences are taken into account, the Hispanic deficit in relation to whites was completely eliminated, and Latinos had a higher rate of political participation than the East Asian "model minority." Whereas in the past, proximity to their native country and residence in rural areas made Mexican-born residents less inclined to naturalize, this largely disappeared with length of residence.

But the importance of recent immigrants in the American political arena was even greater than this suggests. Although they were underrepresented in the voting population because voters must be citizens, even nonnaturalized newcomers gained immediate indirect influence on national elections because, according to the U.S. Constitution, legislative districts must be based on the size of the *overall* population; and since a state's allotment determines the size of its Electoral College votes, this affects presidential elections as well. Because of their relative youth and higher fertility, new immigrants and their offspring accounted for half of the total growth in the U.S. population between 1990 and 2000, and thereby carried considerably weight in the reapportionment process. The 2000 U.S. Census, which reported increasing out-migration of California residents to other states, also revealed to what extent California depended on immigration for the maintenance of its political clout, as the foreign-born accounted for its *entire* population growth between 1990 and 2000. By 2002, Hispanics made up 12.5 percent of the national population compared to 9 percent in 1990, and the findings regarding their shrinking participation deficit in California held for the country at large as well.

A final difference between the two moments arose from the configuration of immigration itself. In the early decades of the twentieth century, from the perspective of the relevant population movements, the United States was in effect an island, whose makeup could be determined by way of remote control. Once decided upon, both Asian exclusion and European restriction were easily implemented by ordinary administrative procedures, even in the face of desperate conditions in the countries of origin. As the century closed, however, while remote control was still functional with regard to most of the world, it simply was not practicable with respect to the neighboring south, in relation to which the erection of exclusionary boundaries posed an unprecedented challenge. To overcome it, the United States would have to venture well beyond immigration policy and undertake a fundamental régime transformation.

"Los Amigos de Bush"

The containment of restrictionism perceptible in the late 1990s was confirmed in the wake of the 2000 election. In keeping with propositions to be inferred from my theoretical argument, the new Republican administration looked upon immigration principally as a welcome source of cheap labor; however, since its political conservatism also mandated commitment to law and order, brazen reliance on undocumented movement was not acceptable, and illegal immigrants should not be rewarded by way of "amnesty." In the cultural sphere, the régime's neoconservative stance was tempered by political opportunism. It was now evident that Hispanics constituted a critical electoral segment in key states, notably California, and that they were far from being irremediably Democratic. Accordingly, the inaugural included an "Amigos de Bush" luncheon at the Mayflower Hotel, with Hispanic leaders including Melquiades R. Marinex, Housing Secretary–designate; and the fiesta went on in the evening with a Hispanic presidential inaugural gala, "Juntos Podemos" ("Together We Can"), at the Omni Shoreham.[11] The crucial importance of political opportunity structures in shaping the administration's orientation is highlighted when one considers the American situation in a comparative perspective, notably in contrast with continental Europe, where they rather favor the adoption of an anti-immigration stance.[12] The Bush strategy clearly paid off: his support among Hispanic men grew from 35 percent in 2000 to 41 percent in 2004, while among women it remained at about the same level, 35 percent;[13] and the election of Antonio Villaraigosa as mayor of Los Angeles in May 2005 further confirmed the emergence of Hispanics as key players in the American political game.

Seizing globalization by the horns, President George W. Bush further undertook to restructure the uneasy relationship between the United States and its southern neighbor. Be it the wiles of history or mere coincidence, a few months earlier, Coca Cola executive Vicente Fox had been elected president of Mexico, marking the end of the protracted hegemony of the Partido Revolucionario Institutional. Fox and Bush were two of a kind, prompting William Safire to prophesy, "A remarkable confluence of personalities and economic forces bids fair to break the logjam along the Rio Grande."[14] Among his boldest initiatives, Fox chose as foreign minister Jorge Castañeda, a well-known leftist academic who, quite surprisingly, affirmed Mexico's commitment to a market-oriented economic policy and promoted "a long-term vision of a NAFTA modeled after the European Union."[15] In one of his first public statements, the Mexican president called for free movement across an open border; however, since this was unlikely to occur in the near future, he urged the United States to institute a large program of temporary work visas, in exchange for which he would strengthen policies to discourage illegal immigration and tighten Mexico's own southern border against Central Americans.

The proposal was evidently inspired by the deal recently negotiated between the European Union and its central and eastern European neighbors aspiring to membership.[16] In response, shortly after taking office, President Bush headed to Mexico to discuss, among other things, the treatment of Mexican workers north of the border, and on April 4, 2001, the two administrations held the first of a series of meetings on international migration.[17] Concurrently, several guest worker proposals were introduced in Congress, including a bipartisan one promoted by California Democratic Representative Howard Berman and Oregon Republican Senator Gordon H. Smith, and another by Senator Phil Gramm. In late April, President Bush met with some of the seventeen Democrats making up the Congressional Hispanic Caucus, several of whom reported later that they were optimistic about working with him but had not received any commitments on amnesty.[18] On May 3, the president hosted the White House's first-ever celebration of the Mexican national holiday, Cinco de Mayo; introduced by his nephew as "Tio Jorge" and sprinkling his remarks with Spanish—"Mi Casa Blanca es su Casa Blanca"—he seized the occasion to announce a version of his weekly radio address in Spanish, immediately prompting Democratic leaders to respond in kind. In his first broadcast, *el Presidente* pledged to cement ties with Mexico, prompting Silvestre Reyes, former INS chief in El Paso and initiator of Operation Crossroads, but now a Democratic representative and chairman of the Congressional Hispanic Caucus, to respond, "Considering there are over 35 million Hispanics in this nation, it is time for the president to show his support through his actions."

As negotiations continued over the summer, President Bush appeared to relent on legalization, prompting the formation of a bipartisan Senate coalition under the leadership of Democrat Majority Leader Tom Daschle, eager to cooperate because legalization "is pro-business, pro-family, and long overdue," while a panel led by Secretary of State Colin L. Powell and Attorney General John Ashcroft undertook the preparation of a plan on border safety and immigration providing on the one hand for a large-scale expansion of guest worker programs, and on the other for a process whereby Mexicans living illegally in the United States could gradually "earn" permanent legal residency.[19] Designed to avoid the appearance of "amnesty" by imposing a fine on applicants, the legalization process was also to include an English requirement as "something which, in order to push this to fruition, they can give to conservatives and others who would be reluctant to embrace the plan, by showing these workers share our language and values."[20] Powell and Ashcroft met with their Mexican counterparts to discuss the subject further in early August, in preparation for a major announcement by President Bush and President Fox at their summit meeting in Washington, scheduled to begin on September 4.

Although the legalization component was said to face opposition from influential Republican congressmen, Mark Krikorian, executive director of the Center for Immigration Studies, saw the handwriting on the wall. Mixing his metaphors, he explained that "Mexicans are the new Soccer Moms," and since there are 8 million of them in the United States, "Any politician is going to go hunting where the ducks are."[21] On September 6, the Mexican president surprised his American hosts by urging a joint meeting of Congress to approve an immigration agreement granting legal rights to millions of undocumented Mexican immigrants by year's end. In response, his host declared publicly for the first time that he hoped to create a route to legalization but called for "a direct and honest assessment of reality," as the immigration issue is "incredibly complex" and it would take much work by his administration to find a solution that Congress can accept.[22]

Although the Bush administration's approach differed somewhat from that of its immediate predecessor, overall it confirmed that the latest immigration settlement would include the naturalization of Spanish as the de facto second American language and the raising to Mexico to privileged status as a soft-boundary neighbor, along with Canada, which benefited from that status all along. This in effect consecrated a boundary shift comparable to what occurred with regard to southern and eastern Europeans half a century earlier.

The Security Challenge

But borders unexpectedly took on renewed significance on September 11, 2001.[23] The tragedy revealed, to the great dismay of analysts and policy makers, that the most immediate and severe threat to American security had little or nothing to do with immigration proper but arose from the process of international *movement*. The challenge this poses is staggering: border inspectors would have to make 1.3 billion correct decisions every year to keep terrorists and their weapons out of the country, including in that count the inspection of ships and cargo containers, of passengers arriving by air, and of persons crossing the borders by land. Some 550 million enter the United States in a given year, amounting to approximately twice its entire population; leaving aside returning citizens as well as daily commuters from Canada and

Mexico with multi-entry passes, documented foreign entrants amount to some 60 million, of whom about half are visitors covered by the Visa Waiver Program, which in 2001 encompassed twenty-nine countries including Canada and all of western Europe, whose nationals were considered unlikely to overstay or to engage in criminal activity.[24] That year, the United States issued 7 million new visas, of which only some 800,000 were awarded to immigrants proper; another 600,000 went to students, and most of the remainder to short-stay tourists and business visitors. Approximately 1 of every 500,000 issued in the two-year period preceding 9/11 went to a hijacker or one of their suspected associates. The task remains staggering even when one narrows scrutiny down to "dangerous" countries: for example, some 120,000 visas were issued to Saudi nationals, of which 15 went to future hijackers—approximately 1 per 8,000, or .0001 percent—and the leading detained suspect charged with crimes related to 9/11 was a Morocco-born French national, admitted without a visa by virtue of his French naturalization.

The prevailing institutional distinction between "visitors" and "immigrants," which the United States shares with others, responds to the contradictory imperatives induced by the contemporary world system. Whereas economic globalization, as well as the expansion of individual rights, has fostered the steady liberalization of procedures governing the international movement of persons, with support from the transportation and tourist industries as well as (in the American case especially) institutions of higher education seeking to attract foreign students, the system's enduring economic inequality and its political organization along Westphalian lines make for acute restrictions on international migration proper. This has resulted in the formation of a differentiated régime, which grants nearly unlimited freedom of short-term international movement to nationals of affluent states, with visitor visas required only of those from emigration-prone countries, in effect the developing world including most of former Communist Europe, while long-term residence involving employment and access to social welfare is universally severely restricted, with intermediary regulations for stays involving study and temporary employment or business activities.[25]

These regulations are largely operationalized by way of "remote control," whereby the relevant authorization must be obtained from consular officials prior to departure and a preliminary border inspection is carried out by the commercial carrier prior to embarkation. Although when political and security concerns enter into play, consular officials may engage in a more elaborate investigation or refer the application for investigation by more specialized bodies, notably intelligence agencies, 9/11 revealed that in the American case the information to which consular officials have access is very limited and that much of the "remote control" task is in fact delegated to travel agencies.[26] Many countries supplement border controls with internal ones, but while the United States was a pioneer in the development of "remote control," with regard to the internal sphere it has remained institutionally at the extreme liberal end of the continuum. Hence concern over foreign intruders has tended to generate ad hoc responses targeting categoric groups, a pattern inaugurated by the Alien and Sedition Acts of 1798 and reenacted in the twentieth century by prohibitions against anarchists as well as later measures against Nazis, persons of Japanese origin, and Communists. As unusual intrusions by the state into the sphere of civil society and private life, these measures stimulated the formation of organizations such as the American Civil Liberties Union, dedicated to their elimination or at least containment by invoking constitutional guarantees and using the judicial apparatus to insure their respect. Consequently, by the end of the Cold War prevailing juridical doctrines sharply circumscribed the capacity of the federal and state governments to limit the personal liberties of U.S. nationals and legal foreign residents in the name of security.

Concern over "terrorism" in the contemporary sense first arose in the course of the Iranian hostage crisis of 1979, when the possibility of militants entering the country disguised as students prompted the INS to require educational institutions to report the comings and goings of foreign students; however, by 1988 forms were piled so high that the agency asked the institutions to stop sending them in.[27] Unease revived following the first attack on the World Trade Center in 1993, prompting consideration of the subject by the Jordan Commission and leading to the stiffening of civil and criminal penalties for illegal entry as well as to the inclusion of provisions for expedited removal in the Illegal Immigration Reform and Immigrant Responsibility Act of 1996 (IIRIRA) and the same year's Antiterrorism and Effective Death Penalty Act. The IIRIRA further mandated the elaboration of a tighter border régime, including an "Integrated Entry and Exit Data System," and extended to state and local police the authority to enforce immigration laws as well as providing for their training to that effect. However, the Clinton administration caved in to pressures from the education and business lobbies to postpone development and implementation of the new régime, and the incoming Bush administration followed suit.[28] Implementation of the mandate was further handicapped by protracted turf wars between the State and Justice Departments.[29]

The first legislative measure explicitly designed to offset the vulnerability exposed by 9/11 was initiated by Attorney General John Ashcroft one week after the attack to allow for the deportation, without a hearing or presentation of evidence, of any alien whom the attorney general had "reason to believe" would "commit, further, or facilitate" acts of terrorism.[30] The Uniting and Strengthening America by Providing Appropriate Tools Required to Intercept and Obstruct Terrorism Act of 2001, an unwieldy title elaborated to produce the bombastic acronym, USA PATRIOT, supported by both parties, was signed by President Bush on October 26, 2001. However, indefinite detention, which evoked the treatment meted out to Japanese Americans during World War II, emerged as a contentious issue, and the enacting compromise included a "sunset clause" providing for the law's expiration in 2005. Among other things, the law imposed a two-year deadline for implementation of the "Integrated Entry and Exit Data System" called for in 1996.[31]

In its initial response to the events, the State Department announced it would subject male visa applicants aged sixteen to forty-five from twenty-six nations in the Middle East, South Asia, Southeast Asia, and Africa to special scrutiny by referring their applications to Washington. This immediately provoked lengthy delays and a sharp drop in applications from those regions to American colleges and universities. The events also triggered a spate of proposals to subject foreign residents to systematic verification. This entailed no mean undertaking, given a mass amounting to 11 percent of the total population, not including millions of temporary visitors. However, given the apparent source of the aggression, for many Americans the distinction that mattered most was between putatively safe immigrants and dangerous ones, identified as "Arabs" or "Muslims," or more diffusely as "Middle Easterners," a designation that often encompassed South Asians.[32] Although the USA PATRIOT Act began with an "expression of the sense of Congress" condemning discrimination against Arabs and Muslims, and despite repeated injunctions by President Bush and other elected officials to avoid blaming groups wholesale, the operationalization of security measures entailed blatant ethnic profiling. After a halting start, in June 2002 the Justice Department published a plan requiring over 100,000 foreign-born Muslim residents to register and be fingerprinted, with new arrivals required to do so after thirty days.[33] The proposal, to be carried out by the federal government with the assistance of state and local law enforcement officials, ignited a raging debate within the administration itself and evoked outrage from civil libertarians and Arab American organizations. The decision to begin detaining asylum seekers from

Iraq and thirty-three other countries, announced on March 17, 2003, evoked harsh criticism from the same quarters.[34] The courts quickly got into the act as well.[35] As of June 2003, it was estimated that about 16 percent of the Arab and Muslim men who came forward to register might face deportation for violating immigration laws; some 500 were fighting deportation in court, but none was charged as a terrorist. The Justice Department's own inspector general subsequently reported that hundreds of the detainees had been mistreated, prompting the department to announce that it would use stricter standards for identifying and incarcerating terrorist suspects.[36]

Although Attorney General Ashcroft continued to seek greater authority under the USA PATRIOT Act, it was in fact the 1996 Antiterrorism and Effective Death Penalty Act, enacted by the Clinton administration in 1996, which emerged as the Justice Department's weapon of choice. The law went into effect in 1998, and as of 2002, more than 75,000 people had been detained under it, many in connection with minor drug crimes that met the definition of "aggravated felonies." In April 2003, the Supreme Court upheld the law's mandatory detention feature, thus reversing the ongoing expansion of immigrant rights and confirming congressional power to limit the rights of permanent residents, putting 11 million "green card" holders on notice that those committing certain offenses might be deported upon completion of their prison sentence.[37] The Justice Department's own inspector general subsequently reported that the INS failed to identify and deport criminal immigrants in a timely fashion, costing millions in unnecessary detention expenses and keeping immigrants in custody beyond their legal sentences. The administration also challenged the tradition whereby the enforcement of immigration laws was considered an exclusively federal domain, and it issued formal proposals to that effect in June 2002.[38] Although opposition was voiced by the civil liberties establishment as well as by conservative libertarians, local authorities began shifting their stance, with Florida the first jurisdiction to enter into a formal partnership with the federal government; by early 2003, a number of police departments had begun arresting people accused of violations of immigration law.[39] Another link between border control and internal law enforcement was established in January 2003, when the State Department opened its visa database of 50 million applicants (including photographs of 20 million), hitherto shared only with immigration officials, to state and local police officers.

The events of 9/11 also precipitated more acute critiques of the border control system as reporters publicized a variety of incidents revealing sloppy practices, and the inspector generals of a number of federal agencies censured them for moving too slowly to overcome leakage.[40] Its order of magnitude can be inferred from the fact that in 2000, the Border Patrol arrested roughly 1 million people trying to sneak into the United States from Mexico, and 12,000 from Canada, including among the latter 254 persons from sixteen Middle Eastern countries. Illegal immigration, which slowed down after 9/11, resumed at its previous level and rose further in 2003 as tariffs on almost all Mexican agricultural imports from the United States were scheduled to end on January 1, jeopardizing the livelihood of some 700,000 small farmers. In early 2003 the INS reported that illegal immigrants jumped by 1 million in less than four years, reaching some 7 million as of January 2000; Mexicans made up 69 percent of the total, compared with 58 percent in 1990. In the light of 9/11, these estimates made for screaming headlines.[41] While unauthorized entry from the south is an old story, initial announcements—subsequently disconfirmed—that several of the hijackers entered surreptitiously across the Canadian border came as an especially frightening revelation, as that line hardly figures in American consciousness as an international divide: albeit twice as long as its Mexican counterpart, with 115 official entry points as against 41, the Canadian border is guarded by only 334 agents, as against some 9,000 in the south.

In early 2002, President Bush asked Congress for an increase of about 20 percent in border security funds and announced plans to operationalize the long-awaited monitoring system. Although there were discussions of a national ID requirement as well, this was dropped for the time being to insure broad bipartisan support for the proposals, which were approved by an overwhelming 97–9 in the Senate and 411–0 (2 voting present) in the House, and were signed into law on May 14, 2002, as the Border Security Act.[42] The following September, the INS reported it was ready on a trial basis to fingerprint arriving foreigners suspected of posing security risks and require them to regularly report their whereabouts and activities; this was subsequently extended to the citizens of eighteen additional countries and scheduled to cover all visitors by 2005; however, the requirement was not applicable to immigrants proper.[43] The fate of the INS, already in question before the events, was sealed in early 2002 when the agency administered itself a coup de grâce by issuing student visa extensions to two of the hijackers six months after they died. Giving up the fight, the Bush-appointed agency head resigned, and on November 25 the president signed a law creating the Department of Homeland Security. Pennsylvania Governor Tom Ridge was swiftly confirmed as its first secretary.[44]

Scheduled to sunset in 2005, the USA PATRIOT Act became the object of a partisan showdown, as the Republicans proposed to make it permanent while the Democrats sought to amend the existing legislation; however, some Senate and House Republicans objected as well, and in mid-2003 a tentative deal was struck whereby the Republicans abandoned their efforts to repeal the sunset provision while the Democrats pulled their own amendments. Renewal of the act was highlighted by President Bush in his 2004 bid for re-election, and upon expiration in mid-2005, it was renewed as a permanent fixture. There is no doubt that the concerns arising from the current international configuration, which are by no means limited to the United States, will foster the development of a tighter international movement régime. In its quest for a more permanent solution, the United States faces a choice: either to elaborate a draconian apparatus of physical and administrative barriers along the longest stretches of relatively open international boundary in the entire world, or to incorporate its two neighbors into a jointly managed "security perimeter," leading to the elaboration of a North American counterpart of the European Schengen system, which originated as an undertaking by the northern tier of European Union members plus Switzerland against the "leaky" Mediterranean South. Following 9/11, the United States and Canada sought to establish a pilot program whereby officials from both countries would team up to check international travelers before leaving for North America from overseas; in return, they would be able to travel more easily between the two countries.[45] A similar security pact with Mexico, whose commerce with the Unites States tripled since 1993 and now ranks second overall, was announced in March 2002, with financial aid for the enhancement of Mexican capacity to be paid for out of the emergency legislation enacted in 2001. However, later in 2002, relations with Mexico hardened after it initially failed to support the United States in the United Nations on Iraq.

Yet it is remarkable that despite the overwhelming support for tighter border control and significant inroads into the civil liberties of resident aliens, notwithstanding continuing pressure by dedicated restrictionists who argue that security considerations mandate a reduced intake, and indications that the growth of the Hispanic population continues at a very high rate—an increase of 9.8 percent in the first two years of the new century—in the wake of 9/11, the United States refrained from severely tightening its immigration policy.[46] This further confirms the fundamental difference between conditions prevailing at the beginning and at the end of the twentieth century.

There was considerable speculation throughout 2003 that the GOP victory in the midterm elections of 2002 and the continued opposition of Mexico to

American policy in Iraq made it unlikely that the guest worker–cum–legalization program discussed on the eve of 9/11 would make any headway. Nevertheless, after a prolonged hiatus, negotiations resumed and by mid-December 2003, Homeland Security Secretary Tom Ridge hinted at a plan to grant the estimated 8–10 million undocumented immigrants some sort of legal status. On January 7, 2004, one week before a scheduled summit meeting of the Mexican and U.S. presidents in Monterrey, Mexico, President Bush proposed a sweeping two-part program that would enable undocumented immigrants in the United States to apply for temporary worker status, with all employee benefits accorded to those legally employed, as well as to travel freely between the United States and their home countries, and to eventually apply for a "green card." Concurrently, the United States would vastly expand its existing "guest worker" program, incorporating into it the unprecedented possibility of using time served toward application for an immigration visa, as had been proposed by the Clinton administration. Commented the *New York Times,* "The president's proposals were designed to appeal to Hispanic groups, a constituency that the White House is focusing on as Mr. Bush seeks re-election this year," but were "expected to face a tough fight in Congress," where conservative Republicans consider programs like this one "nothing more than amnesty for people who have broken the law."[47] Eventually, the proposal for a national ID card was revived as well and made considerable headway within the new securitarian environment. Reactions by Hispanic groups and labor-minded organizations were mixed as well, with many objections raised to the institutionalization of a "guest worker" system, and it was quickly evident that nothing would be done before the 2004 presidential elections. Nevertheless, there was no doubt that movement along these lines would continue, confirming that settlement of the latest immigration crisis will include the institutionalization of a special relationship with Mexico.[48] As of mid-2005, the combination of some form of legalization and a national ID system appeared to provide the makings of a new political trade-off.

"Why Not the Whole World?"

Because international population movements, including refugee flows, are driven by the profound inequality of worldwide demographic, economic, and political conditions, issues arising from immigration and its consequences will remain on the political agenda of affluent democracies for the foreseeable future. What should be done in the face of this challenge? As I have emphasized throughout, the debates that immigration provokes are especially contentious because they implicate disparate spheres of concerns and interests, and also involve both domestic and external policy considerations. Straddling several dimensions, the issues cut across the usual left-right divide, making for strange political bedfellows. Leaving aside the rantings of outright xenophobes, debates often entail "a contest of 'right' versus 'right.' "[49] They pit free-market advocates who welcome an increase in the labor supply as a stimulus to economic growth against others concerned with protecting the job market for indigenous workers, particularly those who are already the most deprived; "humanitarians" who believe affluent democracies have a moral obligation to provide asylum for refugees in need against "realists" who contend that this obligation cannot be discharged because too many refugees are being produced in the world at large; and "cosmopolitans" who believe borders violate the unity of humanity against "nationalists" or "communitarians" who believe that the division of the world into distinct bordered communities is a sine qua non for liberal democracy, and that the viability of such communities would be jeopardized by a very large influx of immigrants, particularly if they are culturally very different from the receivers and impose great demands on collective goods.

For some, the answer is simple: draconian measures are called for to deter the "invaders," especially because by virtue of their origins in the developing world as well as in the unruly Balkans and ex–Soviet Union, they are so different from western receivers as to be "unassimilable"; moreover, it is alleged, experience with recent arrivals from those regions indicates that they insist on maintaining their alien ways, thereby sowing the seeds of future ethnic conflict. Most ominously, this type of reaction has fueled a resurgence of right-wing extremism, especially in Europe.

While the challenges posed by international migration are real and warrant a worldwide reconsideration of prevailing régimes, the resurgence of nativist responses constitutes a more immediate threat to liberal democracy than immigration itself. The most pressing danger is a reenactment of developments triggered by the immigration crisis of the early twentieth century, which prompted a worldwide closing of borders that contributed to the crystallization of political anti-Semitism in Europe as well as of racialist doctrines in the United States and deprived victims of persecution from access to asylum. Moreover, advocates of tighter controls tend to minimize the costs of implementing their policies, not only in financial but also especially in political terms. The elimination of unauthorized immigration would require no less than the transformation of the United States and other affluent democracies into police states, protected by a new iron curtain or a Berlin wall, and the further tightening of asylum procedures would jeopardize the very possibility of providing havens for refugees in need. Rigid adherence to the cultural status quo in the face of pressures to include elements drawn from the cultures of recent immigrants constitutes a self-fulfilling prophecy that renders the incorporation of the newcomers more problematic. Hence the maintenance by the affluent democracies of relatively open borders is a sine qua non for the development of a more liberal world, and is particularly vital for the success of democratizing forces in the developing world and the ex-Communist countries.

While the United States cannot by itself resolve the crisis, it does have the obligation of adopting a normatively desirable policy for its own sake, and thereby also provide suitable leadership for the world at large. The following choices arise:

- *Level of admissions:* Although in theory this ranges from zero to unlimited, in practice it clusters around the low end, with the "traditional immigration countries" somewhat higher than the others. For example, the current U.S. intake amounts to some 0.2 percent of the population annually, as against Canada's 5 percent.
- *Priorities:* Since the number of applicants usually exceeds admissions, triage must take place. Whose needs and interests should be given priority, the applicants' or the receivers'? Current U.S. policy combines several criteria: the primary attachments of its population (family reunion), collective interests of a mercantilist sort (scarce skills), and humanitarian concerns mixed with foreign policy considerations (refugees). What are appropriate proportions?
- *Modalities of incorporation:* Although choices arise only after the intake has taken place, the process is inseparable from immigration proper. Theoretical possibilities (as illustrated historically) range from totally segregated status without rights (slaves) to immediate admission as full members (as in the case of Jews in Israel, or *aussiedler* in Germany). Intermediary situations are more common, involving a range of waiting periods for naturalization and for the acquisition of civil, social, and political rights, as well as between the application of jus sanguinis or jus soli to native-born children of immigrants.

Which principles should guide these policy choices? A recent review has identified "Marxism," "realism," "libertarianism," "liberal egalitarianism"—with a further distinction between "cosmopolitans" and "communitarians"—and "natural law" as the leading perspectives, and suggests that differences among them arise largely from the extent to which they ascribe moral legitimacy to existing institutions, especially the state.[50] In keeping with this, "realists" are wont to advocate quite restrictive immigration (as, for example, George Kennan), whereas "libertarians" usually promote open boundaries (for example, Julian Simon and the *Wall Street Journal*). However, most political theorists dealing with the subject rank as "liberal egalitarians," seeking a compromise between an ethic of rights and consequences.

Much of the debate within this camp revolves around the attribution of different weights to "freedom" and "equality," as well as differing interpretations of the consequences of immigration on these values. For example, "communitarians" argue that since it is well established that cultural heterogeneity is a source of acute political conflict, a democracy is justified in restricting the immigration of very large numbers of people who are very different because of the difficulty of integrating them. Such arguments are made today not only by the extreme nationalist fringe such as Le Pen in France or David Dukes, Pat Buchanan, and Samuel Huntington in the United States, but also by eminently respectable traditionalists such as the late George Kennan and even socially minded liberals such as Michael Walzer.

Beyond this, however, there is an emerging line of contention that cuts across the liberty/equality issue and pertains to both: what is the appropriate unit in relation to which rights and consequences are considered? The debate here divides those who consider these issues from the vantage point of a particular community, and those who would adopt that of the human species as a whole, that is, "nationalists" versus "cosmopolitans." Although the latter perspective has been propelled to the fore in the wake of recent debates over the environment, its importance as a dimension of ethical debate regarding immigration was highlighted nearly a century ago by Henry Sidgwick: "The truth is, that when we consider how far the exercise of this right of exclusion is conducive to the real interest of the State exercising it, or of humanity at large, we come upon the most striking phase of the general conflict between the cosmopolitan and the national ideals of political organization, which has more than once attracted our notice."[51]

I shall conclude with a brief on behalf of the "cosmopolitan" strain of "liberal egalitarianism," tempered by a dose of realism based on an understanding of the contemporary configuration. The choice of starting point itself makes a considerable difference. If one adopts a "realistic" position founded on a world organized into territorial states and a division of the human species into distinct and mutually exclusive communities that are markedly unequal, the fundamental question is, why should any of these communities, and especially the more privileged ones, admit *any* strangers? But if the starting point is a theoretical borderless world, the more radical question arises: what gives a group the right to exclude others? Bruce Ackerman has posed this in terms of a situation involving an explorer landing on a desert island and then refusing access to someone who comes later. If we are to any degree "consequentialists" (as every moral analyst is to some extent), then we are led to ask, what difference do borders make? What is their function?

The answer is twofold. To begin with, under prevailing circumstances, borders are a sine qua non for maintaining affluence and privilege. Brian Barry has pointed out that with free movement, conditions among the rich countries would quickly decline to the level of the less developed ones, and this would apply to politics as well as economics. In addition, borders are necessary to establish and preserve distinctive communities, notably self-governing democracies. Once they are established, international migration entails not merely physical relocation, but a *transfer* from one political entity to another, simultaneously a change of jurisdiction and of membership. We are thus quickly brought to face the two key dimensions of debate in modern political theory, freedom and equality: most obviously, borders constitute a sine qua non for the establishment or the preservation of a liberal (and democratic) political community, but simultaneously constitute an obstacle for the achievement of equality at the global level.

The one is in keeping with the concerns of "communitarians," and the other is of special interest to the "cosmopolitans." In this light, the cosmopolitan position would be significantly bolstered if it could be demonstrated that freedom of movement contributes to the achievement of freedom among the various political communities that constitute the international system.

"Preventive Exclusion" versus "the Melville Principle"

My starting point is the observation that the liberal world order is founded on a striking asymmetry: while the Universal Declaration of Human Rights states, "Everyone has the right to leave any country, including his own," there is no concomitant principle to the effect that "Everyone has the right to *enter* any country." On the contrary, there is a universal and unambiguous consensus on the opposite, namely, that every state has the right to restrict the entry of foreigners. And whereas the liberal international community vehemently objects to the exercise of exclusivist nationalism when it leads to the imposition of barriers on exit or provokes the expulsion of minorities, it voices little disapproval in the face of its less dramatic but nearly universal manifestation in the form of "preventive exclusion."

Brian Barry has argued that there is no good reason why emigration and immigration policies should be symmetrical, given that this is in keeping with a general characteristic of associations, whereby people are free to leave but not free to join; accordingly, there is a presumption in favor of asymmetry rather than symmetry.[52] But this reasoning, which parallels Michael Walzer's, is based on a false analogy. Membership in a political community is different from membership in an association, because the latter is usually not a sine qua non for existence; moreover, if one is excluded from one association, it is possible to join another or even to found a more welcoming one with others who are excluded (as was done, for example, by American Jews who wished to become Masons in the nineteenth century).

But a case can be made for restraining the power to exclude, grounded in the necessity for liberalism to adapt to globalization by developing a more "cosmopolitan" orientation. Questioning national sovereignty as the dominant principle of international organization is in keeping with our dawning awareness of the interdependence of all the segments of the human species, arising from the global nature of the thermonuclear threat and of environmental degradation.

To begin with, the right to leave one's country has come to be recognized as one of the fundamental human rights because it empowers citizens in relation to the state. Most obviously, the ability of citizens to vote with their feet would ultimately leave an oppressive government with no one to rule, and therefore with little choice but to reform in order to secure the consent of its citizens. This eventuality came to pass quite literally in the summer of 1990, when Hungary opened up its border to Austria, providing to masses of East German vacationers the possibility of driving their sputtering Trabants to freedom, and the processes unleashed by this turn of events amounted to a major turning point in world history. Conversely, the experience of the 1930s demonstrates the tragic consequences of *not* having a place to go. Determined to rid Germany and later occupied Europe of the Jews, the Nazis sought initially to expel them; but in the face of their inability to do so, and encouraged by the unwillingness of western democracies to receive them, they resorted to mass murder.

Since the right to leave one's country cannot be exercised unless there is concomitant access to some other one, it follows that adoption of this right, as was done in the Universal Declaration and further in the Helsinki Agreements, imposes on liberal democracies as a whole an obligation to keep their doors open to a substantial extent so as to render movement possible. Minimally, they must accept asylum seekers; and they must acknowledge that as the palette of acknowledged human rights expands, legitimate grounds for asylum do so as well.

The gist of a more radical argument on behalf of open borders was set forth a century and a half ago by Herman Melville, when the Great Hunger drove hundreds of thousands of destitute Irish out of their country, prompting the emergence of a wave of xenophobia on the American side and a spate of proposals for restricting immigration. As against this, Melville, who had recently served as a sailor on an immigrant ship, urged that the door be kept open: "Let us waive that agitated national topic, as to whether such multitudes of foreign poor should be landed on our American shores; let us waive it, with the one only thought that if they can get here, they have God's right to come; though they bring all Ireland and her miseries with them. For the whole world is the patrimony of the whole world; there is no telling who does not own a stone in the Great Wall of China."[53]

Considered more generally, the "Melville principle" suggests that the strict confinement of individuals to membership in the states under whose jurisdiction they happened to be born negates their being as members of a common species, and concomitantly imbues the states in question with an aura of "naturalness" that obfuscates their reality as historical constructs. Descended from common ancestors, in the course of their history humans scattered over the face of the earth by way of untold migrations; and throughout this history, they also constantly organized and reorganized themselves into bounded communities. But what gives the generations alive today a warrant to regard the specific configuration that has resulted from these two processes in our own time as the definitive outcome of history? As empires episodically gave way to national states in the course of the twentieth century, the resulting reorganization also tended to be regarded as definitive; but we now know that this freezing of history proved illusory as a variety of national groups emerged to press claims on behalf of a distinct state of their own. In the same vein, a freezing of the current distribution of political membership by way of prohibitively restrictive immigration policies is contrary to the constitutive principles of a liberal world order because it would in effect confine individuals alive today as well as the generations to come to the jurisdiction of their states of origin, thus vastly enhancing the power of the latter.

From a liberal cosmopolitan perspective, unwanted immigrants are not "invaders," but rather people voting with their feet in support of the "Melville principle," founded on their rights arising from membership in a common species. Concomitantly, the burden of justification must be borne not by those who seek admission in some country, but rather by those who would exclude them. The appropriate question is therefore not "Whom Shall We Admit?" but "Why Not the Whole World?"

The obvious answer is that under present world conditions, in the absence of border controls, the world's affluent countries would be quickly overwhelmed by truly massive flows of international migrants in search of work, social benefits, and safety. Although this is counterfactual, it is highly plausible, as indicated by the long lines that form wherever a possibility of legal admission exists, as well as the proliferation of surreptitious entries. The likelihood that, in the absence of borders, a major redistribution of the world's population would take place is suggested also by theoretical models of migration founded on current and prospective income differentials—to which one might add political conditions as an additional major source of emigration "push." While there is room for debate about the details, there is no gainsaying that movements toward the affluent countries would be extremely large.

This prospect imposes a major constraint on the application of the Melville principle. Upon reflection, it is evident that Melville's generous stance was predicated on the knowledge that Ireland contained but some 6.5 million people, and that there were just so many sailing ships available at any given time to bring the Irish to the United States. In effect, from the perspective of the American side of the Atlantic, prevailing conditions in the world at large kept the mid-nineteenth-century immigration crisis within bounds, even in the absence of restrictive action. But the situation changed dramatically in the final third of the nineteenth century, and continued to evolve in the same direction throughout the twentieth.

What are we to do today in the face of a world that consists of a thousand Irelands, and in which there is in effect an infinite number of ships? Although there are no simple answers, the perspective of cosmopolitan liberalism provides an ethically valid and practical guiding principle. Recognizing that unlimited immigration would jeopardize the material welfare of the receivers without enhancing that of the newcomers, and that it would also jeopardize democratic self-government, we can nevertheless insist that those who would restrict immigration assume the burden of proof regarding its nefarious consequences. To the extent that limits on admission prevail, priority must be given to those in greatest need, people who cannot survive in their country of origin because they are the target of persecution, because of life-threatening violence, or because there is no possible way of making a living. In this light, affluent democracies should forego mercantilist policies that deprive developing countries of precious manpower, but may promote the immigration of less skilled workers, so long as they are prepared to incorporate them. As for the control of unauthorized immigration, they must learn to live with imperfections, which are preferable to most of the draconian solutions being proposed.

The search for guidelines in the formulation of an ethical immigration policy within the framework of liberalism broadly understood for the twenty-first century leads necessarily to a consideration of the situation in the "Irelands" in the world at large. While the erection of barriers against unlimited immigration is warranted as a realistic compromise, the legitimacy of this position is conditional on its linkage with other commitments: as a long-term objective, the affluent democracies must help potential emigrants to live in their own country, and this in turn requires the availability of "bread and peace," sustainable development and trade, as well as respect of human rights and negotiated solutions to domestic and international conflicts. When refugee flows occur, appropriate assistance must be provided to neighboring countries that provide regional havens; and under extreme conditions, humanitarian intervention may be warranted or even constitute an obligation. Because of the interconnectedness of the flows and the interactivity of the policies of all the countries involved, international cooperation in these matters is imperative. As for "bread," while pressure on the borders of the affluent world would be reduced by the development of better opportunities in the countries of origin, this should be envisioned as a medium- to long-term solution because development usually entails displacement, as in the case of Mexican agriculture, and once a flow has been established, economic growth in the sending country does not immediately reduce movement as the immigrant community continues to draw newcomers to itself.

The 9/11 attack confirms what had already been evident from less spectacular manifestations of international terrorism: the growing importance of non-state actors in the contemporary world system. Nevertheless, American responses are being cast primarily within a classically Westphalian framework: calls for a crash program to enhance each state's capacity to police its territorial borders, to identify and neutralize foreign-origin enemies within, and to improve intelligence abroad. Not only does the elaboration of obstacles to international movement clash with the objectives of economic globalization, but globalization in turn provides negative feedback for national security, since it brings about greater population diversity so that, whoever the dangerous group turns out to be, the targeted society is likely to have such people in its midst. Evidence of vulnerability to such attacks enhances the value of protection while downgrading the social costs heightened protection imposes, notably on residents who share an ethnic origin with the putative terrorists or are thought to resemble them. Moreover, interpretations of the conflict as an essentially cultural one, opposing Islamic fundamentalism to western civilization, foster suspicion of Muslims of any kind, much as in the initial years of the Cold War, interpretations of the conflict as an essentially ideological one led many to impugn the loyalty of every left-winger.

Nevertheless, a murderous attack *did* take place, and it is hardly unique; nor is the United States the only target. Moreover, while the military response it provoked disrupted the source network, it is evident that other networks of this sort already exist and that more are likely to come into being. Although over the long term, terrorism is subject to reduction by structural change, and the containment of particular manifestations can be achieved by local intervention, overall the danger will persist for the indefinite future. Under the circumstances, the Westphalian approach still has a lot going for it, despite its archaic character; but it must be updated in light of contemporary conditions. Effective protection is not only desirable in itself, but its reality will also reduce the appeal of blunt and counterproductive Buchanan-like solutions.

To be fully effective, security must not be focused on geographical borders or on the home territory, but projected outward. If there is to be a crash program, it should be directed at the improvement of America's capacity to identify dangerous operations in the making abroad. Contrary to the tendency of going it alone, the development of the appropriate intelligence capability requires cooperation with friendly states that have greater experience in the sphere under consideration. Such intelligence is in turn a prerequisite for the implementation of a more effective screening system for foreign visitors, which is fully possible under existing law. Much can be done to overcome turf wars and to improve the accessibility of relevant information. Beyond this, rather than the border patrol, which has been the major beneficiary of recent investment in border control, priority should be given to consular staffing. As Doris Meissner has pointed out, "Consular work—more a rite of passage than a job requiring substantive expertise—does not enjoy high standing in the hierarchy of responsibilities for U.S. diplomats. Expert senior officers are in short supply and are spread too thin. This model is not tolerable in the face of terrorism. Instead, visa work must be treated as a career specialty. . . . If this work is not suited to Foreign Service careers and rewards, it should be done by a new civil service cadre dedicated to this mission."[54] In the same vein, more can be done to provide advance passenger information so as to improve the security of flights without jeopardizing processing speed.

While vigilance is called for internally as well, nothing has emerged so far to suggest that extraordinary measures are required for this purpose. For the time being, the more urgent internal security task is to provide adequate protection to minorities victimized by the diffuse anger of the uninformed and to insure that in their encounters with American law, they are accorded the full benefit of the procedural rights that constitute one of the major foundations of democracy. Immigrants who feel welcome rarely set out to destroy their new home.

Appendix: Immigration Graphs

All graphics are from the CD-ROM containing a compilation of data on immigration to the United States for the chapter entitled "Immigration," by Robert E. Barde, Susan B. Carter, and Richard Sutch, in Susan B. Carter, Scott S. Gartner, Michael R. Haines, Alan L. Olmstead, Richard Sutch, and Gavin Wright, eds., *Historical Statistics of the United States, Millennial Edition.* New York: Cambridge University Press, 2003.

Number of Immigrants to the United States

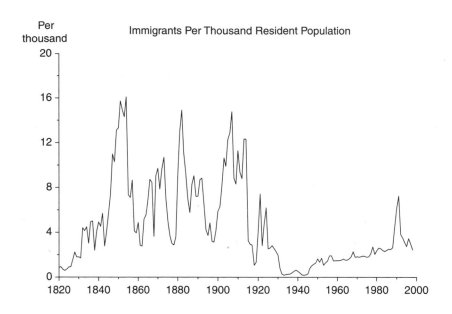

Per
thousand   Immigrants Per Thousand Resident Population

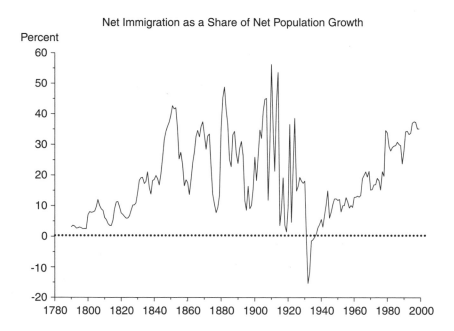

Net Immigration as a Share of Net Population Growth

Percent

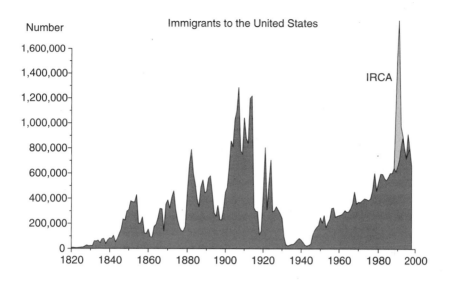

Number — Immigrants to the United States

IRCA

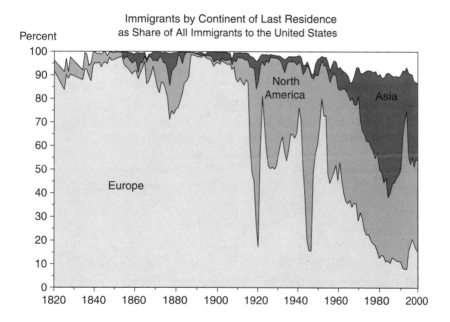

Percent — Immigrants by Continent of Last Residence as Share of All Immigrants to the United States

Europe

North America

Asia

Refugees and Asylees
Granted Permanent Resident Status

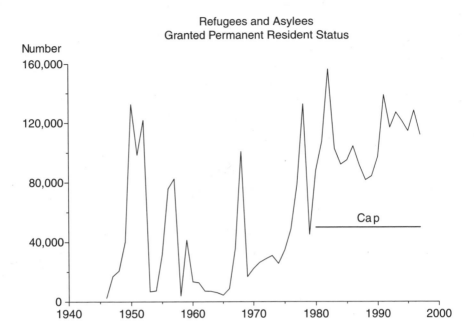

Foreign-Born as a Percent of the Population

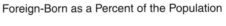

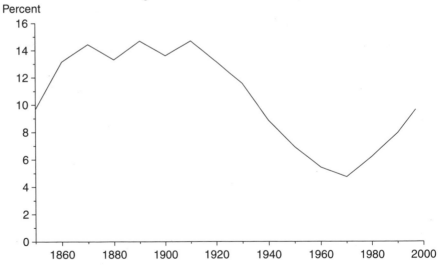

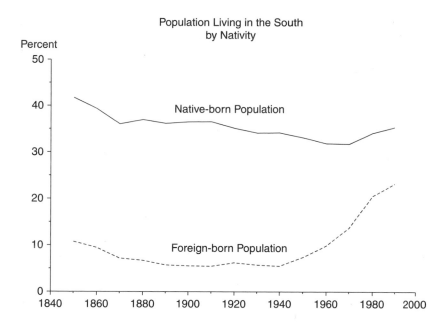

Population Living in the South
by Nativity

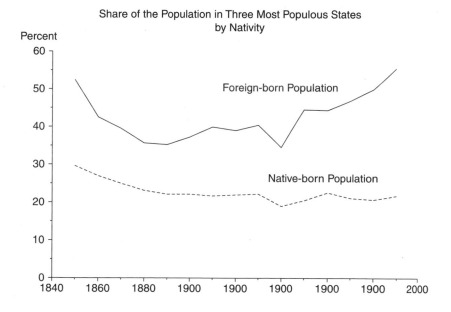

Share of the Population in Three Most Populous States
by Nativity

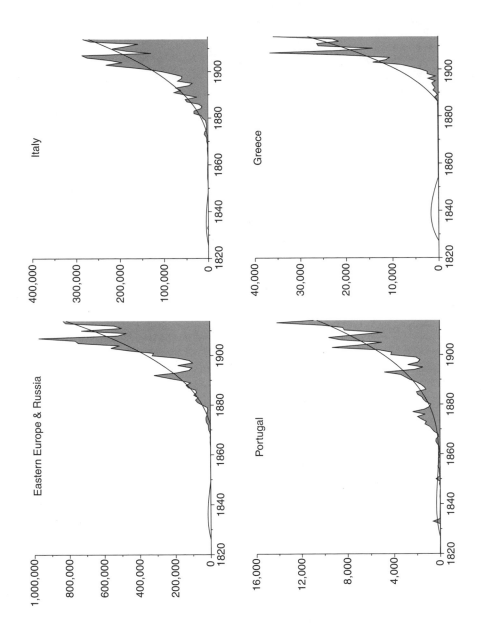

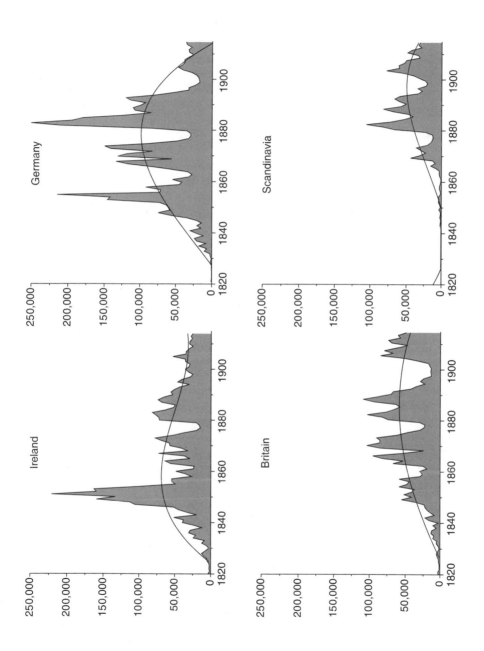

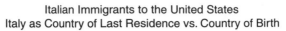

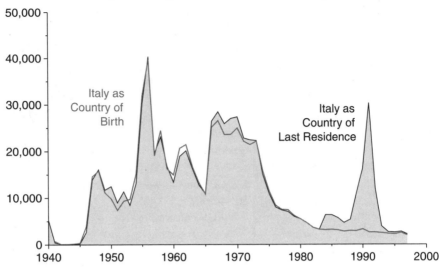

Italian Immigrants to the United States
Italy as Country of Last Residence vs. Country of Birth

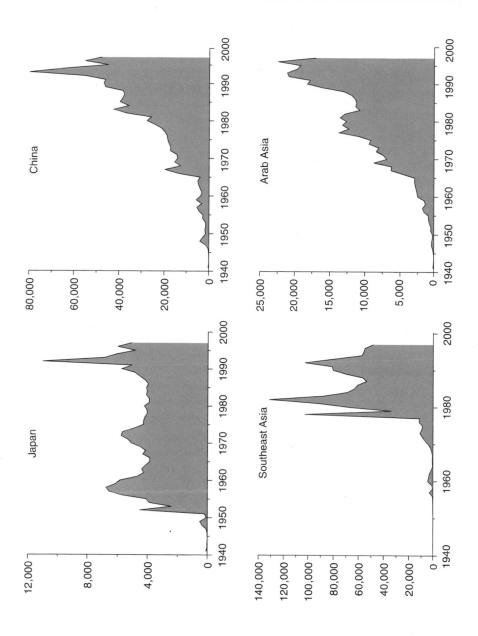

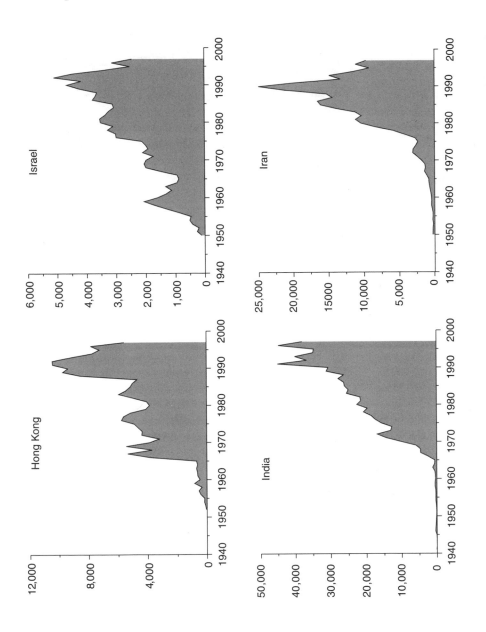

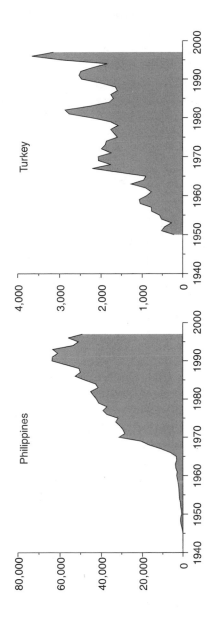

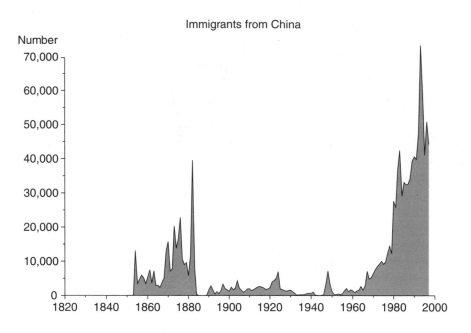

Immigrants from China

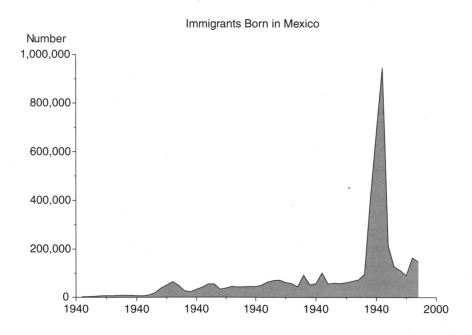

Immigrants Born in Mexico

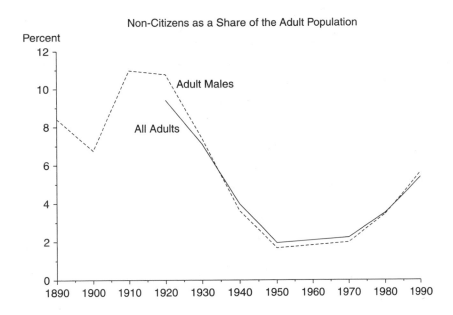

Non-Citizens as a Share of the Adult Population

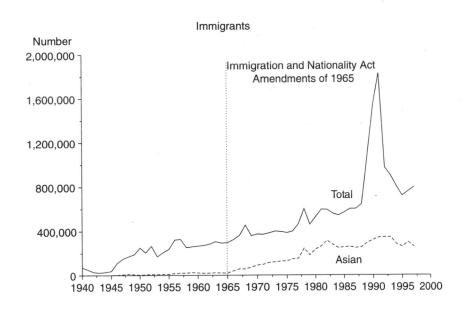

Immigrants

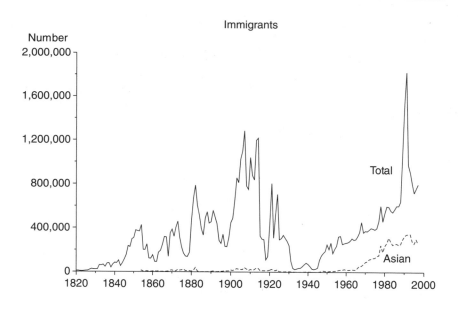

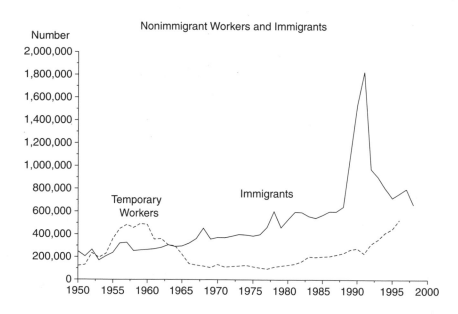

Abbreviations

ACS	American Society for Colonizing the Free People of Color in the United States
AFDC	Aid to Family with Dependent Children
AFL	American Federation of Labor
AICF	American Immigration Control Federation
AJC	American Jewish Committee
CCDP	Citizens Committee on Displaced Persons
CCIR	Citizens' Commission on Indochinese Refugees
CIO	Congress of Industrial Organizations
CIS	Center for International Studies
CRS	Congressional Research Service
DP(s)	displaced person(s)
EVD	Extended Voluntary Departure
FAIR	Federation for American Immigration Reform
GAO	General Accounting Office
GATT	General Agreements on Tariffs and Trade
H-1B	high-skilled temporary visa
H-2	legally recruited foreign seasonal agricultural worker visa
H-2A	temporary workers in agriculture visa
HIAS	Hebrew Immigrant Aid Society
IGC	Intergovernmental Committee [on behalf of refugees]
IIRIRA	Illegal Immigration Reform and Immigrant Responsibility Act of 1996
IIRM	Irish Immigration Reform Movement
INS	Immigration and Naturalization Service
IPL	Immigration Protective League
IQ	intelligence quotient
IR(s)	interpreter releases
IRCA	Immigration Reform and Control Act of 1986
IRL	Immigration Restriction League
IRO	International Refugee Organization
LPC(s)	likely to become a public charge
LPR	legal permanent resident

LULAC	League of United Latin American Citizens
MALDEF	Mexican-American Legal Defense and Education Fund
MIT	Massachusetts Institute of Technology
MP(s)	member(s) of Parliament
NAACP	National Association for the Advancement of Colored People
NAFTA	North American Free Trade Agreement
NAM	National Association of Manufacturers
NGO(s)	nongovernmental organization(s)
NIF	National Immigration Forum
NLIL	National Liberal Immigration League
NRC	National Research Council
NWR	*Niles' Weekly Register*
NYRB	*New York Review of Books*
NYT	*New York Times*
OSSB	Order of the Star-Spangled Banner
RICO	Racketeer Influenced and Corrupt Organizations
SALT	Strategic Arms Limitation Talks
SAW	Special Agricultural Workers
SCIRP	Special Commission on Immigration and Refugee Policy
SSRC	Social Science Research Council
SSI	Social Security Insurance
TANF	Temporary Assistance for Needy Families
TPS	Temporary Protected Status
UFW	United Farm Workers
UNESCO	United Nations Educational, Scientific and Cultural Organization
UNHCR	United Nations High Commissioner for Refugees
UNRRA	United Nations Relief and Rehabilitation Administration
USA PATRIOT Act	Uniting and Strengthening America by Providing Appropriate Tools Required to Intercept and Obstruct Terrorism Act of 2001
USCIR	U.S. Commission on Immigration Reform
USGPO	U.S. Government Printing Office
WSJ	*Wall Street Journal*
ZPG	Zero Population Growth

Notes

1. Themes and Perspectives

1. On "constructing" the nation generally, see Benedict Anderson, *Imagined Communities: Reflections on the Origin and Spread of Nationalism* (London: New Left Books, 1983).

2. On Britain, see Linda Colley, *Britons: Forging the Nation 1707–1837* (New Haven, CT: Yale University Press, 1992). On France, see Colette Beaune, *Naissance de la nation France* (Paris: Gallimard, 1985); and Daniel Nordman, *Frontières de la France. De l'espace au territoire, XVIe-XIXe siècle* (Paris: Gallimard, 1998).

3. On the history of early immigration policy in Canada, Argentina, and Brazil, see Walter Nugent, *Crossings: The Great Transatlantic Migrations, 1870–1914* (Bloomington: Indiana University Press, 1992).

4. See the further discussion in Chapter 2.

5. Maldwyn Jones, *American Immigration* (Chicago: University of Chicago Press, 1960); see also the useful compendium by Edward P. Hutchinson, *Legislative History of American Immigration Policy 1798–1965* (Philadelphia: University of Pennsylvania Press, 1981). On nativism, see Dale T. Knobel, *"America for the Americans": The Nativist Movement in the United States* (New York: Twayne Publishers, 1996).

6. Gerald L. Neuman, "The Lost Century of American Immigration Law (1776–1875)," *Columbia Law Review* 93, no. 8 (December 1993): 1833–901; reprinted in Gerald L. Neuman, *Strangers to the Constitution: Immigrants, Borders, and Fundamental Law* (Princeton, NJ: Princeton University Press, 1996).

7. Smith criticizes Alexander Bickel's celebration of the rights bestowed by the U.S. Constitution as an "idyllic state of affairs," suggesting that the constitutional lawyer's character as "a brilliant Jewish immigrant" is at the root of his overly benevolent assessment. Although I might avail myself of my own standing as a "stateless Jewish immigrant" to claim insight into the international significance of naturalization that is not available to Rogers Smith, I prefer to do so on the basis of comparative and contextual analysis.

8. On the role of the United States in promoting the "exit revolution" in the

early nineteenth century, see Aristide R. Zolberg, "The Revolution of Departures" in Nancy Green and François Weil, Citizenship and Those Who Leave: The Politics of Emigration and Expatriation (forthcoming, Urbana: The University of Illinois Press, 2006.

9. I have elaborated this point in Aristide R. Zolberg, "The Archaeology of Remote Control," in *Migration Control in the North Atlantic World: The Evolution of State Practices in Europe and the United States from the French Revolution to the Inter-War Period,* ed. Andreas Fahrmeir, Olivier Faron, and Patrick Weil (New York: Berghahn.Books, 2003), 195–222.

10. John Higham, *Strangers in the Land; Patterns of American Nativism, 1860–1925* (New Brunswick, NJ: Rutgers University Press, 1955). This was reprinted by Atheneum in 1963, and again by Atheneum in 1969 in a corrected edition with a new preface. The 1963 edition was reissued by Greenwood Press in 1981. A second edition, revised and with a postscript, was published by Rutgers University Press in 1994.

11. Ibid.

12. T.W. Adorno and others, *The Authoritarian Personality* (New York: Harper, 1950); and Gordon W. Allport, *Prejudice: A Problem in Psychological and Social Causation* (New York: Association Press, 1950).

13. The dynamics were first set forth by Richard Hofstadter in his Spencer lecture at Oxford in 1963, published in *Harper's* the following year, and reprinted in Richard Hofstadter, *The Paranoid Style in American Politics* (New York: Knopf, 1965). Within political science, this syndrome was featured in the early work of Gabriel Almond, notably *The American People and Foreign Policy* (New York: Praeger, 1960).

14. Daniel J. Tichenor, "Regulating Community: Race, Immigration Policy, and American Political Development," Brandeis University, Department of Politics, May 1996; and Daniel J. Tichenor, *Dividing Lines: The Politics of Immigration Control in America* (Princeton, NJ: Princeton University Press, 2002). Although in his first chapter Tichenor reviews the period 1776–1896, which here covers five chapters, his effective starting point is post–Civil War Chinese exclusion, and in contrast with my own interpretation arising from the "externalist" framework, he does not stress the role of American expansionism in that episode. I also place much more emphasis on the establishment of "remote control" as a breakthrough innovation of the 1920s.

15. Aristide R. Zolberg, "International Migration Policies in a Changing World System," in *Human Migration: Patterns and Policies,* ed. William H. McNeill and Ruth Adams (Indianapolis: Indiana University Press, 1978), 241–86; and Aristide R. Zolberg, "International Migrations in Political Perspective," in *Global Trends in Migration,* ed. Mary Kritz, Charles Keely, and Silvano Tomasi

(New York: Center for Migration Studies, 1981), 15–51. "Westphalian" refers to the 1648 Treaty of Westphalia, which established the supremacy of individual European sovereigns over their respective territories and the subjects contained therein, and their formal equality under "the law of nations."

16. Kingsley Davis, "The Migrations of Human Populations," *Scientific American* 231, no. 3 (1974): 96.

17. Douglas S. Massey et al., "Theories of International Migration: A Review and Appraisal," *Population and Development Review* 19, no. 3 (September 1993): 431–66.

18. Aristide R. Zolberg, "The Origins of the Modern World-System: A Missing Link," *World Politics* 33, no. 2 (1981): 253–81; Aristide R. Zolberg, " 'World' and 'System': A Misalliance," in *Contending Approaches to World System Analysis,* ed. William R. Thompson (Beverly Hills, CA: Sage, 1983), 269–90; and Aristide R. Zolberg, *Political Forces as Determinants of International Migration* (paper presented at the Rockefeller Study Center in Bellagio [Italy] Workshop on International Migrations held by the International Union for the Scientific Study of Population, March 1986).

19. Although this is a largely neglected subject, many empirical indications are available. For example, U.S. and British immigration restrictions in the 1920s probably deflected much of the movement from eastern and southern Europe to France (and, to a lesser extent, the Netherlands and Belgium), whose foreign population, including notably Armenians, Poles, and Italians, approximately doubled in the 1921–1930 period. Concurrently, much Italian immigration was deflected to South America. Another case in point is emigration from the British West Indies in the post–World War II period. From the 1920s on, British West Indians immigrated to the United States, thanks to the availability of entries under the British quota, undersubscribed by emigrants from the British Isles; numbers are indicated by the fact that among New York City's black population in the 1940 U.S. Census, some 10 percent were foreign-born. Black immigration proved highly disturbing to American segregationists, who had sought in vain to formally restrict it ever since the 1920s; however, in 1952, they successfully enacted a provision within the Walter-McCarran law limiting immigration from each colonial dependency to not more than 100 of the metropolitan country's quota. It is precisely at this time that West Indian immigration to the British Isles, which had hitherto been quite minimal, began to soar; and there is little doubt that the American decision contributed to this shift in direction. Conversely, starting in 1962 Britain began to close its door to people of color, whereas in 1965 the United States dropped its invidious restrictions, effective 1968. Accordingly, West Indian migration was deflected back toward the United States. There were

also many indications of interactivity among asylum applicants to various European countries in the 1980s, and of the deflection of their efforts toward Canada and the United States when the door was closed.

20. Hannah Arendt, *The Origins of Totalitarianism,* new ed. (New York: Harcourt, Brace and Jovanovich, 1973), 278.

21. Yasemin Nuhoglu Soysal, *Limits of Citizenship: Migrations and Postnational Membership in Europe* (Chicago: University of Chicago Press, 1994).

22. Albert O. Hirschman, "Exit, Voice, and the State," in *Essays in Trespassing: Economics to Politics and Beyond,* ed. Albert O. Hirschman (Cambridge: Cambridge University Press, 1981), 246–65; and Margaret Levi, *Of Rulers and Revenue* (Berkeley: University of California Press, 1988).

23. Zolberg, "International Migration Policies in a Changing World System"; and Alan Dowty, *Closed Borders: The Contemporary Assault on Freedom of Movement* (New Haven, CT: Yale University Press, 1987).

24. Aristide R. Zolberg, "The Formation of New States as a Refugee-Generating Process," *Annals of the American Academy of Political and Social Science* 467 (May 1983): 24–38; and Aristide R. Zolberg, Astri Suhrke, and Sergio Aguayo, *Escape from Violence: Conflict and the Refugee Crisis in the Developing World* (New York: Oxford University Press, 1989).

25. Daniel Kubat, *The Politics of Migration Policies: The First World in the 1970s* (New York: Center for Migration Studies, 1979); Wayne A. Cornelius, Philip L. Martin, and James F. Hollifield, *Controlling Immigration: A Global Perspective* (Stanford, CA: Stanford University Press, 1994); Gary P. Freeman, "Modes of Immigration Politics in Liberal Democratic States," *International Migration Review* 19, no. 4 (Winter 1995): 881–902, and "Rejoinder," 909–13; and Grete Brochmann, *European Integration and Immigration from Third Countries* (Oslo: Scandinavian University Press, 1996).

26. Jagdish N. Bhagwati, "Incentives and Disincentives: International Migration," *Weltwirtschaftliches Archiv* 120, no. 4 (1984): 678–701.

27. The use of functionalist language here is intentional. Immanuel Wallerstein, *The Modern World System: Capitalist Agriculture and the Origins of the European World-Economy in the Sixteenth Century* (New York: Academic Press, 1974); Roger Nett, "The Civil Right We Are Not Ready For: The Right of Free Movement of People on the Face of the Earth," *Ethics* 81, no. 3 (April 1971): 212–27; Arghiri Emmanuel, *Unequal Exchange: A Study of the Imperialism of Trade* (New York: Monthly Review Press, 1972); and Elizabeth Petras, "The Role of National Boundaries in a Cross-National Labour Market," *International Journal of Urban and Regional Research* 4, no. 2 (1980): 157–95.

28. Bob Hamilton and John Whalley, "Efficiency and Distributional Implications of Global Restrictions on Labour Mobility: Calculations and Policy Implications," *Journal of Development Economics* 14, no. 1–2 (1984): 61–75.

29. Michael Walzer, "The Distribution of Membership," in *Boundaries: National Autonomy and Its Limits,* ed. Peter G. Brown and Henry Shue (Totowa, NJ: Rowman & Littlefield, 1981); Brian Barry and Robert E. Goodin, eds., *Free Movement* (University Park: Pennsylvania State University Press, 1992); and Joseph Carens, paper on "Membership and Morality: Admission to Citizenship in Liberal Democratic States," German Marshall Fund Conference on Naturalization and the Status of Aliens, Graduate Faculty, New School University, New York City, November 1987.

30. As elaborated, for example, in Adam Przeworski and Michael Wallerstein, "The Structure of Class Conflict in Democratic Capitalist Societies," *American Political Science Review* 76 (1982): 215–38; and Claus Offe, *Contradictions of the Welfare State,* ed. John Keane (Cambridge, MA: MIT Press, 1984).

31. See Chapter 10.

32. Stephen Castles and Godula Kossack, *Immigrant Workers and Class Structure in Western Europe,* 2nd ed. (London: Oxford University Press, 1985); Michael Burawoy, "The Functions and Reproduction of Migrant Labor: Comparative Material from Southern Africa and the United States," *American Journal of Sociology* 81 (March 1976): 1050–87; and Elizabeth Petras, "The Global Labor Market in the Modern World Economy," in *Global Trends in Migration: Theory and Research on International Population Movements,* ed. Mary M. Kritz et al. (New York: Center for Migration Studies, 1981).

33. Michael Piore, *Birds of Passage: Migrant Labor and Industrial Societies* (Cambridge: Cambridge University Press, 1979); and David M. Gordon, Richard Edwards, and Michael Reich, *Segmented Work, Divided Workers: The Historical Transformation of Labor in the United States* (Cambridge: Cambridge University Press, 1982).

34. National Research Council, *The New Americans: Economic, Demographic, and Fiscal Effects of Immigration* (Washington, DC: National Research Council, 1997). It is noteworthy that, in contrast, some European planners in countries with declining populations advocate additional immigration (because immigrants tend to be younger than the general population) as a way of securing additional income for near-bankrupt old age insurance funds.

35. The parallel with "class" is more than metaphoric; as with class, "cultural compromises" can be thought of as "peace settlements" in the wake of "culture wars" pertaining to such matters as the degree of "recognition" of the culture in question, and institutional arrangements in spheres of work, education, and the like. However, contemporary democracies are less well equipped institutionally to deal with cultural matters than with those pertaining to "class," perhaps in part because "culture" has not received the same degree of theoretical elaboration from social scientists dealing with capitalist democracies, whose reluctance to deal with the subject has left a vacuum that is being

filled largely by "cultural studies." As with "class," the question is what intellectual tools are most appropriate for tackling the subject, what information should be relied on to assess putative effects, what are appropriate objectives, and what measures should be used in the evaluation of strategies to achieve them.

36. Aristide R. Zolberg and Litt Woon Long, "Why Islam Is Like Spanish: Cultural Incorporation in Europe and the United States," *Politics and Society* 27, no. 1 (1999): 5–38.

37. My approach owes a great deal to the following works: Clifford Geertz, *The Interpretation of Cultures* (New York: Basic Books, 1973); Benedict Anderson, *Imagined Communities: Reflections on the Origin and Spread of Nationalism* (London: New Left Books, 1983); and Fredrik Barth, ed., *Ethnic Groups and Boundaries* (Boston: Little, Brown, 1969). However, I am putting greater emphasis on "agency" in the form of sustained action by political elites. The notion of a "formula" was suggested by my former colleague Leonard Binder.

38. Rogers Brubaker, *Citizenship and Nationhood in France and Germany* (Cambridge, MA: Harvard University Press, 1992). But whereas Brubaker treats the "ethnic" and "political" foundations of nationality as contrasting ideal types, represented by Germany and France, I am inclined to view them as more or less complementary elements, which can and do coexist.

39. I owe this notion to Barth, *Ethnic Groups and Boundaries* (see note 37).

40. William H. McNeill, *The Rise of the West: A History of the Human Community* (New York: Mentor Books, 1963).

41. Aristide R. Zolberg, "Wanted but Not Welcome: Alien Labor in Western Development," in *Population in an Interacting World*, ed. William Alonso (Cambridge, MA: Harvard University Press, 1987), 36–74. On liminality, see Victor W. Turner, *The Ritual Process: Structure and Anti-Structure* (Chicago: Aldine Publishing Company, 1969).

42. I am grateful to Litt Woon Long for pointing out the distinctiveness of "patrials" as a special category of immigrants and for suggesting how they might fit into this framework. The best-known cases are, of course, Israel and Germany; however, nearly all other countries that had an extensive experience of emigration provide for special arrangements as well, including Italy, Spain, and the United Kingdom.

43. For an exposition of "path dependency," see Kathleen Thelen and Sven Steinmo, "Historical Institutionalism in Comparative Politics," in *Structuring Politics: Historical Institutionalism in Comparative Analysis,* ed. Sven Steinmo, Kathleen Thelen, and Frank Longstreth (New York: Cambridge University Press, 1992), 1–32; and Paul Pierson, "Increasing Returns, Path Dependence, and the Study of Politics," *American Political Science Review* 94, no. 2 (June 2000): 251–67. While sharing in the use, I do not believe it amounts to a testable "theory."

44. A more elaborate discussion of the material of this section is available in Aristide R. Zolberg, "Matters of State: Theorizing Immigration Policy," in *The Handbook of International Migration: The American Experience,* ed. Charles Hirschman, Philip Kasinitz, and Josh De Wind (New York: Russell Sage Foundation, 2000), 71–93.

45. James Q. Wilson, ed., *The Politics of Regulation* (New York: Harper, 1980).

46. Philippe C. Schmitter and Gerhard Lehmbruch, eds., *Trends toward Corporatist Intermediation* (Beverly Hills, CA: Sage, 1979).

47. The Maghrebis in France are a case in point: it is possible to write a detailed account of the politics of French immigration policy in the recent past without any reference to them as organized actors; see, for example, Patrick Weil, *La France et ses étrangers: L'aventure d'une politique de l'immigration de 1938 à nos jours* (Paris: Calmann-Levy, 1991).

48. Keith Fitzgerald, *The Face of the Nation: Immigration, the State, and the National Identity* (Stanford, CA: Stanford University Press, 1996).

49. Aristide R. Zolberg, "From Invitation to Interdiction," in *Threatened Peoples, Threatened Borders: World Migration and U.S. Policy,* ed. Michael S. Teitelbaum and Myron Weiner (New York: Norton, 1995), 117–59.

2. From Empire to Republic

1. My understanding of the Declaration of Independence and of the American Revolution is founded on four key works: Gordon S. Wood, *The Creation of the American Republic, 1776–1787* (1969; reprint, New York: W.W. Norton, 1972); Gordon S. Wood, *The Radicalism of the American Revolution* (1991; reprint, New York: Vintage, 1993); Gary Wills, *Inventing America: Jefferson's Declaration of Independence* (New York: Vintage Books, 1979); and Pauline Maier, *American Scripture: Making the Declaration of Independence* (New York: Alfred A. Knopf, 1997).

2. I am relying here on Herbert Friedenwald, *The Declaration of Independence* (New York: Macmillan 1904), 214–17, 226–29; and Edward Dumbault, *The Declaration of Independence and What It Means Today* (Norman: University of Oklahoma Press, 1950), 104–9.

3. Benjamin Franklin, *Writings,* ed. J.A. Leo Lemay (New York: Library of America, 1987), 357–59.

4. C. Matthew Snipp, *American Indians: The First of This Land* (New York: Russell Sage Foundation, 1991), 10. This range is much higher than the traditional estimate of 1.1 million because of evidence produced by new archeological techniques (Snipp, *American Indians,* 21).

5. Figures are from Campbell Gibson, "The Contribution of Immigration to the Growth and Ethnic Diversity of the American Population," *Proceedings of the American Philosophical Society* 136, no. 2 (1992): 165 n. 6. His source for

Europeans is Hans-Jürgen Grabbe, "European Immigration to the United States in the Early National Period, 1783–1820," *Proceedings of the American Philosophical Society* 133, no. 2 (June 1989): 190–214; and for Africans, Philip D. Curtin, *The Atlantic Slave Trade: A Census* (Madison: University of Wisconsin Press, 1969). For a more recent assessment, see Paul E. Lovejoy, "The Volume of the Atlantic Slave Trade: A Synthesis," *Journal of African History* 23 (1982): 474–501. Another comprehensive review for the period 1700–1775 comes up with similar estimates of 307,400 Europeans and 278,400 Africans; see Aaron Fogleman, "Migrations to the Thirteen British North American Colonies, 1700–1775: New Estimates," *Journal of Interdisciplinary History* 22 (Spring 1992): 691–709.

6. The model was elaborated by Evsey D. Domar, "The Causes of Slavery or Serfdom: A Hypothesis," *Journal of Economic History* 1, no. 30 (March 1970): 18–32. It has been applied to the American situation by Russell Menard, "From Servants to Slaves: The Transformation of the Chesapeake Labor System," *Southern Studies* 16, no. 4 (1977): 355–90; and Peter Kolchin, *Unfree Labor: American Slavery and Russian Serfdom* (Cambridge, MA: Harvard University Press, 1987). Although its explanatory power has been questioned with regard to the transition from white servants to slaves, it retains its full force with regard to the necessity of some form of bondage in situations that combine "free land" and a labor shortage.

7. Richard Colebrook Harris, "The Simplification of Europe Overseas," *Annals of the Association of American Geographers* 67 (1977): 469–83.

8. Charles Verlinden, *The Beginnings of Modern Colonization* (Ithaca, NY: Cornell University Press, 1970); and John H. Parry, *The Discovery of the Sea* (New York: Dial Press, 1974).

9. Noel Deerr, *The History of Sugar* (London: Chapman and Hall, 1949); Sidney Mintz, *Sweetness and Power: The Place of Sugar in Modern History* (New York: Penguin, 1986); and Kolchin, *Unfree Labor*, 40. Colonies were also established to mine precious metals, which might be initially seized by force if a local supply was available, but eventually had to be extracted wherever the deposits happened to be located.

10. Kolchin, *Unfree Labor*, 11. Although the English settlers did enslave some Indians, the proximity of the wilderness and of friendly tribes made it extremely difficult to control them, and the strategy of eliminating the threat of attack by eliminating the Indians themselves negated their use as labor.

11. My categorization of Canada largely follows Harris, "The Simplification of Europe Overseas."

12. Robert Wells, *The Population of the British Colonies in America before 1776: A Survey of Census Data* (Princeton, NJ: Princeton University Press, 1975), 64, 260. The Massachusetts figure is for 1764.

13. Colin McEvedy and Richard Jones, *Atlas of World Population History* (Harmondsworth, UK: Penguin, 1978).

14. E. Anthony Wrigley, "The Growth of Population in Eighteenth-Century England: A Conundrum Resolved," *Past and Present* 98 (1983): 121–50. The population of England and Wales is estimated to have grown from 3.0 million in 1550 to 5.2 million in 1651, at by far the highest rate in Europe.

15. Mildred Campbell, " 'Of People Either Too Few or Too Many': The Conflicts of Opinion on Population and Its Relation to Migration," in *Conflict in Stuart England: Essays in Honour of Wallace Notestein*, ed. William A. Aiken and Basil D. Henning (London: J. Cape, 1960), 171–201; and George Louis Beer, *The Origins of the British Colonial System, 1378–1660* (New York: Macmillan & Co., 1908), 35. The quotation is from Julian H. Franklin (ed and Trans) Jean Bodin, *Sovereignty: Six books of the Commonwealt* (Cambridge: Cambridge University Press, 1992), 85.

16. Henry A. Gemery, "Emigration from the British Isles to the New World, 1630–1700: Inferences from Colonial Populations," *Research in Economic History* 5 (1980): 179–231; and E.G. Ravenstein, "The Laws of Migration," *Journal of the Royal Statistical Society* 48 (June 1885): 167–235.

17. Abbot E. Smith, *Colonists in Bondage: White Servitude and Convict Labor in America, 1607–1776* (Chapel Hill: University of North Carolina Press, 1947), 46. In the mid-seventeenth century, transportation to New England and basic settlement expenses amounted to about £100 for a yeoman family of five, with an annual income of £40–60 pounds a year; the cost for a single servant was about £5, with an annual income of £8 to 12; David Cressy, *Coming Over: Migration and Communication between England and New England in the Seventeenth Century* (Cambridge: Cambridge University Press, 1987), 115–24.

18. Marcus W. Jernagan, *Laboring and Dependent Classes in Colonial America, 1607–1783* (1931; reprint, Westport, CT: Greenwood, 1980); Richard B. Morris, *Government and Labor in Early America* (1946; reprint, New York: Harper Torchbooks, 1965); David W. Galenson, *White Servitude in Colonial America: An Economic Analysis* (Cambridge: Cambridge University Press, 1981); Henry A. Gemery, "Markets for Migrants: English Indentured Servitude and Emigration in the Seventeenth and Eighteenth Centuries," in *Colonialism and Migration; Indenture Labour before and after Slavery,* ed. P.C. Emmer (Dordrecht: Martinus Nijhoff, 1986), 33–54; and Nicholas Canny, "In Search of a Better Home? European Overseas Migration, 1500–1800," in *Europeans on the Move: Studies on European Migration, 1500–1800,* ed. Nicholas Canny (Oxford: Clarendon Press, 1994b), 263–83. For France, see Leslie Choquette, "Recruitment of French Emigrants to Canada, 1600–1760," in *"To Make America": European Emigration in the Early Modern Period,* ed. Ida Altman and James Horn (Berkeley: University of California Press, 1991), 131–71.

19. David W. Galenson, "The Rise and Fall of Indentured Servitude in the Americas: An Economic Analysis," *Journal of Economic History* 46 (1984): 1–8.

20. Smith, *Colonists in Bondage,* 25. It was equally crucial in the settlement of the Caribbean Islands; after sugar was introduced on Barbados, the brightest jewel in the royal crown, its white population grew even more spectacularly from 6,000 in 1636 to 37,200 in 1643.

21. Ernst Van den Boogaart, "The Servant Migration to New Netherland, 1624–1664," in Emmer, *Colonialism and Migration*, 55–71. See also Oliver A. Rink, *Holland on the Hudson: An Economic and Social History of Dutch New York* (Ithaca, NY: Cornell University Press, 1986).

22. Wrigley, "The Growth of Population," 124.

23. Campbell, " 'Of People Either Too Few or Too Many,' " 188. Although the revaluation of English population was translated into policy by the creation of an office to register servant contracts so as to restrict emigration to those of little value to England (1664), it is unlikely that this was effectively implemented; Marilyn C. Baseler, *"Asylum for Mankind": America, 1607-1800* (Ithaca, NY: Cornell University Press, 1998), 35.

24. A. Roger Ekirch, *Bound for America: The Transportation of British Convicts to the Colonies, 1718–1775* (Oxford: Clarendon Press, 1987).

25. Edward P. Thomson, *Whigs and Hunters: The Origins of the Black Act* (New York: Pantheon, 1976).

26. John W. Blake, "Transportation from Ireland to America, 1653–60," *Irish Historical Studies* 3, no. 11 (1943): 267–81.

27. Gemery, "Markets for Migrants," 38.

28. Gemery, "Emigration from the British Isles."

29. The proportion is from Abbot Smith, who goes on to assert that servants "disappeared after 1645"; Smith, *Colonists in Bondage,* 337. The revision is from Cressy, *Coming Over,* 52–54; and Gary B. Nash, *The Urban Crucible: Social Change, Political Consciousness, and the Origins of the American Revolution* (Cambridge, MA: Harvard University Press, 1979), 15.

30. Cressy, *Coming Over,* 66.

31. T. H. Breen and S. Foster, "Moving to the New World: The Character of Early Massachusetts Immigration," *William and Mary Quarterly* 3rd ser., 30 (1973): 189–222; U.S. Bureau of the Census, *Historical Statistics of the United States, Colonial Times to 1970*, series Z, 1–19 (Washington, DC: Government Printing Office, 1971), 156; and David W. Galenson, " 'Middling People' or 'Common Sort?' The Social Origins of Some Early Americans Reexamined," *William and Mary Quarterly* 3rd ser., 35 (1978): 499–524.

32. Campbell, " 'Of People Either Too Few or Too Many,' " 182; Smith, *Colonists in Bondage,* 86; and James H. Cassedy, *Demography in Early America: Beginnings*

of the Statistical Mind, 1600–1800 (Cambridge, MA: Harvard University Press, 1969).

33. Cressy, *Coming Over,* 130ff.

34. Breen and Foster, "Moving to the New World," 201.

35. John Tracy Ellis, *Catholics in Colonial America* (Baltimore: Helicon, 1965), 12, 321–27. In keeping with this reasoning, for example, Charles I did not allow his favorite, the Catholic convert George Calvert, to participate in the Virginia venture, and he granted him a charter for Maryland, far from the French pressure point, only after Virginia was well established as an Anglican colony (1632). Because prospective Catholic settlers were deterred by the requirement of an Anglican oath, as of 1675 they constituted less than one-tenth of the colony's population. The Calverts' charter was revoked and Maryland made into a royal province with the Church of England as its official religion in the wake of the "Glorious Revolution" of 1688.

36. Menard, "From Servants to Slaves," 379. In the last quarter of the seventeenth century, the British Caribbean colonies imported slaves at an annual rate of at least 6,000, and by 1710 slaves constituted over 80 percent of the island population; Curtin, *The Atlantic Slave Trade,* 119, 125; and Galenson, *White Servitude in Colonial America,* table 48b. For the seventeenth century as a whole, they received 263,700 blacks to 174,445 whites, a ratio of approximately 1.5 to 1 (Curtin, *The Atlantic Slave Trade,* 216, table 65).

37. Galenson, " 'Middling People' or 'Common Sort?' "

38. David Brion Davis, *The Problem of Slavery in Western Culture* (Ithaca, NY: Cornell University Press, 1966), 125–262; and Winthrop D. Jordan, *White over Black: American Attitudes toward the Negro, 1550–1812* (Baltimore: Penguin, 1969), 44–98.

39. A.G. Roeber, " 'The Origin of Whatever Is Not English among Us': The Dutch-Speaking and the German-Speaking Peoples of Colonial British America," in *Strangers within the Realm: Cultural Margins of the First British Empire,* ed. Bernard Bailyn and Philip D. Morgan (Chapel Hill: University of North Carolina Press, 1991), 220–83. The response of Brandenburg-Prussia in 1686 expressed the overall norm: "If a government allowed emigration it was to further its own colonies and not to populate those of other states"; John Duncan Brite, "The Attitude of European States toward Emigration to the American Colonies and the United States 1607–1820" (Ph.D. diss., University of Chicago, Department of History, 1937), 198. On European policies more generally, see also Marcus Lee Hansen, *The Atlantic Migration, 1607–1850* (1940; reprint, New York: Harper Torchbooks, 1961).

40. Rink, *Holland on the Hudson,* 156; and Roeber, " 'The Origin.' " On the North Sea networks, see Juliette Roding and Lex Heerma van Voss, eds., *The North Sea and Culture (1550–1800)* (Hilversum, the Netherlands: Verloren, 1996).

41. Brite, "The Attitude of European States," 198.

42. Marianne S. Wokeck, "Harnessing the Lure of the 'Best Poor Man's Country': The Dynamics of German-Speaking Immigration to British North America, 1683–1783," in Altman and Horn, *To Make America,* 204–44.

43. Edward A. Hoyt, "Naturalization under the American Colonies: Signs of a New Community," *Political Science Quarterly* 67 (1952): 263. Unless otherwise indicated, the material on naturalization in this chapter is based on James Kettner, *The Development of American Citizenship, 1608–1870* (Chapel Hill: University of North Carolina Press, 1978), 65–128.

44. The Jewish Naturalization Act of 1753 made it possible for Jews to be naturalized without being received into the Anglican sacrament. See F. Felstenstein, *Anti-Semitic Stereotypes: A Paradigm of Otherness in English Popular Culture, 1660–1830* (Baltimore: Johns Hopkins University Press, 1998).

45. Hoyt, "Naturalization under the American Colonies," 258.

46. Nevertheless, some exceptions were made; Stephen Decatur, a Catholic, was naturalized in 1753. Kettner, *The Development of American Citizenship,* 114 n. 39.

47. Arriving at an average rate of over 50,000 a year for the century as a whole, slaves totaled 5.7–6.0 million for 1700–1810, about 60 percent of the entire historic Atlantic trade. The leading importer was Portugal, which brought some 1.9 million slaves to Brazil alone; Britain was second with 1.7 million, and France followed closely with 1.3 million. The few remaining Dutch colonies in the Caribbean also imported close to half a million Africans.

48. This contradicts the assertion by Parry (*Discovery of the Sea,* 163) that the colonizing nations exported emigrants "at an ever-increasing rate" in the eighteenth century. See the discussion in David Eltis, "Free and Coerced Transatlantic Migration: Some Comparisons," *American Historical Review* 88 (1983): 253; and Henry A. Gemery, "European Emigration to North America, 1700–1820: Numbers and Quasi-Numbers," *Perspectives in American History, New Series* 1 (1984): 303, and 342, table D1.

49. Curtin, *The Atlantic Slave Trade,* 216, table 65; Gemery, "European Emigration," 303, and 342, table D1; Lovejoy, "The Volume of the Atlantic Slave Trade," 484; and Jean-Pierre Poussou, "Les Mouvements Migratoires en France et à partir de la France de la fin du XVe siècle au début du XIXe siècle: Approches pour une synthèse," *Annales de démographie historique* (1970): 53–54.

50. Gemery, "European Emigration to North America," 303, table 3, 308, and 322, table A1(a); Bernard Bailyn, *The Peopling of British North America: An Introduction* (New York: Alfred A. Knopf, 1986); and Bernard Bailyn, *Voyagers to the West: A Passage in the Peopling of America on the Eve of the Revolution* (1986; reprint, New York: Vintage Books, 1988).

51. "During the Walpole era, a period of material progress and substantial tol-eration in England, English immigration slowed to a trickle of indentured servants and transported convicts"; Richard Hofstadter, *America at 1750: A Social Portrait* (New York: Vintage Books, 1973), 19, 24.

52. Smith, *Colonists in Bondage,* 7.

53. G. Moltmann, "The Migration of German Redemptioners to North America, 1720–1820," in Emmer, *Colonialism and Migration,* 105–22; and Wokeck, "Harnessing the Lure."

54. Smith, *Colonists in Bondage,* 5, 92, 110, 152, 163; and Bailyn, *Voyagers to the West,* 262.

55. Ekirch, *Bound for America,* 223, 227.

56. Maldwyn A. Jones, "The Scotch-Irish in British America," in Bailyn and Mogan, *Strangers within the Realm* (Chapel Hill: University of North Carolina Press, 1991), 284–313; and Kerby A. Miller, *Emigrants and Exiles: Ireland and the Irish Exodus to North America* (New York: Oxford University Press, 1985).

57. Miller, *Emigrants and Exiles,* 57.

58. Jones, "The Scotch-Irish," 292.

59. However, Irish Catholic victims of religious persecution, poverty, and forced displacement continued to be shipped mostly to the West Indies as inden-tured servants and convicts; in the middle decades of the eighteenth century, they dominated the lower ranks of the white population (Miller, *Immigrants and Exiles,* 139).

60. Baseler, *"Asylum for Mankind,"* 58–59.

61. Ellis, *Catholics in Colonial America;* David O'Brien, *Public Catholicism* (New York: Macmillan, 1989); and Jay P. Dolan, *The American Catholic Experience: A History from Colonial Times to the Present* (Notre Dame, IN: University of Notre Dame Press, 1992). Contemporaries estimated that perhaps three to four times the 25,000 had arrived from Ireland alone, but that in the absence of clergy and in the face of considerable anti-Catholic pressure, most of the others drifted away into Protestant denominations (Miller, *Emigrants and Ex-iles,* 144; and Ellis, *Catholics in Colonial America,* 377). On the other hand, since it is reasonable to surmise that the growth rate of the population of Irish Catholic origin was of the same order as that of Americans generally, the 25,000 were attributable to a smaller number of immigrants—how small de-pended, of course, on when they arrived.

62. Wrigley, "The Growth of Population in Eighteenth-Century England," 141.

63. L.M. Cullen, "The Irish Diaspora of the Seventeenth and Eighteenth Centu-ries," in Canny, *Europeans on the Move,* 144.

64. Bailyn, *The Peopling of British North America,* 40.

65. Ibid., 37. The "discipline" interpretation is my own.

66. Although there is some lingering confusion as to whether the disallowed act

was designed to attract foreigners, as the sentence's grammatical construction implies, or Scotch settlers, as suggested by leading scholars of the Declaration, the language clearly indicates that its author and presumably his audience were persuaded that legislated incentives contributed to immigration, and concomitantly that in their absence it would decline. See Erna Risch, "Encouragement of Immigration as Revealed in Colonial Legislation," *Virginia Magazine of History and Biography* 45 (1937): 9; Friedenwald, *The Declaration of Independence,* 229; and Dumbault, *The Declaration of Independence,* 105.

67. Emberson E. Proper, *Colonial Immigration Laws* (New York: Columbia University Press, 1900), 75. Proper may have mistaken a proposal for an actual act. His footnote is to page673 of the American Archives, 1774–1775, but in checking on my behalf, Mark Petracca found that the two letters on that page relate only to disputes over colonial naturalization acts. No trace of an act imposing an emigration tax has been found in the records of statutes for the entire period 1773–1775, nor is it mentioned in any of the relevant secondary sources.

68. Brite, "The Attitude of European States," 195.

69. Ibid., 225–302. He provides scattered evidence from Swiss cantons and German principalities that private and even public aid was extended to facilitate the removal of the poor, the lame, the marginals, and the unruly to America.

70. Farley Grubb, "German Immigration to Pennsylvania, 1709 to 1820," *Journal of Interdisciplinary History* 20 (1990): 417–36; and Wokeck, "Harnessing the Lure." The 115,000 is from Grubb; Wokeck suggests it amounted to 13 percent of the total, that is, 65,000 for the period 1683–1783; this is close to the 70,000 suggested by Georg Fertig, "Transatlantic Migration from the German-Speaking Parts of Central Europe, 1600–1800: Proportions, Structures, and Explanations," in Canny, *Europeans on the Move,* 203.

71. On a European scale, German literacy ranked second only to that of the Calvinist Scotch and Dutch. Initially, the Germans were mostly farmers. Although on the eve of independence, this category was twice as large as for English immigrants, by the turn of the nineteenth century the farmers were surpassed by the three retail trades of tailor, butcher, and baker; and the proportion of merchants, clerks, accountants, and doctors rose as well.

72. Risch, "Encouragement of Immigration," 9; Thomas L. Purvis, "The European Ancestry of the United States Population, 1790," *William and Mary Quarterly* 3rd ser., 41, no. 1 (January 1984): 98, table II; and Kettner, *The Development of American Citizenship, 1608–1870,* 99, 103.

73. Cited in Kettner, *The Development of American Citizenship,* 74.

74. In 1753, Parliament granted foreign-born Jews the right to petition for naturalization without being received into the Anglican sacrament; however, the

resulting outcry persuaded the government to repeal the act within a few months; John Gross, "The Waning of Old Stereotypes," *Times Literary Supplement,* May 5, 1995, 13.

75. Roeber, "The Origin of Whatever Is Not English among Us," 265.

76. Kettner, *The Development of American Citizenship,* 106.

77. Bernard Bailyn, *The Ideological Origins,* 203. On British and European state formation in the eighteenth century, see Michael Mann, *The Sources of Social Power* (Cambridge: Cambridge University Press, 1986). I have explored the effects of international conflict in Aristide R. Zolberg, "Strategic Interactions and the Formation of Modern States: France and England," in *The State in Global Perspective,* ed. Ali Kazancigil (London: Gower/UNESCO, 1986), 72–106.

78. Franklin, *Writings,* 357–59.

79. By failing to control his passions and thereby endangering the safety of his children, the king is no longer entitled to be called "father of his people"; Thomas Paine, *Collected Writings* (New York: Library of America, 1995).

80. Franklin, *Writings,* 359.

81. Ibid., 518–30.

82. Ibid., 583.

83. Robert Hughes, *The Fatal Shore: The Epic of Australia's Founding* (New York: Vintage Books, 1988), 54.

84. Franklin, *Writings,* 468.

85. Kettner, *The Development of American Citizenship,* 108; and Maldwyn Jones, *American Immigration* (Chicago: University of Chicago Press, 1960), 44.

86. Wells, *The Population of the British Colonies,* 29; and Cassedy, *Demography in Early America.*

87. Franklin, *Writings,* 367–74. On the significance of Franklin's demographic work more generally, see Alfred O. Aldridge, "Franklin as Demographer," *Journal of Economic History* 9 (1949): 25–44.

88. Franklin, *Writings,* 372.

89. Ibid., 373.

90. Ibid., 373.

91. Ibid., 705.

92. Ibid., 706.

93. Ravenstein, "The Laws of Migration"; see also Douglas S. Massey et al., "Theories of International Migration: A Review and Appraisal," *Population and Development Review* 19, no. 3 (September 1993): 431–66.

94. To hammer the point home, Franklin agitates the specter of feudal privilege, which could be counted upon to evoke in every Briton a vision of the Dark Ages of popery; Franklin, *Writings,* 709.

95. The discussion that follows is based on Frederick Whelan, "Citizenship and

the Right to Leave," *American Political Science Review* 75 (1981): 636–53. He
suggests, "The right to leave one's country—whether for travel, emigration,
or expatriation—falls clearly in the category of the traditional type of civil
rights, although its assertion is evidently new," most explicitly in the Universal
Declaration of Human Rights of 1948 (Whelan, "Citizenship," 639).

96. Ibid., 648.

97. Ibid., 648.

98. Kettner, *The Development of American Citizenship,* 158–66.

99. The characterization as "utterly groundless" is from Joseph J. Ellis, *American Sphinx: The Character of Thomas Jefferson* (New York: Knopf, 1997), 33. "Widely shared" is from Maier, *American Scripture,* 112ff.

100. Wills, *Inventing America,* 89–90.

101. With the French military threat finally out of the way, the more pressing problem stemmed from deteriorating political conditions in the southern colonies. Concurrently, French Canadian landowners perceived an urgent need for protection against the long-standing territorial ambitions of New England and New York, as well as encroachment by American traders into their fur market. For the Roman Catholic clergy, the British crown, which committed itself under the terms of peace to respect freedom of religion, was clearly preferable to the notoriously anti-Papist New Englanders. See McInnis, *Canadian Social and Political History,* 117; Easterbrook and Aitken, *Canadian Economic History,* 133; and Daniel Latouche, *Le Manuel de la Parole* (Sillery, Canada: Editions du Boréal Express, 1977), I, 27–49.

102. Wood, *The Creation of the American Republic,* 42.

103. The charge was again drawn from Jefferson's preamble to the Virginia Constitution, then rewritten by the drafting committee in Philadelphia; Maier, *American Scripture,* 116–17.

104. Kettner, *The Development of American Citizenship,* 104–6.

105. Friedenwald, *The Declaration of Independence,* 229,

106. Hoyt, "Naturalization under the American Colonies," 265. The restrictions on the naturalization of foreigners were not referred to in the first congress's petition to the king (1774), or in the summary view prepared by Jefferson as instructions for the Virginia delegates to that body (Wills, *Inventing America,* 69). However, in that text Jefferson does develop the theory of expatriation as justifying political independence.

107. Julian P. Boyd, ed., *The Papers of Thomas Jefferson* (Princeton, NJ: Princeton University Press, 1950), I:338.

108. As Kettner has emphasized, "Whatever agency admitted them, aliens became subjects by a legal process involving choice, consent, and contract. The kind of volitional relationship between member and community that naturalization implied and familiarized gradually came to dominate Americans' assumptions

about subjectship generally." Beyond this, "If native and adopted subjects shared the same status and the same rights, could not one conclude that their allegiance, too, was the same—contractual, volitional, and legal rather than natural and immutable?" Kettner, *The Development of American Citizenship,* 106–28.

109. Paine, *Collected Writings,* 23. (From *Common Sense,* published February 14, 1776.)

110. Louis Hartz, *The Founding of New Societies* (New York: Harcourt, Brace and World, 1964). For a different critique of Hartz, see Harris, "The Simplification of Europe Overseas."

111. I use 1790 because most of the relevant data refer to the first census as their baseline. The analysis is based on Thomas L. Purvis, "The European Ancestry of the United States Population, 1790," *William and Mary Quarterly* 3rd ser., 41, no. 1 (January 1984): 85–101; this is a critical revision of Forrest McDonald and Ellen Shapiro McDonald, "The Ethnic Origins of the American People, 1790," *William and Mary Quarterly* 3rd series, 37, no. 2 (April 1980): 179–99. The McDonalds rely on the 1931 classification, which gave 60.1 percent English (including Welsh), 17.6 percent Celtic (Scotch, Ulster, and Free State), 8.6 percent German, 6.9 percent other Europeans, and 6.8 percent unassigned. See also Gibson, "The Contribution of Immigration"; and Kolchin, *Unfree Labor,* 20.

112. Roeber, "The Origin of Whatever Is Not English among Us," 221–27.

113. Ellis, *Catholics in Colonial America,* 395; and Dolan, *The American Catholic Experience,* 188.

114. For a detailed treatment of this subject, see D.W. Meinig, *Atlantic America, 1492–1800,* vol. 1 of The *Shaping of America: A Geographical Perspective on 500 Years of History* (New Haven, CT: Yale University Press, 1986), 247ff. He specifies 130 regional-ethnoreligious components as of 1750 for North America as a whole (including the French possessions and the northernmost British territories in what is now Canada).

115. The concept of "plural society" was developed by J.S. Furnivall in *Colonial Theory and Practice: A Comparative Study of Burma and the Netherlands East Indies* (London: Cambridge University Press, 1948), and elaborated later on by M.G. Smith; see in particular M.G. Smith, "Institutional and Political Conditions of Pluralism," in *Pluralism in Africa,* ed. Leo Kuper and M. G. Smith (Berkeley: University of California Press, 1969), 27–66.

116. Nash, *The Urban Crucible,* xii.

117. Franklin, *Writings,* 374.

118. Despite their high literacy and skills, Germans were generally held in contempt by Anglo-Americans as ignorant, stupid, and uninterested in education; Grubb, "German Immigration to Pennsylvania, 1709 to 1820," 430.

119. Franklin, *Writings,* 472.
120. Roeber, " 'The Origin of Whatever Is Not English among Us,' " 243; and Wokeck, "Harnessing the Lure." In 1755, the Pennsylvania Assembly pointed out in an address to the governor, "The German Importations were at first and for a considerable Time of such as were Families of Substance and industrious sober People," but now, "We have reason to believe the Importations of Germans have been for some Time composed of a great Mixture of the Refuse of their People, and that the very Jails have contributed to the Supplies we are burthened with"; reprinted in Edith Abbott, *Historical Aspects of the Immigration Problems* (Chicago: University of Chicago Press, 1926), 702–3.
121. "[O]f the six printing houses in the Province [Pennsylvania], two are entirely German, two half German half English, and but two entirely English; They have one German News-paper, and one half German. Advertisements intended to be general are now printed in Dutch [that is, German] and English"; "[T]he Signs in our Streets have inscriptions in both languages, and in some places only German"; and "They begin of late to make all their Bonds and other legal Writings in their own Language, which (though I think it ought not to be) are allowed good in our Courts, where the German Business so encreases [*sic*] that there is continual need of Interpreters."
122. Michel de Certeau, Dominique Julia, and Jacques Revel, *Une Politique de la Langue: La Révolution Française et les Patois* (Paris: Gallimard, 1975).
123. The garrulous Franklin's silence regarding the Scotch-Irish is not for lack of experience of their troublesomeness, but his discretion may have been induced by the imperatives of political realism: in the absence of a sufficient body of English settlers to provide a political counterweight to the problematic Germans, the Pennsylvanian political leadership had no choice but to co-opt Protestant Celts into the "white Anglo-Saxon" community.
124. Franklin, *Writings,* 474.
125. Aristide R. Zolberg, "From Invitation to Interdiction," in *Threatened Peoples, Threatened Borders: World Migration and U.S. Policy,* ed. Michael S. Teitelbaum and Myron Weiner (New York: Norton, 1995), 117–59.
126. Wood, *The Radicalism of the American Revolution.*
127. Franklin, *Writings,* 646–53.

3. An Acquisitive Upstart

1. Tench Coxe, "An Enquiry into the Best Means of Encouraging Emigration from Abroad, Consistently with the Happiness and Safety of the Original Citizens. Read before the Society for Political Enquiries, at the House of Dr. Franklin, April 20th, 1787," *American Museum* 10 (September 1791): 114. Either neutral or briefly a Loyalist during the Revolution, Coxe became a

member of the Continental Congress in 1788; see *Dictionary of American Biography,* ed. Dumas Malone (New York: Charles Scribner's Sons, 1935), 2: 488–89).

2. The "historical struggle" over immigration appears to have been triggered by a 1928 pamphlet issued by the Immigration Restriction League, and by a critical response by Max J. Kohler. See Kohler's account in *Immigration and Aliens in the United States: Studies of American Immigration Laws and the Legal Status of Aliens in the United States* (New York: Bloch Publishing Co., 1936), 323. For recent attempts to mobilize the founders on behalf of restrictionism, see John Lukacs, *Immigration and Migration: A Historical Perspective* (Monterey, VA: American Immigration Control Foundation, 1986); and Wayne Lutton, *The Myth of Open Borders: The American Tradition of Immigration Control* (Monterey, VA: American Immigration Control Foundation, 1988).

3. Thomas Jefferson, *Notes on the State of Virginia,* ed. William Peden (1787; reprint, Chapel Hill: University of North Carolina Press, 1955).

4. On his intervention at the Convention, see Frank George Franklin, *The Legislative History of Naturalization in the United States: From the Revolutionary War to 1861* (1906; reprint, New York: Arno Press, 1969), 23; and for the 1791 article, see James Madison, *The Papers of James Madison,* ed. William T. Hutchinson et al. (Charlottesville: University of Virginia Press, 1962).

5. For a broadly similar perspective, see Matthew Spalding, "From Pluribus to Unum: Immigration and the Founding Fathers," *Policy Review* 67 (1994): 35–41.

6. Robert H. Wiebe, *The Segmented Society: An Introduction to the Meaning of America* (New York: Oxford University Press, 1975), 130.

7. Hansen, *The Atlantic Migration, 1607–1850* (1940; reprint, New York: Harper Torchbooks, 1961), 53.

8. Karl Polanyi, *The Great Transformation: The Political and Economic Origins of Our Time* (1944; reprint, Boston: Beacon Press, 1957).

9. Maldwyn A. Jones, "The Background to Emigration from Great Britain in the Nineteenth Century," *Perspectives in American History* 7 (1973): 12. The act is 25 Geo. III, c. 67.

10. Maldwyn Jones, *American Immigration* (Chicago: University of Chicago Press, 1960), 67.

11. Reprinted in *Niles' Weekly Register* (hereafter, *NWR*), November 27, 1819.

12. Norman Macdonald, *Canada 1763–1841: Immigration and Settlement: The Administration of Imperial Land Regulations* (London: Longmans, Green, and Co., 1939).

13. The established estimate for the Loyalist population is 450,000; Paul H. Smith, "The American Loyalists: Notes on Their Organization and Numerical Strength," *William and Mary Quarterly* 3rd ser., 25 (April 1968): 259–77. The

figure of 100,000 Loyalist emigrants (for example, Rogers Smith, *Civic Ideals: Conflicting Visions of Citizenship in U.S. History* [New Haven, CT: Yale University Press, 1997], 89), appears to be a "stylized fact"—a term coined by Henry A. Gemery, "European Emigration to North America, 1700–1820: Numbers and Quasi-Numbers," *Perspectives in American History,* new ser. 1 (1984): 313. Recent demographic accounts indicate that some 26,000 immigrated to Canada as of 1783, rising to perhaps 40,000 altogether (Gemery, "European Emigration," 312); an unknown number moved to Britain, some of whom subsequently re-immigrated to British North America. More recently, Christopher Moore has asserted that the conflict "drove at least fifty thousand colonial Americans into exile for the sake of their beliefs"; Christopher Moore, *The Loyalists: Revolution, Exile, Settlement* (Toronto: Macmillan of Canada, 1984), 9. The comparison with France is from Robert R. Palmer, *The Struggle,* vol. 2 of *The Age of Democratic Revolution: A Political History of Europe and America, 1760–1800* (Princeton, NJ: Princeton University Press, 1964), 188.

14. William S. Livingston, "Emigration as a Theoretical Doctrine during the American Revolution," *Journal of Politics* 19, no. 4 (1957): 591–615; and Gerald Neuman, *Strangers to the Constitution: Immigrants, Borders, and Fundamental Law* (Princeton, NJ: Princeton University Press, 1996), 23.

15. Smith, *Civic Ideals,* 93. He also points out that the issue of Loyalists intervened in debates on citizenship, including the question of whether American-born children of persons who left were citizens by virtue of jus soli (154).

16. This episode was referred to in a news story headed "For Nova Scotia Blacks, Veil Is Ripped from Past," *New York Times* (hereafter, *NYT*), October 8, 1999, 11. Nova Scotia still has an isolated black minority of 18,000 people.

17. Editor's comment to James Madison, "Population and Emigration," in *The Papers,* Vol. 14, 122.

18. James H. Cassedy, *Demography in Early America: Beginnings of the Statistical Mind, 1600–1800* (Cambridge, MA: Harvard University Press, 1969), 207–29.

19. Jefferson, *Notes on the State of Virginia,* 84; and Madison, *Papers.*

20. U.S. Bureau of the Census, *Historical Statistics of the United States, Colonial Times to 1970* (Washington, DC: Government Printing Office, 1975), 97. The history referred to is William J. Bromwell, *History of Immigration to the United States* (1856; reprint, New York: Arno Press, 1969). The "quarter of a million" was reproduced by Edward Young in his *Special Report on Immigration* (Washington, DC: U.S. Department of the Treasury, Bureau of Statistics, 1872). The Bromwell-Young data were challenged by E. P. Hutchinson, "Notes on Immigration Statistics of the United States," *Journal of the American Statistical Association* 53 (December 1958): 969. A slight variant (234,000) is provided by Campbell Gibson, "The Contribution of Immigration to United States Population Growth: 1790–1970," *IMR* 9, no. 2 (Summer 1975): 171, table 4.

21. "Hardly more than a trickle" is from Hansen, *Atlantic Migration,* 71 (this refers to the period 1783–1815 only). "Limited" is from Jones, *American Immigration,* 64. "[F]or several decades" is from James H. Cassedy, *Demography in Early America: Beginnings of the Statistical Mind, 1600–1800* (Cambridge, MA: Harvard University Press, 1969), 207 (citing Jones as his source).

22. The two major sources for the new estimates are Henry A. Gemery, "European Emigration"; and Hans-Jürgen Grabbe, "European Immigration to the United States in the Early National Period, 1783–1820," *Proceedings of the American Philosophical Society* 133, no. 2 (June 1989): 190–214. On the basis of population projections, Gemery estimates a minimum of 400,000; on the basis of passenger lists from ships landing in Philadelphia, and inferences from them to the national level, Grabbe estimates 366,000 (1783–1820).

23. Grabbe, "European Immigration," 198–200.

24. Campbell Gibson, "The Contribution of Immigration to United States Population Growth: 1790–1970"; and Campbell Gibson, "The Contribution of Immigration to the Growth and Ethnic Diversity of the American Population," *Proceedings of the American Philosophical Society* 136, no. 2 (1992): 32–35. My percentages are somewhat higher than Gibson's because I use white rather than total population, and because recent research has boosted immigration estimates for the period 1780–1820.

25. Hansen, *Atlantic Migration,* 52; and Bernard Bailyn, *Voyagers to the West: A Passage in the Peopling of America on the Eve of the Revolution* (1986; reprint, New York: Vintage Books, 1988), 1988. More generally, Brinley Thomas has suggested that immigration preceded rather than followed waves of economic growth in the United States before the Civil War; Brinley Thomas, *Migration and Economic Growth: A Study of Great Britain and the Atlantic Economy* (London: Cambridge University Press, 1973).

26. In a footnote, Madison demonstrates the evils of slavery by pointing to the much lower rate of natural increase among Africans, and further of the slave trade, as indicated by the negative rate in the British West Indies (118).

27. Benjamin Franklin, *Writings* ed. J.A. Leo Lemay (New York: Library of America, 1987), 1098–102, letter dated August 12, 1784.

28. Drew McCoy, *The Elusive Republic: Political Economy in Jeffersonian America* (Chapel Hill: University of North Carolina Press, 1980), 155–56.

29. Robert F. Berkhofer Jr., "Jefferson, the Ordinance of 1784, and the Origins of the American Territorial System," *William and Mary Quarterly* 3rd ser., 29 (1972): 232. The negotiated cession of state lands to the national government also served to maintain land prices by reducing competition among sellers.

30. Peter Onuf, *Statehood and Union: A History of the Northwest Ordinance* (Bloomington: Indiana University Press, 1987), 37.

31. Coxe, "An Enquiry," 115.

32. On the place of land in republican theory, see Gordon S. Wood, *The Radicalism of the American Revolution* (1991; reprint, New York: Vintage, 1993), 234. My understanding of the development of the land system is drawn from Marshall Harris, *Origin of the Land Tenure System in the United States* (Ames: Iowa State College Press, 1953), 310–411; Onuf, *Statehood and Union;* and Donald William Meinig, *Continental America, 1800–1867*, vol. 2 of *The Shaping of America: A Geographical Perspective on 500 Years of History* (New Haven, CT: Yale University Press, 1993), 236–63.

33. Harris, *Origins of the Land Tenure System,* 310. In the decades following the Revolution, all the new states abolished primogeniture and entail where they existed, either by statute or in their constitutions; they also recognized the equal rights of daughters and widows in inheritance and possession of property (Wood, *The Radicalism of the American Revolution,* 183).

34. Jones, *American Immigration,* 42. Nevertheless, in the wake of the Revolution, various states made land grants to returning soldiers, often using land confiscated from Loyalists for this purpose.

35. Accordingly, Franklin informed "Those Who Would Remove to America" in 1784, even as the first of the national land ordinances was in preparation, that whereas in the past governments provided land grants and other material advantages by way of encouragement to strangers, they no longer do so beyond "what are derived from good Laws & Liberty"; Franklin, *Writings,* 977–78.

36. Alexander Hamilton, "Report on the Subject of Manufactures" (1791), in *The Papers of Alexander Hamilton,* ed. Harold C. Syrett et al. (New York: Columbia University Press, 1961–1987), X, 233, 254.

37. The measures provided for the western lands to be surveyed and formed into townships of equal size, each divided into 36 sections of 640 acres each, and sold at auction in units of not less than a section and at a price of no less than a dollar an acre. They also swept away most of the remnants of the old order and firmly institutionalized freehold tenure. These arrangements were confirmed by the Northwest Ordinance of 1787, which banned primogeniture and also excluded slavery and other forms of servitude from the states that would emerge from the region. The basic land and governance arrangements were replicated for the Southwest in 1790, but with the provision of slavery as a possibility.

38. The estimated average farm acreage in the North in 1800 was 125–150; Stanley Lebergott, "The Demand for Land: The United States, 1820–1860," *Journal of Economic History* 45, no. 2 (June 1985): 185, table 1.

39. Hansen, *American Immigration,* 58, 62.

40. Macdonald, *Canada 1763–1841,* 90.

41. John C. Miller, *The Federalist Era, 1789–1801* (New York: Harper & Row, 1960), 183–84.

42. Meinig, *Continental America,* 44.

43. Marilyn C. Baseler, *"Asylum for Mankind": America, 1607-1800* (Ithaca, NY: Cornell University Press, 1998), 246.

44. Franklin, 980–81.

45. Hamilton, "Report on Manufactures," 230–340.

46. Ibid., 266.

47. Ibid., 271.

48. Ibid., 296.

49. Jones, *American Immigration,* 69.

50. David M. Gordon, Richard Edwards, and Michael Reich, *Segmented Work, Divided Workers: The Historical Transformation of Labor in the United States* (Cambridge: Cambridge University Press, 1982); and Michael Piore, *Birds of Passage: Migrant Labor and Industrial Societies* (Cambridge: Cambridge University Press, 1979).

51. On this subject generally, see Aaron S. Fogleman, "From Slaves, Convicts, and Servants to Free Passengers: The Transformation of Immigration in the Era of the American Revolution," *Journal of American History* 85, no. 1 (June 1998): 43–76.

52. Gary B. Nash, *The Urban Crucible: Social Change, Political Consciousness, and the Origins of the American Revolution* (Cambridge, MA: Harvard University Press, 1979), 320; and Sharon Salinger, "Colonial Labor in Transition: The Decline of Indentured Servitude in Late Eighteenth Century Philadelphia," *Labor History* 22 (Spring 1981): 183–91.

53. Robert J. Steinfeld, *The Invention of Free Labor: The Employment Relation in English and American Law and Culture, 1350–1870* (Chapel Hill: University of North Carolina Press, 1991), 115; and Morris, *Government and Labor in Early America* (1946; reprint, New York: Harper Torchbooks, 1965), 322 n. 25.

54. David Brion Davis, *The Problem of Slavery in the Age of Revolution, 1770–1823* (Ithaca, NY: Cornell University Press, 1975), 480–82. However, such incidents may have been the work of opportunistic labor recruiters; see for example the incident reported in Steinfeld, *The Invention of Free Labor,* 165; and also Wood, *The Radicalism of the American Revolution,* 184.

55. Steinfeld, *The Invention of Free Labor,* 133.

56. G. Moltmann, "The Migration of German Redemptioners to North America, 1720–1820," in *Colonialism and Migration: Indenture Labour before and after Slavery,* ed. P. C. Emmer (Dordrecht: Martinus Nijhoff, 1986), 106. See also Farley Grubb, "Redemptioner Immigration to Pennsylvania: Evidence on Contract Choice and Profitability," *Journal of Economic History* 46, no. 2 (June 1986): 407–18.

57. Farley Grubb, "The Auction of Redemptioner Servants, Philadelphia, 1771–1804: An Economic Analysis," *Journal of Economic History* 48, no. 3 (September 1988): 589 n. 14.

58. Farley Grubb, "The Incidence of Servitude in Trans-Atlantic Migration, 1771–1804," *Explorations in Economic History* 22 (July 1985): 337. Older estimates were as high as two-thirds; Morris, *Government and Labor,* 322 n. 29. On redemption assistance, see Erna Risch, "Immigrant Aid Societies before 1820," *Pennsylvania Magazine of History and Biography* 60 (1936): 15–33; and G. Moltmann, "The Migration of German Redemptioners to North America, 1720–1820," in Emmer, *Colonialism and Migration,* 105–22.

59. Moltmann, "The Migration," 117.

60. John Duncan Brite, "The Attitude of European States toward Emigration to the American Colonies and the United States 1607–1820" (Ph.D. diss., University of Chicago, Department of History, 1937).

61. Coxe, "An Enquiry," 114–17.

62. Gerald Neuman has pointed out that within the framework of social contract theory, which guided reasoning in these matters, "The notion of an alien's entering the country requires a shift of attention from the society as a union of individuals to the occupation of territory by a society"; Neuman, *Strangers to the Constitution,* 13–14.

63. Robert Hughes, *The Fatal Shore: The Epic of Australia's Founding* (New York: Vintage Books, 1988), 41.

64. Aaron S. Fogleman, "From Slaves, Convicts, and Servants to Free Passengers: The Transformation of Immigration in the Era of the American Revolution," *Journal of American History* 85, no. 1 (June 1998): 60; and A. Roger Ekirch, "Great Britain's Secret Convict Trade to America, 1783–1784," *American Historical Review,* 89 (1984): 1285.

65. A. Roger Ekirch, *Bound for America: The Transportation of British Convicts to the Colonies, 1718–1775* (Oxford: Clarendon Press, 1987), 233–37.

66. Franklin, *Writings,* 1142–44.

67. Edith Abbott, *Immigration: Selected Documents and Case Records* (Chicago: University of Chicago Press, 1924), 102–4; Morris, *Government and Labor,* 327; Jones, *American Immigration,* 67; Roy L. Garis, *Immigration Restriction: A Study of the Opposition to and Regulation of Immigrants into the United States* (New York: Macmillan, 1927), 22; and Gerald Neuman, "The Lost Century of American Immigration Law (1776–1875)," *Columbia Law Review* 93, no. 8 (December 1993): 1841–43.

68. Jefferson, *Notes on the State of Virginia,* 133.

69. See, for example, Kerby A. Miller, *Emigrants and Exiles: Ireland and the Irish Exodus to North America* (New York: Oxford University Press, 1985), 169.

70. Edith Abbott, *Historical Aspects of the Immigration Problems* (Chicago: University of Chicago Press, 1926), 708–11.

71. Palmer, *The Struggle,* 191. This was well known in the United States; see for example James Madison, "Population and Emigration (Published in the *Na-*

tional Gazette, Philadelphia, Nov. 19, 1791," in *The Papers of James Madison,* ed. Robert A. Rutland, Thomas A. Mason, et al. (Charlottesville: University Press of Virginia, 1791), 14:120.

72. Benjamin J. Klebaner, "State and Local Immigration Regulation in the United States before 1882," *International Review of Social History* 3 (1958): 269–95.

73. Neuman, "The Lost Century," 1842. He comments that "to draw a clear distinction between the exclusion of criminals and the exclusion of the undesired poor would be anachronistic."

74. Abbott, *Immigration,* 105.

75. Robert Greenhalgh Albion, *The Rise of the New York Port, 1815–1860* (New York: Charles Scribner's Sons, 1939), 336–53. My account of legislation is reconstructed from materials in Klebaner, Neuman, and Abbott, *Immigration,* 104.

76. For the suggestion of such an effect, see Klebaner, "State and Local Immigration regulation," 284 n. 45, 288–89. I discuss this more extensively in Aristide R. Zolberg, "The Archaeology of Remote Control," in *Migration Control in the North Atlantic World; The Evolution of State Practices in Europe and the United States from the French Revolution to the Inter-War Period,* ed. Andreas Fahrmeir and Patrick Weil (New York: Berghahn Books, 2003), 195–222.

77. This curiously adumbrates the German Democratic Republic practice in the mid-1980s with regard to immigrants from the Third World who were allowed to board its national airline, Interflug, without passports or visas, since it was well known that upon landing they would immediately go to the Friedrichstrasse subway station and be admitted to the Federal Republic as refugees.

78. This is based in large part on Davis, *The Problem of Slavery,* especially 120–30, 173, 273; and John Hope Franklin, *From Slavery to Freedom: A History of Negro Americans,* 4th ed. (New York: Alfred A. Knopf, 1974), 85–101.

79. Winthrop D. Jordan, *White over Black: American Attitudes toward the Negro, 1550–1812* (Baltimore: Penguin Books, 1969), 567.

80. In Jefferson, *Notes on the State of Virginia,* as pointed out by Jordan, *White over Black,* 546.

81. Johnson U. J. Asiegbu, *Slavery and the Politics of Liberation, 1787–1861: A Study of Liberated African Emigration and British Anti-Slavery Policy* (London: Longmans, 1969), 1–29. Winthrop Jordan has suggested, "If there was one thread of development which showed how deeply Americans felt about Negroes, it was a campaign which developed in the 1790's especially in Virginia for ridding the state (and the entire nation) of black men"; Jordan, *White over Black,* 542.

82. Floyd J. Miller, *The Search for a Black Nationality: Black Emigration and Colonization 1787–1863* (Urbana: University of Illinois Press, 1975), 1–20; and

Dickson D. Bruce Jr., "National Identity and African-American Colonization, 1773–1817," *Historian* 58, no. 1 (1995): 15–28.

83. As is well known, representation in the House was to be apportioned among the several states "according to their respective numbers," and this would also go into the determination of each state's votes in the Electoral College for the presidency.

84. Chief Justice John Marshall confirmed retrospectively in *Gibbons v. Ogden,* 9 Wheat., 1, 6L, Ed. 23 (1824), 217–18, that "migration" meant ordinary "immigration"; Charles Warren, *The Supreme Court in United States History* (Boston: Little, Brown, 1922), 1:597–99. See also Davis, *The Problem of Slavery,* 126.

85. In *Federalist* No. 42, Madison defends the clause, albeit regretting that the power to prohibit was postponed until 1808, and in the course of rejecting objections, deals with immigration as well: "Attempts have been made to pervert this clause into an objection against the Constitution by representing it on one side as a criminal toleration of an illicit practice, and on another as calculated to prevent voluntary and beneficial emigrations from Europe to America"; Alexander Hamilton, James Madison, and John Jay, Rossiter, Clinton *Federalist Papers* (New York: Signet Classic, 1961), 267. One might reasonably infer from his use of the qualifiers "voluntary and beneficial" that the power to prohibit was meant to cover their opposite, "involuntary and harmful" immigrations. Garis accepts the interpretation set forth by Justice Iredell at the North Carolina convention that Congress was empowered to prohibit both "migrations" and "importations" after 1808, but in the intervening period could tax only the latter, that is, slaves; Garis, *Immigration Restriction,* 60.

86. Aaron S. Fogleman, "From Slaves, Convicts, and Servants to Free Passengers: The Transformation of Immigration in the Era of the American Revolution," *Journal of American History* 85, no. 1 (June 1998), 44, table 1, and 74. By 1793, only Georgia still allowed the legal importation of slaves from Africa; but even this holdout banned imports from the West Indies and Spanish Florida, and finally prohibited African imports in 1798. Estimates range as high as 291,000 for the period 1780–1819; Robert W. Vogel, "Revised Estimates of the U.S. Slave Trade and of the Native-Born Share of the Black Population," in *Without Consent or Contract: The Rise and Fall of American Slavery: Evidence and Methods,* ed. Robert W. Fogel, Ralph A. Galantine, and Richard L. Manning (New York: Norton, 1992), 53–58. Louisiana, where the shortage was especially acute because the Spanish authorities imposed a total ban on imports from 1795 to 1800 in fear of insurrection, managed to import several thousand in 1806 and 1807; Paul F. Lachance, "The Politics of Fear: French Louisianans and the Slave Trade, 1786–1809," *Plantation Society* 1, no. 2 (June 1979): 180, 189.

87. Richard B. Morris, ed., *Encyclopedia of American History* (New York: Harper & Row, 1976), 757.

88. Empirical details of this section are drawn from Frank George Franklin, *The Legislative History of Naturalization in the United States: From the Revolutionary War to 1861* (1906; reprint, New York: Arno Press, 1969); James Kettner, *The Development of American Citizenship, 1608–1870* (Chapel Hill: University of North Carolina Press, 1978); and Paul Rundquist, "A Uniform Naturalization: The Congress and the Court in American Naturalization, 1865–1952" (Ph.D. diss., University of Chicago, 1975).

89. Smith, *Civic Ideals,* 97–98.

90. Palmer, *The Age of Democratic Revolution,* 1:224.

91. Jefferson, *Notes on the State of Virginia,* 134.

92. Ibid., 85.

93. Palmer, *The Age of Democratic Revolution,* 1:223. My abbreviated presentation of the theoretical side is based on the extensive discussion in Neuman, *Strangers to the Constitution,* 3–15; and in Smith, *Civic Ideals,* 71–86.

94. Neuman, *Strangers to the Constitution,* 11.

95. For example, in Philadelphia alone, around the turn of the new century admissions to U.S. citizenship—which pertained to adult males only, as wives and children benefited from derivative naturalization—averaged over 300 a year; Edward C. Carter II, "Naturalization in Philadelphia, 1789–1806: A 'Wild Irishman' under Every Federalist's Bed—Revisited Twenty Years Later," *Proceedings of the American Philosophical Society* 133, no. 2 (1989): 175–89.

96. Smith, *Civic Ideals,* 155–59, 169–70, 192–94.

97. Because jus soli provides automatic citizenship to the children of immigrants born in the host country, it is generally regarded in contemporary immigration debates as an "open" doctrine, associated with a "civic" conception of nationality, in contrast with the more "closed" jus sanguinis, which is associated with an "ethnic" conception; Rogers Brubaker, *Citizenship and Nationhood in France and Germany* (Cambridge, MA: Harvard University Press, 1992). However, these characterizations are misleading with regard to the period under consideration, and have been questioned to some extent with regard to Europe as well; Yves Lequin, ed., *La Mosaïque France. Histoire des étrangers et de l'immigration en France* (Paris: Larousse, 1988), 36–42. On the entire subject, see also Peter H. Schuck and Rogers M. Smith, *Citizenship without Consent: Illegal Aliens in the American Polity* (New Haven, CT: Yale University Press, 1985).

98. Thomas Paine, "The Rights of Man. Part Two (1792)," in *Collected Writings* (New York: Library of America, 1995), 554–55.

99. Michel de Certeau, Dominique Julia, and Jacques Revel, *Une politique de la langue: La Révolution française et les patois* (Paris: Gallimard, 1975).

100. Hamilton, Madison, and Jay, *The Federalist Papers,* 38. Obviously limiting

himself to the white population, Jay probably had in mind an encompassing "WASP" nationality that included most of the population originating in the British Isles as well as anglicized Netherlanders (such as himself), whose ancestral country had evolved from a trade rival into a "sisterly" kingdom at the time of the Glorious Revolution a century earlier, amounting altogether to 88.7 percent of whites.

101. Paine, "The Rights of Man. Part Two," 554–55.
102. Smith, *Civic Ideals,* 84.
103. Benjamin Rush singled out "[t]he equal share of power it holds forth to men of every religious sect" as the first of the "peculiarities in this government, which cannot fail of being agreeable to Europeans, who are disposed to settle in America," adding that "[a]s the first fruits of this perfection in our government, we already see three gentlemen of the Roman Catholic church, members of the legislature of the United States"; Benjamin Rush, *Essays, Literary, Moral and Philosophical: Edited, with an Introductory Essay by Michael Meranze* (1906; reprint, Schenectady, NY: Union College Press, 1988), 118.
104. Smith, *Civic Ideals,* 129.
105. Jones, *American Immigration,* 80–81.
106. South Carolina, for example, which had a "free and white" qualification for naturalization and required a longer residence than most others, must give equal status to Pennsylvania citizens naturalized after one month, or to pacified Indians who had become citizens of Massachusetts; Hamilton, Madison, and Jay, *Federalist Papers,* 269–70.
107. Rundquist, "A Uniform Naturalization." It was not clear whether states could grant naturalization to foreigners with respect to their own citizenship, even after Congress determined a "uniform rule," as the colonies had often done in relation to Britain; and if so, what would be the relationship between this and U.S. citizenship. Moreover, as the rules of suffrage continued to be determined by the states, persons who did not yet qualify for naturalization under federal law might be granted the right to vote, whereas some of the U.S. naturalized might be denied it. With regard to voting practices during this period, see Jamin B. Raskin, "Legal Aliens, Local Citizens: The Historical, Constitutional and Theoretical Meanings of Alien Suffrage," *University of Pennsylvania Law Review* 141 (1993): 1393–469. Voting rights for alien white men of property were fairly common in the colonial period and survived the Revolution; and in 1789 the 1st Congress reenacted the Northwest Ordinance, which gave freehold aliens who had been residents for two years the right to vote for representatives to the territorial legislature. This stance was maintained as the territories made their transition to statehood.
108. Franklin, *Legislative History of Naturalization,* 38.
109. Wood, *Radicalism of the American Revolution,* 260.

110. This point is emphasized by Garis, *Immigration Restriction*, 22. Massachusetts, for example, prohibited their return.

111. Paine, *Collected Writings*, 554.

112. James Morton Smith, *Freedom's Fetters, American Civil Liberties* (Ithaca, NY: Cornell University Press, 1956).

113. Higham, *Strangers in the Land*, 2nd ed., rev., 7. See also David Bennett, *The Party of Fear: From Nativist Movements to the New Right in American History* (Chapel Hill: University of North Carolina Press, 1988), 22.

114. Stanley Elkins and Eric McKitrick, *The Age of Federalism* (New York: Oxford University Press, 1993), 590. The authors based their judgment on the fact that the program was not endorsed by Adams and was enacted by narrow margins. See also Smith, *Civic Ideals*, 128.

115. I elaborate this in Aristide R. Zolberg, "International Engagement and American Democracy: A Comparative Perspective," in *International Influences on American Political Development*, ed. Ira Katznelson and Martin Shefter (Princeton, NJ: Princeton University Press, 1999). My understanding of the revolutions and wars of the late eighteenth century as a global Atlantic process is drawn from Palmer, *The Age of Democratic Revolution*, vols. 1 and 2. For American developments, I have relied mainly on Miller, *The Federalist Era*; Elkins and McKitrick, *The Age of Federalism*; Robert H. Wiebe, *The Opening of American Society: From the Adoption of the Constitution to the Eve of Disunion* (New York: Alfred A. Knopf, 1984); and James Roger Sharp, *American Politics in the Early Republic: The New Nation in Crisis* (New Haven, CT: Yale University Press, 1993).

116. Ronald P. Formisano, "Deferential-Participant Politics: The Early Republic's Political Culture, 1789–1840," *American Political Science Review* 68 (1974): 473–87.

117. Palmer, *Age of Democratic Revolution*, 1:514; Hansen, *Atlantic Migration*, 58–59; and Paul F. Lachance, "Les Vaincus de la révolution haïtienne en quête d'un refuge: De Saint-Domingue à Cuba (1803), de Cuba à la Nouvelle-Orléans (1809)," *Revue de la société haïtienne d'histoire, de géographie, et de géologie* 54, no. 126 (March 1980): 15–30. According to Lachance, a final wave of between 18,000 and 30,000 refugees reached Cuba in 1803; however, they were subsequently expelled. In 1809–1810, 9,059 of them arrived in New Orleans, including 2,731 whites, 3,102 free persons of color, and 3,226 slaves. Immigration from the Caribbean amounted to some 35,800 for the period 1783–1815, about 10 percent of the total.

118. Grabbe, *European Immigration to the United States*, 192, table 1, and 194, table 2.

119. David Wilson, *Immigrant Radicals in the Early Republic* (Ithaca, NY: Cornell University Press, 1998), 51.

120. Aliens must register with the authorities and turn in their weapons, the king-in-council might prevent them from landing and direct those authorized to do so to live in a particular district, and they could be deported for good cause as defined by law enforcement officials rather than by the courts.

121. Smith, *Civic Ideals,* 161.

122. Franklin, *The Legislative History of Naturalization,* 49–71; and Smith, *Civic Ideals,* 160–62. Although the act arose from a bill reported by a committee chaired by Madison, there is no record of its initial provisions.

123. 3rd Congress, sess. II, ch. 20, "An Act to establish an uniform rule of Naturalization; and to repeal the act heretofore passed on that subject," January 29, 1795. Madison expressed a preference for "the government" over "the constitution," on the grounds that one might be loyal and yet prefer another system than one he helped design. Although there was also some sentiment for requiring the applicant to produce two reliable witnesses to his loyalty, this failed of passage.

124. Philip S. Foner, ed., *The Democratic-Republican Societies: 1790–1800: A Documentary Sourcebook of Constitutions, Declarations, Addresses, Resolutions and Toasts* (Westport, CT: Greenwood, 1976 456) and Elkins and McKittrick, *The Age of Federalism,* 456.

125. Ibid., 55.

126. A. C. Roeber, "Citizens or Subjects? German-Lutherans and the Federal Constitution in Pennsylvania, 1789–1800," *Amerikastudien* 34, no. 1 (1989): 53.

127. As of 1797, the United States also appeared on the edge of war with Britain, and averted this Charybdis only to nearly founder on the French Scylla. Anti-French feeling, fanned by the *Directoire's* hostile stance toward the evidently pro-British American administration, reached a climax in mid-1798. Meanwhile, contrary to Republican expectations, Britain did not succumb to revolution, and Federalist participants in the naturalization debate were quick to attribute this to its vigorous repression of dissenters.

128. Elkins and McKittrick, *The Age of Federalism,* 695.

129. Edward C. Carter II, "A 'Wild Irishman' under Every Federalist's Bed: Naturalization in Philadelphia, 1789–1806," *Pennsylvania Magazine of History and Biography* 94 (July 1970): 331–46; Edward C. Carter II, "Naturalization in Philadelphia, 1789–1806: A 'Wild Irishman' under Every Federalist's Bed—Revisited Twenty Years Later," *Proceedings of the American Philosophical Society* 133, no. 2 (1989): 175–89; and Maurice Joseph Bric, "Ireland, Irishmen, and the Broadening of the Late Eighteenth Century Philadelphia Polity (Pennsylvania)" (Ph.D. diss., Johns Hopkins University, 1991).

130. Carter, "A Wild Irishman" (1970); 345; and Foner, *The Democratic-Republican Societies.*

131. Baseler, *Asylum for Mankind,* 244. The 1794 statement was in a letter to John Jay dated November 1.

132. This and the following quotes are from "Debate on the Proposal to Impose a Tax of $20 on Certificates of Naturalization," *Annals of Congress,* 5th Congress (1797–1790), 1:422–30 (reprinted in Abbott, *Historical Aspects of Immigration,* 711–16).

133. Baseler, *Asylum for Mankind,* 244; and Elkins and McKitrrick, *The Age of Federalism,* 279.

134. Smith, *Freedom's Fetters,* 22; and Elkins and McKittrick, *The Age of Federalism,* 694.

135. Smith, *Freedom's Fetters,* 35–47, 49, 67; and Neuman, *Strangers to the Constitution,* 41, 216. Newcomers must register with the clerk of the district court or with an authorized registrar of aliens within forty-eight hours of entry, resident aliens must report within six months after the bill became law, each registrant must be given a certificate of report, and the secretary of state must maintain a centralized record of all naturalizations.

136. Elkins and McKittrick emphasize that the law would not have been passed at all had it not been for Republican insistence after the modifications noted, and that it thus became "virtually a Republican measure."

137. Heaton, "The Industrial Immigrant," 519.

138. Smith, *Freedom's Fetters,* 52.

139. See, for example, Thomas Jefferson's draft of the Kentucky Resolutions, November 1798, in *The Political Thought of American Statesmen: Selected Writings and Speeches,* ed. Morton J. Frisch and Richard G. Stevens (Itasca, IL: F. E. Peacock, 1973), 15–16. In his response, John Marshall points out among other things that the "Alien" Acts do not interfere with a states' right to admit whom it pleases (prior to 1808), since Virginia had already enacted its own act against dangerous aliens (ibid., 108–9). I am grateful to my late colleague Jacob Landynski for bringing this exchange to my attention.

140. Commenting that "immigration policies have long been a matter of high-level concern," the *NYT* (on August 4, 1987) reported that a browser in the National Archives found a 1798 letter from President John Adams to Secretary of State Thomas Pickering, expressing reluctance to grant a passport to Pierre Samuel Dupont de Nemours "or any other French philosophers in the present situation of our country" on the grounds that "[w]e have had too many French philosophers already." Dupont de Nemours nevertheless did immigrate the following year and went on to found an industrial empire (E17).

141. Elkins and McKittrick point out that the final version was much less drastic than what the extremists sought, and "represented a substantial liberalization of the common law of seditious libel as it then stood"; Elkins and McKittrick, *The Age of Federalism,* 592.

142. Smith, *Freedom's Fetters,* 24–25, 159, 163.

143. Foner, *The Democratic-Republican Societies,* 24.

144. Hugh Henry Brackenridge, *Modern Chivalry,* ed. and intro. by Claude M.

Newlin (1792–1815; reprint, New York: American Book Company, 1937), 6. Brackenridge, initially an ardent Republican supporter of the French Revolution, veered to conservatism after writing a firsthand account of the Whisky Insurrection.

145. Paul A. Gilje, *The Road to Mobocracy: Popular Disorder in New York City, 1763–1834* (Chapel Hill: University of North Carolina Press, 1987), 129. The occasion was the celebration of Saint Patrick's Day on Monday, March 18 (because the proper saint's day fell on a Sunday).

146. See also Elkins and McKittrick, *Age of Federalism,* 695.

147. Palmer, *Age of Democratic Revolution,* 2:537; Jones, *American Immigration,* 88–89; and Elkins and McKittrick, *Age of Federalism,* 695–96.

148. Elkins and McKittrick, *Age of Federalism,* 695.

149. Roeber, "Citizens or Subjects?"

150. Franklin, *Legislative History of Naturalization,* 105.

151. Smith, *Civic Ideals,* 139.

152. Carter, "A 'Wild Irishman' " (1970); 343.

4. The American System

1. Richard R. John, "Governmental Institutions as Agents of Change: Rethinking American Political Development in the Early Republic, 1787–1835," *SIAPD* 11 (Fall 1997): 348.

2. Steven Watts, *The Republic Reborn: War and the Making of Liberal America, 1790–1820* (Baltimore: John Hopkins University Press, 1987). Regarding the impact of international involvement on American political development more generally, see Aristide R. Zolberg, "International Engagement and American Democracy: A Comparative Perspective," in *Between Trade and War: International Influences on American Political Development,* ed. Ira Katznelson and Martin Shefter (Princeton, NJ: Princeton University Press, 2002).

3. Gordon S. Wood, *The Radicalism of the American Revolution* (1991; reprint, New York: Vintage, 1993), 369.

4. Reginald C. Stuart, *War and American Thought from the Revolution to the Monroe Doctrine* (Kent, OH: Kent State University Press, 1982), 149.

5. Wood, *The Radicalism,* 316.

6. Roy L. Garis, *Immigration Restriction: A Study of the Opposition to and Regulation of Immigrants into the United States* (New York: Macmillan, 1927), 34.

7. John C. B. Hutchins, *The American Maritime Industries and Public Policy 1789–1914: An Economic History* (Cambridge, MA: Harvard University Press, 1941), 184, 251.

8. Hans-Jürgen Grabbe, "European Immigration to the United States in the Early

National Period, 1783–1820," *Proceedings of the American Philosophical Society* 133, no. 2 (June 1989): 194, table 2 (my percentages).

9. Maldwyn Jones, *American Immigration* (Chicago: University of Chicago Press, 1960), 93.

10. *NWR,* June 23, 1816. I am grateful to Dan Mulcare, Graduate Faculty, New School, for his assiduous assistance in patiently culling Hezekiah Niles's observations relevant to this work.

11. *NWR,* October 19, 1816.

12. In contrast with the previous period, estimates for 1816–1819 generally concur; Hansen, *Atlantic Migration,* 77, 84, 90, 97, 103; and E. P. Hutchinson, "Notes on Immigration Statistics of the United States," *Journal of the American Statistical Association* 53 (December 1958): 969. The office of the mayor of New York enumerated 18,930 between March 1, 1818, and November 1, 1819; Grabbe, *European Immigration,* 14, table 2.

13. *NWR,* September 13, 1817.

14. Unless otherwise indicated, data on U.S. population cited in this chapter are taken from U.S. Bureau of the Census, *Historical Statistics of the United States, Colonial Times to 1970* (Washington, DC: Government Printing Office, 1971).

15. *Annals of Congress* 41:23 (cited in Edward P. Hutchinson, *Legislative History of American Immigration Policy 1798–1965* (Philadelphia: University of Pennsylvania Press, 1981), 23.

16. Robert Greenhalgh Albion, *The Rise of the New York Port, 1815–1860* (New York: Charles Scribner's Sons, 1939), appendix 28, 419.

17. Thomas W. Page, "The Transportation of Immigrants and Reception Arrangements in the Nineteenth Century," *Journal of Political Economy* 19 (1911): 736; Albion, *The Rise of the New York Port,* 10–12; and Rose May Pirraglia, "The Context of Urban Pauperism: Foreign Immigration and American Economic Growth, 1815–1855" (Ph. D. diss., School of Social Work, Columbia University, 1984), 58, table 3 (from William J. Bromwell).

18. *NWR,* August 17, 1816.

19. John Duncan Brite, "The Attitude of European States toward Emigration to the American Colonies and the United States 1607–1820" (Ph.D. diss., University of Chicago. Department of History, 1937).

20. Page, "The Transportation of Immigrants," 732.

21. Max J. Kohler, "An Important European Investigation of American Immigration Conditions and John Quincy Adams' Relations Thereto, 1817–18," *Jahrbuch der Deutschen-Amerikanischen Historischen Gesellschaft von Illinois* 17 (1917): 301, 303.

22. Herbert Heaton, "The Industrial Immigrant in the United States, 1783–1812," *American Philosophical Society Proceedings* 95 (1951): 522–23.

23. I am grateful to Professor Robert Melville of Ripon College for his assistance

in elucidating the significance of the society, which represented a fraction of Scottish landlords seeking to preserve their domanial way of life against market-driven sheepgrazing, a classic Polanyian attempt to "protect society" from the effects of the "great transformation." Highlanders had originally been encouraged to take over the lands of expelled Acadians during the Seven Years' War. In its campaign, the society reported an instance whereby a ship that would have carried 489 slaves under existing regulations transported 700 emigrants to Nova Scotia. For the Highland Society, see A. J. Symon, *Scottish Farming* (Edinburgh: Oliver and Boyd, 1959), 150–51; and T. C. Smout, *A History of the Scottish People* (London: Collins, 1969), 226.

24. Katherine A. Walpole, "The Humanitarian Movement of the Early Nineteenth Century to Remedy Abuses on Emigrant Vessels to America," *Transactions of the Royal Historical Society* 4th ser., 14 (1931): 197–224; Oliver MacDonagh, *A Pattern of Government Growth, the Passenger Acts and Their Enforcement* (London: MacGibbon and Kee, 1961), esp. 54–57; and Oliver MacDonagh, ed., *Emigration in the Victorian Age: Debates on the Issue from 19th Century Critical Journals* (Westmead, UK: Gregg International Publishers, 1973), n.p.

25. Great Britain, Statutes at Large, 43 Geo. III 1803 (44), 189–97.

26. The "humanitarian" characterization is from Walpole, "The Humanitarian Movement," and the "collectivist" from Oliver MacDonagh, who argues that the act "introduced a revolutionary principle to English law, albeit admittedly unnoticed at the time," namely, "interference of the legislature with freedom of contract" (MacDonagh, *A Pattern*, 15). "Cradled in mercantilism" is from MacDonagh as well (64).

27. Maldwyn A. Jones, "The Background to Emigration from Great Britain in the Nineteenth Century," *Perspectives in American History* 7 (1973): 9–10.

28. Moreover, ships engaged in British government service were exempt from the space requirement as well as other regulations providing for passenger comfort and safety. Designed primarily to cover troop transports, this provision could be easily extended to vessels chartered on behalf of officially sponsored colonization schemes.

29. The French Declaration of the Rights of Man guaranteed "free sojourn and free circulation," and the Constitution of 1791 provided "freedom to move about, to remain, and to leave"; Louis Chevalier, "Émigration Française au XIXème Siècle," *Etudes d'Histoire Moderne et Contemporaine* 1 (1947): 127–41.

30. David W. Galenson, "The Rise and Fall of Indentured Servitude in the Americas: An Economic Analysis," *Journal of Economic History* 46 (1984): 13.

31. *NWR*, October 19, 1816; and June 21, 1817.

32. *NWR*, May 4, 1816; May 11, 1816; and November 9, 1816. In a supplement for March–April 1819, *NWR* reprinted extensive instructions from the *NATIONAL INTELLIGENCER* regarding procedures for American naturalization.

33. *NWR*, August 23, 1817. On other occasions, Niles reports with scorn that the

Hessian government has arrested people trying to leave (September 27, 1817) and the imposition of alien laws in Britain and France, requiring travelers to obtain passports prior to departure, and to register with the authorities upon arrival, contrasting this with open conditions in the United States (December 14, 1816; and March 22, 1817).

34. *NWR,* November 29, 1817.

35. Max J. Kohler, *Immigration and Aliens in the United States: Studies of American Immigration Laws and the Legal Status of Aliens in the United States* (New York: Bloch Publishing Co., 1936), 308. The author comments that John Quincy Adams was probably unaware of policy changes resulting from the treaties (reprinted from "An Important European Investigation,"1917).

36. Cited in *NWR,* April 29, 1820, 157–58; the text is more sharply worded than the paraphrase presented by Hansen in *Atlantic Migration,* 96–97. Opposing immigration policy camps in the early twentieth century exploited the ambiguities of Adams's statement to promote contending interpretations of his position; see for example Kohler, *Immigration and Aliens,* 310; and Garis, *Immigration Restriction,* 34. On the broader political context, see Daniel Walker Howe, *The Political Culture of the American Whigs* (Chicago: University of Chicago Press, 1979), 43–68.

37. Arthur Schlesinger Jr., *The Age of Jackson* (New York: Mentor, 1949), 29.

38. Kohler, *Immigration and Aliens,* 317.

39. Hansen, *Atlantic Migration,* 71.

40. Arthur Mann, *The One and the Many: Reflections on the American Identity* (Chicago: University of Chicago Press, 1979), 60–86; and Wilbur Zelinsky, *Nation into State: The Shifting Symbolic Foundations of American Nationalism* (Chapel Hill: University of North Carolina Press, 1988), 225–53. The decline of the German language was explicitly noted by von Fürstenwärther in his report; Kohler, *Immigration and Aliens,* 311.

41. Von Fürstenwärther insisted that the focus of American concern was not on any particular nationality, but rather on the persistence of any island of foreignness in the American sea; cited in *North American Review* 28, no. 3 (July 1820): 12.

42. Ray Allen Billington, *The Protestant Crusade, 1800–1860: A Study of the Origins of American Nativism* (Chicago: Quadrangle Books, 1964), 32–48.

43. *NWR,* June 30, 1821.

44. Adopted Republican Citizens of the city of New York, "Address of 1809," in Abbott, *Historical Aspects of Immigration,* 716–18. The text is reprinted from Henry Bradshaw Fearon, *Sketches of America,* 2nd ed. (London, 1818).

45. Jamin B. Raskin, "Legal Aliens, Local Citizens: The Historical, Constitutional and Theoretical Meanings of Alien Suffrage," *University of Pennsylvania Law Review* 141 (1993): 1412.

46. Garis, *Immigration Restriction,* 33.

47. *Annals of Congress,* 15th Congress, House, 1222; see also Hutchinson, *Legislative History,* 21.
48. U.S. Statutes-at-Large, III, 488–489.
49. Farley W. Grubb, "The End of European Immigrant Servitude in the United States: An Economic Analysis of Market Collapse, 1772–1835," *Journal of Economic History* 54 (December 1994): 819, app. table 1. On the role of the German societies, see Kohler, *Immigration and Aliens,* 312.
50. Kohler, *Immigration and Aliens,* 309.
51. It was reported in the course of congressional debates that one out of five who sailed from Antwerp in the 1817 season died on the voyage. In a similar vein, Niles related, "The heart is sickened with accounts of the suffering of emigrants from Germany . . . through the cold-blooded cruelty and infernal avarice of the masters and owners of passenger-ships" who, after the emigrants "had wholly or partially paid their passages to the United States," dumped them in Lisbon or on one of the Atlantic islands; however, he was relieved that the wrongdoers were not American but chiefly Dutch; *NWR,* April 11, 1818. See also Abbott, *Historical Aspects of Immigration,* 212–13, 216–17.
52. Abbott, *Historical Aspects of Immigration,* 213. Grabbe suggests that a Pennsylvania Passenger Act of 1818, which permitted a maximum of one adult or two children for every two tons' burthen, curtailed German departures.
53. *North American Review* 28 (July 1820): 17. The article was a review of Von Fürstenwärther's report, which Edward Everett later acknowledged he had written (Kohler, *Immigration and Aliens,* 301). The acceptance of redemption by the business community is also suggested by the story reprinted by Niles in 1817, with fulsome comments about the wonderful ways of Providence, of a German runaway boy who made his fortune as a butcher in Philadelphia, and who upon purchasing a redemptioner arriving from Amsterdam to assist him in his business, discovered him to be his own father; *NWR,* October 18, 1817.
54. Abbott, *Historical Aspects of Immigration,* 216–18 (reprinted from *American State Papers,* Class X, "Miscellaneous," Vol. 2, 550–54).
55. The reform entered a new stage in 1811 when Massachusetts prohibited the imprisonment of petty debtors and culminated two decades later in a general abolition; Peter J. Coleman, *Debtors and Creditors in America: Insolvency, Imprisonment, Debt, and Bankruptcy, 1607–1900* (Madison: State Historical Society of Wisconsin, 1974).
56. *Gibbons v. Ogden,* 9 Wheat., 1, 6L, Ed. 23 (1824), 217–18; and Charles Warren, *The Supreme Court in United States History,* vol. 1 (Boston: Little, Brown, 1922), 597–99.
57. Mary Cochran, "A History of Restriction of American Immigration, 1607–1820," (Ph.D. diss., University of Chicago, Department of History, 1930), 220.

58. *Gibbons v. Ogden,* 218.
59. Hansen, *Atlantic Migration,* 101–2. Insisting that "the general attitude toward incoming foreigners was tolerant, if not cordial," Hansen reasons, "Had sentiment been hostile, it would have so expressed itself" in the course of the act's legislative history, and "an attempt would undoubtedly have been made to fix requirements such as to check the flow." In its absence, we are left with an exclusively humanitarian intent: "This legislation arose from a growing realization of the unsafe and unsanitary conditions of transportation," particularly in relation to the Continental traffic, which lacked the sort of passenger protection afforded by United Kingdom regulations with respect to departures from the British Isles. Complementing altruistic concern with the welfare of foreigners was "the need to keep out pestilence."
60. Cochran, "A History of Restriction," 221.
61. *Annals of Congress, House of Representatives,* Dec. 16, 1818, vol. 33, 414–15.
62. For the positive case on behalf of the act's effectiveness, see G. Moltmann, "The Migration of German Redemptioners to North America, 1720–1820," in *Colonialism and Migration; Indenture Labour before and after Slavery,* ed. P. C. Emmer (Dordrecht: Martinus Nijhoff, 1986), 118–19. The number of contracts recorded in Philadelphia dropped from an all-time high of 1,890 in 1817 to 396 in 1818 (following the protective Pennsylvania enactments), 328 the following year, a mere 18 in 1820, and 5 in 1821. Free German landings in Philadelphia reflect an abrupt drop as well, from 2,591 in 1817 to 551 in 1818 and 1,247 in 1819, but only 100 each in 1820 and 1821; Farley W. Grubb, "The End of European Immigrant Servitude in the United States: An Economic Analysis of Market Collapse, 1772–1835," *Journal of Economic History* 54 (December 1994): 818, app. table 1. I obtained free German immigration from deducting the figures Grubb provides for servants from his total; the round numbers resulting for 1820 and 1821 constitute a strange coincidence. In another article, the same author mistakenly gives the figure of 274 for 1817; see Farley W. Grubb, "The Disappearance of Organized Markets for European Immigrant Servants in the United States: Five Popular Explanations Reexamined," *Social Science History* 18 (1994): table 1.4.
63. Murray N. Rothbard, *The Panic of 1819: Reactions and Policies* (New York: Columbia University Press, 1962), 2–15; Douglas C. North, *The Economic Growth of the United States 1790–1860* (New York: Norton, 1966), 182; and Wood, *The Radicalism of the American Revolution,* 313ff.
64. Hansen, *Atlantic Migration,* 102–5.
65. David M. Schneider, *The History of Public Welfare in New York State: 1609–1866* (Chicago: University of Chicago Press, 1938), 296.
66. Ranging from a high of 38.7 percent in 1798 to a low of 28.8 percent in 1814, following a lull in immigration itself; Raymond A. Mohl, *Poverty in New*

York, 1783–1825 (New York, 1971), 86, table 1 (my percentages). For the relationship between immigration and welfare more generally, see also Pirraglia, "The Context of Urban Pauperism." The citation is from Hansen, *Atlantic Migration,* 106.

67. Abbott, *Historical Aspects,* 727.

68. Albion, *The Rise of New York Port,* 336; and Abbott, *Historical Aspects,* 559 (reprinted from the *Second Annual Report of the Manager of the Society for the Prevention of Pauperism in the City of New York,* December 29, 1819).

69. Hansen, *Atlantic Migration,* 104.

70. Pirraglia, "The Context of Urban Pauperism," 58, table 3; and 221, table 6 (my percentages). The crisis was compounded by the state comptroller's decision, when the proceeds of the auction-duty tax enacted in the 1790s reached $72,705, to suspend payments to the city on the grounds that it did not need such large sums for the foreign poor. Although the suspension was subsequently rescinded, the legislature limited the share allocated to the city to $10,000 a year; Mohl, *Poverty in New York,* 114–15.

71. Mohl, *Poverty in New York,* 22.

72. Ibid., 163.

73. *NWR,* September 19, 1819.

74. Benjamin J. Klebaner, "The Myth of Foreign Pauper Dumping in the United States," *Social Service Review* 35 (1961): 302–9. Despite his title, Klebaner confirms, "Some emigrants who had left the north of England for the United States in the spring of 1819 were persons whose passages had been paid by the parish overseers," as was the case also of 600 out of the 16,000 who embarked at Liverpool in 1830. Although he is concerned to demonstrate that the extent of the "dumping" was vastly exaggerated, he does confirm that the practice was real and significant.

75. Edwin C. Guillet, *The Great Migration: The Atlantic Crossing by Sailing Ship since 1770* (Toronto: Thomas Nelson and Sons, 1937), 24.

76. Jones, "The Background to Emigration," 40.

77. Klebaner, "The Myth of Foreign Pauper Dumping," 307.

78. Benjamin J. Klebaner, "State and Local Immigration Regulation in the United States before 1882," *International Review of Social History* 3 (1958): 269–359; Abbott, *Immigration,* 106–10; and Neuman, *Strangers to the Constitution,* 28–34.

79. Edward F. Tuerk, "The Supreme Court and Public Policy: The Regulation of Immigration, 1820–82" (master's thesis, Department of Political Science, University of Chicago, 1951), 4–22.

80. Abbott, *Historical Aspects,* 99–100.

81. Benjamin H. Hibbard, *A History of the Public Land Policies* (New York: Peter Smith, 1939), 100–115.

82. Franklin, *The Legislative History of Naturalization,* 167; and Hutchinson, *Legislative History,* 23–24.

83. Abbott, *Historical Aspects,* 764–65 (reprint of "Report of Select Committee on Allowing Resident Aliens to Hold Real Estate," New York Assembly, Doc. no. 168, 188).

84. U.S. Census, *Historical Statistics,* series C 89–119, 106. Although Grubb estimates that yearly totals for the 1820s were approximately 122 percent higher than reported in the federal statistics, he confirms that there was a large drop from the teen figures; see Farley W. Grubb, "The Reliability of U.S. Immigration Statistics: The Case of Philadelphia, 1815–1830," *International Journal of Maritime History* 11, no. 1 (June 1990): 29–54.

85. Philip J. Staudenraus, *The African Colonization Movement 1816–1865* (New York: Columbia University Press, 1961), 51.

86. *NWR* December 21, 1816 (published as supplement to vol. 15, May 1818, as part of a reprint of the "Report of the Committee to Whom Was Referred the Memorial of the President and Board of Managers of the American Society for Colonizing the Free People of Color of the US, Read in the House of Representatives, April 18, 1818").

87. Staudenraus, *The African Colonization Movement,* 19–51; and Eli Seifman, "The United Colonization Societies of New York and Pennsylvania and the Establishment of the African Colony of Bassa Cove," *Pennsylvania History* 35, no. 1 (1968): 23–44.

88. Christopher Phillips, "The Dear Name of Home: Resistance to Colonization in Antebellum Baltimore," *Maryland Historical Magazine* 91, no. 2 (Summer 1996): 186.

89. *NWR,* October 4, 1817. He reckons that given the constraints imposed by shipping capacity, the maximum feasible rate of removal is 1,500 ten-person families per year, and that it would take thirty-four years to remove merely one-third of the target population. Including transportation, provisions for one year, clothing for two years, and the purchase of 100 acres for each family, plus agricultural implements, the cost of removal would amount to $4,797,500 a year, and total $163,115,000 for 500,000 Negroes over the thirty-four-year period. However, in the intervening period, the remaining population will have increased to 3 million. The cost of achieving a final solution would thus amount to an astronomical $979,030,000. Niles's estimates are drawn from an account in the *United States Gazette.*

90. *NWR,* May 23, 1818.

91. Reprinted in *NWR,* November 8, 1817.

92. In the next issue, Niles returns to a detailed demonstration that emigration will not significantly reduce the Negro population, and reiterates his call for finding a solution at home (*NWR,* November 15, 1817).

93. *NWR*, May 23, 1818.

94. Amos J. Beyan, *The American Colonization Society and the Creation of the Liberian State: A Historical Perspective, 1822–1900* (Lanham, MD: University Press of America, 1991), 50–112.

95. Seifman, "The United Colonization Societies," 26; Albert G. Oliver, "The Protest and Attitudes of Blacks toward the American Colonization Society and the Concepts of Emigration and Colonization in Africa" (Ph.D. diss., St. John's University, 1978); Ella Forbes, "African-American Resistance to Colonization," *Journal of Black Studies* 21, no. 2 (December 1990): 210–23; and Paul A. Gilje, *The Road to Mobocracy: Popular Disorder in New York City, 1763–1834* (Chapel Hill: University of North Carolina Press, 1987),154–55.

96. As reported in *NWR*, November 27, 1819.

97. Oliver, "The Protest and Attitudes of Blacks," 61.

98. Reportedly, several hundred free American Negroes immigrated to Haiti in the 1820s; however, many returned because of their unfavorable reception by the Haitian upper class; see Floyd J. Miller, *The Search for a Black Nationality: Black Emigration and Colonization 1787–1863* (Urbana: University of Illinois Press, 1975), 55, 74–79.

99. John Hope Franklin, *From Slavery to Freedom: A History of Negro Americans,* 4th ed. (New York: Alfred A. Knopf, 1974), 186.

100. Counts range considerably, from a low of 259 (Seifman, "The United Colonization Societies") to 1,420 (Franklin, *From Slavery to Freedom,* 185). Miller speaks of 300 to 400 in the early 1820s alone (see Miller, *The Search for a Black Nationality,* 88). Information on geographical origins is from Marie Tyler McGraw, "Richmond Free Blacks and African Colonization, 1816–1832," *Journal of American Studies* 21, no. 2 (1987): 210.

101. Bruce Rosen, "Abolition and Colonization, the Years of Conflict: 1829–1834," *Phylon* 33, no. 2: 177–92; Seifman, "The United Colonization Societies," 27–32; Miller, *The Search for a Black Nationality,* 90; and Kurt Lee Kocher, "A Duty to America and Africa: A History of the Independent African Colonization Movement in Pennsylvania," *Pennsylvania History* 51, no. 2 (1984): 118–53. The Pennsylvania society was initially a Quaker initiative; although its leader was abolitionist, he believed free blacks could not possibly gain acceptance in the United States. For the South, see Christopher Phillips, "The Dear Name of Home," 194–98.

102. Miller, *The Search for a Black Nationality,* 134–263; Kwando M. Kinshasa, *Emigration vs. Assimilation: The Debate in the African American Press, 1827–1861* (Jefferson, NC: McFarland, 1988), 63; and Phillips, "The Dear Name of Home," 192.

103. Daniel Walker Howe, *The Political Culture of the American Whigs* (Chicago:

University of Chicago Press, 1979), 292; and Oliver, *The Protest and Attitudes of Blacks,* 220–28.

104. Staudenraus, *The African Colonization Movement,* 113, 248.

5. Tocqueville's Footnote

1. Alexis de Tocqueville, *De la démocratie en Amérique* (Paris: Gallimard, 1961), 1:293–94. This is based on the "definitive" 1850 edition, the last published in Tocqueville's lifetime; the translations are my own.

2. Ibid., 290–91.

3. "[W]ith immigration's negative effects limited to one occupation group (skilled workers) in urban places in one region [as against its more pervasive negative impact in the 1880–1925 period], it was difficult to make the case for restriction to a nation that otherwise derived significant benefits from immigration"; Joseph P. Ferrie, *Yankeys Now: Immigrants in the Antebellum U.S. 1840–1860* (New York: Oxford University Press, 1999), 183; Daniel Walker Howe, *The Political Culture of the American Whigs* (Chicago: University of Chicago Press, 1979), 164–65; and Tyler Anbinder, *Nativism and Slavery: The Northern Know-Nothings and the Politics of the 1850s* (New York: Oxford University Press, 1992), 106, 121.

4. Dale T. Knobel, *"America for the Americans": The Nativist Movement in the United States* (New York: Twayne Publishers, 1996), 148.

5. Alfred D. Chandler, *The Visible Hand: The Managerial Revolution in American Business* (Cambridge, MA: Harvard University Press, 1977).

6. Unless otherwise indicated, demographic data in this chapter are taken from U.S. Bureau of the Census, *Historical Statistics of the United States, Colonial Times to 1970* (Washington, DC: Government Printing Office, 1975). For the period 1800–1830 as a whole, an econometric study (based on official data) has estimated the contribution of immigration to white population growth at 9.3 percent; Peter D. McClelland and Richard J. Zeckhauser, *Demographic Dimensions of the New Republic: American Interregional Migration, Vital Statistics, and Manumissions, 1800–1860* (Cambridge: Cambridge University Press, 1982), 101, table A-14. Even if official immigration is raised by half to allow for unchecked arrivals, as suggested by the recent literature, the relative scale of immigration remains very modest.

7. Rose May Pirraglia, "The Context of Urban Pauperism: Foreign Immigration and American Economic Growth, 1815–1855" (Ph.D. diss., School of Social Work, Columbia University, 1984), 58, table 3.

8. Ira A. Glazier, Deirdre Mageean, and Baranabus Okeke, "Socio-Demographic

Characteristics of Irish Immigrants 1846–1851," in *Maritime Aspects of Migration,* ed. Klaus Friedland (Cologne: Bohlau Verlag, 1989), 243–78.

9. Edith Abbott, *Historical Aspects of the Immigration Problems* (Chicago: University of Chicago Press, 1926), 744ff.

10. Thomas L. Nichols, "Lecture on Immigration and Right of Naturalization" (New York, 1845), extracted in Abbott, *Historical Aspects,* 754.

11. For Ireland, see Kerby A. Miller, *Emigrants and Exiles: Ireland and the Irish Exodus to North America* (New York: Oxford University Press, 1985), 280–344; and Joel Mokyr, *Why Ireland Starved: A Quantitative and Analytical History of the Irish Economy, 1800–1850* (London: George Allen & Unwin, 1983). On the shift to families and the expansion to southern Ireland, see Glazier, Mageean, and Okeke, "Socio-Demographic Characteristics," 258–59. For Germany, see Wolfgang Kollmann and Peter Marschalk, "German Emigration to the United States," *Perspectives in American History* 7 (1973): 499–554.

12. Raymond L. Cohn, "Mortality on Immigrant Voyages to New York, 1836–1853," *Journal of Economic History* 44, no. 2 (June 1984): 289–300.

13. Joseph G. Kennedy, Superintendent of Census, *Population of the United States in 1860; Compiled from the Original Returns of the Eighth Census under the Direction of the Secretary of the Interior* (Washington, DC: U.S. Bureau of the Census, 1864), xxviii–xxxii; extracted in Abbott, *Historical Aspects,* 328–33.

14. Pirraglia, "The Context of Urban Pauperism," 58, table 3; and Amy B. Bridges, *A City in the Republic: Antebellum New York and the Origins of Machine Politics* (Cambridge: Cambridge University Press, 1984), 41.

15. In the same year, immigrants amounted to also 44 percent of the population in the three cities of Ohio, 50 percent in Chicago and Milwaukee, 48 percent in Detroit, 61 percent in St. Louis, and 50 percent in San Francisco.

16. To these might be added part of the 6.06 percent born in "British America," which also included French Canadians.

17. See particularly Brinley Thomas, *Migration and Economic Growth: A Study of Great Britain and the Atlantic Economy* (Cambridge: Cambridge University Press, 1973).

18. Chandler, *The Visible Hand,* 63.

19. Ninety percent of workers were native-born in 1849, but only 35 percent in 1855; Ferrie, *Yankeys Now,* 161.

20. Chandler, *The Visible Hand,* 77.

21. Michael F. Holt, "The Politics of Impatience: The Origins of Know-Nothingism," *Journal of American History* 60 (1973): 325.

22. Benjamin H. Hibbard, *A History of the Public Land Policies* (New York: Peter Smith, 1939), 102–3.

23. Ibid., 244.

24. Ibid., 257; see also Taylor, *The Distant Magnet,* 76–80.

25. John C. B. Hutchins, *The American Maritime Industries and Public Policy 1789–1914: An Economic History* (Cambridge, MA: Harvard University Press, 1941), 272.

26. Ibid., 260; and Maldwyn Jones, "The Background to Emigration from Great Britain in the Nineteenth Century," *Perspectives in American History* 7 (1973): 13–14.

27. Hutchins, *The American Maritime Industries,* 262.

28. Jones, "The Background," 14–15; and Herman Melville, *Redburn* (Harmondsworth, UK: Penguin, 1976).

29. Jones, "The Background," 14–15.

30. Abbott, *Immigration,* 27–28; and Taylor, *A Distant Magnet,* 80–81.

31. Bridges, *A City in the Republic;* the data referred to are drawn from 40, table 1; 46, table 3; 55, figure 4; 56, table 4; and 59, table 5.

32. The information in this section is drawn from Ferrie, *Yankeys Now;* the quotation is on 189.

33. A quarter of those who were white-collar or skilled workers in Europe were initially reduced to a lower-status occupation, and this was especially true of the Irish; however, about one-third of the unskilled rose to a higher level. Confirming Tocqueville's more optimistic view, over time immigrants were able to accumulate modest but significant amounts of wealth, but with the British and Germans again doing better than the Irish.

34. Howe, *The Political Culture of the American Whigs,* 157.

35. Matthew F. Jacobson, *Whiteness of a Different Color: European Immigrants and the Alchemy of Race* (Cambridge, MA: Harvard University Press, 1998), 41.

36. On the "Simian race," see L. Perry Curtis Jr., *Apes and Angels: The Irishman in Victorian Caricature* (Washington, DC: Smithsonian Institution Press, 1971). Joel Mokyr suggests similarly that "Ireland was considered by Britain an alien and even hostile country"; "While in Britain poverty was considered the result of economic fluctuations and structural changes in the economy, Irish poverty was viewed as being caused by laziness, indifference, and ineptitude"; Mokyr, *Why Ireland Starved,* 291. An example of transfer from England is A. H. Everett's article "Immigration" published in the influential *North American Review* in 1835, which quotes copiously from an account of the Irish in Britain that appeared in *Blackwood's Magazine* two years earlier; see Abbott, *Historical Aspects,* 444–45.

37. Howe, *The Political Culture,* 150–80.

38. Ibid., 164. The Holy See's adamant opposition to political liberalism was deplored not only by Protestants but also by a beleaguered minority of Catholic thinkers in western Europe, among them the French circle that included Comte de Montalembert and Tocqueville. Indeed, from the perspective of the French public for whom it was intended, *Democracy in America* can be read

as an argument that the Church would be much better off were it to loosen itself from the ties that bound it to regimes of questionable legitimacy such as Louis-Philippe's in France.

39. Vincent P. Lannie, *Public Money and Parochial Education: Bishop Hughes, Governor Seward, and the New York School Controversy* (Cleveland, OH: Case Western Reserve University Press, 1968), 7 n. 14.

40. The "paranoid" interpretation is exemplified by David B. Davis, *The Fear of Conspiracy: Images of Un-American Subversion from the Revolution to the Present* (Ithaca, NY: Cornell University Press, 1971); see notably his dismissal of Samuel F. B. Morse, 54. However, in his original essay, Richard Hofstadter himself qualifies matters somewhat, suggesting that "we need not dismiss out of hand the desire of Yankee Americans to maintain an ethnically and religiously homogeneous society, nor the particular Protestant commitments to individualism and freedom that were brought into play. But the movement had a large paranoid infusion, and the most influential anti-Catholic militants certainly had a strong affinity for the paranoid style"; Richard Hofstadter, *The Paranoid Style in American Politics* (New York: Knopf, 1965), 17.

41. This is central to Knobel's argument; see Knobel, *"America for the Americans,"* 26.

42. Gerald N. Grob, *The State and the Mentally Ill: A History of Worcester State Hospital in Massachusetts, 1830–1920* (Chapel Hill: University of North Carolina Press, 1966), 139, 162–65, 171.

43. Jay Dolan, *The Immigrant Church: New York's Irish and German Catholics, 1815–1865* (1975; reprint, Notre Dame, IN: Notre Dame University Press, 1983).

44. Diana Ravitch, *The Great School Wars: New York City 1805–1973, A History of the Public Schools as Battlefield of Social Change* (New York: Basic Books, 1974); and Leo Hershkowitz, "The Irish and the Emerging City: Settlement to 1844," in *The New York Irish*, ed. Ronald H. Bayor and Timothy J. Meagher (Baltimore: Johns Hopkins University Press, 1996), 26–32.

45. For a brief overview, see Hasia R. Diner, " 'The Most Irish City in the Union': The Era of the Great Migration, 1844–1877," in Bayor and Meagher, *The New York Irish,* 87–106.

46. David Bennett, *The Party of Fear: From Nativist Movements to the New Right in American History* (Chapel Hill: University of North Carolina Press, 1988), 87–88.

47. Carl E. Prince, "The Great 'Riot Year': Jacksonian Democracy and Patterns of Violence in 1834," *Journal of the Early Republic* 5 (Spring 1985): 1–19.

48. Bridges, *A City in the Republic,* 64; Leo Hershkowitz, "The Native American Democratic Association in New York City," *New York Historical Society Quarterly* 46 (January 1962): 41–59; Walter J. Walsh, "Religion, Ethnicity, and History: Clues to the Cultural Construction of Law," in Bayor and Meagher,

The New York Irish, 66; and Robert E. Cazden, "Party Politics and the Germans of New York City, 1834–40," *Yearbook of German-American Studies* 26 (1991): 1–31.

49. Hershkowitz, "The Native American Democratic Association," 45–49.

50. Leo Hershkowitz, "The Irish and the Emerging City: Settlement to 1844," in Bayor and Meagher, *The New York Irish,* 16.

51. Clifford Geertz, "Ideology as a Cultural System," in David E. Apter, ed., *Ideology and Discontent* (New York: The Free Press, 1964), 46–76.

52. Samuel F. B. Morse, *Imminent Dangers to the Free Institutions of the United States through Foreign Immigration* (1835: reprint, New York: Arno Press and the *New York Times,* 1969); and Samuel F. B. Morse, *Foreign Conspiracy against the Liberties of the United States: The Numbers of Brutus* (1835: reprint, New York: Arno Press, 1977).

53. Morse, *Imminent Dangers,* 13.

54. Howe, *The Political Culture of the American Whigs,* 16, 17.

55. Michael F. Holt, *The Rise and Fall of the American Whig Party: Jacksonian Politics and the Onset of the Civil War* (New York: Oxford University Press, 1999), 116–17, 207.

56. Alexander H. Everett, "Immigration," *North American Review* 40 (1835): 460–76; extracted in Abbott, *Historical Aspects,* 442–47. Alexander was the brother of Edward Everett, cited earlier, and himself a prominent Whig politician who subsequently became a Democrat; see *Dictionary of American Biography,* ed. Dumas Malone (New York: Charles Scribner's Sons, 1935), 6:220–21. In the reformist perspective, abnormal behavior stemmed from faulty thinking, induced by nefarious stimuli generated by a bad environment, and could be remedied by appropriate manipulation of the environment, so as to induce new and more desirable patterns of thought; Gerald N. Grob, *The State and the Mentally Ill,* 52–53.

57. Helene S. Zahler, *Eastern Workingmen and National Land Policy, 1829–1862* (New York: Columbia University Press, 1941), 31, 38.

58. Howe, *The Political Culture,* 255.

59. David M. Schneider, *The History of Public Welfare in New York State: 1609–1866* (Chicago: University of Chicago Press, 1938), 296.

60. Pirraglia, "The Context of Urban Pauperism," 221, table 6.

61. *NWR,* July 3, 1830; reprinted in Abbott, *Immigration,* 111.

62. Abbott, *Immigration,* 112.

63. Benjamin J. Klebaner, "State and Local Immigration Regulation in the United States before 1882," *International Review of Social History* 3 (1958): 274.

64. Edward F. Tuerk, "The Supreme Court and Public Policy: The Regulation of Immigration, 1820–82" (master's thesis, Department of Political Science, University of Chicago), 8–9.

65. Abbott, *Immigration,* 112–14.

66. Of the four-man federalist majority inclined to disallow state passenger regulations three years earlier, only Justice Joseph Story remained; three had died, including Chief Justice John Marshall, making room for Jackson appointments.

67. *New York v. Miln, 2 Paine 429; 8 Peters 120 (1834); and 11 Peters 102 (1837).*

68. In a concurrent opinion, Justice Smith Thompson was even more emphatic: "Can anything fall more directly within the police power and internal regulation of a state, than that which concerns the care and management of paupers or convicts or any other class or description of persons that may be thrown into the country, and likely to endanger its safety, or become chargeable for their maintenance? It is not intended by this remark to cast any reproach upon foreigners who may arrive in this country. But if all power to guard against these mischiefs is taken away, the safety and welfare of the community may be very much endangered. Abbott, *Immigration,* 118"

69. For summary coverage of congressional developments, see Edward P. Hutchinson, *Legislative History of American Immigration Policy 1798–1965* (Philadelphia: University of Pennsylvania Press, 1981), 24–34.

70. Abbott, *Immigration,* 127–28. The Committee recommended sanctions of up to $1,000 for masters who took on board, with the intention of transporting them to the United States, aliens in a number of undesirable categories— "idiots," "lunatics," persons who were "incurably diseased" or those who had been found guilty of an "infamous crime."

71. Ibid., 124–27.

72. Klebaner, "State and Local Immigration Regulations," 276.

73. Tuerk, "The Supreme Court," 11. Combining the two prevailing forms of fiscal regulation, it empowered town officials to appoint officers with the authority to require ten-year bonds of $1,000 for lunatics, idiots, aged and infirm persons, as well as paupers; and to collect a head tax of $2.00 for all other aliens landed.

74. Abbott, *Immigration,* 27–28; and Hansen, *Atlantic Migration,* 253. In January 1847 the Common Council of New York City requested from the Almshouse Commissioner's office a report on numbers admitted since the previous September. Describing the dreadful conditions of those seeking assistance, the report explained that the cause was less attributable to conditions in Europe than to the fact that many who were enticed by alluring descriptions of American life became ill and downgraded as a result of the nefarious experience of travel itself. These documents were eventually communicated to Congress along with petitions from the state, the city, and charitable organizations.

75. Hutchinson, *Legislative History,* 35–36. Designed in relation to two-deck

ships, it set this at fourteen feet for the upper "platform"—increased to twenty if the ship passed through the tropics—and at thirty for the bottom "orlop" deck. Children under one were not counted, and those between one and eight reckoned as half-passengers. Penalties were set at $50 as well as up to one year of imprisonment for each violation, with the possibility of seizure in case excess passengers numbered over twenty.

76. George Minot, ed., *States at Large and Treaties of the United States of America,* vol. 9 (Boston: Little, Brown, and Co., 1862), 127–28, 149, 210. Incidentally, a law of January 21, 1848, exempted ships removing blacks on behalf of the African Colonization Society from all of the above requirements.

77. Melville, *Redburn,* 382. Since another American law was passed in 1848, it cannot be ascertained which of the two he meant; but this does not matter for the present point.

78. Hansen, *Atlantic Migration,* 253.

79. Oliver MacDonagh, *A Pattern of Government Growth: The Passenger Act and Their Enforcement* (London: MacGibben and Kee, 1961), 186. Maldwyn A. Jones also concludes that the law's "net effect was to reduce passenger carrying capacity and thus to increase fares. This served both to restrict emigration from ports in Continental Europe and, more significantly, to divert a large proportion of the exodus from Ireland to the cheaper Canadian route"; Maldwyn A. Jones, "Aspects of North Atlantic Migration: Steerage Conditions and American Law, 1819–1909," in Friedland, *Maritime Aspects of Migration,* 324.

80. The decline pertained entirely to arrivals from continental Europe, whose totals for the three successive years were 71,894, 99,937, and 69,455. Under the circumstances, however, it is impossible to distinguish the deterrent effects of American laws from those of revolution in France and Germany, which probably fostered a desire to emigrate but also temporarily disrupted shipping. In those same years, arrivals from the United Kingdom rose from 73,932 to 128,838 and then to 148,095; although there was an increase in 1848, it occurred at a much lower rate.

81. The law was signed on May 17, 1848, and scheduled to go into effect with respect to the Atlantic thirty days later; 30th Congress, sess. I, chap. XLI, 220–23. Again, Hansen sees it merely as a measure beneficial to passengers, "made inevitable" by the loose interpretation of the 1847 act; Hansen, *Atlantic Migration,* 255, 260.

82. The "superficial" requirement was maintained; but whereas the 1847 act distinguished between two decks, the present measure related the requirement to distance between decks. It remained at fourteen feet in the uppermost deck; beyond this, the requirement was raised to sixteen feet should the distance between decks be between five and six feet, and to twenty-two feet should it

be less than five (as against thirty feet for the unventilated "orlop" in two-deck ships).

83. Hansen, in his discussion of the 1855 law, erroneously states that three-deckers were unheard of when the last legislation (that is, the 1848 act) was passed (*Atlantic Migration,* 300). Jones agrees that "[m]atters had . . . been made somewhat worse" by the 1848 act, but views this as an "unintended effect" of the change from tonnage to space requirements—albeit without justifying the characterization; Jones, "The Background," 15. He subsequently modified his earlier interpretation to suggest, "Whether the tonnage check was abandoned specifically in order to help American vessels in the competition for the emigrant trade is not clear; but that, at all events was its effect."; Jones, "Aspects of North Atlantic Migration," 324. Overall, 1480 ships of over 1,000 tons were built in the sixteen-year period of 1831–1846; but 2,858 were then built in the next eleven years, 1847–1857; John G. B. Hutchins, *American Maritime Industries and Public Policy* (Cambridge, MA: Harvard University Press, 1941), 272.

84. Ira A. Glazier, Mageean, and Okeke, "Socio-Demographic Characteristics of Irish Immigrants 1846–1851," 247.

85. Minot (1862), 30th Congress, sess. II, chap. 111, 399–400.

86. Abbott, *Immigration,* 132–37; and Klebaner, "State and Local Regulation," 274.

87. Charlotte Erickson, ed., *Emigration from Europe 1815–1914: Select Documents* (London: A. and C. Black, 1976), 270ff; Klebaner, "State and Local Regulations," 274; Hansen, *Atlantic Migration,* 256, 259; and Tuerk, "The Supreme Court," 13–14. New York, which required payment of a hospital fee ever since 1797, established a $1.00 general head tax in 1847, together with a $300, five-year noncommutable bond for "defectives"; Massachusetts, which had enacted a $2.00 head tax in the wake of the 1837 immigration crisis, with a $1,000 ten-year bond for "defectives," extended the latter to life in 1848; and Louisiana and Texas established similar head taxes when they became ports of entry in 1842–1844.

88. Hansen, *Atlantic Migration,* 260.

89. 7 How. 283, 1849; Charles Warren, *The Supreme Court in United States History* (Boston: Little, Brown, 1922), II, 171–282; and Charles Hames and Foster Sherwood, *The Role of the Supreme Court in American Government and Politics, 1835–1864* (Berkeley: University of California Press, 1957), 152–53. See also Gerald L. Neuman, *Strangers to the Constitution: Immigrants, Borders, and Fundamental Law* (Princeton, NJ: Princeton University Press, 1996), 45–47.

90. Abbott, *Immigration,* 152.

91. Ibid., 156.

92. Neuman, *Strangers to the Constitution,* 45, 47. The minority considered the

laws in question as a legitimate exercise of police power; among them, Chief Justice Roger Taney argued that in the absence of positive exercise by Congress of its regulatory authority over immigration, the states had concurrent powers in that domain.

93. Klebaner, "State and Local Regulations." The dilemma is well illustrated by Massachusetts. In 1850, after the Supreme Court decision, the state replaced its $2.00 general head fee with a $1,000 life-bond commutable into a $2.00 cash payment, keeping the $1,000 noncommutable life bond for "defectives." However, a Committee concluded two years later that as a consequence, Massachusetts-bound immigrants came through New York or Portland, so that other states benefited from the shipping business and bond income, while Massachusetts ended up with lunatics and paupers anyway. The legislature then reduced the "defectives" bond from life to ten years, and the other from $1,000 and life to $300 and five years—keeping the $2.00 commutation fee. In 1855, after the Know-Nothing Party swept the state, the legislature moved to raise the commutation fee; but this was successfully opposed by Boston's Board of Trade on the grounds that it would destroy "a large part of the city's commerce" and give New York City and Portland a position of preference.

94. Frank George Franklin, *The Legislative History of Naturalization in the United States: From the Revolutionary War to 1861* (1906; reprint, New York: Arno Press, 1969), 266.

95. The Preemption Act of 1841 gave squatters the right to settle on and improve up to 160 acres of unappropriated—but already surveyed—public lands, and later buy them at the minimum price without competition. It was coupled with a plan for distributing federal lands to the states. Albeit falling short of the free land to which western settlers and eastern workingmen aspired, it was a step away from a view of the public domain primarily as a source of revenue for the national government. The right was extended to qualified citizens—family heads, men over twenty-one, and widows; and, over the opposition of Henry Clay and others, extended to aliens who had filed a declaration of intention. Reflecting the interests of their new clientele, the Democrats subsequently attempted, without success, to eliminate even this minimum requirement so as to render the right immediately accessible to all newcomers; see Zahler, *Eastern Workingmen and National Land Policy,* 13–49; and Hibbard, *A History of the Public Land Policies,* 136–65. Opposition surfaced in New York in 1848 to the renewal of a law allowing aliens to hold real estate. In the course of debate, advocates of renewal argued "that we should [not] seek to bribe or compel any to be naturalized, who do not desire to do so." The law was renewed (Abbott, *Historical Aspects,* 763–66).

96. Abbott, *Historical Aspects,* 99.

97. Hibbard, *A History of Land Policies,* 360, 368.

98. Ibid., 370.
99. Zahler, *Eastern Workingmen and National Land Policy,* 162.
100. Abbott, *Historical Aspects,* 781; cited from Congressional Globe, 32nd Congress, first session, April 1852.
101. Hibbard, *A History of Land Policies,* 377–78.
102. Although the U.S. Constitution specifically empowered Congress to enact a uniform naturalization law, an early Supreme Court decision established that the states retained concurrent powers, but that state requirements could not exceed national ones. However, in *Chirac v. Chirac* (1817), Marshall stated that the Constitution and congressional legislation "virtually repealed" state naturalization laws; and this doctrine was reasserted at the circuit court level in 1829; Paul Rundquist, "A Uniform Naturalization: The Congress and the Court in American Naturalization, 1865–1952" (Ph.D. diss., University of Chicago, 1975), 1–20.
103. This account is based on the detailed chronicle of Frank George Franklin, *The Legislative History of Naturalization in the United States: From the Revolutionary War to 1861* (1906; reprint, New York: Arno Press, 1969), 189–300; and it is confirmed by Hutchinson, *Legislative History,* 25–46.
104. Holt, *The Rise and Fall,* 191, 204.
105. Franklin, *Legislative History,* 242.
106. Hutchinson, *Legislative History,* 34–35.
107. Knobel, *"America for the Americans,"* 99–101.
108. David Potter, *The Impending Crisis, 1848–1861* (New York: Harper, 1976), 255. The metaphor is John C. Calhoun's, as cited by Potter. While relying mainly on Potter, I have also incorporated aspects of Michael F. Holt, "The Politics of Impatience: The Origins of Know-Nothingism," *Journal of American History* 60 (September 1973): 309–31; and Anbinder, *Nativism and Slavery.*
109. Potter, *The Impending Crisis,* 241. The Whigs were torn asunder by their inability to resolve what Michael Holt has identified as their persistent dilemma. Tyler Anbinder has argued instead that the northern Whigs' failure is attributable to their insufficient commitment to antislavery, providing an opportunity for the Know-Nothings to attract antislavery Northerners, but acknowledges that "these citizens would not have become Know Nothings had they not also sympathized with its anti-Catholic agenda" (Anbinder, *Nativism and Slavery,* xiii). From the present perspective, these contending interpretations are complementary rather than mutually exclusive.
110. Consequently, "The millstone around the neck of the northern Whigs in 1852 was not the loss of the southern wing of their party; it was a volume of immigration which in four years exceeded Scott's total popular vote. The Whigs knew that this reservoir of potential new votes would soon overwhelm them" (Potter, *Impending Crisis,* 245–46).

111. Holt, "The Politics of Impatience," 322, 325. See also Michael F. Holt, *The Political Crisis of the 1850's* (New York: John Wiley and Sons, 1978).

112. Unless otherwise indicated, the following account is based on Knobel, *"America for Americans,"* 91–115.

113. Potter, *The Impending Crisis,* 250; and Bridges, *A City in the Republic,* 317.

114. Potter, *The Impending Crisis,* 247.

115. American historians have been slow to recognize this relationship, Potter suggests, not only "because they have been confused by a complicated situation," but also because "it has been psychologically difficult, because of their predominantly liberal orientation, for them to cope with the fact that anti-slavery, which they tend to idealize, and nativism, which they scorn, should have operated in partnership" (Potter, *The Impending Crisis,* 252).

116. Ibid., 250.

117. Hansen, *Atlantic Migration,* 303; and Holt, "The Politics of Impatience," 325.

118. Knobel, *"America for the Americans,"* 94.

119. Potter, *The Impending Crisis,* 250–51.

120. Oliver MacDonagh, *A Pattern of Government Growth,* 269. The report was communicated to President Franklin Pierce, who passed it on to the Senate with an accompanying message urging appropriate action (Abbott, *Immigration,* 40).

121. Roy L. Garis, *Immigration Restriction: A Study of the Opposition to and Regulation of Immigrants into the United States* (New York: Macmillan, 1927), 44.

122. Abbott, *Immigration,* 41; and *Congressional Globe.*

123. In light of subsequent collaboration between the U.S. Treasury and the shippers in drafting new regulations, this abrupt departure from hitherto lax enforcement practices may have been a ploy by the Pierce administration to render the shippers more amenable to some departure from the permissive status quo, a change necessitated by the Know-Nothing challenge in an election year.

124. Citing affidavits supplied by the mayor of New York in support of his petition as well as data revealing the high incidence of foreign criminals in state institutions, Senator James Cooper of Pennsylvania asserted on January 25 that dumping, "which is as unjust as it is unfriendly, must be put to an end by legislation, if it cannot be accomplished by negotiations"; taking federal authorities to task for their inactivity, he insisted that "Congress has the power to make such regulations as will effectually close the door against the admission of this class of immigrants; and it will be recreant to one of its highest duties if it should fail to exercise it." *Congressional Globe,* 33rd Congress, 2nd. sess., 389–91, as quoted in Abbott, *Historical Aspects,* 602, 604.

125. Although William Henry Seward's stand on behalf of the Irish ever since his tenure as governor rendered him politically vulnerable, the state's Whig boss,

Thurlow Weed, had secured his safe reelection in 1854 for another six-year term. However, Seward's stand may well have cost him the Republican nomination in 1856, if not in 1860; see Potter, *The Impending Crisis,* 246–47 and n. 41; and Vincent P. Lannie, "Alienation in America: The Immigrant Catholic and Public Education in Pre-Civil War America," *The Review of Politics* 32 (1970): 505 and n. 6.

126. Although the minimum volume was now only 2 tons per passenger (as against 2.5 tons from 1819 to 1848), the law imposed the new requirement of a minimum distance of six feet between decks, and increased the allotment of superficial feet aboard three-deckers from fourteen (as it was since 1848) to sixteen. They were also detailed provisions concerning ventilation, food, and water.

127. Abbott, *Historical Aspects,* 720.

128. Furthermore, "A great difficulty in enforcing this law . . . arose from the transitory nature of the testimony required to convict; for immigrants could not be detained without suffering hardship, so that witnesses were usually lacking at the final trial"; Thomas W. Page, "The Transportation of Immigrants and Reception Arrangements in the Nineteenth Century," *Journal of Political Economy* 19 (January–December 1911): 742–43; the quotes are from 43rd Cong. Senate Exec. Doc. no. 23, 158; and *Cong. Record,* 13, 3,015–21.

129. Anbinder, *Nativism and Slavery,* 247–78; see also the earlier cited comment from Knobel on nativist achievements, *"America for the Americans,"* 147–48.

130. Abbott, *Immigration,* 160–61.

131. Ibid.; quoted from the *Boston Daily Advertiser,* May 16, 1855, and reprinted in *The Citizen,* New York City, May 26, 1855.

132. Abbott, *Immigration,* 163.

133. Klebaner, "State and Local Regulations," 287 n. 3.

134. Abbott, *Historical Aspects,* 467.

135. Ibid., 478–82.

136. Hansen, *Atlantic Migration,* 304–5; J. A. S. Grenville, *Europe Reshaped 1848–1878* (Ithaca, NY: Cornell University Press, 1980), 200–25; and United Kingdom, General Records Office, *External Migrations,* 32 and 95.

137. Walter Nugent, *Crossings: The Great Transatlantic Migrations, 1870–1914* (Bloomington: Indiana University Press, 1992), 27–37.

138. The total value of exports (excluding gold and silver) rose from $203 million in 1853 to $237 million in 1854, then declined slightly in 1855, but surged to $281 million in 1856. Ship traffic expanded concomitantly. The total number of inbound U.S. vessels, which normally filled their decks with immigrants, rose steadily over the period, from 4,004 in 1853 to 4,385 in 1856 (U.S. Bureau of the Census, *Historical Statistics,* 451, 538).

139. However, in his subsequent term as governor of Massachusetts, Banks gave full vent to his nativist inclinations (Grob, *The State and the Mentally Ill,* 187).

140. Franklin, *Legislative History,* 278.

141. 34th Congress, 1st sess., H. or R., Report no. 359, August 16, 1856. All the following quotes are from that document, 17, 22, 23, 26–28.

142. The peroration is worth quoting in full: "Is it not then of the first and highest importance, now that the land is flooded with foreign infidels, who, taught at home to repudiate everything to be revered in human institutions, have already here raised the black standard of atheism, and declared a war of extermination against the faith which supported our ancestors in establishing the republic, and hope with animates us for the future—is it not, in view of all this, the sacred duty of all Americans who love their country, and mean to perpetuate its institutions, to imitate the illustrious example of their sires, and to insist upon having their children taught in our schools the lessons of wisdom to be found only in the Bible, and thus have that Holy Book as one of the textbooks of our public schools?" (34th Congress, 1st sess., H. or R., Report no. 359, August 16, 28–29).

143. Klebaner, "State and Local Regulations," 287; and Tuerk, "The Supreme Court," 35.

144. Potter, *The Impending Crisis,* 253; Ray Allen Billington, *The Protestant Crusade, 1800–1860: A Study of the Origins of American Nativism* (Chicago: Quadrangle Books, 1964), 421; and Hansen, *Atlantic Migration,* 203.

145. Potter, *The Impending Crisis,* 259. It has also been suggested that the Republicans were able to secure a large block of German votes, as mediated by Carl Schurz; George M. Stephenson, *A History of American Immigration* (Boston: Ginn and Co., 1926), 131. In 1856, Millard Fillmore's attacks on John Fremont appeared overly prosouthern, alienating many potential supporters in the North, and the fear that he might help elect Fremont by drawing away previously Democratic voters further reduced his support. In the end, the American Party obtained only 22 percent of the popular vote and a mere 8 electoral votes (Maryland); although most of its support came from the South, Fremont did obtain 21 percent in New York, 24 percent in New Jersey, 33 percent in California, and 18 percent in Pennsylvania.

146. Eric Foner, *Free Soil, Free Labor, Free Men: The Ideology of the Republican Party before the Civil War* (New York: Oxford University Press, 1971), 236.

147. Potter, *The Impending Crisis,* 253, 348.

148. Cited in Anbinder, *Nativism and Slavery,* 267.

149. Potter, *The Impending Crisis,* 259.

6. Seward's Other Follies

1. 38th Congress, 1st sess., H. of R., Report no. 56, "Foreign Emigration," April 16, 1864, 1.

2. Charlotte Erickson, *American Industry and the European Immigrant, 1860–1885* (Cambridge, MA: Harvard University Press, 1957), 143.

3. Morton Keller, *Affairs of State* (Cambridge, MA: Harvard University Press, 1977).

4. See, for example, Roger Daniels's recent *Guarding of the Golden Door: American Immigration Policy and Immigrants since 1882* (New York: Hill and Wang, 2004), as indicated by the title of Chapter 1, "The Beginnings of Immigration Restriction, 1882–1917."

5. Alfred D. Chandler, *The Visible Hand: The Managerial Revolution in American Business* (Cambridge, MA: Harvard University Press, 1977).

6. Edith Abbott, *Historical Aspects of the Immigration Problems* (Chicago: University of Chicago Press, 1926), 831. On the association, see Iver Bernstein, *The New York City Draft Riots: Their Significance for American Society and Politics in the Age of the Civil War* (New York: Oxford University Press, 1990), 163.

7. Bell, "The Attitude of Organized Labor toward Immigration," 9.

8. Richard B. Morris, ed., *Encyclopedia of American History* (New York: Harper & Row, 1976), 276.

9. Marcus Lee Hansen, *The Atlantic Migration, 1607–1850* (1940; reprint, New York: Harper Torchbooks, 1961), 305.

10. Benjamin H. Hibbard, *A History of the Public Land Policies* (New York: Peter Smith, 1939), 382.

11. Maldwyn Jones, *American Immigration* (Chicago: University of Chicago Press, 1960), 172–73.

12. These and the following citations are from 38th Congress, 1st sess., Senate Report no. 15, February 18, 1864.

13. His duties covered protection of the immigrants, including enforcement of the Passenger Act, as well as facilitation of their dispersal throughout the country. The bill specifically prohibited the appointment to these offices of persons involved in land sales or connected with transportation companies. As its advocates set forth when the bill came up for second reading in the Senate on March 2, 1864, for a mere $50,000 in annual expenditure, the program might increase immigration by 100,000 able-bodied persons in the first year, an increment of about 60 percent, and by still more within a short time; Congress. Globe, 38th Congress, 1st sess., Senate, March 2, 1864, 55.

14. Congress. Globe, 38th Congress, 1st sess., Senate, March 21, 1864, 865.

15. 38th Congress, 1st sess., H. of R., Report no. 56, "Foreign Emigration," April 16, 1864, Report no. 56. The House's proposal was labeled H.R. 411.

16. Congress. Globe, 34th Congress, 1st sess., H. of R., 1673, 1802.

17. Congress. Globe, 34th congress, 1st sess., Senate, 2510, 3292, 3368, 3388.

18. Erickson, *American Industry*, 143.

19. Abbott, *Historical Aspects,* 155.

20. Erickson, *American Industry,* 185–86; and Emerson D. Fite, *Social and Industrial Conditions in the North during the Civil War* (New York: Peter Smith, 1930), 191–92.

21. As quoted from an American Immigration Company pamphlet in Congress. Globe, 36th Congress, 1st sess., Senate, July 23, 1866, 4041.

22. Bell, "The Attitude of Organized Labor toward Immigration," 10.

23. Congress. Globe, 36th Congress, 1st sess., Senate, 4043.

24. Mary Beard, *The American Labor Movement: A Short History* (New York: Macmillan, 1928), 68; and Andrew Gyory, *Closing the Gate: Race, Politics, and the Chinese Exclusion Act* (Chapel Hill: University of North Carolina Press, 1998), 20–23.

25. John R. Commons et al., *History of Labour in the United States,* vol. 2 (New York: Macmillan, 1926), 117–18.

26. Bell, "The Attitude of Organized Labor," 15; and Espen Thorud, "Labor and Immigration Policy: The U.S. Case in Theoretical Perspective" (master's thesis, Department of Political Science, University of Chicago, 1982). Andrew Gyory insists that historians have exaggerated labor's anti-immigration stance, and argues forcefully that eastern workers and organized labor more generally objected to "importation" rather than immigration; Gyory, *Closing the Gate,* 70. Although he cites a number of statements in which the distinction is made, my own reading is that labor tended to view *most* of the ongoing immigration as "importation." Tichenor insists that the Knights of Labor's international orientation "made the movement more concerned with attaining the solidarity of all workers, regardless of nationality," but concedes that its posture toward large-scale European immigration was "ambivalent"; Daniel J. Tichenor, *Dividing Lines: The Politics of Immigration Control in America* (Princeton, NJ: Princeton University Press, 2002), 70.

27. Charlotte Erickson, "Why Did Contract Labour Not Work in the 19th Century United States?" in *International Labour Migration: Historical Perspectives,* ed. Shula Marks and Peter Richardson (London: Routledge,1984), 50.

28. For example, from 1870 on, the Burlington and Missouri River Railroad Co. maintained a general agent over European affairs with subagents in Glasgow, Liverpool, and London, and expended considerable amounts on advertising; Hibbard, *A History of the Public Land Policies,* 234. In 1871, the Pennsylvania Railroad organized the American Steamship Co. between Liverpool and Philadelphia, as well as the International Navigation Co. between Antwerp and continental ports; Chandler, *The Visible Hand,* 153. See also Philip Taylor, *The Distant Magnet: European Emigration to the U.S.A.* (London: Eyre and Spottiswoode, 1971), esp. 145–66.

29. Congress. Globe, 39th Congress, pt. 2, Senate, 1758. The grounds invoked

were that the Bureau of Immigration established within the U.S. Department of State was "an utter failure," that its object "was entirely perverted," that it was too closely connected with "an immigrant aid society chartered by the State of Connecticut," and that it duplicated the activities of offices established by the western states.

30. Congress. Globe, 39th congress, pt. 2, 1858; pt. 5, 505.

31. "Reportedly" because although Commons et al. state that "the agitation started at this time doubtless led to repeal," they provide no evidence for this contention; Commons et al., *History of Labour in the United States,* 2:118.

32. Edward P. Hutchinson, *Legislative History of American Immigration Policy 1798–1965* (Philadelphia: University of Pennsylvania Press, 1981), 53–54.

33. Max J. Kohler, *Immigration and Aliens in the United States: Studies of American Immigration Laws and the Legal Status of Aliens in the United States* (New York: Bloch Publishing Co., 1936), 315.

34. Rogers M. Smith, *Civic Ideals: Conflicting Visions of Citizenship in U.S. History* (New Haven, CT: Yale University Press, 1997), 313.

35. Congress. Globe, 40th Congress, 2nd sess., H. of R., Report of the Committee on Foreign Affairs, 97–99.

36. 40th Congress, 2d sess., H. of R., Report no. 76, "Encouragement of Emigration," July 3, 1868, 3. The proclamation became law on July 27, 1868. The United States subsequently negotiated a series of treaties providing for mutual recognition of naturalization processes (Germany in 1868, and Great Britain in 1870); Smith, *Civic Ideals,* 313.

37. Ronald Takaki, *A Different Mirror: A History of Multicultural America* (Boston: Little, Brown and Co., 1993), 192; the reference is to a memoir submitted to the U.S. Senate by Aaron H. Palmer.

38. Ibid., 194.

39. Coolidge, *Chinese Immigration* (New York: Henry Holt, 1909), 498.

40. Sucheng Chan, *The Bittersweet Soil: The Chinese in California Agriculture, 1860–1910* (Berkeley: University of California Press, 1986), 6–31.

41. Most of the emigrants originated in five small regions of the maritime southeast within Fukien and Kwangtung Provinces, as well as the island of Hainan, where peasants were being uprooted by more acute rural poverty arising from a spurt of population growth; the upheavals of the Opium Wars and the Taiping Rebellion contributed to the "push" as well. The pull was organized by Portuguese, Dutch, and British colonizers; in addition, some 80,000–100,000 workers were shipped to work the guano deposits on the offshore islands of Peru, with an estimated survival rate of less than one-third, and about 150,000 were sent to the sugar plantations of Cuba as substitutes for African slaves. See Farley M. Foster, "The Chinese Coolie Trade, 1845–1875," *Journal of Asian and African Studies* 3, nos. 3–4 (July–October 1968): 257–70; and Marianne Bastid-Bruguière, "Currents of Social Change," in *The Cam-*

bridge History of China, II, Part 2, ed. Denis Twitchett and John K. Fairbank (London: Cambridge University Press, 1980), 582–86, 591–93.

42. Curtis T. Henson Jr., *Commissioners and Commodores: The East India Squadron and American Diplomacy in China* (Tuscaloosa: University of Alabama Press, 1982), 82–83; Robert J. Schwendinger, "Coolie Trade: The American Connection," *Oceans* (1981): 38–44; Foster, "The Chinese Coolie Trade"; Sing-wu Wang, *The Organization of Chinese Emigration, 1848–1888: With Special Reference to Chinese Emigration to Australia* (San Francisco: Chinese Materials Center, Inc., 1978); and Shih-Shan H. Tsai, "Preserving the Dragon Seeds: The Evolution of Ch'ing Emigration Policy," *Asian Profile* 7, no. 6 (December 1979): 496–506. On the Indian side, see Hugh Tinker, *A New System of Slavery: The Export of Indian Labour Overseas, 1830–1920* (London: Oxford University Press, 1974).

43. Patricia Cloud and David W. Galenson, "Chinese Immigration and Contract Labor in the Late Nineteenth Century," *Explorations in Economic History* 24 (1987): 22–42.

44. On the importance of preexisting attitudes, see Stuart Creighton Miller, *The Unwelcome Immigrant: The American Image of the Chinese, 1785–1882* (Berkeley: University of California Press, 1969).

45. Attempts to elucidate the truth in these matters therefore figured prominently in the extensive investigations generated by contemporaneous policy makers, as well as in the subsequent historiography on Chinese immigration and exclusion. Coolidge went to great lengths to show that the "coolie" label was inappropriate (Coolidge, *Chinese Immigration*, 41); see more generally Cloud and Galenson, "Chinese Immigration and Contract Labor." The debate was revived in 1964 when Gunther Barth argued that the Chinese flow to the United States was patterned by techniques generated in the extensive traffic between China and Malaysia in the first half of the nineteenth century, so that the "coolie" label was not entirely inappropriate (Gunther Barth, *Bitter Strength* (Cambridge: Harvard University Press, 1964), 76). His contention was subsequently challenged by much of the new literature on Asian Americans cited elsewhere in this chapter.

46. James C. Scott, *The Moral Economy of the Peasant: Rebellion and Subsistence in Southeast Asia* (New Haven: Yale University Press, 1976).

47. Alexander Saxton, *The Indispensable Enemy: Labor and the Anti-Chinese Movement* (Stanford, CA: Stanford University Press, 1971), 178.

48. Otis E. Young Jr., *Western Mining* (Norman: University of Oklahoma Press, 1970).

49. On the Tingley bill, see Barth, *Bitter Strength*, 136–39; and Hudson N. Janisch, "The Chinese and the Courts, 1850–1902" (Ph.D. diss., Law School, University of Chicago, 1971), 6–8.

50. Robert F. Heizer and Alan J. Almquist, *The Other Californians: Prejudice and*

Discrimination under Spain, Mexico, and the United States to 1920 (Berkeley: University of California Press, 1971), 92–119. Although California was admitted as a free state, it was argued that even manumitted slaves would remain dependent on their owners.

51. "[T]hough with complexions in some instances approaching to fair, their whole physiognomy but a slight removal from the African race"; text accompanying the reproduction from *Hutchings' Illustrated California Magazine* in Heizer and Almquist, *The Other Californians,* following 166.

52. Sandmeyer, *The Anti-Chinese Movement in California,* 43 (from Assembly Journal, 1855, appendix).

53. Between 1849 and 1862, the Democrats elected six out of six governors, elected seven of eight senators, and controlled all but one session of the legislature; Tichenor, *Dividing Lines,* 90–91.

54. Barth, *Bitter Strength,* 133–46; Janisch, "The Chinese and the Courts," 5–10; and Sandmeyer, *The Anti-Chinese Movement in California,* 42.

55. The case was *People v. Hall;* Charles J. McClain, *In Search of Equality: The Chinese Struggle against Discrimination in Nineteenth-Century America* (Berkeley: University of California Press, 1994), 70. He cited as his authority Chancellor Kent, who had expressed doubt back in 1826 as to whether "any of the tawny races of Asia" could be admitted to citizenship. Murray's political affiliation is from Sandmeyer, *The Anti-Chinese Movement in California,* 45. See also Paul Rundquist, "A Uniform Naturalization: The Congress and the Court in American Naturalization, 1865–1952" (Ph.D. diss., University of Chicago, 1975), 91; and Heizer and Almquist, *The Other Californians,* 129, 229–34.

56. On the denunciations in Britain, see Tinker, *A New System of Slavery:* Britain took the protectionist lead with an 1855 Passenger Act that subjected its vessels to inspection and prohibited them from carrying Chinese laborers to foreign ports.

57. Foster, "The Chinese Coolie Trade," 262, 266.

58. Jules Davids, ed., *American Diplomatic and Public Papers: The United States and China,* series I, 1846–1860 (Wilmington, DE: Scholarly Resources, Inc., 1973), xxxiii; Kwang-Ching Liu, *Americans and Chinese: A Historical Essay and a Bibliography* (Cambridge, MA: Harvard University Press, 1968), 7–8; Ta Jen Liu, *A History of Sino-American Diplomatic Relations, 1840–1974* (Taipei: China Academy, 1978), 42; and Tsai, "Preserving the Dragon Seeds."

59. Lucy M. Cohen, *Chinese in the Post-Civil War South: A People without a History* (Baton Rouge: Louisiana State University Press, 1984), 35–39.

60. Hutchinson, *Legislative History of American Immigration,* 44, 48.

61. However, even earlier than he found; John Torpey, *The Invention of the Passport: Surveillance, Citizenship, and the State* (Cambridge: Cambridge University Press, 1999), 99.

62. Cole, "Chinese Exclusion," *California History* 57 (1978), 14.

63. Sandmeyer, *The Anti-Chinese Movement in California,* 43.

64. Takaki, *A Distant Mirror,* 197; and Cole, "Chinese Exclusion," 14.

65. Barth, *Bitter Strength,* 117; and Saxton, *The Indispensable Enemy,* 60.

66. Hutchinson, *Legislative History,* 52–66.

67. Immanuel C. Y. Hsu, "Late Ch'ing Foreign Relations, 1866–1905," in *Cambridge History of China,* ed. Denis Twitchett and John K. Fairbank (London: Cambridge University Press, 1980), 73–74; Davids, *American Diplomatic and Public Papers,* I:xxiii–xxiv, 49; and William M. Armstrong, *E. L. Godkin and American Foreign Policy, 1865–1900* (New York: Bookman, 1957), 119.

68. Jules Davids, ed., *American Diplomatic and Public Papers: The United States and China,* series 2, 1861–1893 (Wilmington, DE: Scholarly Resources, Inc., 1979), xiii, 1, 9, 21.

69. Cole, "Chinese Exclusion," 16.

70. William M. Armstrong, "Godkin and Chinese Labor: A Paradox in 19th Century Liberalism," *American Journal of Economics and Sociology* 21 (1962): 93.

71. Rundquist, *A Uniform Naturalization,* 30.

72. Sandmeyer, *The Anti-Chinese Movement,* 46.

73. Rundquist, *A Uniform Naturalization,* 21–43.

74. See also Daniels, *Guarding of the Golden Door,* 14–15.

75. I am especially grateful to Bill Ong Hing for making me aware of the key role of gender strategy in this matter; see Bill Ong Hing, *Making and Remaking Asian America through Immigration Policy, 1850–1990* (Stanford, CA: Stanford University Press, 1993).

76. Saxton, *The Indispensable Enemy,* 10.

77. Ibid., 59, 71.

78. Cohen, *Chinese in the Post-Civil War South,* 26.

79. Barth, *Bitter Strength,* 188.

80. In the Commissioner's 1866 Report to Congress; Cohen, *Chinese in the Post-Civil War South,* 50.

81. Miller, *The Unwelcome Immigrant,* 150.

82. Barth, *Bitter Strength,* 195; Cohen, *Chinese in the Post-Civil War South,* 72; and Gyory, *Closing the Door,* 31–36.

83. Cohen, *Chinese in the Post-Civil War South,* 107.

84. Barth, *Bitter Strength,* 203–7.

85. Thorud, *Labor and Immigration Policy,* 105–23; and Saxton, *The Indispensable Enemy.*

86. Miller, *The Unwelcome Immigrant,* 169.

87. Ibid., 183; and Saxton, *The Indispensable Enemy,* 105, 209.

88. Some of the most prominent included a San Francisco lodging house ordinance (1870), a special tax on Chinese laundries (1873), and the shearing of prisoners' queues in the county jail.

89. The California case reference is *In re Ah Fong,* 1 F. Cas. 213, 216–16 (1874);

before the U.S. Supreme Court, it became *Chy Lung v. Freeman;* Charles J. McClain, *In Search of Equality: The Chinese Struggle against Discrimination in Nineteenth-Century America* (Berkeley: University of California Press, 1994), 60–62.

90. *Chy Lung v. Freeman,* 92 U.S. 275, 181 (1876); Lucy E. Salyer, *Laws Harsh as Tigers: Chinese Immigrants and the Shaping of Modern Immigration Law* (Chapel Hill: University of North Carolina Press, 1995), 5; and Coolidge, *Chinese Immigration.*

91. Cole, "Chinese Exclusion," 24.

92. Stephen Skowronek, *Building a New American State: The Expansion of National Administrative Capacities, 1877–1920* (Cambridge: Cambridge University Press, 1982), 41; and Keller, *Affairs of State,* 74, 171–76.

93. Jean Heffer, *Le Port de New York et le commerce extérieur américain, 1860–1900* (Paris: Publications de la Sorbonne, 1986), 48, 160.

94. Walter Nugent, *Crossings: The Great Transatlantic Migrations, 1870–1914* (Bloomington: Indiana University Press, 1992), 31.

95. Brinley Thomas, *Migration and Economic Growth: A Study of Great Britain and the Atlantic Economy* (London: Cambridge University Press, 1973).

96. Abbott, *Historical Aspects,* 656–85.

97. Morrel Heald, "Business Attitudes toward European Immigration, 1880–1900," *Journal of Economic History* 13 (1953): 293–94.

98. Abbott, *Historical Aspects,* 841. In the absence of a federal agency to encourage immigration, vigorous promotional efforts were launched by western states; and after the demise of the American Emigrant Company, recruiting agents for the private sector steadily expanded the domain and scope of their activities; Erickson, *American Industry,* 6–63.

99. John Higham, *Strangers in the Land; Patterns of American Nativism, 1860–1925* (New Brunswick, NJ: Rutgers University Press, 1955), 33.

100. This is nicely detailed in Gyory, *Closing the Gate,* 76–91.

101. Miller, *The Unwelcome Immigrant,* 151, 158, 189. On the spread of racial ideas and their elaboration in America, see Reginald Horsman, *Race and Manifest Destiny: The Origins of American Racial Anglo-Saxonism* (Cambridge, MA: Harvard University Press, 1981), esp. 157–85.

102. *Statutes-at-Large,* 18, pt. 3, ch. 141, 477–78.

103. Davids, *American Diplomatic and Public Papers* Series 1, xiii, 38.

104. This is covered in detail by Tichenor, *Dividing Lines,* 98–104; see also Sandmeyer, *The Anti-Chinese Movement in California,* 57.

105. Saxton, *The Indispensable Enemy,* 113–40.

106. Tuerk, "The Supreme Court and Public Policy: The Regulation of Immigration, 1820–82," 36–39. M.A. thesis, Department of Political Science, University of Chicago, 1951.

107. In 1872, for example, the National Board of Trade unanimously adopted a resolution initiated by its Boston affiliate condemning both the New York practice and the proposed national tax.

108. *Henderson v. Mayor of New York*, 92 U.S. 259, 23 L. Ed. 543 (1875).

109. Keller, *Affairs of State*, 173–76.

110. "In addition to the wealth which some of them bring, they bring still more largely the labor which we need to till our soil, build our railroads and develop the latent resources of the country in its minerals, its manufactures and its agriculture. Is the regulation of this great system a regulation of commerce? Can it be doubted that a law which prescribes the terms on which vessels shall engage in it, is a law regulating this branch of commerce?"; *Henderson*, 548.

111. Tuerk, "The Supreme Court and Public Policy" 61.

112. Davids, *American Diplomatic and Public Papers*, Series 1, xiiii, 87, 94, 108–10, 124–25.

113. Coolidge, *Chinese Immigration*, 179–233; and Kohler, *Immigration and Aliens*, 131–48, 251–62, 263–74; 392–93.

114. *U.S. v. Wong Kim Ark*, 167 U.S., 1898; and Rundquist, *A Uniform Rule*, 107–14.

115. Hing, *Making and Remaking Asian America*, 48, table 3.

116. U.S. Bureau of the Census, *Historical Statistics of the United States*, 450.

117. Jones, *American Immigration*, 250.

118. *Congressional Record*, 47th, 1st, House, July 1, 1882, 5572–73. In June 1882, it adopted regulations that prevented steamships from using the lowermost ("orlop") deck for passenger transportation—as was the case for sailing ships—only to have this vetoed by the president on the grounds that it would render many recently built ships with an added "spart deck" above the main deck useless and generally hinder emigration. A modified bill to allow for passenger accommodations on three decks became law on August 4, 1882; see *Statutes-at-Large*, 22, ch. 374, "An Act to Regulate the Carriage of Passengers by Sea." When opponents charged that the new version had been written by the steamboat companies, the measure's sponsor in the House conceded that representatives of that industry "were present at the meeting of the [drafting] committee and acquiesced in what the committee had done," and assured his colleagues that by virtue of this, "they will no longer fight the bill"; *Congressional Record*, 47th, 1st, House, July 22, 6367–68.

119. Hutchinson, *Legislative History*, 79–80; and *Congressional Record*, 47th, 1st, House, June 19, 5106. In an earlier version, the bill provided that the expenses of deportation were to be charged by the secretary of the treasury "to the nation to which such person belongs, or from which such person came to the United States" and eventually reimbursed to the fund.

120. *Statutes-at-Large,* 22, ch. 376, 1882, "An Act to Regulate Immigration." Although the measure provoked considerably debate, this centered mostly on the improper behavior of New York Representative Jan Van Voorhis (*Congressional Record,* 47th, 1st, House, June 19, 5105–13; June 21, 5179; June 27, 5404–15).

121. Hutchinson, *Legislative History,* 80.

122. Martin Shefter, "Trade Unions and Political Machines: The Organization and Disorganization of the American Working Class in the Late Nineteenth Century," in *Working-Class Formation: Nineteenth Century Patterns in Western Europe and America,* ed. Ira Katznelson and Aristide R. Zolberg (Princeton, NJ: Princeton University Press, 1986), 58.

123. Erickson, *American Industry,* 150.

124. Richard L. Ehrlich, "Immigrant Strikebreaking Activity: A Sampling of Opinions Expressed in the *National Labor Tribune, 1878–1885,*" *Industrial and Labor Relations Review* 27 (1973): 533.

125. Erickson, *American Industry,* 151.

126. Gwendolyn Mink, *Old Labor and New Immigrants in American Political Development* (Ithaca, NY: Cornell University Press, 1986), 62–64.

127. Ibid., 106.

128. Ibid., 12–13.

129. 48th Congress, 1st session, H. of R., Report no. 144, "To Prohibit the Importation of Foreign Contract Labor into the United States, etc.," February 23, 1884, 2.

130. Ibid.

131. My emphasis on this dimension of immigration policy somewhat parallels that of Keith Fitzgerald, *The Face of the Nation: Immigration, the State, and the National Identity* (Stanford, CA: Stanford University Press, 1996). However, he sets its origins around World War I and limits it to Mexican *braceros.*

132. *Congressional Record,* 48th Congress, 1st sess., H. of R., vol. 15, 5349, June 19, 1884.

133. 48th Congress, 1st session, H. of R., Report no. 144, 8. However, his only mention of contracts refers to engagements after the immigrants landed.

134. Michael Piore, *Birds of Passage: Migrant Labor and Industrial Societies* (Cambridge: Cambridge University Press, 1979), 149.

135. Werner Sombart, *Why Is There No Socialism in the United States?* (White Plains, NY: M. E. Sharpe, 1976). For an elaboration of this point, see Aristide R. Zolberg, "How Many Exceptionalisms?" in Katznelson and Zolberg, *Working-Class Formation.*

136. David M. Gordon, Richard Edwards and Michael Reich, *Segmented Work, Divided Workers: The Historical Transformation of Labor in the United States* (Cambridge: Cambridge University Press, 1982); a similar argument is set forth by Piore in *Birds of Passage.*

137. Albert O. Hirschman, *Exit, Voice, and Loyalty: Responses to Decline in Firms, Organizations, and States* (Cambridge, MA: Harvard University Press, 1970). Mobilization involves the inducement of "voice"; exclusion can be thought as "preventive exit."

138. Gerald Rosenblum, *Immigrant Workers: Their Impact on American Labor Radicalism* (New York: Basic Books, 1973).

139. Cited in Mink, *Old Labor and New Immigrants,* 71.

140. Here, I disagree with Erickson's dismissive concluding observation that "[t]he shift in argument from a practical to a racialist basis which took place during the fight for the Foran Act marked the virtual end of the practical and critical discussions of the immigration question which had been so frequent in the infant labor movement of the previous twenty years" (Erickson, *American Industry,* 186).

141. Coolidge, *Chinese Immigration,* 370; and Chan, *The Bittersweet Soil.*

142. Coolidge, *Chinese Immigration,* 384.

143. Monica Boyd, "Oriental Immigration: The Experience of the Chinese, Japanese, and Filipino Populations in the United States," *International Migration Review* 5, no. 1 (1970–1971), 47.

144. Raymond Buell, "The Development of the Anti-Japanese Agitation in the United States," *Political Science Quarterly* 37 (December 1922): 602–38, and *Political Science Quarterly* 37 (March 1923): 57–81.

145. Lawrence A. Cardoso, *Mexican Emigration to the United States, 1897–1931* (Tucson: University of Arizona Press, 1980); and Colin McEvedy and Richard Jones, *Atlas of World Population History* (Harmondsworth, UK: Penguin, 1978), 291.

146. Friedrich Katz, *The Secret War in Mexico: Europe, the United States, and the Mexican Revolution* (Chicago: University of Chicago Press, 1981), 7.

147. Coolidge, *Chinese Immigration,* 330. Writing in the early 1960s, when the *bracero* program was still in effect, Armstrong drew the same parallel: "A modified, twentieth century counterpart of the Cheap Labor Treaty is the contract labor agreement between the United States and the Republic of Mexico" (Armstrong, "Godkin and Chinese Labor," 93 n. 5).

148. Victor S. Clark, "Mexican Labor in the United States," *Bulletin of the U.S. Bureau of Labor* 78 (September 1908): 466–522.

149. Manuel Garcia y Griego, "The Importation of Mexican Contract Laborers to the U.S., 1942–1964: Antecedents, Operation, and Legacy," in *The Border That Joins: Mexican Migrants and U.S. Responsibility,* ed. P. G. Brown and Henry Shue (Totowa, NJ: Rowman & Littlefield, 1983), 55.

150. The number of Mexican-born enumerated by the U.S. Census approximately doubled from 103,000 in 1900 to 222,000 in 1910; David E. Lorey, *United States–Mexico Border Statistics since 1900* (Los Angeles: University of California, Los Angeles, Latin American Center, 1990).

7. "An Intelligent and Effective Restriction"

1. Edward P. Hutchinson, *Legislative History of American Immigration Policy 1798–1965* (Philadelphia: University of Pennsylvania Press, 1981), 95, 98.
2. Jacob Riis, *How the Other Half Lives; Studies among the Tenements of New York* (New York: C. Scribner's Sons, 1890); and David Bennett, *The Party of Fear: From Nativist Movements to the New Right in American History* (Chapel Hill: University of North Carolina Press, 1988), 171–79.
3. Henry Cabot Lodge, "The Restriction of Immigration," *North American Review* 152 (January 1891): 13.
4. Hutchinson, *Legislative History,* 101.
5. Richard L. McCormick, *The Party Period and Public Policy* (New York: Oxford University Press, 1986), 281.
6. Paul Kleppner, *Continuity and Change in Electoral Politics, 1893–1928* (New York: Greenwood Press, 1987), 42.
7. John Hawks Noble, "The Present State of the Immigration Question," *Political Science Quarterly* 7, no. 2 (June 1892): 236.
8. Kleppner, *Continuity and Change in Electoral Politics.*
9. Philippe C. Schmitter, "Interest Intermediation and Regime Governability in Contemporary Western Europe and North America," in *Organizing Interests in Western Europe,* ed. Suzanne D. Berger (Cambridge: Cambridge University Press, 1981), 285–327.
10. Daniel T. Rodgers, *Atlantic Crossings: Social Politics in a Progressive Age* (Cambridge, MA: Harvard University Press, 1998).
11. E. G. Ravenstein, "The Laws of Migration," *Journal of the Royal Statistical Society* 48, no. 2 (1885): 167–235; and 52, no. 2 (1889): 241–305.
12. The gap is well illustrated in Paul Bairoch, "International Industrialization Levels from 1750 to 1980," *Journal of European Economic History* 11 (1982): 35–74, esp. tables 8 and 9.
13. Leslie Moch, *Moving Europeans: Migration in Western Europe since 1650* (Bloomington: Indiana University Press, 1992), 104–60.
14. Europe's less developed regions accelerated their growth: between 1850 and 1914, the population of the Polish lands escalated most dramatically from 13 million to 30 million, not including 3.6 million emigrants; European Russia increased from 75 million to 125 million, with 8 million departures—5 million to the tsar's eastern lands, and 3 million to the west, mostly overseas; and Italy expanded from 25 million to 39 million, with a net emigration of some 4 million.
15. A good demonstration of how these factors operated in the Italian case is provided by Anna Maria Martellone, "Italian Mass Emigration to the United

States, 1876–1930: A Historical Survey," *Perspectives in American History* new series, 1 (1984): 379–423.

16. John Torpey, *The Invention of the Passport: Surveillance, Citizenship, and the State* (Cambridge: Cambridge University Press, 1999), 77, 103–4.

17. Walter Nugent, *Crossings: The Great Transatlantic Migrations, 1870–1914* (Bloomington: Indiana University Press, 1992), 103.

18. Betty Caroli, "The United States, Italy and the Literacy Act," *Studi Emigrazione* 13, no. 41 (March 1976): 3–22.

19. Sucheng Chan, "European and Asian Immigration into the United States in Comparative Perspective, 1820s to 1920s," in *Immigration Reconsidered: History, Sociology, and Politics,* ed. Virginia Yans-McLaughlin (New York: Oxford University Press, 1990), 50.

20. Estimates for the period 1834–1937 range from about 31 million to as high as 45 million, including over 4 million to Malaya alone. See Hugh Tinker, *A New System of Slavery: The Export of Indian Labour Overseas, 1830–1920* (London: Oxford University Press, 1974); Eric R. Wolf, *Europe and the People without History* (Berkeley: University of California Press, 1982), 371.

21. For a theoretical elaboration, see Aristide R. Zolberg, "The Formation of New States as a Refugee-Generating Process," *Annals of the American Academy of Political and Social Science* 467 (May1983): 24–38. The most thorough historical overview of the subject is Michael R. Marrus, *The Unwanted: European Refugees in the Twentieth Century* (New York: Oxford University Press, 1985).

22. Hannah Arendt, *The Origins of Totalitarianism* (New York: Harcourt, Brace, Jovanovich, 1973), 269–90.

23. Simon Kuznets, "Immigration of Russian Jews to the United States: Background and Structure," *Perspectives in American History* 9 (1975): 35–124.

24. In the period 1871–1913, whereas the United Kingdom's railroad network grew only from 21,558 km to 32,623 km, Austria-Hungary's soared from 6,112 to 22,981, Russia's from 10,731 to 62,300, Norway's from 359 to 3,085, and Italy's from 6,429 to 18,873; B. R. Mitchell, *European Historical Statistics 1750–1970* (New York: Columbia University Press, 1976), 583–84, table G1.

25. As of 1873, seventeen companies were operating 173 ships totaling over 500,000 tons between New York and Europe, with the largest ship around 4,000 tons; but by 1914, Hamburg-Amerika alone operated 442 ships adding up to 1.4 million tons, with the largest vessel over 50,000 tons; Jean Heffer, *Le port de New York et le commerce extérieur américain* (Paris: Publications de la Sorbonne, 1986), 169, graph 19; and Nugent, *Crossings,* 51, 59.

26. Nugent, *Crossings,* 31, 41, 85. Of the 1.8 million who left Austria between 1870 and 1910, nearly three-quarters used Hamburg or Bremen.

27. Computed from Nugent, *Crossings,* 14, table 3.

28. Ibid., 150.

29. Ibid., 43, table 9 (based on Ferenczi and Wilcox). Composition is reckoned on the basis of decennial intercontinental emigration in proportion to national population.

30. Julian L. Simon, "Basic Data concerning Immigration into the United States," *Annals of the American Academy of Political and Social Science* 487 (September 1986): 12–56.

31. Mark Wyman, *Round-Trip America: The Immigrants Return to Europe, 1880–1930* (Ithaca, NY: Cornell University Press, 1993), 9–12. Precise quantitative information on the subject is sparse because the United States and other receiving countries did not keep systematic track of exits.

32. Richmond Mayo-Smith, "The Control of Immigration," *Political Science Quarterly* 3, nos. 1, 2, 3 (March, June, September 1888): 46–77, 197–225, 409–24.

33. Henry Sidgwick, *Elements of Politics* (London: Macmillan, 1891). For a detailed discussion of his perspective, see Aristide R. Zolberg, "Keeping Them Out: Ethical Dilemmas of Immigration Policy," in *International Ethics in the Nuclear Age,* ed. Robert J. Myers, Ethics and Foreign Policy Series, vol. 4 (Lanham, MD: University Press of America, 1987), 261–97.

34. Max Weber, "Enquête sur la situation des ouvriers agricoles à l'est de l'Elbe: Conclusions prospectives," *Actes de la Recherche en Sciences Sociales* 65: 65–69; and Reinhard Bendix, *Max Weber: An Intellectual Portrait* (1960; reprint, Berkeley: University of California Press, 1977), 14–23.

35. Torpey, *The Invention of the Passport,* 112.

36. Michael S. Teitelbaum and Jay M. Winter, *Fear of Population Decline* (New York: Academic Press, 1985). Leading the way was France, which reached a stable population level as early as 1850; England began to experience a fertility decline around 1890, Switzerland around 1905, and Germany around 1910. In relation to world population, Europe's proportion peaked around World War I and then began to decline. The United States and Japan reached their maximum share a few decades later; E. A. Wrigley, *Population and History* (New York: McGraw-Hill, 1969), 205.

37. Geoffrey Barraclough, *An Introduction to Contemporary History* (Harmondsworth, UK: Penguin, 1967), 65, 80–81.

38. Francis A. Walker, *Discussions in Economics and Statistics,* ed. Davis R. Dewey (1899; reprint, New York: B. Franklin, 1970), 124.

39. Charles Franklin Emerick, "A Neglected Factor in Race Suicide," *Political Science Quarterly* 25, no. 4 (December 1910): 638–55.

40. For example, the author of a spirited defense of the newcomers in 1900 insists, "So far as individual race traits are concerned, it would seem that there is no especial trouble to be apprehended from the mass of our newest immigrants.

But beyond race traits we must look at certain general processes at work";
Kate Holloday Claghorn, "Our Immigrants and Ourselves," *Atlantic Monthly*
86 (October 1900): 539.

41. John Stuart Mill contributed to the philosophical respectability of the subject
with his notion of "ethos." Foundational texts include Ernest Barker, *National
Character and the Factors in Its Formation* (London: Methuen, 1927); and Salvador de Madariaga, *Anglais, Français, Espagnols* (Paris: Gallimard, 1930),
commissioned by the League of Nations. Woodrow Wilson, "like most of the
people of his time, believed that each 'race,' or ethnic group, had national
characteristics that all of its members possessed"; Hans Vought, "Division and
Reunion: Woodrow Wilson, Immigration, and the Myth of American Unity,"
Journal of American Ethnic History 13, no. 3 (1994): 32.

42. This process has stimulated a vast outpouring of literature, starting with Oscar
Handlin's now classic *Race and Nationality in American Life* (New York: Doubleday, 1957), and including the stimulating recent work by Matthew Frye
Jacobson, *Whiteness of a Different Color: European Immigrants and the Alchemy
of Race* (Cambridge, MA: Harvard University Press, 1998), especially 39–91.

43. John W. Chambers II, *The Tyranny of Change: America in the Progressive Era,
1900–1917* (Rutgers, N.J.: Rutgers University Press, 1988), 57, 60, 109–10.

44. J.P.N., "Walker, Francis Amasa," in *Dictionary of American Biography,* ed.
Dumas Malone (New York: Charles Scribner's Sons, 1935), 10:342–44.

45. U.S. Bureau of the Census, *Twenty Censuses: Population and Housing Questions
1790–1980,* October (Washington, DC: U.S. Government Printing Office,
1979). The 1870 Census merely recorded whether or not a person's father
and mother were of foreign birth; country of birth was specified from 1880
onward.

46. Francis A. Walker, "Immigration," *Yale Review* 1 (August 1892): 125–45; the
author's opposition to Chinese restriction is discussed on 143.

47. Barbara M. Solomon, *Ancestors and Immigrants: A Changing New England Tradition* (Cambridge, MA: Harvard University Press, 1956), 71, 118.

48. Edward W. Bemis, "Restriction of Immigration," *Andover Review* 9 (March
1888): 251–64. It is noteworthy that his biography is silent on the issue of
his authorship of the idea of the literacy test; see "Bemis, Edward W.," in
Encyclopedia of American Biography (New York: American Historical Society,
1931), 48:168. Bemis went on to earn a reputation as an appraiser of public
utility properties and as a consultant to cities; he subsequently aroused the
ire of University of Chicago President William Harper and local business
interests because of his activities in the Civic Federation, and was fired for
his political activities; Dorothy Ross, *The Origins of American Social Science*
(Cambridge: Cambridge University Press, 1991), 133.

49. Noble, "The Present State," 233, 242.

50. Mayo-Smith, "The Control of Immigration"; and Richmond Mayo-Smith, *Emigration and Immigration: A Study in Social Science* (1890; reprint, New York: Charles Scribner's Sons, 1912). The present citations are from the original articles, 1, 46. In light of his immigration book's standing, it is noteworthy that the *Dictionary of American Biography* memorialist takes the unusual step of minimizing it as much less significant than Mayo-Smith's earlier *Science of Statistics* because "he argues from the *a priori* assumption that American political ideals may be treated as a standard"; W.R.L., "Mayo-Smith, Richmond," in Malone, *Dictionary of American Biography,* 8:467–68.

51. Mayo-Smith explicitly refers to Herbert Spencer in Richmond Mayo-Smith, "Assimilation of Nationalities in the United States, I, II," *Political Science Quarterly* 9, nos. 3–4 (September–December 1894): 426–44, 649–70. On the subject more generally, see Richard Hofstadter, *Social Darwinism in American Thought* (1955; reprint, Boston: Beacon Press, 1992).

52. Going beyond Bemis, he includes in the alien camp not only the American-born children of immigrants who retain "foreign blood and in a good many cases the foreign language and customs," but also southern negroes, "who are as much an alien element in our civilization as are the foreign-born themselves." Reckoning in this manner, he reaches the worrisome conclusion that "we have a total of 21,503,537, or more than two-fifths of the entire population, who on account of race or birth or blood are in reality alien to our American population." Among undesirable whites he singles out most of the Irish, many Germans—now that the domain of emigration encompasses some of the less developed parts of the Empire—as well as southern Italians, Hungarians "who seem to be but little superior to the Chinese in civilization," and French Canadians, whose wants "have been reduced to a point where low expenses no longer indicate economy, but lower civilization." Arabs loom over the horizon as well.

53. Sidgwick, *Elements of Politics.*

54. This was further elaborated in Francis A. Walker, "Restriction of Immigration," *Atlantic Monthly* 67 (1896): 822–29.

55. Noble, "The Present State of the Immigration Question," 232.

56. Richard Gambino, *Vendetta* (New York: Doubleday, 1977); and Marco Rimanelli and Sheryl Lynn Postman, eds., *The 1891 New Orleans Lynching and U.S.-Italian Relations* (New York: Peter Lang, 1992). See also the discussion in Jacobson, *Whiteness of a Different Color,* 57.

57. Henry Cabot Lodge, "Lynch Law and Unrestricted Immigration," *North American Review* 152 (1891): 602–12.

58. Edward N. Saveth, *American Historians and European Immigrants, 1875–1925* (New York: Columbia University Press, 1948), 40, 43, 49, 157.

59. Franz Boas, *The Mind of Primitive Man* (New York: Macmillan, 1911).

60. Roland P. Falkner, "Some Aspects of the Immigration Problem," *Political Science Quarterly* 19, no. 1 (March 1904): 32–49.

61. E. A. Goldenweiser, "Walker's Theory of Immigration," *American Journal of Sociology* 18, no. 3 (November 1912): 342–51. He cites a demonstration by the "careful statistician" Walter F. Willcox that the number of children per 1,000 women ages 15–44 in fact fell steadily in every decade since 1800, suggesting that the decline reflected "the steady industrialization and urbanization of the continent."

62. Walter F. Willcox, "The Distribution of Immigrants in the United States," *Quarterly Journal of Economics* 20, no. 4 (August 1906): 523–46.

63. Mayo-Smith, "Assimilation of Nationalities in the United States, I, II."

64. Malone, *Dictionary of American Biography,* 8:468.

65. Sarah E. Simons, "Social Assimilation. Part I. Principles," *American Journal of Sociology* 6, no. 6 (May 1901): 790–822; Sarah E. Simons, "Social Assimilation. Part II. Illustrations," *American Journal of Sociology* 7, no. 3 (November 1901): 385–404; and Sarah E. Simons, "Social Assimilation. Part II. Illustrations-Concluded," *American Journal of Sociology* 7, no. 4 (January 1902): 539–56. She nevertheless concludes, "There is no doubt that immigration to the United States should be restricted in the case of non-assimilable elements. . . . Cases in point are the Chinese, on the one hand, and the French-Canadians and the Italians, on the other" (542). Incidentally, she is surprisingly confident with regard to the assimilation of Negroes, partly on the basis of "the great work" of Booker T. Washington at Tuskegee, as well as of Indians.

66. Solomon, *Ancestors and Immigrants,* 174.

67. Daniel J. Tichenor, *Dividing Lines* (Princeton, NJ: Princeton University Press, 2002).

68. Claudia Goldin, "The Political Economy of Immigration Restriction in the United States, 1890 to 1921," in *The Regulated Economy: A Historical Approach to Political Economy,* ed. Claudia Goldin and Gary D. Libecap (Chicago: University of Chicago Press, 1994), 223–57.

69. Ashley S. Timmer and Jeffrey G. Williamson, *Racism, Xenophobia or Markets? The Political Economy of Immigration Policy Prior to the Thirties,* NBER Working Paper 5867 (Cambridge, MA: National Bureau of Economic Research, 1996). In relation to an "Immigration Policy Index" based on a ten-point scale, where a positive score denotes a pro-immigration policy, the United States dropped by 2 points between 1865 and 1885, and by another 2.5 between 1885 and 1917. By their own reckoning, in the first period, two-thirds of the change can be attributed to falling relative incomes of the unskilled; however, they concede that "[t]he 2.5 point drop from 1885 to 1917 was due only in small part to rising inequality. Furthermore, the residual is very large during this

period, confirming the views of American historians who stress non-market forces" (28). One might wonder, incidentally, how the unskilled could have acquired the political clout necessary to enact restrictive policies during either of those periods.

70. Alan E. Kessler, "Immigration, Internationalization and Domestic Response, 1850–1930: Toward an Explanation for the Rise of Restriction in the 'New World'" (paper presented at the Conference on Migration Controls in 19th Century Europe and America June 25–26, 1999, Sorbonne, Paris), 28.

71. Goldin, "The Political Economy of Immigration Restriction," 253–56.

72. Surprisingly, in light of general Brahmin attitudes, the president of Harvard University, Charles W. Eliot, remained committed to open immigration; Jennings L. Wagoner Jr., "Charles W. Eliot, Immigrants, and the Decline of American Idealism," *Biography* 8, no. 1 (1985): 25–36. However, he gradually lost faith in America's capacity for cultural assimilation and advocated instead a rigid form of cultural pluralism, whereby each group would preserve its distinct identity, to the point of explicitly rejecting intermarriage—a strategy that would naturally insure the survival of his own insular caste amidst a multicultural archipelago. Despite Eliot's prominence, there are no indications that this was ever taken up as a policy proposal.

73. Solomon, *Ancestors and Immigrants,* 105.

74. The Carnegie citation is from Elizabeth Sanders, *Roots of Reform: Farmers, Workers, and the American State, 1877–1917* (Chicago: University of Chicago Press, 1999), 90.

75. Morrell Heald, "Business Attitudes toward European Immigration, 1880–1900," *Journal of Economic History* 13 (1953): 291–304.

76. Mink, *Old Labor and New Immigrants,* 17–18. "Split labor" was coined by Edna Bonacich to denote a form of labor segmentation founded on racial or ethnic differentiation; Edna Bonacich, "A Theory of Ethnic Antagonism: The Split Labor Market," *American Sociological Review* 37 (October 1972): 547–59. See also Aristide R. Zolberg, "How Many Exceptionalisms?" in *Working-Class Formation: Nineteenth Century Patterns in Western Europe and the United States,* ed. Ira Katznelson and Aristide R. Zolberg (Princeton, NJ: Princeton University Press, 1986), 397–455.

77. Claudia Goldin, "The Political Economy of Immigration Restriction" in Goldin, Claudia, and Libecap, Gary (eds) *The Regulated Economy* (Chicago: University of Chicago Press, 1994, 223–257; and Hatton, Timothy J. and Williamson, Geoffrey G., *The Age of Mass Migration: Causes and Economic Impact* (New York: Oxford University Press, 1998), 174.

78. The data on union membership are from Sanders, *Roots of Reform,* 5.

79. A. T. Lane, "American Labour and European Immigrants in the Late Nineteenth Century," *American Studies* 11, no. 2 (1977): 244.

80. John Bodnar, *The Transplanted: A History of Immigrants in Urban America* (Bloomington: Indiana University Press, 1985), 94. Although American workers resorted to violence, a systematic study of urban conflicts during this period indicates that their outbursts were directed more often against blacks than against immigrants; Susan Olzak, "Labor Unrest, Immigration, and Ethnic Conflict in Urban America, 1880–1914," *American Journal of Sociology* 94, no. 6 (May 1989): 1303–33.

81. Andrew T. Lane, "American Trade Unions, Mass Immigration, and the Literacy Test: 1900–1917," *Labor History* 25 (Winter 1984): 5–26; and the same author's more comprehensive account, *Solidarity or Survival: American Labor and European Immigrants, 1830–1924* (Westport, CT: Greenwood Press, 1987). See also Robert Asher, "Union Nativism and the Immigrant Response," *Labor History* 23, no. 3 (1982): 325–48.

82. Bernard Bailyn et al., *The Great Republic: A History of the American People,* 4th ed. (Lexington, MA: D. C. Heath and Co., 1992), 2:187; National Civic Federation, Immigration Department, "Facts about Immigration," report of proceedings of a conference, September 24 and December 12, 1906, New York City (New York, 1907).

83. Stan Vittoz, "World War I and the Political Accommodation of Transitional Market Forces: The Case of Immigration Restriction," *Politics and Society* 8, no. 1 (1978): 60.

84. Claudie Weill, "Le débat sur les migrations ouvrières dans la Deuxième Internationale," *Pluriel,* no. 13 (1978): 55–73.

85. Paul Kleppner, *Continuity and Change in Electoral Politics, 1893–1928* (New York: Greenwood Press, 1987). The term "de-alignment" arises in relation to the concept of "re-alignment," until recently hegemonic among political scientists specializing in the United States. In short, thinking has shifted from the somewhat simplistic notion of the division of American history into successively similar "party systems," to the idea of a pre-party period (from the founding to 1838), followed by a "party period" of 1838–1893, within which a genuine "realignment" occurred in 1853. See Byron E. Shafer, ed., *The End of Realignment: Interpreting American Electoral Eras* (Madison: University of Wisconsin Press, 1991), especially the essay by Joel Silbey.

86. Joel Silbey, *The American Political Nation 1838–1893* (Stanford, CA: Stanford University Press, 1991), 234.

87. Richard J. Jensen, *The Winning of the Middle West: Social and Political Conflict, 1888–1896* (Chicago: University of Chicago Press, 1971), 306.

88. As of 1890, "intentioners"—immigrants who had taken out what were commonly referred to as their "first papers"—constituted less than 1 percent of the eligible national electorate, but as much as 16 percent in North Dakota and 8 percent in Wisconsin as well as Minnesota. A survey of Michigan farm

laborers in June 1894 revealed that although half were themselves immigrants, 62 percent claimed that further immigration would hurt them economically; Richard Jensen comments, "No wonder the people of Michigan voted 4 to 1 in 1894 to discourage further immigration by requiring full citizenship of voters" (227). Wyoming followed suit the same year, Minnesota in 1896, and North Dakota in 1898. The elimination of alien suffrage was completed in 1926, in Arkansas; Kleppner, *Continuity and Change in Electoral Politics,* 166.

89. Rowland T. Berthoff, "Southern Attitudes toward Immigration, 1865–1914," *Journal of Southern History* 17 (1951): 351.

90. Robert Singerman, "The Jew as Racial Alien," in *Anti-Semitism in American History,* ed. David A Gerber (Urbana: University of Illinois Press, 1987), 103–28; see also Barbara Solomon, *Ancestors and Immigrants.*

91. Max J. Kohler, *Immigration and Aliens in the United States: Studies of American Immigration Laws and the Legal Status of Aliens in the United States* (New York: Bloch Publishing Co., 1936), viii.

92. This section is based on Judith S. Goldstein, *The Politics of Ethnic Pressure: The American Jewish Committee as Lobbyist, 1906–1917* (Ph.D. diss., Columbia University, 1972; reprint, New York: Garland Publishing, 1990); Naomi W. Cohen, *Not Free to Desist: The American Jewish Committee 1906–1966* (Philadelphia: Jewish Publication Society of America, 1972); and Henry Beardsell Leonard, *The Open Gates: The Protest against the Movement to Restrict European Immigration, 1896–1924* (Ph.D. dissertation, Columbia University, 1972; reprint, New York: Arno Press, 1980).

93. Rivka Shpak Lissak, "The National Liberal Immigration League and Immigration Restriction, 1906–1917," *American Jewish Archives Journal* 47 (1995): 197–246.

94. Kleppner, *Continuity and Change in Electoral Politics,* 89. There is a similar ambiguity with regard to the Catholic stance on Prohibition and related matters; as Norman Clark has observed, although many in the movement itself were anti-Catholic, "Catholics were never unified on the issue, and they saw no reason why they should be"; Norman H. Clark, *Deliver Us from Evil: An Interpretation of American Prohibition* (New York: Norton, 1976), 187.

95. In a letter to Jacob Epstein, which was published in the *New York Herald;* John Tracy Ellis, *The Life of James Cardinal Gibbons: Archbishop of Baltimore, 1834–1921* (Milwaukee, WI: Bruce Pub. Co., 1952), 2:533–35. I am grateful to Philip Gleason for this information as well as for more general suggestions concerning the Catholic stance on the subject. The cardinal's 1888 involvement is from Berthoff, "Southern Attitudes toward Immigration," 339.

96. David Joseph Goldberg, *Discontented America: The United States in the 1920s* (Baltimore: Johns Hopkins University Press, 1999), 147. The general characterization of the Catholic stance is from Jay P. Dolan, *The American Catholic*

Experience: A History from Colonial Times to the Present (Notre Dame, IN: University of Notre Dame Press, 1992), 300–1, 356.

97. Thomas Henderson, *Tammany Hall and the New Immigrants: The Progressive Years* (New York: Arno Press, 1976), 56.

98. Victor Safford, *Immigration Problems: Personal Experiences of an Official* (New York: Dodd, Mead and Co., 1925), 185.

99. Since these developments have been thoroughly studied, I focus mostly on the political dynamics. Unless otherwise indicated, my account is based on Solomon, *Ancestors and Immigrants;* Higham, *Strangers in the Land;* Hutchinson, *Legislative History;* and Tichenor, *Dividing Lines.*

100. Lucy E. Salyer, *Laws Harsh as Tigers: Chinese Immigrants and the Shaping of Modern Immigration Law* (Chapel Hill: University of North Carolina Press, 1995), 70.

101. On this turning point, see also the discussion in Torpey, *The Invention of the Passport,* 101–3.

102. Hutchinson, *Legislative History,* 413–14.

103. U.S. Bureau of the Census, *Twenty Censuses, Population and Housing Questions 1790–1980,* October (Washington, DC: U.S. Government Printing Office, 1979), 29.

104. Thomas M. Pitkin, *Keepers of the Gate: A History of Ellis Island* (New York: New York University Press, 1975), 23.

105. Berthoff, "Southern Attitudes toward Immigration," 345; Howard Markel, *Quarantine! East European Jewish Immigrants and the New York City Epidemics of 1892* (Baltimore: Johns Hopkins University Press, 1997). Markel argues that the New York episodes illustrate a tension "between the modern science of bacteriology and the politics of nativism"; but Sherwin B. Nuland has questioned how much assurance existed at that time regarding the science; Sherwin B. Nuland, "Hate in the Time of Cholera" (review of *Quarantine!* by H. Markel), *New Republic,* May 26, 1997, 32–37. After the epidemic was traced to the French S.S. *Massilia,* sailing from Marseilles, some 1,200 fever victims and healthy Russian Jewish passengers were rounded up from their East Side tenements and quarantined on North Brother Island, up the East River and downwind from the city's garbage dump at Riker's Island, in improvised ramshackle accommodations without any provision for kosher food.

106. Isaac Hourwich, "The Economic Aspects of Immigration," *Political Science Quarterly* 26, no. 4 (December 1911): 615.

107. The secretary of the treasury also reported that a commission that had looked into consular inspection concluded that it was not feasible and that it was therefore preferable to leave responsibility for returning excludables in the hands of the shippers.

108. Peter H. Schuck, *Citizens, Strangers, and In-Between: Essays on Immigration and*

Citizenship (Boulder, CO: Westview, 1998), 20–24; the citation is from *Nishgimaru Ekiu v. United States,* 142 U.S. 651, 659 (1892).

109. William Preston Jr., *Aliens and Dissenters: Federal Suppression of Radicals, 1903–1933* (Cambridge, MA: Harvard University Press, 1963), 11. The relevant case is *Fong Yue Ting v. United States.*

110. Senate, Committee on Immigration, *Report no. 290 (to Accompany S. 2147),* 54th (1st, 1896), 1.

111. House of Representatives, 54th, 1st, Committee on Immigration and Naturalization, *Report no. 1079, Amending the Immigration Laws (to Accompany H.R. 7864),* April 2, 1896, 2.

112. Sanders, *Roots of Reform,* 90, 131, 132.

113. Bailyn et al., *The Great Republic,* 2:174, 176.

114. Inspectors were to be furnished with copies of the Constitution, "printed on numbered uniform pasteboard slips, each containing not less than 20 or more than 25 words of said Constitution printed in the various languages of the immigrants in double small pica type." The several sets were to be "kept in boxes made for that purpose and so constructed as to conceal the slips from review." Having drawn a slip from the appropriate language box, the immigrant must "read, and afterwards write out, in full view of the immigration officers, the words printed thereon." In case of failure, the inspector must "keep a certified memorandum of the number of the slip which the said immigrant failed to read or copy out in writing"; *Congressional Record,* 54th Congress, 2nd sess., House, 1897, 2667–68.

115. I am inferring this from developments related in the next paragraphs.

116. A prominent restrictionist commented that a principal reason for the veto was concern to maintain friendly relations with Canada, and that Cleveland subsequently remarked that "if he had known as much about immigration at the time as he did later, he would have signed the bill in spite of its objectionable features"; Henry P. Fairchild, "The Immigration Law of 1924" *Quarterly Journal of Economics* 31 (1917): 460.

117. Hutchinson, *Legislative History,* 128. While the House passed the bill over the president's veto by a strong margin, the Senate took no action and so the measure died. Senator Lodge and his House teammate reintroduced their respective bills on the first day of the first session of the 55th Congress (March 15, 1897), with newly elected President William McKinley's explicit endorsement and the American Federation of Labor (AFL) now on record in support as well. Although economic expansion resumed in mid-1897, the bill cleared the Senate in January 1898 (45–28, 16 not voting); however, the measure died again when a number of Republicans in the House broke party discipline in the face of opposition from immigrant constituents, employers, as well as steamship companies, and voted against taking up the Senate bill (December

14, 1898; 101–104, 150 not voting). In mid-1898 Congress established a nonpartisan commission to recommend legislation "to meet problems presented by labor, agriculture, and capital," including immigration.

118. Michel Foucault, *Surveiller et Punir: Naissance de la Prison* (Paris: Gallimard, 1975).

119. Pitkin, *Keepers of the Gate,* 32.

120. Bronwen J. Cohen, "Nativism and Western Myth: The Influence of Nativist Ideas on the American Self-Image," *Journal of American Studies (Great Britain)* 8, no. 1 (1974): 27.

121. N. Cohen, *Not Free to Desist,* 41–53; and Kohler, *Immigration and Aliens in the United States,* 48.

122. Joel Perlmann, " 'Race or People': Federal Race Classifications for Europeans in America, 1898–1913" (working paper, Levy Economics Institute, Bard College, January 2001). I am grateful to Victoria Hattam and Margo Jefferson for bringing this paper to my attention. See also Patrick Weil, "The Modes of Control in American and French Immigration Policy (1): The Rise and Fall of Racial Distinctions in American Immigration Policy 1898–1952" (paper presented at a conference on Migration Controls in 19th Century Europe and America, June 25–26, 1999, Paris), 7, 18.

123. John R. Jenswold, "Leaving the Door Ajar: Politics and Prejudices in the Making of the 1907 Immigration Law," *Mid-America* 67, no. 1 (January 1985): 6.

124. Rogers M. Smith, *Civic Ideals: Conflicting Visions of Citizenship in U.S. History* (New Haven, CT: Yale University Press, 1997), 443.

125. There had been a Jewish cabinet member in the Confederate government, Judah Benjamin, who served at different times as attorney general, secretary of war, and secretary of state. Although Hearst lost the election, he won four out of the five Jewish-dominant assembly districts; Henderson, *Tammany Hall and the New Immigrants,* 112.

126. Straus resigned from its board, but walked daily to his office with fellow member Cyrus Adler, assistant secretary of the Smithsonian. The newly organized NLIL entered the fray as well by seeking exemptions for immigrants whose only reason for coming to the United States was to avoid persecution; proposed as an amendment by Representative Lucius Nathan Littauer, this precocious element of refugee policy was initially accepted but subsequently deleted from the House bill.

127. Jenswold, "Leaving the Door Ajar," 17.

128. Cohen, *Not Free to Desist,* 41–53.

129. Paul S. Peirce, "The Control of Immigration as an Administrative Problem," *American Political Science Review* 4, no. 3 (August 1910): 389. This appears to be the only article on immigration proper in the first twenty-five years of the

APSR (1906–1930), as ascertained by a JSTOR (electronic journal storage search).

130. Tomas Amalguer, *Racial Fault Lines* (Berkeley: University of California Press, 1994), 186.

131. Perlmann, " 'Race or People.' "

132. Neill was another of the Progressive economists, instrumental in the background investigations that led to legislation in meatpacking, child labor, and conservation, who subsequently became a labor mediator. His primary concern was probably with the impact of immigration on wages and labor standards (personal communication from Philip Gleason, March 22, 2000). The AJC failed to secure the appointment of one of its own; Cohen, *Not Free to Desist,* 47.

133. One of the Commission's major preoccupations was to establish a reliable classification of immigrants by origin; see Perlmann, " 'Race or People' "; and Mae M. Ngai, *"Impossible Subjects: Illegal Aliens and the Making of Modern America"* (Princeton: Princeton University Press, 2004), 58–60.

134. The racist stereotypes were emphasized exclusively by Oscar Handlin in a statement submitted to the 1952 Presidential Commission on Immigration Hearings, which forms the basis of "Old Immigrants and New" in Handlin, *Race and Nationality in American Life* (New York: Doubleday, 1957), 74–110.

135. *Commission,* abstract, 47; and *Commission,* reports, I, 25.

136. Jeremiah W. Jenks and W. Jett Lauck, *The Immigration Problem: A Study of American Immigration Conditions and Needs* (New York: Funk & Wagnalls, 1912).

137. Emily Greene Balch, "The Immigration Problem," *Political Science Quarterly* 27, no. 3 (September 1912): 549–52.

138. Referring the reader to another piece where Lauck develops this thesis "with more freedom and more interestingly," Balch also suggests that "[w]orth considering on the other side" is an article by Dr. Isaac Hourwich that appeared in the *Political Science Quarterly* itself a few months earlier.

139. Isaac A. Hourwich, "The Economic Aspects of Immigration," *Political Science Quarterly* 26, no. 4 (December 1911): 615–42; a book version was subsequently published as Isaac A. Hourwich, *Immigration and Labor* (New York: G. P. Putnam's Sons, 1912). On the AJC's commissioning, see Cohen, *Not Free to Desist,* 48.

140. See on the critical side Robert F. Foerster, "Hourwich's Immigration and Labor," *Quarterly Journal of Economics* 27, no. 4 (August 1913): 656–71; as well as a review of the second edition by Henry Pratt Fairchild, "Population and Migration," *American Economic Review* 12, no. 3 (September 1922): 523–24; and, on the other, Max J. Kohler, "Some Aspects of the Immigration Problem," *American Economic Review* 4, no. 1 (March 1914): 93–108.

141. Cohen, *Not Free to Desist,* 50.

142. One immigration advocate demonstrated that the proportion debarred from landing climbed steadily after the accession of Williams, reaching an unprecedented 6.1 percent in January 1911, after which "the percentage tended downwards, as protests began to be effective, and Secretary Nagel," Straus's successor at the Department of Commerce, "gave public expression to his more reasonable views, and Congressional investigations began to be threatened"; Kohler, *Immigration and Aliens,* 46–65 (originally published in "The Editorial Review," August 1911).

143. The secretary did not resort to that argument in his public message; in a striking divergence from the Commission's perspective, he asserted, "We need labor in this country, and the natives are unwilling to do the work which the aliens come over to do," and further, that reports of the new immigrants' lesser assimilation were vastly exaggerated; ibid., 164–65.

144. Vought, "Division and Reunion," 33.

145. Sidney L. Gulick, *The American Japanese Problem: A Study of the Racial Relations of the East and the West* (New York: Charles Scribner's Sons, 1914), 284–85. Annual admissions would be limited to a number equivalent to 5 percent of the American citizens originating from each land, including both the naturalized and their American-born progeny.

146. Joseph O'Grady, ed., *The Immigrants' Influence on Wilson's Peace Policies* (Lexington: University of Kentucky Press, 1967); and Henderson, *Tammany Hall and the New Immigrants,* 176–79.

147. Edward George Hartmann, *The Movement to Americanize the Immigrant* (New York: Columbia University Press, 1948).

148. Alan M. Kraut, *The Huddled Masses: The Immigrant in American Society, 1880–1921* (Arlington Heights, IL: Harlan Davidson, Inc., 1982), 157.

149. *New Republic,* April 8, 1916, 254–55.

150. "The responsibility of the state for the welfare of its individual members is progressively increasing. The democracy of to-day is intolerant of disease, degeneracy, poverty. It cannot permit these social ills to be aggravated by excessive immigration. The complicated governmental problems of a modern democratic nation demand the intelligent attention of the whole public. And this implies the necessity of a considerable degree of homogeneity. We permit at our peril the planting on our soil of unassimilable communities." *New Republic,* April 8, 1916, 254–55.

151. The Jewish welfare organizations acknowledged that they could live with the outcome; following the collapse of the dreadful tsarist regime soon afterward, they anticipated that the Jewish exodus would very much slow down; Kohler, *Immigration and Aliens,* 119, reprinted from *American Law Review* 51, no. 3 (May–June 1917), 23 ; and Cohen, *Not Free to Desist,* 53.

152. Leo Lucassen, "The Great War and the Origins of Migration Controls in Western Europe and the United States (1880–1920)," in *Regulation of Migration: International Experiences,* ed. Anita Boecker et al. (Amsterdam: Het Spinhuis, 1998), 58; and John Torpey, *The Invention of the Passport,* 105–16.

153. Torpey, *The Invention of the Passport,* 112.

154. Bureau of Immigration, U.S. Department of Labor, *Annual Report of the Commissioner General of Immigration to the Secretary of Labor* (Washington, DC: Government Printing Office, 1919), 65–68. The State Department pointed out in a retrospective publication that this had already been achieved with regard to Chinese exclusion under the act of 1882, which required consular officers to examine "persons of the Chinese race claiming to belong to a class not debarred from the United States, such as students, travelers, and merchants, and to pass upon the correctness of certificates showing such status"; U.S. Department of State, *The Immigration Work of the Department of State and its Consular Officers* (Washington, DC: Government Printing Office, 1934), 2. Subsequently, as we have seen, various proposals for advance inspection surfaced within Congress, but no legislation ensued "because it was uncertain how foreign governments would regard such inspection of their citizens," and development along these lines was limited to the sphere of health; Darrell Hevenor Smith and H. Guy Herring, *The Bureau of Immigration: Its History, Activities, and Organization* (Baltimore: Johns Hopkins University Press, 1924), 10, 16. For the latter, see Alan M. Kraut, *Silent Travelers: Germs, Genes, and the "Immigrant Menace"* (New York: Basic Books, 1994), 67–77.

155. Graham H. Stuart, *The Department of State: A History of Its Organization, Procedure, and Personnel* (New York: Macmillan, 1949), 251, 354–55.

156. U.S. Department of State, *The Immigration Work,* 3.

157. Carlos Rico, "Migration and U.S.-Mexican Relations, 1966–1986," in *Western Hemisphere Immigration and United States Foreign Policy,* ed. Christopher Mitchell (University Park: Pennsylvania State University Press, 1992), 221–83, 243. The devastating effects of a decade of revolution (1910–1921) occasioned wholesale flight to the United States, not only of threatened upperclass Mexicans but also of masses of *campesinos* uprooted by the collapse of agriculture in their homeland.

158. Lawrence A. Cardoso, *Mexican Emigration to the United States, 1897–1931* (Tucson: University of Arizona Press, 1980), 86 in diss.

159. Hutchinson, *Legislative History,* 169.

160. Fairchild.

8. A Nation Like the Others

1. The estimate of the effectiveness of Prohibition is from Mark H. Moore, "Actually, Prohibition Was a Success," *NYT,* October 16, 1989, A21.

2. The impact of the restrictive legislation is elaborated in Aristide R. Zolberg, "Matters of State: Theorizing Immigration Policy," in *The Handbook of International Migration: The American Experience,* ed. Charles Hirschman, Philip Kasinitz, and Josh De Wind (New York: Russell Sage, 1999), 71–93.

3. Maurice Davie, *World Immigration* (New York: Macmillan, 1936), 390.

4. André Siegfried, *America Comes of Age* (New York: Harcourt, Brace and Company, 1927 and 1929), 3.

5. A. B. Wolfe, "The Population Problem since the World War: A Survey of Literature and Research (Continued)," *Journal of Political Economy* 36, no. 6 (December 1928): 670.

6. Frederick Lewis Allen, *Only Yesterday: An Informal History of the Nineteen-twenties* (1931; reprint, New York: Bantam Books, 1952).

7. John Higham, *Strangers in the Land: Patterns of American Nativism, 1860–1925* (New Brunswick, NJ: Rutgers University Press, 1955). See especially Desmond King, *Making Americans: Immigration, Race, and the Origins of the Diverse Democracy* (Cambridge, MA: Harvard University Press, 2000); and Mae Ngai, *Impossible Subjects: Illegal Aliens and the Making of Modern America* (Princeton, NJ: Princeton University Press, 2004).

8. In a letter to Husband, May 23, 1927; from the archives of the American Jewish Historical Society, as cited in Joel Perlmann, " 'Race or People' " (unpublished paper, 2001).

9. Here I explicitly disagree with Keith Fitzgerald, who argues that "the failure to restrict labor was not an act of the state. It came about because of the absence of state autonomy and capacity"; Keith Fitzgerald, *The Face of the Nation: Immigration, the State, and the National Identity* (Stanford, CA: Stanford University Press, 1996), 254 n. 5. Such absence is not a given, but the outcome of a process involving choice.

10. Leo Lucassen, "The Great War and the Origins of Migration Controls in Western Europe and the United States (1880–1920)," in *Regulation of Migration: International Experiences,* ed. Anita Boecker et al. (Amsterdam: Het Spinhuis, 1998), 58; and John Torpey, *The Invention of the Passport: Surveillance, Citizenship, and the State* (Cambridge: Cambridge University Press, 1999), 105–16.

11. Imre Ferenczi, "An Historical Study of Migration Statistics," *International Labour Review,* no. 20 (September 1929); cited in Stan Vittoz, "World War I and the Political Accommodation of Transitional Market Forces: The Case of Immigration Restriction," *Politics and Society* 8, no. 1 (1978) 63.

12. George M. Stephenson, *A History of American Immigration* (Boston: Ginn and Co., 1926), 172; and Sheldon Morris Neuringer, *American Jewry and United States Immigration Policy, 1881–1953* (1969; reprint, New York: ARNO Press, 1980), 134.

13. Neuringer, *American Jewry,* 125–28. 344).

14. Michael Marrus, *The Unwanted: European Refugees in the Twentieth Century* (New York: Oxford University Press, 1985), 52.

15. A. B. Wolfe, "The Population Problem since the World War: A Survey of Literature and Research," *Journal of Political Economy* 36, nos. 5–6 (October–December 1928): 671.

16. Wolfe, "The Population Problem," 534; John Maynard Keynes, *The Economic Consequences of the Peace* (New York: Harcourt, Brace, & Howe, 1920); and E. A. Ross, *Standing Room Only?* (New York: Century Co., 1927).

17. Wolfe, "The Population Problem," 672.

18. David Joseph Goldberg, *Discontented America: The United States in the 1920s* (Baltimore: Johns Hopkins University Press, 1999), ch. 7, 141–66.

19. Ibid., 68.

20. Norman H. Clark, *Deliver Us from Evil: An Interpretation of American Prohibition* (New York: Norton, 1976), 129.

21. William Preston Jr., *Aliens and Dissenters: Federal Suppression of Radicals, 1903–1933* (Cambridge, MA: Harvard University Press, 1963), 228.

22. Nancy MacLean, *Behind the Mask of Chivalry: The Making of the Second Ku Klux Klan* (New York: Oxford University Press, 1995).

23. Clark, *Deliver Us from Evil,* 135.

24. Higham, *Strangers in the Land,* 391. Gary Gerstle has pointed out that John Dewey only once protested against the 1924 law and "turned away from his personal involvement with immigrants," and that Horace Kallen also "became disillusioned with diversity"; cited by Desmond King, *Making Americans,* 30–31.

25. Stanley Coben, *Rebellion against Victorianism: The Impetus for Cultural Change in 1920s America* (New York: Oxford University Press, 1991), 58.

26. Important works in this vein are Roy L. Garis, *Immigration Restriction: A Study of the Opposition to and Regulation of Immigrants into the United States* (New York: Macmillan, 1927); and Madison Grant and Charles Stewart Davidson, eds., *The Founders of the Republic on Immigration, Naturalization and Aliens* (New York: C. Scribner's Sons, 1928).

27. Leon J. Kamin, *The Science and Politics of I.Q.* (Potomac, MD: L. Erlbaum Associates with John Wiley, 1975), 15–32; and Daniel J. Kevles, *In the Name of Eugenics: Genetics and the Uses of Human Heredity* (New York: Knopf, 1985).

28. Madison Grant, *The Passing of the Great Race or, the Racial Basis of European History: New Edition Revised and Amplified with a New Preface by Henry Fairfield Osborn* (New York: C. Scribner's Sons, 1919). vii, ix. The characterization of Scribner's is attributed to the literary critic Malcolm Crowley (Cobden, *Rebellion,* 53).

29. T. Lothrop Stoddard, *The Rising Tide of Color against White World-Supremacy; With an Introduction by Madison Grant* (New York: C. Scribner's Sons, 1920).

30. Roy Garis, *Immigration Restriction,* 239. Late twentieth-century defenders of

the IQ tradition have asserted that "the testing community did not generally view its findings as favoring restrictive immigration policies like those in the 1924 Act, and Congress took virtually no notice of intelligence testing in making its decision"; Mark Snyderman and R. J. Herrnstein, "Intelligence Tests and the Immigration Act of 1924," *American Psychologist* 38 (September 1983): 986–95. However, recent research indicates clearly that the selective findings noted were assiduously channeled to the congressional immigration committees and invoked in support of their proposals; Lynne Getz, "Biological Determinism in the Making of Immigration Policy in the 1920s," *International Science Review* 70, nos. 1–2 (1995): 26–33.

31. *Nation,* March 2, 1921, 330–31.
32. *Nation,* October 18, 1922, 404.
33. *New Republic,* August 17, 1921, 314; and April 30, 1924, 242.
34. See, for example, book reviews in *American Journal of Sociology* 31, no. 1 (July 1925): 122; 32, no. 1 (July 1926): 149–50; 32, no. 2 (September 1926): 300–3; 34, no. 2 (September 1928): 376–82; and 34, no. 4 (January 1929): 742; *American Historical Review* 22, no. 4 (July 1917): 842–44; 30, no. 3 (April 1925): 570–73; *Political Science Quarterly* 39, no. 3 (September 1924): 502–5; and *Journal of Negro History* 10, no. 1 (January 1925): 102–3.
35. Casey Walsh, "The Social Science Research Council and Migration Studies (1922–1930)" (unpublished paper, September 30, 1997); and Casey Walsh, "Eugenics, the SSRC Migration Committee, and Manuel Gamio" (paper presented at the 10th Reunion de Historiadores, November 19–22, 2000, Fort Worth, Texas), 5.
36. Paul Kleppner, *Continuity and Change in Electoral Politics, 1893–1928* (New York: Greenwood Press, 1987), 141, 196.
37. Lawrence H. Chamberlain, "The President, Congress, and Legislation," *Political Science Quarterly* 61, no. 1 (March 1946): 55. As it happens, Professor Chamberlain was subsequently my freshman adviser at Columbia University.
38. Charles W. Eagles, "Congressional Voting in the 1920s: A Test of Urban-Rural Conflict," *Journal of American History* 76, no. 2 (1989): 528–34.
39. David Burner, *The Politics of Provincialism: The Democratic Party in Transition, 1918–1932* (1968; reprint, Cambridge, MA: Harvard University Press, 1986), 73, 106.
40. At its May 1919 convention, it countered congressional proposals for suspending immigration for a period of years with the observation that the United States was more likely to suffer an outflow of population than an inflow; National Association of Manufacturers, *Proceedings of the 1919 Convention* (Chicago: NAM, 1919).
41. The Inter-Racial Council, *Proceedings: National Conference on Immigration* (New York: Inter-Racial Council, 1920).
42. Kleppner, *Continuity and Change in Electoral Politics,* 44.

43. Henry Beardsell Leonard, *The Open Gates: The Protest against the Movement to Restrict European Immigration, 1896–1924* (master's thesis, Northwestern University, 1967; reprint, New York: Arno Press, 1980), 249.

44. Goldberg, *Discontented America,* 30.

45. Garis, *Immigration Restriction,* 150.

46. Ibid., 162–68.

47. U.S. Department of State, *The Immigration Work of the Department of State and Its Consular Officers* (Washington, DC: Government Printing Office, 1934), 3.

48. A. Dana Hodgdon, "Extension of Administrative Authority in Immigration Regulation," *American Foreign Service Journal* 8, no. 2 (February 1931): 45–49; and U.S. Department of State, *The Immigration Work,* 3.

49. Although some of the "Canadians" were recent arrivals from Europe, most were, as in the past, Quebeckers coming to work in New England timber and industry.

50. Paul S. Taylor, "Some Aspects of Mexican Immigration," *Journal of Political Economy* 38, no. 5 (October 1930): 609–15.

51. Edith Abbott, "Immigration Restriction: Economic Results and Prospects," *American Economic Review,* 17, no. 1 (March 1927): 128–29.

52. Taylor, "Some Aspects of Mexican Immigration," 612.

53. Nicholas Lemann, *The Promised Land: The Great Black Migration and How It Changed America* (New York: Vintage, 1992), 15.

54. Goldberg, *Discontented America,* 103–16.

55. Max J. Kohler, *Immigration and Aliens in the United States: Studies of American Immigration Laws and the Legal Status of Aliens in the United States* (New York: Bloch Publishing Co., 1936), 153.

56. U.S. Bureau of the Census, *Historical Statistics of the United States, Colonial Times to 1970,* series C 25–73 (Washington, DC: Government Printing Office, 1975), 46–47.

57. Unless otherwise indicated, statistical information on Mexican movement is drawn from Davie E. Lorey, *United States–Mexico Border Statistics since 1900* (Los Angeles: University of California, Los Angeles, Latin American Center, 1990); and Davie E. Lorey, *U.S.-Mexico Border Statistics since 1900: 1990 Update* (Los Angeles: University of California, Los Angeles, Latin American Center Publications, 1993), see especially 40, table 120.

58. David Montejano, *Anglos and Mexicans in the Making of Texas, 1836–1986* (Austin: University of Texas Press, 1987); and Camille Guerin-Gonzales, *Mexican Workers and American Dreams: Immigration, Repatriation and California Farm Labor, 1900–1939* (New Brunswick, NJ: Rutgers University Press, 1994), 43.

59. Vittoz, "World War I," 73; and Harvey A. Levenstein, "The AFL and Mexican Immigration in the 1920s: An Experiment in Labor Diplomacy," *Hispanic American Historical Review* 48 (May 1968): 206.

60. The precise magnitude of settlement is difficult to establish because the 1930 U.S. Census lumped together Mexican aliens and their American-born children, and also identified Mexicans as a "race," thereby excluding thousands of old-stock Americans of Spanish origin all over the Southwest.

61. Statement of Professor Roy L. Garis, "Immigration from Countries of the Western Hemisphere," *Hearings before the Committee on Immigration and Naturalization,* House of Representatives, 71st Congress, 2nd sess., March 14, 1930.

62. The debate over the suitability of Mexicans for citizenship has been examined by Clare Sheridan, "Contested Citizenship: National Identity and the Mexican Immigration Debates of the 1920s" (paper presented at the Annual Meeting of the American Political Science Association, September 3–6, 1998, Boston).

63. Cited by Davie, *World Immigration,* 209.

64. Mexican ambivalence is illustrated by Manuel Gamio, *Mexican Immigration to the United States* (Chicago: University of Chicago Press, 1930).

65. Manuel Garcia y Griego, "The Importation of Mexican Contract laborers to the U.S., 1942–1964: Antecedents, Operation, and Legacy," in *The Border That Joins: Mexican Migrants and U.S. Responsibility,* ed. P. G. Brown and Henry Shue (Totowa, NJ: Rowman & Littlefield, 1983), 53.

66. "Admission of Mexican Agricultural Laborers," *Hearings before the Committee on Immigration,* U.S. Senate, 66th Congress, 2nd sess., 1920, 4.

67. Robert A. Divine, *American Immigration Policy, 1924–1952* (New Haven, CT: Yale University Press, 1957).

68. Davie, *World Immigration,* 218.

69. Carey McWilliams, *Factories in the Field: The Story of Migratory Farm Labor in California* (1935; reprint, Berkeley: University of California Press, 2000), 125–26.

70. This was candidly acknowledged by Henry Pratt Fairchild in "The Immigration Law of 1924," *Quarterly Journal of Economics* 38 (August 1924): 659–60.

71. Levenstein, "The AFL and Mexican Immigration in the 1920s," 210.

72. James J. Davis, *Selective Immigration* (St. Paul, MN : Scott-Mitchell Publishing Co., 1925), 206, 207–14.

73. Details of the legislative process are taken from various issues of *Interpreter Releases,* mimeographed bulletin, January–June (New York City: Foreign Language Information Service, 1924). Comprehensive accounts can be found in Higham, *Strangers in the Land;* and Divine, *American Immigration Policy.* More recent accounts emphasize the construction of racial and ethnic categories: Mae Ngai, "The Architecture of Race in American Immigration Law: A Reexamination of the Immigration Act of 1924," *Journal of American History* 86, no. 1 (June 1999): 67–92; and King, *Making Americans,* 199–228.

74. Neuringer, *American Jewry,* 161.

75. Ibid., 153.

76. Edward P. Hutchinson, *Legislative History of American Immigration Policy 1798–1965* (Philadelphia: University of Pennsylvania Press, 1981), 190 (from *Congressional Record,* 65:5568).

77. Stephen Wagner, "The Lingering Death of the National Origins Quota System: A Political History of U.S. Immigration Policy, 1952–1965" (Ph.D. diss., Harvard University, 1986), 8, 15; Higham, *Strangers in the Land,* 321; Clinton Stoddard Burr, *America's Race Heritage: An Account of the Diffusion of Ancestral Stocks in the United States during Three Centuries of National Expansion and a Discussion of Its Significance* (New York: National Historical Society, 1922). The reference to Trevor's role is from Ngai, *Impossible Subjects,* 24–25.

78. The amendment was introduced by Senator Thomas Sterling of South Dakota after his proposal to divide national quotas into "commonly recognized and well-defined distinct racial groups" was rejected by Senator David Reed as unworkable. However, for other than quota purposes, immigrants identified as Jewish continued to be classified as "Hebrew" rather than according to the countries of their birth; Wagner, "The Lingering Death," 14, 47.

79. Vittoz, "World War I," 64–65.

80. In a preface to a symposium on immigration published by the NAM magazine in February 1923, the organization's president asserted, "The quota should be determined with the ultimate object of obtaining net immigration and not according to the present method which causes a deficit of labor in many instances," and further advocated abolition of the literacy test. Other contributors argued in the same vein, pointing out among other things that the literacy test barred many farmers or women servants. The commissioner-general of immigration stood out as the lone voice of restriction; *American Industries* 23, no. 7 (February, 1923); and 23, no. 8 (March 1923): 22. See also Alfred D. Chandler, *The Visible Hand: The Managerial Revolution in American Business* (Cambridge, MA: Harvard University Press, 1977), 456.

81. Leonard, *The Open Gates,* 263; Kohler, *Immigration and Aliens in the United States,* 24 (originally a letter to *NYT,* January 9, 1924). Even the two Jewish congressmen on the Immigration Committee, Samuel Dickstein of New York and Adolph Sabath of Chicago, conceded the necessity of limiting immigration in some fashion; Leonard, *The Open Gates,* 243–49.

82. Neuringer, *American Jewry,* 133.

83. Higham, *Strangers in the Land,* 304, 392 n. 11.

84. David J. Hellwig, "Black Leaders and United States Immigration Policy, 1917–1929," *Journal of Negro History* 66, no. 2 (Summer 1981): 110–27.

85. Cited in Lawrence B. Davis, *Immigrants, Baptists, and the Protestant Mind* (Urbana: University of Illinois Press, 1973), 189.

86. Robert E. Park, "Book Reviews," *American Journal of Sociology* 34, no. 2 (September 1928): 377.

87. Ngai, "The Architecture of Race," 67.

88. Garis, *Immigration Restriction*, 228, 247.

89. In a 1926 statement cited in Neuringer, *American Jewry*, 196.

90. As quoted in Ira De B. Reid, *The Negro Immigrant: His Background, Characteristics and Social Adjustment, 1899–1937* (New York: Columbia University Press, 1939), 32.

91. Wagner, "The Lingering Death," 8.

92. For Asians, race trumped nationality or place of birth, so that a Cuban-born Cuban citizen of even part Chinese ancestry, for example, was inadmissible.

93. Ian Haney Lopez, *White by Law: The Legal Construction of Race* (New York: New York University Press, 1996). With regard to Jews, for example, in his 1939 work on *The Negro Immigrant,* Ira De B. Reid invokes John Dollard's recent use of "caste" for elucidating the situation of Negroes, and suggests en passant that it is applicable to Jews as well (28). Construction of the Jews as powerful global manipulators was a basic element of early twentieth-century anti-Semitism; see, among others, the discussion in David Wyman, *Paper Walls: America and the Refugee Crisis* (Amherst: University of Massachusetts Press, 1968), 14–23.

94. Policy regarding the Philippines is fully discussed by Mae Ngai, *Impossible Subjects*, 247–314.

95. This factor has been largely left out of accounts in the often invidious comparisons of their achievements with those of African Americans; see notably, the widely touted work of Thomas Sowell, *Migrations and Cultures: A World View* (New York: Basic Books, 1996).

96. Ngai, *Impossible Subjects,* 54; and Burr, *America's Race Heritage.*

97. Ngai, *Impossible Subjects,* 58–60.

98. This aspect is especially emphasized in John F. McClymer, "The Federal Government and the Americanization Movement, 1915–1924," *Prologue: The Journal of the National Archives* 10, no. 1 (1984): 23–41. The classic account of Americanization is Edward George Hartmann, *The Movement to Americanize the Immigrant* (New York: Columbia University Press, 1948). For a recent update, see King, *Making Americans,* 85–126; however, he ignores the fact that Americanization implied, willy-nilly, that white immigrants were *assimilable.*

99. The ratios are my reckoning from numbers cited in *American Foreign Service Journal.* Northern and western Europe quotas totaled 140,899, with demand was estimated at 395,197; for southern and eastern Europe, they totaled 20,447, with demand estimated at 1,585,756.

100. The commissioner of immigration suggested in his report for 1919, "The matter of having representatives of the Immigration Service permanently stationed at consular offices and elsewhere in foreign countries has been fre-

quently discussed, but not until the excellent results of the passport-visé [*sic*] system appeared, were the advantages of the proposal so clearly established," and therefore suggested that "to a considerable extent the immigration laws would be valuably supplemented in times of peace if a system modeled" on the one currently in effect "could be permanently adopted" and that the bureau had undertaken to prepare a plan to that effect; Bureau of Immigration U.S. Department of Labor, *Annual Report of the Commission General of Immigration to the Secretary of Labor* (Washington, DC: Government Printing Office, 1919), 3.

101. Daniel J. Tichenor, *Dividing Lines: The Politics of Immigration Control in America* (Princeton, NJ: Princeton University Press, 2002), 102.

102. Victor Safford, *Immigration Problems: Personal Experiences of an Official* (New York: Dodd, Mead and Co., 1925), 192.

103. William Barnes and John Heath Morgan, *The Foreign Service of the United States: Origins, Development, and Functions* (Washington, DC: Historical Office, Bureau of Public Affairs, U.S. Department of State, 1961), 158, 188; Graham H. Stuart, *The Department of State: A History of Its Organization, Procedure, and Personnel* (New York: Macmillan, 1949), 185–87; Hodgdon, "Extension of Administrative Authority," 45–49, 84–86; and Davie, *World Immigration,* 400. The development of the new regulatory system has not yet been the subject of serious historical study.

104. Fitzgerald, *The Face of the Nation,* 132. The amalgamated service numbered 641, with consular officers outnumbering former diplomatic officers by approximately five to one; in its first year, they visaed some 657,968 alien passports; U.S. Department of State, *The Immigration Work,* 1. Since visitors' visas provided an entry wedge, the consuls had authority to deny them to persons whom they suspected of seeking to enter permanently. This was upheld as early as 1926 by Judge Charles M. Hough of the U.S. District Court, District of Vermont; *American Foreign Service Journal* 4, no. 1 (1927): 12.

105. *American Foreign Service Journal* 3, no. 7 (1926): 226.

106. Alcott W. Stockwell, "Our Oldest National Problem," *American Journal of Sociology* 32, no. 5 (March 1927): 742–55.

107. Higham, Clifford Alan Perkins, *Border Patrol: With the U.S. Immigration Service on the Mexican Boundary 1910–54* (El Paso: Texas Western Press, 1978), 90–91.

108. Perkins, *Border Patrol,* 90–91.

109. Davie, *World Immigration,* 400–1.

110. Perkins, *Border Patrol,* 65.

111. Lawrence A. Cardoso, *Mexican Emigration to the United States, 1897–1931* (Tucson: University of Arizona Press, 1980), 162–94; and Juan Ramon Garcia, *Operation Wetback: The Mass Deportation of Mexican Undocumented Workers in 1954* (Westport, CT: Greenwood, 1980), 100–8.

112. H. R., Committee on Immigration and Naturalization, "Immigration Border Patrol," 71st Cong., 2nd sess. (January 15, 1930), 8.

113. During the war, the facilities had been used to intern German ship crews as well as enemy aliens, while the U.S. Army took over the hospital; and in 1919–1920 they were turned into a deportation center for expelled radicals. Ellis Island then resumed its traditional role as an inspection center for incoming lower-fare passengers. Thomas M. Pitkin, *Keepers of the Gate: A History of Ellis Island* (New York: New York University Press, 1975), 120; and Harlan D. Unrau, *Ellis Island Statue of Liberty National Monument: Historic Resource Study (Historical Component),* vol. 3 (Washington, DC: Government Printing Office, 1984), 892–99.

114. Modifications that were enacted included the granting of nonquota status to aliens who served in the armed forces during the war, as well as their spouses and unmarried children under eighteen; to the wife and children under eighteen of alien ministers and professors who entered the United States before July 1, 1927; to Spanish citizens resident in Puerto Rico at the time of the American occupation; and to women who lost their U.S. citizenship prior to September 22, 1922, by reason of marriage to an alien, but who were no longer married at the time of their application (Hutchinson, *Legislative History,* 198, 200, 203). The platforms are quoted in Rita J. Simon, *Public Opinion and the Immigrant: Print Media Coverage, 1880–1980* (Lexington, MA: D.C. Heath, 1985), 22.

115. Frank C. Bowen, *A Century of Atlantic Travel: 1830–1930* (Boston: Little, Brown, & Co., 1930), 374–75.

116. They included reducing the quotas, making aliens register and carry identity cards, enacting a constitutional amendment excluding them from the population count for apportionment, and imposing a test in American standards by a U.S. Commission before the prospective immigrant left his native land; *American Foreign Service Journal* 9, no. 1 (1932): 17; and Davie, *World Immigration,* 390.

117. Cited in Getz, "Biological Determinism," 29.

118. Levenstein, "The AFL and Mexican Immigration," 212–19.

119. Francisco Rodriguez Balderrama and Raymond Rodriguez Balderrama, *Decade of Betrayal: Mexican Repatriation in the 1930s* (Albuquerque: University of New Mexico Press, 1995), 18. The interest basis for the split within the South and Southwest is emphasized also by Clare Sheridan in "Contested Citizenship."

120. McWilliams, *Factories in the Field,* 127. McWilliams contests the "homer" view and points out that the farm workers generally did not return to Mexico at the end of the harvest but hibernated in Little Mexicos throughout urban southern California, as indicated by the high proportion of charitable expenditures attributable to Mexican cases (149–50).

121. As set forth in a consular conference convened in Mexico City in February

1929; Hodgdon, "Extension of Administrative Authority," 45–49, 84–86. A similar policy was applied to Canada following consular conferences in Ottawa, Montreal, and Halifax. A measure providing for new categories of deportable aliens appears to have targeted Mexicans as well. See also Hutchinson, *Legislative History,* 195, 197, 200, 207, 211; Davie, *World Immigration,* 409; and Balderrama and Balderrama, *Decade of Betrayal,* 61.

122. Divine, *American Immigration Policy,* 65–66. Although in May 1930 a Mexican quota bill received overwhelming support in the Senate (56–11), it failed to clear the House Rules Committee after President Herbert Hoover threatened to veto the measure. A bill providing for a 90 percent reduction of the quotas was passed by the House twice in 1931 and might have made it through the Senate had the legislative session not ended before it came to a vote; Wyman, *Paper Walls,* 3; and Hutchinson, *Legislative History,* 210–54.

123. Divine, *American Immigration Policy,* 78.

124. *American Foreign Service Journal* 7, no. 11 (1930): 412.

125. Richard Breitman and Alan M. Kraut, *American Refugee Policy and European Jewry, 1933–1945* (Bloomington: Indiana University Press, 1987), 15.

126. U.S. Department of State, *The Immigration Work,* 1, 4. Nonimmigrant visas were reduced as well, from 69,920 to 51,805.

127. Ibid., 1, 10; and *American Foreign Service Journal* 9, no. 7 (1932): 286.

128. Niles Carpenter, "The New American Immigration Policy and the Labor Market," *Quarterly Journal of Economics* 45, no. 4 (August 1931): 720, 722–23.

129. As committee chair, Dickstein was also able to fend off further attempts to reduce quota numbers. Concurrently, another Jewish representative from New York, Emmanuel Celler, who assumed the chairmanship of the House Judiciary Committee, introduced a bill to extend quota exemptions to parents over fifty-five and husbands of American citizens who had wed between June 1, 1928, and July 1, 1933; however, despite perennial attempts over the next several years, only the husband provision made it into law.

130. The State Department's annual report for 1934 emphasizes "the relatively permanent character of the restrictive effect of the immigration laws, as now administered, on immigration from Mexico"; U.S. Department of State, *The Immigration Work,* 12–24. Data are taken from Lorey, *United States–Mexico Border Statistics since 1900, 1990 Supplement,* 104, table S18.

131. Recent estimates range from 365,000 for 1929–1932 (Guerin-Gonzales, *Mexican Workers and American Dreams,* 94) to 1,000,000 (Balderrama and Balderrama, *Decade of Betrayal,* 122).

132. For a contemporaneous account, see Helen W. Walker, "Mexican Immigrants and American Citizenship," *Sociology and Social Research* 13, no. 5 (1929): 465–71.

133. O. Douglas Weeks, "The Texas-Mexican and the Politics of South Texas," *American Political Science Review* 24, no. 3 (August 1930): 623. In Los Angeles, for example, the growing cost of relief in the Mexican quarter prompted calls to repatriate the unemployed. When federal officials pointed out that many of the families involved had American-born children, who were citizens, and also insisted on public hearings and formal orders of deportation, local officials quickly devised an alternative: Mexicans receiving charity were made to signify their willingness to return to Mexico, so that repatriation could be presented as a policy designed solely for relief of the destitute "even . . . in cases where invalids are removed from the County Hospital in Los Angeles and carted across the line"; Carey McWilliams, "Getting Rid of the Mexican," *American Mercury* 28 (March 1933): 322–24. McWilliams suggests elsewhere that the deportations were also designed to discourage Mexican efforts to organize labor unions (McWilliams, *Factories in the Field,* 129).

134. Abraham Hoffman, *Unwanted Mexican Americans in the Great Depression: Repatriation Pressures 1929–1939* (Tucson: University of Arizona Press, 1974), 91.

135. Guerin-Gonzales, *Mexican Workers and American Dreams,* 85–86. See also R. Reynolds McKay, "The Impact of the Great Depression on Immigrant Mexican Labor: Repatriation of the Bridgeport, Texas, Coal Miners," *Social Science Quarterly* 65, no. 2 (June 1984): 354–63. The Mexican government pledged to provide transportation into the interior and offered returnees the prospect of resettlement in agricultural colonies, but largely failed to implement its promises.

136. The improvement is noted by Balderrama and Balderrama, *Decade of Betrayal,* 64.

137. Cited in Divine, *American Immigration Policy,* 92.

138. Wyman, *Paper Walls,* 31.

139. Marrus, *The Unwanted,* 126–207.

140. A pioneer scholarly work was David Brody, "American Jewry, the Refugees and Immigration Restriction (1932–1942)," *American Jewish Historical Society* 45 (1956): 219–47.

141. Wyman, *Paper Walls;* Henry L. Feingold, *The Politics of Rescue: The Roosevelt Administration and the Holocaust, 1938–1945* (New Brunswick, NJ: Rutgers University Press, 1970); Barbara McDonald Stewart, *United States Government Policy on Refugees from Nazism 1933–1940* (1969; reprint, New York: Garland, 1982); and Friedman, *No Haven for the Oppressed.*

142. Important works include Neuringer, *American Jewry;* Fred Lazin, "The Response of the American Jewish Committee to the Crisis of German Jewry, 1933–1939," *American Jewish History* 48, no. 3 (March 1979): 283–304; David S. Wyman, *The Abandonment of the Jews: America and the Holocaust 1941–1945*

(New York: Pantheon, 1984); Alan M. Kraut and Richard D. Breitman, "Anti-Semitism in the State Department, 1933–44: Four Case Studies," in *Anti-Semitism in American History,* ed. David A. Gerber (Urbana: University of Illinois Press, 1987), 167–97; Breitman and Kraut, *American Refugee Policy and European Jewry;* Monty Noam Penkower, *The Jews Were Expendable* (Detroit, MI: Wayne State University Press, 1988); and Henry L. Feingold, *Bearing Witness: How America and Its Jews Responded to the Holocaust* (Syracuse, NY: Syracuse University Press, 1995). See also *NYT,* March 21, 1984, A1, B4.

143. *NYT,* March 21, 1984, A1, B4. The report was prepared by Professor Seymour Pinger on behalf of an unofficial group of thirty-four Jewish Americans,

144. For Britain, the leading work in this vein is Bernard Wasserstein, *Britain and the Jews of Europe 1939–1945* (Oxford: Clarendon Press, with the Institute of Jewish Affairs, London, 1979); and on Canada, Irving Abella and Harold Troper, *None Is Too Many: Canada and the Jews of Europe* (New York: Random House, 1983).

145. William D. Rubinstein, *The Myth of Rescue: Why the Democracies Could Not Have Saved More Jews from the Nazis* (London: Routledge, 1997), x.

146. Ibid., 37.

147. Stephen D. Krasner, "Sovereignty: An Institutional Perspective," *Comparative Political Studies* 21 (April 1988): 67.

148. Paul Pierson, "Increasing Returns, Path Dependence, and the Study of Politics," *American Political Science Review* 94, no. 2 (June 2000): 251–67.

149. I am relying heavily on the balanced account of Breitman and Kraut, *American Refugee Policy and European Jewry.* However, a thorough understanding of the American role requires greater attention to the changing nature of the challenge, arising not only from the evolving situation in Germany but also at the international level, including the responses of other states in Europe and overseas, as well as of the League of Nations.

150. Unless otherwise indicated, all the population data in this section are based on "Demographic Aspects of German Jewry 1933–1945," and "Demographic Aspects of German-Jewish Emigration," in *Jewish Immigrants of the Nazi Period in the U.S.A.,* ed. Herbert A. Strauss (New York: K. G. Saur, 1987), 144–54.

151. Maurice R. Davie, *Refugees in America: Report of the Committee for the Study of Recent Immigration from Europe* (New York: Harper & Brothers, 1947), 7.

152. Schacht's role is discussed in Gordon A. Craig, *Germany 1866–1945* (New York: Oxford University Press, 1978), 633.

153. See, for example, the conversations reported by Victor Klemperer, *I Will Bear Witness: A Diary of the Nazi Years, 1933–1941* (New York: Random House, 1998).

154. Klemperer, *I Will Bear Witness,* 18.

155. H. H. Ben-Sasson, ed., *A History of the Jewish People* (Cambridge, MA: Harvard

University Press, 1976), 1009–10. Widely criticized by Jews and others committed to a boycott of German products, the agreement contributed to an internal crisis within the Zionist movement.

156. In addition, immigrant professionals faced guildlike requirements imposed by their American counterparts, notably in medicine. Eastern European Jews who had immigrated to Germany and not yet acquired German nationality were deterred by the restrictive quotas for their countries of origin, notably Poland.

157. Cited in Daniel J. Tichenor, "Regulating Community: Race, Immigration Policy, and American Political Development," Brandeis University, Department of Politics, May 1996, 326.

158. Neuringer, *American Jewry,* 216 (cited from American Jewish Committee archives, March 31, 1933).

159. My understanding of political dynamics in this period is based on David Plotke, *Building a Democratic Political Order: Reshaping American Liberalism in the 1930s and 1940s* (New York: Cambridge University Press, 1996), esp. chs. 3–5, 77–161; and David M. Kennedy, *Freedom from Fear: The American People in Depression and War, 1929–1945* (New York: Oxford University Press, 1999), 102–28.

160. Breitman and Kraut, *American Refugee Policy,* 15–18.

161. Fitzgerald flags this as marking the emergence of foreign policy concerns within the sphere of immigration policy (Fitzgerald, *The Face of the Nation,* 163–73); however, we have already encountered earlier manifestations of this process, notably the Gentlemen's Agreement regarding Japanese immigration (1907) and resistance to the imposition of quotas on Mexican immigration (1924–1930).

162. The concept "habitus" is from Pierre Bourdieu, *Distinction: A Social Critique of the Judgment of Taste* (Cambridge, MA: Harvard University Press, 1984).

163. The State Department's anti-Semitism is a major theme of the literature referred to earlier. The perspective of the generation in question is well illustrated by the discussion of immigration in George F. Kennan, *Around the Cragged Hill: A Personal and Political Philosophy* (New York: W. W. Norton, 1993), 151–55; see also comments on Kennan by Gordon F. Wood, "All in the Family," *New York Review of Books* 48, no. 3 (February 22, 2001): 12–13. A close and balanced scrutiny of the subject, including a discussion of Carr, is provided in Kraut and Breitman, "Anti-Semitism in the State Department."

164. Fitzgerald, *The Face of the Nation,* 165. Perkins also appointed an Ellis Island Committee of Citizens to review immigration procedures with an eye to their liberalization; but although the Committee was able to promote greater consideration of due process in deportation cases, its proposals regarding admission required legislative action, which foundered on the usual obstacles.

165.. Anti-Semitism is amply documented by its manifestations in contemporaneous media, ranging from the popular press to the novels of Ernest Hemingway and F. Scott Fitzgerald, and was subject to rudimentary measurement. In surveys conducted by the American Institute of Public Opinion in 1938 and 1939, about 20 percent of respondents said they thought there is likely to be a widespread anti-Semitic campaign in this country, and 12 percent said they would support it; Hadley Cantril, ed., *Public Opinion, 1935–1946* (Princeton, NJ: Princeton University Press, 1948), 381–82. More generally, see David A. Gerber, ed., *Anti-Semitism in American History* (Urbana: University of Illinois Press, 1987); and with regard to high culture, the account in James Atlas, *Bellow: A Biography* (New York: Random House, 2000), 59–99.

166. Kennedy, *Freedom from Fear,* 231. Anti-Semitism was by no means a preserve of the political right, as indicated by the prominence of the Rothschilds in the traditional mythology of the left.

167. Lazin, "The Response of the American Jewish Committee," 291–93.

168. Breitman and Kraut, *American Refugee Policy,* 227.

169. At the 1933 convention of the American Federation of Labor, the rank and file rejected a resolution on behalf of special admission for German refugees, and the organization adhered to this position for the remainder of the decade; Tichenor, *Dividing Lines,* 162, 165.

170. The constituted international community's refugee regime was rudimentary, limited to the creation of an ad hoc organism for resettling refugees from Russia in the wake of the revolution, and hesitating attempts by the Institut de Droit International to define "refugees" as a concept in international law; Jacques Vernant, *The Refugee in the Post-War World* (London: George Allen and Unwin, 1953), 24.

171. Claudena Skran, *Refugees in Inter-war Europe: The Emergence of a Regime* (Oxford: Clarendon Press, 1995), 135.

172. In the same vein, in 1935 he asked for approval of a treaty providing for American affiliation with the World Court at The Hague (Kennedy, *Freedom from Fear,* 233).

173. Doc. 140, December 27, 1935, in *Jewish Immigrants of the Nazi Period in the U.S.A.,* vol. 4, ed. Herbert A. Strauss (Munich: K. G. Saur, 1992), pt. 2, 290–94.

174. Breitman and Kraut, *American Refugee Policy,* 80; and Stewart, *United States Government Policy,* 187. It should be noted that Stewart is the daughter of High Commissioner McDonald.

175. Breitman and Kraut, *American Refugee Policy,* 46, 50.

176. Related by Friedman, *No Havens for the Oppressed,* 56.

177. *NYT* cited a "high European authority" to the effect that "[e]very Jew east, north and south of Switzerland must be rated now as a potential refugee.

They number 5,000,000 to 6,000,000, excluding Russia"; July 10, 1938, E3. In the course of 1938, Rumania's royal dictatorship deprived about one-third of the country's 600,000 Jews of their citizenship, while Hungary, which initially had some 225,000 and acquired another 150,000 when it annexed parts of Czechoslovakia, drastically reduced their participation in economic and cultural life. Polish anti-Semites also seized the opportunity to intensify their own long-standing campaign against the 3 million of them at home; in June 1937, a pogrom erupted in Czestochowa, whose population was one-third Jewish, and in the summer of 1938, the government itself launched a virulently anti-Semitic radio campaign. See also Skran, *Refugees in Inter-War Europe,* 206–16.

178. Neuringer, *American Jewry,* 229.

179. Stewart, *United States Government Policy,* 282. My discussion of Evian is based on Stewart's account, 280–316, as well as coverage in *NYT.* I am especially grateful to Yannet Lathrop for tracking this down.

180. *NYT,* July 5, 1938, 11.

181. *NYT,* July 3, 1938, 8. The initial wording specified "condemned," but this was rejected by the resolutions committee as overly strong; the delegates also called for a ten-year suspension of all immigration.

182. Cited by Rubinstein, *The Myth of Rescue,* 50.

183. *NYT,* July 4, 1938, 12.

184. *NYT,* July 4, 1938, 13.

185. In fact, 20,301 immigration visas were issued in fiscal year 1938 (79 percent of the quota); Breitman and Kraut, *American Refugee Policy,* 50.

186. *NYT,* July 8, 1938, 1, 7.

187. Catholic organizations estimated that the refugees to date included 10,000 "so-called non-Aryan Catholics," dependent on the charity of their religious brethren in various countries, and that some 50,000 remained to be dealt with inside the Greater Reich (*NYT,* July 10, 1938, E3).

188. *NYT,* July 7, 1938, 1, 8. A subsequent report suggested that German officials had tentatively offered to allow Austrian Jews to leave with 20 percent of their goods as an inducement to speed up emigration, and that as many as 50,000 might depart before the end of the year if appropriate arrangements could be made (*NYT,* July 9, 1938, 1).

189. *NYT,* July 14, 1938, 15.

190. Ibid., 20. In contrast, the *New York Herald Tribune* wondered whether the Intergovernmental Committee on behalf of refugees (IGC) would not be making things worse by helping the Nazis achieve their objectives, and in the same vein Assistant Secretary of State George Messersmith feared that its existence might inspire Poland to undertake a deliberate push-out as well. AFL President William Green, who had joined the newly organized Congress of

Industrial Organizations (CIO) in forming a Labor League for Human Rights, praised the president for his initiative and denounced Nazi anti-Semitism, but restated his opposition to the admission of any refugees beyond quota limits; Tichenor, *Dividing Lines,* 376.

191. August 3, 1938; cited in Feingold, *Bearing Witness,* 96.
192. Friedman, *No Haven for the Oppressed,* 83.
193. For example, in Saul Bellow's early novel, *Dangling Man* (New York: Putnam, 1947).
194. Friedman, *No Haven for the Oppressed,* 3, 57.
195. Stewart, *United States Government Policy,* 313. The "stepping stone" interpretation is from Skran, *Refugees in Inter-War Europe.*
196. November 23, 1938; on display at the Holocaust Museum, Washington, D.C.
197. Stewart, *United States Government Policy,* 316, 357.
198. The parallel is noted by Feingold, *Bearing Witness,* 76–77.
199. Stewart, *United States Government Policy,* 427.
200. Figures on Britain vary somewhat. In what is generally considered the definitive work on the subject, A. J. Sherman initially stated 50,000, but raised this in a subsequent edition to 60,000–70,000; Marion Berghahn has estimated 80,000 for the period extending to the end of World War II (citations from Rubinstein, 27, and n. 37). The Netherlands and Belgium similarly liberalized their immigration policies somewhat, and Australia also announced that it would admit 5,000 refugees a year over a three-year period; Skran, *Refugees in Inter-War Europe,* 222.
201. Kennedy, *Freedom from Fear,* 416.
202. Wyman points out that, in contrast, a year later Congress extended refuge to British children on a nonquota basis (Wyman, *Paper Walls,* 119–20); however, it should be noted that the latter action was much easier to achieve since it was evident that the children were "visitors" who would eventually return to their families in Britain.
203. Feingold, *Bearing Witness,* 117–36.
204. Beitman and Kraut, *American Refugee Policy,* 74.
205. Figures for Palestine are from Rubinstein, *The Myth of Rescue,* 31; see also Ben-Sasson, *A History of the Jewish People,* 1010.
206. Breitman and Kraut, *American Refugee Policy,* 74.
207. Hutchinson, *Legislative History,* 254.
208. Breitman and Kraut, *American Refugee Policy,* 241. The information about the IGC meeting is from Feingold, *Bearing Witness,* 99.
209. For example, former Ambassador James Bullitt claimed that most Nazi spies in France had been refugees, while the *Saturday Evening Post* reported that the Nazis maintained a school in Prague where their spies learned to speak Yiddish and even underwent circumcision; the Soviets were reported to be engaging in similar practices (Wyman, *Paper Walls,* 194).

210. Davie, *Refugees in America,* 31. "Unblocking" meant that if a person who applied earlier was unable to leave, the next person on the list who had travel documents and an exit permit would be granted a visa without delay.

211. Wyman, *Paper Walls,* 194.

212. Feingold, *Bearing Witness,* 166, 225.

213. Following the onset of deportations from the unoccupied zone of France in mid-1942, a group of relief agencies obtained from Prime Minister Pierre Laval an exemption for those holding U.S. visas. Seeking to preempt enactment of a measure providing asylum for all residents of France fleeing persecution, the State Department agreed to award tourist visas to 5,000 children. But Laval stalled under pressure from his German allies, who feared the children would be used for propaganda. In the intervening period, Allied troops landed in North Africa, and on November 11, Germany moved troops into the unoccupied zone, thereby eliminating any possibility of shipping the children out directly. However, an undetermined number were smuggled out by way of Spain and Portugal; Breitman and Kraut, *American Refugee Policy,* 161–64. The INS claim is from Rubinstein, *The Myth of Rescue,* 35; he cites this number from a Department of Justice typescript, but adds, "The figures given here differ significantly from those presented in many other accounts of Jewish refugee migration to the United States" (224 n. 59).

214. Friedman, *No Haven for the Oppressed,* 140.

215. Although the heated historical debate extends to the issue of possible wartime actions in this sphere, notably the bombing of Auschwitz and railroad lines leading to the death camps, I shall limit myself here to matters pertaining to immigration policy.

216. Breitman and Kraut, *American Refugee Policy,* 246.

217. The segment on the Bermuda Conference is based on Penkower, *The Jews Were Expendable,* 102–19. Early in January 1943, Foreign Secretary Anthony Eden secured cabinet authority to that effect, but an aide-mémoire calling for a conference was initially dismissed by Assistant Secretary Breckinridge Long as an attempt to dump the problem in America's lap.

218. Friedman, *No Haven for the Oppressed,* 163–64.

219. Ibid., 186.

220. Davie, *Refugees in America,* 31.

221. Friedman, *No Haven for the Oppressed,* 126

222. Ibid., 189; and Breitman and Kraut, *American Refugee Policy,* 188.

223. Feingold, *The Politics of Rescue,* 266, 294; and Breitman and Kraut, *American Refugee Policy,* 247.

224. Fred W. Riggs, *Pressures on Congress: A Study of the Repeal of Chinese Exclusion* (New York: King's Crown Press, 1950); and Hutchinson, *Legislative History,* 264–65.

225. Divine, *American Immigration Policy,* 104.

226. Breitman and Kraut, *American Refugee Policy,* 10.

227. Fitzgerald reaches a similar conclusion regarding the determinative weight of the bureaucratic process, but exaggerates the extent to which the State Department's rigid stance was attributable to its concern to avoid offending Germany, as against commitment to immigration restriction pure and simple; Fitzgerald, *The Face of the Nation,* 162–63.

228. The references to Smull Zygelbojm are from Penkower, *The Jews Were Expendable,* 117; and Feingold, *Bearing Witness,* 259, Friedman reports that Elie Wiesel in retrospect advocated civil disobedience to secure American intervention following information about the death camps, but suggests that this would have been viewed as seditious behavior jeopardizing American fighting men abroad (Friedman, *No Haven for the Oppressed,* 153).

9. The Ambiguities of Reform

1. On the importance of bipartisanship, see notably Stephen C. Schlesinger, *Act of Creation: The Founding of the United Nations* (Boulder, CO: Westview Press, 2003).

2. Keith Fitzgerald, *The Face of the Nation: Immigration, the State, and the National Identity* (Stanford, CA: Stanford University Press, 1996), ch. 7, 206–28.

3. My account of legislative developments during this period largely parallels Tichenor's in *Dividing Lines,* which should be consulted for additional details; however, I place much greater emphasis on the linkage between "main-gate" and "back-door" policy, and on the significance of the liberal camp's endorsement of a Western Hemisphere ceiling as early as 1953; Daniel J. Tichenor, *Dividing Lines: The Politics of Immigration Control in America* (Princeton, NJ: Princeton University Press, 2002).

4. Harold Vatter, *The U.S. Economy in the 1950's: An Economic History* (New York: W. W. Norton, 1963), 9; William E. Leuchtenburg, *A Troubled Feast: American Society since 1945* (Boston: Little, Brown, 1973), 70; and William Issel, *Social Change in the United States, 1945–1983* (New York: Schocken, 1985), 87. Historical Abstracts, series A 195–209, 14; A 95–122, 11; C 185–217, 65; Cited in Leuchtenburg, *A Troubled Feast,* 42, 125.

5. Arturo Morales Carrion, *Puerto Rico: A Political and Cultural History* (New York: W. W. Norton, 1983), 288, 347.

6. Marty Jezer, *Dark Ages: Life in the United States, 1945–1960* (Boston: South End Press, 1982), 215. Between 1948 and 1961, the number of production workers in manufacturing declined by about 1.5 million, while white-collar workers in the same industries increased by about the same number.

7. For example, from 1947 to 1961 employment in the textile sector declined by 35 percent; Leuchtenburg, *A Troubled Feast,* 45.

8. Vatter, *The U.S. Economy,* 222; Leuchtenburg, *A Troubled Feast,* 79; C. Wright

Mills, *White Collar: The American Middle Class* (New York: Oxford University Press); and William H. Whyte, *The Organization Man* (New York: Simon & Schuster, 1956).

9. As American society became more affluent, farm workers remained among the poorest. While the poor shrank from some 51 percent of the population in the 1930s—an increase from the pre-Depression period—to only 21 percent in 1961, as of 1968 there were still an estimated 25 to 30 million Americans below the poverty line, one-fourth of them farm workers; Leuchtenburg, *A Troubled Feast,* 48.

10. Ibid., 83.

11. Tichenor, *Dividing Lines,* 203.

12. Eric F. Goldman, *The Crucial Decade and After: America, 1945–1960* (New York: Vintage Books, 1986), 21.

13. Sheldon Morris Neuringer, *American Jewry and United States Immigration Policy, 1881–1953* (1969; reprint, New York: ARNO Press, 1980), 343–44. As a case in point, he cites the fact that Henry Pratt Fairchild could still write in 1947, without creating much of a stir, that "America was built step by step, piece by piece by colonists from England, from Holland, from France, from Sweden and by their descendants generation after generation. . . . The recent immigration has had an infinitesimal part in shaping its development"; Henry Pratt Fairchild, *Race and Nationality: As Factors in American Life* (New York: Ronald Press, 1947), 17, 43. Fairchild maintained, as he had two decades earlier, that because the nation is the indispensable large social group, its solidarity is imperative, and since this is weakened by differences arising from immigration, entry must be severely restricted.

14. Sociologist Clyde Kyser, in *The Annals of the American Academy of Social and Political Science* 256 (March 1949): 128–29 (cited by Neuringer, *American Jewry,* 344).

15. Hadley Cantril, ed., *Public Opinion* (Princeton, NJ: Princeton University Press, 1946), 95, 477. The survey on a Catholic as president took place in 1937 and 1940.

16. Bernard Bailyn et al., *The Great Republic: A History of the American People,* 4th ed. (Lexington, MA: D. C. Heath and Co., 1992), 2:438; the quote is from the commander of the West Coast military district in charge of the operation. According to a 1942 survey, 93 percent of the American public approved of the decision with regard to Japanese aliens, and 59 percent with regard to the native-born; Cantril, *Public Opinion,* 380.

17. Notable early scholarly works include Eugene Rostow, "The Japanese American Cases: A Disaster," *Yale Law Journal* 54 (1945): 489–504; and Morton Grodzins, *Americans Betrayed: Politics and the Japanese Relocation* (Chicago: University of Chicago Press, 1949).

18. Cantril, *Public Opinion,* 381.

19. Ronald H. Bayor, "Klans, Coughlinites and Aryan Nations: Patterns of American Anti-Semitism in the Twentieth Century," *American Jewish History* 76, no. 2 (December 1986), 181–98.

20. Cantril, *Public Opinion,* 384.

21. Gordon W. Allport, *ABC's of* Scapegoating (New York: Anti-Defamation League of B'nai Brith, 1948); and Theodor W. Adorno et al., *The Authoritarian Personality: Studies in Prejudice* (New York: Harper, 1950).

22. Ruth Benedict, *Patterns of Culture* (Boston: Houghton Mifflin, 1934); and Margaret Mead, *Coming of Age in Samoa* (New York: Modern Library, 1953). Although Mead's interpretation of Samoan culture is now deemed highly questionable, this in no way reduces its validity as a document in American intellectual history.

23. Otto Klineberg, *Race and Psychology* (Paris: UNESCO, 1951).

24. Neal Gabler, *An Empire of Their Own: How the Jews Invented Hollywood* (New York: Crown, 1988), 349–50. A similar theme was tackled in *Crossfire,* where a murderer with anti-Semitism as his explicit motive is pictured as a psychopath, reflecting Franz Alexander's psychoanalytic interpretation of racism; however, it should be noted that in Richard Brooks's source novel, *The Brick Foxhole* (Garden City, N.Y., 1945), the victim was homosexual.

25. Richard Hofstadter, *The Paranoid Style in American Politics* (New York: Knopf, 1965). The title essay was originally published in *Harper's,* November 1964.

26. The observation about Gunnar Myrdal's introduction was made by Issel, *Social Change,* 152. The most tragic confrontation took place in Detroit, where some 500,000 newcomers had arrived since 1940, including 60,000 blacks, resulting in 34 deaths, 25 of them black. Ralph Ellison, *Invisible Man* (New York: Random House, 1952).

27. This segment is based on research by Brad Usher. The following works were consulted: P. Adler, "The 1943 Zoot Suit Riots: Brief Episode in a Long Conflict," in *An Awakened Minority: The Mexican Americans,* 2nd ed., ed. M. P. Servin (Beverly Hills, CA: Glencoe Press, 1974); M. Mazon, *The Zoot Suit Riots: The Psychology of Symbolic Annihilation* (Austin: University of Texas Press, 1984); and George J. Sanchez, *Becoming Mexican: Ethnicity, Culture, and Identity in Chicano Los Angeles, 1900–1945* (New York: Oxford University Press, 1995). As the barrio expanded, the Los Angeles media attributed responsibility for the city's growing problems of juvenile delinquency to these *pachucos* and "Zoot Suiters." The "zoot suit" was subsequently identified with youth culture more generally. Remarkably, the ten-day-long riots produced no fatalities or major casualties. Peace returned after military commanders declared the barrio off-limits to servicemen, and the City Council subsequently declared zoot suits a "public nuisance."

28. Samuel Lubell, *The Future of American Politics* (New York: Harper & Brothers,

1952), 81; and Stephen Wagner, "The Lingering Death of the National Origins Quota System: A Political History of U.S. Immigration Policy, 1952–1965" (Ph.D. diss., Harvard University, 1986), 410ff.

29. Rita J. Simon, *Public Opinion and the Immigrant: Print Media Coverage, 1880–1980* (Lexington: D. C. Heath, 1985), 133–56.

30. Edwin Harwood, "American Public Opinion and U.S. Immigration Policy," *Annals of the American Academy of Political and Social Science* 487 (September 1986): 202–3.

31. Issel, *Social Change,* 154, 157.

32. Will Herberg, *Protestant-Catholic-Jew: An Essay in American Religious Sociology,* rev. ed. (Garden City, NY: Doubleday Anchor, 1960).

33. Lawrence H. Chamberlain established in 1946 that Congress had exercised controlling influence over the substance and passage of all nine pieces of immigration legislation enacted between 1880 and 1940, and demonstrated more generally that Congress had been very much underrated by political scientists as an innovator in policy making; Lawrence H. Chamberlain, *The President, Congress and Legislation* (New York: Columbia University Press, 1946), 454. A 1970 study confirmed that "Congress has continued its dominance over immigration legislation"; Ronald C. Moe and Steven C. Teel, "Congress as Policy-Maker: A Necessary Reappraisal," *Political Science Quarterly* 85, no. 3 (September 1970): 446.

34. Gerald Marwell, "Party, Region and the Dimensions of Conflict in the House of Representatives, 1949–1954," *American Political Science Review* 61, no. 2 (June 1967): 380–99.

35. David Plotke, *Building a Democratic Political Order: Reshaping American Liberalism in the 1930s and 1940s* (New York: Cambridge University Press, 1996), 192.

36. Herbert McCloskey, Paul J. Hoffmann, and Rosemary O'Hara, "Issue Conflict and Consensus among Party Leaders and Followers," *American Political Science Review* 54, no. 2 (June 1960): 406–27.

37. I am relying largely on Wagner, "The Lingering Death," esp. 237: "No Senator rivaled his influence over immigration policy, and the Eisenhower Administration, wary of antagonizing him, dispensed with the services of one of his conspicuous opponents, refrained from calling for the abolition of the national origins system, and failed to press hard even for the lesser charges it did advocate."

38. Colin McEvedy and Richard Jones, *Atlas of World Population History* (Harmondsworth, UK: Penguin Books, 1978), 64. They attribute the surprisingly high birthrate of the Netherlands to rivalry between the Protestant and Catholic communities.

39. The Irish had the benefit of a relatively large U.S. quota of 17,853, and were

also welcome in the overseas "White Commonwealth" countries; although the Dutch had a much smaller quota of 3,153, they too had alternative possibilities, notably Canada, which actively solicited their settlement; and the Spaniards as well as Portuguese, while sharply restricted under the national origins system, could go to South America or Africa (for example, Angola or Mozambique). Although some of the Italian Mezzogiorno's "push" was absorbed by the rapidly developing industrial centers of the North, and emigrants could also go to South America (such as Argentina), Italian demand for U.S. visas vastly exceeded the very limited supply of 5,802 a year.

40. Robert A. Divine, *American Immigration Policy, 1924–1952* (New Haven, CT: Yale University Press, 1957), 157.

41. Maurice Davie, "What Shall We Do about Immigration?" (1946) in *The Papers of Maurice R. Davie,* ed. Ruby Jo Reeves Kennedy (New Haven, CT: Yale University Press, 1961), 102–3. He went on, "The problems it poses can be solved only through international cooperation. In dealing with them the United States, which has emerged as the most powerful nation, must take a leading part." Hence, from the American perspective, "the problems of post-war migration is more than a domestic question; it is international."

42. Michael R. Marrus, *The Unwanted: European Refugees in the Twentieth Century* (New York: Oxford University Press, 1985).

43. Elizabeth G. Herzog, "Patterns of Controversy," *Public Opinion Quarterly* 13, no. 1 (Spring 1949): 50.

44. Cantril, *Public Opinion,* 387, 1087, 1089. When reworded as "Do you think the United States should let any of these displaced persons enter this country?" the yes's dropped to 36 percent, and the no's rose to 58.

45. Jacques Vernant, *The Refugee in the Post-War World* (London: George Allen and Unwin, 1953), 24–53.

46. Leonard Dinnerstein, *America and the Survivors of the Holocaust* (New York: Columbia University Press, 1982); Neuringer, *American Jewry.*

47. Ellen Percy Kraly, "U.S. Refugee Policy and Refugee Migration since World War II," in *Immigration and U.S. Foreign Policy,* ed. Robert W. Tucker, Charles B. Keely, and Linda Wrigley (Boulder, CO: Westview Press, 1990), 76; and Dinnerstein, *America and the Survivors of the Holocaust,* 263.

48. Gil Loescher and John A. Scanlan, *Calculated Kindness: Refugees and America's Half-Open Door, 1945 to the Present* (New York: The Free Press, 1986), 13–14. In response to a question that asked how they would vote on refugee legislation if serving in Congress, 72 percent of the American public still said they would vote against letting additional refugees enter; Harwood, "American public opinion and U.S. immigration policy," 204.

49. Divine, *American Immigration Policy,* 157.

50. Neuringer, *American Jewry,* 288. The odd figure arose from the belated ad-

dition of a quota for 2,000 Czechs following the February 1948 Communist coup in Prague. Provisions designed to minimize Jewish participation included limiting eligibility to persons who had entered DP camps by December 22, 1945, which disqualified survivors who initially returned to Poland but were subsequently driven back to Germany by anti-Semitic violence; setting aside 30,000 for *Volksdeutsche*; reserving half of the visas for persons originating in annexed territories (that is, the Baltic Republics and eastern Poland); and imposing occupational priorities for which Jews were unlikely to qualify, including farm laborers (up to 30 percent), construction workers, physicians, and scientists. However, the latter provision was broadened in the process of congressional trade-offs to also include tailors.

51. Ibid., 297.
52. Wagner, "The Lingering Death," 33. The latter charge was based on the erroneous assumption that most DPs from the Baltics were Protestant.
53. Concurrently, Britain launched a "Westward Ho!" program of its own for DPs, with Canada as well as Australia following suit. Although all three were also concerned to minimize their Jewish intake, the resettlement of groups from eastern and central Europe constituted a significant departure from the hitherto almost exclusively English-speaking sources of Commonwealth immigration.
54. Bernard Lemelin, "Emmanuel Celler of Brooklyn: Leading Advocate of Liberal Immigration Policy, 1945–52," *Canadian Review of American Studies* 24, no. 1 (Winter 1994): 81–111; and Wagner, "The Lingering Death," 35–38.
55. Kraly, "U.S. Refugee Policy," 76. Jewish organizations estimated that about 16 percent of the entries were allocated to Jews.
56. Marty Jezer, *Dark Ages: Life in the United States, 1945–1960* (Boston: South End Press, 1982), 158–59.
57. Manuel Garcia y Griego, "The Importation of Mexican Contract Laborers to the U.S., 1942–1964: Antecedents, Operation, and Legacy," in *The Border That Joins: Mexican Migrants and U.S. Responsibility,* ed. P. G. Brown and Henry Shue (Totowa, NJ: Rowman & Littlefield, 1983), 49–98; 81st Congress, 2nd sess., Senate Report 1515, "The Immigration and Naturalization Systems of the U.S. Report of the Committee on the Judiciary pursuant to Senate Resolution 137 (80th/1st)," April 1950 (referred to hereafter as "Senate Report 1515"), 573; and Richard B. Craig, *The Bracero Program: Interest Groups and Foreign Policy* (Austin: University of Texas Press, 1971).
58. Juan Ramon Garcia, *Operation Wetback: The Mass Deportation of Mexican Undocumented Workers in 1954* (Westport, CT: Greenwood, 1980), 142–43.
59. Craig, *The Bracero Program;* Garcia y Griego, "The Importation"; Manuel Garcia y Griego, *The Bracero Policy Experiment: U.S.-Mexican Responses to Mexican Labor Migration, 1942–1955* (Ph.D. diss., Department of History, Univer-

sity of California, Los Angeles, 1988); Kitty Calavita, *Inside the State: The Bracero Program, Immigration, and the I.N.S.* (New York: Routledge, 1992); and David G. Pfeiffer, "Braceros from the Mexican Side," in *Mexican Workers in the United States: Historical and Political Perspectives,* ed. George Kiser and Martha Kiser (Albuquerque: New Mexico University Press, 1979), 65–82.

60. Senate Report 1515, 665.

61. Pfeiffer, "Braceros from the Mexican Side," 65–82.

62. *Congressional Record* 97:7163, as cited in Craig, *The Bracero Program,* 75; see also Edward P. Hutchinson, *Legislative History of American Immigration Policy 1798–1965* (Philadelphia: University of Pennsylvania Press, 1981), 301–2. Under section 8 of the 1917 Immigration Act, it was a misdemeanor to bring in or harbor an alien not duly admitted by an immigration officer; and this was upgraded to a felony during the "wetback" crisis of 1948. However, in the intervening period, the Supreme Court had held there was no enforceable law against harboring an illegal immigrant. Several bills to that effect were therefore introduced in the 82nd Congress. On the G.I. Forum, see Calavita, *Inside the State.*

63. Senate Report 1515, 661.

64. Calavita, *Inside the State,* 80, 92–93, 147.

65. Senate Report 1515. This section relies heavily on two unpublished dissertations available from University Microfilms (Ann Arbor, MI): Marius Albert Dimmitt Sr., "The Enactment of the McCarran-Walter Act of 1952" (Ph.D. diss., Modern History, University of Kansas, 1970); and Wagner, "The Lingering Death."

66. Marion T. Bennett, *American Immigration Policies: A History* (Washington, DC: Public Affairs Press, 1963); the Lehman staff member's appreciation is from Wagner, "The Lingering Death," 42.

67. Wagner, "The Lingering Death," 47 n. 72.

68. Dimmitt, "The Enactment," 171.

69. Neuringer, *American Jewry,* 342.

70. Wagner, "The Lingering Death," 47. The subsequent decline was attributed to "maltreatment during the period of World War II," and to the INS commissioner's order to cease recording them as "Hebrew."

71. *NYT,* March 2, 1949, 25.

72. Neuringer, *American Jewry,* 377.

73. William S. Bernard, ed., *American Immigration Policy: A Reappraisal* (New York: Harper, 1950). Reviews of the Bernard book in various social science journals emphasized its partisan character; see, for example, G. Wallace Chessman, review, *Journal of Economic History* 12, no. 1 (Winter 1952): 83–85; and E. P. Hutchinson, review, *American Sociological Review,* 15, no. 2 (April 1950): 314–15. An exception is R. A. Schermerhorn, who characterized it as "a study designed to acquaint the public and Congress with inherent

fallacies and misconceptions in the American immigration policy following the discriminatory quota law and National Origins Act"; R. A. Schermerhorn, review, *American Journal of Sociology* 56, no. 1 (July 1950): 110–12.

74. 82nd Congress, 1st sess., Senate, "Joint Hearings before the Subcommittee of the Committee on the Judiciary on S. 716, H.R. 2379, H.R. 2816," March 6–April 7, 1951, 352 (hereafter, Hearings 1951).

75. This contention was in turn challenged by Roy L. Garis in a generally denunciatory review of Bennett's book in *Journal of Southern History* 16, no. 3 (August 1950): 402–5.

76. These proposals were variously featured in the Bernard report, in a bill introduced by Emmanuel Celler in the House in early 1951, and in a substitute bill introduced by Senators Hubert Humphrey and Herbert Lehman after Walter-McCarran was reported favorably in early 1952.

77. As in the past, they also shied from direct confrontation, leading Rita Simon to express retrospective outrage: "The failure of *Commentary,* a publication of the American Jewish Committee, to run even a single article on McCarran-Walter specifically, or on immigration policy generally, during the first eight years following World War II seems extraordinary"; Simon, *Public Opinion and the Immigrant,* 162.

78. Neuringer, "The Lingering Death," 350; and Dimmitt, "The Enactment," 177.

79. Dimmitt, "The Enactment," 173, 186–90.

80. Bennett, *American Immigration Policies,* 177, 179.

81. This includes even the German expellees admitted under the various DP laws, since according to American practice, they would be assigned to the quota of their country of birth, mainly the USSR, Poland, the Baltic Republics, and Czechoslovakia. As Marion Bennett observed in 1963, "While the restrictionists were able to prevent a basic change in the quota and national origins formulas, they were unsuccessful in preventing such broad exceptions through nonquota and preference quota loopholes as to weaken these formulas in the effects both upon the numbers and kinds of immigrants. This . . . leads to the inescapable conclusion that immigration restriction was not such a prominent feature of public law in the years 1953–1960 as previously was the case"; ibid., 211.

82. Harwood, "American Public Opinion," 204.

83. In a New York speech in mid-October; Neuringer, *American Jewry,* 361.

84. President's Commission on Immigration and Naturalization, *Whom We Shall Welcome* (Washington, DC: U.S. Government Printing Office, 1952); this aspect was highlighted in a review by Simon Marcson in *American Journal of Sociology* 61, no. 1 (July 1955): 95–96. The Commission also recommended the creation of a new and independent immigration agency instead of the existing division between the Justice and State Departments.

85. 83rd Congress, 1st sess., *Immigration and Citizenship Act of 1953,* August 32,

1953 (S. 2585), Statement relative to S. 2585 presented by Senator Lehman, *Congressional Record,* August 3, 1953, 11225; see Louis L. Jaffe, "The Philosophy of Our Immigration Law," *Law and Contemporary Problems* 21, no. 2 (1956): 358–75.

86. Cited in Wagner, "The Lingering Death," 300.

87. Nathan Glazer, *Law and Contemporary Problems* 21, no. 2 (1956): 401–12.

88. Wagner, "The Lingering Death," 158, 161. The change of majority in both houses of Congress for the first time since 1932 made little difference with regard to immigration policy. McCarran's Republican successor, Arthur Watkins of Utah, had conditioned his acceptance of the chairmanship on the retention of Richard Arens as staff counsel, and replied to the president's letter that his colleague's act operated "much better than expected." The new Republican House subcommittee chair was similarly beholden to Walter.

89. Garcia, *Operation Wetback,* 81–96. The legalization process was accomplished by having Mexicans run back to the border, put one foot on Mexican soil, and then dart back to be admitted officially. However, recruitment stopped at the end of the month because the comptroller general ruled that funds could not be used for recruitment in the absence of an agreement.

90. Calavita, *Inside the State,* 60; and Garcia, *Operation Wetback,* 212.

91. Lorey, *U.S.-Mexican Border in the Twentieth Century,* 105, table S19.

92. Loescher and Scanlan, *Calculated Kindness.*

93. The resulting Refugee Relief Act of 1953 provided for 214,000 admissions, including 45,000 escapees from Communism, 60,000 Italians, 17,000 Greeks, and 17,000 Dutch. President Dwight Eisenhower appointed as administrator the State Department's restrictionist Robert C. Alexander, who was very slow in setting up the administration and admitting beneficiaries; Neuringer, *American Jewry,* 383; Wagner, "The Lingering Death," 221; and Hutchinson, *Legislative History,* 332. Reflecting established alignments, the House vote was 221–185, with the winning side composed of 132 Democrats, 74 Republicans, and 1 independent, as against 74 Republicans (nearly all from the Midwest) and 111 Democrats (nearly all from the South) The Senate passed the bill by a voice vote, with McCarran against it.

94. With the help of blood tests and a "confession program" exposing false genealogies, eventually some 30,000 were legalized. Consequently, despite the 105 annual quota, 42,935 Chinese immigrants entered the United States between 1944 and 1960, of whom two-thirds were either wives (16,935) or persons eligible under the Refugee Relief Act of 1953 (10,376); Mae M. Ngai, "Legacies of Exclusion: Illegal Chinese Immigration during the Cold War Years," *Journal of American Ethnic History* 18, no. 1 (Fall 1998): 3–35. The pursuit of such claims was facilitated by the destruction of the San Francisco Hall of Records following the earthquake and fire of 1906.

95. This meant that on a per capita basis, Canada hosted over five times more Hungarians than the United States.

96. Arthur A. Markowitz, "Humanitarianism versus Restrictionism: The United States and the Hungarian Refugees," *International Migration Review* 7 (1973): 46–59.

97. The recommendations included among other things changes in the baseline that would increase quota admissions to 300,000, the pooling of unused visas, and the elimination of the 2,000 ceiling on the Asia-Pacific region. However, in response to the declaration of 1960 as the "World Refugee Year," Eisenhower did secure an expansion of the attorney general's parole authority to admit refugees under the mandate of the UNHCR, then still limited to Europe, on a "fair share" basis, defined as one for every four taken in by others (Act of July 14, 1960). By the end of the year, 5,144 persons had been found admissible under this act.

98. Harry N. Rosenfield, "The Prospects for Immigration Amendments," *Law and Contemporary Problems* 21, no. 2 (1956): 405.

99. Donald J. Kingsley, "Immigration and Our Foreign Policy Objectives," *Law and Contemporary Problems* 21, no. 2 (1956): 299–310.

100. David M. Reimers, "An Unintended Reform: The 1965 Immigration Act and Third World Immigration to the United States," *Journal of American Ethnic History* 3, no. 1 (Fall 1983): 9–28.

101. Harwood, "American Public Opinion," 204.

102. The characterization is from Bennett, *American Immigration Policies,* 192.

103. Wagner, "The Lingering Death," 343–44.

104. The data in this paragraph are drawn from McEvedy and Jones, *Atlas of World Population History.*

105. "If Castro's policies created the potential for mass exodus, U.S. policies made the exodus possible"; Richard F. Fagen, R. A. Brody, and T. J. O'Leary, *Cubans in Exile: Disaffection and the Revolution* (Stanford, CA: Stanford University Press, 1968), 102.

106. The 1962 Migration and Refugee Assistance Act was devised to alleviate the costs incurred by localities.

107. Abba P. Schwartz, *The Open Society,* with a foreword by Arthur Schlesinger Jr. (New York: Morrow, 1968). The author was subsequently appointed as administrator of the State Department's Bureau of Security and Consular Affairs. The observation regarding his relationship with Walter is from Wagner, "A Lingering Death," 370–73.

108. Bennett, *American Immigration Policies,* 255.

109. Ibid., 264.

110. Lorey, *U.S.-Mexican Border,* 105, table S19.

111. Unless otherwise indicated, the information in this section is drawn from

Interpreter Releases, mimeographed bulletin, vols. 40–42 (New York City: Foreign Language Information Service, 1963–1965).

112. Bennett, *American Immigration Policies,* 272–73.

113. Wagner, "The Lingering Death," 377. Although Abba Schwartz claimed the proposal's paternity, he appears to have been overshadowed by the more dynamic Justice Department under the president's brother.

114. Ibid., 381. He refused to schedule a hearing because the McCarran-Walter law provided for a Joint Committee on Immigration, which he would be in a position to head, but ever since 1952 the Senate had refused to appoint its members. Subsequent developments indicate he also had misgivings about the substantive aspects of the proposal. Nevertheless, despite his obstructionism, upon his death Feighan was commemorated by *NYT* as "Architect of '65 Immigration Law" (March 20, 1992, A21).

115. Wagner, "The Lingering Death," 393–94. On Valenti's role more generally, see the profile, "The Personal Touch," *New Yorker,* August 13, 2001, 42–59.

116. Simon, *Public Opinion and the Immigrant,* 79–95.

117. Wagner, "The Lingering Death," 423.

118. *Senate Hearings, S. 500,* February 10, 1965, 19, 56, 123.

119. *Senate Hearings, S. 500,* AFL-CIO testimony, March 15 and June 8, 1965, 640; and Farm Bureau Federation testimony, June 16, 735.

120. Reportedly, the formula was the result of an agreement between Ervin Dirksen and Attorney General Nicolas Katzenbach on the day the Western Hemisphere amendment was rejected in the House (Wagner, "A Lingering Death," 442–43, based on an interview with Senator Kennedy senior staff member Jerry Tinker). Dirksen subsequently stated explicitly that Western Hemisphere restriction was the price that the administration agreed to pay for his support; *NYT,* October 29, 1968, A12.

121. Sheila Patterson, *Immigration and Race Relations in Britain 1960–1967* (Oxford: Oxford University Press, 1969).

122. Hutchinson, *Legislative History,* 377.

123. Reimers, *Still the Golden Door?* (New York: Columbia University Press, 1985), 80–81.

124. Christopher Mitchell, ed., *Western Hemisphere Immigration and United States Foreign Policy* (University Park: Pennsylvania State University Press, 1992); Loescher and Scanlan, *Calculated Kindness;* Norman L. Zucker and Naomi Flink Zucker, *The Guarded Gate: The Reality of American Refugee Policy* (San Diego, CA: Harcourt, Brace, Jovanovich, 1987); Jorge I. Dominguez, "Cooperating with the Enemy? U.S. Immigration Policies toward Cuba," in Mitchell, *Western Hemisphere Immigration,* 31–88; and Fagen, Brody, and O'Leary, *Cubans in Exile,* 102.

125. Anna O. Law, "Shifting Ethnic Alliances: The Politics of American Immigra-

tion Reform" (paper presented at the Annual Meeting of the American Political Science Association, September 1999, Atlanta, Georgia),15, 21–22. Law cites Lawrence Fuchs to the effect that the lottery proposal was "an attempt to legalize the illegal Irish population since many of the illegal Irish had missed the eligibility cutoff date for the 1986 amnesty program" (21). See also Debra L. DeLaet, *U.S. Immigration Policy in an Age of Rights* (Westport, CT: Praeger, 2000), 81.

126. Reimers, *Still the Golden Door?* 253–63.

10. The Elusive Quest for Coherence

1. Official figures cited in this section are from Immigration and Naturalization Service (INS), *1998 Statistical Yearbook of the Immigration and Naturalization Service* (Washington, DC: INS, 2002), table 1. Another 145,000 visas were added to the Western Hemisphere allocation in 1977–1981 as the result of a lawsuit by applicants who claimed they were turned down because 145,000 visas had been mistakenly issued to Cuban refugees (*Silva v. Levi*); nearly 80 percent of the extra admissions were allocated to persons born in Mexico, more than half of them women.

2. A notorious example of the "wool-pulling" school is Peter Brimelow, *Alien Nation: Common Sense about America's Immigration Disaster* (New York: Random House, 1995).

3. Gabriel Chin, "The Civil Rights Revolution Comes to Immigration Law: A New Look at the Immigration and Nationality Act of 1965," *North Carolina Law Review* 75, no. 1 (November 1996): 273–345.

4. Select Commission on Immigration and Refugee Policy (SCIRP), *U.S. Immigration Policy and the National Interest,* staff report, April 30 (Washington, DC: Select Commission on Immigration and Refugee Policy, 1981), 28.

5. Charles B. Keely, "Measuring the Effect of Labor Certification," *International Migration Review* 4, no. 2 (1969–1970): 87–98. Among those reporting occupations, "professionals" and "managers" hovered around 12 percent in the years immediately prior to the change; they rose to 12.4 percent in 1966, 13.7 percent in 1967, and 12.8 percent in 1968, but with a much higher proportion for most Asian and African countries.

6. Ellen Percy Kraly, "U.S. Refugee Policy and Refugee Migration since World War II," in *Immigration and U.S. Foreign Policy,* ed. Robert W. Tucker, Charles B. Keely, and Linda Wrigley (Boulder, CP: Westview, 1990), 73–98, especially 77–78, table 6.1.

7. Accordingly, as of 1980, the waiting list for visas reached 1,088,063, for an annual allocation of 270,000; the most oversubscribed category was the fifth preference, covering adult brothers and sisters of U.S. citizens and their fam-

ilies, with a waiting list of 507,756 for an annual 64,800; U.S. Department of State, Bureau of Consular Affairs, Visa Office, SCIRP staff report (from unpublished data), 377.

8. Jeffrey S. Passell and Karen A. Woodrow, "Geographic Distribution of Undocumented Immigrants: Estimates of Undocumented Aliens Counted in the 1980 Census by State," *International Migration Review* 18, no. 3 Fall 1984): 642–71.

9. Campbell J. Gibson and Emily Lennon, Population Division, U.S. Bureau of the Census, *Historical Census Statistics on the Foreign-Born Population of the United States: 1850–1990,* working paper 29, February (Washington, DC: U.S. Bureau of the Census, 1999), table 1, rounded at one decimal. The foreign-born population does not include persons born outside the United States with at least one parent who is an American citizen.

10. Gibson and Lennon, *Historical Census Statistics,* table 2; and U.S. Department of State, SCIRP staff report, 28. The yearly average for the 1980s as a whole escalated to 166,000 because of legalizations from 1987 to 1990.

11. "Overstayers" include persons entering the United States on tourist, business, and student visas, as well as those who do not require visas for temporary visits (including citizens of Canada, Australia, New Zealand, and most western European countries).

12. Augustin Escobar Latapi et al., "Factors That Influence Migration," in *Migration between Mexico and the United States: Binational Study,* vol. 1 (Mexico City and Washington, DC: Mexican Ministry of Foreign Affairs and U.S. Commission on Immigration Reform, 1998), 163–250. In reality, "demand-pull" factors are difficult to separate from "supply-push" ones, since demand for immigrant labor develops as a function of its availability as a cheaper alternative to domestic labor, while supply itself develops as a function of the availability of opportunities abroad. The notion of "system" is elaborated in Aristide R. Zolberg and Robert C. Smith, *Migration Systems in Comparative Perspective: An Analysis of the Inter-American Migration System with Comparative Reference to the Mediterranean-European System* (New York: International Center for Migration, Ethnicity, and Citizenship, 1996).

13. Colin McEvedy and Richard Jones, *Atlas of World Population History* (Harmondsworth, UK: Penguin, 1978), 291–93, http://www.library.uu.nl/wesp/populstat/Americas/mexicoc.htm. Quite unusually for a developing country, in the early part of the twentieth century Mexico's population actually declined, from 15.2 million in 1910 to 14.4 million in 1920, as a consequence of a bloody civil war followed by a deadly influenza pandemic and the onset of substantial emigration to the United States. Its subsequent dramatic expansion was attributable to the persistence of a high fertility rate of about 6.5 children born per woman until the early 1970s, while infant mortality and

the overall death rate sharply decreased; Geoffrey McNicoll, "Institutional Analysis of Fertility Transition," in *The Reader in Population and Development,* ed. Paul Demeny and Geoffrey McNicoll (New York: St. Martin's Press, 1998), 171. Although "population pressure" in the developing world does not automatically translate into increased emigration to the United States, proximity and networks play an important role; Mary M. Kritz, "Population Growth and International Migration: Is There a Link?" in *Global Migrants, Global Refugees: Problems and Solutions,* ed. Aristide R. Zolberg and Peter M. Benda (New York: Berghahn Books, 2001), 19–41.

14. The *ejido* system instituted in the 1930s set off an era of rural prosperity that fostered an expansion of agricultural production at an annual rate of 5.7 percent from 1940 to 1965, enabling most of the expanding rural population to survive on its own land; Lourdes Arizpe, "The Rural Exodus in Mexico and Mexican Migration to the United States," in *The Border That Joins: Mexican Migrants and U.S. Responsibility,* ed. Peter G. Brown and Henry Shue (Totowa, NJ: Rowman & Littlefield, 1983), 162–83. As in Ireland or Flanders earlier, larger families had an advantage because they could maximize their income by diversifying the activities of male members, some of whom stayed put while others migrated within Mexico or to the United States. GNP more than doubled from about $500 in 1973 to $1,100 in 1979, and after a slight setback, resumed its growth and passed the $2,000 mark in 1984, reaching $3,320 in 2000. By 2000, agriculture accounted for only 23 percent of the labor force and 9 percent of GDP.

15. The road network expanded rapidly in the 1950–1980 period, totaling 237,000 kilometers in 2000; World Bank, *The Transport Sector in Mexico: An Evaluation,* http://wbln0018.worldbank.org/oed/oeddoclib.nsf: 06/30/1998. Literacy reached 90 percent in 2000.

16. Gerardo Otero, "Neoliberal Reform and Politics in Mexico: An Overview," in *Neoliberalism Revisited: Economic Restructuring and Mexico's Political Future,* ed. Gerardo Otero (Boulder, CO: Westview Press, 1996), 1–25; and Gustavo del Castillo V., "NAFTA and the Struggle for Neoliberalism: Mexico's Elusive Quest for First World Status," in *Neoliberalism Revisited: Economic Restructuring and Mexico's Political Future,* ed. Gerardo Otero (Boulder, CO: Westview Press, 1996), 27–42.

17. Gary Gereffi, "Mexico's 'Old' and 'New' Maquiladora Industries: Contrasting Approaches to North American Integration," in *Neoliberalism Revisited: Economic Restructuring and Mexico's Political Future,* ed. Gerardo Otero (Boulder, CO: Westview Press, 1996), 85–105.

18. Harris N. Miller, "The Right Thing to Do: A History of Simpson-Mazzoli," *Journal of Contemporary Studies* 7 (Fall 1984): 59.

19. Lawrence Fuchs, "The Reactions of Black Americans to Immigration," in *Im-*

migration Reconsidered: History, Sociology, Politics, ed. Virginia Yans-McLaughlin (New York: Oxford University Press, 1990), 302.

20. Between 1970 and 1980, self-identified Hispanics grew from 9.1 million, of whom 4.5 million were of Mexican birth or descent, to 14.6 million, including 8.7 million of Mexican origin. Among the four states bordering Mexico—Arizona, California, New Mexico, and Texas—the latter grew from 11.3 percent of the population to 16.7 percent. David E. Lorey, ed., *United States–Mexico Border Statistics since 1900* (Los Angeles: University of California, Los Angeles, Latin American Center, 1990), 7–8, table 100; 39, table 119; 41, table 122. Some of the statistical increase probably reflected better enumeration.

21. On the emergence of Mexican political action groups (and other Latino groups), see Louis DeSipio, *Counting the Latino Vote: Latinos as a New Electorate* (Charlottesville: University Press of Virginia, 1996).

22. John A. Garcia, "The Political Integration of Mexican Immigrants: Examining Some Political Orientations," *International Migration Review* 21, no. 2 (Summer 1987): 386.

23. On the formation of MALDEF and the role of the Ford Foundation, see Karen O'Connor and Leo Epstein, "A Legal Voice for the Chicano Community: The Activities of the Mexican American Legal Defense and Educational Fund, 1968–82," *Social Science Quarterly* 65, no. 2 (1984): 245–56; and Maurilio Vigil, "The Ethnic Organization as an Instrument of Political and Social Change: MALDEF, a Case Study," *Journal of Ethnic Studies* 18, no. 1 (1990): 15–31.

24. Cited in Michael Eduardo Cortés, "Policy Analysis and Interest Groups: The Case of Immigration Reform" (Ph.D. diss., Public Policy, University of California, Berkeley, 1992), 320. More militant groups included the Crusade for Justice, founded by Rodolfo Gonzales in Denver in 1965, and Reies Lopez Tiherina's Alliance of Land Grants, launched in the 1960s to reopen the question of Spanish and Mexican land grants.

25. The policy director of La Raza related that he concluded on the basis of his own research that the costs of discrimination would outweigh the benefits of deterring illegals. Nevertheless, he acknowledged, "We had a constituency on our board and some organizations that wanted to know what the big deal was about employer sanctions. 'Why are you wasting so much time opposing this?,' they said. 'These people are taking our jobs!' [By then, there were] fewer lefties on our board who dealt with everything in ideological terms. And we [had] old-line farmworker folks . . . who always view the undocumented as the enemy" (Cortés, "Policy Analysis," 357).

26. Peter Skerry, in a 1987 article, as cited by ibid., 315. Skerry elaborated his views in *Mexican Americans: The Ambivalent Minority* (Cambridge, MA: Harvard University Press, 1993).

27. Roger Waldinger, *Through the Eye of the Needle: Immigration and Enterprise in New York's Garment Trades* (New York: New York University Press, 1986). For the West Coast, see Wayne A. Cornelius, "The Role of Mexican Labor in the U.S. Economy: Two Generations of Research" (paper presented at the Annual Directors' Meeting of PROFMEX, July 27, 1984, Cozumel, Mexico).

28. James G. Gimpel and James R. Edwards Jr., *The Congressional Politics of Immigration Reform* (Boston: Allyn & Bacon, 1999), 112, and 113, table 4.4.

29. Daniel J. Tichenor, *Dividing Lines: The Politics of Immigration Control in America* (Princeton, NJ: Princeton University Press, 2002), 219–41; and Gimpel and Edwards, *Congressional Politics,* 117–18. After Peter Rodino moved into the chair of the House Judiciary Committee, an office that brought him national prominence in the course of the Nixon impeachment hearings, his successor within the Immigration Subcommittee, Joshua Eilberg, again pushed for employer sanctions, with strong support from the NAACP and organized labor, but over the opposition of Hispanic subcommittee members as well as some members of the Black Caucus, and of course representatives from agricultural districts. In response to these efforts, the Ford administration's Domestic Policy Council came down cautiously in favor of employer sanctions, but coupled this with an expansion of the H-2 program and increased funds for border enforcement.

30. DeSipio, *Counting the Latino Vote,* 45. The National Latino Immigrant Survey and the Latino National Political Survey established in the late 1980s that among U.S. citizens, 66 percent of Mexican Americans and 70 percent of Puerto Ricans were Democrats, as against 20 percent Republican.

31. Reimers, *Still the Golden Door?* 95. The Department of State objected to a ceiling on the traditional "Good Neighbor Policy" grounds. Accordingly, Chairman Rodino introduced an amendment raising the cap for Canada and Mexico to 35,000; this was evidently a face-saving device for those who wanted Mexico to have extra slots, as Canada did not come anywhere near using its allotment. However, objectors pointed out that countries in the Western Hemisphere were already unduly privileged, since the region contained only 9 percent of world population but received 41 percent of all the visas.

32. Gay P. Freeman and Frank D. Bean, "Mexico and U.S. Worldwide Immigration Policy," in *At the Crossroads: Mexico and U.S. Immigration Policy,* ed. Frank D. Bean et al. (Lanham, MD: Rowman & Littlefield, 1997), 27.

33. Reimers, *Still the Golden Door?* 88. P.L. 94–571 also eliminated the exemption of labor certification for parents of U.S. citizens or resident aliens under twenty-one, putting in effect an end to the practice of birthing on U.S. soil. In 1976, Congress also eliminated the physician preference from the Immigration and Nationality Act.

34. Shortly before, the Ford administration granted a change of status to Cuban

refugees, who took up much of the Western Hemisphere quota at the expense of all others; this cleared up some of the backlog, much as the Refugee Relief Act had done with displaced persons in 1953.

35. Michael C. LeMay, *Anatomy of a Public Policy: The Reform of Contemporary American Immigration Law* (Westport, CT: Praeger, 1994), 35.

36. For example, the director of the Maricopa County Organizing Project (MCOP) in Arizona, which César Chávez had supported, sent him an open letter urging him "to stop all actions that would create a greater division among workers (undocumented and documented)," provoking the UFW to dismiss MCOP as being "a bunch of students and do-gooders whose jobs were not being threatened"; Majka, Inda, and Majka,Theo, *Farmworkers,Agribusiness, and the State* (Philadelphia: Temple University Press, 1982), 259, 262. While the Hispanic organizations remained opposed, the UFW, which had joined the AFL-CIO and settled with the growers in 1970, continued to insist on them, and its actions were in turn criticized by advocates for the undocumented.

37. Gil Loescher and John A. Scanlan, *Calculated Kindness: Refugees and America's Half-Open Door, 1945 to the Present* (New York: The Free Press, 1986), 78.

38. As of 1975, the United States had taken in only 26 out of 12,224 Chileans fleeing the right-wing coup of 1973, Reimers, *Still the Golden Door?* 189. However, several hundred more were admitted after Carter came to power.

39. The principal sources for this section are Alan Dowty, *Closed Borders: The Contemporary Assault on Freedom of Movement* (New Haven, CT: Yale University Press, 1987); and Loescher and Scanlan, *Calculated Kindness.*

40. I am grateful to Stephen Burg for explaining the dynamics of Soviet policy in this sphere.

41. According to William Safire, Henry Kissinger told him and Robert Haldeman in preparation for negotiations in Moscow to say nothing about the issue while there, pointing out, "How would it be if Brezhnev comes to the United States with a petition about the Negroes in Mississippi?" Cited in Loescher and Scanlan, *Calculated Kindness,* 92.

42. Jeremey Azrael suggested at the time that the Soviet leadership may have welcomed this choice because of Arab objections to substantial immigration into Israel (personal communication; Chicago, June 1967).

43. Dowty, *Closed Borders,* 204.

44. Jewish emigration persisted as a bargaining chip between the superpowers; in 1978–1979, for example, Moscow granted over 50,000 Jewish exit visas to insure congressional approval of SALT II. A similar pattern arose with regard to Soviet citizens of German ancestry, whose exit was linked to diplomatic and trade negotiations with the Federal Republic of Germany.

45. My understanding of the political dynamics of the Indochinese situation owes a great deal to Astri Suhrke; see Aristide R. Zolberg, Astri Suhrke, and Sergio

Aguayo, *Escape from Violence: Conflict and the Refugee Crisis in the Developing World* (New York: Oxford University Press, 1989), 160–73.

46. Reimers, *Still the Golden Door?* 176.

47. The notion of an "alliance" is based on my own observations and informal conversations with officials in 1982–1989. They organized a blue-ribbon Citizens' Commission on Indochinese Refugees, modeled after the post–World War II Citizen's Commission on Displaced Persons.

48. Although an advisory panel suggested that many "fled primarily because of . . . economic and social conditions" rather than because of persecution, the State Department's regional specialists insisted that "there existed strong foreign policy reasons for developing a long-range refugee program"; Loescher and Scanlan, *Calculated Kindness,* 128. China responded to discrimination against the Sino-Vietnamese by cutting off aid to Vietnam, and the deterioration of the relationship between the two countries in turn placed the target group in yet greater jeopardy.

49. Ibid., 145–46. Following on an earlier demand that the British authorities in Hong Kong had made of China, the partners also pressured Vietnam into pledging that it would make every effort to stop "illegal departures." Criticized by human rights advocates as "undercutting the right of people facing persecution to move out of danger and flee their country," this abruptly reduced the outflow and prompted greater cooperation from the first asylum countries.

50. Arnold H. Leibowitz, "The Refugee Act of 1980: Problems and Congressional Concerns," in *The Global Refugee Problem: U.S. and World Response,* ed. Gil D. Loescher and John A. Scanlan, *Annals of the American Academy of Political and Social Science* (May 1983): 163–71; and Deborah Anker, "The Development of U.S. Refugee Legislation," in *In Defense of the Alien,* ed. Lydio Tomasi, vol. 6 (New York: Center for Migration Studies, 1984), 159–66.

51. Arthur C. Helton, "Political Asylum under the 1980 Refugee Act: An Unfulfilled Promise," in Tomasi, *In Defense of the Alien,* 6:201–6. This was in keeping with international law and the practices of other liberal states.

52. Gimpel and Edwards, *Congressional Politics,* 125–28. They indicate that the estimated probability of voting "yes" on the conference report was .74 for Democrats as against .24 for Republicans, and .65 for nonsouthern versus .28 for southern (132, table 4.7).

53. Kraly, "U.S. Refugee Policy," 77–78, table 6–1; after 1986, various issues of *Refugee Reports.*

54. Jorge I. Dominguez, "Cooperating with the Enemy? U.S. Immigration Policies toward Cuba," in *Western Hemisphere Immigration and United States Foreign Policy,* ed. Christopher Mitchell (University Park: Pennsylvania University Press, 1992), 31–88; see also Robert L. Bach, "The Cuban Exodus: Political

and Economic Motivations," in *The Caribbean Exodus,* ed. Barry B. Levine (New York: Praeger, 1987).

55. Josh De Wind and Michael K. Baldwin, *International Aid and Migration: A Policy Dialogue on Haiti* (Washington, DC: Commission for the Study of International Migration and Cooperative Economic Development, 1990); Terry L. McCoy, *U.S. Policy and the Caribbean Basin Sugar Industry: Implications for Migration* (Washington, DC: Commission for the Study of International Migration and Economic Development, 1990); and Alex Stepick, "Unintended Consequences: Rejecting Haitian Boat People and Destabilizing Duvalier," in Mitchell, *Western Hemisphere Immigration,* 125–56.

56. This did not entail their recognition as refugees, which would have been politically problematic, because of the absence of numerical restrictions on immigration from the independent states of the Western Hemisphere at the time and their ability to meet the "qualitative" requirements then in force.

57. Terry L. McCoy, *U.S. Policy and the Caribbean Basin Sugar Industry: Implications for Migration* (Washington, DC: Commission for the Study of International Migration and Economic Development, 1990).

58. Reimers, *Still the Golden Door?* 193.

59. Christopher Mitchell, "U.S. Foreign Policy and Dominican Migration to the United States," in Mitchell, *Western Hemisphere Immigration,* 89–124.

60. Although it received the largest quota allocation, which amounted to approximately half the regional total, its export tonnage to the United States dropped from an average of 815,335 tons in 1975–1981 to about one-fourth that level at the end of the 1980s; McCoy, *U.S. Policy and the Caribbean Basin Sugar Industry.*

61. Sergio Aguayo and Patricia Weiss Fagen, *Central Americans in Mexico and the United States* (Washington, DC: Center for Immigration Policy and Refugee Assistance, Georgetown University, 1987); Zolberg, Suhrke, and Aguayo, *Escape from Violence,* ch. 8, 204–24 (largely authored by Sergio Aguayo); and Lars Schoultz, "Central America," in Mitchell, ed., *Western Hemisphere Immigration and United States Foreign Policy,* 157–220.

62. President Ronald Reagan later repeated Carter's request to have Fidel Castro take back criminals, threatening to cut down future immigration from Cuba unless he did so. About 200 were repatriated before the Cuban government announced in 1985 that it was suspending the agreement because of the creation of Radio Marti—a broadcasting station established in the United States by Cuban exiles to promote the anti-Castro cause. By 1988, only 125 of Marielitos interned at arrival were still in custody, but several thousand others had been arrested and convicted of crimes committed in the United States. The United States and Cuba reached a new agreement in 1987 to deport many of these prisoners in return for U.S. willingness to accept political

prisoners; however, prisoner riots in Atlanta and Oakdale prompted the United States to suspend deportations and review individual cases. Deportations resumed the following year.

63. Schoultz, "Central America," 178.

64. As of January 31, 1982, 7 claims had been granted, 165 were denied, and over 8,900 were still pending. Following a critique by the UNHCR, in September 1983 the Reagan administration informed Congress that it would admit 200 Salvadorans as refugees. Advocates urged that Salvadorans, as well as Haitians, be accorded EVD, which had been granted to Iranians unable to return home after the Khomeini takeover in 1978–1979, as well as to Ugandans, Ethiopians, and Nicaraguans. However, the government refused, despite a plea from the Salvadoran president in 1978. The advocates then sought to write EVD for Central Americans into law, but succeeded only in 1990 (see below).

65. SCIRP, *U.S. Immigration Policy.*

66. Unless otherwise indicated, this section is based on *Congressional Weekly*; reports in the daily press, particularly *NYT*; publications of concerned interest groups, particularly *Forum Information Bulletin* and *FAIR/Immigration Report*; and informal interviews with key actors in the legislative process over several years, notably Senator Alan Simpson; his chief aide, Richard Day; Senator Edward Kennedy's chief aide, Jerry Tinker; and Ms. Doris Meissner, later INS commissioner.

67. Lawrence H. Fuchs, "The Immigration Reform and Control Act of 1986: A Case Study in Legislative Leadership and Pluralistic Politics, a Triumph for the Civic Culture" (paper presented at the annual meetings of the American Political Science Association, September 1987, Chicago), 8. The senators were Charles Mathias (D-MD), Dennis DeConcini (D-AZ), Edward Kennedy (D-MA), and Alan Simpson (R-WY); the representatives were Peter Rodino (D-NJ), Elizabeth Holtzman (D-NY), Robert McClory (R-IL), and Hamilton Fish (R-NY). Cabinet members included Secretary of State Cyrus Vance, Attorney General Benjamin Civiletti, Secretary of Labor Ray Marshall, and Secretary of Health, Education, and Welfare Patricia Harris. The public members included Joaquin Otero, head of the ALF-CIO Brotherhood of Railway and Airline Clerks, a Cuban American who was also president of the Labor Council for Latin American Advancement; Judge Cruz Reynoso, of the California Court of Appeals, a Mexican American; Rose Ochi, assistant to the mayor of Los Angeles, a Japanese American; and Reuben Askew, former governor of Florida.

68. In the course of its tenure, the commission organized seven task forces, examined fifty briefing and background papers prepared by an extensive staff, held a dozen regional hearings with nearly 700 witnesses as well as 24 sem-

inars with specialized scholars, and sent out 14 issues of its newsletter. At a series of meetings between July and November 1980, the commissioners cast straw ballots on 74 decision memoranda. A draft report of SCIRP's recommendations emerged on January 27, 1981, after 25 hours of discussion and voting. The commissioners considered some 140 recommendations altogether, ranging from work with other nations and international organizations to develop a better understanding of international migration (approved unanimously) to the English language requirement for naturalization (2 were absent; 2 voted for its elimination altogether, 2 for retaining it with existing exemptions for the elderly, and 9 for broadening the exemptions). Most of the votes were close to unanimous, but there were noteworthy divisions on a few issues: the use of identification for the purpose of employer sanctions (9–7 on behalf of maintaining existing identification, 8–7 on behalf of developing more secure documents), and the future of the fifth preference pertaining to brothers and sisters of citizens (9 for maintaining the preference for all siblings, 7 for limiting it to unmarried ones).

69. SCIRP, *U.S. Immigration Policy,* 3; see also Fuchs, "The Immigration Reform and Control Act of 1986," 10.
70. LeMay, *Anatomy,* 37.
71. Freeman and Bean, "Mexico and U.S. Worldwide Immigration Policy," 29; based on Andrew Herschkowitz, "American Political Institutions and Policymaking: The Select Commission on Immigration and Refugee Policy" (Ph.D. diss., Department of Government, University of Texas, Austin, 1994).
72. See Barry R. Chiswick, ed., *The Gateway: U.S. Immigration Issues and Policies* (Washington, DC: American Enterprise Institute for Public Policy Research, 1982).
73. Mark Miller, "Continuities and Discontinuities in Immigration Reform in Industrial Democracies: The Case of the Immigration Reform and Control Act of 1986," *International Review of Comparative Public Policy* 1 (1989): 131–51.
74. Philip L. Martin, *Harvest of Confusion: Migrant Workers in U.S. Agriculture* (Boulder, CO: Westview Press, 1988); and Philip L. Martin, "Harvest of Confusion: Immigration Reform and California Agriculture," *International Migration Review* 24, no. 89 (Summer 1990): 69–95.
75. Franklin S. Abrams, "American Immigration Policy: How Strait the Gate?" in *U.S. Immigration Policy,* ed. Richard R. Hofstetter (Durham, NC: Duke Press Policy Studies, Duke University Press, 1984), 118, 123, 135. The labor analysts cited are, respectively, David North and Allen LeBel, and Wayne Cornelius.
76. Tichenor, *Dividing Lines,* 242–62.
77. Nicholas Laham, *Ronald Reagan and the Politics of Immigration Reform* (Westport, CT: Praeger, 2000), 81–84. This work provides a useful detailed over-

view of the administration's activities, but exaggerates its role in the making of the Immigration Reform and Control Act of 1986.

78. Laham, *Ronald Reagan*, 40–124. Although the White House may have remained silent because it wanted those in the business community who opposed Simpson's proposal to hear his complaints, it maintained a passive stance on the subject of immigration throughout the Reagan era and after Vice President George Bush became president. See also Schuck, *Citizens, Strangers, and In-Between*, 105–6, and 397 n. 59 (based on an interview with Richard Day).

79. The Task Force also dealt with the refugee crisis. While agreeing to allow Cuban and Haitian "entrants" to apply for permanent status after two years' residence, they differed on whether to detain arrivals during processing.

80. Gimpel and Edwards, *Congressional Politics*, 152–53. In the sphere of immigration policy, whereas in the mid-1960s recorded votes were called for about one-third of the time, the proportion rose steadily until by the mid-1990s they were requested three-quarters of the time; moreover, floor divisions reflected ever-narrower majorities. Although they interpret this as "a clear sign that immigration matters have become increasingly controversial" because of its evolution into a redistributive issue, heightened partisanship was a more general phenomenon, and I believe that the more controversial character of immigration issues was attributable to the increasing prominence of the identitarian dimension.

81. As he reminisced in 1997, "I was stuck. I said, 'How did you put me on there?' and Senate Majority Leader Howard Baker said, 'Oh, Alan, you are the junior Republican." Based on an interview on the occasion of a lecture at the Institute of International Studies, University of California, Berkeley; see http://www.globetrotter.berkeley.edu/conversations/Simpson.

82. Related by Schuck, *Citizens, Strangers, and In-Between*, 104 (from an interview with Lawrence Fuchs).

83. See especially Leon Bouvier and Lindsey Grant, *How Many Americans? Population, Immigration, and the Environment* (San Francisco: Sierra Club Books, 1994).

84. SCIRP, *U.S. Immigration Policy*, 411–12; and Laham, *Ronald Reagan*, 36. Senator Simpson later mocked Hispanic organizations as groups that "have no members, they just get their money from the Ford Foundation by playing the violin, pleading, and saying that there's discrimination rampant through the country." However, he acknowledged their effectiveness: "People listened to them. . . . Their purpose was to build their constituency, and you do that in Washington regardless of what constituency it is. Whether it's the NRA or the NEA or the whatever, you do that by frightening your members"; see http://www.globetrotter.berkeley.edu/conversations/Simpson.

85. Harris N. Miller, "The Right Thing to Do: A History of Simpson-Mazzoli," *Journal of Contemporary Studies* 7 (Fall 1984): 64. The two held unusual joint hearings, at which I testified to the continued ability of the United States to incorporate diverse immigrants.

86. Immigration and Naturalization Service (INS), *1998 Statistical Yearbook of the Immigration and Naturalization Service* (Washington, DC: INS 2002), table 1.

87. Seeking to paper over the cracks, Jack Otero, the AFL-CIO's representative on SCIRP, "tried to protect member interests by continuing the Federation's traditional restrictionist stance, while minimizing disagreement among member unions, and minimizing hard feelings among current and potential nonunion coalition partners who opposed employer sanctions and other new restrictions"; Fuchs, "The Reactions of Black Americans to Immigration," in Yans-McLaughlin, *Immigration Reconsidered,* 298–99. Black resentment was directed especially at Indochinese and Cuban refugees, who benefited from special assistance programs; in the same vein, illegal aliens were characterized in an *Ebony* article as a "Big Threat to Black Workers" (Fuchs, "The Reactions of Black Americans to Immigration," 303). See also Cortès, "Policy analysis," 443.

88. Cortès, "Policy Analysis," 429.

89. Leah Haus, "Openings in the Wall: Transnational Migrants, Labor Unions, and US Immigration Policy," *International Organization* 49, no. 2 (Spring 1995): 285–313.

90. Majka and Majka, *Farmworkers,* 274.

91. Cose, *Nations of Strangers,* 194.

92. I am grateful to Brad Usher for his assistance in tracing the origins of the Federaion for American Immigration Reform (FAIR). "Opposition to immigration led some to develop links with conservative groups, especially in the West"; see Robert Gottlieb and Peter Dreier, "The State: Sierra Club Wrestles with the Nativism in Environmentalism," *Los Angeles Times,* March 1, 1998, 6. According to Ruth Conniff, "Extreme Right ideology has been sifting into the environmental movement for some time"; see Ruth Conniff, "The War on Aliens: The Right Calls the Shots," *Progressive,* October 1993, 22–29 (citing Chip Berlet of Political Research Associates in Cambridge, Massachusetts, who reported that there had been a rebirth of "Green Nazis" in Germany as well).

93. Garrett Hardin, *Biology: Its Human Implications* (San Francisco: W. H. Freeman, 1949; new editions in 1966 and 1978). On Hardin more generally, see Alexander Cockburn, "Commentary: A Big Green Bomb Aimed at Immigration; Remember Eugenics? Sierra Club Revives Its Propaganda about Population Growth," *Los Angeles Times,* October 2, 1997, B9. Garrett Hardin's "The Tragedy of the Commons" was reprinted in his *The Immigration Dilemma: Avoiding the Tragedy of the Commons* (Washington, DC: Federation for Amer-

ican Immigration Reform, 1995). All the citations that follow are drawn from the latter work. Invited to present a paper on immigration at the 1974 meetings of the American Association for the Advancement of Science, Hardin responded with "Living on a Lifeboat," which pictures rich nations as heavily loaded lifeboats surrounded by sinking vessels filled with the world's poor, some of whom seek to survive by climbing abroad one of the privileged crafts. On connections between environmentalism and restrictionism more generally, see Gottlieb and Dreier, "The State," 6; and Conniff, "The War on Aliens."

94. Mary Elizabeth Brown, *Shaper of the Great Debate on Immigration: A Biographical Dictionary* (Westport, CT: Greenwood Press, 1999), 260–74; Conniff, "The War on Aliens"; and Jean Stefancic, "Funding the Nativist Agenda," in *Immigrants Out! The New Nativism and the Anti-Immigrant Impulse in the United States,* ed. Juan F. Perea (New York: New York University Press, 1997), 119–35. The Stefancic account is based largely on James Crawford, *Hold Your Tongue: Bilingualism and the Politics of "English Only"* (Reading, MA: Addison-Wesley, 1992). A similar conflict arose within the Petoskey Regional Group of the Sierra Club, which he founded in 1970.

95. Tanton subsequently convened U.S. English, FAIR, and like-minded organizations into a WITAN—short for the Old English "witenagemot," or council—initially hosted by Governor Richard Lamm of Colorado; however, revelation of the anti-Hispanic tone of his convening memorandum led to the resignation of U.S. English Executive Director Linda Chavez, followed by other prominent board members, including Walter Cronkite. Chavez also denounced the reprinting by a member of Tanton's network of Jean Raspail, *The Camp of the Saints* (1973; reprint, Petoskey, MI: Social Contract Press, n.d.; discussed in the next chapter), which she denounced as "without doubt the most vehemently racist book I have ever read"; see Cose, *A Nation of Strangers,* 194.

96. The Pioneer Fund, founded in 1937 by eugenicist Harry H. Laughlin, also financed studies by Arthur Jensen and others alleging the intellectual inferiority of blacks.

97. Conniff, "The War on Aliens," 25. It subsequently spun off the Center for Immigration Studies directed by David E. Simcox, director of the State Department's Office of Mexican Affairs in 1977–1979, who also signed on as one of the incorporators of U.S. English in 1988.

98. At the markup stage, Kennedy managed to broaden legalization to cover all those who arrived before January 1, 1982, but failed in his attempt to provide the Secretary of Labor with more control over temporary workers.

99. Miller, "The Right Thing to Do," 71; and Gimpel and Edwards, *Congressional Politics,* 136. Attributing this outcome to Mexican objections to a tightening of the border at a time when the United States had become dependent on that country for oil, the *NYT*'s John Crewdson concluded that it would be

best to "Leave well enough alone" but suggested it was just as well, because "the immigration reform proposals were bound to prove unworkable." Crewdson, *The Tarnished Door: The New Immigrants and the Transformation of America* (New York: Times Books, 1983), 332.

100. *Plyler v. Doe,* 457 U.S. 202 (1982); Cortés, "Policy analysis," 383, 350–51; and Fuchs, "The Reactions of Black Americans," 298–99.

101. By the end of the year, the minimum wage in Mexico had lost three-quarters of its dollar value while the peso value of U.S. wages soared. The situation was repeated five years later, when Mexican wages dropped again after a year of record inflation rates; the heightened presence of women within the migratory flow may have reflected growing economic distress as well. Katharine M. Donato, "U.S. Policy and Mexican Migration to the United States, 1942–92," *Social Science Quarterly* 75, no. 4 (December 1994): 713, Table 2, and 714.

102. Fuchs, "The Immigration Reform and Control Act of 1986," 24.

103. According to Roybal, as reported by Martin Tolchin in *NYT,* November 30, 1983; Robert Pear, *NYT,* January 19, 1984, A10; Miller, "The Right Thing to Do," 73; and Fuchs, "The Immigration Reform and Control Act of 1986," 25.

104. Fuchs, "The Immigration Reform and Control Act of 1986," 26. Simpson again complained of lack of support from the White House, which remained silent as the Office of Management and Budget published an estimate of the high costs of sanctions and legalization.

105. As reported by Bill Keller, *NYT,* July 21, 1984.

106. Tichenor, *Dividing Lines,* 262.

107. *Forum Information Bulletin* 3, no. 1 (March 19, 1984): 11.

108. In an attempt to secure broader Hispanic support, at Barney Frank's initiative the bill was further amended to prohibit employers from discriminating against legal aliens in hiring or recruitment (404–9). Enactment of the bill in effect killed the prospects of H.R. 4904, sponsored by Roybal, which, in an attempt to make border control more acceptable to Hispanics, provided for amnesty without employer sanctions, calling instead for stricter enforcement of the appropriate labor laws as well as reinforcement of INS services.

109. "The final vote . . . was like a suspense novel, as its fate teetered back and forth during the final 15-minute roll call. 'No' votes outnumbered the 'yes' until just a few seconds before the end, when the tally tied at 210 and Congressional arm-twisting on the floor obtained the few more votes that led to victory."; LeMay, *Anatomy,* 43 (from Rossana Perotti, "Resolving Policy Conflict: Congress and Immigration Reform" [Ph.D. diss., University of Pennsylvania, 1989], 165). The count was 125 Democrats and 91 Republicans versus 138 Democrats and 73 Republicans.

110. Miller, "The Right Thing to Do," 73.

111. B. Lindsay Lowell, Frank D. Bean, and Rodolfo O. De la Garza, "The Dilemmas of Undocumented Immigration: An Analysis of the 1984 Simpson-Mazzoli Vote," *Social Science Quarterly* (1985): 118–27.

112. Miller, "The Right Thing to Do," 78 n. 1.

113. *NYT*, October 12, 1984.

114. Tichenor, *Dividing Lines*, 261. In the same vein, LeMay views the final phase leading to the enactment of IRCA as an instance of the "integrative bargaining model" (LeMay, *Anatomy*, 52). The model is set forth in Thomas Dye, *Understanding Public Policy*, 7th ed. (New York: Prentice Hall, 1992).

115. This colorful locution is borrowed from Senator Simpson's declaration of October 10, 1986 (see citation below).

116. Tichenor reports that Simpson and Kennedy worked closely together on this occasion and instructed their staffs to cooperate, a partnership that continued for the rest of the decade; I can confirm this from personal observation of relations between their respective chiefs of staff, Richard Day and Jerry Tinker, at several conferences and workshops in the early 1990s. On at least one occasion, they shared a family vacation.

117. Miller, "Continuities and Discontinuities," 137.

118. *NYT*, April 18, May 24, and June 14, 1985. Senator Simpson's critique of the Chamber of Commerce appeared in a *NYT* op-ed, August 10, 1982, A27.

119. *NYT*, July 18, 1985, A12; and *Economist*, September 28, 1985, 24.

120. Robert Pear in *NYT*, May 4, 1986.

121. As a California assemblyman from a liberal Los Angeles district, Berman was one of the architects of the 1975 California Agricultural Labor Relations Act, which provided state protection for the UFW's organizational efforts. In 1980 the UFW leadership supported his bid for the state assembly speakership; however, he lost the race when two Chicano assemblymen switched to Willie Brown, who they thought would be in a better position to support the interests of urban Chicanos (Majda and Majda, *Farm Workers*, 271).

122. *NYT*, February 15 and 21, and April 29, 1986; *Wall Street Journal*, May 14, 1986; and *FAIR Immigration Report*, May 1986.

123. First, the amnesty was extended to any illegal aliens who could prove they had been working in agriculture for at least twenty full days from May 1, 1985, to May 1, 1986. Second, the government would be authorized to admit more agricultural workers if the Departments of Labor and Agriculture determined there was a shortage of labor for farms producing fruits and vegetables; after working in agriculture at least forty days in each of their first two years, these workers would be admitted to permanent resident status, like ordinary immigrants. They would then qualify for citizenship after five years' residence, also like ordinary immigrants, but on the condition that they work in agriculture for at least forty days a year during this period. It was worked

out with the conservative Lungren and both Berman and Panetta on the House Democratic side, as well as with Simpson and Wilson on the Republican side of the Senate and Paul Simon and Howard Metzenbaum for the Democrats.

124. Reported on July 1. Another survey cited in *US News and World Report* found that 51 percent favored a decrease. Making a special effort to tap Hispanic opinion, the survey established, not surprisingly, that Hispanics were much more favorable to immigration than whites, with only 31 percent favoring a decrease as against 52 percent; blacks were slightly closer to Hispanics than to whites on this issue (39 percent); mirroring this, 61 percent of Hispanics thought immigration should be the same or increased, as against 39 percent of whites, with blacks again in the middle (52 percent).

125. There were 296,697 admissions in 1965 and 621,444 in 1983, the latest available at the time; apprehensions numbered 110,371 and 1,251,357.

126. Rodino said he continued to support the compromise but would allow the House to vote on a motion to delete it, while Speaker Thomas "Tip" O'Neill remained unconvinced; *New York Times,* September 19, 1986. With the administration's antidrug campaign swinging into action, both Attorney General Edwin Meese and INS Commissioner Alan Nelson again linked drugs to illegal immigration and urged O'Neill to put the bill to a vote. On September 17, Senator Simpson once again obtained assurance from the president that he would not veto the bill; Fuchs, "The Immigration Reform and Control Act of 1986," 41.

127. *NYT,* October 9, 1986.

128. Overall, 30 more Democrats and 29 fewer Republicans supported the measure than in 1984; yet despite heavy Democratic support (168 for it, 61 against it), it would not have passed without the contribution of a sizable minority of Republicans (62 for it, 105 against it).

129. Pear in *NYT,* October 10, 1986; and Fuchs, "The Immigration Reform and Control Act of 1986," 38.

130. *NYT,* October 12, 1986.

131. Shirley J. Smith, Roger G. Kramer, and Audrey Singer, *Characteristics and Labor Market Behavior of the Legalized Population Five Years following Legalization,* prepared by the Division of Immigration Policy and Research as the Department of Labor's Submission to the Administration Report Effects of the Immigration Reform and Control Act, May (Washington, DC: Bureau of International Labor Affairs, U.S. Department of Labor, 1996), 63.

132. Anna O. Law, "Shifting Ethnic Alliances: The Politics of American Immigration Reform" (paper presented at the Annual Meeting of the American Political Science Association, September 1999, Atlanta, Georgia), 23.

133. *NYT,* October 16, 1986; and Fuchs, "The Reactions of Black Americans to Immigration," 305. The four Hispanics who voted in favor were all elected to

the House in 1984, and hence none had voted on the measure in 1983 or 1984.

134. *NYT,* October 17, 1986.

135. It became Public Law 99–603. In addition to the text, see: House Committee of the Judiciary, *The Immigration Reform and Control Act of 1986: A Summary and Explanation,* 99th Cong., 2nd sess. December 1986, Serial no. 14.

136. *NYT,* October 19, 1986, E22.

137. Fuchs, "The Immigration Reform and Control Act of 1986," 43. I was a discussant on the panel.

138. *FAIR/Immigration Report* 7, no. 2 (November 1986).

139. *NYT,* October 16, 1986.

140. Most of this took the form of studies commissioned by the U.S. government and conducted by the Program for Research on Immigration Policy established by the RAND Corporation and the Urban Institute with initial support from the Ford Foundation. Preliminary findings were discussed at conferences held in Guadalajara, Mexico (May 1989), and Washington, D.C. (July 1989). Major results were published in Frank D. Bean, Georges Vernez, and Charles B. Keely, *Opening and Closing the Doors: Evaluating Immigration Reform and Control* (Santa Monica, CA, and Washington, DC: Rand Corporation and the Urban Institute, 1989); Susan González Baker, *The Cautious Welcome: The Legalization Programs of the Immigration Reform and Control Act* (Santa Monica, CA, and Washington, DC: Program for Research on Immigration Policy, the RAND Corporation, and the Urban Institute, 1990); and Frank D. Bean, Barry Edmonston, and Jeffrey S. Passel, eds., *Undocumented Migration to the United States: IRCA and the Experience of the 1980s* (Washington, DC: Urban Institute Press, 1990). These publications form the basis for the present account.

141. In particular, the choice of 1982 rather than date-of-act as the cutoff for eligibility emerged as a serious problem for many families, as in many cases the husband had come to the United States before other members; the U.S. Catholic Conference therefore appealed to President Reagan to allow ineligible spouses and children who were in the country as of November 6, 1986, to be allowed to remain and work until the legalized family member became eligible to pass on a family reunification preference under the established system. In October 1987 the INS relaxed the rules somewhat, alleviating the situation of some 100,000, and the following year the courts ordered further liberalizations; González Baker, *The Cautious Welcome,* 6–9. The cases were *Gutierrez v. Ilchert* and *Catholic Social Services v. Meese* (both 1988).

142. For example, *Haitian Refugee Center Inc., et al., v. Nelson, et al.* (1988), leading to a review of some 21,000 applications.

143. Smith, Kramer, and Singer, *Characteristics and Labor Market Behavior.* For LAWs, the figures were 88, 6, and 6; and for SAWs, 84, 14, and 2.

144. Bean, Edmonston, and Passel, *Undocumented Migration,* 86, table 2A, and 87, table 2B. They ranged from 219.2 percent of the estimated eligible in Houston, thanks to the mobilization of Central Americans by "sanctuary" activists, to only 51.9 percent in New York City, whose illegal population consisted mostly of overstayers, many of whom did not consider themselves qualified or, in the case of Europeans, did not intend to settle permanently in the United States.

145. Immigration and Naturalization Service, *Annual Report 1992* (Washington, DC: Government Printing Office, 1994), 10, table 2.1; 16, table 3.2; and 23.

146. Bean, Edmonston, and Passel, *Undocumented Migration,* 50, 78–80.

147. Expenditures over the seven years of the program amounted to $3.5 billion, averaging $1,167 per eligible person, mostly covering medical services for pregnant women, children, and the elderly and handicapped, as well as emergency care. Only 29 percent of the legalized aliens were high school graduates or better, and 85 percent had a limited knowledge of English, ranging from a high of 92 percent in Texas to only 58 percent in Florida, where many of the legalized originated from the English-speaking Caribbean. Although as of 1992 nearly one-quarter of a sample of legalized aliens still reported knowing no English whatsoever, the proportion able to speak English on the phone had risen from 60 percent to 71 percent, and 36 percent now reported speaking English at home or being able to speak it "well or very well," with men and younger people of both sexes substantially more fluent than older adult women, in keeping with long-standing patterns among immigrants; Susan González Baker, "The 'Amnesty' Aftermath: Current Policy Issues Stemming from the Legalization Programs of the 1986 Immigration Reform and Control Act," *International Migration Review* 31, no. 1 (Spring 1997): 16, appendix A, table 3.2, and 90, table 3C. Overall, "classes did perform a valuable function by welcoming legalization applicants into American society and encouraging their further efforts at self-improvement. . . . To the extent that mandatory English training encouraged other investments in human capital, they were indeed successful"; Bean, Edmonston, and Passel, *Undocumented Migration,* 78.

148. González Baker, "The 'Amnesty' Aftermath," 18.

149. Immigration and Naturalization Service, *Annual Report 2002,* table 46; see also Immigration and Naturalization Service, "Petitions for Naturalizations Filed, Persons Naturalized, and Petitions for Naturalizations Denied, Fiscal Years 1907–2000," http://www.ins.usdoj.gov/graphics/aboutins/statistics/00yrbk_NATZ/Natz2000tables.pdf.

150. LeMay, *Anatomy,* 99.

151. Bean, Edmonston, and Passel, *Undocumented Migration,* 51, 73.

152. Ibid., 73–74; LeMay, *Anatomy,* 119; and Michael Fix, ed., *The Paper Curtain: Employer Sanctions' Implementation, Impact, and Reform* (Washington, D.C.:

Urban Institute Press, 1991), 91. Acknowledging that some discrimination was taking place, Richard W. Day, Senator Simpson's chief of staff, suggested that this might be overcome by employer education; George Vernez, ed., *Immigration and International Relations: Proceedings of a Conference on the International Effects of the 1986 Immigration Reform and Control Act (IRCA)*, May, Rand Corporation JRI-02 and UI Report 90–7 (Santa Monica, CA, and Washington, DC: Program for Research on Immigration Policy, the Rand Corporation, and the Urban Institute, 1990), 16–20.

153. Bean, Vernez, and Keely, *Opening and Closing the Doors*, 46–47; and State of New York Task Force, *The Human Cost of Employer Sanctions* (Albany: State of New York, 1989).

154. Bean, Vernez, and Keely, *Opening and Closing the Doors*, 84.

155. Immigration and Naturalization Service, *Annual Report 2000* (Washington, D.C.: Immigration and Naturalization Service, 2002), 21, table 8.

156. Freeman and Bean, "Mexico and U.S. Worldwide Immigration Policy," in Bean et al., *At the Crossroads*, 32, table 1.3.

157. As pointed out by Kitty Calavita in her review of Bean, Edmonston, and Passel, *Undocumented Migration*, in *Contemporary Sociology* 21, no. 4 (July 1992): 489.

158. Keith Crane et al., *The Effect of Employer Sanctions on the Flow of Undocumented Immigrants to the United States*, RAND Corporation JRI-03 and UI Report 90–8, April (Santa Monica, CA, and Washington, DC: RAND Corporation and the Urban Institute, 1990). In any case, conclusions based on apprehension were inherently misleading because field studies revealed that immigrants kept trying to cross the border until they made it, so the relevant variation to be measured was the number of tries, not of apprehensions; however, these tries were not recorded in official statistics, which did not keep track of repeaters.

159. Crane et al., *The Effect of Employer Sanctions*, 71.

160. Katharine M. Donato, Jorge Durand, and Douglas S. Massey, "Stemming the Tide? Assessing the Deterrent Effects of the Immigration Reform and Control Act," *Demography* 29 (1992): 139–57; Donato, "U.S. Policy and Mexican Migration"; and Reimers, *Still the Golden Door?* 250 (citing Wayne Cornelius).

161. Demetrios G. Papademetriou et al., *Employer Sanctions and U.S. Labor Markets: First Report*, prepared by the Division of Immigration Policy and Research as Part of the Department of Labor's Submission to the President's First Report on the Implementation and Impact of Employer Sanctions, July (Washington, DC: Bureau of International Labor Affairs, U.S. Department of Labor, 1991), xii, xviii.

162. Freeman and Bean, "Mexico and U.S. Worldwide Immigration Policy," 34.

163. John K. Hill and James E. Pearce, "The Incidence of Sanctions against Employers of Illegal Aliens," *Journal of Political Economy* 98, no. 1 (February 1990): 28–44.

164. Bean, Vernez, and Keely, *Opening and Closing the Doors*, 1989, 43; and Jason

Juffras, *Impact of the Immigration Reform and Control Act on the Immigration and Naturalization Service,* RAND Corporation JR-09 and UI Report 91–08, January (Santa Monica, CA, and Washington, DC: Program for Research on Immigration Policy, the RAND Corporation, and the Urban Institute, 1991).

165. Fix, *The Paper Curtain,* 322–23.

166. According to the Department of State, 1.4 million applications were received during a seven-day registration period in January 1987; Ireland received 3,112 visas, Canada 2,078, and Great Britain 1,181 (Law, "Shifting Ethnic Alliances," 22).

167. Ibid., 23.

168. Gimpel and Edwards, *Congressional Politics,* 182–83. An EVD bill cleared the Senate subcommittee in July 1987 as well as its House counterpart, despite opposition from the new Republican subcommittee minority leader, Pat Swindall of Georgia; with southern Democrats generally adopting an anti-immigration stance, the bill got through the House but died in the Senate, and in any case would have run into a presidential veto. Similarly, the House Judiciary Committee approved a six-month extension of the IRCA legalization programs, which were scheduled to expire in May 1988, but this was defeated in the Senate, where Senator Simpson led the opposition.

169. In keeping with SCIRP recommendations, the bill also doubled the number of preference visas for relatives of permanent resident aliens (second preference), which had extensive backlogs, but narrowed the category to include only spouses and unmarried children under 26, and also limited the fifth preference to *unmarried* brothers and sisters of citizens, so as to limit "chaining."

170. Reimers, *Still the Golden Door?* 256 n. 10.

171. Gimpel and Edwards, *Congressional Politics,* 180.

172. Demetrios G. Papademetriou et al., *The Effects of Immigration on the U.S. Economy and Labor Market: Immigration Policy and Research,* report 1, May (Washington, DC: Bureau of International Labor Affairs, U.S. Department of Labor, 1989), 179–89, 200. The concluding chapter is specifically credited to Papademetriou.

173. See, for example, Barry Chiswick, "Mexican Immigrants: The Economic Dimension," *Annals of the American Academy of Political and Social Science* 487 (September 1986): 92–113, and George J. Borjas, *Friends or Strangers: The incorporation of Immigrants in the U.S. Economy* (New York: Basic Books, 1990).

174. The report explained that "[i]mmigration reduces the marginal product, and thus the wages, of those natives that most resemble immigrants," but simultaneously "increase[s] the average earnings of higher-skilled workers and the profits returned to capital." In this perspective, "By becoming the guarantor of low wage labor, the government intervenes to provide, in effect, a wage subsidy."

175. *Congressional Quarterly Almanac,* 1989, 265–73; Daniel J. Tichenor, "Regulating Community: Race, Immigration Policy, and American Political Development," Brandeis University, Department of Politics, May 1996, 517; and Reimers, *Still the Golden Door?* 256–57. At a conference on IRCA held in Guadalajara, Mexico, in May 1989, Latinos charged that current efforts to reform legal immigration were driven by nativism, notably the introduction of English language points, and Asians strongly objected to the ceiling on relatives as an attempt to retract the new opportunities that opened to them after many decades of exclusion. However, in his keynote address to the conference, Senator Simpson's chief of staff, Richard W. Day, defended the proposal by pointing out that "no matter what we do with legal immigration reform, we will eventually evolve a point system designed to try to select immigrants that will be more in the national interest rather than selecting them through a family connection. Since the law changed in 1965, the skill and education levels of immigrants to the United States have dropped"; Vernez, *Immigration and International Relations,* 20, 44.

176. Message from Secretary of Labor Elizabeth Dole to Richard Darman, August 25, 1989, cited by Tichenor, *Regulating Community,* 519 (from L. Fuchs archives, Brandeis University, Waltham, MA).

177. The bill also established another commission and required the president and Congress to reexamine visa allocations every three years.

178. The full text is reprinted in U.S. Congress, House, Subcommittee on Immigration, Refugees, and International Law. *Immigration Act of 1989: Hearings (Part 1),* 101st Cong. (1989), 114–48.

179. U.S. Congress, *Immigration Act of 1989: Hearings (Part 1),* 381. The paper is David M. Reimers, "An Unintended Reform: The 1965 Immigration Act and Third World Immigration to the United States," *Journal of American Ethnic History* 3, no. 1 (Fall 1983): 9–28.

180. Gimpel and Edwards, *Congressional Politics,* 187; and Reimers, *Still the Golden Door?,* 258.

181. Tichenor, *Regulating Community,* 519.

182. Ibid., 520.

183. LeMay, *Anatomy,* 143–49.

184. Gimpel and Edwards, *Congressional Politics,* 194.

185. The vote was 264 to 118, with 50 not voting, and with the Democrats voting 3:1 for approval and the Republicans 1.5:1. LeMay, *Anatomy,* 141, 147; *Congressional Record,* House, October 27, 1990, H-12360; *Congressional Record,* Senate, October 26, 1990, S-17106; *Congressional Quarterly Weekly,* November 3, 1990, 3753; Joyce C. Vialet and Larry M. Eig, *Immigration Act of 1990 (P.L. 101–649),* CRS Report no. 90–601 EPW, December 14 (Washington, DC: Congressional Research Service, U.S. Library of Congress, 1990); Joyce C. Vialet, *Immigration and Related Legislation Enacted in the 101st Con-*

gress, 1989–1990 (Washington, DC: Congressional Research Service, U.S. Library of Congress, 1990); and Debra L. DeLaet, *U.S. Immigration Policy in an Age of Rights* (Westport, CT: Praeger, 2000), appendix C, 133–38.

186. In the final House vote, five members of the Hispanic Caucus who opposed IRCA now voted yes, and not a single one voted no. Among the Black Caucus, five who voted no on IRCA voted yes, along with eight others; one shifted from yes to no; two did not vote.

187. A slightly higher level of 700,000 was provided for in the intervening period to accommodate pending applications; Hong Kong was granted extra visas for residents working for American companies, and was to be treated as a separate nation after 1994. See Vialet and Eig, *Immigration Act of 1990;* Vialet, *Immigration and Related Legislation Enacted in the 101st Congress, 1989–1990* (Washington, DC: Congressional Research Service, U.S. Library of Congress, 1990; and DeLaet, *U.S. Immigration Policy,* Appendix C, 133–38.

188. First preference: unmarried adult children of U.S. citizens (23,400); second preference: spouses and unmarried children of permanent residents, of which 75 percent must be set aside for spouses and minor children (114,200); third preference: married adult children of U.S. citizens (23,400); and fourth preference: brothers and sisters of adult U.S. citizens (65,000).

189. First preference: immigrants of outstanding ability (40,000); second preference: professionals with advanced degrees or immigrants with exceptional abilities (40,000); third preference: skilled workers or unskilled workers for whom there is a shortage; fourth preference: special immigrants, including religious workers (10,000); and fifth preference: investors (10,000). The visas allotted to unskilled workers cannot rise above 10 percent, and applicants in the second and third preferences require certification from the Department of Labor that native workers are not available. These preferences also covered the workers' families.

190. It transferred exclusive jurisdiction to naturalize from federal and state courts to the attorney general, and also amended substantive requirements for naturalization: the state residency requirement was reduced to three months, added another ground for waiving the English language requirement, and lifted the permanent bar to naturalization for aliens who applied to be relieved from U.S. military service on grounds of alienage if they previously served in the country of their nationality. The law also eliminated the ban on homosexuals and members of Communist parties, and accorded American citizenship to Filipino World War II veterans.

191. Cited in DeLaet, *U.S. Immigration Policy,* 77; on public opinion more generally, see Thomas Espenshade and Karen Hempstead, "Contemporary American Attitudes toward U.S. Immigration," *International Migration Review* 30 (1996): 535–70; and George J. Sanchez, "Face the Nation: Race, Immigration, and

the Rise of Nativism in Late Twentieth Century America," *International Migration Review* 31, no. 4 (Winter 1997): 1009–30.

192. Tichenor, *Dividing Lines*, 274. and Reimers, *Still the Golden Door?* 261.

193. DeLaet, *U.S. Immigration Policy*, 79, 89.

11. Why the Gates Were Not Shut

1. Philip Q. Yang, *Post-1965 Immigration to the United States: Structural Determinants* (Westport, CT: Praeger, 1995), 180–82.

2. Peter Andreas, "The Making of Amerexico: (Mis)Handling Illegal Immigration," *World Policy Journal* (Summer 1994): 46.

3. Peter Andreas, *Border Games: Policing the U.S.-Mexico Divide* (Ithaca, NY: Cornell University Press, 2000), 39.

4. Alene H. Gelbard and Marion Carter, "Mexican Immigration and the U.S. Population," in *At the Crossroads: Mexico and U.S. Immigration Policy,* ed. Frank D. Bean et al. (Lanham, MD: Rowman & Littlefield, 1997), 117–23.

5. Jorge Durand, Douglas Massey, and Grace Kao, "Hispanics in America at the Year 2000," *Social Science Quarterly* 81, no. 1 (Spring 2000): 55–57.

6. Christopher Mitchell, "U.S. Border Control: The Case of Miami" (paper presented at the Conference on Border Control, State Power, and Economic Integration, June 4–6, 1999, Cambridge, Massachusetts, Harvard University, Weatherhead Center for International Affairs).

7. Finally on September 18, 1994, as paratroopers from the 82nd Airborne Division began to load, an agreement with the Haitian military was negotiated by former President Jimmy Carter, Senator Sam Nunn, and General Colin Powell. General Raoul Cedras departed, making way for the restoration of Jean-Bertrand Aristide, and the confined Haitians could be returned without angering the administration's political allies.

8. With the Cuban Americans divided, the United States engaged in quick diplomatic negotiations with Cuba, resulting in an agreement to allow 20,000 Cubans to enter yearly as ordinary immigrants, in exchange for which Cuba undertook to discourage rafters and subsequently agreed to accept without reprisals unauthorized emigrants picked up by U.S. vessels on the high seas; an additional provision was made to include Cubans in the 1995 visa lottery.

9. It subsequently came to light that one of those charged overstayed his tourist visa, applied for asylum, and became a follower of Sheikh Omar Abdel Rahman in Jersey City, New Jersey, who himself obtained a "green card" despite being on a watch list regarding his involvement in terrorist activity because U.S. consulates lacked information available in Washington that would have blocked his entry. After his green card was revoked, Sheikh Abdel

Rahman applied for asylum, and his case was under consideration when the bomb went off.

10. The *Golden Venture* was used as a cover illustration for a reissue of Jean Raspail, *The Camp of the Saints* (1973; reprint, Petoskey, MI: Social Contract Press, n.d.). The mastermind of the operation, Lee Peng Fei of Taiwan, was captured in Thailand in 1995 and brought to the United States for trial on federal charges of manslaughter and alien smuggling. He pleaded guilty in March 1998 and was sentenced on June 19; twenty-one others who pleaded guilty to various charges received terms ranging from less than a year to ten years in prison. A similar incident made prime time on the West Coast shortly afterwards, when the freighter *Pai Chang* dumped its human cargo near the Golden Gate Bridge and then led the Coast Guard on an eight-hour chase in San Francisco Bay.

11. Simon and Lynch, "A Comparative Assessment of Public Opinion Toward Immigrants and Immigration Politics," *International Migration* Review 33 (1999), 458. In one 1993 poll, for example, 59 percent as against 31 percent thought immigration had been a good thing in the past, but with regard to the present, the proportions were almost precisely reversed: 29 percent good versus 60 percent bad.

12. Thomas J. Espenshade and Maryann Belanger, "U.S. Public Perceptions and Reactions to Mexican Migration," in Bean et al., *At the Crossroads,* 227. The dramatic surge of support for reduction is confirmed by the more reliable National Election Study (NES) surveys, according to which the "reducers" rose from 49 percent in 1992 to 66 percent two years later.

13. Reviewing opinion trends from 1965 onward, Gregory A. Huber and Thomas J. Espenshade observed that the percentage of reducers was highly correlated with the unemployment rate; Gregory A. Huber and Thomas J. Espenshade, "Neo-isolationism, Balanced-Budget Conservatism, and the Fiscal Impacts of Immigrants," *IMR* 31, no. 4 (Winter 1997): 1031–54; and see also Thomas Espenshade and Karen Hempstead, "Contemporary American Attitudes toward U.S. Immigration," *International Migration Review* 30 (1996): 535–70.

14. Simon and Lynch, "A comparative Assessment," 455–67 (based on a June 1993 *CBS News/NYT* poll).

15. Jack Citrin et al., "Public Opinion toward Immigration Reform: The Role of Economic Motivations," *Journal of Politics* 59, no. 3 (August 1997): 859, 873, 876–77. They suggest further that the domain of immigration policy thus "constitutes another case in which narrow self-interest is not a significant influence on preference formation" and confirms "the impact of enduring values and identifications on mass opinion about public policy questions."

16. Peter Burns and James G. Gimpel, "Economic Insecurity, Prejudicial Stereotypes, and Public Opinion on Immigration Policy," *Political Science Quarterly* 115, no. 2 (2000): 201–25.

17. Those judging Latinos too numerous climbed to 69 percent, Asians to 62 percent, Africans to 47 percent, but Europeans only to 36 percent. The poll data under discussion are drawn from John S. Lapinski, Pia Peltola, and Alan Yang, "The Polls, Trends: Immigrants and Immigration," *Public Opinion Quarterly* 63 (1997): 356–93.

18. I constructed these scores by subtracting the percentage attributed to each group as a source of problems from the percentage it received as a source of benefits in a Gallup Poll of July 1993, reproduced in Lapinski, Peltola, and Yang, "The Polls," 366.

19. Jeff Diamond, "African-American Attitudes towards United States Immigration Policy," *IMR* 32, no. 2 (Summer 1998): 468. In the Latino National Political Survey of 1989–1990, over 75 percent of Mexican American citizens agreed that there were too many immigrants, virtually the same proportion as whites and Puerto Ricans, and somewhat higher than Cuban American citizens. In the same vein, a 1995 study of Latinos in four states found persisting opposition to current levels of immigration, with a slight majority supporting legislation to reduce the legal intake; Rodolfo O. de la Garza and Louis DeSipio, "Interests Not Passions: Mexican-American Attitudes toward Mexico, Immigration from Mexico, and Other Issues Shaping U.S.-Mexico Relations," *IMR* 32, no. 2 (Summer 1998): 410.

20. Citrin et al., "Public Opinion," 869, 877.

21. Lapinski et al., "The Polls," 358, 374, 376.

22. M. V. Hood III and Irwin L. Morris, "Amigo o Enemigo? Context, Attitudes, and Anglo Public Opinion toward Immigration," *Social Science Quarterly* 78, no. 2 (June 1997): 311. However, whites living in California were more negative, leading the authors to speculate that this arose from living in a state with many Hispanics and Asians but not in close contact with them, and to suggest that "there is a limit to the potentially liberalizing influence of the racial context."

23. Caroline J. Tolbert and Rodney E. Hero, "Race/Ethnicity and Direct Democracy: An Analysis of California's Illegal Immigration Initiative," *Journal of Politics* 58, no. 3 (August 1996): 806–18; and Hero and Tolbert, "A Racial/Ethnic Diversity Interpretation of Politics and Policy in the States of the U.S.," *American Journal of Political Science* 40, no. 3 (August 1996): 851–71. For another study that emphasizes the importance of ethnicity as a determinant of policy outcomes, see Yeuh-Ting Lee, Victor Ottati, and Imtiaz Hussain, "Attitudes toward 'Illegal' Immigration into the United States: California Proposition 187," *Hispanic Journal of Behavioral Sciences* 23, no. 4 (November 2001): 430–33.

24. Charles R. Chandler and Yung-Mei Tsai, "Social Factors Influencing Immigration Attitudes: An Analysis of Data from the General Social Survey," *Social Science Journal* 38 (2001): 185. On the language issues, see Raymond Tata-

lovich, *Nativism Reborn? The Official English Language Movement and the American States* (Lexington: University of Kentucky Press, 1995); and Tatalovitch, "Official English as Nativist Backlash," in *Immigrants Out! The New Nativism and the Anti-Immigrant Impulse in the United States,* ed. Juan F. Perea (New York: New York University Press, 1997), 78–102.

25. Thomas C. Wilson, "Cohort and Prejudice: Whites' Attitudes toward Blacks, Hispanics, Jews, and Asians," *Public Opinion Quarterly* 60, no. 2 (Summer 1996): 253–74. He suggests that anti-Semitism may increase as the result of cohort succession as well.

26. "By 1996, the immigrant concept was given specific content, and respondents' prejudices toward Latinos could be more precisely linked to attitudes on immigration policy. . . . The magnitudes of the coefficients do not greatly change, but the extent to which Hispanic prejudice explains immigration attitudes clearly does" (Peter Burns and James Gimpel, "Economic Insecurity, Prejudicial Stereotypes, and Public Opinion" *Political Science Quarterly,* 115 no.2, 212). They emphasize that this is contrary to the results proclaimed in *Congressional Politics,* the study Gimpel coauthored with Edwards on the basis of data from the early 1980s (223). The puzzling contradiction between generally declining levels of prejudice, indicated among other things by increased racial and ethnic intermarriage, and increasing hostility to immigrants has been noted by Frank D. Bean and colleagues, who have tried to resolve it by arguing that the growing concern over immigration is a response to "an increasingly fragile sense of the social contract"; Frank D. Bean et al., "Immigration and the Social Contract," *Social Science Quarterly* 78, no. 2 (June 1997): 263.

27. Huber and Espenshade, "Neo-isolationism."

28. The following account is selective and analytic. A useful compendium of short statements by representatives of various positions has been provided by Nicholas Capaldi, ed., *Immigration: Debating the Issues* (Amherst, MA: Prometheus Books, 1997); on the restrictionist side, see Perea, *Immigrants Out!* For a collection emphasizing integration, see Tamar Jacoby, ed., *Reinventing the Melting Pot: The New Immigrants and What It Means to Be American* (New York: Basic Books, 2004).

29. Daniel Choi, "Border Lines. An Immigration Debate Guide," *New Republic,* September 13, 1993; and Michael Lind, "American by Invitation: A Conservative Call to Arms on a Coming Issue," *New Yorker,* April 24, 1995, 107–13.

30. Choi, "Border Lines"; and Peter Schuck, "The Great Immigration Debate," *American Prospect,* Fall 1990, 101.

31. Julian Simon, *The Economic Consequences of Immigration* (Cambridge, MA: Basil Blackwell, 1989); earlier papers by Julian Simon include "Immigrants,

Taxes, and Welfare in the United States," *Population and Development Review* 10 (1984): 55–60; and "Basic Data concerning Immigration into the United States," *Annals of the American Academy of Political and Social Science* 487 (September 1986): 12–56. The *Wall Street Journal*'s position was set forth in editorials of February 1 and July 3, 1990; the latter called for a constitutional amendment establishing "open borders."

32. George J. Borjas, *Friends or Strangers: The Incorporation of Immigrants in the U.S. Economy* (New York: Basic Books, 1990), 6, 8, 12, 17, 19, 22; like Simon, Borjas set forth his arguments in earlier articles throughout the 1980s.

33. George J. Borjas, *Heaven's Door* (Princeton, NJ: Princeton University Press, 1999), 207.

34. Vernon M. Briggs Jr., *Mass Immigration and the National Interest* (Armonk, NY: M. E. Sharpe, 1992), 7. Earlier statements of his position were set forth, among others, in Vernon M. Briggs Jr., *Immigration Policy and the American Labor Force* (Baltimore: Johns Hopkins University Press, 1984). Briggs was a member of the National Council on Employment Policy from 1977 to 1987 and served as its chair in the last two years.

35. The basic materials include Donald Huddle, "Immigration and Jobs: The Process of Displacement," *NPG Forum* (May 1992): 6; *The Cost of Immigration* (Washington, DC: Carrying Capacity Network, 1993, updated 1994); and *A Critique of the Urban Institute's Claims of Cost Free Immigration: Huddle Findings Confirmed* (Washington, DC: Carrying Capacity Network, 1994).

36. Peter Skerry, "Beware of Moderates Bearing Gifts," *National Review,* February 21, 1994, 46.

37. Huber and Espenshade, "Neo-isolationism," 1053. The maldistribution was confirmed by research conducted on behalf of the National Research Council; see Barry Edmonston and Ronald Lee, eds., *Local Fiscal Effects of Illegal Immigration: Report of a Workshop* (Washington, DC: National Academy Press, 1996); and James P. Smith and Barry Edmonston, eds., *The New Americans: Economic, Demographic, and Fiscal Effects of Immigration* (Washington, DC: National Academy Press, 1997), discussed below.

38. Michael Fix and Jeffrey S. Passell, *Immigration and Immigrants: Setting the Record Straight* (Washington, DC: Urban Institute, 1994).

39. Joyce C. Vialet and Larry M. Eig, *Immigration and Federal Assistance: Issues and Legislation,* CRS Issue Brief, updated May 30, 1996 (Washington, DC: Congressional Research Service, Library of Congress, 1996).

40. Leon F. Bouvier and Lindsey Grant, *How Many Americans? Population, Immigration and the Environment* (San Francisco: Sierra Club Books, 1994). I am grateful to Bill Broder for initially bringing the Sierra Club affair to my attention. For details, see Robert Gottlieb and Peter Dreier, "The State: Sierra Club Wrestles with the Nativism in Environmentalism," *Los Angeles Times,* March

1, 1998, 6; and Lisa Duran, "Scapegoating Immigrants: Environmentalists Debate Population Policy," *Denver Post,* April 7, 1996, D4. Other reports consulted include the *Los Angeles Times,* September 29, October 6, and October 7, 1997; and March 1, March 15, March 16, March 21, April 23, April 26, May 1, and May 5, 1998; the *San Francisco Chronicle,* March 25, 1998; and the *Manchester (UK) Guardian,* October 1, 1997, 15, and March 18, 1998, 11. I am grateful to Rachel Schwartz for help in gathering this information. According to Ruth Conniff, "Extreme Right ideology has been sifting into the environmental movement for some time"; see Ruth Conniff, "The War on Aliens: The Right Calls the Shots," *Progressive,* October 1993, 22–29 (citing Chip Berlet of Political Research Associates in Cambridge, Massachusetts, who reported that there had been a rebirth of "Green Nazis" in Germany as well).

41. Nicholas Eberstadt, "Population Change and National Security," *Foreign Affairs* (Summer 1991): 115–31. The article is drawn from a paper presented to a U.S. Army Conference on Long Range Planning; Michael T. Teitelbaum, "The Population Threat," *Foreign Affairs* (Winter 1992–1993): 63–78.

42. Paul Kennedy, *Preparing for the Twenty-first Century* (New York: Vintage, 1993), 44.

43. Matthew Connelly and Paul Kennedy, "Must It Be the Rest against the West?" *Atlantic Monthly,* December 1994, 61–91; and Robert Kaplan, "The Coming Anarchy," *Atlantic Monthly,* February 1994, 44–76. The Raspail novel *The Camp of the Saints,* initially published in France in 1973, was published by Scribner's in 1975 and subsequently reprinted. When first published in the United States, it evoked dismissive outrage from mainstream reviewers. For a more extended discussion, see Aristide R. Zolberg, "Introduction," in Zolberg and Peter Benda, eds., *Global Migrants, Global Refugees: Problems and Solutions* (New York: Berghahn Books, 2001), 1–19.

44. Myron Wiener, "Security, Stability, and International Migration," *International Security* 17, no. 3 (Winter 1992–1993): 95; and Myron Wiener, *The Global Migration Crisis: Challenge to States and to Human Rights* (New York: HarperCollins, 1995). The article was subsequently incorporated in a volume in a popular college-level political science text series. While disagreeing with the late Myron Wiener on this issue, I retain the highest regard for him as my teacher and was happy to collaborate on one of his immigration/refugee projects.

45. This concern emerged in France but subsequently spread to Germany and Europe as a whole; see Michael S. Teitelbaum and Jay M. Winter, eds., *Fear of Population Decline* (New York: Academic Press, 1985).

46. Amartya Sen, "Population: Delusion and Reality," *New York Review of Books,* September 22, 1994, 63. In fact, the Asian and African shares of world population are presently still below their 1650 or 1750 level.

47. Lawrence Auster, *The Path to National Suicide: An Essay on Immigration and Multiculturalism* (Monterey, Va.: American Immigration Control Foundation, 1990).

48. George F. Kennan, *Around the Cragged Hill: A Personal and Political Philosophy* (New York: W. W. Norton, 1993).

49. Peter Brimelow, *Alien Nation: Common Sense about America's Immigration Disaster* (New York: Random House, 1995); see also Peter Brimelow, "America's Assisted Suicide," *National Review,* November 1996, 65–67. On Harry Evans, see Jacob Weisberg, *New York Times,* April 24, 1995: 24.

50. Weisberg, *New York,* 24. The publication figure is from David Reimers, *Unwelcome Strangers* (New York: Columbia University Press,1998), 157.

51. Daniel Kanstroom, "Dangerous Undertones of the New Nativism: Peter Brimelow and the Decline of the West," in Perea, *Immigrants Out!* 303. Linda Bosniak has suggested that unlike Patrick Buchanan, "Brimelow is not regarded as a fringe political actor" but is "an establishment conservative with 'insider' credentials"; Linda Bosniak, " 'Nativism' the Concept: Some Reflections," in Perea, *Immigrants Out!* 286–87, 296.

52. Lind, "American by Invitation," 24.

53. Stephan Thernstrom, "Has the Melting Pot Begun to Boil?" *Washington Post,* April 2, 1995, 1, 10; Linda Chavez, "Nativists Still Scapegoat Immigrants," *Denver Post,* June 4, 1995, D4; Nathan Glazer, "The Closing Door," 15–20 (his response to Brimelow is based on the 1992 article); and Peter D. Sahlins, "Take a Ticket," *New Republic,* December 27, 1993, 13–15.

54. Samuel P. Huntington, *Who Are We? The Challenges to America's National Identity* (New York: Simon & Schuster, 2004).

55. 103rd Congress, 1st Session, House Report 103–216, *The Immigration and Naturalization Service Overwhelmed and Unprepared for the Future,* Second Report by the Committee on Government Operations together with Additional Views (Washington: U.S. Government Printing Office, 1995), 10, 11, 13, 15, 22. The 1990 law "significantly broadened the enforcement authority of INS personnel, and included new deportation procedures intended to expedite the deportation process"; the agency's budget more than tripled between 1975 and 1990, thanks in part to the creation of user fee programs; and its staff increased by 70 percent. Nevertheless, the report found that "there are serious management problems which plague INS and have interfered with its ability to do its job." Witnesses singled out "the lack of good leadership" as the most important problem, arising from the fact that the "senior, politically-appointed layer of management" lacked "both substantive knowledge and adequate managerial competence. As a result, implementing policy, even once it is set, is difficult if not impossible."

56. A February 1989 special audit determined that the INS had lost such control

of its fiscal year 1988 funds "that we could not determine . . . if the agency was in violation of the Anti-Deficiency Act." This was further confirmed in a General Accounting Office (GAO) report, which also found that the INS lacked information, did not have the resources to collect it, and exercised little or no control over the security of the information it did have. It was "often indifferent" to training, failed to supervise employees involved in critical decisions, and mismanaged its appropriations, now amounting to over $1 billion.

57. Thomas J. Espenshade, "Does the Threat of Border Apprehension Deter Undocumented U.S. Immigration?" *Population and Development Review* 20 (1994): 871–92; Andreas, *Border Games*, 90–98; and Timothy Dunn, *The Militarization of the U.S.–Mexico Border, 1978–1992. Low-Intensity Conflict Doctrine Comes Home* (Austin: Center for Mexican American Studies, University of Texas Press, 1994), 152–56.

58. Philip G. Schrag, *A Well-Founded Fear: The Congressional Battle to Save Political Asylum in America* (New York: Routledge, 2000), 17–36. Unless otherwise indicated, data are from various issues of *Refugee Reports*. Applications rose steadily from 56,310 in 1991 to 154,464 in 1995, with the backlog climbing concurrently from 137,046 to 464,121. As the number of "defensive" applicants vastly exceeded the jail space the INS could secure with its limited budget, many were let go; when their hearing finally came up, many applicants failed to show up altogether, and others disappeared after being turned down.

59. Ibid., 43.

60. The appointment was made on June 19, 1993, and Meissner was confirmed the following October. I should record my longtime association with Doris Meissner, who served as an adviser on a refugee study I conducted in the 1980s in collaboration with Astri Suhrke and Sergio Aguayo, and was a guest of the International Center for Migration, Ethnicity, and Citizenship.

61. Tichenor, *Dividing Lines,* 278; and Gimpel and Edwards, *Congressional Politics,* 216–20. George Sanchez has suggested that Jordan's presence deflected potential charges of racism directed at the stringent provisions of the policy recommendations"; George Sanchez, "Face the Nation: Race, Immigration, and the Rise of Nativism in Late Twentieth Century America," *IMR* 31, no. 4 (Winter 1997): 1017.

62. Among others, Democratic Senator Harry Reid of Nevada and Republican Richard Selby of Alabama teamed up to propose the Immigration and Stabilization Act of 1993 (S. 1351), which was supported by FAIR as a "landmark piece of legislation," which set an overall ceiling of 300,000 for all types of immigration, increased funding for the INS, imposed tighter asylum procedures, and provided for the speedy deportation of alien criminals. Reid in-

troduced his proposal again the following year with his fellow Nevadan Democrat James Libray cosponsoring in the House; David M. Reimers, *Unwelcome Strangers: American Identity and the Turn against Immigration* (New York: Columbia University Press, 1998). With regard to illegal immigration, Senator Simpson again introduced a bill for summary exclusion, which even Senator Kennedy appeared to accept, albeit with greater procedural protections; Schrag, *A Well-Founded Fear,* 45.

63. 103rd Congress, 1st session, House Document 103–124, "Proposed Legislation: Expedited Exclusion and Alien Smuggling Enhanced Penalties Act of 1993. Message from the President of the United States, July 27, 1993" (Washington, DC: U.S. Government Printing Office, 1993); and Office of the President, *Accepting the Immigration Challenge: The President's Report on Immigration* (Washington, DC: U.S. Government Printing Office, 1994), iv.

64. David Spener and Kathleen Staudt, "Reconstructing La Frontera: Debordering and Rebordering Processes between the United States and Mexico" (paper presented at the Annual Meeting of the Latin American Studies Association, Los Angeles, December 1998).

65. William J. Clinton, Office of the President, *Accepting the Immigration Challenge: The President's Report on Immigration* (Washington, DC: U.S. Government Printing Office, 1994), iii, vi, viii.

66. Their author provided his own account in David A. Martin, "Making Asylum Policy: The 1994 Reforms," *Washington Law Review* 70 (1995): 725.

67. Frank Bean et al., "Illegal Mexican Migration and the United States/Mexico Border: The Effects of Operation Hold the Line on El Paso/Juarez" (Washington, DC: U.S. Commission on Immigration Reform, 1994), 123–29.

68. Gary P. Freeman, "Can Liberal States Control Unwanted Migration?" *Annals of the American Academy of Political and Social Science* 534 (July 1994): 17–30.

69. U.S. Commission on Immigration Reform, *U.S. Immigration Policy: Restoring Credibility. A Report to Congress. Executive Summary,* September (Washington, DC: U.S. Commission on Immigration Reform, 1994), 5–17.

70. Gimpel and Edwards, *Congressional Politics,* 217.

71. H. Eric Schockman, "California's Ethnic Experiment and the Unsolvable Immigration Issue: Proposition 187 and Beyond," in *Racial and Ethnic Politics in California,* ed. Cain Preston, Bass (1998), 249–50.

72. Jack Miles, "Blacks vs. Browns: The Struggle for the Bottom Rung," *Atlantic Monthly* 270, no. 4 (1992): 60; *NYT,* August 25, 1993, A1; *Congressional Quarterly Researcher,* 846; *Wall Street Journal,* January 18, 1994, B1; and *NYT,* January 2, 1994, 4:3.

73. *USA Today,* April 8, 1994: 3; Sanchez, "Face the Nation," 1011. In 1986 and 1987 the Republican governor vetoed—against the advice of a bipartisan blue-

ribbon commission he had helped to appoint—an extension of the state's mandatory bilingual education law, thus allowing it to "sunset."

74. *NYT,* October 30, 1994, E3 (Ashley Dunn reporting; statistical analysis provided by Andrew A. Beveridge from the U.S. Census Bureau and Richard Lovelady of the Sacramento Census Data Center). In fact, census data indicated that of Mexicans who arrived from 1980 to 1990 (both legal and undocumented), only 1.7 percent were on public assistance, compared with 4.8 percent for the Los Angeles population as a whole, and 4.4 percent for the entire United States.

75. Karin MacDonald and Bruce E. Cain, "Nativism, Partisanship, and Immigration: An Analysis of Prop. 187," in *Racial and Ethnic Politics in California,* vol. 2, ed. Preston and Bass, 286 (citing Lubenow).

76. *NYT,* May 21, 1994, A12; *Los Angeles Times,* September 19, 1993, A1, A28; and Miles, "Blacks vs. Browns," 63.

77. *Time,* October 3, 1994, 47.

78. Ashley Dunn, "In California, the Numbers Add Up to Anxiety," *NYT,* October 30, 1994.

79. My understanding of the place of Proposition 187 within the Californian political configuration was vastly enhanced by the tutoring of Brad Usher, graduate student in the Department of Political Science, New School University. Basic information is drawn from Philip Martin, "Proposition 187 in California," *IMR* 29, no. 1 (Spring 1995): 255–63; and Peter H. Schuck, *Citizens, Strangers, and In-Betweens: Essays on Immigration and Citizenship* (Boulder, CO: Westview, 1998), 149–62. Although in withholding public education from children of mandatory school age, the initiative explicitly challenged the Supreme Court's 1982 ruling, the sponsors hoped that its passage would prompt a reconsideration of the issue by the court.

80. Robert Scheer, "The Dirty Secret behind Proposition 187," *Los Angeles Times,* September 2, http://www.robertscheer.com/l_natcolumn/94_columns/0929 94.htm. Former INS Commissioner Alan C. Nelson commented similarly that California had brought the problem upon itself by its earlier attitude "that illegal immigration was O.K."; *NYT,* October 15, 1994: A1, 10 (Joel Brinkley reporting); and Michael Alvarez and Tara L. Butterfield, "The Resurgence of Nativism in California? The Case of Proposition 187 and Illegal Immigration," *Social Science Quarterly* 81, no. 1 (March 2000): 167–79.

81. Susan González Baker, "The 'Amnesty' Aftermath: Current Policy Issues Stemming from the Legislation Programs of the 1986 Immigration Reform and Control Act," *IMR* 31, no. 1 (Spring 1997): 5–27.

82. Skerry, "Beware of Moderates Bearing Gifts," 47.

83. *NYT,* May 21, 1994, A12; and MacDonald and Cain, "Nativism," 286.

84. For example, *Time* magazine hailed it as "truly a referendum for the 1990s. . . .

In a country built by immigrants, it is a measure of the deep dissatisfaction with the generosity of the welfare state that the public has seized on aliens as the enemy within" (October 3, 1994, 46–47).

85. *NYT,* October 6, 1994, A29, and October 29, 1994, A19.

86. *Time,* October 31, 1994, 39.

87. Anonymous official quoted in *Time,* October 3, 1994, 47.

88. *NYT,* September 19, 1994, A11, B3; October 15, 1994, A10 (Joel Brinkley reporting); and October 21, 1994, A1; and *Time,* October 3 and November 28, 1994.

89. On October 26, Michael Huffington himself was hit by a scandal echoing the "nannygate" that beset the administration following the appointments of Zoe Baird and Kimba M. Wood, when the *Los Angeles Times* revealed that his daughters had been cared for from 1989 to 1994 by an illegal immigrant (*NYT,* October 28, 1994, A3, and October 29, 1994, A23). The San Francisco *Free Press,* put out by striking workers of the *Chronicle* and *Examiner,* subsequently reported that Senator Dianne Feinstein had employed an illegal Guatemalan housekeeper in the early 1980s as well (*NYT,* November 4, 1994, A7, and November 5, 1994, A11, B. Drummond Ayres Jr. reporting).

90. Ralph Armbruster, Kim Geron, and Edna Bonacich, "The Assault on California's Latino Immigrants: The Politics of Proposition 187," *International Journal of Urban and Regional Research* 19, no. 4 (1995): 662.

91. Facing an election of their own, President Carlos Salinas and his hand-picked successor, Ernesto Zedillo Ponce de Leon, sought to make up for promoting NAFTA over the qualms of their nationalistic compatriots by assailing Proposition 187 as misguided and xenophobic, and promising to fight it in the courts; *NYT,* November 3, 1994, A2, and November 14, 1994 (Tim Golden reporting).

92. *NYT,* October 16, 1994, A10, and October 27, 1994, A1, A27.

93. *NYT,* October 31, 1994, A3 (B. Drummond Ayres Jr. reporting). The first endorsement of any candidate for governor by the paper in a quarter of a century, it was hotly contested by some Hispanic staff members. *NYT,* October 21, 1994, A9.

94. Alvarez and Butterfield, "The Resurgence of Nativism."

95. Schockman, "California's Ethnic Experiment," 267.

96. MacDonald and Cain, "Nativism," 256; and Schockman, "California's Ethnic Experiment."

97. Lina Y. Newt, "Why Some Latinos Supported Proposition 187: Testing Economic Threat and Cultural Identity Hypotheses," *Social Science Quarterly* 81, no. 1 (March 2000): 180–93. A number of studies have pointed to a Chicano history of tenuous relations with Mexican immigrants; see for example H. L. Browning and Rodolfo de la Garza, eds., *Mexican Immigrants and Mexican-*

Americans: An Evolving Relation (Austin: CMAS Publications of the University of Texas, 1986). According to a Latino National Political survey, 75.2 percent of Mexican Americans interviewed agreed that there were "too many immigrants"—a higher proportion than among whites; Rodolfo de la Garza et al., *Latino Voices: Mexicans, Puerto Ricans, and Cuban Perspectives on American Politics* (Boulder, CO: Westview Press, 1992), 110.

98. MacDonald and Cain, "Nativism," 284; see also Alvarez and Butterfield, "The Resurgence of Nativism," 172.

99. *Time,* November 21, 72–73, and November 28, 1994, 36; and *NYT,* November 18, 19, and 20, 1994.

100. She explained that "Proposition 187's requirements directly regulate immigration by creating a comprehensive scheme to detect and report the presence and affect the removal of illegal aliens. . . . The state is powerless to enact its own scheme to regulate immigration." She also struck down section 8, which would have excluded illegal immigrants from public postsecondary institutions. These rulings set in motion a protracted legal battle; Schockman, "California's Ethnic Experiment," 258–59. See also Debra L. DeLaet, *U.S. Immigration Policy in an Age of Rights* (Westport, CT: Praeger, 2000), 106.

101. Jeffrey Rosen, "Citizens," *New Republic,* November 21, 1994, 42. However, the Supreme Court eroded the distinction in the 1970s and 1980s by holding that aliens are entitled to many of the benefits that previously had been reserved for citizens alone. Rosen goes on to invoke Schuck and Smith's "liberal case" for "reinvigorating a consensual ideal of citizenship"; Peter H. Schuck and Rogers M. Smith, *Citizenship without Consent: Illegal Aliens in the American Polity* (New Haven, CT: Yale University Press, 1985).

102. Kitty Calavita, "The New Politics of Immigration: 'Balanced-Budget Conservatism' and the Symbolism of Proposition 187," *Social Problems* 43, no. 3 (August 1996): 285.

103. *Time,* October 3, 1994, 47.

104. Louis DeSipio, *Counting the Latino Vote: Latinos as a New Electorate* (Charlottesville: University Press of Virginia, 1996), 59, 62, 87.

105. John A. Garcia, "The Political Integration of Mexican Immigrants: Examining Some Political Orientations," *International Migration Review* 21, no. 2 (Summer 1987): 372–89.

106. Susan Gonzaléz Baker, "Su voto es su voz: Latino Political Empowerment and the Immigration Challenge," *PS: Political Science and Politics* 29, no. 3 (September 1996): 465–68.

107. Schockman, "California's Ethnic Experiment," 261.

108. I am grateful to William A. Gordon, graduate student in the Department of Political Science, Graduate Faculty, New School University, for his painstaking assistance on this segment. Unless otherwise indicated, the information is drawn from various issues of *Interpreter Releases.*

109. Roy Beck, "Right of Silence?" *National Review,* July 11, 1994, 27–35.

110. Lamar Smith and Edward R. Grant, "Immigration Reform: Seeking the Right Reasons," *St. Mary's Law Journal* 28 1–15 (1997); Gimpel and Edwards, *Congressional Politics,* 213; and Dick Kirschten, "Second Thoughts," *National Journal,* January 21, 1995.

111. Schrag, *A Well-Founded Fear,* 70.

112. Reimers, *Unwelcome Strangers,* 134. Howard Berman subsequently introduced an administration bill, the Immigration Enforcement Improvements Act, providing for tough measures to discourage illegal entry and overstaying; Tichenor, *Dividing Lines,* 282.

113. Stephen Chapman, "Old Arguments on Immigration," *St. Louis Post-Dispatch,* June 12, 1995, B7.

114. U.S. Commission on Immigration Reform, *Legal Immigration: Setting Priorities,* June (Washington, DC: U.S. Commission on Immigration Reform, 1995), 70–80. The dissenter was Warren Leiden, who advocated maintenance of the established family reunion system.

115. Other recommendations pertained to naturalization, including, on the one hand, measures for speeding up the process but, on the other, more stringent verification procedures.

116. Cited in Gimpel and Edwards, *Congressional Politics,* 225.

117. Kirschten, "Second Thoughts"; and Schrag, *A Well-Founded Fear,* 58.

118. He lost his bid for reelection as Republican whip to Trent Lott; earlier, his motion opposing renewal of the Lautenberg Amendment on the grounds that it had become "for the most part an immigration program in refugee clothing" effect lost by a humiliating 85 to 15 and cost him a number of friends; Schrag, *A Well-Founded Fear,* 52.

119. Ibid., 65; and Gimpel and Edwards, *Congressional Politics,* 239–41.

120. Reimers, *Unwelcome Strangers,* 133; and Gimpel and Edwards, *Congressional Politics,* 216.

121. Roberto Suro, *Watching America's Door: The Immigration Backlash and the New Policy Debate* (New York: Twentieth Century Fund, 1996), 8–9.

122. Gimpel and Edwards, *Congressional Politics,* 246, 262.

123. Ibid., 236–38. A multidimensional analysis revealed a restriction/expansion dimension at work as well, with Republicans mostly restrictionist, but less concentrated on this than on the partisan dimension. They also point out that African Americans somewhat surprisingly voted with Hispanics against restriction, despite their economic interest in the matter.

124. Schrag, *A Well-Founded Fear,* 60, 88.

125. Ibid., 105–15; the author himself was instrumental in the creation of the CPA.

126. Joyce C. Vialet and Larry M. Eig, *Alien Benefit Eligibility Provisions in H.R. 4* (Washington, DC: Congressional Research Service, Library of Congress, 1996).

127. Cited in *Immigration Review* 73, no. 48 (December 20, 1996): 1750 [reprinted from the issue dated April 17, 1995].

128. While final Senate deliberations were pending, the INS released statistics indicating a 10 percent drop in admissions for fiscal year 1995, with a comment from Commissioner Meissner that this shows "the system can work." However, the INS subsequently acknowledged that its report of a drop in admissions was a fluke, and that projected figures for the coming year were in fact up; Reimers, *Unwelcome Strangers,* 140.

129. Thomas J. Espenshade, Jessica L. Baraka, and Gregory A. Huber, "Implications of the 1996 Welfare and Immigration Reform Acts for US Immigration," *Population and Development Review* 23, no. 4 (December 1997): 775. Legal immigrants already in the United States (hitherto subject to "deeming" for their first three years) also remained eligible at the state's discretion, but newcomers were ineligible for the first five years, except for emergency medical assistance, after which eligibility was again at the state's discretion.

130. Larry M. Eig and Joyce C. Vialet, coordinators, *Immigration Enforcement Legislation: Overview of House and Senate-Passed H.R. 2202,* CRS Report for Congress (Washington, DC: Congressional Research Service, Library of Congress, July 1, 1996); and Joyce C. Vialet and Larry M. Eig, *Alien Eligibility for Benefits under H.R. 3734, Welfare Conference Agreement* (Washington, DC: Congressional Research Service, Library of Congress, 1996), 96–617 EPW, updated August 1, 1996. Gary Freeman is among those who interpret the law as not primarily restrictionist (personal communication).

131. *Los Angeles Times,* August 11, 1996 (Patrick J. McDonnell reporting).

132. Barney Frank and Howard Berman charged that, in a departure from tradition, the Republicans excluded the minority Democrats from conference negotiations and completely rewrote the bill on their own (from an interview with Gimpel and Edwards, *Congressional Politics,* 280).

133. Ibid., 283.

134. Kathleen M. Moore, "U.S. Immigration Reform and the Meaning of Responsibility," *Studies in Law, Politics, and Society* 20 (2000): 126.

135. Reimers, *Unwelcome Strangers,* 143.

136. T[homas] H[umphrey] Marshall, *Citizenship and Social Class, and Other Essays* (Cambridge: Cambridge University Press, 1950).

137. Moore, "U.S. Immigration Reform," 138.

138. Cited by ibid., from Cong. Rec. House, September 25, 1996, H11080 (emphasis added by Moore).

139. The Social Security Administration reckoned that of an estimated 818,000 noncitizen SSI recipients, of whom two-thirds lived in California, New York, and Florida, approximately half a million would lose their benefits as well as their Medicaid eligibility, which in many states is tied to SSI, by the fall of

1997; 1 million receiving food stamps and 600,000 with full Medicaid coverage would do so as well; Espenshade, Baraka, and Huber, "Implications of the 1996 Welfare and Immigration Reform Acts," 775.

140. Michael Fix and Jeffrey S. Passel, *Trends in Noncitizens' and Citizens' Use of Public Benefits following Welfare Reform: 1994–97,* March (Washington, DC: Urban Institute, 1999), 10.

141. Gimpel and Edwards, *Congressional Politics,* 284; and DeLaet, *U.S. Immigration Policy,* 106–8.

142. Moore, "U.S. Immigration Reform," 145. The benefits included TANF, SSI, Medicaid, and food stamps. In California, 23.7 percent of the recently naturalized got Medicaid, compared with 8.2 percent of the general population.

143. *NYT,* editorial, June 26, 2001, A16.

144. Justice Department investigators subsequently reported that citizenship was granted in some cases before the INS received criminal background checks from the FBI (www.CNN.com, August 1, 2000). The matter remained on the agenda as of mid-2005.

145. Stephen H. Legomsky, "Fear and Loathing in Congress and the Courts: Immigration and Judicial Review," *Texas Law Review* 78, no. 7 (June 2000): 1616.

146. Moore, "U.S. Immigration Reform," 140.

147. *Reno v. American-Arab Anti-Discrimination Committee* (525 U.S. 471 1999).

148. Ronald Schmidt Sr., *Language Policy and Identity Politics in the United States* (Philadelphia: Temple University Press, 2000); Raymond Tatalovich, *Nativism Reborn? The Official English Language Movement and the American States* (Lexington: University of Kentucky Press, 1995); and Robert D. King, "Should English Be the Law?" *Atlantic Monthly,* April 1997, 55–64. See also "English Language Constitutional Amendments," Hearings before the Subcommittee on Civil and Constitutional Rights of the Committee on the Judiciary, House of Representatives (May 11, 1988), Serial no. 120 (1989).

149. James Crawford, "Disaster at the Polls," http://ourworld.compuserve.com/homepages/JWCRAFORD/BECh13.htm, 13.

150. Cited in Robert Warren, "Annual Estimates of the Unauthorized Immigrant Population Residing in the United States and Components of Change: 1987 to 1997," September, draft version (Washington, DC: Office of Policy and Planning, U.S. INS, 2000), 3. The estimates were based on the U.S. Census Bureau's annual Current Population Survey (CPS), Three years later, the agency announced that, on the basis of the Census Bureau's annual CPS, it revised the estimate to 5.1 million as of January 1997.

151. My estimate for 2000 is reached by adding 405,000 (105,000 × 3) to the INS 1997 level. The Census Bureau estimate of residual foreign-born in 1990 is cited in Joe Costanzo et al., *Evaluating Components of International Migration:*

The Residual Foreign-Born, Working Paper no. 61, January (Washington, DC: Population Division, U.S. Census Bureau, 2002).

152. A. Dianne Schmidley, *Profile of the Foreign-Born Population in the United States: 2000,* U.S. Census Bureau Current Population Reports no. P23–206, December (Washington, DC: U.S. Census Bureau, 2001). For consistency, I have rounded all millions and percentages to the nearest decimal; Frederick W. Hollman et al., *U.S. Census Bureau Measurement of net international migration to the United States,* U.S. Census Bureau Population Division Working Paper no. 51, December (Washington, DC: U.S. Census Bureau, Population Division, 2001). Concurrently, Census Bureau researchers reached an alternative estimate of 8.1 million by adding legal immigration, refugees, net unauthorized migration, and net temporary migration for a total of 10.8 million, and subtracting emigration amounting to 2.7 million.

153. Kevin E. Deardorff and Lisa M. Blumerman, *Evaluating Components of International Migration: Estimates of the Foreign-Born Population by Migrant Status in 2002,* U.S. Bureau of the Census Population Division, Working Paper no. 58, December (Washington, DC: U.S. Bureau of the Census, Population Division, 2001); and Costanzo et al., *Evaluating components of international migration.* They deducted from the total foreign-born population (33.1 million), the estimated "survived legal immigrants" (21.6 million), and temporary migrants (such as students and H-1B workers, .8 million), producing an estimate of 8.7 "residual foreign born" (RFB). These were assumed to be undercounted by 15 percent, producing a "true" level estimate of 10.2 million. From this, they deducted a "known component" of 1.8 million (for example, asylum applicants and others in a quasi-legal situation). At the same time, using the recent 2000 enumeration and following the "residual method"—deducting from the total foreign-born population immigrants who could be accounted for and correcting for undercounting—other researchers from the same project estimated that some 4.9 million were added in the 1990s, representing an increment of some 129 percent over the 1990 level. Taking into consideration undercounts, the estimate rises to 5.5 million. As the researchers acknowledge that the RFB include some "quasi-legal migrants" ("in process" cases of various sorts), the estimate of unauthorized population proper is in the range of 4.0–4.5 million, a result consistent with the one reached by the "residual" method. The "residual foreign born" of 2000 were younger than those of 1990 (40.0 percent aged 18–29 in 2000 versus 32.8 percent in 1990), more male (54.2 percent versus 48.4 percent), and much more Mexican (44.5 percent versus 26.8 percent); Marc Perry et al., *Evaluating Components of International Migration: Legal Migrants,* Working Paper no. 59, January (Washington, DC: Population Division, U.S. Census Bureau, 2002), 14. Another team sought to estimate annual legal immigration by reevaluating the admis-

sion data reported by INS, which, according to the agency itself, "do not convey a meaningful indication of any demographic concept" because, among other things, they encompass a large number of "adjustees" who entered the country at some earlier time. By assigning these adjustees to the year of actual entry and taking into account mortality as well as emigration, the team estimated net legal immigration for the 1990s at 7.5 million, to which might be added another 950,000 "quasi-legal" immigrants (persons who initiated a request for change of status, with likely positive outcomes), for a total of 8.45 million, consistent with its earlier estimates. This represented an increase of approximately 60 percent over the net legal intake of the 1980s, with a slight increase of the Hispanic component from 30.2 percent to 32.5 percent. Other researchers from the same project subsequently came up with 8.4 million "implied" unauthorized residents in 2000, suggesting a net addition of 4.6 million for the decade, double the bureau's own earlier estimate and nearly three times the INS figure.

154. "Number of Foreign-Born Up 57 percent since 1990, According to Census 2000," June 4, 2002, http://www/census.gov/Press-Release/www/2002/cb02cn117.html.

155. Tables 4 in NS reports for 1998 and 2000, (covering new entrants and adjustments, but excluding IRCA legalizations); the percentages do not add up to 100 because miscellaneous categories have been omitted. Although the bureau did not break down legal immigration by categories, INS reports indicated that whereas in 1991 qualifying relatives of citizens and permanent residents accounted for 64.4 percent of admissions, as against 8.4 percent employment-related admissions and 19.8 percent refugees and asylees, in 2000 the proportions were, respectively, 86.6, 12.6, and 7.8 percent.

156. The information that follows is from *Refugee Reports,* August 25, 1995, August–September 1999, 16. The fiscal year 1996 level of refugee admittances was 90,000, an 18 percent decrease from the previous year, half of it allocated to the former Soviet Union and 25,000 to Southeast Asia. Only 76,000 were actually admitted, and in the next year the level was reduced by another 13 percent to 78,000, with Southeast Asia the major loser. However, it was raised again to 83,000 the following year to provide for 25,000 from former Yugoslavia, and returned to 91,000 in fiscal year 1999, including 13,000 Kosovars as well as additional Africans. Both the level and distribution pattern persisted for the remainder of the administration's tenure. Concurrently, advocates continued to press for the regularization of specific groups. In November 1997, the president signed the Nicaraguan Adjustment and Central American Relief Act, which allowed some who entered before December 1, 1995, to adjust to permanent resident status, and enabled Salvadorans, Guatemalans, and certain eastern Europeans and former Soviets who arrived before 1990 to apply

for suspension of deportation under the more lenient rules that existed prior to IIRIRA. Regarding asylum, the 1996 law's filing deadline of twelve months from arrival, unless delayed by extraordinary circumstances, contributed to a substantial drop in applications amounting to 72 percent from fiscal year 1994 to fiscal year 1999; concurrently, however, cases were processed faster and the proportion of approvals increased by 16 percent (*Refugee Reports,* December 31, 1997, 5–7; and February 2000, 2). Between 1989 and 1997, a total of 95,889 cases were turned down and 22,482 approved, an overall rate of 19 percent, with Somalia, Bosnia, Sudan, Afghanistan, Burma, Iraq, and Ethiopia obtaining the highest. As against this, in fiscal year 1998 alone, 228,010 cases were denied or referred and 63,332 were approved, an overall rate of 21.7 percent, with Syria added to the top group while Ethiopia and Afghanistan dropped out. However, the administration also continued to grant "temporary protected status" to some persons already in the country (and most of these grants were subsequently extended so as to constitute, in effect, full-scale admission), including Liberians, Rwandans, Bosnians, and Somalis in 1996, as well as Sudanese, Sierra Leoneans, and Burundians the following year.

157. Office of Policy and Planning, U.S. Immigration and Naturalization Service (hereafter, INS), *Estimates of the Unauthorized Immigrant Population Residing in the United States: 1990 to 2000,* January 31 (Washington, DC: Office of Policy and Planning, U.S. Immigration and Naturalization Service, 2003). Using the Census 2000 enumeration of foreign-born and taking into consideration undercount, the agency adopts as its baseline an estimated net overall immigration of 13.5 million for the decade. Given 8.0 million net legal immigrants, this indicates a net addition of 5.5 million unauthorized to the 3.5 million said to be living in the United States in 1990. The "primary reason" cited for the revision was the raising of estimated net entries from Mexico by about 1.2 million; INS, *Estimates,* 2. The 1.6 million figure is my own "residual" inference: table C indicates 3.6 million left altogether; about 1.2 million; INS, *Estimates,* 2.

158. 40.9 percent emigrated, 32.0 adjusted to legal status, 9.7 left and reentered legally, 5.8 percent died, and only 11.6 percent were removed by the INS; INS, *Estimates* 10, table C.

159. One need not be an expert statistician to wonder about the curious coincidence that the final tally for the decade was a neat 100 percent net increase in illegal immigrants, that is, 3.5 million left over from the 1980s plus a net 3.5 million added in the 1990s, making for an even 7.0 million in 2000.

160. *NYT,* July 10, 2001, WK3.

161. *St. Louis Post-Dispatch,* December 17, 1996 (Maggie Gallagher reporting). While some remain determined to stem the tide, "many major conservative

voices seek to head the debate off at the pass. Linda Chavez and *The Wall Street Journal's* influential Paul Gigot recently publicly warned the GOP that even raising the issue may alienate 'culturally conservative' Hispanic voters, one of the fastest-growing ethnic groups." The *NYT's* California correspondent commented similarly a year later, "The California Republican Party, the mighty army that helped propel Richard Nixon and Ronald Reagan to the White House, now finds itself facing a big problem: It is rapidly losing ground among the fastest-growing group in the electorate of the nation's most populous state, Hispanic voters. Expressed in either English or Spanish, the arithmetic is clear"; *NYT,* December 9, 1997, A1 (Todd S. Purdum reporting).

162. Peter Brimelow and Ed Rubenstein, "Electing a New People," *National Review,* June 16, 1997.

163. Jack Citrin and Benjamin Highton, *How Race, Ethnicity, and Immigration Shape the California Electorate* (San Francisco: Public Policy Institute of California, 2002), 4, 23.

164. Schockman, "California's Ethnic Experiment," 261.

165. Dubbed "English for the Children," Proposition 227 required all public school instruction to be conducted in English but mandated the spending of $50 million per year for ten years on the training of tutors for limited English proficient (LEP) students. Although Unz himself had opposed Proposition 187 and rejected Wilson's support in an effort to disassociate opposition to bilingual education from nativism, and even though some Hispanics shared doubts about the benefits of bilingual education as practiced in local schools, many felt targeted by the measure.

166. Schmidt, *Language Policy,* 18–19; Crawford, "Disaster at the Polls"; and James Crawford, "The Campaign against Proposition 227: A post Mortem," http://brj.asu.edu/archives/1v2/articles/Issue1Crawford.html.

167. As against 59 percent for independents and only 47 percent for Democrats. Hispanics disapproved by 63 percent, but this was much less than the 87 percent who opposed Proposition 187, fostering renewed debate regarding their educational preferences. These data are from the *Los Angeles Times*–CNN exit poll, *Los Angeles Times,* June 4, 1998. Recent immigrants with children in bilingual education were far more likely to oppose. The Asian percentages were respectively 57 and 47; males supported Prop. 227 64–36, females 57–43; voters grew more anti-bilingual with age, recent immigrants with children in bilingual education were far more likely to oppose it, but the relationship of education and income to support was curvilinear, being highest in the middle. Overall, Latino opposition was less intense than for Proposition 187 (as mentioned, 87 percent against it).

168. Citrin and Highton, *How Race, Ethnicity, and Immigration,* 43, 77; and *NYT,* January 16, 1999, A8 (Todd S. Purdum reporting).

169. Following the 1998 election, the U.S. District Court granted California a temporary delay on its Proposition 187 appeal on the grounds that the new governor, Gray Davis, might adopt a different policy. In April 1999, Speaker Antonio Villaraigosa asked the court to mediate the issue, and a deal was struck at the end of July, whereby the governor agreed to drop the appeal on the grounds that most of Proposition 187's intent was covered by the federal laws passed in 1996—except for the banning of education for illegal children, which had in any case been declared unconstitutional in 1982—while those who had sought to prevent the measure from taking effect in turn agreed to drop their lawsuits against the state. Davis subsequently obtained another thirty-day suspension of proceedings in order to clarify whether he was obligated to defend the measure; *Los Angeles Times,* March 25 and 29, 1999, and April 3, 1999; *Contra Costa Times,* April 12, 1999; and *NYT,* July 30, 1999. The U.S. District Court subsequently dismissed most of Proposition 187, leaving only two minor items establishing criminal penalties for creating, using, and selling false documents to conceal a person's illegal immigration status.

170. Citrin and Highton, *How Race, Ethnicity, and Immigration,* 28, 31; Thomas Rivera Policy Institute, press release, February 29, 2000, http://www.trpi .org/press/022800.html.

171. *Washington Post,* December 12, 1996.

172. U.S. Commission on Immigration Reform, *1997 Report to Congress: Becoming an American: Immigration and Immigrant Policy,* September (Washington, DC: U.S. Commission on Immigration Reform, 1997), xvii–xix, 224–25. The Carnegie Endowment's Demetrios Papademetriou concurred that the brothers and sisters preference should be eliminated, albeit "on pragmatic grounds," as there was already an 1.8 million backlog in this category, increasing by 100,000–150,000 a year, yet only 60,000 could be accommodated. Further criticizing the labor certification as "inefficient, ineffective, costly, useless," he proposed to develop a system whereby people should come "because prospectively they will contribute substantially to the United States," assessed through such proxies as education, age, experience, and personal and professional adaptability, along Canadian and Australian lines; Klusmeyer, "Immigration Challenges," 246.

173. Smith and Edmonston, *The New Americans.*

174. Most notably, George J. Borjas, who had served as a member of the research panel, subsequently insisted that residential clustering reflected not merely a desire to be near co-ethnics but also a tendency on the part of less skilled immigrants to settle in the states that offer the highest benefits.

175. Gimpel and Edwards, *Congressional Politics,* 315.

176. Cited in the *Chicago Tribune,* April 3, 2000, CISNEWS@cis.org (Mike Dorning reporting).

177. Including a new bureau within the Justice Department for border and interior enforcement; an undersecretary of state for citizenship, immigration, and refugee admissions within the State Department; an Agency for Immigration Review for independent repeals of administrative decisions; and a transfer of the enforcement of immigration-related employment standards to the Labor Department. A few months earlier, the GAO had issued a report of its own, which found that although the INS had made some progress, many long-standing issues had yet to be adequately addressed. However, rather than restructuring the agency to separate enforcement and service functions, it recommended clarifying existing lines of accountability and communication and improving the INS's financial accounting, budget, as well as resource allocation process; U.S. General Accounting Office, *INS Management: Follow-Up on Selected Problems,* GGD-97–132, July (Washington, DC: U.S. General Accounting Office, 1997).

178. *NYT,* January 21, 1998, A12 (Eric Schmitt reporting). Under congressional pressure, the administration then established a Restructuring Office and contracted with yet another firm to develop a blueprint, published as U.S. Immigration and Naturalization Service, *A Framework for Change: The Immigration and Naturalization Service,* April (Washington, DC: U.S. Immigration and Naturalization Service, 1998). As the confrontation rankled on, the Carnegie Endowment's study group came up with a median solution, a new, independent, Cabinet-level agency for immigration and citizenship affairs that would consolidate a wide array of functions now scattered among several federal departments; Demetrios G. Papademetriou, T. Alexander Aleinikoff, and Deborah Waller Meyers, *Reorganizing the U.S. Immigration Function: Toward a New Framework for Accountability,* no. 7 (Washington, DC: International Migration Policy Program, Carnegie Endowment for International Peace, 1998), vi, vii.

179. William J. Krouse, "Immigration and Naturalization Service Reorganization and Related Legislative Proposals," Congressional Research Service Report RS20279, updated July 24 (Washington, DC, Library of Congress, 2001), 3. In March 2000, the subcommittee again approved legislation to dismantle the INS, but the Judiciary Committee again failed to act.

180. *Chicago Tribune,* April 2, 2000, CISNEWS@cis.org (Mike Dorning reporting).

181. In 1998 the legislators raised the cap by 75 percent, from 65,000 to 115,000, but the quota was used up by midyear, prompting calls for yet another increase. In early 2000, a pair of Democrats proposed allowing international students to work in the United States after graduating, while Senator Spencer Abraham proposed raising the H-1B cap to 195,000 a year until 2002; with the benefit of bipartisan backing, the measure was subsequently approved by the Judiciary Committee.

182. *Wall Street Journal,* May 31, 2000 (Marjorie Valbrun reporting).

183. An alternate House bill, vehemently opposed by business, would have lifted

the ceiling entirely on six-year visas, but condition them on the employers' paying the immigrants at least $40,000 and not using them to replace Americans on their payrolls; *New York Times,* October 3, 2000 (Associated Press). Vernon Briggs warned that if the endorsement occurred, "working people— especially those on the lower rungs of the economic ladder—will have lost the support of the most effective champion they ever had"; Vernon Briggs, *Immigration and American Unionism* (Ithaca, NY: Cornell University Press, 2001). As against this, the National Immigration Forum's Frank Sharry explained that immigrants are complementary to native workers rather than a substitute for them, and that "a liberalized system will lead to more order and control." Characterizing the Executive Council's decision as "a surprising turnabout," contrary to its 1986 stance, the *NYT* called for rejection as "[a]mnesty would undermine the integrity of the country's immigration laws and would depress the wages of its lowest-paid native workers"; *NYT,* February 22, 2000, A22. See also *Wall Street Journal,* February 10 and May 31, 2000.

184. George W. Bush was viewed "as a nonpolarizing figure whose successful outreach to Hispanic voters in Texas might translate well here"; *New York Times,* February 28, 2000, A1 (Todd S. Purdum reporting). A California news paper explained similarly that "Republicans with national ambitions are disinclined to follow former California Governor Pete Wilson's lead"; *Sacramento Bee,* March 7, 1999.

185. *NYT,* January 16, 1999, A8 (Todd S. Purdum reporting)

186. "We wouldn't have had a 187 in my state," he declared in March 1999, playing up his success at appealing to Hispanic voters in Texas and casting himself as an inclusive candidate who would not be tugged to the right (*Sacramento Bee,* March 7, 1999). The following June, in the course of his first swing through California as a declared presidential candidate, he again cast himself as more temperate than most Republicans leaders both in California and Washington on two ballot measures that had roiled his party, immigration and affirmative action (*NYT,* June 30, 1999, A20; *Washington Post,* October 15, 1999).

187. *NYT,* January 16, 1999, A8 (Todd S. Purdum reporting). The executive director of the nonpartisan National Association of Latino Elected and Appointed Officials (NALEAO) drew the contrast between the two candidates, pointing out that the Texan spoke fluent Spanish and had generally good relations with Hispanic voters because "he gets it, he understands what Latinos mean to the future of his state."

188. Unless otherwise indicated, the Bush citations are taken from http://www .issues2000.org/Celeb/George_W_Bush_Immigration.htm. This is obviously a partisan source, but precisely for that reason, it constitutes a reliable indicator of what the candidate wanted the public to hear.

189. *NYT,* January 15, 2000, A15 (Don Van Natta Jr. reporting). Univision, the dominant Spanish-language network, never took in more than $500,000 in political advertising dollars during a campaign season until 1998, but when Gray Davis attacked the GOP for anti-immigrant activities, its political revenue shot up to $8 million, and it was now estimated that at least $20 million would be spent in the current year; *San Jose Mercury News,* January 21, 2000.
190. *Washington Times,* January 14, 2000 (Ralph Z. Hallow reporting).
191. *NYT,* February 28, 2000, A1 (Todd S. Purdum reporting).
192. Cited in the *Chicago Tribune,* April 3, 2000, CISNEWS@cis.org (Mike Dorning reporting).
193. It was also pointed out that 6 in 10 Hispanic voters supported a successful initiative to limit marriage to heterosexual couples, which Democrats opposed by a like margin; *NYT,* March 8, 2000, A27 (Todd S. Purdum reporting); see also Steven Greenhouse, "Guess Who's Embracing Immigrants Now," *NYT,* March 5, 2000, WK4.
194. http://www.mc.org/GOPInfo/Platform/2000platform4.htm; and http://www.issues2000.org/Celeb/Republican_Party_Immigration.htm.
195. http://www.issues2000.org/Celeb/Democratic_Party_Immigration.htm. The bulk of the remainder went to Ralph Nader.
196. *NYT,* July 15, 2001, A1 (Erich Schmitt reporting).
197. *NYT,* October 22, 2000, A16 (Eric Schmitt reporting); and December 13, 2000, A12 (Robert Pear reporting).
198. *NYT,* April 8, 2001, WK5 (Eric Schmitt reporting).

Conclusion: National Design in a Globalizing World

1. Orlando Patterson, *Slavery and Social Death: A Comparative Study* (Cambridge, MA: Harvard University Press, 1982).
2. Arthur Mann, *The One and the Many: Reflections on the American Identity* (Chicago: University of Chicago Press, 1979).
3. Albert O. Hirschman, "Exit, Voice, and the State," in Albert O. Hirschman, *Essays in Trespassing: Economics to Politics and Beyond* (Cambridge: Cambridge University Press, 1981), 246–65.
4. David M. Kennedy, *Freedom from Fear: The American People in Depression and War, 1929–1945* (New York: Oxford University Press, 1999), 712.
5. For an elaboration of this concept, see Aristide R. Zolberg, "Wanted but Not Welcome: Alien Labor in Western Development," in *Population in an Interacting World,* ed. William Alonso (Cambridge, MA: Harvard University Press, 1987), 36–74.
6. Richard D. Alba and Victor Nee, *Remaking the American Mainstream: Assimilation and Contemporary Immigration* (Cambridge, MA: Harvard University Press, 2003).

7. Samuel P. Huntington, *Who Are We? The Challenges to America's National Identity* (New York: Simon & Schuster, 2004).

8. James G. Gimpel and James R. Edwards Jr., *The Congressional Politics of Immigration Reform* (Boston: Allyn & Bacon, 1999), 298. Partisanship remains a statistically significant explanatory variable for most immigration votes in the 104th Congress even if formerly Democratic southern seats are counted as Democratic.

9. Ibid., 306.

10. The following calculations are from data in Jack Citrin and Benjamin Highton, *How Race, Ethnicity, and Immigration Shape the California Electorate* (San Francisco: Public Policy Institute of California, 2002).

11. *NYT*, January 19, 2001, A3.

12. Martin Schain, Aristide R. Zolberg, and Patrick Hossay, eds., *Shadows over Europe* (New York: Palgrave, 2002).

13. *NYT*, December 22, 2004, A27.

14. *NYT*, April 2, 2001, A15.

15. Editorial, *NYT*, May 12, 2001, A14.

16. In his first visit to California as Mexican president-elect to deliver the keynote address at the Mexican American Legal Defense and Educational Fund (MALDEF) Los Angeles Awards dinner in November 2000, Vicente Fox declared, "We recognize that an integrated North America is here to stay," and said he would support both Mexicans who apply for U.S. citizenship and naturalized Mexican Americans who want to regain their Mexican citizenship; Associate Press dispatch, November 10, 2000 (Erica Werner reporting);http://www/sfgate.com.cgi-bin/article.cgi?file=/news/archive/soooo/11/10/state01 12EST02http://www/sfgate.com.cgi-2.

17. In late March 2001 President Fox returned to California, where he announced to farm workers that he would press for amnesty on their behalf, as well as for a major guest worker program. Although President Bush reportedly still opposed outright amnesty, Foreign Relations Committee Chairman Jesse Helms, working closely with ranking minority member Joseph Biden, responded positively to Foreign Minister Jorge Castañeda's invitation to a get-together with his committee's counterpart in Mexico City (with the agenda to include drug flows, migration, as well as amnesty) and the formation of a joint "migration working group" to review proposals; *NYT*, April 3, 2001, A10, A12.

18. *NYT*, April 23, 2001, A12; May 5, 2001, A9; and May 6, 2001, A36.

19. *NYT*, July 11, 2001, A1 (Eric Schmitt reporting). The plan included a guest worker program limited to temporary visits as well as a more controversial one that would provide a road to permanent residency status for some of the millions of undocumented Mexican immigrants already in the United States. In response to criticism from Democrats and labor unions for focusing on

Mexico exclusively, the administration said it would make it clear that the guest worker plan is "Mexico first, not Mexico only," opening the door for similar programs involving other countries; *Washington Post,* September 1, 2001, A8 (Mike Allen, staff writer).

20. *Washington Post,* September 1, 2001, A8 (Mike Allen, staff writer).

21. *Washington Times,* August 17, 2001. An August poll indicated that only 28 percent supported making it easier for illegals to become citizens while 67 percent opposed, and another poll on the eve of the September meeting reported that a majority found amnesty a bad or very bad idea; *USA Today/CNN/Gallup poll,* from CIS archives (accessed at www.cis.org). However, as the meeting neared, White House officials said that hopes for reaching a specific agreement by its conclusion "have been dashed by the difficulty of working out the mechanics, and by opposition on Capitol Hill to broad amnesty for illegal workers." Senator Phil Gramm still objected to a guest worker plan that led to amnesty, permanent residency status, or citizenship, while Republican representatives F. James Sensenbrenner and George W. Gekas opposed any reform until the INS was overhauled. The slow pace "came as an acute disappointment to some of those close to Bush" and to Republican officials who believe "that a successful guest worker program could help make inroads with Hispanic voters, a top priority of the White House political apparatus"; *Washington Post,* September 1, 2001, A8 (Mike Allen, staff writer).

22. The *NYT* editorialized that the pomp and circumstance of the occasion could not mask diminished expectations of the Mexican president's state visit to Washington, now that both American and Mexican economies have stalled, and that while Fox's immigration timetable may make for good politics in Mexico, President Bush needs more time to build political support on this side; *NYT,* September 7, A14.

23. For a fuller discussion of these issues, see Aristide R. Zolberg, "Guarding the Gates," in *Understanding September 11,* ed. Craig Calhoun, Paul Price, and Ashley Timmer (New York: The New Press, 2002), 285–89; and "Immigration and Security," in *ABC Clio Encyclopedia of Migration* (forthcoming, 2005).

24. These figures are taken from Annual Reports of the Immigration and Naturalization Service (Washington, DC: Immigration and Naturalization Service, various years); I am grateful to Fred Cocozelli for his assistance in gathering the appropriate data.

25. Rare exceptions include "patrials," notably Jews "returning" to Israel.

26. This was notoriously the case during the Cold War, when persons wishing to visit Communist countries, especially for purposes of academic research or journalistic inquiry, had to file their requests well in advance, while the United States required even visitors from allied countries to declare under oath that they were not affiliated to "subversive" organizations.

27. In any case, the system hardly proved an effective deterrent as many schools

in effect practiced open enrollment and sent out the form required to obtain a visa ("I-20") to anyone who paid an application fee. Moreover, the INS took 6–12 months to report to the schools whom they should be expecting, and the schools in turn were not required to confirm their arrival, unless asked by the INS, which occurred rarely.

28. In 2001, a Justice Department report found that the INS mismanaged a $31 million program to electronically record entries and exits of noncitizens, and that the job would take four more years and an additional $57 million to complete; Nicholas Confessore, "Borderline Insanity," *Washington Monthly,* February 2002. Karl Rove, who had final authority on immigration issues and was determined to move more Hispanics into the GOP column, secured the appointment of James Ziglar, a libertarian with no immigration experience, as head of INS, with Stuart Anderson, formerly of the libertarian CATO Institute and Senator Spencer Abraham's chief of staff, as his policy director.

29. Since visas must be awarded abroad, the function devolves upon the State Department; however, control of entry at the border proper falls within the sphere of domestic policing, then controlled by the INS, housed in the Justice Department. Although in recent years consular officials gained access to an INS database with 5.7 million names of individuals with past immigration problems, this does not cover first-time applicants. Moreover, the FBI refused to open its own database either to the INS or to the State Department, and neither of the agencies that regulate admissions had access to data from intelligence agencies that monitor threats emanating in the outside world. No action was taken with regard to the development of federal-local linkages, as the Justice Department's legal counsel opined that the Constitution precluded such arrangements, while local police argued that involvement in immigration enforcement would interfere with their basic obligations.

30. This account is drawn from Melanie Nezer, "The New Antiterrorism Legislation: The Impact on Immigrants," *Refugee Reports* 22, no. 11 (November 2001): 1–8.

31. The USA PATRIOT Act gives law enforcement agencies broader powers to pursue terrorists through search warrants and eavesdropping, and provides for the possibility of holding aliens without charges for up to six months, with the possibility of renewal, subject to a review that puts the burden of proof on the government to demonstrate that the alien's release will threaten national security, the safety of the community, or any person; Rosemary Jenks, "The USA PATRIOT Act of 2001: A Summary of the Anti-terrorism Law's Immigration-Related Provisions," December (Washington, DC: Center for Immigration Studies "Backgrounder," 2001). It further expanded the definition of terrorism, which was already a ground for denying admission and for deportation, to include use of any "weapon or dangerous device" with the intent

to endanger persons or cause damage to property; limited judicial review to habeas corpus issues; authorized a tripling of the number of Border Patrol personnel, customs personnel, and immigration inspectors along the northern border: provided for improved monitoring technology; and granted INS and State Department personnel access to FBI files for the purpose of checking the criminal history of visa applicants.

32. The size of these groups itself became an object of controversy. "Arabs" and "Muslims" overlap only in part because until recently, the U.S. population of Arab origin was overwhelmingly Christian, as illustrated by former White House Chief of Staff John Sununu and former Michigan senator and energy secretary Spencer Abraham, as well as the late scholar and public intellectual Edward Saïd.

33. On November 13, 2001, the Justice Department announced it would pick up and question some 5,000 Middle Eastern men 18 to 33 who entered the country legally on student, visitor, or business visas—but not as immigrants—since January 1, 2000. Although officials said the interviews were intended to be voluntary and the people sought are not considered suspects, the move was sharply criticized by civil liberties organizations as a "dragnet approach that is likely to magnify concerns of racial and ethnic profiling"; *New York Times,* November 14, 2001, B8. While the roundup resulted in the incarceration of numerous Middle Easterners for violations of immigration regulations, mostly by way of overstaying, which was likely to lead to their deportation, there were no indications that it netted any suspects related to the 9/11 events. In January 2002, the Justice Department announced a new effort to find and deport people who ignored deportation orders, beginning with the tracking down of several thousand men from Muslim and Middle Eastern countries.

34. *NYT,* June 4, 2002, A1 (Eric Schmitt reporting); *NYT,* June 6, 2002, A30; and see also the David Cole, "Misdirected Snooping Doesn't Stop Terror," *NYT,* op-ed, June 4, 2002, A19. The inclusion of Pakistanis set off an unusual rush of asylum seekers to Canada, which sent them back to the United States with an appointment, usually about a month later; and in January 2003, the foreign minister of Pakistan flew to the United States to protest in person.

35. A federal judge ruled as early as April 2002 that the detention of a Jordanian student constituted a misuse of the material witness statutes; although the Justice Department not only appealed the decision, but also even issued a regulation barring state and local governments from releasing the names of detainees, the following August Judge Gladys Kessler of the Federal District Court in Washington, D.C., declared that secret arrests are odious to a democratic society and ordered the Bush administration to release most of the names within fifteen days. Later that month, the Federal Appeals Court in

Cincinnati declared that the practice of holding deportation hearings in secret was unlawful, that they must be open unless the government or the detainee can persuade a judge that interests of the highest order are at stake, and that the press and public enjoy First Amendment rights of access to them.

36. U.S. Department of Justice, Office of the Inspector General, *The September 11 Detainees: A Review of the Treatment of Aliens Held on Immigration Charges in Connection with the Investigation of the September 11 Attacks,* April (Washington, DC: U.S. Department of Justice, 2003).

37. http://www.supremecourtus.gov/opinions/02pdf/01–1491.pdf. The case involved Hyung Joon Kim, who came to the United States in 1984 at age five, became a lawful resident two years later, and in 1997, at age eighteen, was convicted of petty theft and sentenced to three years' imprisonment. Upon release from state prison, he was detained by the INS under the 1996 law on the grounds that his criminal record made him deportable. In January 2002, the Federal Appeals Court for the Ninth Circuit in California ruled 3–0 that the law violated the constitutional guarantee of due process because it makes no provision for release on bail of those who present no danger of threat or flight. The court relied on two U.S. Supreme Court decisions of June 2001, which ruled that the federal government cannot deport resident immigrants who have been convicted of certain crimes without a court hearing, and that keeping immigrants who had been ordered deported in indefinite detention if no country would accept them was a violation of the due process clause of the Fifth Amendment. It is noteworthy that the INS expressed doubts about the law from the outset, and that the Justice Department's own general counsel advised against it as late as 2001. Similar challenges were pending in Cincinnati, Denver, New York, and Richmond.

38. In many localities, notably New York City, the police have been explicitly forbidden from cooperating with federal officers, on the grounds that this would interfere with the performance of their basic functions. This doctrine prevailed within the Justice Department as well, and was reaffirmed by its legal counsel following 9/11.

39. *NYT,* June 2, 2002, A21 (Eric Schmitt reporting).

40. In the same vein, that same month the GAO recommended strengthening of the visa process as an antiterrorism tool; GAO, *Border Security: Visa Process Should be Strengthened as an Antiterrorism Tool,* October (Washington, DC: U.S. General Accounting Office, 2002).

41. *Washington Post,* October 25, 2001, A24; and Kevin E. Deardorff and Lisa M. Blumerman, *Evaluating Components of International Migration: Estimates of the Foreign-Born Population by Migrant Status in 2000,* Working Paper no. 58, December (Washington, DC: U.S. Bureau of the Census, Population Division, 2001). The bureau calculated that in 2000, there were some 8.7 million aliens

in the United States who were neither temporary visitors nor legal immigrants; however, as the total includes some in a quasi-legal status waiting to have their cases adjudicated, it reckoned illegal immigrants proper at between 7 and 8 million, which is close to the earlier INS estimate of 7.5 million. Although a subsequent breakdown by nationality indicated that half of them originated in North and Central America, with Mexico alone providing 44 percent, many headlines chose to emphasize that "115,000 Middle Eastern Immigrants Are in the U.S. Illegally." Joe Costanzo et al., *Evaluating Components of International Migration: The Residual Foreign Born*, Working Paper Series no. 61, December (Washington, DC: U.S. Census Bureau, Population Division, 2001); and *NYT*, January 23, 2002, A10.

42. One of the most criticized features was the "Visa Express," whereby consulates delegated visa authority to travel agencies, notably in Saudi Arabia, without interviews. In December, the State Department's own inspector general reported that little had changed since 9/11 and that the system for issuing nonimmigrant visas remained too lax and poorly financed to screen out determined terrorists. The department launched a new visa system, in development since 2000, at the Winter Olympics of early 2002. Student visas were singled out for special concern in light of reports that most of the terrorists were "intellectuals," and in light of the by-now notorious fact that such visas can be obtained by registering in a wide range of institutions. The new system increased immigration inspectors and investigators, required universities to keep better track of foreign students, and heightened scrutiny of visa applications from countries deemed dangerous. The FBI and the CIA must also share more information with the State Department, which issues visas, and the government will meld certain databases. The federal government will have to issue machine-readable and tamper-resistant visas and travel documents imprinted with biometric identifiers such as fingerprints or retina scans. The Association of International Educators supported the bill in its final form, as did the National Immigration Forum and La Raza. A presidential commission will examine the use of the proposed electronic data systems to see if it infringes on privacy rights. Facing congressional scrutiny, in July 2002 the State Department announced it had ordered a review of its visa-issuing procedures, with special inspection teams due to go out in the fall.

43. Although the Justice Department would not disclose the criteria its agents will use, it was widely assumed that visitors from Arab and Islamic nations will receive the closest scrutiny. Many of them were already singled out for extra investigation before leaving home, making for considerable delays, particularly for students. Government scientists further recommended a combination of facial recognition and fingerprint scanning technologies as federal standards for identity documents to be issued to foreigners starting in 2004, as man-

dated by the USA PATRIOT and the Border Security Acts. A new system of airport profiling was suggested as well, whereby passengers would be assigned a risk level, encrypted in their boarding passes. The State Department's visa information campaign was featured under the title "Secure Borders, Open Doors"; see http://www.unitedstates.visas.gov.

44. On January 22, 2003. Despite the transfer of immigration from the Department of Justice, the proposed division between enforcement and services prevailed. The Bureau of Border Security gained full authority over all aspects of border enforcement, while immigration services, including asylum, were placed under the Bureau of Citizenship and Immigration Services. The spirit of the department's founding was reflected in the appointment of Asa Hutchinson, currently in charge of drug enforcement, as undersecretary for border and transportation security, and of Michael J. Garcia, who had made his reputation by prosecuting the planners of the 1993 World Trade Center bombing, as head of the Bureau of Immigration and Customs Enforcement. In keeping with the political wooing of Hispanics, Eduardo Aguirre Jr., vice president and chief operating officer of the Export-Import Bank, was made acting director of the Bureau of Citizenship and Immigration Services. In March 2003, the CIA team leader who caught double agent Aldrich Ames came out of retirement to take charge of the new department's intelligence bureau. A panel of technology and security experts recommended in October 2002 that the administration develop a system to share intelligence gathered in the United States and abroad among local, state, and federal agencies, while developing guidelines to protect against abuses; rather than the FBI, this should be entrusted in the domestic intelligence center within the new department; see *Protecting America's Freedom in an Information Age*.

45. In the wake of 9/11, the Canadian government itself fast-tracked legislation to tighten security at points of entry, and it was reported that the courts would authorize racial profiling for this purpose; they also sought authority to return asylum seekers who entered from the United States; *National Post*, October 10, 2001. Within the framework of NAFTA, Canada continued to push aggressively a plan that would eventually allow more than 7,000 trucks each day to pass the border uninspected (using a version of EZ-Passes) and would allow companies with regular freight traffic across the border to undergo security prescreening. It had already begun to phase in a program for U.S. truckers, enabling them to enter without inspection if they work for recognized companies that have been screened, such as General Motors.

46. On the contrary, in March the House approved renewal of a measure enacted in 2000 that facilitated the legalization of Mexican illegal immigrants (Section 245(i), which expired in April 2001), but despite sponsorship by thirty senators ranging from Helms to Kennedy, the provision did not survive in the final state.

47. *NYT*, January 7, 2004.
48. President Bush also indicated that Mexicans would be exempt from the mandatory reporting procedures to be imposed on all foreigners.
49. Michael Teitelbaum, "Right versus Right: Immigration and Refugee Policy in the United States," *Foreign Affairs* 59, no. 1 (Fall 1980): 22.
50. Terry Nardin, "Alternative Ethical Perspectives on Transnational Migration," in *Freedom of Movement*, ed. Brian Barry and Robert E. Goodin (University Park: Pennsylvania State University Press, 1992), 267–76. It should be clear that "liberalism" is meant here in the philosophical, and not current political, sense.
51. Henry Sidgwick, *Elements of Politics*, 4th ed. (London: Macmillan, 1919), 309.
52. Brian Barry, "The Quest for Consistency: A Sceptical View," in *Free Movement*, ed. Brian Barry and Robert Goodin (University Park: Pennsylvania State University Press, 1992), 284.
53. Herman Melville, *Redburn* (Harmondsworth, UK: Penguin Books, 1976), 382.
54. Meissner, "After the Attack," 4.

Index

Abbott, Edith, 23
Abolitionists, 104
Aborigines, 26
Abortion, 17
Accepting the Immigration Challenge, 401
ACLU. *See* American Civil Liberties Union
ACS. *See* American Society for Colonizing the
    Free People of Color in the United States
Act of Union (Scotland, 1701), 48
Act to Encourage Immigration, 172, 180
Adams, John, 80, 88, 93
Adams, John Quincy, 105, 106, 107
"A Defense of Americans" (Franklin), 42
Adler, Cyrus, 236
Adorno, Theodore, 6, 299
Advisory Committee on Refugees, 287
AFDC. *See* Aid to Family with Dependent
    Children
Affirmative action, 369
AFL-CIO, 331, 359, 413, 428
AFL. *See* American Federation of Labor
Africa: colonization by free American Negroes
    interpreted as attempt at ethnic cleansing,
    192; colonization of, 120–124; Negroes
    returned to, 120; slave trade of, 27, 29, 78;
    workers imported from, 1, 27
African Americans. *See* Death, social; Ellison,
    Ralph; Negroes
African Colonization Society, 158
African Union Society, 77
Agricultural industry, 33, 114
Aid to Family with Dependent Children
    (AFDC), 416
AJC. *See* American Jewish Committee
Alabama-Chattanooga railroad, 183
Alamo, 133
Alien and Sedition Acts, 70, 87, 444
Alien Bill, 90

Alien Enemies, 93, 94
Alien Friends Act, 93, 94, 95, 96
Alien Laws, 96
Aliens: friendly v. dangerous, 88; incorporation
    of, 38; national surveillance of, 94
Allen, Frederick Lewis, 244
Allport, Gordon W., 6, 299
Alms Houses (New York), 140
Amendments: Fifteenth Amendment (U.S.
    Constitution), 182; Fourteenth Amendment
    (U.S. Constitution), 361, 412, 419; Gallegly
    Amendment, 417; language constitutional,
    403
America Comes of Age (Siegfried), 244
American Business for Legal Immigration, 413
American Civil Liberties Union (ACLU), 365,
    374, 444
American Committee on Italian Immigration,
    379
American Economic Association, 199
American Emigrant Company, 166, 172–173,
    174
American Enterprise Institute, 355, 377
American Farm Bureau Federation, 332
American Federation of Labor (AFL), 218, 219,
    256, 297
American Foreign Service Journal, 265
American Immigration Policy: A Reappraisal,
    314
American Indians, 86, 100; removal of, 117–
    118
Americanism, 110, 238, 330
Americanization, 107–110, 263–264, 298, 433
American Jewish Committee (AJC), 222, 230,
    235, 236, 274, 314
American Joint Distribution Committee, 282
American Journal of Sociology, 215, 265
American Legion, 305